Nicholas I
Emperor and Autocrat of All the Russias

Riasanovsky, for it was his book, *Nicholas I and Official Nationality in Russia*, which first stirred my fascination with the character of Nicholas I. Finally, my thanks go to my wife Patti, to whom this book is dedicated, and who first directed my attention to the interest which the personality of Nicholas I had for the non-specialist in Russian history.

Institutions as well as individuals have aided me greatly in this work. The International Research and Exchanges Board has supported me as an exchange scholar to the Soviet Union, and the Fulbright-Hays Faculty Research Abroad Program has supported my research both in the Soviet Union and in Poland. Generous grants from the American Philosophical Society, the American Council of Learned Societies and Northern Illinois University have also aided me in this work, as did a summer research associateship from the Russian and East European Center at the University of Illinois. Archivists and librarians at the Central State Historical Archive in Leningrad, the Central State Archive of the October Revolution in Moscow, the Saltykov–Shchedrin Public Library, the Lenin Library, the Public Records Office, the British Museum, the University of Warsaw Library, the Library of Congress, the Sterling Memorial Library at Yale University, the Columbia University Library and the University of Illinois Library have helped me greatly in locating and using the materials which went into my research. Without their generous efforts on my behalf, the research for this book could not have been undertaken. To all of them I owe a special debt which formalistic acknowledgement and thanks such as this can never repay.

W. Bruce Lincoln
DeKalb, Illinois

balanced historical perspective. For Nicholas's reign was a good time for many Russians, and some looked back upon it with a sense of longing, even nostalgia. It was, after all, the last time in Imperial Russia's history when things were certain and predictable. Russia stood at the pinnacle of her power during those years, and Russian society was plagued by few of the self-doubts that would begin to tear the old order apart in the half-century after Nicholas's death. As the Baroness Frederiks, who had lived at Nicholas's Court as a child, wrote in the 1880s, when looking back upon his reign after some three decades of social turmoil, which had seen the emancipation of the serfs and the beginnings of the Industrial Revolution in Russia, 'during the lifetime of Nikolai Pavlovich, Russia had great and noble stature . . . [and] he heaped still greater glory upon her. Everyone and everything bowed down before him and before Russia!'[1]

The obligations one incurs in undertaking a study such as this are, of course, immense. My greatest debt is to three historians whom one must hold in awe for their broad knowledge of Russia's history and culture: Professor Leopold Haimson, who first directed my attention to the era of Nicholas I as a fruitful area for study, and whose patience as a graduate adviser and teacher will always be remembered by those who have studied with him; Professor Marc Raeff, who for a number of years has provided me with encouragement, helpful advice and criticism far in excess of what one can reasonably expect from any friend or scholar; and Professor Petr Andreevich Zaionchkovskii of Moscow State University, who for more than a decade has been my mentor when I have visited the Soviet Union, and has directed my attention to many helpful research materials in Moscow and Leningrad. Special thanks are also due to the late Professor J. B. Hoptner and to Professor Albert Resis, colleagues of mine at Northern Illinois University, with whom I have spent many profitable hours in discussing Russia's past. Likewise, two of my former doctoral students, Professors Lee Congdon and Jo Ann Ruckman, have given me much help as critics and as friends.

Over the past few years, I have profited greatly from discussions with a number of scholars in the United States and abroad. In this regard, Samuel Baron, Ludwik Bazylow, Daniel Brower, Michael Cherniavsky, Ralph Fisher, Jacob Kipp, Sidney Monas, Daniel Orlovsky, Franciszka Ramotowska, Edward Thaden, and George Yaney are at the top of what is, to my good fortune, a rather lengthy list. Peter Carson at Penguin Books encouraged me to write this book on Nicholas I; Tamara P. K. Lincoln shared with me many of the trials and difficulties related to the writing of this present work; and Professor Patricia Good read much of it in an earlier form. I owe a special debt, too, to Professor N. V.

Preface

Perhaps no ruler left more of an impression upon nineteenth-century Russia than did the Emperor Nicholas I, for the origins of nearly every major change or event during the last century of Romanov rule can be traced to his reign. Certainly Nicholas was an imposing figure. Many Russians admired, even venerated him; others saw him as the personification of oppression. But none who lived during his thirty-year reign could remain indifferent to the force of his personality and the system which he developed.

Yet, despite his importance as Emperor of Russia, Nicholas I has been much neglected by historians. There has been only one serious scholarly biography of him in Russian, that written by M. Polievktov in 1918. In Western languages, the best work is that by the German scholar Theodor Schiemann, also written in the early twentieth century, though Schiemann's work is heavily orientated towards Nicholas's foreign policy. A brief monograph by Constantin de Grunwald, *Le Tsar Nicolas Ier*, was translated into English some two decades ago, though Grunwald's work, like Schiemann's, focuses mainly on foreign affairs. Only the excellent work of Professor N. V. Riasanovsky, *Nicholas I and Official Nationality in Russia, 1825–1855*, begins to unravel the complex personality of Nicholas I, but Riasanovsky focuses primarily upon the ideology of Official Nationality, which Nicholas and his advisers created, rather than upon a comprehensive study of the Emperor and his policies.

Given the paucity of historical works about Nicholas I, Russians and Westerners alike tend to base their view of him upon the unflattering, though admittedly often dramatic, portraits that emerge from such monumental autobiographical and memoir accounts as those by Aleksandr Herzen, I. I. Panaev, P. V. Annenkov and a number of others who suffered from the ravages of censorship during his reign. As such, their accounts are biased, often bitter, and what emerges from them is an untempered portrait of a cruel, perhaps even mentally unbalanced, tyrant.

This present study, among other things, redresses the balance to some extent in Nicholas's favour. Certainly it is not intended as an apology for Russia's firm, sometimes cruel, Emperor. It is, however, an effort to view Nicholas as his contemporaries saw him and, given the distance of some 150 years since his accession, to place him and his policies in a more

Contents

FOR PATTI

First Midland Book Edition 1980

Manufactured in the United States of America

Library of Congress Cataloging in Publication Data

Lincoln, W. Bruce.
    Nicholas I.

    Bibliography: p.
    Includes index.
    1.   Nicholas I, Emperor of Russia, 1796-1855.
2.   Russia—Kings and rulers—Biography.   3.   Russia—
History—Nicholas I, 1825-1855.   I.   Title.
DK210.L56   947'.07'0924   [B]   77-15764
ISBN 0-253-34059-4
        0-253-20254-X pbk. 2 3 4 5 82 81 80

W. Bruce Lincoln

———

Nicholas I
Emperor and Autocrat of
All the Russias

———

Indiana University Press
Bloomington and London

A Note on
Russian Names
and Dates

The spelling of Russian names may present some difficulties to the more casual reader. Nevertheless, I have avoided Anglicizing most Russian proper names and have used Russian spellings for all but the names of Emperors and such well-known place names as Moscow and St Petersburg. Thus, for example, Nicholas I's younger brother is referred to as the Grand Duke Mikhail Pavlovich, rather than Michael Paulovich, and the Emperor's wife is Aleksandra Fedorovna, not Alexandra Theorodovna. In transliterating these and all other Russian names and phrases, I have used a somewhat modified version of the Library of Congress system of transliteration.

Dates, too, sometimes present a problem to the reader of Imperial Russian history because, between 1700 and 1918, Russians used the Julian, rather than the Gregorian, calendar. During the nineteenth century, this meant that Russian dates were twelve days behind those in the West. Thus, for example, Nicholas I's accession, 14 December 1825 according to the Russian calendar, occurred on 26 December 1825 when reckoned by the calendar in use in Western Europe.

This difference in dates is of no real import when writing about Russian internal affairs; it does become a matter of some consequence, however, in a discussion of Russian foreign policy. In an effort to minimize the difficulty, I have used the Western calendar when discussing European events, and Russian dates when dealing with events which occurred in Russia itself. In cases where confusion between the two might arise – as, for example, in the case of events in Russian Poland – I have indicated both dates.

Part One

Prologue

---

*'For lo, these many centuries, we have seen
our monarch as our supreme judge
and have recognized his benevolent will as
the highest authority . . . In Russia, the
sovereign is the living law: he shows
favour to the good and punishes the
wicked . . . In the Russian monarch all
powers are joined; our government is paternal
and patriarchal. Autocracy is the
bulwark of Russia'*

N. M. KARAMZIN, COURT HISTORIAN
IN THE REIGN OF ALEXANDER I

I

1825:
The Emperor is
Dead!
Long Live the
Emperor!

'Even if I shall be Emperor
for only one hour
I shall show myself worthy
of the honour'

NICHOLAS I, ON THE MORNING
OF HIS ACCESSION

For the people of St Petersburg the morning of 19 November 1825 seemed in no way unusual. As always, Russia's capital awakened gradually, as if reluctant to face the cold of another winter morning. First to appear on the city's streets were its labourers, wrapped in worn sheepskins to fend off the biting wind. Along with them came the capital's many favour-seekers, unfortunates who, through a stroke of ill-fortune, mismanagement or outright profligacy, had fallen upon hard times and hoped to restore their fortunes by begging favours from high officials or great noblemen. All came bearing petitions: one urging a favourable resolution of a generation-long lawsuit, another seeking a position in the civil service or the army for himself, a son or a relative. Still others begged some special privilege, and here and there a widow might appear to plead for a supplement to her meagre pension, or for a place in one of the capital's élite schools or Guards regiments for her son. Although the official or grandee to whom they would direct their pleas rarely appeared before midday, those who sought his favours had to be at his anteroom by six o'clock in the morning to secure an advantageous place near the entrance to his reception chambers.[1]

Next to appear were the capital's countless scribes and copyists, men who spent their lives perched upon high stools at their dimly lit desks in St Petersburg's chanceries, where they copied and re-copied documents in fine, elegant copper-plate. In the pale light of the waning northern night, this army of petty clerks scurried through the city's side-streets to be at their places, buried deep in the warrens of the capital's many government offices, by nine o'clock.[2] Merchants began to stir somewhat later since shops in the centre of the city did not open much before mid-day. Their clientele, the aristocratic and high official families, usually did not venture abroad much before noon, having sought the comfort of their beds not long before the labourers and petitioners had arisen.

The early-morning hours thus belonged to those who worked in trade, laboured in workshops or at copy-desks, or sought favours from the powerful and the rich. From midday until nightfall, the city was shared by rich and poor alike. As evening came on, however, the city streets would alter their character. Those who had spent the day in labour made their weary way homeward to their lodgings in the city's poorer quarters or on its outskirts, while the main streets, already bathed in watery lamplight, became the domain of the capital's aristocrats, high officials and dashing army officers. St Petersburg's social season was at its height, and all vied to receive and be received. Wrapped in heavy cloaks of rich furs, great lords and ladies sped in elegant equipages on their way to theatres or the city's many splendid palaces of green, turquoise or pink which lined the embankments of the Moika, the Fontanka and the Neva.

1. *The Death of an Emperor*

Not even those members of the Imperial family who were in St Petersburg in mid November 1825 had any inkling of the crisis about to burst upon them. Within less than a month, Russia would see two emperors proclaimed, the flower of her nobility rise in revolt and the sound of cannon and musket fire would echo just outside the Winter Palace itself. Some fourteen hundred miles to the south, in the small port town of Taganrog on the Sea of Azov, the final act of a drama that would profoundly affect the lives of them all was drawing to a close. There Russia's Emperor Alexander I, a conqueror of Napolean and liberator of Paris, lay at death's door.

Despite the fact that, in theory at least, the conduct of all affairs of state hinged upon his personal decision, Alexander's absence from his capital was not itself surprising to most Russians. Ever since Napoleon's Grand Army had been driven, freezing and bleeding, from Russia's soil at the end of 1812, he had often left his capital for long periods. During 1813 and 1814, Alexander had ridden with Russia's armies as they fought their way along the battle-torn road which led from the Empire's western frontiers through Warsaw, thence to Lützen, Bautzen, Dresden and, finally, to Leipzig where, in a colossal battle of the giants, the Allies had dealt Napoleon that shattering blow which had forced him to sign the first Peace of Paris in May 1814. The year 1815 had found Alexander again in Paris after Napoleon's second defeat, at Waterloo, and during the next decade he had visited the West several times to discuss the fate of post-Napoleonic Europe with other monarchs and statesmen.

But if Russians had become used to seeing their Emperor leave his capital for months at a time, no one understood very clearly why he had chosen to spend the winter of 1825 in the remote and sleepy town of Taganrog. Several factors, however, may have contributed to his decision. Because of her poor health, the Empress Elizaveta Alekseevna found it difficult to spend winters in St Peterburg's harsh climate and imperial physicians had urged her to spend that winter in Italy or southern France. But the delicate state of Russia's relations with the Ottoman Empire made it doubtful whether Alexander could have accompanied his empress to the West in the winter of 1825, and so they may well have settled upon southern Russia as an alternative. Indeed, his relations with the Ottoman Empire, and the need to make certain that his southern armies were ready for war, were in themselves important reasons for Alexander to visit the south. As he had written the previous year, 'there are rumours that the ruinous spirit of free-thinking and liberalism will flood or, indeed, is already flooding, our armies', and he saw this as the work of 'the greater part of the staff and higher command officers'.[3] It is quite possible that he went to the south in the autumn of 1825 so as to evaluate the threat of this danger among the troops stationed along Russia's southern frontier.

The loyalty of his army in the south may have been especially important to Alexander at this point because there is at least circumstantial evidence to indicate that he was about to launch a new offensive against the Ottoman Empire, and that part of his reason for going to the south was to 'move to a forward command post in preparation for a vigorous new policy to solve the Eastern Question'.[4] Certainly, his rigorous inspection of his southern forces, and the fact that he took his Chief of Staff, General Baron I. I. Dibich, with him, lend some weight to this view. Equally important, he had spent much of the year in a series of complex negotiations with Western powers on the question of Greece and the Danubian principalities of Wallachia and Moldavia and, as a result, may have concluded that, in Russia's best interests, he must take decisive military action against the Ottoman Empire.[5]

During the last three months of his life, Alexander inspected Russia's southern military forces and naval installations, as well as hospitals and religious establishments, with considerable care. In fact, it was while he was visiting St George's Abbey near Simferopol in the Crimea that he suffered the first symptoms of the illness which would cause his death. Alexander may have contracted typhoid during his inspection tour,[6] for he had visited soldiers stricken with typhoid during those last weeks of his life, or it may have been some form of malaria. By 14 November, several days after he had returned to Taganrog, Alexander's condition had taken a marked turn for the worse, and, at the urging of Prince P. M. Volkonskii, the Empress begged her husband to take the last sacraments. Alarmed that his condition was viewed as so serious, Alexander summoned Sir James Wylie, the English physician in his entourage, whose prescriptions he had stubbornly refused since he had first become ill on 31 October. 'In what condition am I, really?' Alexander asked. 'Am I, then, near my end?' Wylie replied with equal directness: 'Yes, Sire. Your Imperial Majesty has rejected my prescriptions. I now speak not as a physician, but as an honest man. It is my duty as a Christian to tell you that you have no time to lose.'[7] By early the next morning, Alexander was so ill that the Empress immediately summoned the archpriest Feodotov to hear his confession, and Dibich, now thoroughly alarmed, wrote to warn the Dowager Empress Mariia Fedorovna in St Petersburg that the Emperor was very ill.[8]

Although the Empress and most of his entourage believed on 15 November that Alexander would not live out the day, he still lingered on and, on the morning of the 17th, his condition improved. Even Sir James Wylie, who had been so certain of the Emperor's impending death two days earlier, admitted that there was still a chance that he might recover. As Elizaveta Alekseevna wrote to the Dowager Empress:

Today, thanks to the Supreme Being, there is a very decided amendment in the state of the Emperor. Even Sir James Wylie considers the case of the invalid more satisfactory. But he is feeble in the extreme . . . Dear Mama, pray with us; pray . . . that God may be pleased to grant the recovery of our beloved sufferer.[9]

Wylie was mistaken, for fever had damaged Alexander's brain and there was no hope for his full recovery. Alexander I, upon whom the Imperial Senate, the State Council and the Holy Synod had once bestowed the epithet 'The Blessed', died at 10.50 on the morning of 19 November.

Alexander was dead, but no one in St Petersburg knew as yet that he was even seriously ill. A special courier, galloping night and day from the Crimea, could not reach Russia's capital with Dibich's first message until the evening of 25 November. Then, the next morning, the more optimistic letter arrived which the Empress had written on 17 November.[10] To celebrate their Emperor's apparent escape from the jaws of death, and to pray for his further recovery, the Imperial Family ordered two special masses for the morning of 27 November. One was to be attended by the capital's civil officials and military officers and would be held in the spacious Aleksandr Nevskii Monastery. A second, for the Imperial Family, the Court and a few of the highest dignitaries, would be celebrated in the Winter Palace chapel.[11]

On the morning of 27 November, the Winter Palace chapel's dark blue walls, covered with the flickering lights of many candles placed before ancient icons, resounded with chants of gratitude and hope. During the course of the service, however, the Dowager Empress's valet knocked at the chapel door. The Grand Duke Nikolai Pavlovich hastened outside and, in an anteroom, found General Count M. A. Miloradovich, the Military Governor-General of St Petersburg. 'From Miloradovich's appearance,' he noted in his diary, 'I . . . [saw] that all was lost, that everything was finished, that our Angel was no longer on this earth!'[12] Only then did St Petersburg learn what had happened eight days earlier in Taganrog. Alexander I was dead, and Russia had been without an emperor for more than a week.

2.   *Constantine I, Emperor of All the Russias*

The news which Count Miloradovich brought to the imperial chapel during the dark, early-morning hours of 27 November set in motion a series of events that were to plunge Russia into a three-week crisis. Overcome with grief, Nikolai Pavlovich approached the priest with word of what he had just learned. Solemnly the priest took the crucifix in his hands and covered it with crêpe. To the Dowager Empress he spoke in solemn tones: 'Man must bend to the decrees of God.'[13] Everyone in the chapel thus learned of Alexander's passing. The Grand Duke left the chapel for only a moment to see that his mother, who had fallen into a faint, had proper attendants. He spoke to his wife in urgent tones: 'See to our Mother and I will go to do my duty.'[14] He hastened back to the chapel. As he noted in his diary, word of Alexander's death marked 'the end of my happy existence which *he* [Alexander] had created for me! To serve him, to serve his memory, his will, it is to this that I shall devote the remainder of my days – my entire existence!'[15]

Nikolai Pavlovich's first act to serve his brother's memory was to fall on his knees before the altar and there, before the highest court and state dignitaries of the Empire, to swear allegiance to his brother Konstantin

Pavlovich as the new Emperor, Constantine I. He then arose, demanded that all in the chapel follow his example, and left immediately to administer the oath to the Preobrazhenskii Imperial Guards regiment, that morning on guard duty at the Winter Palace. He also ordered the officer of the day in the palace, General A. N. Potapov, to see that the main palace guard swore its allegiance to Constantine, sent his adjutant to administer the oath to the Corps of Engineers which he commanded, and ordered General A. I. Neidhardt to ride immediately to the Aleksandr Nevskii Monastery with orders that the oath should be given to all of the other Imperial Guards regiments as well.[16]

In less than half an hour after word of Alexander's death had reached the Winter Palace, Nikolai Pavlovich, Count Miloradovich, General Adjutant Prince V. B. Trubetskoi and many other leading statesmen and officers who were part of the imperial suite had sworn allegiance to the Emperor Constantine I, and the process of administering the oath to all of the élite troops in the capital was under way.[17] Only after these measures had been taken did Nikolai Pavlovich return to his mother's apartments. The Dowager Empress had regained consciousness, and when she learned what had transpired during the previous half-hour she was dismayed: 'Nicholas, what have you done? Did you not know that there is another manifesto which names you as heir-apparent?'[18] For Mariia Fedorovna, like Alexander's closest confidants Count A. A. Arakcheev, Prince A. N. Golitsyn and the Metropolitan of Moscow, Filaret, knew the full contents of the secret manifesto which Alexander had signed more than two years before in which he had decreed that Nikolai Pavlovich, and not the Grand Duke Konstantin, should rule Russia after his death.

Historians are almost unanimous in faulting Nikolai Pavlovich for so hastily taking the oath to his elder brother after he received news of Alexander's death. Some have argued that he did not even know of the secret manifesto of 1823 which designated him heir-apparent, or that, while he knew of its existence, he did not know its precise contents. In retrospect it appears quite certain that, while Nikolai Pavlovich may not have known its precise wording, he did know that Alexander I had expected him to be Russia's next Emperor. The Dowager Empress's secretary, G. I. Villamov, recorded in his diary as early as 16 March 1807 that Mariia Fedorovna knew 'the throne will go to Grand Duke Nikolai and for this reason his education is especially close to her heart';[19] the Academician Heinrich Storch, in a memorandum of 1810 to the Dowager Empress, referred to Nikolai Pavlovich as the person 'who will one day probably rule us';[20] and the historian P. I. Bartenev noted in 1896 that there was in the Hermitage a medal portraying Nikolai Pavlovich with the inscription 'Tsesarevich Nikolai, 10 January 1809', the very day when all members of the Imperial Family were known to have been closeted with the Dowager Empress for several hours.[21]

Furthermore, some time before 1813, when discussing with his younger brother the need for him to be diligent in pursuing his studies, Alexander I had urged him to 'complete your education, become as much as possible worthy of that position which you will in time come to occupy: this will be the sort of service to our beloved fatherland that an heir to the throne should perform'.[22] Finally, according to the accounts of both Nikolai Pavlovich and his wife, the Grand Duchess Aleksandra Fedorovna, Alexander I had announced at a small family dinner on 13 July 1819 that he would some day retire from his duties as Emperor and that he regarded Nikolai Pavlovich and not Konstantin Pavlovich as his heir.[23] The young couple recorded their reactions to this announcement in considerable detail, and both seem to have greeted the news with some dismay. As Nikolai Pavlovich recalled a number of years later:

The conversation ended and the Emperor departed. My wife and I remained in a position which I can liken only to that sensation which would strike a man going calmly along a comfortable road sown with flowers, and which always has marvellous scenery, when suddenly there yawns wide beneath his feet an abyss into which an irresistible force draws him without allowing him to step back or to turn aside. That is the exact portrayal of our terrible position.[24]

There is, then, considerable evidence to indicate that Nikolai Pavlovich knew he had been chosen to succeed Alexander I, and that the Imperial Family, and those who shared their most intimate confidence, knew it as well. Yet on the morning of 27 November the young Grand Duke immediately swore allegiance to his elder brother as Constantine I. Was it perhaps fear of the Imperial Guards' displeasure that made him take the oath to Constantine rather than assume the crown himself? It was certainly true that Nikolai Pavlovich was not popular with the Imperial Guards though it is not clear just how aware of it he was at that point. But neither was Constantine over-popular with them. He had been away from the capital for nearly a decade when Alexander's death occurred, and was a man notorious for his temper and tendency to brutality.

The dislike of him by the Guards alone, however, would probably not have been enough to prevent Nikolai Pavlovich from assuming the crown on 27 November. He was unpopular because he enforced rigidly all of the regulations, but he did so because he considered it his duty. Had he felt that duty required him to mount the Russian throne at the moment he learned of Alexander's death, there is no reason to think he would not have done so. Quite the contrary, when he assumed the crown some two weeks later, Nikolai Pavlovich knew full well that a revolt among the

Guards was brewing, yet he did his duty as he saw it without hesitation. Clearly neither the question of how much Nikolai Pavlovich knew about the secret manifesto, nor his apprehension about what response his accession might provoke among the Imperial Guards, can explain his initial refusal to assume the crown. The explanation must be sought elsewhere.

Most crucial to understanding Nikolai Pavlovich's actions are his concepts of duty and legitimacy. He was particularly conscious of the need for legitimacy and order in the Russian state. Most of all, he was determined to fulfil his duty as an obligation which he placed above all others. In this context we must review briefly the succession crises which the Russian state had suffered for more than a century since 1722, when Peter the Great had decreed that Russia's Emperor could choose his successor and not be bound by traditional laws of inheritance. Yet Peter had died suddenly in 1725 before designating a successor, and in the resulting series of succession crises, commonly called palace revolutions, the Imperial Guards had played a decisive part in determining who would sit upon the Russian throne. Catherine I, Peter II, Anna Ivanovna, the regent Anna Leopoldovna, Elizabeth I and Catherine II all had ascended the throne as the result of such palace revolutions between 1725 and 1762.

To regularize the situation, Nikolai Pavlovich's father, Paul I, who had been kept from the throne for more than three decades by his mother Catherine II, took steps to re-establish a law of succession on 5 April 1797, when he decreed that the succession in Russia would be by hereditary descent through the male line. The simple whim of the autocrat could thus no longer alter it, and Alexander had, in fact, violated his father's law when, on 16 August 1823, he had signed the secret manifesto declaring that Konstantin Pavlovich had renounced his rights to the Russian throne in favour of his younger brother. According to the law of 1797, Nikolai Pavlovich could indeed become Emperor provided Alexander I had no heirs and Konstantin Pavlovich died or renounced the throne. But therein lay the difficulty. For only Konstantin Pavlovich had the right to designate his successor, and for that action to appear legal in a state which had suffered numerous succession crises and in which there was a growing concern for legality, it was necessary that he do so publicly rather than by an agreement whose exact contents were hidden from all but six individuals in the Empire.

Since his elder brother was thus regarded as the legitimate heir by the succession law of 1797, and by almost everyone in authority in Russia, Nikolai Pavlovich could do little else than take an oath of allegiance to Constantine I. The laws of the Empire required it, and his own sense of legitimacy demanded it. And if there was any doubt about who was considered to be the rightful heir in the public eye, it was only necessary to remember that, throughout Alexander's last illness, courtiers bearing reports about his condition had been dispatched even more frequently to Konstantin Pavlovich in Warsaw than to the Dowager Empress in St Petersburg. As a result, Konstantin Pavlovich learned of his brother's death a full two days before it was known in the Winter Palace. Alexander's wife, Baron Dibich and those of his suite who had accompanied him to Taganrog, all regarded Konstantin Pavlovich as the rightful heir to the throne, and thus took what they considered to be appropriate measures to inform him before anyone else of his brother's condition.

It was most probably all of these factors which Nikolai Pavlovich had in his mind when replying to his mother when she reproached him. 'If there is such a manifesto,' he told her, 'it is not known to me; no one knows of it. But we all know that our master, our legitimate sovereign, is my brother Constantine and we have fulfilled our duty, come what may!'[25] Until Constantine should publicly renounce his title to the throne, the young Grand Duke had no legitimate right to assume the crown and his duty lay in swearing allegiance to his elder brother. As he wrote to Constantine a few days later:

I have sworn the oath to you. Could I, according to any human understanding, have acted otherwise? Could I, forgetting my honour and my conscience, have placed the state, our beloved motherland, in such a difficult position? This would have meant scorning my sacred duty both in regard to you, my master, and in regards to our motherland . . . I, alas, know you well enough so as not to doubt what the result of my actions will be . . . All is in order . . . [but] hasten here for the love of God.[26]

Convinced that he had fulfilled his duty to Constantine, to God and to the memory of Alexander I, Nikolai Pavlovich then returned at about midday to his wife and mother in their Winter Palace apartments.

Nikolai Pavlovich was not alone in thinking that he had acted properly that morning. Alexander I had ordered that copies of his secret manifesto be deposited with the Imperial Senate, the State Council and the Holy Synod, and had written on the sealed envelopes, 'In the event of my death to be opened before proceeding to anything else.' The only man in St Petersburg who knew what these envelopes contained, however, was Prince A. N. Golitsyn, and as soon as he had learned of Alexander's death, he had hastened to Prince P. V. Lopukhin, the president of the Imperial State Council, to urge that the council be summoned into session at once. Once Alexander's secret manifesto had been opened and read, at least two members of the council – the Minister of Justice,

D. I. Lobanov-Rostovskii, and the Minister of Public Instruction, A. S. Shishkov – immediately insisted that the wishes of the dead emperor, even though expressed formally in an imperial manifesto, could not alter the established order of succession. Until he came to St Petersburg and formally renounced the throne, they argued, the State Council must recognize Constantine as their legitimate sovereign, as Nikolai Pavlovich had already done. Prince Lobanov-Rostovskii and Shishkov were joined in their arguments by St Petersburg's Military Governor, Count Miloradovich, who had already taken the oath to Constantine in the Winter Palace chapel that morning. Miloradovich now urged his fellow council members to do likewise.[27]

Nikolai Pavlovich added similar arguments, and the State Council agreed to reassemble that evening to take the oath to Constantine. By that time all the Guards regiments had also hailed Constantine as Emperor, and instructions had been issued to Prince D. V. Golitsyn, Governor-General of Moscow; and to General A. A. Zakrevskii. Governor-General of Finland, to see that the officials and troops in those areas took the oath as well.[28] Within a few days, Constantine had been proclaimed Emperor in Russia's old and new capitals, in the Duchy of Finland, and, as the necessary instructions reached them, in other areas of the Empire.[29]

The Grand Duke Konstantin Pavlovich, who, on the morning of 27 November was proclaimed as the Emperor Constantine I, possessed a personality that was many-sided and complex. Several contemporaries have left portraits of him, and there is a remarkable agreement about his appearance and character. One observer, D. V. Davydov, remarked that

he had a physiognomy which struck everyone by its originality and by the total absence of any pleasant expression. Try to imagine a face with a minuscule nose that turned sharply upward at the end, a face on which a thick growth of hair at two points above the eyes took the place of normal eyebrows. The flesh below the bridge of the nose was decorated with several small, light hairs, which were scarcely noticeable when he was calm, but which, like the eyebrows, stood erect during moments of anger.[30]

Another observer of Russian Court life at the turn of the century considered Konstantin Pavlovich to be 'a son worthy of his father: the same eccentricities, the same severity, and the same turbulence, distinguish him; but he will never possess . . . his capacity, though he promises in time to equal and even surpass him in the art of manoeuvring a dozen automatons'.[31]

Like his father Paul I, Konstantin Pavlovich was often brutal, although this was somewhat tempered by his deference and affection for his parents, and by his complete submissiveness and loyalty first to Alexander I and later to Nikolai Pavlovich after he had ascended the throne as Nicholas I. The French traveller, the Marquis de Custine, was among those to comment that Konstantin Pavlovich had an extremely cruel turn of mind. He recorded how, on one occasion, to demonstrate the discipline of Russia's troops for a foreign observer, Konstantin Pavlovich pierced the foot of one of his generals with his sword while the general remained standing rigidly at attention.[32]

De Custine's portrait may be overdrawn, since no other sources appear to mention this incident. But other and more reliable accounts of the Grand Duke's excesses are quite plentiful. During the critical days of late November and early December 1825, many Russians must have shared the apprehensions which Countess M. D. Nesselrode confided in a letter on 6 December 1825, in which she expressed fears that, should Konstantin Pavlovich assume the Russian crown, his reign would create 'a kingdom of distrust, spying, [and] a vast sea of pettiness, of agonizing captiousness'.[33] The historian A. E. Presniakov has characterized him as 'a typical representative of the "Gatchina School", addicted to ceremonial parades', and 'one of the most vivid representatives of autocratic militarism'.[34]

Even so, Konstantin Pavlovich, though every inch a tyrant, had insisted from the moment of Alexander I's accession in 1801 that should the throne ever come to him, he would not accept it.[35] As the years passed, he became even more persistent in insisting he would never reign, and he became increasingly aloof from other members of the Imperial Family and from Russian affairs. In 1814, he became the commander-in-chief of Russian forces in Poland, where he served as Russia's viceroy in all but name and, in early 1820, he divorced Anna Fedorovna, the wife from whom he had lived apart for nearly two decades. Within two months, he had married the Polish Countess Joanna Grudzinska in a morganatic marriage which excluded their children from inheriting the Russian throne, and less than a year later, he told his youngest brother, the Grand Duke Mikhail Pavlovich, that he considered Nikolai Pavlovich to be the heir apparent.[36]

Konstantin Pavlovich soon took formal steps to remove himself from the Romanov line of succession. During the Christmas holidays in 1821, he came to St Petersburg and told both Alexander I and the Dowager Empress that under no circumstances would he ever accept the Russian throne. Two weeks later, on 14 January 1822, he restated his position in an official letter. Alexander then procrastinated for more than a year, but finally drafted the secret manifesto designating Nikolai Pavlovich as heir on 16 August 1823. The succession issue thus seems to have been settled to the satisfaction of the two elder brothers whatever considerable doubts there were about the legality of this procedure in the minds of some Russian statesmen when, on 27 November 1825, they learned what had been done.

But even though he had been proclaimed Russian Emperor, Constantine would simply have nothing to do with the Russian crown, and for nearly a week no one in St Petersburg was even certain where he might be found. In fact, Constantine had an almost psychotic fear of the Imperial title. Just a few moments after he learned of Alexander's death, he encountered N. N. Novosil'tsev, one of his brother's most trusted councillors. Assuming that the Grand Duke was now Russia's Emperor, Novosil'tsev had addressed him as 'Your Imperial Majesty'. Constantine explained, with considerable anxiety and persistence, that he had renounced the throne several years before in favour of his younger brother, and when Novosil'tsev, still at something of a loss, referred to him again by his Imperial title, the Grand Duke flew into a rage. 'For the last time,' he shouted, 'I ask you to desist, and remember that our one and only sovereign and Emperor is now Nikolai Pavlovich.'[37] But Constantine's anger at Novosil'tsev was mild in comparison to the rage which he vented upon his own adjutant, P. A. Kolzakov, who entered the room only a few moments after Novosil'tsev hurried away. Not knowing otherwise, Kolzakov also greeted the Grand Duke as 'Your Imperial Majesty'. This time Constantine's fury knew no limits. He hurled himself upon the unfortunate officer, seized him by the front of his uniform and roared: 'All right! Shut up! How can you dare speak such words? Do you know what you are exposing yourself to? Do you realize that for this you can be put in chains and sent to Siberia? Consider yourself under arrest and surrender your sword!'[38]

Constantine's refusal to have himself recognized even briefly as Emperor of course baffled his brothers, Russia's statesmen and all who served him. The fact that he had rejected any notion of being Alexander's successor almost from the moment when he learned of his father's murder in 1801 has led some commentators to conclude that he refused the crown out of cowardice. Yet Constantine had displayed considerable valour on the battlefield and had clearly put his life in danger on a number of occasions. He was not a coward, and the reasons for his fear of the Imperial title are far more complex than such clear-cut explanations would indicate. Although we cannot explain his behaviour with real certainty, there appear to have been a number of factors. Certainly his deep sense of inferiority in relation to his elder and younger brothers, all of whom he regarded as more educated and better prepared to rule, was one of them. 'I must say,' he once remarked to some friends, 'that, turning all of her attention to my brother Alexander, the Empress Catherine did not devote herself to me at all during my childhood.'[39] And, if he felt ignored by his grandmother, he felt equally neglected by his mother, Mariia Fedorovna, whose four sons had been born in two groups some two decades apart. Alexander I had been born in 1777, and Konstantin Pavlovich in 1779, while the younger sons, Nikolai and Mikhail, had been born in 1796 and 1798. Soon after the birth of her younger sons, Mariia Fedorovna had been widowed and had become Dowager Empress while her eldest son ruled. No longer burdened by imperial duties, she devoted her years as dowager to the education of her two youngest sons, while Konstantin Pavlovich, already a young man at the time of his father's death, was left to go his own way.

To understand Constantine's personality and attitudes more fully, one must also consider the fact that he may well have been impotent throughout most of his life,[40] and that his first marriage, in which he and his wife lived apart for the last two decades of their union, had been a catastrophe from beginning to end. No children resulted from it, but Constantine's desire for heirs was so intense that at one point he supposedly claimed as his own the child of a certain Madame Friedriks, the wife of the Police Chief of Dubno.[41] Constantine's probable impotence, his disastrous first marriage, and his longing for heirs must be kept in mind when we examine his relationship with Countess Grudzinska.

The countess, who became Princess Lowicza when she wed the Grand Duke in 1820, already had several children by an earlier marriage and provided him with the sort of family life which he evidently craved. Further, she must have provided him with a measure of emotional security which he had not known before, for, as one observer commented, 'the woman who could soften, and almost transform, a character so ferocious and imperious as that of Constantine, must have been herself truly amiable ... Under her influence, he learned self-control, and became a welcome guest even at the Court of the stiff and formal Frederick Augustus, King of Saxony.'[42] But Princess Lowicza was often in poor health and it was necessary for her to visit a number of spas in Germany every year. The Grand Duke went with her and, at least in her company, gave himself up to the joys of family life. Although his mien on the parade-ground remained as brutal and as rigid as before, his marriage thus evidently added a dimension to his life which he had long desired. One thus might well suppose that he was not willing to see this woman, towards whom 'he never dropped the tenderness of the lover, but became daily more and more attached',[43] placed in the painful position of a wife who could not reign as Empress were he to accept the crown.

All of these factors must thus be considered in explaining Constantine's passionate and furious rejection of the crown. Most of all, while he saw himself as an utterly devoted servant of his elder brother Alexander I and, later, of his younger brother Nicholas I, he may well not have felt himself able to deal with the demands of ruling the Russian Empire. Yet, perhaps equally important, the recently found family happiness which he had discovered in his marriage to the Princess Lowicza may have been too precious at this time of his life for him to place the woman he loved in an awkward position. In any case, he considered that the succession question had been settled by Alexander's manifesto of 1823. On the day after he learned of his brother's death, he wrote to Nikolai Pavlovich that he would not accept the throne. But Constantine's letter did not arrive in St Petersburg until the morning of 3 December, some six days after he had been proclaimed as Emperor.[44] When he learned on 2 December that he had been proclaimed Emperor, he left no doubt about his position. 'My resolve is unshakeable and sanctioned by the spirit of my benefactor, Emperor, and Master [Alexander I],' he wrote to Nikolai Pavlovich. 'I cannot accept your invitation to come more quickly to you, and I tell you that I will go even further away if everything is not arranged in conformity with the will of our deceased Emperor.'[45] Constantine would not occupy the throne to which he had been proclaimed, and Russia thus was still without an Emperor.

Given Russia's political tradition, and the fact that the entire concept of autocracy rested upon a theological as well as a secular base, it was inconceivable that the Empire should have been without an Emperor for two full weeks. Yet Nikolai Pavlovich was still not willing to accept the imperial crown on the basis of Alexander's secret manifesto and Constantine's personal letters. The succession turmoil of the past century, and the possibility of another palace revolution, must have haunted him, for, by early December, Count Miloradovich had made him vividly aware of his unpopularity with the Imperial Guards regiments in the capital. Should it seem that he was in any way usurping Constantine's throne, Miloradovich warned, there was serious risk of revolt.[46] Therefore, although Nikolai Pavlovich knew by 3 December that he must be Russia's next Emperor, he urged Constantine to come to St Petersburg and publicly renounce the throne or, at the very least, to send a formal manifesto of abdication so that his own assumption of the imperial crown might be orderly and appear as legitimate as possible.[47]

Nikolai Pavlovich thus devoted the nine days from 3 to 12 December to urging formal renunciation or abdication upon his elder brother in a series of personal letters which were carried back and forth between Warsaw and St Petersburg by their youngest brother, the Grand Duke Mikhail. Yet for reasons that have never come to light, Constantine refused to leave Warsaw and, despite even the pleas of his mother, he refused so much as to send an abdication manifesto. It has been suggested recently by Soviet scholars that, despite his renunciation of the throne in 1822, Constantine still cherished secret hopes of wearing the crown and that he may have considered using the Polish army, nearly 100,000 men strong, to enforce his claim. Such an argument implies that he refused to abdicate, or even come to St Petersburg, because he was preparing his forces in Poland to support his seizure of the throne.[48] But while it is true that Constantine might have been able to use the Polish forces under his command for such a purpose, it is improbable that he planned to do so. His self-imposed isolation from Russian internal affairs, his relationship with Princess Lowicza, his first reactions to the news of Alexander's death, would all argue against such a theory. And, if Constantine had wanted the crown, it was, in fact, his for the asking. Nikolai Pavlovich had proclaimed him Emperor only moments after he had learned of Alexander's death, and had he wanted the imperial title, he needed only go to St Petersburg and instal himself in the Winter Palace.

3. *'Emperor . . . At the Price of My Subjects' Blood'*

Thus, in early December 1825, Russia faced the impossible situation of having an Emperor who refused to recognize himself as such, and who would not even formally abdicate the throne which he did not want to occupy. Realizing that he must soon take the crown even without Constantine's formal abdication, Nikolai Pavlovich had begun to prepare an accession manifesto on 9 December. We cannot know how long this state of affairs would have continued had outside forces not intervened. The impasse was broken very early on the morning of Saturday, 12 December, by the arrival from Taganrog of Baron A. A. Frederiks, a colonel in the Life Guards of the Izmailovskii Regiment and an adjutant to Baron Dibich, the Chief of Staff, who had accompanied Alexander I on his last southern journey.[49]

Dibich had sent Colonel Frederiks from Taganrog to deliver a packet of secret reports marked 'of extreme urgency',[50] and once he had broken the seals on the packet, Nikolai Pavlovich immediately recognized the reason for Dibich's concern. Dibich's dispatches included a report from Alexander I's aide-de-camp, General Count Chernyshev, which contained information so damaging and so potentially explosive that Chernyshev had written out the report himself rather than give it to a secretary and chance a tear in the curtain of secrecy which he and Dibich had drawn around the information they had gathered.[51] With the help of informers, especially I. V. Sherwood and A. I. Maiboroda, Dibich and Chernyshev had uncovered a plot among the officers in Russia's southern army.

Sherwood, an Englishman born in Kent in 1798, had been brought to Russia by his parents at the age of two. He had later entered the Russian army, and while serving in the south had learned of certain secret societies and had reported them to Alexander I. But Sherwood's report had been based on the most superficial sort of hearsay evidence and Alexander had dismissed it as being of no great consequence. Maiboroda, a captain in the southern army, was much more intimately involved in the secret Southern Society of conspirators and was for a time even a confidant of its leader, Colonel P. I. Pestel'. He had learned a great deal more of their plans to overthrow the autocracy and had reported their designs to Alexander. But Alexander had initially discounted Maiboroda's accusations because he thought that the captain was simply seeking to advance his own career. Further disclosures, most notably those made by General Count I. P. Witt, had led Alexander to investigate the charges of Maiboroda and Sherwood more fully, and eventually had enabled Chernyshev and Dibich to disclose the entire Southern Society and its connections with the so-called Northern Society that was centred in St Petersburg itself.[52]

Historians differ as to when Nikolai Pavlovich first learned that secret societies, comprised of young army officers and officials who represented the flower of the Empire's aristocratic youth, existed in Russia for the purpose of overthrowing the autocracy. From his diary, it would appear that he first learned of this 'terrible plot' on the morning of 12 December, when he read Dibich's report. His first thought was that 'most stern measures' must be taken. He sent for Prince A. N. Golitsyn, whom he had consulted about the succession question, ordered his adjutant Colonel V. A. Perovskii to search for N. M. Murav'ev, a captain on the Guards General Staff whom Dibich had named as a leading conspirator in St Petersburg, and summoned Count Miloradovich and a number of military commanders in the city to the Winter Palace for discussions. Most important, Nikolai Pavlovich decided he must mount the throne even without Constantine's abdication. His young wife recorded the event in her diary late that very afternoon:

And so I write in this diary for the first time as Empress. My Nikolai returned and knelt before me in order to be the first to greet me as Empress. Constantine does not want to issue a manifesto and holds firmly to his former decision.[53]

Once he had decided that he must lose no time in assuming the crown, Nikolai Pavlovich hastened to complete his accession manifesto. The day before he had consulted M. M. Speranskii who had, during the years just before Napoleon's invasion of Russia, been Alexander I's closest adviser. Speranskii had fallen from favour on the eve of Napoleon's invasion,[54] but had since been allowed to return from exile to St Petersburg. Because of his expertise in legal matters, Nikolai Pavlovich sought his advice. The man who played the most important role in preparing this document, however, was N. M. Karamzin, Russia's Court Historian and author of the monumental *History of the Russian State*, who was a firm defender of autocracy and the existing social order. Karamzin was a welcome guest at the Winter Palace: in fact, he had been there on the day when word of Alexander's death reached St Petersburg. As Nikolai Pavlovich noted in his diary that day, the Dowager Empress, terribly distraught at news of her eldest son's death, became 'much more calm after a conversation with Karamzin'. Karamzin had been at the Winter Palace nearly every day since then, and on at least one occasion had taken tea with Nikolai Pavlovich and his wife. The Grand Duke had begun to discuss his manifesto with him on 9 December; they had discussed it again two days later and, on 12 December, Karamzin and Speranskii completed the final version.[55]

Nikolai Pavlovich's conviction about the need for haste in ending the interregnum, now entering its fourth week, was further strengthened later that evening. In his diary, the Grand Duke recorded the evening's episode with only the cryptic comment that 'Rostovtsev [a junior lieutenant in the Guards] came with a letter and left';[56] but, in fact, what Rostovtsev had done was to report that there was a broad conspiracy afoot in St Petersburg itself to overthrow the autocracy, and that a number of Guards officers were involved. Rostovtsev has been accused of revealing the Northern Society's plans to Nikolai Pavlovich for reasons of personal gain,[57] because he wished, as it were, 'to light a candle both to God and to the Devil'.[58] But it is much more probable that he did so out of a deep loyalty to the throne and that his revelations about the Northern Society caused him a great deal of personal anguish. Certainly that is what his close friend, Prince E. P. Obolenskii, believed, and although Obolenskii suffered many years' exile for his part in the Decembrist revolt, the two men remained close friends until Rostovtsev's death in 1860 since the prince believed in the nobility of his friend's motives in reporting the plot.

What Rostovtsev revealed about the conspiracy in St Petersburg was evidently no more than Nikolai Pavlovich had already learned from Dibich's urgent dispatches that morning. But Rostovtsev's revelations were an important factor in spurring him to action because of what the young lieutenant had to say about the temper of the Guards in St Petersburg. Rostovtsev had urged Nikolai Pavlovich 'either to refuse the throne or to wait for a formal . . . renunciation from the Tsesarevich' if he wished 'to prevent bloodshed'.[59] The Grand Duke therefore concluded that time was of the essence, that it was necessary for him to act 'not losing a moment, with full powers, and . . . with decisiveness'.[60] Nikolai Pavlovich had thus decided by the evening of 12 December that he must order the oath of allegiance to be taken to him on the morning of the 14th. He signed the manifesto announcing his accession the next morning, but back-dated it to Saturday, 12 December, the day of his decision. The manifesto carefully detailed the passage of events since word of Alexander's death had reached St Petersburg: the proclamation of Constantine as Emperor, Constantine's refusal of the crown and, finally, Nikolai Pavlovich's decision to become Emperor in his stead. Equally important, he ordered the immediate publication of Alexander I's secret manifesto of 16 August 1823, that named him heir apparent, the letters dated 14 January and 2 February 1822, in which Konstantin Pavlovich renounced the throne, and the letters which Konstantin Pavlovich had sent to the Dowager Empress and to him on 26 November 1825, affirming his decision not to reign.[61] By doing so, Nikolai Pavlovich hoped to make clear that his elder brother would, under no circumstances, accept the Russian crown, and that his determination to renounce the throne was, in the language of the manifesto itself, 'absolute and irrevocable'.

Nikolai Pavlovich had only twenty-four hours left in which to make all necessary preparations for his accession, and he was quite certain that he would face a revolt that morning. Once the manifesto announcing his accession as the Emperor Nicholas I had been prepared and signed, the most pressing need was to decide what measures should be taken in the capital to deal with the threatening revolt. So, to decide what steps would be most effective, Nikolai Pavlovich summoned the Minister of War, General A. I. Tatishchev, to ask his advice. Tatishchev proposed that any known conspirators who could be found in the capital should be put into prison immediately. But Nikolai Pavlovich refused to see his reign begin with a flurry of arrests and therefore rejected the general's advice: 'No, do not do it. I do not wish the oath [to me] to be preceded by arrests. Think of what an ugly impression we should make on everyone.' Tatishchev pointed out that, if the arrests were not made, then the chances for a revolt would be greater. 'Then let it be so,' responded the Grand Duke. 'The arrests then will astonish no one; people will not then regard them as unjust or arbitrary.'[62]

Until 13 December, Constantine's absolute refusal to accept the crown, and Nikolai Pavlovich's plan to proclaim himself Emperor on the following day, were closely guarded secrets known to almost no one outside the Winter Palace. Apart from the Imperial Family and their personal secretaries, only Nikolai Pavlovich's most trusted adjutants, General A. Kh. Benkendorf and Colonel V. F. Adlerberg, St Petersburg's Military

Governor-General, Count Miloradovich, the Minister of War, Tatishchev, the State Council President, Prince P. V. Lopukhin, and a very few others knew of what was in store. To make certain that his accession would not be opposed by the Empire's senior statesmen, Nikolai Pavlovich informed the Foreign Minister, Count K. V. Nesselrode, of his plans on the morning of 13 December, and then asked Prince Lopukhin to summon a special and secret meeting of the State Council that evening. The Grand Duke Mikhail Pavlovich was expected to return from Warsaw that afternoon, and Nikolai Pavlovich planned that both of them would tell the State Council that Constantine had absolutely renounced the throne. Since Constantine had told Mikhail Pavlovich of this personally during the latter's stay in Warsaw, Nikolai Pavlovich hoped that it would add further legitimacy to his claim and put to rest suspicions that he might be usurping the throne. This was particularly necessary, he believed, since there were rumours afoot that Constantine had not renounced the throne but was being held in chains somewhere on the road between Warsaw and St Petersburg.[63]

In response to Nikolai Pavlovich's request, the State Council assembled in the Winter Palace for an unprecedented evening session.[64] When all of the twenty-three members present in the capital at the time had assembled, Prince Lopukhin announced that the Grand Duke would attend the meeting but would arrive later. Then began several hours of anxious anticipation while the council sat awaiting the Grand Duke's arrival.

At eleven o'clock, Nikolai Pavlovich ordered dinner to be served to the members while they sat in the chamber. Dinner was finished, the hour of midnight came and went, and still they sat.[65] Nikolai Pavlovich appeared shortly after midnight, but he came alone. He had awaited his younger brother's arrival from Warsaw for the entire day and half the night, and since it was already 14 December had concluded that he must address the council without him. Addressing the silent assembly, the Grand Duke reviewed the unprecedented events of the past two weeks. He reminded the council that he had been the first to swear allegiance to Constantine, that he had urged them to do likewise, that Constantine had refused the imperial crown and that there was now no alternative but for him to become Emperor himself. He then asked them to approve his actions, remarking that 'today, I request you to take the oath; tomorrow I shall command you'.[66] This statement, in fact, set the tone for his relationship with the State Council throughout the entire course of his thirty-year reign. As he told Baron M. A. Korf some years later, 'The Council exists . . . solely for the purpose of conscientiously giving me its view on those questions about which I seek such opinions: no more and no less . . .'[67]

The stage was thus set for the final act of the drama, but we should now turn to the conspiracy brewing among some of the younger Guards officers. Ever since Russia's armies had returned from Western Europe after their victories over Napoleon in 1812–15, there had been growing in Russia a number of secret societies composed of men whose ambition was to improve Russian life and to make it conform more to that which they had experienced in the West.[68] There were, in fact, three secret societies which were involved to some extent in the events of 14 December 1825. Two of them – the Southern Society and the Society of the United Slavs – took no part in the revolt in Russia's capital itself, though when a distorted version of the events reached them later that month, soldiers and officers of the Chernigov and Poltava regiments loyal to these two groups began to march northward, only to be stopped in a bloody encounter with loyal government forces near Belaia Tserkov in the Ukraine. It was the third society, the Northern Society, which played the central role in the events of 14 December in St Petersburg itself.

The Northern and Southern Societies, as well as the Society of the United Slavs, were the offspring of the Union of Welfare which had been active in Russia between 1818 and 1821 and which was itself an outgrowth of an earlier organization known as the Union of Salvation. We know very little of this first organization, though we know a good deal more about its successor, the Union of Welfare. Both organizations were modelled upon the *Tugendbund*, a German patriotic society of the Napoleonic period which had striven for Prussian spiritual and national regeneration. They also embodied a mixture of the ideals of freemasonry in its Russian form,[69] of German Romanticism, and some of the ideals of the eighteenth-century Enlightenment. Originally, it would seem that these groups of young officers and Russian patriots, motivated by what they had seen in the West, had hoped to promote social and political progress in the Empire within the framework of the established order.

These young aristocrats were initially imbued with a deeply romantic attachment to the person of Alexander I. Especially in the case of their leaders, they had reached maturity in time to march with Russia's victorious armies to the West where they had seen their Emperor emerge as a heroic figure. Alexander's liberal pronouncements in the West, his even-handed treatment of France, and his generosity to the Polish Kingdom, had all given them hope that he would treat Russia in a like manner. Such men were well exemplified by Tolstoi's character Nikolai Rostov in *War and Peace*, a young man who had rushed to join the colours at an early age in 1812, and whose romantic attachment to the Emperor was so intense that he was struck nearly speechless at the sight of him in the distance. These young men, then, at first had absolute faith in the autocracy as the social and political corrective force best able to right the wrongs which they perceived in the Russian state and society. If only the Emperor knew of the evils which flourished in his Empire, they believed that he would right them immediately. Therefore the young members of the Unions of Salvation (1816–18) and of Welfare (1818–21) saw it as the purpose of their societies to advise their Emperor about the injustices in Russian society. Surely a ruler who had urged Louis XVIII to grant the Charter of 1814 to France, and who had granted a constitution to the Polish Kingdom over which he had just begun to rule, would do no less for their beloved Russia.

But they soon became bitterly disillusioned with the Emperor whom they had idolized. When they returned to Russia after the wars, they found that General Count A. A. Arakcheev, a martinet notorious for his cruelty, was gaining more and more influence in the direction of Russia's internal affairs. With Arakcheev's rise came also a new institution, the military colonies, which were to serve as Russia's first line of defence, reduce the Empire's military costs and enable soldiers to spend part of their time in agriculture rather than in endless parade drill. But under Arakcheev's stewardship, the colonies became living monuments to brutality, cruelty and inefficiency.[70] Furthermore, the long-anticipated constitution for Russia did not materialize, and Alexander seemed more concerned about Western European issues than about Russian problems. The evils of serfdom continued unabated and, in fact, increased. And the growing bureaucracy, which the nobility had always seen as an impersonal force interposing itself between the Emperor and his most loyal subjects to the great detriment of both, continued to rule the land.

Since, by virtue of their natures and their military training, these young men sought action rather than contemplation, they became increasingly impatient as the years passed. The year 1820 served as a critical watershed in crystallizing their opinions when Alexander I ordered the brutal suppression of the so-called 'Semenovskii Revolt'. It had not, in fact, been a revolt at all, but simply a case where junior officers refused to follow the sadistic and cruel orders of their commander, Colonel G. E. Schwartz, on the parade ground.[71] Furthermore, in the same year, Alexander had agreed to the use of force in suppressing revolts against the Habsburg monarchy in Naples, as well as to the strict suppression of dissent in Russia's military colonies.

Because the young officers' idolization of their Emperor had been so intense, their disillusionment was all the more bitter. As a result, by the beginning of 1821, they came to reject their earlier 'advisory' role and began to regard themselves as conspirators. They would no longer seek change through autocracy, but would destroy it so as to replace it with

some variety of constitutional government. Such realizations came as an
intense psychological shock for many of the members of Russia's secret
societies and, when reorganization of the Union of Welfare along con-
spiratorial lines was proposed in 1821, a number of them could not
accept such a course and took no further part.[72] Those who remained
were to become the leaders of the secret societies of which the Northern
and Southern Societies were the most important.

The division between these two societies, and, indeed, the reason for
forming them in the first place, was initially geographical. The Northern
Society was centred in Moscow and, particularly, St Petersburg, while
the Southern Society had its centre at the headquarters of the Second
Army in the Ukraine. In both cases, their views were as yet unfocused,
and while their members shared a belief in progress and social justice and
a common love of Russia, they had not yet determined how their aims
should be institutionalized. However, the differences which separated the
groups in the north and the south soon became far more serious than the
geographical ones, especially as they began to formulate programmes and
to draft institutional patterns for a future Russia. The Northern Society,
whose leading theoretician was N. M. Murav'ev, a young captain in the
Guards, soon came to favour some type of constitutional monarchy, while
the Southern Society, dominated by the powerful, forceful and brilliant
personality of Colonel P. I. Pestel', sought the creation of a republic.[73]

Their divergent visions of Russia's future appear to have kept both
societies apart between 1821 and 1825, though in 1824 they did agree to a
plan of common action: if one group began a revolt, the other would
follow. Their differences, however, were in fact more over means than
over ends by the time that the death of Alexander I occurred. Murav'ev
still proposed a constitutional monarchy, though one in which the
monarch would have very limited powers,[74] while Pestel' still urged a
republic. But Pestel' proposed to implement his republic by means of a
temporary dictatorship,[75] something which Murav'ev found abhorrent.
As he wrote in 1821:

The experience of all peoples and all times shows that Autocratic Power is
destructive both for rulers and for society. It is in agreement neither with the
laws of our holy faith nor with the bases of sound reason. It is impossible to
tolerate as the basis of government the arbitrary will of a single individual. One
cannot accept the notion that all rights belong to one side and all obligations
belong to the other.[76]

This basic disagreement over the role that dictatorial power would
play in the transition from autocracy to a constitutional government
seems to have been the factor which kept Murav'ev and Pestel' apart.

This was the situation in which the secret societies found themselves when they learned of Alexander's death. Pestel' still had not completed the definitive draft of his programme, *Russkaia Pravda* (*Russian Law*), and Murav'ev would only put the final formulation of his constitutional ideas on paper when he was in the Peter-Paul Fortress awaiting his sentence. But the momentary disarray of the forces of order resulting from more than three weeks without an Emperor seemed to them too good an opportunity to let slip away. Furthermore, the authorities were closing in on the secret societies. Dibich and Chernyshev in the south had already begun a series of arrests which would soon sweep even Pestel' himself into their net. Although news of the arrests in the south was not yet fully known in the north, the succession crisis seemed an ideal moment for an uprising. The members of the Northern Society therefore planned a revolt in connection with Nikolai Pavlovich's accession. When the Guards were asked to take the traditional oath of allegiance to Nicholas I, they would inform the rank and file that Constantine was their lawful Emperor, that his younger brother was attempting to usurp the throne, and then would order the men under their command to march to the centre of the city to defend Constantine's right to the throne. In reality, they planned to do away with the autocracy and to implement some sort of constitutional order in its stead.

The strength of the conspirators was not, however, spread evenly through all of the Guards regiments in the capital. They were especially strong among the junior officers of the Moskovskii Regiment, the Grenadier Life Guards and the Marine Guards, but had much less support elsewhere. Most important, they had very little following in one of the oldest Guards regiments – the Preobrazhenskii – nor did they have the support of the artillery, the Horse Guards or the Chevalier Guards. And when the conspirators had approached the commander of the Semenovskii Guards regiment, General S. P. Shipov, a close friend of the Southern Society's leader Colonel Pestel', he had bluntly refused his support, telling one of the conspirators, Prince S. P. Trubetskoi, that Nikolai Pavlovich was 'an enlightened European, while Constantine was a malicious barbarian'.[77] Thus it was clear by the evening of 13 December that the conspirators could not hope for support in their revolt from any but a few regiments, a situation which led one of their leaders, Prince Trubetskoi, to comment that 'this is a hopeless undertaking from which nothing but ruin will result'.[78] Nevertheless, they decided to push ahead with their plans, despite the almost certain defeat that awaited them. As the poet K. F. Ryleev said on the evening before the revolt, 'I am certain that we shall suffer ruin, but our example will remain. We shall sacrifice ourselves for the future freedom of our motherland.'[79]

The conspirators, whom history would remember as the 'Decembrists', thus prepared to act on the morning of 14 December. They expected to suffer defeat since they had now learned that Nikolai Pavlovich knew something of their plot. But, as one of the conspirators commented, they preferred to 'be taken on the [Senate] Square than in our beds'.[80] Nikolai Pavlovich, however, was by no means certain of what the morning of 14 December would bring, and, as he said to his close friend and aide-de-camp, General Benkendorf, 'perhaps by this evening, neither of us will still be among the living, but, at least, we will die in fulfilling our duty'.[81] With these doubts in their minds, both the Grand Duke and the conspirators began to assemble their forces in the early-morning hours of 14 December, and prepared to do their duty as their consciences dictated.

December the 14th was a Monday, an unlucky day according to Russian superstition. The temperature that morning was some eight degrees below freezing, and an icy wind, which cut through all but the warmest clothing and inflicted severe pain on exposed skin, swept in from the Gulf of Finland. It was a morning on which it would be misery to be anywhere but in the shelter of a well-heated room, with the windows sealed and heavy curtains drawn against the cold.

Nikolai Pavlovich had arisen well before dawn to meet all the generals and colonels of the Imperial Guards whom he had ordered to assemble at 5 a.m. at the Winter Palace.[82] He stood before them, explained that Constantine's unalterable decision had forced him to ascend the throne, and ordered them to swear allegiance to him as Emperor. That being done, he addressed to them an ominous warning: 'After this, you will answer to me with your heads for the tranquillity of the capital. As far as I am concerned, even if I shall be Emperor for only one hour, I shall show myself worthy of the honour.'[83]

The new Emperor's initial impressions were that all was going well in the capital that morning. The senior Guards officers had assured him of their loyalty, and by 7 a.m. the members of the Imperial Senate and the Holy Synod had been in their appointed places to take the oath to him.[84] Somewhat later, Count Miloradovich arrived at the Winter Palace and, as Military Governor-General of the city, reported that all was quiet. Soon after Miloradovich had made his report, the commander of the Imperial Horse Guards, aide-de-camp General A. F. Orlov, arrived to say that his regiment had taken the oath. Orlov was followed by the commander of the Guards' artillery, Major-General I. O. Sukhozanet, with word that his troops had sworn the oath as well, though a few junior officers had expressed the fear that Mikhail Pavlovich was being kept under arrest because he did not support the transfer of power from Constantine to Nicholas.[85] Sukhozanet, a rigid disciplinarian and absolutely loyal to the throne, reported that he had had these officers arrested. But Nicholas tended to be more lenient. His younger brother had at that moment arrived from Warsaw, and he ordered him to go to the Guards' artillery and to explain that Constantine had told him personally that he would not accept the crown.[86] But the impression of general calm and order was not to last long. Shortly before noon, Major-General A. I. Neidhardt, Chief of Staff of the Guards Corps, arrived breathless from his gallop. He reported: 'Sire, the Moskovskii Regiment is in full revolt. [Brigade Commander-General V. N.] Shenshin and [Regimental Commander-General Baron P. A.] Frederiks have been seriously wounded and the rebels are marching towards the Senate!'[87]

Confusion had reigned at the barracks of the Moskovskii Regiment that morning. Being especially strong among the regiment's junior officers, the conspirators had managed to convince the rank and file not to take the oath to Nicholas by arguing that Constantine had not re-nounced the throne but was being held prisoner, together with his youngest brother, the Grand Duke Mikhail Pavlovich, somewhere on the road from Warsaw to St Petersburg. Having gained the confidence of the regiment's rankers, Staff Captain M. A. Bestuzhev had issued them with live ammunition instead of the blank charges which they usually carried, and the regiment, some seven hundred strong, prepared to march towards the Senate Square where the conspirators had agreed to assemble their forces.[88]

When the conspirators started to lead the troops of the Moskovskii Regiment from their barracks, Generals Shenshin and Frederiks, to-gether with Colonel P. K. Khvoshchinskii, tried to turn them back. To prevent the plot from being foiled after its initial success, Bestuzhev tried to shoot Frederiks, only to have his pistol misfire.[89] A moment later, Prince Shchepin-Rostovskii, another Staff Captain in the regiment, had drawn his sabre, dealt the Baron a severe head wound, and only the intervention of Mikhailo Kuzmin, Frederiks's personal servant, had saved him from death.[90] Shchepin-Rostovskii then turned upon General Shenshin, slashed him with his sabre, and then attacked Khvoshchinskii. The colonel dodged aside, so avoiding the main force of the blow and being only struck in the back with the flat of the Prince's sabre.[91] Within the space of a few moments, three senior officers of the Moskovskii Regiment had fallen beneath the weapons of the insurgents.

The die was cast. The expected and feared revolt had begun. On his first day as Emperor, if he was to remain upon the Russian throne, Nicholas I would have to crush an insurrection led by young officers representing some of the greatest noble families in the Empire. For an officer who had never yet seen combat, the young Emperor conducted

himself with considerable presence of mind. He sent General A. I.
Neidhardt to the Horse Guards barracks with orders that they mount
and remain in readiness for further instructions, while he ordered
General S. S. Strekalov to assemble the First Battalion of the
Preobrazhenskii Guards in front of the Winter Palace.[92] Finally, he
detailed another aide-de-camp, Colonel A. A. Kavelin, to hasten to the
Anichkov Palace and bring the Empress and their children to the Winter
Palace where the Guard was heavier.[93] Nicholas then turned to leave the
Palace so as to lead the Preobrazhenskiis against the insurgents on the
Senate Square. On the stairs he met one of his adjutants, General S. P.
Apraksin, the commander of the Chevalier Guards, and 'sharply reminded
him that his place was . . . with his troops'.[94] Reaching the square in
front of the Winter Palace, Nicholas found the Preobrazhenskiis, selected
from among the tallest and most handsome men in the Empire, drawn up
in ranks awaiting his command. Accompanied by his aides, Generals
P. V. Kutuzov and S. S. Strekalov, and by Colonels N. D. Durnovo,
V. A. Perovskii and V. F. Adlerberg, Nicholas took his place at the head
of his soldiers. As he later recalled, 'This was an unparalleled moment in
my life! No artist can portray the heroic, honourable, and calm appearance
of this, the truly greatest battalion in the world, at such a critical moment.'
He then gave the order; 'To the attack in columns!'[95] and the first of the
many troops who would remain loyal to him that day sprang into action.

When the Preobrazhenskiis had marched some 300 metres to the point
where the Nevskii Prospekt intersected the Admiralty Boulevard,
Nicholas learned that their weapons were as yet unloaded. Stopping and
giving the order to load muskets with combat ammunition, he also
dispatched Colonel Perovskii to the Horse Guards barracks with orders
that they meet him at St Isaac's Square, not far from the Senate Square,
by now held by the rebels.[96] It was at that moment that Prince A. M.
Golitsyn from the General Staff galloped up with word that Count
Miloradovich, who had gone to the Senate Square to calm the insurgents,
had been mortally wounded. Miloradovich, who had fought through some
fifty battles untouched by any enemy weapon, died from a Russian
bullet fired from the pistol of P. G. Kakhovskii, a retired lieutenant who
had joined the conspirators. From a vantage point in the crowd, where
the muzzle of his weapon almost touched his quarry, the young ex-
lieutenant had pressed the pistol to the count's side, just under his Cross
of St Andrew, and had fired at point-blank range.[97] Thus Miloradovich,
who possibly more than any other figure in St Petersburg governing circles
had feared the possibility of revolt, and who had, as a result, perhaps
over-emphasized the extent of disaffection among the Guards, was the
first of only two men to fall on the government's side that day. Ironically,

the other casualty among the loyal forces, Colonel N. K. Stürler, commander of the Grenadier Life Guards, would also die from a ball fired by Kakhovskii's weapon later that afternoon.[98]

Since Orlov's Horse Guards had not yet reached St Isaac's Square, Nicholas halted his Preobrazhenskiis, posting guards on their flanks to prevent the rapidly gathering populace of St Petersburg from mixing with them. During this time, he clearly heard shouts of, 'Hurrah for Constantine!' coming from the ranks that the Moskovskii Regiment and the other insurgents had formed on the Senate Square. It was only a matter of minutes before Orlov and his Horse Guards arrived. Nicholas then began to see to the disposition of his forces, posting the Horse Guards, the Preobrazhenskiis and the recently arrived Chevalier Guards at various points around the Senate Square.[99] While the troops were moving into position, he ordered his adjutant and close friend, Colonel V. F. Adlerberg, to return to the Winter Palace and, if necessary, to take his wife, the Dowager Empress and the Imperial children out of St Petersburg to their summer residence at Tsarskoe Selo some twenty miles away, escorted by a squadron of Chevalier Guards to ensure their safety. He then sent for the Guards' artillery to advance from its barracks and to take up positions within sight and range of the Senate Square.[100]

Nicholas had not acted a moment too soon in ensuring the safety of the Imperial Family. A portion of the Grenadier Life Guards, in disarray and without officers except for one rebel lieutenant, N. A. Panov, had marched to the Winter Palace in hopes of seizing them. Only the timely arrival of loyal troops had prevented their plan from succeeding. As Nicholas recalled some years later, when he wrote his recollections of the day's events, 'if the Sapper Battalion had been delayed by only a few minutes, then the Palace and all of Our family would have been in the hands of the rebels'.[101] Nicholas encountered these same rebel Grenadier Life Guards near the General Staff Headquarters only moments after they had turned away from the Winter Palace, though he did not know at the time what their earlier intentions had been. In response to his order to halt, the Grenadiers replied: 'We are for Constantine!' 'Very well,' Nicholas supposedly responded, pointing to the Senate Square, 'your place is over there!'[102] Most ironically of all, because they did not recognize their new Emperor, the rebel Grenadier Guards, who a few moments before had been foiled in their efforts to seize the Imperial Family, marched directly past the young ruler whom they were hoping to overthrow. Had but one soldier recognized him, Nicholas would have fallen into the hands of the insurgents.

Now that it had become generally clear which army units were loyal to him and which were not, Nicholas prepared to deal with the rebels.

He had assembled a vastly superior force: the Horse Guards, the Preobrazhenskiis and the Semenovskiis holding the advanced positions, while the Izmailovskiis (who had at first seemed on the verge of joining the rebellion but who had been brought safely into the vicinity of the square by Nicholas's aide-de-camp, General V. V. Levashov), the Chevalier Guards and the Chasseur Guards were held in reserve.[103] It was already nearly three o'clock, and in the northern winter would be dark within an hour or so. The situation on the square was becoming increasingly tense as the rebels, having stood there for more than four hours, began to fire their weapons at random. Few injuries had as yet been inflicted upon by-standers or loyal troops, but, when the Grand Duke Mikhail Pavlovich had advanced to the rebels in an effort to convince them to surrender, a civil servant who had joined the Decembrists, I. I. Pushchin, suggested to one of his comrades, the poet V. K. Küchelbecker, that he ought to 'graze' him with a shot from his pistol. Küchelbecker aimed and pressed the trigger, but the weapon misfired and Mikhail Pavlovich retreated.[104] To make the situation more potentially explosive, the workmen who were building St Isaac's Cathedral began to throw pieces of firewood at the loyal troops,[105] and the large crowd of civilians, which had assembled to watch the spectacle, began to mingle with the insurgents. As the French journalist J. H. Schnitzler recalled, Nicholas was

displeased at the presence of so many idle spectators. He advanced . . . and several times requested the crowd to retire. 'Do me the favour,' he said, 'to return home. You have nothing to do here.' They retired a few steps, and then, impelled by curiosity, returned. I did the same, and near me some old women remained, in equally flagrant disobedience, repeating, 'He comes to ask us himself! And how politely, too!'[106]

Nicholas therefore resolved that decisive measures must be taken. He ordered first a cavalry attack against the insurgents. The Horse Guards, resplendent in their red-collared white uniforms, their brass helmets glinting dully under the darkening winter sky, attacked in squadrons against the massed rebel force, but because their horses were not properly shod for attacks over icy pavements, they were unable to gain the momentum necessary for a charge, and slid rather than galloped towards their objective. The rebels fired into the ranks of the attacking cavalry and wounded a number of them, including Colonel O. O. Velliot, who lost an arm to a musket ball fired by one of the mutineers in the Moskovskii regiment.[107] As Nicholas later recalled, 'they could accomplish nothing because of the confined space, the icy pavement and, in particular, because they did not have sharpened sabres'.[108] Indeed, because they were more prepared for parades than for combat, all the cavalry that day answered the Emperor's summons with unsharpened parade-ground sabres.

After the Chevalier Guards had been ordered to the attack and had suffered a similar setback, Nicholas finally made the decision that he had postponed from the moment he had arrived at St Isaac's Square. With the greatest reluctance, he decided that the artillery must be used against the insurgents. It is generally agreed by scholars who have studied the events of this fateful day that the young Emperor tried to avoid bloodshed by every means possible, and that throughout the entire day he had not ordered any of his troops to fire. In fact, when his aide-de-camp, General K. F. Tol had exclaimed, gesturing towards the rebels, that 'grape [shot] is what they want! . . . The only way to put an end to this is to turn the cannon upon this rabble,'[109] Nicholas had rejected his advice. Only after his aide-de-camp, General Prince I. V. Vasil'chikov, had pleaded, 'Sire, there is not a moment to lose! You can do nothing else! You must give the order to fire!'[110] did Nicholas conclude that there was no other way to end the uprising before nightfall. Turning sadly to his aide-de-camp, Nicholas posed a fateful question. 'Would you have me spill the blood of my subjects on the first day of my reign?' 'Yes, sire,' the Prince replied, 'to save your Empire.'[111] With this, the artillery was given orders to load their weapons.

But Nicholas was unwilling to turn field-guns upon his subjects without making one final effort to convince them to lay down their weapons. He therefore sent Major-General I. O. Sukhozanet to tell them that the artillery was to be brought into action if they did not surrender immediately.[112] Sukhozanet had no success in convincing the rebels. He returned to the command post to report, and Nicholas then gave the order: 'The guns to fire in order beginning from the right flank.'[113] Twice, Nicholas countermanded his own order and the guns remained silent. The third time, the guns roared one after another, most of them throwing shot into the centre of the insurgent mass. It was only moments before the rebels broke ranks and sought to escape the deadly iron hail that fell in their midst. Staff Captain M. A. Bestuzhev sought to rally them on the ice of the Neva River in an effort to lead them against the Peter and Paul Fortress whose guns could command not only the Admiralty, the Senate and the Synod, but the Winter Palace itself. But Nicholas's gunners turned their cannon on the frozen surface of the Neva and the ice began to crack after only a few balls had broken through. The rebels then broke and dispersed in all directions.[114]

Nicholas did not even remain to see the final moments of the action. As soon as it became clear that the insurgents' resistance was broken, he turned and hurried to the Winter Palace where his wife and mother, who had refused to leave for Tsarskoe Selo, had remained to await the outcome. But even before he returned to his Empress, Nicholas had issued the last orders for dealing with the catastrophe that had taken place that day. To his trusted aide-de-camp General Benkendorf, soon to become head of Russia's new Gendarmerie, the Third Section, Nicholas gave the order to comb Vassilevskii Island and arrest all conspirators who could be found; to another aide-de-camp, General Prince I. V. Vasil'chikov, he gave the same task on the other side of the Neva, where the Winter Palace, the Admiralty and all the government offices were located.[115] All suspected of being involved were to be arrested and brought to Nicholas, who slept not at all but remained in the Winter Palace throughout the night as the first prisoners were brought in. Prince Eugene of Württemberg remarked that Nicholas was like Caesar that night,[116] as dispatches from Vasil'chikov and Benkendorf poured in. 'My rooms were much like a general headquarters during a campaign,' Nicholas later recalled. 'Everywhere they were rounding up fleeing soldiers.'[117]

According to the best recollections of Nicholas and of Prince Eugene of Württemberg, the first prisoner to be brought in was Prince D. A. Shchepin-Rostovskii, the Staff Captain from the Moskovskii Regiment who had wounded two generals and a colonel with his sabre. He appeared before his Emperor in bespattered and torn full-dress uniform, his epaulettes having been ripped from his shoulders after his arrest.[118] As Nicholas recalled the scene, 'We had suspected that he was the main leader of the revolt; but from his very first words one could be assured that he was only a blind weapon of others.'[119] After Shchepin-Rostovskii, a continuous procession of prisoners was brought before Nicholas, but the most dramatic event of the night came only later. Nicholas soon learned from one of the Bestuzhev brothers that Prince S. P. Trubetskoi had been acknowledged as leader of the rebels before the revolt began. Trubetskoi was not easily found, and it was only after some considerable searching that Nicholas's aides learned that he had taken refuge in the home of his brother-in-law, the Austrian ambassador Count Lebzeltern, who agreed to his arrest only after direct requests had come from Foreign Minister, Count Nesselrode, and from Nicholas himself. Trubetskoi began his interview with Nicholas by maintaining that he knew nothing of the conspiracy. But when Nicholas showed him evidence to the contrary, the man who had been the Decembrists' choice to lead their hoped-for new government completely lost his nerve. When the Grand Duke Mikhail Pavlovich entered Nicholas's rooms later that night, he saw Trubetskoi on his knees before his Emperor, tearfully begging for his life.[120]

Throughout that night, the following day and the next night, Nicholas and his aides questioned one prisoner after another. At one point, soon after he had first returned to the palace, Russia's new Emperor took up his pen and wrote: 'Dear, dear Constantine. Your will has been done: I am Emperor, but, my God, at what a price! At the price of my subjects' blood!'[121] When Nicholas had left the Winter Palace on the morning of the revolt, his crown had sat awkwardly and he did not know if he would live to see night fall. He had returned to the Winter Palace an Emperor, the conqueror of a revolution. And this would have far-reaching consequences for his reign. Emerging victorious from the Decembrist revolt, he came to see himself as the champion of order both at home and abroad. Convinced that if he could defeat revolution in Russia, he could also destroy it abroad, Nicholas defended the established order in Western Europe both in 1830 and in 1848. As the result of his efforts, he would become known well before the end of his reign as the 'Gendarme of Europe'.

2

The Education
of a
Drill-Master

*'Here [in the army] there is order . . . All things
flow logically, one from the other. No one here
commands without first learning to obey. No one
rises above anyone else except through a
clearly defined system. Everything is subordinated
to a single, defined goal, and everything has
its precise designations. That is why I shall always
hold the title of soldier in high esteem. I regard
all human life as being nothing more than service
because everyone must serve'*

NICHOLAS I

1. The Birth of a Grand Duke

The prince who ascended Russia's throne on 14 December 1825 was a
striking figure of a man. As the Marquis de Custine described him:

he is taller than ordinary men by half a head . . . [with] a Grecian profile . . .
a straight and perfectly formed nose, a finely shaped mouth, and a noble countenance which is shaped in a rather elongated oval. He has a military air about him
which is rather more Germanic than Slavic. His carriage and attitudes are
naturally imposing . . . The Emperor Nicholas is more sincere [than his brother
Alexander I] but has a habitual expression of severity which sometimes gives
the impression of harshness and inflexibility. However, if he is less charming
[than his late brother] he is more firm. The Emperor Nicholas . . . desires to
be obeyed where others desire to be loved.[1]

The ladies at the British Court were infatuated with him when he visited England in 1816, and one of them remarked at the time that 'he is devilish handsome; he will be the handsomest man in all of Europe'.[2]

All who encountered him agree that Nicholas looked every inch the autocrat, a man above men who seemed born to rule an empire that covered one sixth of the earth's surface and stretched from the Polish border nearly 7,000 miles eastward to the Pacific. Like the far-flung holdings of Britain in the nineteenth century, the sun never really set upon the Russian Empire; as evening descended upon its Western frontier, the dawn was already colouring the sky along its Pacific shores. The vastness of its steppes, its forests of birch and pine, its snow-covered wastes, seemed limitless. The journey overland from one end of the Empire to the other took over a year. And, within this vast domain, one man held sway over millions, most of whom were serfs of noblemen or of the state, and all of whom, from the greatest lord to the poorest beggar, were subject to the autocrat's will. Not without reason did the imperial anthem speak of the Emperor as 'reigning in glory, for the glory of us all'.

Yet Nicholas had not been born to rule this vast domain. Born on 25 June 1796, he came into a family which already had two adult sons. His eldest brother, the Grand Duke Aleksandr Pavlovich, who would ascend the throne as Alexander I some five years later, was already nearing nineteen, and his second brother, the Grand Duke Konstantin Pavlovich, was only two years younger. As a third son, it is hard to imagine that anyone expected Nicholas to reign one day, although his grandmother, the Empress Catherine II, was more prophetic than she could have known when, on the day of his birth, she wrote to the *philosophe* Melchior Grimm that 'his brothers will prove to be dwarfs before this colossus'.[3] Indeed, Nicholas possessed a commanding presence from the very first. According to the Empress's account, he was just over two feet in length at birth, and as she wrote to Grimm in the same letter, 'his hands are only a bit smaller than my own'. As had been the case with her two elder grandsons, whose schooling she had entrusted to the Swiss tutor LaHarpe in the hope of educating them as enlightened princes, Catherine oversaw Nicholas's upbringing from the moment of his birth and took great pride in his development. When he was two weeks old, she again wrote to Grimm that, 'Nicholas is already eating gruel . . . It is extraordinary! He takes stock of everyone and turns his head just as I do.'[4] But Catherine died less than five months after Nicholas's birth, and it was his parents – the militaristic Emperor Paul I and the regal and proper Empress Mariia Fedorovna – who saw to his training and education. Paul set the tone for his infant son's upbringing on the day after Catherine's death when he appointed him to his first military command. At just over four months, Nicholas became a colonel in the Imperial Horse Guards: his education as a drill-master seemed assured.[5]

Nicholas's early life was spent in the company of governesses and nannies, most of them women of foreign birth, while his mother, now the reigning Empress, saw him only for a few minutes each day.[6] Perhaps the most influential of all the women who dominated his childhood was his nurse, Miss Jane Lyon, the daughter of a Scottish artist who had been brought to Russia by Catherine some years earlier. Miss Lyon was a woman of unusually bold and decisive character. She had been imprisoned by Polish rebels for some months in Warsaw during the uprising of 1794, and she never tired of relating tales about the ill-treatment she suffered at their hands,[7] a fact which probably accounted in part for Nicholas's negative attitude towards the Poles when he became Emperor.[8]

Besides Miss Lyon, two Baltic German noblewomen, both from military backgrounds, served as Nicholas's first teachers. His governess, Madame Iulia Adlerberg, was the wife of a colonel who had commanded the Vyborg Musketeer Regiment, and the sister of a general who fell in the 1812 campaign against Napoleon. Nicholas's head governess, Madame Charlotte Lieven, was the daughter of Baron Haugreben, and was made a Countess by Paul I for her part in the Grand Duke's upbringing.[9] As Nicholas's elder sister, the Grand Duchess Mariia Pavlovna, described her:

Madame Lieven had little of what one would call literary schooling, but was possessed of a sharp and penetrating wit, sound common sense, and a natural shrewdness as is rarely met with . . . She had a natural talent for command . . . She spoke German as it is commonly spoken in the Baltic provinces; Russian she spoke indifferently . . . and French imperfectly. Her solicitude towards us has always been unflagging, and we are very attached to her.[10]

The appointment of women from military backgrounds as governesses for the infant Nicholas was part of a broader phenomenon that emerged in Russia during the reign of Paul I. The transposition to Russian soil of the familial and proprietary concepts of Prussian militarism, and the evolution of its particularly virulent Russian form, is a problem that has been too little studied. The genesis of this phenomenon can perhaps be found in the attitudes of the Emperor Peter III, who had been Duke of Holstein before the Empress Elizabeth named him her heir and brought him to Russia in 1742. But Peter's reign was brief; he sat on the Russian throne only from 1761 to 1762. Moreover, his Holstein sympathies and his admiration of Frederick the Great had offended the Russian nobility who, as a result, murdered him and elevated to the throne his wife Catherine, herself a German princess from Anhalt-Zerbst. Catherine's reign, however, was a time of 'Russian-ness', despite her foreign origins. To be sure, she brought the ideas of the French *philosophes* into fashion and, as a result, the Russian nobility became more Europeanized than ever before. But it was also during her reign that Russians began to take pride in their own accomplishments. Particularly in the army, a Russian, rather than a German, spirit prevailed.

With the accession of Paul I in 1796, the pendulum swung once again in the direction of German influence, partly because the Empress Mariia Fedorovna was herself a Württemberg princess, partly because Paul was especially proud of the Holstein legacy of his father Peter III, and most of all, because of Paul's admiration of all things Prussian, especially the Prussian army. Paul I in a sense institutionalized his Prussian militaristic sympathies in his succession law of 1797[11] which set Russia's entire Imperial Family outside the normal framework of civil and public law.[12] The Russian Imperial Family thus lived its separate life within the isolated milieu of the Court where it was especially susceptible to the influence of those foreign princes and princesses who married into it. As we have seen, when Alexander I decreed in 1820 that the offspring of any union between a member of the Imperial Family and someone who did not belong to a reigning dynasty forfeited all dynastic rights and privileges, members of the Romanov family were thus forced to seek marriages with members of ruling families in Europe. This, in turn, strengthened further the German connections of the Romanov dynasty, and hence the German influence at Court, because of the large number of ruling families in Germany by comparison with other countries in Europe. As a result, the first half of the nineteenth century saw Russian grand dukes and grand duchesses enter into marriages with a number of German families. Alexander I married a princess from Baden. Nicholas I would marry a Prussian princess. Konstantin Pavlovich's first wife was a princess of Saxe-Coburg, while Nicholas's younger brother, Mikhail Pavlovich, married a Württemberg princess. Nicholas's eldest son, the future Alexander II, would marry a princess from Hesse-Darmstadt.

Nicholas's exposure to the militaristic atmosphere predominant at the Russian Court came very early.[13] He formally appeared at Court for the first time on 2 February 1798, when he was just over eighteen months old, at the ceremony held to celebrate the birth of his younger brother, Mikhail. Nicholas's first recollections must thus have been of the military, of rigid court ceremonies and of a mother who enforced the most stringent demands of court etiquette upon his brief meetings with her. Indeed, Nicholas and Mikhail saw their mother rarely, and there was one month in

1798 in which, according to the journal of the grand ducal *fourriers*, she spent not more than six or seven hours with them. Such parental affection as the young grand dukes received came mainly from the Emperor him-self, who, in free moments, would play with them, calling them his 'little sheep'. But in the rigid protocol of the Russian Court, such moments were rare because every moment of the day was planned and accounted for. Paul I generally had moments free for his younger children only while his hair was being dressed.

Given the heavy demands which court ceremonial and etiquette placed upon their parents, Nicholas and Mikhail were left mainly to the care of their nurse and governesses, who brought the militaristic atmosphere of the Court into the nursery itself. From her experiences in Poland in 1794, Miss Lyon obviously could tell exciting tales in which the Polish rebels were villains and her Russian rescuers were the heroes who had freed her from seven months of captivity.[14] Given Nicholas's deep affection for his nurse – until her death in 1842 he always called her his 'lioness',[15] a pun which he coined rather early – these tales must have impressed him with the heroism of Russia's soldiers and as an example worthy of emulation. Perhaps equally important, as we saw earlier, both Madame Lieven and Madame Adlerberg came from Baltic German families which had a tradition of loyal service to Russia's rulers, and which had risen high because of their success in military affairs. They owed their position in society to their families' military exploits, and both of them, as was common in the Court of Paul I, bore the military ranks of their husbands.[16] It is difficult to imagine that these women did not talk of military affairs in the young Grand Duke's presence, and, as he became old enough to comprehend, to amuse him with tales of military valour.

The first moral precepts to which Nicholas and Mikhail thus were exposed were ones which stressed the virtues of duty to the Emperor (a characteristic of Baltic Germans which once led Nicholas to remark that 'the Russian nobles serve the state; the Germans serve *us*!'[17]) and military heroism, combined with an emphasis upon correct behaviour, dignity and the control of emotion which they perceived in the actions of their mother – a type of rigid self-control that would later lead a number of observers to comment on Nicholas's inner coldness. Queen Victoria once remarked that Nicholas was a man who 'seldom smiles, and when he does the expression is *not* a happy one', and that the expression of his eyes was 'formidable, and unlike anything I ever saw before'.[18] The Marquis de Custine wrote that 'he cannot smile at the same time with his eyes and his mouth; a disharmony which denotes a perpetual constraint'.[19]

2. *'Lieber Herzens – Papa' Lamsdorf*

Emphasis upon things military took a more concrete form as Nicholas grew from infancy into childhood. When he was just over two years old, he was given his first toy musket. A few months later, in December 1798, he and his brother received four wooden swords and, just before that, they were given field drums, which they both dearly loved. In April 1799, when he was not yet three, Nicholas wore military uniform for the first time: the crimson uniform of a colonel in the Imperial Horse Guards.[20] Even more important, however, it was at this time that men rather than women began to rule his life. In November 1800, Paul I appointed as governor for his young sons a general – Count M. I. Lamsdorf – who boasted no intellectual accomplishments whatsoever, but had pleased Paul as Governor of Courland and as director of the First Cadet Corps. The Emperor's conversation with Lamsdorf when he told him of his new duties, presaged things to come and, it is symbolic of the continued militaristic German influence which surrounded Nicholas, that his father and his first governor discussed his education in German. 'I have chosen you as governor for my sons,'[21] the Emperor told Lamsdorf at an audience which took place at six in the morning;[22] and, when the general tried to refuse the position, Paul continued: 'If you do not wish to undertake this for me, then you must do it for Russia; but I will only ask that you do not make out of my sons good-for-nothing rascals as are the German princes.'[23]

Thus it was that a man of little learning, who had risen to some prominence as a result of his Emperor's favour, and whose only pedagogical experience involved instilling military discipline in the young men of the First Cadet Corps, came to occupy the most influential position in forming Nicholas's character. Lamsdorf assumed his duties when the Grand Duke had just passed from infancy into childhood. When he retired from his post, his charge would have become a man. Quite possibly it was Lamsdorf more than any other individual who created the future ruler, though Nicholas himself did not have very warm recollections of him. In 1831 he recalled that:

Count Lamsdorf instilled in us only the feeling of fear; such fear and certainty of his omnipotence, in fact, that our mother assumed only secondary importance in our understanding. This arrangement deprived us completely of any filial confidence in our mother, into whose presence we were only rarely admitted alone and then, only as if some sort of sentence was being passed upon us. Incessant changes in the personnel of our entourage instilled in us from our earliest childhood the habit of searching for weaknesses in them in order to turn them to our advantage . . . Fear, and efforts to escape punishments, occupied my mind more than anything else.[24]

As Miss Lyon's daughter, Madame Vecheslovaia, later described Lamsdorf on the basis of what her mother had told her, he was 'perfidious, egotistical, haughty, and narrow', and spent much of the time, when their paths crossed in the nursery, in attempting to seduce the twenty-year-old red-haired beauty who was still his charge's nurse.[25]

On the night of 11 March 1801, less than four months after he had appointed Lamsdorf as governor for his two youngest sons, Paul was murdered. His eldest son, now Alexander I, assigned the task of overseeing his younger brothers' education to his mother, Mariia Fedorovna, who became Dowager Empress. It would seem that it was she who was most influential in keeping Lamsdorf at his post, which appears somewhat surprising in view of her strict emphasis on proper behaviour and her insistence that all demands of court etiquette be observed. The Dowager Empress's preference for the ageing general, despite his lecherous behaviour in the nursery, can perhaps only be explained by the fact that his simple German burgher ways may have struck a responsive chord in her heart. Throughout the many years in which he governed the lives of her youngest sons, she wrote him many letters, continually referring to him as 'Lieber Herzens-Papa', and it seems that she found some particular comfort in having someone near by who, like herself, felt awkward with the Russian language and could share her middle-class '*Hausfrau*' tastes.

Lamsdorf's appointment had breached the feminine wall which surrounded Nicholas and his younger brother Mikhail from birth. Not long afterwards, in 1803, Miss Lyon and Mesdames Adlerberg and Lieven were all replaced by men who would seek to educate the young grand dukes in a manner befitting imperial princes. Historians have frequently argued that, in supervising the education of her younger sons, the Dowager Empress sought to isolate them from the military life which had become so pervasive during her husband's reign. In fact, she was very much a part of the militarism which pervaded all aspects of court life, and she shared many of its values. One of her favourite retreats was a small cottage at Krasnoe Selo, where the Russian army held its summer manoeuvres and where she loved to stay while her husband and, later, her sons, reviewed their armies and watched the progress of their war games.[26] But the Dowager Empress did not want her younger sons to grow up as coarse, crude drill-masters, who emulated the manner which superiors usually adopted towards their inferiors at that time. This was especially clear in a letter which she wrote to her sons on the eve of their departure to the West in early 1815, in which she exhorted them always to remember that they were princes and to act accordingly. As she cautioned them:

I hope, my dear children, that the military regimen, which you will see everywhere, will not cause you to become crude and coarse, severe or peremptory. It develops that sort of characteristic among everyone, but such is totally unbecoming to individuals of your birth and station who, even at those moments when it is necessary to curb errors, ought to use only a tone of exalted firmness, which has incomparably more influence than impulsiveness or rage.[27]

It was evidently in an effort to eliminate such rude and coarse behaviour, so associated with the army at the time, that Mariia Fedorovna stressed in her protestations that she did not want her sons to be influenced by military life. Above all, she wished to instil in them that type of regal behaviour and carriage which she herself so prized in royalty and which accounted for her rigid adherence to court etiquette to such a degree that it had required the intervention of the Emperor himself in 1799 before Nicholas was allowed to have as playmate the son of his governess Madame Adlerberg.[28] Mariia Fedorovna's efforts to instil in her sons that type of behaviour which she valued was evident in her choice of adult companions for them beginning in their earliest years, for she chose Major-General Akhverdov and Colonels Arsen'ev and Ushakov, men noted for their civility, manners and education. These officers, who have been described by Nicholas's personal friend, Baron M. A. Korf, as men who, in comparison to Lamsdorf, 'were . . . vastly more educated than he and knew several languages and sciences',[29] were expected to disapprove of any rude or coarse behaviour on the part of the grand dukes and report it to their mother.

Akhverdov, Arsen'ev and Ushakov, however, could not themselves be expected to provide their young charges with the sort of broad education which the Dowager Empress regarded as necessary for imperial princes. Therefore, between 1803 and 1809, to provide Nicholas with what she called his 'gymnasium' education, she engaged a number of special tutors. Nicholas studied political economy with Professor Storch, and Professor Adelung taught him Latin, Greek and German. Both men were celebrated scholars but monumental pedants. M. Puget d'Yverdon, a native of Lausanne, served as Nicholas's tutor in French, and also taught him and his younger brother history. Puget quickly learned that the two boys were not at all interested in the distant past and that they were completely uninspired by his tales of ancient Greece and Rome. But when Puget switched the topic of his lessons to the French Revolution, their interest was quickly aroused. Nicholas, in fact, showed particular attention in history when it dealt with something that fired his enthusiasm. Before long he had learned many of the important facts of Russia's military history by heart, and the history of revolutionary France excited his interest in a similar manner.

Nicholas's views about the French Revolution, even in his pre-adolescent years, contrasted sharply with those of his eldest brother and, in both cases, the influence of a childhood tutor was significant. Alexander's tutor, the Swiss republican LaHarpe, had sought to instil in his student an admiration for the ideals of revolutionary France. Alexander was very much a part of the eighteenth-century Enlightenment tradition, and he saw a number of positive features in the Revolution of 1789. He regarded Napoleon as a gravedigger of some of the best features of the French Revolution, and his animosity towards him was a major factor in Russia's participation in the campaigns of 1805–7 against France. On the other hand, Puget painted the Revolution to the younger Russian grand dukes in 'the most hideous shades imaginable', and while his eldest brother regarded Napoleon as an evil tyrant, Nicholas came to view him as something of a hero since he had brought about 'the triumph of order over anarchy'.[30]

Perhaps even more significant than his view of Napoleon was Nicholas's appraisal of Louis XVI's conduct during the early days of the Revolution. Even at the age of ten, the young Grand Duke had clearly begun to exhibit traits and attitudes that would be very characteristic of Nicholas the Emperor, and he one day told Puget that 'King Louis XVI did not do his duty and for this he was punished. To be weak does not mean that one is merciful. Louis XVI was faced with what was, in fact, a conspiracy disguised under the false name of liberty. He would have spared his people a great deal of misery if he had not spared the conspirators.'[31] Such words were indeed prophetic, for Nicholas reacted in precisely this manner towards the Decembrists. Not only did he crush the revolt (while insisting that it gave him great pain to do so), but he also imposed severe punishments upon those responsible. For it was Nicholas's view that mercy towards the conspirators of 14 December might have brought a revolution which would have caused distress on a vast scale. To be merciful to the mass of his subjects, Nicholas felt it necessary to deny mercy to the few who, in his opinion, had sought to inflict revolutionary suffering upon the many.

But even though he learned some useful lessons from Puget's tales of the French Revolution and found some momentary excitement in his studies of Russia's military past, studies were for Nicholas an almost unmitigated misery. His mentors' journals reflected their continual frustration at having to teach a child who in no way valued traditional learning. In 1805, one entry in the journals kept by Akhverdov, Ushakov and Arsen'ev noted that 'he is curious, attentive to that which is told to him, and eager to understand things. But when he must work at something himself, his diligence is of very brief duration, and ends by degenerating into inattention.' Two years later, the same sort of comment focused upon Nicholas's dislike for any sort of sustained thought. 'His lessons, especially those which require some serious thought, are, for the most part, never better than mediocre.'[32]

The situation became even more unbearable, in Nicholas's view, after 1809 when his 'gymnasium' education ended and his so-called 'university' education began. Adelung continued to teach him Greek, Latin and German as well as the fundamentals of logic. Storch continued his lectures on political economy. Professor Kukolnik was invited to teach him natural law, while Professor Balugianskii tried to provide Nicholas with some notion of the history of law. In addition, there were new tutors to teach him about higher mathematics, the sciences and English, and it would seem, from Nicholas's recollections, that these lessons were all a torment. Nearly four decades later, in 1847, when discussing the education of his own sons with their tutor Baron M. A. Korf, Nicholas recalled his own schooldays with a great deal of pain:

I remember how those two men tormented us . . . Kukolnik and the now-dead Balugianskii meant well . . . and were very learned, but they were the most insupportable pedants imaginable. One lectured to us about Roman, Greek, and God only knows what other kinds of laws, in a mixture of all sorts of languages, of which we understood not even one well; the other talked about some sort of imaginary 'natural' law. In addition, they sent Storch to us with lectures about political economy that were certain to put you to sleep.[33]

These scholars only spoke about the theory of law, but made little effort to draw practical conclusions from their lectures, and as Baron Korf once noted, 'the science of jurisprudence remained completely outside the school experience' of Nicholas and his younger brother.[34] In fact, Nicholas's understanding of practical legal matters was so vague when he ascended the Russian throne that, in a remark to the Swedish ambassador, he implied a belief that authorities could not arrest criminals in a state governed by a constitution. In explaining to the ambassador about the many arrests which followed the Decembrist revolt, Nicholas remarked that, 'in a country such as ours, which, to our good fortune, is not a constitutional state, arrests can take place in a completely legal manner'.[35]

For Nicholas and his younger brother, the school room was a torment not soon to be forgotten. The two brothers sought to escape the deadening atmosphere of their tutors' lectures by sketching caricatures of them, but knowing that the day of reckoning would come in which they would be expected to demonstrate a knowledge of all the material which they were supposed to have committed to memory 'without any use for the future'. And, in the background, there always stood Lamsdorf the 'omnipotent' who, as Nicholas later recalled, 'frequently punished me very painfully with a rod during the lessons themselves'.[36]

The only relief which Nicholas and his brother found was in their fascination with the army, and this occupied all their leisure moments. The two boys took turns acting as each other's adjutant, reporting to each other when they awakened in the morning. Their games were strenuous, even violent, and as Nicholas's mentors once noted in their journals, 'in his games, he [Nicholas] almost always ends up hurting himself or injuring others; his games are too boisterous and are far too full of rude manners and bad behaviour'.[37] Nicholas and his brother devoted many of their free moments to building fortresses in their rooms out of chairs, and sometimes constructed even more realistic fortresses out of earth in the palace gardens. And whenever he built some sort of imaginary abode for his nurse or his governesses, Nicholas always took care to place 'cannon' around it 'for defence'.[38]

Indeed, as a child, Nicholas appears to have been deeply preoccupied with defence. When still under the care of Miss Lyon, he used to grow pale when he met army officers because they might take him 'prisoner'.[39] Perhaps the murder of his father by army officers when he was not yet five years of age had left a deeper scar than anyone suspected. Certainly 'defence' was the key word in many of his policies as Emperor. He sought to defend the state from sedition and revolution, and to shield his subjects from ideas which he regarded as harmful. Most of all, he sought to defend Russia from Europe – from its constitutions, its revolutions and the breakdown of its *ancien régime* mores. Indeed, this notion of defence would sharply differentiate Nicholas's foreign policy from that of Alexander I. For while Alexander saw Russia as part of Europe, Nicholas would regard his Empire as unique and different from the West. For him, the abstract Western concepts of law and legality, which Kukolnik, Balugianskii and Storch had tried so unsuccessfully to instil in him as a youth, had only a limited application to Russia. As he once told Korf, when discussing the education of his own sons, 'the best theory of law is a well-intentioned morality, but it ought to exist in one's heart, independent of abstractions, and have as its base religion'.[40]

Nicholas's childhood preoccupation with defence soon took the form of serious studies about fortifications in which General Akhverdov was particularly helpful. He loved to draft designs for fortresses and buildings, a talent which he was helped to develop by Colonel Gianotti, who was retained to teach him about fortifications and the tasks of military engineers. As a child, Nicholas often began discussions of military affairs with phrases such as 'we engineers',[41] and throughout his life the military engineers would be one of his greatest passions. Nicholas founded a school for military engineers in the gloomy fortress palace surrounded by a moat, which his father had once inhabited in St Petersburg. And Nicholas's first active command in the army would be in the engineers when they were just beginning to be regarded as an important part of the Russian military establishment.

3. The Drill-Master Takes the Field

Napoleon's invasion of Russia in the late spring of 1812 brought both joy and sadness to Nicholas. Since it never seemed to enter his head that Napoleon might be victorious, the invasion was for him an opportunity for Russia's armies to cover themselves with new glories and heroism. This year also brought him some relief from the dullness of the classroom, but to his dismay he had to wait yet two more years before he could join the army in the field. Some two decades later, Nicholas still remembered the anguish of being unable to join in Russia's defence:

Finally, the year 1812 began; this fateful year changed our situation . . . The departure of the Emperor for the army was for the two of us a bitter blow . . . We remained behind, but everything around us took a different form. Everyone was concerned with our common affair and things went easier for us. All of our thoughts were with the army.[42]

Nicholas and Mikhail burned to join Russia's heroic defenders in the field, but their mother was firm. 'You, Michael,' she commented at one point, 'are too young to be a soldier; and you, Nicholas, in spite of your impatience, which I understand and am gratified for, must be retained for other things. Holy Russia will not lack for defenders.'[43]

But even though Napoleon's invasion freed Nicholas from the demands of his schoolmasters for the moment, he was forced to keep at his studies while the Russian army drove Napoleon from Russia and marched on to Paris without him. It was a bitter pill, for he yearned above all to be with Russia's armies. As he recalled not long after he had become Emperor, 'military studies alone occupied me passionately. Only in them did I find consolation and a pleasing occupation in keeping with the inclination of my spirit.'[44] At that point in his youth Nicholas was convinced that a military career was the only proper occupation for a nobleman or a non-reigning prince, and when one of his tutors assigned him to write an essay 'to prove that military science is not the only service for a nobleman, but that other occupations are for him just as honourable and useful', he refused to write anything at all, so firmly did he believe that there was no way to defend such a proposition.[45]

Passion for the army would be a characteristic of Nicholas as Grand

Duke and as Emperor, and the intensity of his love for the army comes
through again and again in his writings. Apart from letters to his wife,
Nicholas's prose nearly always had a stilted and moribund quality about
it except when it was about the army. Only then did he write about such
exalted notions as honour, love and spirit. And it was characteristic of
Nicholas the soldier that he summed up his view of life quite succinctly
in discussing the army. In describing his admiration for military life on
one of his visits to Prussia to see his betrothed, the Princess Charlotte, he
wrote:

Here [in the army] there is order . . . All things flow logically one from the
other. No one here commands without first learning to obey. No one rises above
anyone else except through a clearly-defined system. Everything is subordinated
to a single, defined goal, and everything has its precise designations. That is
why I shall always hold the title of soldier in high esteem. *I regard all human
life as being nothing more than service because everyone must serve.*[46]

Only at the beginning of 1814 did Alexander I finally give his younger
brothers the long-awaited permission to join the army in the field. It was
a moment of intense happiness for Nicholas as they prepared for their
departure. As he later recalled, 'I cannot even begin to describe our
happiness or, more accurately, our mad joy. We began to live and, in a
single moment, crossed the threshold from childhood into the world,
into life.'[47] Yet, for their mother, it was a time of deep sadness. She had
given more than a decade of her life to the education of her younger sons,
as if, in her limited way, she hoped to emulate and perhaps even surpass
the accomplishment of her mother-in-law Catherine II, who had scorned
her and taken from her the upbringing of her two eldest sons. But Mariia
Fedorovna had never been able to break down the barrier which separated
her from her youngest sons. The obstacle had been created by her own
reserve and obsession with correct form. It was perhaps indicative of what
must have been for her an unending agony of alienation from her children
that she could not draw them to her for her parting words but, instead,
confined all of her intense feelings to a lengthy letter which she gave
them on the eve of their departure. Her letter, written in the French she
loved, but with the German syntax and rigidity that she could never
abandon, flowed on for page after page and, despite its emotional quality,
she focused directly upon those very flaws in her sons' character that
would become intensified with time.

Military trifles concern you more than they should [she wrote]. You must
earnestly seek that exalted knowledge that makes great leaders of men . . . and
you must be concerned with everything, paying particular attention to those
things which have as their object the welfare of the common soldier, which is

so often neglected and sacrificed to the elegance of uniforms, to useless military exercises . . . and to the ignorance of their commanders. Finally . . . you must learn the manner of Princes . . . and thus merit the esteem of your Sovereign, your country, and your associates . . . Never be hasty in your judgements . . . either about men or about things. Of all judgements, that of other men is the most difficult and will demand from you the most attention . . . Observe . . . and reflect upon the character of individuals, but do not judge them until you have solid evidence upon which to base your conclusions![48]

Nicholas and Mikhail thus set out to join the Russian army in the West late in the winter of 1814. Their suite was made up of men who had been their companions for a decade: Generals Savrasov, Aledinskii, and Arsen'ev, Colonel Gianotti, a German doctor, Rühl, and, finally, General Count Lamsdorf, plus the aide-de-camp, General P. P. Konovitsyn, assigned to them by Alexander himself. The two grand dukes left St Petersburg thirsting for glory and the sound of battle. But because of Lamsdorf's penchant for leisurely travel, and Alexander's refusal to have them near any actual military engagements, they did not reach Paris until early June, after the peace had been signed.

The days which Nicholas spent in the French capital during the summer of 1814 were significant for Nicholas in that he made two life-long friendships. The first was with V. F. Adlerberg, the son of his former governess, and a childhood playmate separated from him a number of years before to attend the Pages Corps but now an officer in the Lithuanian Guards Regiment. In 1817, Adlerberg would be named one of the Grand Duke's adjutants. The second friendship was perhaps even more important. It was with Lieutenant-General I. F. Paskevich, a daring young officer who had risen rapidly to command the Second Grenadiers Division as a result of his valour on the battlefield. From the moment of their first acquaintance, Paskevich was one of the men whom Nicholas most admired. Indeed, at one point later in his life, Nicholas commented that, 'I respect this man as only a son can respect a father',[49] and his letters to Paskevich, whom he made first a count and then a prince, were filled with filial respect.[50] Clearly Paskevich was a model whom Nicholas wished to emulate. He was brave to the point of recklessness, and had personally led bayonet charges, even as a Major-General, during the earlier Napoleonic wars. But Paskevich was a mediocre strategist, and a pedantic military commander who placed more emphasis upon parade-ground precision than upon combat training. He was a poor example to follow and in many ways shared that same infatuation with military trivia so characteristic of Paul I and Lamsdorf, Nicholas's first and 'second' fathers.

The grand dukes returned to Russia in late 1814 after visiting several

European courts, including that of Prussia, where Nicholas first met his future wife, the Princess Charlotte. It would be one of those rare dynastic arrangements which blossomed into genuine love, but Nicholas did not pledge his heart to the young princess until the following year. After a brief stay at the Prussian Court, the brothers returned to Russia where their mother sent them back to the schoolroom. But the tie had been weakened and Nicholas's education now took a different turn as he devoted much time to the study of military science. Under the tutelage of General Oppermann, he planned various campaigns for which his mentor provided him with a detailed critique.[51]

But his time in the classroom was to be brief. Not long after his return to St Petersburg, Napoleon escaped from Elba and raised a new army to challenge the Allies. In May 1815, Nicholas returned again to Western Europe, sent on his way with another lengthy letter of maternal counsels.[52] After commending him and his younger brother to the care of their 'dignified and respectable second father General Lamsdorf', the Dowager Empress urged her sons to be on guard against adopting that brusque and crude type of behaviour which she found so objectionable among army officers trained in her dead husband's 'Gatchina school', and begged them to 'close your ears to all adulation and flattery and never trust men who flatter your baser passions and who may even encourage such in you in order to court your favour'.

Yet the grand dukes' ties to their mother had not yet been completely severed. From St Petersburg she urged Alexander to return her sons to their studies as soon as possible, and he did so later in 1815. Nicholas thus slowly and reluctantly made his way back to Russia by way of Baden, Frankfurt, Leipzig and, of course, Berlin. By early October, the two brothers were in the Prussian capital, and for a brief space Nicholas wooed the Princess Charlotte with uncharacteristic passion. Both were in love for the first time and gave themselves up to the youthful joy of romance.[53] It was the only time in his life that Nicholas wrote poetry, though it was devoted, significantly enough, not to his beautiful companion, but to his love for the Russian people and the glory of his brother Alexander. For the moment, as the tall and slender Russian Grand Duke, and the romantic and starry-eyed Prussian princess wandered through the picturesque Potsdam countryside, the rest of the world was forgotten, and it was there, on the Pfaueninsel, that Nicholas proposed to his princess that autumn.[54]

Then, having announced his betrothal to the Princess Charlotte, he returned to Russia at the end of the year. His studies during the winter of 1815–16 were much more of the type to prepare a prince to rule, and perhaps may serve as evidence that Alexander had already begun to consider the nineteen-year-old Grand Duke as his heir. During the last winter of his studies, Nicholas was no longer the schoolboy trying by all means to avoid his duties. On occasion, he even seemed almost like a ruler questioning his advisers, a change of attitude very evident in the reports his tutors made about his work. Professor Balugianskii, whom Nicholas regarded as one of the 'most insupportable pedants imaginable',[55] instructed him about state finances that winter, and his comments bear witness to the fact that Nicholas had begun to take his work seriously. According to Balugianskii, the lessons were made 'very interesting by the questions which His Imperial Highness posed', and, on occasion, the Grand Duke 'of his own free will continued the lesson for yet half an hour more'.[56]

It is hard to say what Nicholas learned for the future from Balugianskii's lectures, though state finances would always be a matter to which he devoted much energy after he became Emperor. He also must have learned a good deal from the course in Russian history which his companion General Akhverdov read to him that winter. Akhverdov read lectures on the reigns of Ivan the Terrible, and the Time of Troubles,[57] lessons which must have impressed upon Nicholas the catastrophic consequences of weakness on the part of an autocrat. In Ivan the Terrible, he saw an autocrat who ruled Russia cruelly but firmly. The succession of weak rulers who followed, however, must have seemed to him a direct cause for Russia's defencelessness at the beginning of the seventeenth century when the nation became so weak that the Poles occupied Moscow itself.

The spring of 1816 brought an end to Nicholas's schoolroom days once and for all. If he were to be a military commander, then he first must become better acquainted with his command in the broadest sense. Therefore the Emperor and Dowager Empress sent him on a lengthy tour of Russia, a journey of some 7,000 kilometres (about 4,350 miles) travelled in approximately three months, which took him to the south into the Crimea and through many of Russia's western and south-western provinces. During these travels he kept a journal, and from it one can see emerging in the twenty-year-old Grand Duke several of the faults and virtues of Nicholas the Emperor. He was energetic and anxious to do well, qualities which, as Emperor, would lead him to continual and rapid inspections of his 'command'. Probably no other Russian Emperor since Peter the Great would be so conscientious about trying to learn the true state of affairs in his Empire. On this first journey, he moved quickly from place to place in an effort to uncover abuses of authority and incompetence, and seemed at times almost overwhelmed by the shortcomings he found and the poverty he witnessed.

In Porkhovo [he wrote in his diary] the nobility is sufficiently numerous but they live almost like peasants. The jail and the hospital are in such a terrible condition that it is sinful not to mention it. It is a dilapidated wooden hut consisting of three low-ceilinged storerooms, almost without windows or ventilation in which . . . in two rooms, there are sixty-six prisoners, without food or clothing, suffocating in fetid air, with no distinctions being made as to the nature of their crime and their ages.[58]

Although concern for the welfare of criminals was worthy of a benevolent prince, the faults in Nicholas's attitudes were not so much to his credit, and would be even less worthy in a ruler. Throughout his journal, his dislike of Jews, Poles and other minority groups was vividly evident.[59] Polish serfowners were, to his mind, the worst, the most demanding and the most oppressive masters in the Empire. He considered them disloyal to Russia because they had sworn allegiance to Napoleon, and he saw as seditious their efforts to spread the ideas of Roman Catholicism among the Russian peasantry. Almost as bad as the Poles, in his view, were the Tatars.

There is nothing poorer and more lazy than these southern Tatars [he wrote]. If the Crimea was not in Tatar hands, then everything would be entirely different, for where there are Russian or Little Russian serfowners and settlers . . . there is grain. In other words, they utilize the wealth with which this land is blessed.[60]

Nicholas's excessive concern with the most petty details of military affairs also boded ill for Russia's future. Certainly, he had not heeded his mother's admonition two years earlier when she had warned him that 'military trifles concern you more than they should'.[61] Even as sympathetic an observer as Baron Korf, to whom Alexander II gave the task of compiling materials about Nicholas as Emperor, was appalled by this aspect. Critical value-judgements about Nicholas were rare for Korf, for he revered him excessively and regarded him as the ideal ruler. Yet even Korf was shocked by Nicholas's lack of concern for serious military affairs as a Grand Duke, and commented that, in the journal which he kept in 1816, 'almost all comments related only to unimportant *externalia* of military service, uniforms, parade drill, marching, and so forth *and did not concern a single essential matter of military organization, administration, or the moral spirit and attitude of the rank and file.* Even about such an important aspect of military affairs as *musketry practice, there is not a single mention.*'[62]

Perhaps it was almost as indicative of the sorry state of affairs in Russia that when Alexander II read Korf's lines, he wrote in the margin: 'This was not his [Nicholas's] fault for, with the ending of the war in 1815 until his accession to the throne [in 1825] no one gave any thought to this matter.'[63] Nevertheless Nicholas had become what his mother had feared: a princely drillmaster.

4. Marriage Vows

Nicholas's education on Russia ended late in the summer of 1816, and when he returned to St Petersburg in late August his days of study were past. But the world of Russia was only part of that which the Emperor Alexander wanted him to see. Nicholas's earlier visits to Europe had been brief, and much time had been spent with the army. Alexander now wanted him to see Europe more extensively as a traveller rather than as a royal military officer. Therefore, just more than two weeks after Nicholas returned to St Petersburg, the Emperor sent him to Western Europe where he would remain for some eight months, four of which would be spent in England.

The main purpose of Nicholas's journey to the West was clear from a memorandum which Alexander ordered the Foreign Minister, Nesselrode, to draft for him: the Emperor wanted his younger brother to observe the constitutional state order of England, but he also wanted him to understand clearly the limited applicability which such ideas could have for Russia. On the eve of his departure, Nesselrode urged Nicholas to remember that England's institutions were above all the product of her unique historial experience and, by implication, pointed out one of the fundamental political lessons that would later guide Nicholas as Emperor of Russia: that as a result of its unique historical development, every nation possessed institutions that were peculiarly its own and that it was the ruler's task to cherish such and to defend them from those who would forget the nation's past and seek to graft alien borrowings upon it.[64] For Nicholas this would come to mean that he had a God-given duty and an historical mission to preserve and protect autocracy in Russia, and he would ascend the Russian throne as autocracy's champion.

Alexander need not have feared that his younger brother might become enamoured of British institutions. By all accounts, Nicholas found the aristocratic side of English life delightful. He enjoyed the company of the Duke of Wellington; he spent five pleasant days with the Prince Regent at Brighton;[65] and he excited considerable favourable comment from the ladies at Court.[66] But if he enjoyed the company of England's gentlemen and ladies, he was completely nonplussed by its political institutions. Nicholas travelled extensively in England and during four months saw much of English political and economic life, for he had arrived at a time of social and political unrest. He was in England at the time of the riot at Spa Fields in December 1816, and when the attack was made upon the Prince Regent the following February. The totality of England's political life – its clubs, its meetings, the public demonstrations – was to Nicholas incomprehensible and appalling. As he commented to his aide-de-camp, General P. V. Golenishchev-Kutuzov: 'If ever, to our great misfortune, some sort of evil force should bring to us these clubs and meetings, which make more noise than achievements, I would beg God to repeat the miracle of the confusion of the tongues or, better still, to deprive all those who abuse it in such a way of the gift of speech.'[67]

There was no such duality in his attitudes towards Prussia which he revisited in the spring of 1817. At Berlin and Potsdam he was in his element – the world and situation he understood best: that of military parade command. In honour of Nicholas's coming marriage to his daughter, the Prussian king made him the chief of the Third Brandenburg Cuirassier Regiment, an honour which overjoyed the young prince more than anything that had happened during the entire course of his journey. He was filled with immense pleasure and pride when he himself led his regiment before the Prussian king in a military review that spring.[68]

Nicholas returned to St Petersburg in late April 1817, to prepare for the reception of his bride-to-be. In early June he was at the Prussian border to greet his betrothed, and on 9 June 1817, the Princess Charlotte crossed into Russia to be greeted by Nicholas 'at the head of his soldiers'.[69] Escorted by a Cossack Guard, she entered Russia to become the Grand Duchess Aleksandra Fedorovna. Ten days later, she entered the capital city of the Empire which she would one day rule as the wife of Nicholas I.

Her first descriptions of her new country focused upon the army, and provide further evidence of the militaristic attitudes becoming so ingrained as the Imperial Family continued to marry Germans. The young woman was homesick, lonely and overwhelmed by her strange surroundings. But she found solace in the appearance of the Imperial Guards. She recalled of the day of her entry into St Petersburg:

I was delighted to see again the Semenovskii, Izmailovskii, and Preobrazhenskii Regiments which I remembered from a military review in Silesia . . . during the armistice of 1813. And when I saw the Chevalier Guards drawn up near the Admiralty, I could not restrain a small cry of pleasure because they reminded me of my beloved Guards of the Berlin Regiment. I did not even think that I would one day be the honorary commander of this regiment.[70]

For a young woman not yet out of her teens to find an antidote to her homesickness in the comforting appearance of regiments drawn up in parade formations indicates that Nicholas had found a woman in harmony with his own views. Nor was it a passing fancy. Two years later, when the

Grand Duchess spent three weeks at Krasnoe Selo, where Nicholas's regiments held their summer training manoeuvres, she commented that, 'these three weeks passed far too quickly for me, so pleasing did I find this military life'.[71]

Perhaps the best portrait that we have of Nicholas on the eve of his marriage has been supplied by the memoirist F. F. Vigel', who witnessed the young couple's ceremonial entrance into St Petersburg. Vigel' wrote with the advantage of hindsight, but his portrait of the young Grand Duke is still revealing. According to Vigel':

Russians at that time knew little about him. Scarcely having emerged from adolescence, he had spent two years on campaigns in the West. He then had spent a third year travelling throughout Europe and, on his return, he began to command the Izmailovskii Guards Regiment. He was uncommunicative and cold; all of his devotion was to his duty and, in fulfilling it, he was too severe, both with himself and with others. In the regular features of his fair, pale countenance, there was visible a certain rigidity, a certain instinctive severity. The cloud, which in his first adult years overshadowed his brow, seemed an omen of all the misfortunes which afflicted Russia during the time when he was on the throne . . . The most terrible criminal horrors would shake the world during his reign . . . No one knew, no one thought about his destiny at this time. But many regarded him unfavourably . . . To tell the truth, absolutely no one liked him.[72]

Such a public image was unfortunate since it was not in keeping with Nicholas's true character. His wife, and those who observed him in his family circle, found him warm and open-hearted.[73] And the homesick and lonely young Prussian princess found him the ideal husband. As she recalled her marriage day, 1 July 1817, 'I felt myself very, very happy when our hands joined. With complete confidence and trust, I gave my life into the hands of my Nicholas and he never once betrayed this trust.'[74] But Nicholas, as Vigel' noted, placed his duty above all else and, most of all, saw his duty in soldierly terms. To him, this required that he present a cold, impersonal, brusque image to all in Russia but those closest to him.

There is an even more vivid indication of the same attitude in Nicholas's younger brother. As the historian Presniakov noted, when Mikhail Pavlovich visited Western Europe, he was very affable and likeable. But when he returned to Russia, 'he changed his clothing at the border for a tight-fitting military dress uniform, spoke to his image in the mirror before which he was arranging his clothing, saying, "Farewell, Mikhail Pavlovich", and once again assumed that harsh and rigid image by which he was known in Russia'.[75] Certainly there were also elements of this attitude in Nicholas's manner. Those who met him in the West found him charming, but all detected an underlying severity which he could never lose completely. As Queen Victoria described him when he visited England in 1844:

He is certainly a *very striking* man; still very handsome; his profile is *beautiful*, and his manners *most* dignified and graceful; extremely civil – quite alarmingly so, as he is full of attentions and *politenesses*. But the expression of the *eyes* is *formidable*, and unlike anything I ever saw before . . . He seldom smiles and when he does the expression is *not* a happy one.[76]

Even Aleksandra Fedorovna noted this characteristic quite early in her life with Nicholas in St Petersburg. 'It is true that my Nicholas's appearance was far too serious for his twenty-one years, especially when he appeared publicly at balls,' she wrote. 'We both were truly happy and content only when we found ourselves alone in our apartments, and he then was very tender and loving towards me.'[77]

The Grand Duchess spent her first years in Russia trying to learn the language and customs of her adopted country under the tutelage of the poet V. A. Zhukovskii, whom she characterized as being 'too much of a poet to be a good tutor'. 'Instead of working assiduously at grammar,' she recalled, 'some chance word would give him an idea and this idea would, in turn, put him in mind of a poem which would then serve as a subject for discussion, and the lesson would thus pass in this manner.'[78] Meanwhile Nicholas continued in his role as parade-ground commander. Shortly after his marriage he became the head of the Corps of Engineers, and also commanded a Guards brigade composed of the Izmailovskii Regiment and the Guards Chasseurs. For eight years the young couple had few cares and enjoyed the company of each other and that of their close family circle, including various German relatives who visited them. It was not until October 1818 that they entertained formally for the first time when, on the occasion of the birthday of the Crown Prince of Prussia, they opened the social season in St Petersburg with a ball for the high society of the capital.[79]

The close Prussian connections which Nicholas developed as a result of his marriage stimulated further his reputation as a drill-master. Yet it cannot be over-emphasized that in their infatuation with Prussian militarism, the Russians adopted only its external manifestations. Nicholas was not alone in his love of the parade-ground, and this tendency to evaluate the army in terms of its appearance was already undermining the effectiveness of Russia's land forces even before he ascended the throne. The Russian army were becoming parade-ground performers rather than an effective fighting force. As the Prussian General Ludwig von Nazmer commented when he accompanied Aleksandra Fedorovna to Russia in 1817: 'to our good fortune, all junior officers, without exception, are unfit, and the major portion of officers in the higher ranks are also not much better. Only a few generals reflect upon their true calling, but the vast majority, on the other hand, think that they have achieved everything if they succeed in satisfactorily leading their regiment in a ceremonial parade march past the Emperor.' General von Nazmer noted that Alexander I had 'a passion for military trivia',[80] and this interest in uniforms, parades and rank was perhaps most dramatically reflected by the fact that when Nicholas's and Aleksandra's first son, the future Alexander II, was born on 17 April 1818, Alexander I's first act was to appoint him chief of the Lifeguards Hussar Regiment.[81]

The extent to which his life between 1817 and 1825 prepared Nicholas to assume the crown is questionable, to say the least. Historians have assumed that Alexander made little effort to prepare his younger brother for possible future duties.[82] And it is true, of course, that during these years, Nicholas held only military commands, and never set foot in the State Council. Yet, in retrospect, Nicholas himself regarded this as helpful preparation for ruling an empire. As he later recalled, 'this time [involved with petty military matters] was . . . a priceless experience for learning about people'.[83] Although Nicholas received a far from ideal preparation for ruling Russia, he was as well, if not better, prepared for assuming the Russian crown than were most of his immediate predecessors. Alexander I had had no practical experience in governing before he was suddenly lifted to the throne by the assassination of his father in 1801, and in fact he probably knew a good deal less about conditions in the Empire than did Nicholas. Alexander, after all, had been educated by the Swiss republican LaHarpe, whose ideals bore little relation to the situation in Russia at the beginning of the nineteenth century, and he had matured in the near-hermetically sealed world of the St Petersburg *haute societé*, which was more European than Russian. While a Grand Duke, Nicholas's father Paul I had been kept in semi-isolation at Gatchina by his mother Catherine II, where he whiled away his idle hours by drilling the troops under his command. And Catherine II herself, if we are to believe her own account of her life as a Grand Duchess,[84] read widely in the writings of the early French *philosophes*, but had no practical experience in governing before she ascended the throne. Much the same can be said of Catherine's husband Peter III, Peter's aunt and predecessor the Empress Elizabeth and, indeed, every Russian ruler of the eighteenth century, including Peter the Great. In fact, the first Russian Emperor conscientiously to school his heir in the art of governing the Empire was Nicholas himself.

Nicholas, then, was certainly no worse prepared to govern Russia than were his imperial predecessors. One might even argue that he was in a better position to rule than were either his grandmother or his elder brother. Both of these monarchs found their early years on the throne especially difficult as they tried to reconcile the ideas which they had extracted from their readings of the *philosophes* with the situation which they discovered in Russia after they ascended the throne. Nicholas, on the other hand, was troubled by no such philosophical illusions or conflicts. As we have seen, he had rejected Western political systems as inapplicable to Russia long before he came to the throne, and he sought to isolate Russians from such ideas from the beginning of his reign. Indeed, as he reportedly once told Prince P. P. Gagarin, 'I must tell you that I do not like to send . . . [young men needing technical training] abroad. Young people return from there with a spirit of criticism which, perhaps with good reason, makes them find the institutions of their own country inadequate.'[85]

Further, and again unlike Alexander I and Paul I, Nicholas had had considerable experience in the West before he became Emperor. Not only had he been there during the closing days of the campaigns of 1814 and 1815, but he had visited England and had spent much time in Germany. Indeed, during the period between his marriage in 1817 and his accession eight years later, Nicholas spent one entire year in Prussia, leaving St Petersburg on 13 September 1820 and returning only on 10 September 1821. Some of his biographers regarded such lengthy absences from Russia as poor training indeed for an Emperor.[86] But given Alexander I's concern about Russia's place in Europe, and his earlier efforts to acquaint his younger brother with European politics and political systems, one could as easily argue that Nicholas's visit to Germany for an entire year was designed to acquaint him further with the European situation. Even as early as August 1815, Alexander reportedly acquainted Nicholas with the text of the Holy Alliance, saying that, 'I like to think that one day you will also be its most firm defender'. Nicholas's comment on that occasion was already characteristic of Nicholas the Emperor. After expressing delight at seeing 'Russia announce to Europe an era of religion, peace, and justice', he added, 'I have never thought that any system could be better than that by which Kings were delegated by Providence to govern the masses.'[87] Two fundamental elements of Nicholas's view of the role of ruler were clearly expressed in this brief comment. First, he believed that rulers received their power to govern from God, and that it should never be otherwise. Nearly as important, he saw Russia as being the supreme force of morality and justice which should dictate to Europe the policies that were in Europe's best interests.

When he ascended the throne, therefore, Nicholas's attitudes towards both Russia and the West were well-defined and featured none of the grandiose notions or troublesome dreams that had played upon the minds of Catherine and Alexander. He had no desire whatsoever to project the image, especially in the West, of being a philosopher on the throne (as had Catherine at the beginning of her reign). Nor did he have any pretensions to being an enlightened emancipator of Europe (as had Alexander). Nicholas would be perfectly content to follow a far more conservative policy in his relations with the West, and to defend the existing order both at home and abroad.

Perhaps Nicholas would rule more single-mindedly as an autocrat than his immediate predecessors because he was more at ease with his self-image and knew precisely on which side of the Western European–Russian frontier he stood. While Catherine to some extent, and Alexander to a far greater degree, were cosmopolitan in outlook, Nicholas saw himself as first of all a Russian. For him, Russia and the West were not synonymous terms, and he sought to separate Russia's spiritual and intellectual life from that of the West rather than blur the distinction. As Emperor, his first concern was to do his duty as he defined it,[88] and he defined his duty in terms of what he knew and understood best: life as the military commander of all Russia.

Nicholas also faced problems that were even more serious than those which had confronted Catherine, Paul or even his brother. Russia faced the challenge posed by the rapidly industrializing nations of Western Europe, led by England, with an under-developed industry and a backward social and economic order. Further, the Empire's aristocracy, traditionally the pillar of the throne, was rapidly on the way to economic ruin because of the devastation caused by the Napoleonic invasion of 1812 and their extravagant tastes for Western luxury goods which, in most cases, far exceeded their ability to pay for them from their estate incomes. Finally, Russia's internal administration had been seriously neglected during the last years of Alexander I's reign under the capricious hand of the martinet General Count A. A. Arakcheev; the Empire's laws were filled with ambiguities and contradictions; procedures in the Empire's courts were ineffective and corrupt; and the Russian nation was burdened with a vast internal debt as the result of a highly inflated paper currency. Such problems were well known to the Imperial Family, and they regarded them partly as the result of Alexander I's lengthy absences from Russia. In November 1815, when the Emperor had been absent from Russia for more than a year, the young Grand Duchess Anna Pavlovna would write that, 'the least political error can have the most fatal consequences here. You know how internal affairs go badly and each day one learns of new details'; to which the Dowager Empress added, 'I am not able to repeat frequently enough how very essential it is that he [Alexander] should return as soon as possible.'[89]

Nicholas was made painfully aware of all these difficulties on that day of his accession when the flower of Russia's noble youth sacrificed itself in an ill-fated attempt to bring down the autocracy. His first task as Emperor was to examine the grievances which these young men laid before him in their 'confessions' during the next several days and nights as each one was brought before the ruler whom they had sought to destroy. The cumulative effect of the tales they told, both to Nicholas and to the Imperial Investigating Commission which later questioned them, was to paint a vast panorama of abuses and crimes at all levels of Russian life. To be sure, Nicholas would punish the Decembrists severely. But he listened to what they had to say. He soon had their testimony compiled, and a digest of it prepared. Throughout the next three decades the volume would never leave his desk.[90]

Part Two

———

Genesis

———

'Not by daring and rash dreams, which are
always destructive, but gradually, and
from above, laws will be issued, defects
remedied, and abuses corrected. In this
manner all modest hopes for improvement,
all hopes for strengthening the rule of
law, and for the expansion of true
enlightenment, and the development of
industry, will be gradually fulfilled.
The legitimate path, open for all, will
always be taken by Us with satisfaction.
For We do not have, and cannot have,
any other desire than to see Our Motherland
attain the very heights of happiness
and glory pre-ordained for her by
Providence.'

NICHOLAS I, IN HIS CORONATION MANIFESTO

———

3

The Genesis of the Nicholas System

*'I have never thought that any system
could be better than
that by which Kings were delegated
by Providence to govern
the masses'*

NICHOLAS I, WHILE STILL A GRAND DUKE

Late in the afternoon of 14 December 1825, Nicholas returned from the Senate Square, victor over what he regarded as sinister forces of revolution in Russia. He was now autocrat of all the Russias, or, as he viewed himself, their 'commander'.[1] Among Russia's intellectuals, as the memoirist F. F. Vigel' remarked, 'no one liked him'.[2] But the attitude of many in St Petersburg was perhaps summed up best by Countess M. D. Nesselrode at the end of December: 'The Emperor Nicholas proved . . . that he was capable of governing some fifty million subjects . . . In a few hours, by his courage, his presence of mind, and his firmness, he managed to win the hearts and the confidence of the army, [and] the inhabitants of his capital.'[3]

Nicholas inherited a state that was far from being in good order. For more than a century, Russia's only claim to recognition by the powers of Western Europe had rested upon her armies, the forces which had crushed Charles XII of Sweden at Poltava in 1709, which had stood at the gates of Berlin in 1761, which had marched through northern Italy with the legendary commander Suvorov in 1799, and which had ridden along the Champs-Elysées in 1814 and 1815. But in 1825, Russia's liabilities far outnumbered her assets. In the short space of a decade, Europeans had come to view her as the champion of reaction rather than the liberator of

Europe. Perhaps even more important, by 1825, a number of cancers gnawed at the very vitals of the Empire and had begun to sap her vitality. An unwieldy bureaucracy, corrupt and notoriously incompetent, had emerged to administer the Emperor's domains. To be sure, it was not large by Western European standards since there were only about 1·3 officials per 1,000 inhabitants in Russia as compared with 4·1 per 1,000 in England and 4·8 per 1,000 in France.[4] But, unlike England and France, only a small portion of Russia's population encountered the bureaucracy on a regular basis. Most Russians were peasants, many of whom never encountered a state official in the course of their lives. Those who confronted state officials most frequently were the nobles, of whom there were some 720,000. On this basis, since there were some 65,000 officials in the Empire, the ratio of officials to those who dealt with them most frequently was 11·8 per 1,000, and even if we consider the other class which encountered state officials with some frequency, the merchants, the ratio was still higher than anywhere in the West. For those Russians who had to deal with the Empire's officials, the bureaucracy must thus have seemed ponderous indeed. And it seemed even more so because the aristocracy in Russia regarded the bureaucracy with particular disapproval since it had come to interpose itself between them and the throne, thereby disrupting the traditional ties between ruler and his chosen favourites, the nobility, who served as his bulwark.[5]

But the bureaucracy was only one of many illnesses from which Russia suffered at this time. Perhaps even more important, the entire fabric of Russian society was permeated with an arbitrariness which left subordinates at the mercy of their superiors. This was the case from the peasant grovelling before his master's bailiff, to the great nobleman, himself perhaps the master of thousands of serfs, forced to hear himself addressed only in the most familiar terms by his Emperor. Such arbitrariness had the effect of increasing tension in Russian society and masked many faults from the men who had the power to correct them. Since subordinates' positions depended utterly upon the whim of their superiors, they sought to please them in any way possible. As a result, Russia's most serious problems were hidden from the Empire's statesmen and, most of all, from the Emperor himself.

Part of this arbitrariness was, of course, the result of the autocratic system in Russia, where the Emperor, in theory at least, had absolute power. But it was also the product of the erosive institution of serfdom where the master had absolute power over his serfs. Indeed, many of the problems which Nicholas's Empire faced on the day of his accession were connected with serfdom. Certainly, if Russia was going to compete with the post-Napoleonic West, which had lived through the French Revolution of 1789 and was now going though the Industrial Revolution, she would be distinctly disadvantaged by having to do so with an obsolete social and economic order. But the most powerful class in the Empire, the nobility, relied for its financial sustenance upon serfdom, and Nicholas well knew what consequences a direct attack upon that institution could bring. His own father had been murdered by powerful nobles opposed to his policies. Perhaps even more frightening, the nobility was already in serious economic difficulties as a result of the Napoleonic wars and their own financial irresponsibility. Their demands for loans were already a serious drain on a state treasury that was itself in precarious financial condition, and an attack on serfdom could easily cause an economic crisis among the nobility of such overwhelming proportions that the state might not survive the added burden.

Thus the plight of the enserfed peasantry, the misery of the common soldier, the precarious condition of the state's finances and the Empire's entire economic system all demanded attention. So did the economically impoverished nobility, the Empire's underdeveloped industry and Russia's unfavourable balance of trade with the West. And the bureaucracy needed to be reformed so that it would administer the Empire in the interests of the state as a whole and serve as an instrument for expressing the Emperor's will. Beyond that, the Empire needed a courts system which worked smoothly, fairly, and efficiently; it required a system of taxation which did not fall mainly upon the poorest elements; and it needed an army which did not consume the lion's share of the state budget. But Nicholas could not attack these many problems directly and institute the monumental reforms which the Empire needed. For one thing, he was convinced of the basic soundness of the existing order. For another, he was unwilling to relinquish any of his immense autocratic power. And yet, even had he been willing to share his power, there was no group in the Empire which could have used it well. The nobility was largely dominated by self-interest, a fact which Alexander I had learned very quickly when he considered the possibility of introducing a constitution in Russia early in his reign. At the same time, it was clear that neither could the bureaucracy be given added power to act independently. The aristocracy would probably never have tolerated such a move on the part of the Emperor. Yet even had it been possible to grant the bureaucracy power to deal directly with some of Russia's problems, to have done so would have been to court catastrophe. The mass of Russia's officials feared any change, either progressive or conservative, for they feared that it would burden them with tasks that they could not, or would not, learn to perform.[6]

Nicholas's solution to the many problems which his Empire faced was to create the 'Nicholas system', in which absolute monarchy in its most extreme form became the sanctioning political principle. Trusting neither the nobility nor public opinion, he sought to deal with all of Russia's problems himself or, like an efficient military commander, through the offices of his adjutants, his ministers. The Nicholas system was not, of course, an innovation in Russia. Rather, it was the culmination of the Empire's entire political experience since at least the beginning of the eighteenth century, cloaked in religious precepts dating from a much earlier time to endow it with the highest possible legitimacy. Nearly all of the institutional elements which Nicholas introduced into his system had earlier antecedents. But it was Nicholas who brought them together into a unified system – into what would be Imperial Russia's last attempt to govern on the basis of an absolutist police state with no concessions to any individual elements of society.

But Nicholas had had little experience in governing before he ascended the throne, and despite his lengthy tour of Russia in 1816, he knew far too little about Russian conditions. His first task, therefore, was to seek information about the true state of his 'command' from those who had tried to seize it from him. With this in mind, he began to question closely the Decembrists who were so critical of the existing order in Russia that they had sought to overthrow it and establish a more representative form of government in its place.

1. *The Grand Inquisitor*

Nicholas was certainly no coward, but there is no doubt that the events of 14 December impressed indelibly upon him that, as Russia's Emperor, his life would always be in danger. Unlike his father Paul I, he did not as a result barricade himself into a stronghold. In fact, he often appeared in just those places where death could have come most easily, as, for example, when he went to St Petersburg's Haymarket in the summer of 1831 to calm the city's masses, thrown into a panic by an outbreak of cholera.[7] But the knowledge that he might well suffer a fate similar to that of his father always remained in the back of Nicholas's mind and, quite probably, increased after 1831 when Polish patriots, furious and bitter at his revocation of Poland's constitution and the ruthless manner in which he crushed the revolt of 1830–31, openly plotted his assassination. Even as late as 1844, an armed Pole was apprehended at Windsor Castle when Nicholas visited it in June, and the need to assure his personal safety was one of the major concerns of Queen Victoria and her ministers.[8] In 1835, Nicholas was sufficiently apprehensive about his personal safety to draft a testament of advice for his heir, the future Alexander II, should he be assassinated when he visited the Prussian king that summer.[9] And, even in 1841, after the Nicholas system had become firmly fixed in Russia for nearly a decade, Baron M. A. Korf recounted the tale of a young nobleman who had written in a letter (subsequently read by the police) that it was necessary to assassinate Nicholas 'for the general good' of Russian society.[10] Yet there was a certain fatalism about Nicholas. After all, as one observer once remarked, 'the Emperor of Russia is a military commander and each one of his days is a day of battle'.[11] Personal danger was a part of any commander's lot, and Nicholas therefore shrugged off any concern which his advisers might express about his personal safety with comments such as, 'God is my protector, and if I am no longer needed for Russia, then He will take me to His bosom!'[12]

But, if the Decembrist revolt made Nicholas aware of personal danger which he chose to ignore, it also made him acutely conscious of the need to learn more about the state of his 'command'. He believed it essential to know what had driven such fine young men as the Decembrists to decide upon so drastic a form of action. From his point of view, after all, most of them had everything to lose and very little to gain since, in many cases, they had brilliant careers before them. Of the 289 young men who would ultimately be punished for their part in the conspiracy, twenty-two were the sons of generals, and ten the sons of colonels. Thirty-eight had fathers who had reached at least the fifth rank (which conferred hereditary noble status and was half-way between the ranks of colonel and general) in the Empire's civil service. Of that number, thirteen were the sons of senators, seven of provincial governors, two of state ministers, and one the son of a statesman who sat on the Imperial Russian State Council.[13]

There was also an element of self-justification in Nicholas's efforts to get to the very bottom of the Decembrist conspiracy. Count Miloradovich had impressed upon him how very unpopular he was with the army, the institution in Russia which he loved above all else, and Nicholas perhaps wanted to convince himself that he was not as unpopular as the revolt made it appear. In fact, there was something almost plaintive in his remark reported by Countess Nesselrode to her brother that, 'I know that I have been a disagreeable brigade commander, an unbearable "division-naire" . . . But now . . . I shall change.'[14] Certainly the fact that the Decembrists had revolted at the moment of his accession made it very clear that they, at least, found him objectionable as a ruler, and some of Nicholas's comments to them as they were brought before him smacked strongly of efforts at self-justification. The tension which Nicholas must have felt during his efforts to question the conspirators was perhaps best expressed by his younger brother when he remarked:

... for us, it is not only a physical fatigue, but a mental strain as well; it cuts one to the heart. These gentlemen speak of horrors with *sang-froid*, as if they had been within their full rights. *Are we low fellows and these gentlemen honourable men, or is it the other way round?*[15]

Most important of all, however, Nicholas feared that the revolt was a far-reaching conspiracy which threatened the very fabric of the state. As he commented to the French ambassador, La Ferronnays, '. . . it is not an army revolt [which we have to deal with here] but a vast conspiracy which, through abject crime, strives to attain absurd ends'.[16] He had even more reason to think so within three weeks when, on 30 December, the two Murav'ev-Apostol brothers and M. P. Bestuzhev-Riumin led the Chernigov regiment in revolt in the distant Ukraine and were halted only after three days in a bloody encounter with loyal troops at Belaia Tserkov. In fact, Nicholas feared that some of the Empire's most prominent statesmen were involved. Among others, M. M. Speranskii, one of those he had consulted about drafting his accession manifesto; General P. D. Kiselev, the commander of a portion of the Second Army in the south; and Admiral Mordvinov all had to convince Nicholas of their innocence. As Nicholas wrote to Konstantin Pavlovich in Warsaw later that month, 'I have a very firm suspicion . . . that all this reaches into the State Council itself, in particular to Mordvinov.'[17]

To investigate the background of the revolt, and to question the accused more systematically, Nicholas appointed an Investigating Commission on 17 December 1825. Reflecting his view of himself as Russia's 'commander', most of the commission was made up of his adjutants, for it would always be Nicholas's first action in time of crisis to send his adjutants to make on-the-spot investigations. Prince A. N. Golitsyn, State Secretary D. N. Bludov, and the Commission's secretary, A. D. Borovkov, a civil servant from the War Ministry, were the only civilians. Of the rest, Generals P. V. Golenishchev-Kutuzov, A. Kh. Benkendorf, V. V. Levashov, A. N. Potapov, A. I. Chernyshev, and Colonel V. F. Adlerberg were all imperial aides-de-camp. Baron I. I. Dibich was Nicholas's Chief of Staff, and the Commission's president, General A. I. Tatishchev, was Minister of War.[18] In all, the Investigating Commission questioned some 579 individuals suspected of being involved in the Decembrist movement, and 289 of these were later dealt out sentences ranging from death to reassignment to other places of service, usually in more remote areas of the Empire.[19]

The Investigating Commission sat for just over five months. Its work was remarkably thorough, aided greatly by the extreme candour with which a number of the Decembrists revealed plans, associations, even innermost thoughts. For, like most in Russia at the time who criticized the established order, the Decembrists saw the Emperor as having the power to correct the many abuses and shortcomings from which Russian society suffered. Beginning with A. N. Radishchev, who first openly challenged the established order with the publication of his *Journey from St Petersburg to Moscow* in 1790, until the failure of the emancipation of 1861 disillusioned Russia's intellectuals, all critics of the established order placed their hopes for reform and change in the Emperor. And, for those of the Decembrists who did not do so, threats of torture, inquisitions held late at night, damp cells and heavy chains were evidently used to gain cooperation.[20]

Thus the Decembrists, many having little thought for their personal fates, poured out denunciations of abuses and flaws in Russian society which were overwhelming in their breadth. Indeed, they spared no one as they tore away the coverings from the many social and economic sores which festered in the very heart of their homeland. The absence of a code of laws in Russia, the hopelessly complex court procedures, the ruinous tax burden which weighed upon the shoulders of the peasantry, the tyranny of local officials, the corruption at all levels of state administration, all were part of the Decembrists' criticism. It had been the government itself which had first pronounced the words 'freedom and emancipation' when it sought to free Russian soil of the French invaders and to emancipate Europe from the yoke of Napoleon. But, said the men who stood accused, such words had no meaning for the Russians who fought for them. As many soldiers said after they returned to Russia from Europe, 'we spilled our blood for the salvation of our homeland but we must again labour as slaves in our masters' fields; we delivered our motherland from the tyrant [Napoleon], but our masters once again tyrannize us!'[21]

The Investigating Commission was empowered only to investigate the Decembrist conspiracy, and its task was complete once its members gave their final report to Nicholas on 30 May 1826. The sentences of the Decembrists were decided upon and announced by a Supreme Criminal Court, especially appointed by Nicholas, which first met on 3 June 1826, to consider the Investigating Commission's findings and to determine the fates of those judged guilty. Interestingly enough, although Nicholas assigned the task of investigating the conspiracy to his adjutants, the formal task of judging the extent of the Decembrists' guilt and assigning punishments was left largely in the hands of civil officials, although some of the appointees to the Supreme Criminal Court did hold military rank. The majority of the court, however, was made up of the Empire's leading statesmen: Prince P. V. Lopukhin (President of the State Council), the Minister of Justice, Prince D. I. Lobanov-Rostovskii, Prince A. B. Kurakin, Prince S. N. Saltykov, Count Lieven, Count Golovkin, Senators

Baranov, Bolgarskii and Lavrov, and the aides-de-camp, Generals Count Lambert, Count Borozdin and Balashov.[22]

After examining the amassed evidence, the Court determined that the five Decembrists judged most guilty should be quartered and that another thirty-one should be beheaded, although Nicholas later commuted all but five capital sentences to imprisonment. On 12 July 1826, all the accused were brought before the Supreme Criminal Court in groups, divided according to how extensive their involvement in the conspiracy was judged to be, and had their sentence read to them. Colonel Pavel Pestel', the leader of the Southern Society; P. G. Kakhovskii, the man who had shot Governor-General Count Miloradovich; S. I. Murav'ev-Apostol and M. P. Bestuzhev-Riumin, who had led the revolt of the Chernigov regiment in the south; and K. F. Ryleev, were sentenced to death by hanging. At three o'clock on the morning of the following day, 13 July, these five were led out on to the square for execution. Their badges of rank were stripped from their uniforms, their swords were broken over their heads, even their uniforms were taken away. Clad in loose robes, they were led up to the scaffold. Nooses were adjusted around their necks and the stools upon which they stood were kicked away. It was a tragic end to their equally tragic effort to win freedom for Russia, for the men who had already suffered a great deal were inadvertently caused to suffer further. In three cases the nooses slipped and the victims fell to the floor of the scaffold. Murav'ev-Apostol, his leg broken in the fall, cried out as his executioners lifted him and his two companions up to be hanged yet a second time: 'Poor Russia! Here we don't even know how to hang a man properly!'[23]

The trial and execution of the Decembrists was over. And, as the bodies of the five who had been hanged were buried in a secret (and still undiscovered) place, the remainder of those judged guilty began their journeys to exile. General A. Kh. Benkendorf, who served for nearly two decades as the head of Nicholas's Third Section, the Empire's secret police, remarked that, 'never before in Russia had there been a court of law which was allowed greater independence' than that which tried the Decembrists.[24] But, in fact, the court never tried, but simply condemned, and the Decembrists never even knew that they had been tried, let alone found guilty, until 12 July when they were told their sentences. Certainly independent thought was not one of their judges' virtues. Prince Lopukhin, the Supreme Criminal Court's president, was almost stone deaf, while Nicholas himself remarked to his mother that Prince Lobanov-Rostovskii was, 'stupid'.[25] Clearly, the court was designed to act only as an extension of Nicholas's own will and he was inclined neither to mercy nor kindness. As he wrote to Konstantin Pavlovich during the height of the investigations; 'We . . . must seek revenge for Russia and for our national honour. For such [criminals] there can be no mercy!'[26] He was even more vehement in his comments to the French ambassador:

The leaders and the instigators of the conspiracy will be dealt with without pity, without mercy. The law demands retribution and, in their cases, I will not use my power to grant mercy. I will be unbending; it is my duty to give this lesson to Russia *and to Europe*.[27]

There was thus more to Nicholas's insistence that the Decembrists be severely punished than personal hatred or revenge. Revenge must be 'for Russia' and for 'national honour'. In his opinion, the law itself demanded 'retribution'. Most of all, however, Nicholas saw it as his duty to give 'a lesson to Russia and to Europe'. As a man, he could feel sympathy for the accused and their families. But as an Emperor, as the Autocrat of All the Russias, he was convinced that he must be 'unbending'. Thus he could grant a generous pension to Ryleev's wife,[28] and yet send her husband to the gallows. And he could write to his mother quite honestly of his dismay that Prince S. G. Volkonskii, the son of one of her ladies-in-waiting, had been condemned to twenty years' hard labour, but his duty as Emperor dictated his course:

. . . this unfortunate cannot be saved . . . It is possible that . . . [his mother] will come here to witness the disgrace of her unworthy son! What a terrible thought – all the more so because I can do nothing to soften his punishment.[29]

Nicholas's close involvement in the proceedings against the Decembrists has caused historians to remark on the flagrant violations of legality involved. It has been said that, 'rarely has there been a judicial case in which defendants suffered more savage and inequitable punishment than that of the Decembrists'.[30] It is certainly true that Nicholas served as prosecutor, judge, jury and executioner for the Decembrists, and, in the context of Western law, a greater violation of the principles of legality could hardly be imagined. Yet it is necessary to put the Decembrists' conspiracy and trial into the context of Russian life and legality at the time, not so much to excuse Nicholas's conduct, as for what such conduct can tell us about his view of the role which the autocrat should play in state affairs. To Nicholas, the Decembrists were traitors of the worst sort, especially since they had contemplated the ultimate crime, tsaricide. His letters to Konstantin Pavlovich in Warsaw make this especially clear:

The more our investigation progresses, the more horrors are revealed before our very eyes. One must see everything and hear with one's own ears all of these monsters in order to believe all of these horrors.

One cannot hurry things because it would be terrible to lose a single thread [of this conspiracy].

It is impossible to ever thank God enough for His help in preserving us from all of these horrors which they had planned for us.[31]

The fact that the Decembrists were mainly army officers only made their crime worse in Nicholas's eyes since the army should be loyal above all else to its supreme commander, the Emperor. As Russia's supreme commander, he was horrified at what the Decembrists had intended. And, if we recall Nicholas's comments as a child about Louis XVI's conduct in 1789, that, 'he would have spared his people a great deal of misery if he had not spared the conspirators,'[32] we can see that he believed that the welfare of his command and of his subjects demanded firmness. He feared the consequences such a revolt could have upon Russia's position in Europe, not only because Russia stood as a champion of legitimacy, but also because Russia's army was her only claim to membership in the European community. His mother, the Dowager Empress, supposedly spent the last hours of the revolt itself wailing, 'What will Europe say?'[33] and Nicholas shared much the same concern. Less than a week after the revolt had been crushed, he summoned the French ambassador, La Ferronnays, to an audience to tell him, 'Today I want only to give you the means to calm the anxiety which the madness of our Russian liberals could arouse in Paris and you may guarantee [to your superiors] that it will be a very long time before they will be in any condition to repeat this sort of attempt again.'[34]

Yet Nicholas's close involvement with the questioning of the Decembrists was not a product only of his horror at their revolt. He knew well that conditions in Russia were far from ideal and he sought to learn from interviews with the Decembrists. One of his first acts after the investigation, trial and sentencing was to ask for a digest of their testimony about Russia's shortcomings, a task given to the secretary of the Investigating Commission, A. D. Borovkov, who drafted a digest notable for its bluntness. This painted a vast panorama of abuses, of a Russia where 'the strong and informers flourish, but where the poor and innocent suffer'.[35] And a measure of Nicholas's sincerity in wanting to learn the true state of his command can be found in the fact that for his digest, blunt and frank though it was, Borovkov rose rapidly in the service and in just more than a decade was made a senator.[36] Nicholas kept throughout his reign Borovkov's digest on his desk, and referred to it frequently.[37]

The revolt, however, had left an indelible mark upon him and would condition his attitude towards all questions of change throughout his years of rule. 'No one can fully comprehend that burning pain which I feel and will continue to feel throughout the rest of my life whenever I remember this day,' he told La Ferronnays.[38] He would always greet news of any irregularity or minor disorder with the comment that, 'these are my friends of the fourteenth' at work again,[39] and he would never be able to trust fully either the nobility or educated public opinion, for he identified both to some degree with the Decembrists. As a result, Nicholas sought to take a more direct part in government, and to assume more responsibility for Russia's day-to-day welfare, than any monarch since Peter the Great. In doing so, Nicholas did precisely what N. M. Karamzin had warned his elder brother against some fifteen years earlier in 1810:

... at the present time, the nobility, dispersed throughout the realm, assist the monarch in the preservation of peace and order; by divesting them of this supervisory authority, he would, like Atlas, take all of Russia upon his shoulders. Could he bear it? A collapse would be frightful.[40]

Nicholas would bear the burden for nearly three decades before the collapse began. And during those years he would take his task seriously – perhaps more seriously than any other Russian monarch. Governing his Empire was, for Nicholas, a daily chore and one to which he devoted nearly every waking hour. That the burden was ultimately too heavy would be evident in the collapse which Russia would suffer in the Crimean War, and in the fact that when Nicholas died at the age of fifty-eight, he would have become an old man whose exhausted organism had not the strength left to fight off a common cold.

2. The New Reign Begins

Historians sometimes divide Nicholas's reign into narrow periods of 'quasi-reform' (1825–30), 'strict conservatism' (1830–48), and a 'system of reaction' (1848–55).[41] Others tend to see the reign in more unified terms, separating its beginning from its latter years in terms of 'significant results' of the reign both at home and abroad in the first fifteen years as opposed to diplomatic defeats and growing tension at home which characterized the latter years.[42] Yet it is important most of all to see the continuity in the reign of Nicholas I; to see it from beginning to end as the creation, development and ultimate failure of an integral system: the Nicholas system in which Nicholas sought to create a personal absolutism so pervasive in nature that he, and those who served as the direct extension of his power, would touch the lives of all in Russia. Nicholas perhaps expressed his aspirations best in the coronation manifesto which he issued on 13 July 1826, the day the five Decembrists were executed and the remainder sent into exile. In proclaiming his desire to serve the welfare of Russia, Nicholas decreed:

Not by daring and rash dreams, which are always destructive, but gradually, and from above, laws will be issued, defects remedied, and abuses corrected. In this manner all modest hopes for improvement, all hopes for strengthening the rule of law, for the expansion of true enlightenment, and the development of industry, will be gradually fulfilled. The legitimate path, open for all, will always be taken by Us with satisfaction. For We do not have, and cannot have, any other desire than to see Our motherland attain the very heights of happiness and glory preordained for her by Providence.[43]

As we have seen, Nicholas ascended the Russian throne with his attitudes about his role as autocrat clearly defined. As Russia's supreme commander, he bore responsibility to his subjects and to God for all that was done within his command. In his view, the Russian autocrat had awesome and far-reaching responsibilities. He must serve as a model of devotion and piety and must conduct himself in a manner that would 'serve as a living example to all'. He should be 'gentle, courteous, and *just*' in the sense of being merciful, yet also firm. He should be 'benevolent and approachable to all unfortunates' but 'must not squander treature'. He should not seek conflicts with foreign powers, but 'must always defend the dignity of Russia'. Above all, he must remember that he was Russian. That, Nicholas once commented, 'means everything'.[44]

Nicholas's view of autocracy comprised the heart of his system, for he was in every sense its personification. His views closely paralleled those which the historian Karamzin had expressed some years earlier in his *Memoir on Ancient and Modern Russia* on the eve of Napoleon's invasion.[45] 'In Russia, the Sovereign is the living law. He favours the good and punishes the bad . . . A soft heart in a monarch is counted as a virtue only when it is tempered with the sense of duty to use sensible severity.' The 'monarch must follow his conscience and nothing else'. But, Karamzin also cautioned, 'forgiveness is praiseworthy in a Sovereign only when extended to offences of a personal or private nature, and not to offences which impinge upon the interests of society'. 'In the Russian monarch concentrate all the powers: our government is fatherly, patriarchal,' and the Emperor's 'sacred person symbolizes the fatherland'. But even though Karamzin considered the autocrat a sacred symbol of the fatherland and answerable only to God, he insisted that, as ruler, he could be neither capricious nor arbitrary; the Emperor must always serve the interests of Russia. These were sentiments which Nicholas often echoed himself, and, in fact, while lying on his deathbed, his last words to his son would reportedly be: 'I shall ascend to pray for Russia . . . Serve Russia!'[46]

Karamzin was perhaps Nicholas's closest adviser during the first weeks of his reign. Beginning in the earliest days of the interregnum, Karamzin came regularly to the Winter Palace, and it would seem that Nicholas wanted very much to appoint him, a man who had been highly critical of Alexander I's efforts to create new political institutions for Russia, to a ministerial post. Karamzin had exhorted Alexander to pay 'more attention to men than to forms', to remember that 'one of the worst political evils of our time is the absence of fear', and that 'skill in choosing and handling men is the foremost among the skills which a Russian sovereign must possess'.[47] Such sentiments must have appealed to Nicholas, who had heard similar injunctions since the days of his childhood and youth. Indeed, in 1814, his mother's parting words to him, as he departed to join the Russian army in the West, had been to remember that, 'of all judgements, that of other men is the most difficult and will demand from you the most attention'.[48] And Nicholas himself regarded his early days on active service, the years just before he received his first active command in 1818, as valuable for 'the priceless practice for learning about men'.[49]

But Karamzin's failing health made it impossible for him to accept a government post, and Nicholas soon released him from service with a princely annual pension of 50,000 roubles.[50] Nevertheless, he sought Karamzin's advice in a number of appointments, the most prominent of which were D. N. Bludov (a member of the Investigating Commission and later Minister of Justice, Minister of the Interior and a count); D. V. Dashkov (later Minister of Justice); and S. S. Uvarov (later a count, who served first as rector of St Petersburg University and later as Minister of Public Instruction). These men had been close associates of Karamzin in the Arzamas circle,[51] a literary society which had often served as a vehicle through which writers expressed their mutual admiration. The poet Pushkin was perhaps its most famous member, but it also included V. A. Zhukovskii, the poet who first taught Russian to the Empress Aleksandra Fedorovna and later became a tutor to Nicholas's sons.

Karamzin's injunction to pay 'more attention to men than to forms' was something which Nicholas took very much to heart during the early months of his reign. The reactionary Count Arakcheev, Alexander's major adviser in domestic matters, was relieved of his duties, as was the obscurantist M. L. Magnitskii, the rector of Kazan University who had so influenced Alexander's educational policies. Nicholas permitted most of Alexander's other advisers to remain for the time being, though several were of advanced years and soon died or left their posts for reasons of poor health. To those whom he regarded as especially talented, Nicholas gave more responsibilities. Count V. P. Kochubei (later granted the title of prince) continued to serve as he had throughout Alexander's reign. So did Speranskii, and Alexander's talented and efficient Minister of Finance, E. F. Kankrin. But Nicholas's close relationship with Karamzin, who, after all, had never held a high administrative post, set the pattern that would develop further during the next three decades. Nicholas insisted that he keep all decision-making power in his own hands, and relegated only lesser issues to his ministers. This set a precedent which would be followed in the Russian service for many years, and even as late as the 1870s, A. V. Golovnin (Minister of Public Instruction, 1861–6) would still lament that, 'from conversations with our present-day statesmen, it is clear that, because of their absorption in . . . questions and subjects of secondary importance . . . they have absolutely no opportunity . . . to reflect upon things and to gain some perspective on the general state of affairs'.[52]

Nicholas thus relied upon adjutants – men who could serve as a direct extension of his personal will – to advise him on many important issues, and most of these advisers were military men. Virtually all of those upon whom he relied most heavily would be so. In civil affairs, during the early years of his reign, Nicholas turned to Generals A. Kh. Benkendorf, A. I. Chernyshev and V. V. Levashov, as well as General P. A. Kleinmikhel, a man who has been described as 'rude, brutal, and hypocritical', but who was absolutely loyal, even to the extent that much later in the reign he would adopt as his own Nicholas's illegitimate children from a liaison the Emperor contracted after the Empress's illness.[53] It was to these men that Nicholas entrusted many important affairs of state, especially those which he would seek to deal with outside the framework of regular state institutions.

Even before the final episode in the drama of the Decembrists' condemnation had been played out, Nicholas created the first of these personal institutions of administration. On 25 June 1826, his thirtieth birthday, he created the Third Section of His Majesty's Own Chancery to act as the moral and political guardian of all Russia. As one noted historian has indicated, 'the vagueness of the tasks assigned to the Third Section is remarkable indeed'.[54] It was anyone's guess as to what Nicholas meant by his instruction that the Third Section should gather 'information concerning all events, without exception', and no one ever defined who the 'dangerous and suspicious persons' were whom Nicholas urged the Third Section to arrest or exile.[55] Even Benkendorf was somewhat baffled at first, and the oft-quoted though apocryphal tale that Nicholas passed him a white handkerchief with the comment, 'here are your orders [as newly appointed Head of the Third Section]. Take this and wipe away the tears of my people',[56] illustrates the amorphous quality of the secret police organization he created. To Nicholas, the function of the Third Section was self-evident: it was to serve as an extension of his personal will into every corner of the Empire. As Benkendorf expressed it, 'Our Sovereign

... wishes to see in ... [a gendarme officer] just such an Ambassador, just such an honourable and useful representative of the government, as he has in London, Vienna, Berlin, and Paris.'[57] 'The gendarmerie has become the moral physician of the people.'[58]

Under the stewardship of Benkendorf and his immediate successors, the Third Section spread its tentacles over all of Russia. By 1836, a year in which Russia fought no foreign wars beyond the usual annual campaign against the natives of the Caucasus, and faced no internal threats or conspiracies, some 1,631 individuals were kept under police surveillance, 1,080 of them for political reasons. That same year, the Third Section chancery dealt with more than 15,000 petitions and appeals relating to a wide variety of issues: appeals against court decisions, requests for scholarships, requests for tax exemptions, political denunciations and many, many others.[59] The Third Section would later increase its powers and further expand its involvement in the lives of Russians. As social and political opinion began to denounce the abuses of Russia's government, and as Nicholas and his advisers became more fearful of the challenge posed by the revolutions of 1848 in Europe (a threat made more real by the Third Section's discovery of the socialist 'conspiracy' of M. V. Butashevich-Petrashevskii's circle in 1849), surveillance was intensified within state offices themselves. Mail sent from one city to another was opened regularly so that Third Section agents might more accurately gauge public opinion and keep a vigilant look-out for the development of new 'conspiracies'. By the early 1850s, the power and scope of the Third Section's agents would become so pervasive that they even detailed an agent to keep Nicholas's second son, the Grand Duke Konstantin Nikolaevich, under regular surveillance, and on a number of occasions this agent clandestinely examined even the secret files which, as Chief of Russia's navy, the Grand Duke kept in his private office.[60]

This, of course, was done without Nicholas's consent, or even his knowledge, and the discovery of such surveillance upon members of the Imperial Family would undoubtedly have enraged him, so firmly did he adhere to the Fundamental Laws of 1797 which gave to all members of the Imperial Family 'an utterly exclusive position outside the normal bounds of both public and civil law'.[61] The fact that such surveillance of a grand duke was undertaken, even when its discovery would have meant ruin of those who ordered it, is further evidence that not even Nicholas himself was able fully to control the bureaucratic police apparatus which he unleashed in 1826. Perhaps equally important, the Third Section's efforts to guard Russia from internal threats by carrying its surveillance into the bosom of the Imperial Family itself illustrates another funda-mental aspect of the bureaucratic absolutism of the Nicholas system as it would evolve by the latter part of the reign. Since there was an agency designated as Russia's first guardian against internal sedition, then it followed logically that such sedition must exist. Otherwise, there would be no reason for maintaining such an organization. The perpetuation of such an organization obviously involved the livelihoods of a number of officials. As a result they spared no effort in seeking to rout out the threats to Russia's internal order which, in their view, must exist by definition.

Although the Third Section served as 'the moral physician of the people', Nicholas also took steps to make his subjects less susceptible to certain ailments. Some of Nicholas's advisers turned almost immediately after the events of 14 December to the Empire's system of education as a prime cause of the disaffection which led to the revolt. Anonymous accusations that Russia's educational system was guilty of having poisoned the younger generation with dangerous ideas were widespread. Some even went so far as to argue that the Imperial Lyceum at Tsarskoe Selo was a serious threat and should be closed.[62] Most notable in condemning Russia's schools as breeding-grounds of sedition and revolution was General I. V. Vasil'chikov, the imperial aide-de-camp to whom Nicholas had assigned the task of arresting all conspirators who could be found in the central part of the capital on the evening after the revolt. 'The entire contemporary generation is infected,' Vasil'chikov wrote. He urged not only that Kazan and Kharkov Universities be closed, but that the aristocracy's practice of engaging tutors for their children should also be closely examined and curtailed: '. . . home education also is a festering sore to the eradication of which should be devoted all of our resources.'[63] To keep Russia's noble youth pure from the contamination of such ideas, Vasil'chikov urged Nicholas to establish Cadet Corps schools in all provincial capitals, 'where the education so necessary for our time can be combined with military discipline'.[64] Education should be under the control of generals, who, 'with their service and moral principles would represent the best possible guarantee' for instilling unswerving loyalty to the autocracy in the minds of Russia's younger generation.[65]

Nicholas was not prepared to follow so obscurantist a course as that proposed by Vasil'chikov. His advisers were men of 'more thoughtful and sensible conservatism',[66] especially during the early years of his reign. Nevertheless, he was convinced that foreign ideas were to some degree responsible for the Decembrist revolt. As he wrote to his brother Konstantin Pavlovich in early January, 'everything which took place here evidently was . . . the result . . . of foreign influences'.[67] He therefore would seek to attack such influences throughout his reign in an effort to eliminate broader sources of discontent. While the events of 14 December had shown him that he had the necessary resources at his command to crush a similar revolt, he continued to fear more widespread movements such as the mass upheaval led by the Cossack Emelian Pugachev in the 1770s. That was the thought which had plagued his mind from the moment the revolt on the Senate Square had been crushed. On 17 December he had written to his elder brother of his relief that 'there remains only a small amount of disquiet among the masses which, I hope, will be quickly dispersed'.[68] On 11 January 1826, he wrote to him of his concern that 'among the masses there still are circulating rumours that you have not come [to St Petersburg] because you are under arrest in Warsaw and similar nonsense'.[69] Nicholas would always have such fears. In 1849, admittedly when he was particularly fearful of revolution spreading to Russia, he told the Slavophile publicist, Iu. F. Samarin, whom he had ordered arrested and brought into his presence, 'I know that you did not have this intention. But you have let loose among the masses a dangerous idea, suggesting that Russian tsars from the time of Peter the Great acted only according to the suggestions and under the influence of the Germans. If this idea reaches the masses it will produce terrible calamities.'[70]

Nicholas's first step in dealing with the many accusations which he had received about Russia's educational institutions was to limit access to them. His grandson, Alexander III, once subscribed to the position that secondary education for the lower classes was dangerous because it bred 'contempt for parents, dissatisfaction with their own station, and bitterness towards the existing and, in the nature of things, inevitable inequality in the financial position of various social groups'.[71] Nicholas held a similar view. In July 1826, he asked the State Council to pass a law to prevent peasant children from being admitted to schools that might prepare them for further education, which, in turn, might enable them 'to rise above their station'.[72] But, on the advice of V. P. Kochubei, Nicholas changed his tack and ordered that the Minister of Public Instruction act to restrict admissions. As Kochubei told him, a ministerial circular would be preferable to a formal State Council decree, because, 'a law, published by the Council, would become known to all of Europe' and would create an unfavourable impression abroad.[73]

But Nicholas wanted to do more than keep Russia's masses away from potentially dangerous ideas. He also wanted even to keep the élite in Russia free from Western influences. As he told Prince P. P. Gagarin in 1827, he did not like to send young noblemen abroad to be trained, even in such technical subjects as naval affairs, because 'young men return from there with a spirit of criticism'.[74] Even in cases where foreign study was necessary, as in the case of educating new faculty staff for Russia's universities, Nicholas wanted to limit it as much as possible. In 1827, he insisted that students sent abroad must 'absolutely be of pure Russian background', and three years later he decreed that students must study in Russia between the ages of ten and eighteen;[75] a policy which would subject them to the influences which Nicholas regarded as most desirable during their most impressionable years.

Nicholas's creation of the Third Section and his efforts to limit access to education and Western ideas were only reactions to pressures of the moment, a stop-gap effort, as it were, to strengthen Russia's defences against sedition and revolt. Both he and his closest advisers well knew that piecemeal reactions to specific threats could not provide Russia with the social calm, the political stability and the economic progress which were necessary for Russia to attain, as Nicholas had proclaimed in his coronation manifesto, 'the very heights of happiness and glory preordained for her by Providence'. There was no doubt in Nicholas's mind that, to improve conditions in Russia, some adjustment in the Empire's present state would have to be made. The major question was what would have to be done and how it should be accomplished. Certainly Nicholas and his advisers were not opposed to economic progress so long as it was kept within the bounds of preserving autocracy and the existing social system. Only much later in the reign would Russian statesmen argue against alterations of the existing order out of fear that any changes might have dangerous consequences.

3. The Committee of 6 December

To determine just what the state of the Empire was at the time, and what reforms should be considered, Nicholas formed a special committee of his closest advisers on 6 December 1826. Count V. P. Kochubei was its chairman, and the other members were Count P. A. Tolstoi, I. V. Vasil'chikov, Prince A. N. Golitsyn, Baron I. I. Dibich, and M. M. Speranskii. D. N. Bludov and D. V. Dashkov, both soon to rise to ministerial rank, served as the secretaries of the committee. As we would expect several of these members were military men. Vasil'chikov, a cavalry general with a long and brilliant war record, had been wounded at both Borodino and Leipzig. Count P. A. Tolstoi had been an Imperial General aide-de-camp since the days of Nicholas's father. Like Vasil'chikov he had fought with distinction in the Napoleonic Wars, and had also been the Military Governor-General of St Petersburg early in Alexander I's reign. Baron Dibich, who had become an Imperial General aide-de-camp in 1818, and had fought with distinction throughout the Napoleonic Wars, was Chief of Staff when Nicholas ascended the throne, and was instrumental in arresting Decembrists in the south.

Aside from these three, however, the rest of the committee were civil officials who had extensive experience, and were regarded as some of Russia's most prominent statesmen. Count Kochubei had been a member of Alexander I's progressive-minded Unofficial Committee early in his reign, and as such discussed broad programmes of reform in Russia, including some sort of constitutional limitation upon the autocrat's powers. Although Kochubei had grown more conservative, or perhaps simply more realistic, by 1825, he was without doubt one of Russia's leading statesmen and had a great deal of knowledge about the Empire which soon would lead to his appointment as President of the Committee of Ministers, a post in which he would serve from 1827 until his death in 1834.

M. M. Speranskii, as perhaps the leading statesman of Alexander I's reign and the Emperor's closest confidant for a number of years, had drafted far-reaching reform proposals, both for modernizing Russian society and for renovating the administrative machinery of the Empire. He had fallen into disfavour in 1812 when, having become the object of almost universal hatred among the nobility, Alexander was forced to dismiss him in an effort to gain the united support of the Russian aristocracy on the eve of Napoleon's invasion. In trying to improve the quality of administration and government in Russia, Speranskii had attacked some of the nobility's most cherished prerogatives. He had argued that merit must be the determining factor in reaching the higher ranks of the civil service; he had stressed the need for better education among senior officials; and he had attacked some of the aristocracy's favourite schemes for advancement in the service, especially their practice of equating court service with other types of state service duties. Finally, although it is not clear just how widely known his proposals were, Speranskii had drafted plans for a limited and gradual emancipation of the nobility's serfs. He was, in brief, a defender of rational bureaucratic government which the nobility in Russia bitterly opposed since they regarded the bureaucracy as interposing itself between the Emperor and his most faithful servants, the nobility.[76]

Bludov and Dashkov quite probably owed their positions on the Committee of 6 December to the influence of Karamzin, but both were quite well-suited for their assignments. Each had already served in the Russian bureaucracy for nearly a quarter of a century, and had had extensive experience in internal affairs and legal matters. Dashkov was especially well-educated, though Bludov's home education had been of far higher quality than was usual at the time. Bludov had already served his new Emperor loyally as a member of the Investigating Commission, and after the Committee of 6 December completed its work nearly six years later, he would soon become Minister of the Interior. In the same year, 1832, Dashkov would become Russia's Minister of Justice. The remaining member of the committee, Prince Golitsyn, had been in state service for more than thirty years, had held ministerial rank since 1817, and had been one of the Emperor Alexander's closest confidants during the last years of his reign.

Nicholas assigned to the Committee of 6 December the task of undertaking a thoroughgoing survey of the entire state of the Russian Empire, and by its creation he established a pattern for dealing with especially critical state problems which he would follow throughout his reign: rather than rely upon the bureaucracy or upon educated public opinion for advice in bringing about change, he would turn to secret committees composed of his most trusted counsellors. Nicholas regarded the bureaucracy as incompetent, and educated public opinion was something of which he was always wary after the Decembrist revolt. The Committee of 6 December, then, was his first secret committee created for dealing with pressing problems of state. But no other body during the course of his reign would have such broad opportunities for reviewing Russian conditions and for making recommendations for their improvement. All succeeding secret committees would devote their efforts only to portions of the general review which the Committee of 6 December accomplished.

The committee's first task was to examine various reform proposals found among the papers of Alexander I, and then to review all aspects of state administration and set forth rules for its better organization.[77] In directing the committee to proceed in such a manner, Nicholas also set the framework for all subsequent reform. Since he regarded the basic structure and organization of the Russian state as healthy and sound, Nicholas urged only that the machinery of government be tuned more finely so as to function in the most effective manner possible. He never for a moment contemplated fundamental changes in the organization of the state, its administration or Russian society itself.

Perhaps Speranskii stated this view most clearly when he argued that their task was, 'not the full alteration of the existing order of government, but its refinement by means of a few particular changes and additions'.[78] The committee thus examined first the areas of responsibility of all state institutions so as to delineate more precisely the functions of each. They discussed at some length the division of functions and the separation of judicial, legislative and administrative institutions. But all the while, they skirted the major issue. Whenever they came to the fundamental question of providing political guarantees to defend society against arbitrary power, they put it aside and pleaded that it would be dangerous to consider fundamental changes in the existing order.[79]

Typical of the committee's examination of Russia's central institutional structure was its attempt to improve the quality of personnel in the Imperial Senate. The committee was clearly aware that 'the Senate frequently is filled with individuals who have no experience in civil affairs and know neither the national laws nor even the language; men who have spent their entire lives in other fields of endeavour'.[80] Men who had risen to Senatorial rank by 1825 were those who had been educated during the days of Catherine II or Paul I, when noblemen were taught at home by tutors of often dubious merit. Even as late as 1826, after Speranskii's educational requirements for senior officials had been in effect for well over a decade, the censor A. V. Nikitenko noted in his diary that 'among us it is customary to educate young men [noblemen] for the fashionable world' rather than for administrative careers.[81] In fact, even the educational requirements which Speranskii had introduced in 1810, admirable as they were, were not the best training for careers in a government that was called upon to solve increasingly complex problems. For Speranskii's reforms emphasized general education rather than administrative specialization. Thus, even a certificate from an élite school, such as one of the Cadet Corps institutions or the Lyceum at Tsarskoe Selo, meant that even though a young man might have studied a disparate and wide-ranging curriculum, he had little of the specialized knowledge needed to deal with highly complex economic or, in the case of the Senate, legal matters.[82]

What they found to be true of the Senate was, of course, also true of the state administration at provincial level. The problem of poorly educated officials who, despite high birth, had learned many of their tasks through a kind of 'on the job training' programme,[83] required basic solutions. But the Committee of 6 December proposed to deal with the problem of incompetent Senators by opening up Senate membership to men of the fourth civil rank (High State Councillor) rather than to only men of the higher third, second and first ranks. This proposal Nicholas himself rejected because, as he noted, 'there is no certainty of finding in the rank of High State Councillor people who are more knowledgeable and talented in civil affairs'.[84]

In proposing reforms of the central government, then, the committee dealt only with narrow technical changes and adjustments. In the end, it acted to perpetuate the very state order that it had been called upon to investigate. It also took a position that would become increasingly characteristic of the Nicholas system in its discussion of local administration. Here they stressed the need for a surveillance that was 'not personal and despotic like [that] ... of the Governors-General ... but ... continual on the basis of firmly established rules [which would have] not only the means to certify disorders and abuses, but to end them; to halt abuses not after months and years, but to nip them in the bud; to hold officials strictly accountable and to bring the guilty to trial'.[85] This was the same view that underlay Nicholas's creation of the Third Section, and it demonstrated a fundamental weakness in Russian attitudes towards local administration and the methods of governing such a vast state. Most important, Russia suffered from a backward judiciary which provided no solid foundation upon which to erect an efficient system of administrative law. In other European states, the problem of controlling local officials fell into the domain of administrative law and were dealt with by the legal system as such. But in Russia, statesmen were forced to deal with what was basically the juridical problem of control as an administrative rather than a legal issue, and surveillance thus became the most essential means for preserving the state's administrative power. Russia's entire system of local administration at the accession of Nicholas I was, and continued to be, based upon a false hope that the relationship between central and local organs of government could be reduced to a matter of form and not of power.[86]

Beginning with the recommendations of the Committee of 6 December, and continuing throughout his reign, Nicholas and his advisers would seek to centralize further the governmental process and extend the power of the central bureaucracy as far as possible into the Russian countryside. But this required a functionally professional civil service that could be relied upon to execute commands in a stable and consistent manner. And this Nicholas was never able to achieve. As one official noted, 'bureaucracy as a disciplined, corporate body, which serves defined political ends, does not exist in Russia'.[87] Equally important, the sort of centralization which Nicholas and his advisers sought from the very beginning – something similar to the direct chain of command in the army – required swift and reliable communications. And in an Empire as vast as Russia, where railways would not be seriously developed until well into the second half of the nineteenth century, and where roads were pitifully inadequate because they were in poor repair and turned into seas of mud in the spring and autumn, it was impossible to have the sort of communications demanded by the military-like centralization which Nicholas regarded as the ideal.

The clear ordering of relationships between all social groups in his Empire was something which Nicholas insisted upon from the very outset. Just as the relationship between men of different ranks was clearly specified in the army, so Nicholas strove to achieve an equal clarity for the relationships between various social groups in Russia. He thus directed the committee to define more precisely the relationships between nobles and serfs as well as clarifying the rights and privileges of the nobility. As one might expect from a body whose members were of high aristocratic rank, the Committee of 6 December concentrated first on the question of the nobility in Russia. In particular, they wished to prevent men of lower social origin from gaining access to the nobility through service. They therefore recommended that noble status be granted only by imperial charter, and that men who won high rank in the service be given membership in a specially created group known as 'esteemed citizens'.[88] In so doing, they were still grappling with the problem which had troubled the Russian nobility ever since Peter the Great had introduced the Table of Ranks in 1722, and thereby opened access to noble rank through service in the military or the bureaucracy. Throughout the eighteenth century, the Russian nobility had always felt uneasy about ennoblement simply through formal service and bureaucratic procedures, and insisted that something more than a document signed by a clerk in the Office of Heraldry was needed to make a man or his family legitimately noble.[89] But although the Committee of 6 December sought to limit access to the nobility, they made no effort to gain political rights for that class to protect its privileged position. Indeed, they insisted that Russia's population ought to be given 'no political rights whatsoever'.[90] Such lack of interest in political rights, even for their own class, was again typical of attitudes which the nobility had held from the beginning of the eighteenth century. So long as its dominant position in the countryside was assured, the nobility did not feel the need for political rights to enable them to defend their privileges from attacks by the ruler. Their position had been momentarily challenged by Paul I at the end of the eighteenth century, but until the emancipation of 1861 deprived them of their absolute and arbitrary power in the countryside, Russia's nobility did not demand any sort of political representation as a class.

As far as the peasantry was concerned, the Committee of 6 December did little except to resurrect Speranskii's proposal, made nearly two decades earlier, that serf-owners be prohibited from selling their peasants apart from the land so as to institute what Speranskii had called 'true serfdom'. In this the peasantry would be bound to the land rather than to their owners. But, Speranskii and the other members of the committee insisted, the regulating of serf–master relationships should be undertaken very gradually, and they proposed little beyond urging improvements in the administration of the peasants under the stewardship of the state treasury in the hope that this might serve as an example and induce the nobility to treat their own peasants better.

Moderate as they were, none of the proposals for reform and change made by the Committee of 6 December ever became reality. But the committee's work, even its existence, was significant because its approach to the problems of government, its view of the Russian state and society and its attitudes towards change, embodied the essence of the system which Nicholas and his advisers would soon create. Suspicion of educated public opinion, distrust of the regular bureaucracy, stress upon the need for only minor adjustments in the state order and insistence that all changes, no matter how slight, be made very gradually so as not to disturb the social equilibrium, best characterized this approach. While Nicholas and his advisers regarded educated opinion as politically un-reliable and dangerous, and viewed the bureaucracy as ineffectual, they considered Russia's state order to be fundamentally viable. This meant that the most critical problems facing Russia – serfdom, economic back-wardness and stagnation – would be dealt with in the dark reaches of chancery conference rooms during the three decades when Nicholas sat upon the Russian throne. Yet, while Nicholas and his advisers sought to shroud their actions in secrecy, they felt it essential to have as open a view as possible into the minds and actions of Russians. Surveillance – 'to end abuses not after months and years, but to nip them in the bud', but also, as in the case of the Third Section, to serve as a moral guardian for all of Russia – became a fundamental aspect of the Nicholas system. Thus the state shut itself off from educated society by means of secret commit-tees while educated public opinion withdrew deeper into the recesses of the small circles of intellectuals which began to form in the 1830s and 1840s. Both became alienated from Russian reality: the state by a nearly impenetrable wall of bureaucratic formalism, and educated opinion by its fear of coming to grips with the real problems which Russia faced.

4. First Efforts at Reform

Neither the Committee of 6 December's failure to propose concrete solutions to the very real problems which confronted Russia, nor the fact that its members were far from sharing the Decembrists' criticism of the existing order, prevented Nicholas from taking certain steps to improve conditions in his Empire during the early years of his reign. Most im-portant, he allowed no favourites to gain the sort of ascendancy in internal affairs enjoyed by Arakcheev or Prince Golitsyn during Alexander I's last years. For Nicholas uncompromisingly regarded ministers of state as agents to implement his decisions, as extensions of his imperial will.

Nevertheless, Nicholas proceeded cautiously, and fear of disrupting the delicate balance of social and economic forces in Russia seems once again to have been one of his prime concerns. Important also was his realization that he knew little of the business of ruling and needed time to acquaint himself with the intricacies of Russian state affairs. Therefore he followed very closely the advice he would one day give his son about how a newly crowned Emperor should govern. Summon the State Council and tell them that everything was to be preserved and continued as before 'without even the slightest changes', he counselled his son. Next wait a year or two before even making changes in ministerial personnel, so as 'to become well acquainted with state affairs and with individuals . . . Then,' Nicholas commanded, 'begin to *rule*.'[91]

Only after his first year on the throne did Nicholas begin to examine the state which he had inherited when he created the Committee of 6 December. Only after that had been done did he begin to replace the high-ranking personnel he had inherited from his brother. Arakcheev had already withdrawn from state affairs even before Nicholas had formally assumed the reins of power. Since Golitsyn's influence on state affairs had depended more upon his personal relationship with Alexander than upon his position as Director of the Postal Department, the change of rulers removed him from his influential position in state affairs. A number of Alexander's other senior advisers were quite aged, and in 1827 Nicholas began to replace them with more vigorous men. In April 1827, Prince Lopukhin, the President of the State Council died and Nicholas replaced him with Count V. P. Kochubei, a man who, at the age of fifty-nine, was some fifteen years younger. Likewise, in 1827, Nicholas replaced the seventy-year-old Prince Lobanov-Rostovskii as Minister of Justice with the younger and more energetic Prince A. A. Dolgorukov; and in 1828 he replaced A. S. Shishkov as Minister of Public Instruction with Count K. A. Lieven, a man some thirteen years younger. V. S. Lanskoi, like Shishkov aged seventy-four, was replaced by General A. A. Zakrevskii, a man twenty-nine years his junior.

Nicholas kept some of Alexander's ministers at their posts, but these were of notable ability. Count K. V. Nesselrode, who had become Foreign Minister in 1814, continued to serve until the end of Nicholas's reign, and E. F. Kankrin, whom Nicholas made a count in 1829, continued as Minister of Finance until 1844. Beyond this, Nicholas set out to reorganize the Russian navy and restore it to the power it had held under Catherine II in the last third of the eighteenth century.[92] In 1828 he appointed a general aide-de-camp, Prince A. S. Menshikov, to reform the navy, despite the fact that Menshikov had no experience whatever in naval affairs and had refused a naval appointment under Alexander I precisely because he did not have the necessary expertise.[93]

Menshikov's appointment as Naval Chief of Staff was an outstanding example, by no means isolated, of Nicholas's habit of appointing generals aide-de-camp to deal with critical state problems. His appointment of General Benkendorf to head the Third Section was another example.

Indeed, Nicholas soon began to use His Majesty's Own Chancery as something like a personal 'General Staff' in an effort to bypass the regular bureaucracy and to assign critical state problems to agencies over which he could exercise direct personal control. When he ascended the throne, His Majesty's Own Chancery consisted mainly of one small bureau, whose functions were loosely defined as having to do with questions which required the Emperor's personal attention. Under Nicholas, this section ultimately evolved into an organization which had control over civil service promotions and positions. But much more important was the manner in which the young Emperor expanded the Chancery to deal with a whole range of problems and state affairs by creating, in 1826, the Third Section, and, in 1828, the Fourth Section to administer charitable and educational institutions in the name of his mother, the Dowager Empress.

Beyond these sections of His Majesty's Own Chancery, Nicholas created others to deal with especially difficult problems of state. Later we will see how he used the newly created Fifth Section in 1835 as something resembling a 'General Staff for Peasant Affairs'. Most important, at the beginning of his reign, even before he created the Third Section, Nicholas had formed a Second Section on 31 January 1826, to deal with the problems of codifying the laws of the Empire, a problem which had defied the best efforts of Russia's Emperors since the time of Peter the Great. Every monarch since had sought to codify the Empire's laws, for Russia had had no law code after that issued by Tsar Aleksei Mikhailovich in 1649. Because legislation in Russia was by imperial decree, and since the number of such decrees vastly increased beginning with Peter the Great, Russia was forced to function throughout the eighteenth and first quarter of the nineteenth century with no clearly defined body of laws. This created many serious problems for Russian subjects and officials alike. Since no one could demonstrate what laws governed a particular situation, officials who had access to files of imperial decrees in the inner recesses of St Petersburg's chanceries could be completely despotic in their behaviour, especially since the decrees were often contradictory and could be interpreted in many different ways.

Although the Second Section was headed from the start by the prominent jurist, M. A. Balugianskii, one of Nicholas's childhood tutors, much of the impetus for its creation came from Speranskii, who presented a proposal for codifying the Russian laws to Nicholas on 26 January 1826. Speranskii urged that the state should seek three goals in dealing with the law: first, the collection and publication of all decrees issued since 1649; secondly, using the collection as a basis, the compilation of a digest of laws to facilitate access to the law for all who needed reference to them; finally, the drafting of a new law code, using the digest of laws as a guide, which would harmonize the existing Russian legal forms with the new concepts needed to meet the needs and demands of a modern society.[94] Nicholas, however, would support only the first two tasks. He wanted to clarify regulations and procedures and to tune the state administrative machinery more finely so that it would function in an ideal manner. But he wanted no part of fundamental changes in the social and political amalgam which had emerged in Russia during the course of the previous century. Further, he tended to equate new law codes with the *philosophes* and with revolutionary developments in late eighteenth-century France,[95] and rejected such as dangerous for Russia.

The task which Speranskii proposed was immense. He had at first thought that the compilation of a collection of laws and the codification of a digest based upon them would take less than three years. In fact, it took more than twice as long.[96] Most complex of all, in the early stages of the work, all the decrees and laws issued since 1649 had to be collected together. Certain of the Empire's decrees and laws, up to the end of Catherine II's reign, had never even been printed, being circulated only in manuscript form to the central governmental bureaux to which they applied.[97] And, equally difficult, before the establishment of the State Council as 'the focal point of all affairs of the central administration' in 1810,[98] there had been no single source of legislation in the Russian Empire. Laws and decrees were issued by a variety of government agencies 'in the name of the Emperor', as well as by the Emperor himself, with the result that many decrees were scattered throughout governmental offices both in the capital and in the provinces.[99] From the beginning of the eighteenth century, Russian law had thus been 'created by the arbitrary and capricious decisions of the sovereign and of various government bodies for specific and individual cases, without regard to general concepts, legal traditions, and precedent'.[100] Anyone who seriously undertook the task of codifying the Russian law would first have to become familiar with this disparate mass of legal material created in the course of nearly two centuries. Only then would it be possible to create from it a digest of laws.

The work which Speranskii, Balugianskii and the Second Section undertook between 1826 and 1830 was aided to some extent by the efforts of a Commission on Laws created by Alexander I and headed by Baron G. A. Rosenkampf. Rosenkampf had first searched systematically through the archives for decrees and had ordered the compilation of a preliminary register of earlier legislation. On the basis of this work, he and his assistants had succeeded in preparing a brief *Systematic Survey of Existing Laws of the Russian Empire with the Foundations of Law Derived from Them*, a collection of some fifteen volumes published between 1815 and 1822. Alexander I had not shown much interest in the commission's work, and had allowed it to stagnate. Yet despite its limited and technical nature, Rosenkampf's *Systematic Survey* was an important step in paving the way for Speranskii and his assistants.[101]

The Second Section of His Majesty's Own Chancery, officially created at the end of January 1826, began to meet regularly in April.[102] It owed much of its success to Speranskii's talents at bureaucratic organization, for it was far more efficiently set up than other governmental offices in St Petersburg at the time. Its members were specialists: jurists and young men with some legal training, even though institutions to train such individuals would not be founded in Russia until later in Nicholas's reign. Given the vast amount of material to be sifted, the speed with which the Second Section worked was amazing. By 1828 the first volume of the *Complete Collection of the Laws of the Russian Empire* was ready for printing, and by 1830 the first series of the *Complete Collection*, comprising forty-five volumes supposedly including all laws in Russia until December 1825 was complete.[103] Urged on by Speranskii's driving personality, and stimulated to further labour by Nicholas's own interest,[104] the Second Section completed a fifteen-volume *Digest of the Laws of the Russian Empire* by 1 January 1833. Two years later, this *Digest* became effective as the sole authoritative source of law.[105] For the first time in almost two centuries, the Russian Empire had a code of laws which, at least to some degree, reflected its existing political, social and administrative realities.

Even so, we have to note that the *Complete Collection of Laws* was not as complete as its title indicated. A number of secret decrees and acts were not included, these materials being kept behind locked doors and Nicholas's permission being needed for the publication of each item. He refused to allow many of them to be published, and he made his decisions not on the basis of juridical considerations, but on the basis of what he regarded as politically most expedient.[106] Important legislative material was thus excluded, partly because Nicholas regarded the collection as a historical source rather than an active code of laws (that function was filled by the *Digest*, which contained only laws still in force). And history, for Nicholas, was more important for what he wished to have remembered than for recording what actually occurred.

Whatever its shortcomings, the compilation and codification of the Empire's laws was hailed throughout most of the nineteenth century as one of the most significant feats in Russia before the Great Reforms. Nicholas made Speranskii a count, and the careers of several who worked under his tutelage advanced rapidly, especially those of Bludov, Dashkov and Baron Korf. And there is no question as to the significance of their labours. For the first time most major legislative acts were brought together in one place, published and made accessible to all who needed to refer to them. As Speranskii's most important biographer has described the result of the Second Section's work:

Jurisprudence, the study and history of law became possible. Judges and administrators were provided with a relatively reliable source book, and their interpretations and decisions could be checked by reviewing authorities (something that had been almost impossible in the past, as every court and office had a different and incomplete set of legal sources) . . . Codification was . . . another means for creating a *Kulturgemeinschaft* in the existing *Staatsgemeinschaft* of the Empire. Again it showed Speranskii's belief that far-going social and economic processes can be introduced and helped along by administrative measures.[107]

The publication of the *Complete Collection of the Laws* and its accompanying *Digest* also struck at the heart of bureaucratic caprice and arbitrariness. To be sure, the simple publication of the Empire's laws did not end the tyranny which officials imposed upon those who came into contact with them. But their arbitrariness could no longer continue unchecked, for it was possible to review their decisions in the light of a clearly existing body of law. An important step had been taken towards introducing clear-cut notions of legality into the lives of Russians.

The publication of the *Complete Collection of the Laws* and its *Digest* was a critical step in the genesis of the Nicholas system. Nicholas, as we have seen, sought to transfer responsibility for all problems in Russia to himself or those who served him as adjutants. On one level, this meant that the positions of ministers came to be far more like imperial adjutants than had been the case before. Nicholas now required written and oral reports from them on a regular basis, and regarded it as his business to know about even very minor problems. But minister-adjutants were usually empowered only to deal with the day-to-day problems of administration. Hence Nicholas appointed his special adjutants, all highly trusted advisers, to deal with particularly pressing issues, and formed them into such secret committees as the Committee of 6 December – a committee that was so secretive that when the Minister of Finance, Kankrin, was called before it, he was not told its purpose, and did not know (or, at least, felt called upon to act as if he did not know) of its existence.[108]

Rather than rely upon the regular bureaucracy in Russia, Nicholas in some cases institutionalized the use of adjutants to deal with special problems of state, particularly in his creation of the Third Section under General Benkendorf. This agency embodied another fundamental principle of the Nicholas system: the use of extensive and intensive surveillance. Everything in Russia was to function according to clear-cut rules and regulations, just as Nicholas's ideal form of organization, the army, was supposed to function. That it did not do so is, of course, obvious, and

Nicholas undertook further efforts throughout his reign to make society and the machinery of government function as he thought they should.

But the measures which Nicholas and his advisers implemented to create the so-called Nicholas system were only part of the system as a whole. Together with his efforts to regularize Russian administration and society, Nicholas also sought to create a system of foreign policy which more accurately reflected his view of Russia, Western Europe and the relationship he believed should exist between the two. Unlike his brother Alexander, Nicholas knew very clearly which side of the Russian–Western European frontier he stood upon, and his policies towards the West could be characterized as far more defensive than those of his elder brother. Therefore we should now turn our attention to the genesis of the Nicholas system as it related to the Empire's foreign policy: specifically to Western Europe, to the Kingdom of Poland and to the Near East.

4

The Heritage
of the
Holy Alliance

'I am fully satisfied with all of my foreign relations,
and everything that has come to pass is
completely in agreement with my wishes . . .
[All this seems] to me to insure, in a perfect
manner, our security and our defensive position'

NICHOLAS I, TO
FRIEDRICH WILHELM III IN 1833

Alexander I once remarked to Chateaubriand that 'now there no longer exists an English policy, a French, Russian, Prussian, or Austrian policy; there is now only one common policy which, for the welfare of all, ought to be adopted in common by all states and all peoples'.[1] Russia's Emperor devoted the last decade of his life to an effort to create just such a 'concert of Europe', and he viewed his Holy Alliance as the most important element in making such a dream a reality. The Holy Alliance, however, was not something unique to Alexander's outlook; it embodied sentiments which were quite widespread in Europe at the time. Some time before, François Baader had urged a closer identity between politics and religion as the only cure for the evils of the French Revolution, and Chateaubriand's *Génie du Christianisme* had argued similar principles. Even Napoleon had supposedly at one point thought in terms of some such universal pact.[2] Alexander himself had been very much a part of this current of opinion for at least a decade before the final defeat of Napoleon. As early as September 1804, he had sent N. N. Novosil'tsev to England to argue for an alliance against Napoleon in which, once France was defeated, the victors would agree to a system of collective security, arbitration of disputes rather than resort to war and something resembling a league of nations.[3] Although the Third Coalition failed to defeat Napoleon,

Alexander returned to these principles again in 1812 when he spoke of his plans for European sovereigns 'to live like brothers, aiding each other in their need, and comforting each other in their adversity'.[4]

But when Alexander sought to incorporate such principles into his Holy Alliance in 1815, they reflected his own growing mystical-pietist outlook. As such, they hardly seemed appropriate to the increased antagonism and suspicion emerging among Napoleon's conquerors. Viscount Castlereagh characterized the Holy Alliance as a 'piece of sublime mysticism and nonsense',[5] and confessed that when Alexander first showed the draft to him and to the Duke of Wellington, 'it was not without difficulty that we went through the interview with becoming gravity'.[6] The Habsburg statesman, Prince Metternich, who would later seek to subvert the Holy Alliance to his own ends, first called it 'ringing and empty'.[7]

In fact, the cynicism with which European statesmen greeted Alexander's statements that 'Christian charity and peace . . . must have an immediate influence on the councils of princes and guide all their steps', reflected a rapidly growing suspicion about Russia's aims throughout Europe. The situation was not unlike that which the Allies faced more than a century later when the end of the Second World War approached. As in 1945, Russia in 1815 stood poised on the Eastern frontier – a colossus with vast human resources and the largest army on the continent – and demanded a greater role than ever before in European affairs. European statesmen feared that this new power might at one stroke destroy the equilibrium so recently re-established after the defeat of Napoleon. As the Whig politician Thomas Creevey wrote, many Europeans feared that Russia planned 'to make Constantinople the seat of her power and to re-establish the Greek Church upon the ruins of Mohammedanism', and that Europe would witness a 'new crusade . . . by a new and enormous Power . . . brought into the field by our own selves, and one that may put our existence at stake to drive out again'.[8]

Some of Europe's senior statesmen were perceptive enough to discredit the wild rumours of Russian expansionist schemes, and both Wellington and Castlereagh urged a policy of trust and peace. Castlereagh, especially, recognized that growing anti-Russian sentiment was inevitable 'against a State as powerful as Russia has latterly become', but continued to insist that 'the true interests of Russia dictate a pacific policy'. Metternich, however, sought at every turn to play upon Europe's fears of Russia and to turn them to the advantage of his government. Thus, in March 1817, he proposed that Great Britain join Austria in curbing Russia's 'ambitions' in Spain, as well as in the Near East, a proposal which Castlereagh rejected out of hand. Metternich's apprehensions about Russian policy, the British Foreign Secretary insisted, were not justified 'either in degree or in proximity', and he refused to discuss any such 'measures of precautionary policy upon speculative grounds' because he regarded them as dangerous and a threat to European unity.[9]

But Castlereagh's dispassionate view of European affairs and his careful estimate of how little of the Russian threat was real and how much was either an invention of Metternich's or, as one historian has remarked, 'a gigantic bluff on the part of Russia herself',[10] was certainly not characteristic of many European statesmen. Distrust of Russia's ambitions was becoming an ever-growing wedge, splitting East and West. Thus, the just equilibrium which Castlereagh had sought to create by the Treaty of Chaumont in March 1814, and the need for 'Christian charity and peace' to guide the steps of princes which Alexander had spoken of in presenting the text of the Holy Alliance in September the following year, were threatened by new forces and sentiments emerging in post-Napoleonic Europe.

A major threat to the 'concert of Europe', conceived in the terms proposed by Castlereagh and Alexander I, was the machinations of Metternich and his desire to use the Holy Alliance to shore up the already flimsy structure of the Habsburg Empire. Metternich's actions had already gone a long way towards creating a deep distrust of Alexander's intentions. Equally important, however, the Russian Emperor himself sought to impose static principles upon a dynamic and rapidly changing world. Certainly Alexander had not conceived of his Holy Alliance as an instrument of reaction and oppression when he proposed it. But he was ill-prepared by education or experience to deal with the changing realities in Europe after the French Revolution and the Napoleonic Empire. Alexander had been educated in the best tradition of the Enlightenment as an enlightened monarch, as one of those select few who, by force of will and personality, could mould the destiny of nations and peoples. Yet while such a view may have been well-suited to eighteenth-century Europe, it was (or would soon become) an anachronism in the Europe which emerged after the defeat of Napoleon.

The early nineteenth century had seen the first stirrings of nationalistic sentiments in the hearts of many European peoples ruled too long by others; and the union of these aspirations with the convictions of liberalism spelled the failure of Alexander's and Castlereagh's hopes for a stable and peaceful Europe. Alexander thus saw his vision of 'one common policy which, for the welfare of all, ought to be adopted in common by all states and all peoples' come into direct conflict with the liberal sentiments he had once cherished. Inevitably, as nationalistic challenges to the stability and order of Europe broke out in Spain, Naples and Greece during the decade following the Congress of Vienna, Alexander saw his Holy Alliance become identified with the forces of reaction. A combination of Europe's growing fears of the Russian colossus, and Russia's increased identification with the forces of reaction and the *status quo* in Europe, caused Alexander's image to change quickly from that of Europe's liberator to something very close to the image which his younger brother Nicholas would assume fully: the gendarme of Europe.

The personalities of the great statesmen of the Napoleonic era continued to hold the failing 'concert of Europe' together for several more years. But, in the late summer of 1822, Castlereagh committed suicide and was replaced as Britain's Foreign Secretary by Sir George Canning, a man whom Metternich once characterized as a 'malevolent meteor'; Canning fully reciprocated Metternich's dislike, once referring to the Austrian statesman as the 'greatest rogue and liar in Europe, perhaps in the civilized world'.[11] This mutual antagonism further weakened the already precarious unity among the European allies. Canning sought a middle course between despotism and revolution in European politics, and to achieve that end moved quickly to dissociate Britain from the Holy Alliance. He thus refused to accept the Verona Conference's decision to intervene in Spanish internal affairs in September 1822, and in 1823 and 1824 declined even to attend proposed European conferences on the Spanish and Eastern Questions. Castlereagh's death and his replacement by Canning thus dealt the 'concert of Europe' a blow from which it seemed unlikely to recover. But the concert soon suffered further shocks which made its demise a certainty. The Prussian statesman, Prince K. A. von Hardenberg, another of the great protagonists of the Vienna Congress, also died in 1822. And, three years later, Alexander followed Castlereagh and von Hardenberg to the grave, leaving his younger brother to face a Europe becoming rapidly divided and increasingly suspicious of Russia.

The heritage of the Holy Alliance – the challenge of nationalistic movements to the stability of Europe, the diplomatic schemes of Metternich and the failure of the conference system which become so evident after Canning's appointment – was the legacy which fell to Nicholas when he ascended his brother's throne. Equally important, once the more calm and reasonable Castlereagh was no longer there to inject a note of common caution into Western chancelleries, apprehensions about Russia's motives grew at an alarming rate. For the vision of the Russian colossus, poised with endless reserves of manpower to fall upon Europe, and, particularly, upon Constantinople, remained ever-present in the minds of Europeans.

Yet if Europeans, particularly at Metternich's urging, saw Russia as an ever-present threat, the young Emperor Nicholas saw Europe as an equally great danger to the domestic tranquillity of his Empire. To him and to his advisers, the Decembrist revolt was clearly an attack by the French Revolution upon Russia. General Benkendorf was especially insistent in his arguments that French 'revolutionaries' had come to Russia in the late eighteenth and early nineteenth centuries, seeking positions as tutors in noble households, and had spread their 'poison' among the Russian aristocratic youth, thereby making them all the more susceptible to the corruption of French revolutionary ideas when they went with Russia's armies to the West in 1813–15.[12] And Nicholas himself saw the threat in equally real terms. 'Everything which took place here [on 14 December] evidently was . . . the result . . . of foreign influences,' he wrote to his brother.[13] 'We . . . must seek revenge for Russia and our national honour.'[14] Nor, in Nicholas's view, was the Decembrist revolt the last attack by revolutionary Europe. In fact, it was only a beginning. Revolutionary France posed such threats not only in 1825, but again in 1830–31, and yet again in 1848. And, to Nicholas, these were very real threats indeed. In his view, revolution *had* come to Russia from France in 1825. It came again in 1830–31 by way of Poland, and France's warm support of the Polish revolutionaries in those years seemed further evidence of the threat. And Nicholas saw himself as facing revolution from Europe and, especially, from France, again in the late 1840s. The revolt of the Polish peasants in Galicia in 1846 was only a beginning. Before long, Nicholas's armies would face the revolution in Hungary and in Russia itself in the form of the Kyrillo–Methodius Society in 1846–7, and the circle of M. V. Butashevich-Petrashevskii in 1849.

But revolutionary France comprised only one part of the threat which, in Nicholas's view, Europe posed to Russia. Besides the broad European sympathy for Poland's revolutionaries, there was also the threat posed by an expansionist Britain who, because of her suspicions about Russia, never came to understand that his policy towards the Ottoman Empire was to prevent other states from seizing lands along Russia's borders, not to seize more territory for Russia herself. Beyond this, there was what Nicholas saw as the ever-present threat which Western ideas continually posed to the established order, a threat of which he was perpetually aware as a result of the diligent (and, sometimes, self-serving) efforts of the censorship apparatus of his government.

Nicholas therefore followed a much more conservative and defensive policy towards the West than had his brother. While Alexander I had seen Russian security as being very much tied to her part in a European-wide system adhered to by all monarchs, Nicholas, at the beginning of his reign, was content to leave the Europeans much more to themselves, and to call upon the principles of the Holy Alliance to defend the *status quo* throughout the West. Foreign policy in regard to Western Europe was therefore something which occupied considerably less of Nicholas's attention than has often been thought. Western authors[15] have tended to see him in terms of his foreign policy precisely because they reflect Western apprehensions about Russia, for Western Europeans have been fearful of the Russian threat since the early eighteenth century. Yet Nicholas seems to have been concerned about the West only in so far as it posed a threat to the domestic tranquillity of Russia. He thus involved himself and his government with European domestic affairs to a lesser degree than had his elder brother.

1. The Emperor-Diplomat

Nicholas inherited as Foreign Minister Count K. V. Nesselrode, whom the Prussian statesman, Baron vom Stein, once characterized as a man who had 'neither a homeland, nor a native language and . . . has not one single fundamental feeling; his father was a German adventurer, and God only knows who his mother was; he was educated in Berlin and serves in Moscow'.[16] There was considerable factual truth in vom Stein's description, but the Prussian minister failed to include Nesselrode's most important characteristic: his deep loyalty to the Russian masters whom he served for more than half a century. Under Alexander I, Nesselrode had become a diplomat of special commissions, an instrument of the Emperor's personal policy, and had carried out secret negotiations with those men who would ultimately betray Napoleon: Caulaincourt and Talleyrand. From 1814 onwards, he had directed Russia's Foreign Office, and would continue to do so until the end of Nicholas's reign. But even though he rose to become State Chancellor of the Russian Empire under Nicholas, Nesselrode still remained to a large degree a State Secretary for diplomatic affairs. To be sure, he carried out much of Russia's foreign policy, but his actions were always very much those of an imperial adjutant. The extent to which Nicholas regarded him as such was especially evident from the fact that he sometimes carried on important negotiations without Nesselrode's participation, as, for example, when he went to England in 1844 for the purpose of improving relations with that country. Even more than under Alexander, Nesselrode was an agent of his Emperor's will rather than a policy-maker, although he was not without influence in Russian state affairs.

Nicholas was thus very much his own foreign minister from the moment of accession. It was directly to him that Western ambassadors were summoned to receive an account of the Decembrist revolt, and in the few days that followed Nicholas exhibited many of the traits which would come to characterize his diplomacy. His manner was one of outward frankness and candour. As he told the assembled members of the diplomatic corps, 'I will tell you without reservation all further information which I may obtain, for my wish is that the entire truth be known in Europe as well as in Russia.'[17] Nicholas gave foreign ambassadors the impression of taking them still further into his confidence by more intimate conversations which he had with some of them. The French ambassador, Comte de la Ferronnays, reported to his superiors in Paris that Nicholas met him privately on several occasions after the revolt,[18] and when he spoke, 'he took my hand, pressing it firmly, as if he wished to impress upon me the sincerity of his words . . . Dismissing my colleagues,' La Ferronnays continued, 'he put his arm around my shoulder and led me into his private study.'[19] This sort of behaviour flattered the vanity of those ambassadors with whom Nicholas dealt. As La Ferronnays reported, 'the candour . . . which reigned there [at the audience] touched us all greatly and we took leave of him, unanimous in the admiration which he had inspired in us'.[20]

There was an element of sincere friendship in the relationship which Nicholas had with a number of the diplomatic corps of St Petersburg. But he never allowed such friendships to interfere with the performance of his duty or with the state policy which he believed Russia should follow. Most of all, it would seem that Nicholas wanted peace with Europe. His militarism, so much a part of his everyday life, and which conditioned his attitudes to many of the problems he faced at home, was not the sort of aggressive militarism which demanded conquests and glory in foreign wars. The militaristic views which Nicholas held meant, most of all, an emphasis upon order and regularity. As one observer would note later in his reign, St Petersburg had become a city where order and regularity reigned supreme.[21]

Nicholas emphasized his desire for peace from the very first. As he told La Ferronnays during the first week of his reign, 'assure your King that my only wish is to follow the example of my brother, that my basic principles are the same as his, and that I am inspired by a single wish to preserve the peace'.[22] He emphasized his peaceful intentions even more strongly a few weeks later. Speaking with the Vicomte de Saint-Priest, he commented:

I know very well that, in view of the fact that I am only twenty-nine years old, and that I have just ascended the throne . . . [foreign statesmen] impute to me military leanings and the desire to mark the beginning of my reign with some sorts of military victories . . . But they misjudge me. I love peace and recognize its value and necessity, both for Russia . . . and for Europe.[23]

Even though Nicholas may have desired peace and hoped to avoid war, events soon forced new diplomatic problems. In July 1826, just as he arrived in Moscow for his coronation, he received word that the Persian army under Prince Abbas Mirza had invaded Russia's domains in the Caucasus and had occupied Lenkoran, Elizavetpol and Karabag.[24] The Persian attack posed no direct threat to Russia's security, though it was irritating at a time when she was seeking to subjugate the mountaineers of that region. Certainly Nicholas could not ignore the challenge. As he commented at the time, 'this unfortunate matter is for me unbearable, like an undigestible appetizer'.[25] The Persians' success was especially annoying coming at the time of his coronation and just a few months after the Decembrist revolt. 'Could anyone be more unfortunate?' he exclaimed to General Paskevich at a brief private meeting. 'I am just crowned and here are the Persians occupying several of our provinces. Does Russia lack men capable of defending her dignity?'[26]

Nicholas placed the blame for Persia's initial successes upon General A. P. Ermolov, a rough infantry officer and a hero of the campaigns of 1812–15, who was generally unconcerned about the parade-ground performance of his troops and demanded instead that his army be an efficient fighting force. Ermolov was popular with his soldiers, and this may well have aroused Nicholas's suspicions since he wanted no one to challenge his authority with the army. Further, the fact that Ermolov and Nicholas's close friend and confidant Benkendorf were implacable enemies did little to help Ermolov's cause. At a time when Nicholas had just finished hearing from many Decembrists a searing indictment of arbitrariness and tyranny in the Russian government, Benkendorf's statements that Ermolov 'for ten years has ruled the region [the Caucasus] with all the despotism and improvidence of a Turkish pasha'[27] did little to raise him in Nicholas's opinion. Most of all, Nicholas suspected Ermolov of sympathy towards the Decembrists, an unforgivable breach of trust. Baron Dibich had defended Ermolov in the strongest terms against Nicholas's suspicions,[28] and even the Investigating Commission had found nothing to implicate him in the conspiracy. But the fact that he supposedly gave preferential treatment to those Decembrists sent to the Caucasus kept Nicholas's distrust alive.[29]

Ermolov was one of the most decorated heroes in the Russian army, and his command record was unblemished. For some time he had been urging his superiors in St Petersburg to send reinforcements in anticipation of just such a Persian attack as occurred in July 1826.[30] But no one in St Petersburg could believe that Persia would risk such an undertaking. Abbas Mirza's attack thus hardly took Ermolov by surprise. What is puzzling is that it seems to have found him totally unprepared. Evidently he had taken Alexander I's firm assurances about Persia's peaceful motives too much to heart. Whatever the reasons for this lack of preparation Nicholas regarded Abbas Mirza's successes as clear evidence that Ermolov had not done his duty, especially since the general persistently refused to comply with orders to mount an immediate offensive. While Nicholas exhorted him that 'you and fifteen thousand Russians seem to be a sufficient guarantee of success',[31] Ermolov refused to attack, fearing that a campaign against the Persians might well expose Tiflis, Georgia's capital.[32] Rather than take into account the factors which weighed in Ermolov's decision, Nicholas simply chose to regard him as a 'man who sees falsehood as virtue if it can work to his advantage'.[33]

The Emperor proposed to deal with the problem in the Caucasus, not by sending Ermolov the reinforcements he had requested, but by sending General Paskevich, one of his close friends and most trusted commanders, to make an on-the-spot assessment of Ermolov's command capabilities. But Paskevich went to the south reluctantly, for he and Ermolov were bitter rivals. As he told Dibich before his departure, 'I know Ermolov. He would not give me even a company to command.'[34] To allay Paskevich's reluctance, Nicholas ordered that he assume command of Russia's forces in the field while Ermolov continued as supreme commander of the Caucasus region, thus setting the stage for several months' bickering over command decisions.[35]

Paskevich arrived at Elizavetpol on 10 September, just after the Russians had reoccupied the city following Major-General Prince Mandatov's brilliant victory over the Persians at Shamkhor. Mandatov's victory marked the first Russian offensive against the Persians, and the fact that he defeated an enemy force outnumbering his own by five to one seemed to Nicholas further evidence of Ermolov's incompetence. Paskevich immediately took command of the troops in the field himself, and within a week had routed Abbas Mirza's main force, thereby further undermining Ermolov's position. While Paskevich won victories and the Emperor sang his praises, Ermolov received further reprimands.[36] The issue of command in the Caucasus was finally settled in early 1827 by Dibich, whom Nicholas sent to Tiflis in February. Obviously Nicholas hoped to catch Ermolov unaware and to prove the truth of Benkendorf's accusations and his own suspicions. 'I am telling only you [of Dibich's impending arrival],' he wrote to Paskevich on 31 January 1827. 'His arrival ought to be unexpected and therefore I ask you to keep this in the utmost secrecy and, when he arrives, not to show that you knew of it in advance.'[37] Nicholas's attitude put Dibich in a very delicate position since he considered Ermolov a competent commander and was reluctant to recommend his dismissal. Yet Nicholas was not prepared to hear much good said of the 'old lion', as Dibich called him.[38] Ermolov was to be removed, Nicholas ordered Dibich, but 'without any fuss or scandal'.[39]

Ermolov had already seen that he had no hope of retaining his command, and on 3 March sent Nicholas a letter asking to be relieved, stating that 'my ability to command is paralysed by the thought that I am not able to fulfil Your commands'.[40] Ermolov was thus removed from command responsibilities on 28 March, and replaced by Paskevich. He was told nothing except that he was relieved of command and was to return to Russia. As he confided to his diary, 'I am not retired from the service, nor am I sent on leave. It is not said if I will remain in the army or not.' Ermolov remained in Tiflis for yet another month and left for Russia at the end of April. So complete was Nicholas's antipathy towards the fallen commander, and so great was Paskevich's arrogance, that, as Ermolov bitterly remarked, 'the new authorities here did not have the courtesy even to give me an escort which is not refused to anyone who is leaving'.[41]

Paskevich had had a reputation for great valour, even rashness, ever since the early battles of the Napoleonic wars. He now pressed the campaign against the Persians in the same manner. The Persians suffered one defeat after another, and on 2 October 1827 the major stronghold of Erivan fell to Russian attack. Paskevich entered the city in triumph and reported to Nicholas:

The standards of Your Imperial Majesty float above the walls of Erivan. The keys to this much-renowned fortress . . . together with the loyalty and gratitude of its inhabitants, delivered from their pretended defender and their cruel oppressors – all this, Sire, I hasten to lay at Your feet. The soldiers of Your Imperial Majesty have again covered themselves with the glory of victory.[42]

By late January 1828, the last fortress had fallen, the road to Tehran lay open before the Russians and the Persians sued for peace.[43] At midnight, between 9 and 10 February, Paskevich and Abbas Mirza signed the Treaty of Turkmanchai, Russia received the khanates of Erivan and Nakhichevan as well as an indemnity of some 20 million roubles.[44] Paskevich had urged Nicholas to demand even more, especially Azerbaijan,[45] but Nicholas wished to follow a conciliatory policy towards Europe and realized that British interests in India would be threatened by a Russian annexation of Azerbaijan. Perhaps equally important, as Paskevich's biographer has pointed out, Nicholas's strict view of dynastic legitimacy would not allow him to violate the territorial integrity nor the dynastic order of a legitimate state.[46] For his part in defeating the Persians, Nicholas rewarded Paskevich with a grant of a million paper roubles (approximately 250,000 silver roubles), and, as the decree of the Imperial Senate stated, 'We grant unto him and his heirs the title of Count of the

Russian Empire, and ordain that henceforth he shall be called Count Paskevich-Erivanskii.'[47]

Peace had come. But not for long. The Eastern Question, so much a tinderbox throughout the nineteenth century, flared into war at the moment Russia concluded peace in Persia.

When Nicholas spoke with several European ambassadors soon after his accession, one of the first topics they raised was the Eastern Question and, particularly, the question of Greece. Several years before, the Greeks had revolted against their Ottoman masters and their struggle for independence had caught the popular imagination of all Europe. The British Romantic poet, Lord Byron, went to join the Greek patriots, and died of rheumatic fever in 1824 while working for their cause. Even Nicholas's wife, the young Grand Duchess Aleksandra Fedorovna, had been caught up in the drama, and wrote to her father, the Prussian king, Friedrich Wilhelm III, in early December 1821 that 'the cause of the Greeks cannot be compared to that of other revolutionaries: it seems fine and just to me, and of a kind to fill the minds of youth with enthusiasm'.[48]

Alexander I, however, had proceeded cautiously in dealing with the Greek crisis, although during the last year of his reign the failure of the Petersburg Conventions to resolve the issue had led him to declare that he reserved for himself the right to deal with it and other problems connected with the Ottoman Empire as he thought fit.[49] The fact that Alexander had not taken any direct action to deal with the Greek revolt at the time of his death, but appeared to be planning some new military operations against the Ottoman Empire, made European diplomats particularly interested in his younger brother's attitudes on the subject.[50] But Nicholas was a more practical statesman than his elder brother had been during the last years of his life. When pressed on the subject of the Greeks and the Near East by Saint-Priest in January 1826, Nicholas stated his general views quite clearly.

My brother left me some extremely important matters to deal with and the most important of all is the Eastern Question . . . I must, without fail, bring this matter to a rapid conclusion, or otherwise it will become for me a source of grave complications . . . I will be happy to reach an agreement with all of my allies on this question, the importance of which, both for them and for Russia, I vividly recognize. But . . . if they cannot or will not act in concert with me and thus force me to it, then my behaviour will be absolutely different from that of the Emperor Alexander and I will consider it my duty to put an end to the matter . . . I want peace in the East. Indeed, I need peace . . . But, let me repeat: if even one of my allies should betray me, then I will be obliged to act alone and you can be certain that this will not trouble me in the least.[51]

Saint-Priest now knew that he was dealing with a different sort of diplomat from Alexander I. Nicholas had a very winning manner when he wished to charm his listener. And he could be disarmingly candid. But he was, above all, the Autocrat of All the Russias, and the intricacies of diplomatic manoeuvring did not appeal to him. He rarely engaged in duplicity, for his *ancien régime* sense of honour bound him to commitments once made. He made his position immediately clear, and expected others to do the same. And, as far as the Eastern Question was concerned, Nicholas never sought territory in the Balkans at the expense of his enemies or his allies. He stressed this point in his conversations with Saint-Priest. 'I will give you my word of honour,' he said (and, for Nicholas there was no stronger guarantee), 'that I do not want, do not desire, and do not plan to add a single inch of territory [in the Near East] to the holdings of Russia, which is already large enough as it is. I am prepared to give in this case whatever formal guarantees are desired.'[52] But, as he would repeat throughout his reign, Nicholas would allow no other European power to expand its influence in that area either. As he told Lord Aberdeen when he visited England in 1844, 'I do not claim one inch of Turkish soil, but neither will I allow that any other shall have an inch of it.'[53]

In Nicholas's view, the sources of conflict between Russia and the Ottoman Empire could most easily be separated into two categories. Into one group fell all of the difficulties specifically related to the situation in Greece, where Greek patriots continued to challenge the suzerainty of the Sultan. The second category was broader in scope, but its definition was perhaps more specific, for it included what Nicholas regarded as violations by the Turks of the obligations imposed upon them by a number of treaties with Russia,[54] the most important being the treaties of Kuchuk-Kainardji (1774), Jassy (1791) and Bucharest (1812). Nicholas regarded the Greek question as an all-European problem, and so, in his conversations with Saint-Priest, he urged all European powers to join in seeking a common and effective solution. On the question of the Ottoman Empire's violation of its treaties with Russia, however, Nicholas would brook no interference by European statesmen. He regarded this as a matter which concerned no one but Russia and the Turks,[55] and he would not even discuss his views about it with his allies.[56]

While Nicholas thus spoke of his willingness to discuss the Greek question with the powers of Western Europe to seek to bring about a rapid resolution, he proceeded to take up secretly what he regarded as the far more pressing issue: the Porte's violation of various treaty commitments. Central to this problem was the Sultan's refusal to evacuate Turkish troops from the Danubian principalities of Wallachia and

Moldavia, as he had agreed to do a number of years earlier, and his failure to implement the conditions of the Treaty of Bucharest in regard to Serbia. Alexander I had engaged in protracted negotiations with the Sultan over these issues, and they had produced little result. But Alexander, after all, had tended to place less emphasis upon the Eastern Question during the last decade of his reign as he directed most of his attention to European affairs. Nicholas's priorities were very different. He had been deadly serious when he told Saint-Priest in January 1826 that he regarded the Eastern Question as 'the most important of all'. Therefore, where Alexander had negotiated with the Sultan over these issues, Nicholas followed the direct approach of a military commander.

On 24 March 1826, he ordered his representative in Constantinople to deliver an ultimatum to the Sultan: within not more than six weeks, Turkish troops must be evacuated from the Danubian principalities; the conditions of the Bucharest Treaty in regard to Serbia must be fulfilled; the Serbian deputies being held under arrest in Constantinople must be released; and Turkish representatives must be dispatched to one of the Russian border towns so as to conclude the discussions which Alexander's diplomats had carried on without result with the Sultan's ministers between 1816 and 1821.[57] Should the Sultan not agree to his demands, Nicholas stated, he would order his representative to leave Constantinople the moment the deadline passed, and, he concluded, 'it should not be difficult for the ministers of the Sultan to foresee the rapid consequences of such an event'.[58]

As one historian has characterized it:

[This] fearsome ultimatum fell upon the Porte like a thunderbolt. News about the circumstances surrounding the accession of Emperor Nicholas to the throne had given it [the Porte] hopes for a domestic revolt in Russia which would not give her Emperor a chance to think about a foreign war. Then suddenly this thunderous blow fell precisely from the quarter whence they least expected it.[59]

The Sultan's reply came within a month. Russia's first three demands not only were agreed to, but they had already been fulfilled by the time that the reply was delivered to the Russian representative in Constantinople. Further, the Sultan declared, the discussions which Nicholas demanded could begin as soon as the Russians informed him where the meeting would take place.[60] On 1 July, therefore, discussions between Russian diplomats and the representatives of the Sultan began at the town of Akkerman. At Akkerman, Nicholas presented a second ultimatum to the Turks in the form of a draft agreement. As his representatives Count M. S. Vorontsov and Count A. I. Ribeaupierre informed the

Sultan's delegates, the draft must be agreed to by 26 September. Should the Turks fail to do so, Nicholas declared, he would withdraw his representatives and then would take whatever measures were 'deemed necessary by our law, interests, and honour'.[61] Lacking firm allies among the Western powers since he was at odds with them over the Greek question, the Sultan acceded to Nicholas's demands and, on 25 September 1826, signed the Akkerman Convention. The Turks thus agreed to observe earlier treaty obligations and to grant Russian merchantmen free passage through the Straits and the right of navigation in Turkish waters.[62]

Nicholas had managed to impose his will upon the Sultan in the most blunt manner imaginable, for his demands had come at just the moment when the nations of Western Europe were supporting the cause of the Greeks against their Ottoman rulers. Nicholas himself had little sympathy for the Greek cause. As he later remarked to Count Zichy, Austria's ambassador in St Petersburg,

I abhor the Greeks, although they are my co-religionists; they have behaved in a shocking, blamable, even criminal manner; I look upon them as subjects in open revolt against their legitimate sovereign; I do not desire their enfranchisement; they do not deserve it, and it would be a very bad example for all other countries if they succeeded in establishing it.[63]

But despite his dislike of the Greeks, Nicholas did not hesitate to use their cause, for which there was considerable sympathy in the West, to advance Russia's own interests in dealing with the Sublime Porte.

Indeed, discussion of the Greek question with Western Powers had preceded Nicholas's diplomatic offensive against the Sultan. On 18 February 1826, the Duke of Wellington had arrived in St Petersburg to congratulate Nicholas on his accession. The Iron Duke was empowered by the British government to negotiate on the Greek issue, and he found Nicholas more than willing to do so. On 10 March he thus recognized the legitimacy of Russia's demands concerning the Danubian principalities,[64] though, at the time, he did not know of the ultimatum which Nicholas would present to the Sultan a fortnight later. Certainly Wellington's declaration improved Russia's position in dealing with the Turks; it was strengthened even further on 23 March, the day before the Russian representatives presented their ultimatum in Constantinople, when Nesselrode and Wellington, together with Count Lieven, Russia's ambassador to the Court of St James's, signed the St Petersburg Protocol by which they agreed that the Sultan must grant Greece full autonomy in internal affairs and the right to be governed by rulers of the Greeks' own choosing. Greece was to be guaranteed independence in conducting foreign trade and her subjection to the Porte was to be strictly tributary.[65] Just over three months later, on 24 June (6 July) 1827, this agreement became an international convention when, in London, France added her signature.[66] Britain, France and Russia were now arrayed against the Porte, although Metternich fumed[67] and Prussia, following his lead, remained aloof.

In keeping with their joint resolution to settle the Greek question, Britain, France and Russia ordered their representatives at Constantinople to present a collective note on 4 (16) August, informing the Sultan of the London Convention and making formal demands upon him to settle the Greek issue in the manner the three powers had agreed upon. Two weeks later, the Turks replied, refusing to meet the Allied demands. Control of events then passed from the diplomats into the hands of a joint Russian, French and British naval squadron off the Morea commanded by Sir Edward Codrington. In late July (7 August), Codrington had been instructed to 'intercept all ships freighted with men and arms destined to act against the Greeks'. At the same time, he was cautioned to prevent his measures from 'degenerating into hostilities'. To Codrington, a blunt naval officer from the Napoleonic Wars, such instructions were incomprehensible. He sought clarification from Sir Stratford Canning, Britain's ambassador at Constantinople. Canning's reply told Codrington what he wanted to know: 'the prevention of supplies is ultimately to be enforced, if necessary . . . by cannon shot'.[68]

Canning's reply reached Codrington while his fleet lay off the coast of the Morea in the vicinity of Navarino Bay. Each day Codrington and the Russian and French admirals under his command had watched as clouds of smoke proclaimed the vengeance which the Turkish-Egyptian armies of Ibrahim Pasha were wreaking upon the Greeks. Finally, on 8 (20) October, they decided to 'put a stop to atrocities which exceed all that has hitherto taken place'. Verbal remonstrances with the Turks soon degenerated into scattered cannon fire; the cannon fire soon developed into a major battle. By nightfall, allied naval forces had destroyed the Turkish-Egyptian fleet. As one witness put it, 'the Bay of Navarino was covered with their wrecks'.[69]

If the Sultan had had any doubts as to what measures the Allies were prepared to take to settle the Greek question, the battle of Navarino quickly dispelled them. According to Russia's ambassador to the Porte, Count Ribeaupierre, 'the Navarino affair angered the Sultan to such an extent that he intended, without a declaration of war, to kill us all [the Allied ambassadors] in retribution for the destruction of the Turkish fleet'. In fact, the Dragoman of the Porte did threaten Ribeaupierre with imprisonment only to be told that should he do so, Russia's Emperor would take such a revenge against the Turks that 'not one single stone would be left standing upon another in Constantinople'. Faced with such threats, Ribeaupierre and his French and British counterparts decided in early December that further negotiations with the Porte on the Greek question were useless. On 5 (17) December they weighed anchor and left Constantinople.[70]

Nicholas regarded the turn which events had taken in the autumn and early winter of 1827 as the logical outcome of the common policy he had followed with England and France on the Greek question. He noted in a letter to his brother Grand Duke Konstantin Pavlovich that what had taken place at Navarino proved 'how much our resolve to put an end to this affair is serious and . . . how sincere . . . is the sense of common purpose among our three countries in dealing with this delicate matter'.[71] Konstantin Pavlovich was far more suspicious of Russia's allies, however. In contrast to his brother's enthusiasm for the victory, he cautioned,

I can only deplore the motives and the results and the incalculable consequences of this naval victory. The English, in true Machiavellian fashion, knew how to profit from the situation of the Russians and the French who, in any case, being driven into a corner, could do nothing else except join in the battle so as not to be accused of cowardice or timidity. The Russians fell into this position because of their sincerity; the French did so because of their stupidity. Only the English acted for their self-interest by destroying the fleet [which might have threatened them at some future time].[72]

There was some truth in this. Metternich, of course, was furious, for the joint action threatened to undermine the strict principles of legitimacy which he had conspired to establish among the Allies ever since 1814. To Count Apponyi he wrote:

the event of October 20th [the Navarino battle] begins a new era for Europe . . . Everything is changed. The Ottoman Empire has ceased, for the moment, to belong to itself . . . What effect will be produced? . . . We may infer that the Sultan will decide, in consequence of the sanguinary affront he has just received, to resist everything.[73]

To restore the balance of forces which Admiral Codrington's attack upon the Turkish fleet had disrupted, Metternich sought to undermine the union between France, England and Russia. He hoped to use public opinion as his weapon.

In his comments to Nicholas about the situation in the West, Konstantin had been especially disparaging about the role of public opinion in influencing state policy. 'Public opinion,' he wrote to Nicholas, 'is a plague, and if governments submit to it and act according to it, then there are no longer any limits since it is also as changeable as the wind.'[74] Metternich shared similar sentiments, but he clearly saw the use to which public opinion could be put. He knew that the British were far from pleased at Paskevich's seizure of Erivan, 'which event will certainly make a contrary impression in London',[75] and he was also convinced that in Britain 'the public voice is less and less in favour of the Navarino affair'. 'The English cabinet,' he added, 'will certainly be ready to bargain for . . . pacification,' since public opinion 'must be shocked by an act which all the sophistries in the world can never represent as lawful'.[76] Thus he believed that the British would pull back from a war with the Ottoman Empire over the Greek question. As he noted confidently, 'liberalism has not yet succeeded in introducing itself into the figures of the counting houses'.[77] Without British support, Metternich believed that the French would also draw back from war, especially in view of their political situation. 'Reports from Paris show only the greatest confusion in both ideas and things,' he reported to his Emperor at the end of November.[78] In sum, Metternich concluded, only Russia was a real threat to peace in the Near East. Nesselrode, he learned, had written to Count Tatishchev, the Russian ambassador in Vienna, '*Vive la force!* It is might which rules the world nowadays . . . This is how Carnot and Danton, and afterwards their imitators, thought and spoke.'[79]

Metternich's judgements were not based only upon wishful thinking or the unfounded hope that public opinion could turn the course of state policy in France and Britain. During the autumn of 1827, several other events also served to advance his cause. First, Canning died in July and was eventually replaced by the Duke of Wellington. And even though Wellington had signed the Petersburg Protocol in March of the previous year, his attitudes towards Britain's alliance with Russia had changed significantly. During the months before Canning's death, he had openly disputed the wisdom of the Foreign Secretary's course in the Near East. Once he had succeeded Canning, Wellington's major concern was 'to preserve the independence and integrity of the Ottoman Empire'.[80] Britain thus adopted a more conciliatory tone towards the Sultan which the Russians saw as something of a betrayal of their common cause.[81]

But Britain's change of heart was not the only alteration in the international situation. In early January, the unpopular Villèle ministry fell in France, and the new ministry of Martignac, despite the fact that its foreign minister was Nicholas's personal friend La Ferronnays, was determined to follow a more cautious course.[82] The Grand Duke Konstantin Pavlovich had thus been partly correct in his scepticism on the possibilities of extended joint action by France, Britain and Russia in the Near East. By the end of 1827, Nicholas was left to face the Ottoman

Empire virtually alone, though once hostilities did begin, England and France took some measures against the Sultan since they were not disposed to leave the entire settlement of the Eastern Question in Russian hands. In July 1828, they concluded a protocol agreeing to immediate joint action against the forces of Ibrahim Pasha in the Morea; and while the British Admiral Sir Pulteney Malcolm negotiated in Egypt with Mehemet Ali for the withdrawal of Egyptian forces from the Morea, a French expeditionary force of some 14,000 men under General Maison landed at Petalidi. The efforts of the French and British commanders soon succeeded in arranging the immediate evacuation of Egyptian forces from the Morea, and a protocol concluded in London on 16 November 1828, placed the Morea and the Greek islands under Allied protection. Four months later, on 22 March 1829, another protocol stated that Greece would become an autonomous but tributary state governed by a prince to be selected by the British, French and Russians.

But the Anglo-French efforts after hostilities began did not mean that they supported Russia energetically during the last months of 1827. Once Russia was left without staunch allies in the West, the Porte almost immediately disavowed the Akkerman Treaty. And, on 8 (20) December 1827, the Sultan exhorted all Muslims everywhere to wage a Holy War against Russia:

This war will not be . . . a political struggle for territory and frontiers . . . For us lies ahead a struggle for the faith and for our national existence. Each of us, whether rich or poor, great or small, must look upon this struggle as a sacred duty.[83]

Nicholas had pressed the Ottoman Empire too long and too hard. Although he had shown great talent in charming foreign diplomats in his entourage, he was unable to imagine himself in the position of his opponent. Convinced that he was right and knew what was best for the world, he had forced the Sultan in 1826 and 1827 to bow to humiliating ultimatums. He now was about to reap the bitter harvest he had sown.

2. *The Emperor-Commander*

War did not come immediately after the Sultan's December declaration, however. Although Nicholas put his army on a war footing at that time, he only gradually became convinced that war could not be avoided. 'I shall not be the one to begin it,' he had written to his brother on 23 November. And despite the Sultan's declaration of a Holy War a few days later, Nicholas still held back. Part of the reason, of course, was that he undoubtedly wished to wait for spring before launching a campaign. Quite probably, too, he was awaiting the conclusion of peace in the Trans-caucasus with the Persians. Certainly he wanted to be able to throw Paskevich's battle-hardened troops against the Turks in the East if need be, and once it became clear that peace would soon come in the Trans-caucasus, grew more resolute in his attitude towards the Turks. 'My decisions have been made; they are irrevocable,' he wrote to Konstantin on 17 February 1828. But Nicholas may have hoped that Russia's peace with the Persians might cause the Sultan to reconsider his call for a Holy War. In mid March, just after he received news of the Turkmanchai Treaty, he had written to his brother: 'I hope that this news will influence the Turks and perhaps will make them more prudent so as not to let war break out.'[84]

But there was no turning back. By early April Nicholas had begun to pose before Europe as being forced into war because the Sultan had closed the Straits to Russian commercial shipping and thereby threatened his Empire with economic disaster. 'The produce of our soil cannot be sold because everything must pass through that narrow channel of Constantinople, which is closed to my vessels,' he told the Austrian ambassador Count Zichy.[85] Metternich regarded such arguments as 'a parallel with Bonaparte's system',[86] and viewed Nicholas's claim that the 'commerce of Odessa alone has sustained a loss of thirty millions [of roubles]'[87] as simply a ruse by which he hoped to bleed the Porte dry through indemnities after he had won the war. Russia thus formally declared war on the Ottoman Empire on 14 (26) April 1828, and on 25 April, the troops of the Russian Second Army, under the command of General Field-Marshal Wittgenstein, crossed the Pruth River (the scene of Peter the Great's humiliating defeat by the Turks in 1711) into the Danubian principalities. War had begun, but it would seem that Nicholas still hoped that a show of force would compel the Sultan to propose peace negotiations. As he told Count Zichy just more than a week after war had been declared:

If circumstances beyond all human calculations should lead the Porte to accomplish its own destruction, I should deplore it very sincerely. I prefer to believe that this deplorable catastrophe will not take place. I am going to place myself at the head of my army, holding myself in readiness to receive at any instant any overtures which the Sultan may still wish to make.[88]

Nicholas thus seems to have expected that the Turks would yield to an initial show of force. 'Cannon and the bayonet are necessary to frighten them,' he told Count Zichy.[89] But the Sultan did not yield, even though it would appear that he expected nothing but defeat. Indeed, the pessim-ism of the Sultan and his generals was so great that they did little but wage a defensive war, failing to follow up Russian blunders by attacks which might have won them considerable ground. As Metternich commented in September, 'the plan of the Russian campaign shows deficiencies which might have already led to the most disastrous results if the attitude of the Turks had not been purely negative . . . It is clear,' he added, 'that the war was undertaken on the supposition that the Porte would yield to fear.'[90]

In retrospect, there seems to have been a good deal of truth in Metternich's remarks. In 1821, Baron Dibich, then an imperial aide-de-camp, had drafted a daring plan for a campaign against the Turks. At that time, Dibich had argued that the Sultan's forces could be crushed in one campaign provided the Russians began their advance early (not later than 1 March), and that sufficient quantities of manpower were thrown into the attack from the beginning.[91] But the actual campaign of 1828 was vastly different from the one Dibich had proposed seven years earlier. The fact that Nicholas postponed a declaration of war for so long after the Sultan had called for a Holy War may well have given the Turks time to augment their weak army and improve the defences of their Balkan fortresses.[92]

Yet little hindered the initial Russian advance. Firing hardly a shot, Wittgenstein occupied Moldavia and Wallachia and moved to establish the beginnings of a Russian administration there under the direction of F. P. Pahlen.[93] On 24 April, the day before his armies crossed the Pruth, Nicholas appointed Count V. P. Kochubei, Prince A. N. Golitsyn and Count P. A. Tolstoi, to form a Provisional Supreme Commission in St Petersburg which would govern in his absence,[94] and the next day himself left for the front. Anxious to join his troops, to prove himself a commander in battle as well as on the parade ground, Nicholas raced southwards accompanied only by General Benkendorf and his aides-de-camp Potemkin, Read and Suvorov.[95] Travelling night and day, stopping only to review troops along the way, he reached Tiraspol on 5 May. Two days later, on the 7th, Nicholas crossed the Pruth and journeyed on to join his army near Braila that very night.[96] For the first time since Peter the Great had done so in 1711, a Russian Emperor had set foot on Turkish territory.

Nicholas appeared every inch a commander the next morning as he reviewed the Russian troops laying siege to Braila. As one observer described him, 'in his physical appearance, he surpassed all the generals and officers that I have ever seen in the army'.[97] At Braila he was surrounded by a brilliant suite; not only were there his generals, but also a number of foreign officers and other dignitaries. Throughout these days, a festive atmosphere reigned. As Nesselrode wrote to his wife in late June:

If Petersburg society does not know where to gather in the evenings, we do not suffer that dilemma here. We have several open houses. Yesterday, for example, General Vasil'chikov gave a very nice luncheon, and [Count] Blome [the Danish ambassador] provided us with a magnificent supper. As for conversation, I challenge you to find any that is more agreeable than here; it is, from morning to night, an uninterrupted running fire of witticisms, *bon mots*, and pranks.[98]

Nicholas, it would seem, saw little difference between a military campaign and the summer manoeuvres held each year outside the capital at Krasnoe Selo. The similarity became even more evident during the next few weeks as he raced from one part of his army to another, everywhere reviewing his troops and commenting on their parade-ground appearance. 'Gaiety and good health are the order of the day,' he wrote to Konstantin Pavlovich in early June.[99] Nicholas had never seen the bloody battles of the Napoleonic Wars. He did not yet know how brutal real war would be.

To all this was added the glory of victory. Count Paskevich-Erivanskii, fresh from his conquests over the Persians, seized Kars and several other important Turkish fortresses in the east.[100] In the Balkans, the main theatre of war, Russian troops crossed the Danube on 27 May, after being halted for a time by the flood-stage waters.[101] The next day, even before a bridgehead was fully secured, Nicholas also crossed the river.[102] By 17 June, just more than six weeks after they had first crossed the Pruth, Russia's armies had seized six Turkish fortresses. Victory seemed to follow the young Emperor everywhere.

But the heady wine of victory soon began to sour as the inadequacy of Russian preparations began to be felt. Expecting the Sultan to sue for peace well before his armies reached the Danube, Nicholas and his generals had sent far too few men and supplies into the Balkans. As the Turks fell back, gathering their forces as they retreated, Russia's generals found themselves facing larger concentrations of enemy troops, and, at Shumla, were badly outnumbered.[103] Russian troops also suffered dreadfully from the intense summer heat. 'These last few days have been exhausting,' Nicholas wrote to his elder brother. 'There is no water and the temperature has reached forty-four degrees [Réaumur]!'[104] The heat and shortage of water about which Nicholas complained aggravated the condition of the already disease-ridden encampment. Epidemics raged, and even Nicholas, despite what one observer called his 'iron constitution',[105] fell ill and suffered from extremely debilitating attacks of diarrhoea.[106]

The summer of 1828 was therefore the time when Nicholas finally came to know the reality of war. During the early summer months. Commander-in-Chief Field-Marshal Wittgenstein and General Count Dibich, Nicholas's special military adviser, had engaged in a long and acrimonious debate about how the campaign should be waged. Nicholas had settled the dispute by siding with Dibich and ordering that all three major fortresses which lay before them – Shumla, Varna and Silestria – be besieged simultaneously. It was a plan that stretched the meagre Russian resources of men and *matériel* to the limit. And it was here, as the Russians fought under the blazing summer sun, that Nicholas saw men torn apart by cannon shot, split open by sabres and wasted away in their thousands as dysentery gripped their bowels and fever parched them in the broiling heat.[107]

Nicholas had had the opportunity to command in battle himself during these months, and had acquitted himself tolerably well. As the Danish ambassador Count Blome described an attack which Nicholas directed at Shumla on 12 July: 'His Majesty the Emperor himself gave all the commands and the troops executed them with a precision which could not have been more perfect at the Krasnoe Selo manoeuvres. The calm and serene manner in which His Majesty gave his orders was admirable, worthy of a most masterful general.'[108] But even though his calm and bravery under fire won for Nicholas the admiration of those around him, he was still a parade-ground commander, a fact which even his loyal companion General Benkendorf could not help but mention.[109] The summer of 1828 showed Nicholas that he was not cast in the mould of a great general. Never again would he lead troops in the field, and never again would he desert the day-to-day affairs of his Empire to seek glory in battle.

Indeed, if the campaign of 1828 against the Turks in the Balkans had become bogged down during the summer, and if Nicholas had reached the point at which he could no longer live with all the horrors of siege warfare, there were other things to cause him further anxiety. The war with Turkey had never, in fact, been popular in Russia. A. A. Zakrevskii, the Governor-General of Finland and Minister of Interior, was not of the opinion that a war with the Ottoman Empire could serve Russia's interests. 'Better that all your efforts [to prepare for a Balkan campaign] should come to naught,' he wrote to a friend, 'than for us to have a war which would bring no benefit to Russia and, even more, would do her harm in view of her weak condition.'[110] Even Zakrevskii, who was neither an able statesman nor an effective administrator, realized that, following the ruinous financial drain of the Napoleonic Wars, Russia's economic situation was precarious and needed attention. More perceptive statesmen were even more acutely aware of the problem. During January 1828, for example, General P. D. Kiselev had written, 'the state is without funds and industry . . . It may become very much like . . . a colossus with feet of clay.'[111] To be sure, there had been some speculation that a victory over the Turks would enable Russia to collect a large indemnity and that this sum could be used to revive the nation's flagging agriculture and backward industry.[112] This was, in fact, one of Metternich's greatest fears. As he wrote to Count Esterhazy in May 1828, 'he [Nicholas] will impose on the Porte pecuniary charges that will tax its resources to the utmost . . . In a word, the Porte has the choice between death and a prolonged agony.'[113] But certainly, while Nicholas might hope to weaken the Ottoman Empire through financial exactions and thus make the Sultan more amenable to Russia's wishes, no one could have expected that Russia would succeed in exacting a sum vast enough to subsidize her industrial development and pay the colossal expenses of the war as well.

If army generals and senior officials did not favour the war, neither did Russia's masses. If the annual reports which General Benkendorf drafted as head of the Third Section are to be believed, discontent with the war was increasing during the latter half of 1828. The Turkish war had never been presented to the masses in a way which could win their enthusiasm, Benkendorf noted, and this again stands as further evidence that Nicholas had expected it to end almost as soon as it began. As Benkendorf wrote:

For the vast majority of the population the manifesto [declaring war on the Ottoman Empire] said nothing which went to their hearts. It mentioned not one word about Greece, about the Orthodox faith, or about Mother Russia . . . As a result, at the declaration of war, the masses remained passive . . . The departure of the Emperor to join the army increased . . . ferment even further. All groups were unanimous in complaining that the Emperor had exposed himself to the dangers of war.[114]

The extent to which Russians, especially in the capital, regretted Nicholas's absence, and how much Benkendorf was embroidering upon the truth to convince him to leave the Balkans and the war to his generals, we cannot tell. Certainly Benkendorf was fearful of dissent in Russia. He continually referred to those who were unenthusiastic about the war, or who criticized its conduct, as 'frondeurs',[115] and, according to Zakrevskii's account, even he was placed under secret surveillance in the spring of 1829, although he was Minister of the Interior. Benkendorf evidently wanted to know how often Zakrevskii met with the fallen hero General Ermolov, then living on a small estate outside Moscow.[116] Given Ermolov's popularity with the army, perhaps Benkendorf feared that he might become the centre of an army conspiracy. The head of the Third Section thus loudly played the tune that Nicholas's abandonment of administrative matters to seek glory on the battlefield had given rise to a great deal of discontent. In any case, after witnessing the fall of Varna, Nicholas returned to St Petersburg, his efforts to seek glory on the battlefield ended. As the Prussian diplomat Küster reported to his king, 'Europe can at least derive the consolation . . . of knowing that Nicholas will never be a conqueror.'[117]

Once back in St Petersburg, Nicholas proceeded to deal with the war he had left behind with new energy. Russia's armies had been forced to withdraw into winter quarters and much of the ground they had won in the summer would have to be retaken next year. New decisions about the coming campaign would have to be made, and to make them Nicholas formed a special secret committee composed of Count V. P. Kochubei, Count A. I. Chernyshev, Prince I. V. Vasil'chikov and Baron Tol'.[118] Of particular importance in the work of the committee was a memorandum prepared by General Vasil'chikov which found numerous shortcomings in the army's command structure and in the choices of personnel. Vasil'chikov's criticisms, notable for their candour and bluntness, are a rarity among advisers to absolute monarchs. 'The centralization and unity of power is one of the first requirements of a well-organized army,' he wrote. And, as far as the choice of commanders was concerned, Vasil'chikov argued that it could hardly have been worse.

If the Chief of the General Staff lacked experience, the Quartermaster-General not only had even less, but also lacked energy and foresight . . . The Commissariat General was far from having the requisite talents for such a vital post; he was ignorant, incapable of formulating great plans, lacked foresight, and had no idea of what war was about at all.[119]

Following Vasil'chikov's advice, Nicholas removed Field-Marshal Wittgenstein from his post as Commander-in-Chief of the Balkan front. Paskevich continued to direct the campaign against the Ottoman Empire in the East, but Nicholas now gave command in the Balkans to General Count Dibich. Dibich was not popular, either with the army's officer corps or with the populace as a whole (for whom Ermolov remained a national hero). Within the army itself, Dibich was regarded as a careerist and opportunist. As Zakrevskii had written to General Kiselev a number of years earlier, 'Dibich loves only himself and not the service.'[120] But Dibich was energetic, in sharp contrast to Wittgenstein who was far too aged to undertake a combat military command. And, most important, he had shown himself to be absolutely loyal to his Emperor.

Under Dibich's direction the 1829 campaign in the Balkans moved far more energetically and successfully. In early May, Russia's forces once again crossed the Danube to begin a campaign that would prove decisive. At Kulevcha, on 30 May, the Russians dealt the Turkish forces their most serious defeat, though just how much the victory was the result of Dibich's generalship is still an open question. According to one observer at least,

Dibich was some six kilometres away from the field of battle watching its progress through a telescope, certainly not the ideal location for a commander who might need to shift the deployment of his forces at any moment.[121] Less than three weeks later, the Turkish fortress of Silestria fell, and on 5 July Dibich began his march towards the eastern Balkans, heading for Adrianople.[122] But he was not well prepared to cross the mountains. Russian soldiers made the crossing weighed down like beasts of burden, and many fell along the way in the heat. K. I. Zeidlits, a doctor serving with the Russian forces, recalled:

The soldiers became exhausted under the weight of their accoutrements: they had to lug on their backs a haversack, a uniform, a heavy overcoat, a mess tin with water, and rations for ten days, that is, twenty pounds of dried bread crusts . . . Many soldiers died along the march.[123]

Once in southern Bulgaria, Dibich's army began to live off the land. As Zeidlits recalled, 'in the vineyards we gathered unripe maize, small watermelons, and honeydew melons . . . The commander whom I had treated sent me two fresh loaves of bread. To us they seemed like absolute ambrosia.'[124] As a result of better diet, the army's fighting trim improved and the Russians seized Turkish strongholds and key cities in rapid succession. The port city of Burgas fell on 12 July, and in early August the Russians reached Adrianople. At almost the same moment, news reached Constantinople that General Paskevich had seized and occupied the key city of Ezeroum. The road to Constantinople lay open in the west and the last key city had fallen in the east. Dibich's armies were now less than two hundred kilometres from Constantinople itself.

As a result of the Russian victories, the Sultan opened peace negotiations, and on 28 August Russia and the Ottoman Empire signed the Treaty of Adrianople which recognized the Russian claim to Georgia and other Caucasian provinces; gave neutral ships free navigation in the Black Sea and on the Danube; granted practical autonomy to Wallachia and Moldavia under Russian protection; placed Russian merchants in the Ottoman domains under the control of Russian consuls rather than under the control of Turkish authorities; and, finally, recognized the provisions of the London Convention of 1827 with regard to Greece. The actual settlement of the Greek question, however, was left to a conference in London and, on 3 February 1830 (NS), this gathering declared Greece to be an independent monarchical state whose status would be guaranteed by Britain, France and Russia. Nicholas had thus succeeded in forcing his will upon the Porte. The Sultan accepted the disputed treaty clauses and assured access to the Mediterranean for Russian shipping. For the moment, Russia had become the predominant power in the Near East. As Lord Aberdeen commented to Princess Lieven, the sister of General Benkendorf and wife of Russia's ambassador to England, 'Russia dominates the world today; notwithstanding the modesty of your language, you are omnipotent everywhere.'[125]

Russia's prestige and power in Europe had reached new heights and the poor showing of her armies against the Turks during the previous year was momentarily forgotten. Most ironically, the arms of Russia, the bastion of legitimacy, had been the deciding factor in winning independence for the Greeks who had been in revolt for a number of years against their lawful rulers.

3. Revolution Threatens

The agreement reached at the London Conference on 3 February 1830 (NS) pointed the way to the final solution of the Greek question, even though there would be further refinements added in 1832, and the first King of Greece, Otto, a Bavarian princeling, would not ascend the throne until January 1833. Nicholas, however, had been far more concerned with forcing the Ottoman Empire to live up to previous treaties and to assure free access to the Mediterranean for Russian shipping, and as we have seen the Greeks were in his eyes rebels, and their independence something not particularly desirable in itself. The reasons for his declaration of war against the Sultan in 1828 had had little to do with creating an independent Greece.

Metternich held much the same opinion on the subject of the Greek revolt. At every point during the Russo–Turkish campaigns of 1828 and 1829, he had urged the defence of legitimacy and a return to the principles of European unity proclaimed at the defeat of Napoleon.

If the spring of 1829 sees the renewal of war [he warned], and if the same lack of agreement between the principal Courts should be prolonged until that time, Europe will then have to face an awful prospect of troubles and revolutions . . . Will a means of making peace be found? . . . That is the question, and its answer will decide neither more nor less than the maintenance of the old political order in Europe or its fall.[126]

Thus Metternich steadfastly urged the maintenance of legitimacy throughout Europe. 'With this principle alone can general peace be possible,' he told his Emperor.[127] Most important, by 'general peace' Metternich meant stemming the tide of revolution. 'The . . . reproach which I make against you, is the flood-way which, by your deviation from the only correct political principles, you have afforded to the enemies of order,' he told Count Nesselrode at Königswart at the end of July 1830, in criticizing Russia's role in establishing an independent Greece. Although Metternich did not yet know it, two days before, on 28 July (NS), revolution had erupted in Paris. By the 29th the Hôtel de Ville had been seized and the insurgents were masters of the city. On the 30th Louis Philippe was proclaimed King of the French. The revolution in Paris had succeeded almost overnight.[128]

For Nicholas, the July Days in Paris marked the beginning of two years of crises, for he faced two revolutions in the West (in France and Belgium), and one in Poland. Furthermore, there would be a serious cholera epidemic to deal with, as well as revolts in Sevastopol and in the military colonies in Russia's western provinces. By the time these crises had passed, the Nicholas system would have assumed a definitive form. And its form would to some extent be influenced by the crises of 1830–31.

Word of revolution in Paris itself certainly came as no great surprise to Nicholas. As he commented some time after:

We had foreseen this dreadful event for some time and We had exercised nearly all Our means of persuasion that friendship and Our good relations would permit on Charles X and his ministers. All Our efforts were in vain. Thus, We do not hesitate to place the blame [for this revolution] on the illegal acts of Charles X.[129]

This was more than simple hindsight. As early as 3 April 1830, Nicholas had told Dibich that the political situation in France was becoming increasingly volatile and that, 'as painful as it is to say it, it is the folly of the King which is the cause of all this'.[130] And, not long before the outbreak of violence in the streets of Paris, Nicholas had told the French ambassador, Baron de Bourgoing, that Charles X was 'rushing to his destruction'. Nicholas and educated Russian opinion were at one in regarding the arch-reactionary ministry of Polignac, whose fall signalled the beginning of the revolution in Paris, as a government of obscurantists which threatened the peace and order of France, and perhaps even of Europe. As Benkendorf summed it up in his 1830 report on the state of public opinion in Russia, 'it was evident to almost every educated individual that, during recent months, France was governed by mystics and Jesuits'.[131]

Nicholas was in no way disposed to defend Charles X. In his strict legitimist view, he considered that the French king had forfeited his right to the throne by his unprincipled behaviour, by his 'inexplicable folly' and his 'vile advisers'.[132] Nicholas may well have sympathized with Charles's dislike of the Charter of 1814. Indeed, he was facing a similar situation in the Kingdom of Poland, where he was obliged to govern as a constitutional monarch, though this was repugnant to his political principles. But Nicholas believed that once a monarch had given his word to observe faithfully a constitutional charter, he must keep his promise. In his view, every *coup d'état* undertaken by a constitutional monarch (such as that initiated in France by the publication of the five July Ordinances), by definition seriously weakened the credibility of the institution of the monarchy.[133]

Even so, Nicholas would not recognize the revolutionary government established under Louis Philippe as legitimate. 'The [Duke] of Orleans will never be more than a vile usurper,' he wrote.[134] To his mind, only the lawful successor to Charles X could be the legitimate sovereign of France. To violate such a fundamental principle of legitimacy was, in Nicholas's opinion, a dangerous thing indeed. The issue of legitimacy in Europe, and the principles of the Holy Alliance, with which it was intimately connected, formed, in his mind, the very fabric of European stability. He considered such stability a fundamental prerequisite for Russia's own security. 'It is Our duty to think of our security,' he told his brother. 'When I say *ours*, I mean the tranquillity of Europe.'[135]

The fact that Louis Philippe was a 'vile usurper' raised a serious question of principle in Nicholas's mind, but it did not in itself challenge the peace of Europe, and hence Russia's safety. 'As long as the French slaughter each other, it is no concern of Ours,' was the first position which he adopted towards the July Monarchy. Indeed, he argued that the simple fact of Louis Philippe's usurpation of the French throne 'gives Us neither the right nor even the need to intervene with force; Our opposition will be *moral* . . . But,' he added ominously, 'if a revolutionary France thinks to regain her ancient frontiers, that will change Our duty entirely.'[136] To be prepared for such a possibility, he ordered the Grand Duke Konstantin Pavlovich to place the armies of the Polish Kingdom on alert so as to be ready to march if necessary.[137] And, to express his opposition further to the new French régime, he dispatched two of his most trusted adjutants to the Courts of Central Europe. Dibich he sent to Berlin, and General aide-de-camp A. F. Orlov (who little more than a decade later would succeed Benkendorf as head of the Third Section) to Vienna. Together they were to seek grounds for a common policy in respect of the revolutionary government in France. But in Berlin and Vienna they found little support for the non-recognition policy which Nicholas proposed. Although Metternich was also a champion of legitimacy, it was his policy to re-establish order as quickly as possible so as to keep the revolution from spreading, especially to the Habsburg domains in Italy. While Nicholas could better afford to stand on principle, very real and immediate political pressures conditioned Metternich's position. He still feared the Russian menace and, if he were to agree to so drastic a step as refusing to recognize Louis Philippe, then he wanted formal agreements and guarantees that Nicholas was not yet ready to give. Thus, Prussia and Austria both recognized the July Monarchy. In the end, Nicholas had to do likewise.

Nicholas's conduct during the early days of the July Monarchy has often been misunderstood, and historians have often viewed his initial reaction to revolution in Paris as one in which he was ready to march on the West in defence of legitimacy.[138] Yet Nicholas was far too astute a politician to enter such a diplomatic blind alley from which there might later be no escape. Certainly his sense of morality was deeply outraged at Louis Philippe's accession (though he liked the man personally), and he spoke of a campaign in the West. But always he qualified such statements. While he ordered the military governor-general of Kronstadt, Vice-Admiral Rozhnov, to refuse permission to all French ships flying the revolutionary Tricolour to land, an act which could have led to war (though the possibility was highly remote), he allowed himself to be dissuaded from this path with remarkable ease by France's ambassador Baron de Bourgoing. Like any astute statesman, he had tested the ground to see how far the new French government might bend. In the final analysis, Nicholas was not prepared for war with France over the question of who sat upon the French throne, nor did he seriously consider it. 'The principle of legitimacy is what guides me in all cases,' he had told Baron de Bourgoing.[139] And while he would express his outrage and his 'moral opposition' as he felt he must, and while he would use all diplomatic means at his disposal to prevent Louis Philippe's recognition by other powers, he would not intervene directly in France's internal affairs.

Louis Philippe and the July Monarchy soon became exemplars of bourgeois cultural and political values, and it grew very clear that neither the new French king nor his ministers contemplated repeating the experience of republican France in the early 1790s. Indeed, the republic was over almost before it began. As the special French emissary to Vienna, General Belliard, described it, Louis Philippe, before his proclamation as king, 'took General LaFayette by the arm and led him to the balcony; there he embraced him and it was all over with the Republic'.[140] But what about revolutionary ideas? On this question Nicholas took a much more rigid position. As he told Konstantin Pavlovich when he first received the news of revolt in Paris, Russia would know her duty should the revolution spread. He thus reserved to himself the right to intervene in European politics under conditions which he would himself define. In doing so, he articulated the first principles which would lead him and Russia to become regarded as the Gendarme of Europe.

Fears of a revolutionary France following the path taken in the early 1790s thus appeared groundless in the days just after the proclamation of the July Monarchy. A few weeks later, however, the threat suddenly loomed much larger. In Metternich's words, the 'extraordinary influence exercised by the Revolution of July over men's minds far beyond the boundaries of France' began to take hold. On 25 August (NS), one month to the day after the Parisian insurgents had seized the Hôtel de Ville, revolution broke out in Brussels. Crowds gathered for a performance of Scribe's and Auber's opera, *La Muette de Portici*, a portrayal of the Neapolitans' uprising against their Spanish masters, broke into revolt against the rule of the Dutch King William I.

Unlike the July Days in Paris, where the outcome was decided within two days, the revolution in Brussels went on for more than a month. This time Nicholas considered that war was much more a possibility: the major European Powers had all committed themselves to preserving the territorial integrity of the Netherlands in 1814, and King William now requested military support from them. But even though a legitimate sovereign had made a legitimate request for Russian aid, Nicholas would agree to act only in concert with other European Powers or to quell the menace of an expansionist revolutionary France. As he told Konstantin Pavlovich, King William had requested military assistance from the Great Powers, and had 'an incontestable right to do so . . . But,' Nicholas added, 'all that will only move us if the French think about sending even one man to their borders. Then we shall see that this is not just a simple insurrection, but that its source is . . . emanating from Paris.'[141] By early November, the Belgian provinces were lost to the Dutch king and a Belgian National Congress voted to establish an independent monarchy. The European allies once again agreed to accept the inevitable and to seek a resolution of the Belgian issue through negotiations, though a final settlement would not be reached until nearly a decade later.[142]

During the summer and early autumn of 1830, Nicholas had thus seen two revolutionary crises in the West and in each case had followed a moderate course. Although revolutionary régimes in Belgium and France were offensive to his sense of honour and conflicted with his legitimist principles, they at least preserved a monarchical form and no republics had been proclaimed. Nicholas would make no military move so long as he did not find in them the seeds of a new revolutionary menace such as had confronted Europe in the late eighteenth century. As Count Nesselrode once told Metternich, 'the Emperor will never fire a single shot, shed one drop of Russian blood, or spend one half-penny to redeem the errors that have been committed in France'.[143]

One of the reasons why Nicholas maintained such a balanced view when faced by revolutions in Europe was that Russia's house had remained calm and in very good order during the summer and early autumn. As General Benkendorf reported in his annual summary about public opinion in Russia, no 'pernicious ideas' were afoot in the Empire. Certainly a few 'junior Guard officers and reckless individuals . . . [had drunk] the health of Louis Philippe'. But this sort of thing, in Benkendorf's view, 'was limited to simple idle chatter'.[144] There was, to be sure, a certain amount of youthful idealization of the revolution in Paris, for, as Aleksandr Herzen, then a young university student, noted in his autobiography, 'we followed step by step every word [and] every event'.[145] But most of Russian society paid little notice to the July Days.[146] By November 1830 it must have seemed to Nicholas that the revolutionary menace was passing. France had made no effort to export the doctrines of revolution, and although Belgium was 'already looked upon as lost', to use Metternich's phrase,[147] the revolution seemed to be dying out there as well. Events in Europe had not threatened Russia's security. As Nicholas himself commented, 'the geographical position of Russia is so advantageous that it . . . makes her independent of what occurs in Europe; she has nothing to fear'.[148] He could thus look forward to turning his full attention 'to Russia's internal problems, especially to repairing the ravages of the cholera epidemic which had struck the same year.

Then, only days later, revolution struck Nicholas's domains. As Herzen described it, 'suddenly, like a bomb . . . news of the Warsaw insurrection deafened us. This was no longer far away. This was right here at home!'[149]

4. Revolution!

On the night of 17 (29) November 1830, a handful of Polish conspirators set a Warsaw brewery afire as the signal to begin a revolt against Poland's Russian rulers. The flames flared only briefly, and then were extinguished by a watchman. It was a symbolic beginning to an ill-fated revolt which provided Nicholas with the long looked-for excuse to revoke the charter which Alexander I had granted to the Poles in 1815. By the time that the last vestiges of the revolt were crushed a year later, Poland would be more firmly under Russian control than ever.

The causes which led the Poles to revolt were numerous and complex.[150] They were the result both of centuries-long antagonisms between Russian and Pole, and of more pressing immediate concerns. The Warsaw revolt of November 1830 has often been portrayed as an inevitable result of the Russian régime under which Poles had lived for the fifteen years between 1815 and 1830. Yet much had been done during those years to improve living conditions in Poland. As a result, these were somewhat better than in Russia itself. For one thing, the Poles lived under a semblance of a constitutional order which meant that they were not subject to the totally arbitrary whims of the men who governed them. Conditions in the Polish army were considerably better for the rank and file, at least, than for Russians. While their Russian counterparts were obliged to serve for twenty-five years, Polish soldiers served only eight.[151] Beyond this, Alexander I and his advisers had honestly sought ways to bring about a reconstruction of Poland's ruined national economy after the shambles created by the late eighteenth-century partitions and the Napoleonic wars. Nicholas had continued the policy, and while Poland's economic difficulties were by no means solved by 1830, there was enough improvement to show that the Kingdom was on the road to recovery.[152] In short, the more substantial portions of the Polish *szlachta* (nobility) had done relatively well under fifteen years of Russian rule. Nicholas's extravagant claim that Poland 'had attained a state of remarkable prosperity'[153] was, of course, an over-statement, but, although much still needed to be accomplished, there was some cause for optimism alongside the many good reasons for dissatisfaction.

We have already mentioned the age-old antagonism between Russian and Pole. Coupled with this were other factors which made political tensions in Poland increasingly acute during the 1820s. For one thing, Romanticism, the emotional and intellectual foundation of nationalist movements throughout Europe, was especially strong in Poland. The Polish nation had known greatness and power. Polish Renaissance art and culture had at one time dominated Eastern Europe, and Poland's political might had formerly made her a threat to both Russia and Prussia. Poland regarded herself as the last bastion of European civilization on the edge of Asia; Warsaw was, for Poles, the 'Paris of the East'.

Such intense national pride, coupled with a great national literary and musical heritage, assumed a further heroic dimension in the hands of men such as the poet Adam Mickiewicz, the historian Joachim Lelewel and the composer Frederic Chopin. In true Romantic fashion, the virtues most extolled among the Poles were heroism and patriotism. Young men thought not of the nation's economic progress but of mighty deeds in its service. It would be the same throughout the nineteenth century: young men would reject the more solid but dull economic and administrative concerns of their elders in favour of a passionate devotion to the cause of Polonism. As late as 1864, W. A. White, the British resident in Warsaw, captured this spirit very precisely in a report to his superiors in the Foreign Office:

... a Polish boy's idea of glory is to be, as soon as possible, a Conspirator ...
This fiery Polish patriotism is at the same time a conviction and a dominant
passion and brings a portion of each successive generation of Poles to an untimely
grave. The experience of the Fathers is of no avail to the Sons.[154]

Such passionate Romantic sentiments, coupled with nationalist
strivings, were bound to assume an anti-Russian character among the
younger generations of Poles. These feelings were intensified as the result
of events connected with the 1825 Decembrist revolt in Russia. Nicholas's
Investigating Commission in St Petersburg had disclosed a link between
the reconstituted Polish Patriotic Society and the Decembrists' Southern
Society, and although no Poles had been involved in the revolt itself, a
number of them were arrested, including Colonel Seweryn Krzyżanowski,
the leader of the Patriotic Society. Unaccustomed to constitutional
limitations upon his power, Nicholas had insisted that Krzyżanowski and
a number of other prominent Poles be tried for high treason, and it was
only after considerable pressure from his advisers, and especially from the
Grand Duke Konstantin Pavlovich, that he agreed to permit Krzyżanowski
and his fellow officers to be tried by a court of Polish Senators as provided
for by the constitution of 1815.[155] The sentences handed down by the
court were mild. Krzyżanowski was condemned to three years in prison,
others received even briefer terms, and a number were acquitted. Nicholas
accepted the verdict, though he reprimanded the Polish Senators for
their leniency and imposed upon those Poles who possessed Russian
citizenship much harsher sentences.[156] But such behaviour affronted
Polish national honour and marked a turning point in Russo–Polish
relations. Although the initial result of Krzyżanowski's trial and conviction was to make many prominent Poles more wary of connections
with secret societies in the future, the colonel's 'martyrdom' provided a
focal point for young men with heroic and Romantic aspirations.[157]

In December 1828, a full three months before Krzyżanowski's sentence
was confirmed, a number of students at the Cadet School in Łazienki,
less than an hour's stroll from Konstantin Pavlovich's Warsaw residence
at the Belvedere Palace, formed a new conspiracy. The cadets' leader
was a young instructor, the subaltern Piotr Wysocki.[158] Military cadets
were particularly fertile ground for the seeds of revolution in Poland.
True to its long aristocratic tradition, Polish society regarded service in
the army as an important aspect of a young nobleman's education, and
it was by the military rank he earned while serving with the colours that
a Polish nobleman (as well as his future wife) would be addressed for the
rest of his days.[159] To some degree, then (except in the case of titled
aristocrats), the rank which a young man won in the service of Poland
defined his social position. Yet in Poland's relatively small army of some

90,000 men there was little chance for advancement. The cadets at Łazienki, some of whom had already served in the army for more than a decade without promotion, were thus particularly disenchanted with the state of affairs in the late 1820s.[160] For such men – young, fervently patriotic, romantic, anxious to become Poland's new generation of heroes, but seemingly condemned to spend their early adult years in the army's cadet ranks with little prospect of advancement – revolt was an appealing alternative. Nicholas and the Grand Duke Konstantin Pavlovich became for them objects of scorn and hatred. And, to a significant degree, both merited the antipathy of their Polish subjects. It must, in all fairness, be said that Konstantin Pavlovich could be generous and magnanimous on occasion, and that he seems to have had a genuine interest in Polish affairs and a deep affection for the country. But it was his fits of temper and his despotic behaviour which characterized him in the eyes of Poles, and Nicholas received numerous and bitter complaints about him, even from Russians who were serving in the Polish Kingdom.[161]

To the Poles, Nicholas was little better than his elder brother, and what they knew of his conduct was enough to foster a widespread antipathy. His persecution of the Polish Patriotic Society in the first years of his reign was one factor which earned him widespread enmity. His attitude towards Poland's constitution was another. It was not that Nicholas openly violated the constitution: he observed it quite scrupulously,[162] and some historians argue that he was more correct in his observance of its articles than was Alexander I.[163] Nicholas had submitted to what he regarded as the 'pointless ordeal' of being crowned King of Poland in Warsaw; in 1830 he had summoned the Polish National Assembly (*Sejm*), and presided over its opening as prescribed by law. Yet beneath his attitude of rigid correctness, Nicholas had a deep antipathy to the role he was obliged to play, and this did not remain hidden from the Poles. His reluctant agreement to permit Krzyżanowski and his co-defendants to be tried by a Polish court was one obvious instance of his dislike for Poland's constitution, and there were others. He was reluctant to summon the *Sejm* to approve Poland's state budget, and he made no secret of his dislike for its Polish delegates. Nicholas was thus ill at ease as a constitutional monarch in Poland. He regarded it as his duty to observe the constitution to the letter, but was only too happy to revoke it when, in his view, the Poles violated it at the end of November 1830.

The loosely knit band of conspirators who began their attack against the Russians on the night of 17 (29) November 1830 would have suffered defeat within a few hours had they been left to their own devices. Their attack on the Belvedere Palace, their main objective that night, failed for want of manpower and because they did not stay long enough to seek out Konstantin Pavlovich, whom they had hoped to capture. Wysocki could not find a single senior officer in all of Warsaw to head his forces, and many of Warsaw's middle- and upper-class citizens hastened to lock their doors and kept off the streets.[164] Two factors turned the tide in favour of Wysocki and his cadet revolutionaries, neither of which they had foreseen. First was the unexpected support from Warsaw's lower classes; second was the indecisive behaviour of the usually firm and assertive Grand Duke.

Harvests had been poor in Poland in 1830 and the price of grain in Warsaw more than doubled during the second half of the year.[165] To make matters worse, the prices of beer and spirits were raised on the very day the revolt began. These immediate aggravations, as well as a number of other grievances, such as corruption among city officials, led the Warsaw masses to join the revolt almost immediately. City labourers broke into the arsenal and seized some 30,000 muskets. They were soon joined by some of the rank and file of the Polish garrison who were disgruntled by poor rations and the rigid discipline. Within the space of a few hours, a poorly planned military *coup d'état*, begun by a few cadets, had grown into a full-scale revolutionary upheaval.[166] The rebels had at their command some 30,000 untrained civilians, a formidable force in a battle waged in Warsaw's narrow city streets. Konstantin Pavlovich faced them with some 8,700 Polish infantry, 850 Polish cavalry, and thirteen pieces of artillery, in addition to Russian forces under his command which numbered some 4,400 infantry, 2,250 cavalry, and four more guns – in all, more than 16,000 crack troops, well-trained and equipped. But he instantly abandoned all thought of resistance to the rebels, almost without firing a shot.

Konstantin Pavlovich's behaviour during the first day of the revolt is difficult to explain. He abandoned Belvedere Palace immediately and had retreated to the outskirts of Warsaw with the Russian and Polish troops under his command. There he waited for several days, seemingly uncertain as to how he should react to the crisis. He had sufficient forces at his disposal to take some effective measures against the rebels, and this was the course which his adjutants, some of them Polish officers, urged him to follow.[167] But Konstantin Pavlovich seems to have been rendered ineffective by a legal dilemma, particularly by his own view of the precise relationship between Russia and Poland within the larger imperial framework. To his mind, Poland was a separate entity and Russian troops should not be used to put down Polish rebels. As he told his aide-de-camp Władysław Zamoyski, 'not a single Russian will meddle in this matter. The Poles have begun it; it is a Polish affair. Let them settle it among themselves . . . I shall not interfere in it in any way whatsoever.'[168] Beyond that, it would appear that Konstantin was genuinely reluctant to commit to battle the troops he had so meticulously drilled. Fear of spoiling his army's parade-ground appearance had quite probably been a major reason for his refusal to send Polish troops to fight with the Russians against the Turks in 1828. And, as at least one observer commented, in 1830, the Grand Duke expressed similar sentiments during the days just after the Warsaw rising began.[169] In any case, Konstantin Pavlovich determined to leave the solution of the revolt to the Poles, for he apparently believed that the Poles were revolting against the Polish not the Russian authorities. He told Prince Adam Czartoryski and Prince Ksawery Lubecki, two members of the Kingdom's Administrative Council who approached him, 'It is up to you, gentlemen, to employ those measures which you consider most effective for calming this riot.'[170] It is significant that the Grand Duke used the word 'riot' rather than 'revolution' (the term which Nicholas used when he heard of it). He had far under-estimated the incident's seriousness.

While Konstantin Pavlovich was discussing with the Poles what measures they might employ to put down *their* riot, Nicholas knew nothing of what had occurred. Only on the evening of 25 November (7 December) did he finally receive word from his brother of what had taken place in Warsaw some eight days earlier. Nicholas showed none of his brother's hesitation. Loyal officers had been killed, including General Maurycy Hauke, Poland's Deputy War Minister. His duty was clear. The Poles were rebels and must be punished as such. Russia's honour must be defended. 'I will fulfil my duty to our Motherland and to Poland.' he promised.[171] As he told his brother:

I will never give way before force . . . What choice is left to me if the Poles in their blindness persist in their treason and madness . . . ? My position is serious, my responsibility awesome, but I have nothing to reproach myself for as far as the Poles are concerned, and I can be certain that my conscience will never trouble me about it at all.[172]

Nicholas immediately appointed Field-Marshal Count Dibich, the recent conqueror of the Turks in the Balkans, to command his armies in the West, and ordered them to march upon Poland, though he still had not given up hope that the rebels would surrender before war began. As he wrote to Konstantin Pavlovich, 'I fully believe that there are many who have been led astray . . . and it is with this hope that I have again issued an appeal to the loyalty and honour of the [Polish] nation and the army.'[173] He could not have misunderstood the Polish rebels more. To them, the honour of the Polish nation and its army demanded that they fight the Russians as long as breath remained in their bodies. And while Konstantin retreated to the Russian border, the Poles, knowing they could never match the might of Nicholas's armies, raised the red and white flag of Poland and sang 'Poland has not yet perished, while we are still living. What a foreign power has taken from us, we will take back by the sword.'

A number of influential Poles, however, knew well the folly of open rebellion against Russia, and during the early days of December 1830 they sought to re-establish order in Warsaw and end the revolt without confrontation. Prince Adam Czartoryski, one of Alexander I's closest associates and, at one time, a member of the Imperial Russian State Council, was one; Prince Ksawery Lubecki, Minister of Finance in the Kingdom, was another. Perhaps most important, General Józef Chłopicki, a much-adored national hero, shared their views. Unknown to the Warsaw masses, Chłopicki had commented when the revolt had broken out, 'some fools have begun a riot for which we all may have to pay dearly. We ought not to get involved in it.'[174] In an effort to keep the radicals from gaining control, however, Chłopicki declared himself dictator on 5 December (NS) at the head of a Supreme National Council which included Czartoryski. Prince Lubecki and Count Jan Jezierski went at the head of a delegation to St Petersburg in a last effort at reconciliation.[175]

Lubecki and Jezierski found Nicholas in no mood to bargain. While he appealed to the Poles to desist from their 'treason and madness', he was preparing to crush them mercilessly if they did not submit. 'If necessary,' he had already told his assembled Guards, 'you will march to punish these traitors, restore order, and avenge the now-stained honour of Russia.'[176] Nicholas thus gave Lubecki no room to manoeuvre, and their interview on 14 (26) December ended with him telling Dibich, 'well it is war. Marshal, you will leave immediately.'[177] 'I have exhausted every possible means for bringing these madmen to reason,' Nicholas wrote to Konstantin Pavlovich. 'To do more . . . would be incompatible with the honour . . . of this Empire which has been so scandalously insulted.'[178] To the Poles he sent the message that 'the first cannon shot fired by the Poles will kill Poland'.[179]

But Prince Lubecki and the other moderates no longer controlled the course of events. Radical elements in Warsaw were becoming more influential with every day that passed. In early January, Chłopicki resigned as dictator of the Supreme National Council, convinced he could not dissuade his hot-headed colleagues from a disastrous war. The moderates had thus failed to pull Poland back from the brink. Just over a week later, on 13 (25) January 1831, Dibich led his armies into Poland. The same day, the rebels declared that Nicholas was no longer their king and that the Polish throne was vacant. War had begun.

Within the month, the Russian army had swept to the very gates of

Warsaw. There, across the River Wisła from the city's centre, near the suburb of Praga, Dibich on 13 (25) February engaged the Poles in the brutal battle of Grochów which claimed the lives of more than 20,000 Russian and Polish troops. But Dibich was not the intrepid commander Nicholas thought him, and although the Polish defences were on the verge of collapse, he completely misjudged their strength and broke off the battle.[180] Gripped by panic in the face of what seemed certain defeat, Warsaw was saved for the moment; the Russians were not able to fight their way back to the city until September.

Nicholas took Dibich firmly to task for his poor judgement, particularly because he thought that his field-marshal's inability to crush the Poles quickly had made Russia appear ludicrous in the eyes of the West. Further, he was furious about the loss of some 9,000 Russian troops for 'no purpose whatsoever'.[181] He wrote to Dibich in mid April:

All this is truly inexplicable . . . Your continual lack of resolution, your marches and counter-marches, only serve to exhaust and dishearten [the army]. It will lose all confidence in its commander when it sees no other result from its efforts . . . except misery and death . . . For God's sake be firm in your decisions, stop beating around the bush all the time, and try, through some brilliant and daring attack, to prove to Europe that the Russian army is still the same as that which twice marched to Paris.[182]

Russia's armies suffered from more than Dibich's poor generalship, however. As summer approached, its ranks were ravaged by an epidemic of cholera which claimed more Russian lives than did the Polish bullets. It was not until 14 (26) May that Dibich managed to win a major victory against the Poles at Ostrołška, but even that was followed by more inaction and indecisiveness. 'Try to show that you are still the old Zabalkanskii,' Nicholas wrote in late May, referring to the title Dibich had received in commemoration of his Balkan victories.[183] But Dibich never saw this last exhortation from his Emperor. On 27 May (9 June) he died from cholera, and thus escaped the humiliation of being relieved of his command. Nicholas had already decided upon his successor; nearly two months earlier, on 5 April, he had recalled his 'father commander' Field-Marshal Paskevich, from the Transcaucasus. Paskevich now assumed command in Poland.

The cholera had saved Nicholas the trouble of removing an ineffective commander in Poland. Soon, it solved another of his difficulties. The Grand Duke Konstantin Pavlovich, as we have seen, had always presented something of a problem to Nicholas in formulating a Polish policy, both because of his sometimes capricious behaviour, and because of his desire to keep Russia and Poland separate in administrative terms. Just over a fortnight after Dibich's death, cholera claimed the life of the Grand Duke. At four in the afternoon he fell ill. By eight in the evening he was no more.[184] Nicholas was left to pursue a Polish policy of his own. It would be decisive, firm and merciless.

Paskevich assumed his new command on 13 (25) June, in no mood to postpone final victory. By late July he reached the outskirts of Warsaw, this time with more than 78,000 troops and nearly 400 pieces of artillery. He had well over twice as many troops as had the Poles, and nearly four times as many cannon.[185] Faced with inevitable defeat, the Poles sought to delay in protracted negotiations. But there was only one possible outcome: surrender. On 27 August, Nicholas's younger brother, the Grand Duke Mikhail Pavlovich, personally led the Imperial Guards into Warsaw. That night, Paskevich occupied the Belvedere Palace where the revolt had begun nine months earlier. From there, he sent his Emperor another of his famous victory bulletins: 'Warsaw is at the feet of your Imperial Majesty.'[186] 'From this day forth,' Nicholas replied, 'you will be known as the most illustrious Prince of Warsaw.'[187] The war was over. On 22 September (4 October), the tattered remnants of Poland's armies crossed into Prussian territory.[188] Many would not return, but would, instead, become exiles in Paris, heaping abuse upon Nicholas and his advisers from the safety of the Hôtel Lambert.

Nicholas was again King of Poland. The civil liberties, the legal codes, the institutions of local government, and a number of other privileges which the kingdom had received in the constitution of 1815 remained. But the constitution was 'modified' by an Organic Statute which Nicholas signed on 14 (26) February 1832, and the charter itself was placed in the Kremlin Armoury along with other trophies of Russian victories. Poland's separate army, the pride of Konstantin Pavlovich, was abolished. Most significant, Poland was now to be an 'indivisible part' of the Russian Empire,[189] a state of affairs for which Nicholas would obtain Prussian and Austrian approval at Münchengrätz the following year.

5. The Aftermath of Revolution

On a personal level, Nicholas's relations with the Prussian Court were the warmest of any in Europe. He was married to the daughter of the Prussian King Friedrich Wilhelm III, and held honorary commands in the Prussian army. His personal relations with 'Fritz', the Crown Prince, who, in 1840, would become King Friedrich Wilhelm IV, were even closer. Nicholas and Aleksandra Fedorovna had spent the autumn of 1820 and much of 1821 at the Prussian Court, and, early in Nicholas's reign, the Crown Prince had spent nearly a year in St Petersburg.[190]

Nicholas always felt particularly comfortable in Prussian surroundings and it has been said that he saw Friedrich Wilhelm III as a father figure. Certainly the Prussian Court was more to his liking than any other in the West. As he wrote to Dibich just after he and Aleksandra Fedorovna arrived in Berlin for a month's visit in the spring of 1829, 'at last I am relaxing here after four years of labours. Everyone received us not only with joy but with rapture.'[191]

Despite close personal relations with his son-in-law, Friedrich Wilhelm III was far from being a strong supporter of Russia's ventures in the Caucasus, the Balkans and the Near East, areas where Prussia herself had no particularly vital interests at stake. Such a contrast between personal and diplomatic relations is difficult to explain, but one plausible hypothesis is the 'complete dependence of the Berlin cabinet on Vienna in all matters of general policy' at the time.[192] And, conflicts arising from the Eastern Question, as we have seen, had made Nicholas's relationships with Austria less than cordial during the first five years of his reign. Also important, those years had been marked by Russia's warm relations with France and even, on occasion, with Britain, both of whom Metternich suspected of dangerous liberal tendencies.

Yet the final heritage of the Holy Alliance was to establish a unity of interests between Nicholas and the rulers of Prussia and Austria that would endure until the eve of the Crimean War. One key factor in this realignment was the impact which the events of 1830–31 had not only upon Nicholas, but also upon statesmen in Prussia and Austria. A defence of legitimacy, a fear of all political upheavals and an antipathy to all nationalist aspirations not tied to the dominant political and social order became the hallmarks of their union. Conservative nationalism, with its emphasis upon traditional values and the *ancien régime* social order, was elevated into a national (even international) virtue.

The old Quadruple Alliance system of 1814–15, which had been expanded in 1818 to include France, was a thing of the past by the time Paskevich triumphantly laid Warsaw at Nicholas's feet. Metternich had regarded the system as having come to be 'nothing more than a mere phrase' as early as 1826.[193] His sentiment was not shared by Nicholas, or many other statesmen in Europe at the time, however. But there was no doubt that the revolutions of 1830–31 had put the final nail in the coffin of the Holy Alliance system. Two of the major European Powers (France and Britain) were parliamentary governments; the three Eastern Powers were absolute monarchies. That division, which the Allies had sought to gloss over in 1814–15, assumed overriding importance in the wake of the new wave of revolutions in Europe. As Metternich wrote to Count Apponyi in early 1832, 'from the time Liberalism gained the upper hand in France and England, this kind of meeting [conferences between the five Great Powers] began to degenerate ... for it is an attempted compromise between the temper of the Right and the temper of the Left, and these two are mutually destructive of one another.'[194] The three Eastern Powers must combine, Metternich insisted, to construct a solid wall against the threat of revolution. 'There exists in Europe only one issue of any moment,' he wrote, 'and that is Revolution.'[195]

The first note of cooperation between the three Eastern Powers had been struck on 25 July (6 August) 1830, when Nesselrode and Metternich had signed the so-called 'Chiffon de Carlsbad', later adhered to by Prussia, in which Russia and Austria agreed 'to adopt for the general basis of our conduct not in any way to interfere in the internal disputes of France, but, on the other hand, to permit no violation on the part of the French government either of the material interests of Europe, as established and guaranteed by general transactions, or of the internal peace of the various States composing it'.[196] It was what Metternich called a 'feeble, but correct enunciation of principles',[197] but it was a beginning. At the time, however, Nicholas refused to enter into the sort of formal agreement Metternich envisaged which would set forth how the three powers would act in concert.[198] Lack of a concrete agreement as to how to react to the revolutionary events in Europe had led Austria and Prussia to recognize Louis Philippe in a manner which caught Nicholas and Nesselrode by surprise. Nicholas thus began to see the need for a more formal statement of principle more clearly than ever.

The Polish revolt of 1830–31 showed even more dramatically how closely some of the interests of the three Eastern Powers were connected, and made more clear the threat which revolution posed to them all. All three states had Poles living within their boundaries as a result of the partitions of Poland in the late eighteenth century and the settlements of 1814–15. An outbreak of revolution in the Polish territories of one state threatened the stability of all. Beyond that, Prussia especially had a strong economic interest in Poland since Polish markets played an important part in her economic system. These factors, plus their general fear of revolution anywhere in Europe, drew Austria, Prussia and Russia together during late 1832 and early 1833. At the same time, the fact that Britain and France provided a haven and moral encouragement for several thousand Polish émigrés, who had fled the country after Paskevich's victory, served to alienate those two powers even further from Russia. Nicholas, after all, regarded the Polish revolt as a domestic matter, something which concerned no one but Russia. To him, the sympathy for the Poles expressed openly and forcefully in London and Paris, even in the French Chamber of Deputies, was exactly what he had himself so scrupulously avoided in 1830: interference in the internal affairs of another sovereign state. Nicholas was therefore especially receptive to Metternich's view that 'all the efforts of the French Government are persistently directed to weakening foreign countries'.[199]

Metternich believed that France in 1832 resembled 'in many respects, France at the beginning of the Great Revolution'.[200] Nicholas regarded France in much the same manner. To this common view of European politics was added Nicholas's traditionally close personal relations with the Prussian Court and that court's close agreement with Austrian policy. As a result, once the breach between Nicholas and Metternich had been healed, the stage was set for the creation of a close community of interests between the three Eastern Powers. Discussions for a diplomatic agreement between the three courts were first planned to take place at Teplitz in late July or early August, but since Nicholas was unable to leave Russia so soon, only the Emperor Franz and Friedrich Wilhelm III met there between 2 and 4 (14–16) August 1833.[201] When foul weather forced his ship back into the naval base of Kronstadt, Nicholas had to travel overland and reached Germany only in mid (late) August.[202] He consulted first with the Prussian King at Schwedt, but the meeting did little but show him once again that the real key to diplomatic agreements lay with Metternich and not his father-in-law.[203] In fact, the king's unwillingness to discuss hard diplomatic questions so infuriated Nicholas that he suffered a bilious attack and had to retire early that evening.[204]

The most important discussions thus took place between Nicholas, Metternich and the Emperor Franz at Münchengrätz. Because King Friedrich Wilhelm was obliged to be present at previously announced manoeuvres in Magdeburg and Berlin, Prussia was represented by the Crown Prince, Nicholas's brother-in-law.[205] In addition, there were several other Russian statesmen present: Count Nesselrode, Count Orlov, and Russia's ambassador to Vienna, Count Tatishchev. There were also the Austrian Prince Felix von Schwarzenberg and Austria's ambassador to St Petersburg, Count Ficquelmont. It was an impressive gathering, indicative of how much weight the Russians and Austrians attached to the hoped-for outcome.

Discussions began with Nicholas's arrival on 29 August (10 September) and continued until 7 (19) September. During his nine days at Münchengrätz, Nicholas exhibited that charm which had won for him advocates among the foreign diplomatic corps in St Petersburg and which would gain him other adherents on his visits to European courts during the next fifteen years. He showed respect and deference to the ageing Austrian Emperor, flattered Metternich, and charmed his young wife, the Princess Melanie. Indeed, if the Princess's account is correct, the moment Nicholas arrived at the Austrian Court he told Metternich, 'I am come to put myself under the command of my chief. I look to you to give me a hint when I make any mistake.'[206] Metternich returned such flattery in much the same vein. 'The Münchengrätz Conference is ended,' he told Count Benkendorf the next day. 'It used to be that at meetings such as these they would discuss things and scribble on papers for months. But your Emperor has another method. In one hour everything is decided and done with.'[207] Nicholas kept to himself his belief that Metternich had never ceased to be a 'cohort of Satan'.[208]

The heads of state spent much of the time at Münchengrätz in amusements, reviews and banquets, while the major work was done by Metternich and Nesselrode, who spent long hours together.[209] By 6 (18) September the agreements, which Metternich characterized as the 'embodiment, in the simplest terms, of those principles of the law of nations which are least open to dispute',[210] were ready to be signed. Nicholas and his Habsburg counterpart had come to a firm understanding about the Polish and Eastern Questions. The two monarchs thus pledged on 6 (18) September to use all means within their power to preserve the existence of the Ottoman Empire; to defend the Sultan against the attacks of the Egyptian Pasha Mehemet Ali; and, to consult about a mutual course of action should the collapse of the Ottoman Empire come about despite their best efforts to prevent it.[211] The next day the emperors signed a further agreement to guarantee mutually the security of their Polish possessions; to aid each other in the event of disorders breaking out in those provinces; and to extradite political criminals who might take refuge in each other's territory.[212]

Metternich considered that the Münchengrätz resolution rested 'on the surest basis which diplomatic labours can possibly have: the frank conviction of those who frame them ... Never,' he added, 'was conviction more unanimous than that now existing between the two Emperors and their respective Cabinets.'[213] The agreements became binding on Prussia just less than a month later when, on 3 (15) October, the representatives of all three powers signed the Berlin Convention, which proclaimed their adherence to the principles of legitimacy, and their support of non-intervention in internal affairs of sovereign states without express invitation. In the case of such direct invitation by a legitimate sovereign, the three powers would join in opposing the efforts of any other power to prevent such intervention.[214]

For Nicholas, the conclusion of the Münchengrätz and Berlin agreements marked the culmination of eight long years of diplomatic labours designed above all else to protect Russia from the menace of the West. They marked the establishment of the Nicholas system in foreign affairs.

On the day when he signed the first of the Münchengrätz resolutions, Nicholas wrote to his father-in-law,

I am fully satisfied with all of my foreign relations, and everything that has come to pass is completely in agreement with my wishes and in conformity to the principles which I have had the good fortune to hear expressed on the part of Your Majesty, so that all the documents decided upon between the Emperor [Franz] and me, and which will be submitted for the approval of Your Majesty, seem to me to ensure, in a perfect manner, our security and our *defensive position*.[215]

Nicholas later commented that Münchengrätz marked 'an epoch in my life'.[216] Indeed it did. For the moment, the Polish question was settled, defences had been constructed against the menace of revolution and, as we shall see, Russia had gained a predominant position on the Black Sea and in Turkish affairs by the Treaty of Unkiar–Skelessi, signed with the Sultan on 26 June 1833. The Holy Alliance had been a vague system based heavily upon the personal relations between monarchs and ministers, evolved during their common struggle against Napoleon and bound to erode as soon as their common enemy was vanquished. It was now replaced by a system of far more solid commitments. Nicholas had inherited from Alexander I an anomalous situation in Poland, a complex series of conflicts in the Balkans and with the Ottoman Empire, and a threatening situation in the Transcaucasus where Persia was about to fall upon Russia's outlying possessions. By 1833, he had turned this heritage into the more integral commitments of the Nicholas system abroad. The result was a conservative, balanced system, in which legitimacy and the political *status quo* were elevated to the highest level of virtue. Such a system, however, was meant to be neither static nor reactionary, for Nicholas and his advisers favoured progress so long as it took place within the established political system.

Part Three

Absolutism Triumphant

---

*'Russia's past is admirable; her present more
than magnificent; as to her future, it
is beyond the grasp of the most daring
imagination'*

COUNT BENKENDORF

5

The Apogee of Autocracy

'Tsar Nikolai Pavlovich, magnanimous, severe, and upright beyond reproach, was in our eyes a Russian folk hero. In the eyes of contemporaries, his person was sacred; his memory belongs to the ages'

N. M. KOLMAKOV,
A STUDENT AT ST PETERSBURG UNIVERSITY

The 1830s and much of the 1840s comprised what might be called the apogee of autocracy in Russia and marked an era of stability and peace at home and abroad. From 1831 until 1849, Russians faced no major wars and, apart from annual campaigns against the natives of the Caucasus, the Empire was at peace. The turmoil of the Napoleonic era and the unsettled years of the Holy Alliance were past. For the moment, Russia's conflicts with the Ottoman Empire were settled, and the difficulties brought on by the creation of the Polish Kingdom in 1815 were being resolved by Prince Paskevich's firm policies as viceroy in Warsaw. Something resembling a 'Pax Nicholeana' had descended upon Russia and upon Central and Eastern Europe. Russia had embarked upon a period of economic progress and domestic tranquillity.

Yet this is not the view of life under the Nicholas system that emerges from many accounts of the period, for one often reads of the intellectual oppression, the tyranny, the arbitrariness which made such a deep impact on the lives of some. This is, perhaps, partly the result of an over-emphasis upon the Russian radical movement by both Soviet and Western scholars, for much study has been devoted to Russia's dissident intellectuals during these years, and many of the memoir and diary accounts published and translated into Western languages have been those of intellectuals who suffered intensely under the Nicholas system. We therefore more often see this period through the eyes of someone like Aleksandr Herzen, who was finally forced into exile in the West, and wrote one of the greatest of nineteenth-century autobiographies. Or we see it from the viewpoint of people such as I. I. Panaev or V. G. Belinskii, who suffered the frustrations and oppression of official censorship and left bitter accounts. For men like these, there is no doubt but that the apogee of autocracy in Russia was a gruelling and terrible time, just as any period of history may be oppressive and cruel to those who dissent from the established order. And such men suffered continually from persecution by state authorities – from the petty tyranny of censors and surveillance by the secret police – throughout Nicholas's thirty-year reign.

Yet the Nicholas system as it emerged after the revolutions of 1830, and before it was besieged by the stronger revolutionary movements of the mid to late 1840s, had another side to it. We should not minimize the cruelty and terror that men like Herzen or Belinskii suffered because of their dissident beliefs. But, for many in Russia, this was a time to be looked back on with nostalgia, a period when things were certain and life was predictable in a way it never would be again. For those who had even a small stake in the established order, stability was what they most fervently desired. As General A. E. Tsimmerman, who was just beginning a successful career as an army officer in St Petersburg during this period, recalled later in his life, after he had lived through the upheavals of the Great Reforms of the 1860s and the Polish revolution of 1863–4,

... everything went calmly and normally. Society was in an organic period of existence, and no ... great changes could be anticipated ... The entire order seemed as if it would stand for a long time and no dissonances destroyed the general harmony, for there was a conservative, monarchical sentiment in all strata of society, and there seemed to be no possibility of any others.[1]

Baroness M. P. Frederiks, who was a bit younger than Tsimmerman and thus lived her childhood and youth during the apogee of autocracy, recollected:

... during the lifetime of Nikolai Pavlovich, Russia had great and noble stature. He knew how to preserve the enchantment which she possessed before his time, and by his chivalrous, firm, and undaunted character, he heaped still greater glory upon her. Everyone and everything bowed down before him and before Russia![2]

To people such as these, Nicholas and his system embodied precisely those qualities which were best for Russians. As another contemporary observed:

Generally we in Russia are normally much closer to Constantinople and Tehran than to Paris or London. The very understanding of the Russian people about good and evil, about right, about law, and justice, comes closest to that of the eastern peoples. In government, the people respect and particularly want to see strength . . . Our common people love to see in their ruler a powerful and stern sovereign.[3]

Depending on whether individuals opposed the Nicholas system or accommodated themselves to it, Nicholas himself seemed either a villain or a hero. But in either case, he assumed larger-than-life dimensions in the eyes of his contemporaries. As Baron M. A. Korf, one of Nicholas's confidants, later commented:

The central focus of everything was our great Nicholas. His spirit and his personality penetrated everything. He gave real significance and brilliance to everything and all strands of the [state's] many-sided civil activity came together in his hands alone.[4]

There is, of course, no doubt that during the apogee of autocracy, the position of the serfs in the Russian Empire worsened steadily as their masters demanded from them higher payments in cash, kind and labour. It is equally certain that Nicholas was deeply concerned about the plight of the Russian serfs and hoped to improve their position. Indeed, in March 1842 he issued the strongest public indictment of serfdom yet to be made by a Russian ruler when he told the assembled members of his State Council that, 'there is no doubt but that serfdom, in its present form, is an evil for all concerned'.[5] But Nicholas was unable to find a way out of the dilemma posed, on the one hand, by a nobility which opposed any change in the Empire's social and economic relationships, and, on the other, by his own fear of disorder and social upheaval. The apogee of autocracy brought also the beginnings of industrialization to Russia, and with it came all of the sufferings associated with that phenomenon in the West. But the same Nicholas system witnessed the greatest age of Russian literature; it saw the beginnings of modern Russian music and of the Russian classical ballet; and it produced the monumental architecture which gave to St Petersburg the unique character it still possesses.

The question of whether the Nicholas system as it existed between the revolutions of 1830–31 and the mid 1840s was good or evil is perhaps less important than that of what it did or did not accomplish. In his auto–biography, one of Nicholas's most bitter enemies, Aleksandr Herzen, perhaps stated best the problem as some contemporary Russians saw it.

It is oppressive and vile to live in Russia. That is the truth. And all the more so was it oppressive for us because we thought that in other countries it was easier and more pleasant to live. But now we know that there [in the West] it is also oppressive, because there too they have not yet resolved that question on which all of human activity centres – the question about the relationship of the individual to society and of society to the individual.[6]

Nicholas and his advisers sought to resolve the dilemma in one way, while Herzen sought another. To Nicholas and those around him, only an enlightened autocrat, acting in the best interests of all, could transcend the class demands and economic rivalries of various interest groups in the Empire and act for the welfare of Russian society as a whole. Only within the framework of a paternalistic system could the best life for the individual be created. This was the fundamental precept upon which the Nicholas system was founded, and the Nicholas system and the paternalistic personality of Nicholas the Emperor were very intimately connected.

1. Life at the Winter Palace

The years between the revolutions of 1830 and the mid 1840s were thus good ones for Nicholas. As Russia's ruler, his power was undisputed at home and respected abroad. He was surrounded by advisers whom he trusted, men whom he had known since the days of his youth, men with whom he had shared the crises of his accession and early years on the throne, who believed in the glory of Russia and who shared his values. Most of his advisers were men of honour and integrity. Even Count Benkendorf, head of the Third Section, was generally well regarded during the 1830s, because he embodied the values which much of Russian educated opinion espoused and, equally important, did not use the awesome powers of his office for evil or petty purposes.

The men who advised Nicholas in the 1830s served faithfully and mostly devoted themselves to Russia's welfare. Some of them may have had an exalted notion of their importance, and of the positive results which their labours and those of Nicholas had produced. Count Benkendorf, for example, once commented that 'Russia's past is admirable; her present more than magnificent; as to her future, it is beyond the grasp of the most daring imagination'.[7] No one, of course, would accept Benkendorf's view in retrospect, and few in Russia at the time would probably have been so glowing in their praise. But it is important to remember that not just Benkendorf, but even petty officials, saw their labours as being directed towards Russia's welfare. M. P. Veselovskii, a junior official in the St Petersburg offices of the Ministry of Interior during the latter years of Nicholas's reign, recalled many years later that, 'each new document which was produced seemed to me to be a new current of benevolence flowing from [our office near] Chernyshev bridge into the vastness of Russia'.[8] To be sure, there were numerous officials in Russia who cared not at all about what their work was, or what value it had. There were many to whom state affairs, as N. A. Miliutin once cynically remarked about his less responsible associates, were nothing more than, 'a lot of arguments and passing of papers from hand to hand'.[9] But it is significant that, under Nicholas, there were some who shared his ideals of duty and service to the state. These men believed in what they were doing and in the value of the system which Nicholas had created.

These were also good years for Nicholas in terms of his personal life. He was at the peak of his powers, between thirty-five and fifty. He was vigorous and handsome, and not until the very end of his period would age begin to leave its mark. Even as late as 1844, Queen Victoria would describe him as 'a *very striking* man; still very handsome; his profile is beautiful and his manners most dignified and graceful'.[10] He was surrounded by family and friends whom he trusted and loved. His children began to marry only towards the end of these years, and, with the exception of Grand Duke Konstantin Pavlovich, death did not begin to separate Nicholas from his closest friends and advisers until near the end of this period. Speranskii, a great statesman but hardly a close friend, died in 1839; but the first of Nicholas's intimate confidants to leave him would be Benkendorf, who died in 1844.

Nicholas valued such personal relationships greatly, not only for the advice he obtained but for the relationships themselves. He placed an immense value upon those relatively few real friendships he possessed. No matter how pressing state affairs might be, he still found time, for example, to think of the welfare of Baron Frederiks, the officer who had been forced into temporary retirement as a result of the head wound received during the Decembrist revolt. When Frederiks's country estate was threatened by cholera in 1831, Nicholas thought to send a boat to move him and his family to safety.[11] In a similar vein, when Count Benkendorf became seriously ill in 1837, Nicholas found time to visit him almost daily.[12]

Personal friendships were important to Nicholas from the moment when, on 14 December 1825, he had suddenly found himself alone at the summit of the colossal Russian Empire. Even more important were the very close relationships he had with his family: his two brothers Konstantin and Mikhail, his children and, most of all, his wife. Nicholas knew of Konstantin Pavlovich's shortcomings and of his capricious behaviour in Warsaw.[13] He realized that Konstantin's indecisiveness to crush the revolt in Warsaw immediately in November 1830 had led to a crisis which had cost a great deal of treasure and many lives to resolve.

Yet not one word of reproach crept into the letters he wrote to his elder brother.[14] Much the same was true of Mikhail Pavlovich: he was at best little more than a regimental staff officer. He shared all of Nicholas's fascination with military trivia, but never developed the broader view of state affairs which Nicholas possessed. Mikhail could be jovial and good-natured with fellow officers in barrack-room gatherings. Yet his personal behaviour must have caused Nicholas considerable embarrassment. His relationship with his wife, the elegant and intelligent Grand Duchess Elena Pavlovna, was the talk of St Petersburg, especially when, on their wedding day, Mikhail galloped off to review a Guards regiment rather than return to his apartments with his new wife that evening.[15] Some contemporaries considered Nicholas's younger brother immensely boorish and one memoirist recalled how he sometimes entered the elegant salon gatherings, which his wife held on Thursday afternoons, smoking a foul-smelling cigar and accompanied by a huge dog where he would relate crude jokes to any Guards officer who might be present.[16] Such behaviour must have been offensive to Nicholas, whose moral code was quite puritanical and who regarded propriety and good form in public as essential. Yet Nicholas always remained close to his younger brother and put him in positions where he could share the glory which he won for Russia. It was Mikhail Pavlovich, after all, who had led the first regiment of victorious Russian Guards into Warsaw in September 1831, even though the victory belonged to Field-Marshal Paskevich. And Mikhail Pavlovich was the first one whom Nicholas appointed to the Imperial State Council after his accession.[17]

Nicholas's relations with his children, especially during these years, were even closer. There were seven in all: three grand duchesses and four grand dukes. The eldest, Aleksandr, would one day beome Emperor Alexander II, the Tsar-Emancipator, while Nicholas's second son, Konstantin, would play an important part in the naval reforms of the 1850s and the Great Reforms a decade later. Of Nicholas's three daughters, the eldest, the blonde and blue-eyed Mariia, would become Duchess of Leuchtenberg, and the pale, black-haired Olga, Queen of Württemberg; but the youngest, Aleksandra, the image of her mother and possessing considerable musical talent, would die only a year after marrying the Prince of Hesse-Cassel. Later in the reign, Nicholas and Aleksandra Fedorovna had two more sons: Nikolai, who would later become the Russian commander-in-chief in the Russo-Turkish War of 1877–8, and Mikhail, later Inspector-General of the Russian artillery.

Nicholas followed a rigid daily routine which allowed him to spend at least two hours with his children. Each morning he arose early, spent several hours at various tasks and came to the Empress's apartments promptly at ten o'clock, where he spent an hour breakfasting with his family and holding what he called '*la revue de la famille*'.[18] Always the 'father-commander', Nicholas required each of his children to present him with a report on how the previous day had been spent and what progress had been made on studies and other tasks. He examined his children's study books himself and satisfied himself on their progress. He was a firm taskmaster, meted out punishments frequently, and bestowed rewards much more rarely, for, in the upbringing of his children, Nicholas saw himself as training a new generation of Russian leaders. Duty, love of Russia and diligence were the virtues he sought to instil in the young grand dukes and grand duchesses, and an indication of his attitudes can perhaps best be found in the words with which he accompanied punishments: 'It is for the Motherland that you ought to do your duty. It is not I, but the Motherland, who punishes or rewards you; I am here only to carry out her orders and her intentions.'[19] But despite Nicholas's severity, his children were not condemned to the same cold existence which he himself had suffered as a child. For his children, the demands imposed by 'duty' were tempered by parental warmth. And the dullness of the classroom, which Nicholas had known as a youth, was somewhat lessened by the more talented tutors he chose for his children: the poet Zhukovskii, the statesman Baron M. A. Korf, and the reformer and legal expert M. M. Speranskii.

Nicholas was a stern parent, for he was very conscious that he and Aleksandra were founding a dynasty: the dynasty which would, in fact, rule Russia until the Revolution of 1917. Paul I's two eldest sons had died without heirs; Nicholas's younger brother and his wife had several children, but all except one, the Grand Duchess Ekaterina Mikhailovna, died in childhood.[20] Thus fate ordained that it would be Nicholas and Aleksandra Fedorovna who would rear the rulers of nineteenth-century Russia. But although he was stern, Nicholas loved his children deeply and, until they were grown and married, he dined *en famille* at precisely four o'clock every afternoon with the Empress, their children and, perhaps, a few intimate counsellors such as Counts Adlerberg, Benkendorf, Orlov or Kiselev.[21] Such dinners were short – usually no longer than forty-five minutes – after which the Imperial Family and guests, if such were present, retired briefly to the Empress's study for coffee and conversation until Nicholas left to return to his work. Later in the evening they might gather again for readings or for small concerts where Nicholas himself sometimes took part, playing the cornet.[22]

Most of all, Nicholas loved the Empress, 'Mouffy', as he called her. 'God has bestowed upon you such a happy character that it is no merit to love you,' he wrote to her in 1836, nearly twenty years after their marriage.[23] And, when the Winter Palace burned the following year, Nicholas reportedly told an aide-de-camp, 'let everything else burn up, only just save for me the small case of letters in my study which my wife wrote to me when she was my betrothed'.[24] Theirs was an attraction of opposites in many ways: Nicholas, tall, robust, dynamic, and Aleksandra Fedorovna, slender, frail, often in poor health. But their mutual love continued for many years, and only after nearly three decades of marriage would Nicholas take a mistress. This was at a time when he was himself beginning to show the signs of age. He was becoming preoccupied with his health; he perceived the signs of advancing years in his receding hairline and expanding girth; he feared the onset of impotence.[25] To console himself, in an effort to recapture his lost youth, to find the physical solace which the Empress's recurring heart attacks made it impossible for her to provide, he turned to one of her young maids-of-honour, Varvara Nelidova.

But much love still remained between the imperial couple. In 1845, three decades after they had been betrothed, Nicholas would weep when he learned that the court doctors had prescribed for Aleksandra Fedorovna a visit to Palermo in an attempt to regain her health. 'Leave me my wife,' he begged the physicians,[26] and, when he learned that she must go, he began to plan how to join her there, even if for only a brief time. If physical love was forbidden by the Empress's physicians, the comradeship between them remained. Nicholas's letters were always filled with tenderness and with the many details which she loved to read about costumes and furnishings, uniforms and reviews, at courts he visited. And it was in Aleksandra Fedorovna's company that Nicholas continued to seek refuge from the cares of state. 'Happiness, joy, and repose – that is what I seek and find in my old Mouffy,' he once wrote.[27]

Nicholas always found a sympathetic listener and a devoted companion in the shelter of Aleksandra Fedorovna's apartments. The two shared deep feelings of trust and confidence and, when she recalled the day of her marriage, Aleksandra Fedorovna could write some years later that, 'with complete confidence and trust I gave my life into the hands of my Nicholas and he never once betrayed this trust . . . We were both truly happy and content when we found ourselves alone in our apartments,' she added.[28] For most of their lives together, Nicholas was entirely deserving of such confidence and trust. Such flirtations as he engaged in at court were no more than that. 'He clings to the strange notion of marital fidelity,' one woman at Court commented.[29] The Empress held to such notions even more firmly. For her, Nicholas was always the prince who had wooed her in the Potsdam countryside and on the Isle of Peacocks in the late summer and early autumn of 1815. Only for Nicholas's dashing aide-de-camp, the handsome cavalry general Aleksei Orlov, did she at one time have some tender, though most probably no more than platonic feelings.[30]

The centre of Nicholas's private life was thus his family, an intimate and closed haven to which few others were admitted, and into which the pomp, splendour and immense opulence of the Imperial Court did not penetrate. For Nicholas, who possessed vast wealth as a sovereign, lived a frugal and spartan existence. While Aleksandra Fedorovna's quarters were elegant and richly decorated, Nicholas himself worked in very modest surroundings: a small room with a cot and the straw-filled leather pallet upon which he always slept, a desk, a sofa, a few chairs, tables and various personal mementoes.[31] Family, a few friends and immense amounts of work thus comprised Nicholas's daily life in the Winter Palace.

2. Nicholas and His Advisers

During that decade and a half which separated the revolutions of 1830 and the beginning of the upheavals in Austrian Galicia in 1846, Nicholas was served by the best counsellors of his reign. Among them were Prince A. S. Menshikov, regarded by many as well-educated and intelligent, who served as Head of the Russian Admiralty during most of the reign; Count Nesselrode, Foreign Minister for more than four decades by the time of Nicholas's death; General (later Count) P. D. Kiselev, a close adviser, and Minister of State Domains for the last two decades of the reign, whom Nicholas called his 'Chief of Staff for Peasant Affairs';[32] Count Benkendorf, Head of the Third Section and, until the early 1840s, Nicholas's regular companion on his many lightning inspections of his 'command'; D. V. Dashkov, who had served loyally on the Investigating Commission of 1826, and was Minister of Justice from 1832 until a few months before his death in 1839, who enjoyed a reputation for being 'personally incorruptible in the face of all temptations and who combined great erudition with an absolute passion for work', even though he may have been 'a bit peculiar and shy in his social relationships';[33] D. N. Bludov (later a count), who served as Minister of Justice, Minister of the Interior and President of the State Council's Department of Laws for more than two decades; Count A. G. Stroganov, a Minister of the Interior at the age of forty-four, distinguished in the minds of some by a 'noble and firm character and a purity and firmness of principles' which were considered 'very rare, even among officials of the highest rank';[34] and S. S. Uvarov (later a count), who served for some sixteen years in the difficult post of Minister of Public Instruction and formulated the ideological expression of the Nicholas system. There were also Count

E. F. Kankrin, Minister of Finance until 1844, the year before his death, who, more than any other, tried to keep the Empire on a firm financial basis; L. A. Perovskii (made a count in 1849), who served throughout the entire reign, first as Minister of Court Lands and then as Minister of the Interior; Nicholas's 'father-commander' Prince Paskevich; and several others.

Nicholas thus had the advice and counsel of a number of men to whom he was very close personally during these years to aid him in his efforts 'to see Our Motherland attain the very heights of happiness and glory pre-ordained for her by Providence'.[35] This was an important, almost essential element in his work as Russia's ruler, for although he insisted upon making most important decisions himself, he nevertheless consulted a number of trusted advisers before reaching any final decision.[36] With men such as these he was sometimes remarkably open-minded. On other occasions, he expected to be told only what he wished to hear. But, in either case, Nicholas was very much involved with the day-to-day business of governing Russia, more so than any other Russian ruler since Peter the Great. Therein, as we have said, lay the virtue of Nicholas as a monarch and the critical flaw in the Nicholas system.

Since Nicholas insisted that all decision-making power be vested in him alone, the path which Russia took during the critical second quarter of the nineteenth century, when the nations of Western Europe were industrializing, beginning to construct railway networks and modernizing the armaments and tactics of their armies, was determined most of all by the Emperor himself. Nicholas's ability to deal with the many very serious problems which his Empire faced hinged upon two critical elements: the quality of his ministers and the information which they provided to him; and his own ability to make the right decisions in respect of the problems which he and Russia faced. In both cases, the functioning of these two critical elements was flawed, and the manner in which Russia was governed during the apogee of autocracy reflected this fact very dramatically. Nicholas and, in most cases, the men who served him sought to do their best for Russia. But they suffered from many very human short-comings. In particular, Nicholas created (or caused to be created) for himself a vast amount of unimportant work by insisting that he know about the most minute details of many problems, especially when they concerned the military or technology. His own emphasis upon such matters led his ministers and advisers to do likewise. If the Emperor demanded to know all the details of a matter with which he dealt, it was their task also to know if they wished to win his approval. But they often lacked the necessary specialized knowledge and expertise, and, equally important, were so overwhelmed with minor matters that they never had the opportunity to reflect upon any broader scheme. As a result, the nearly superhuman task of modernizing the Russian Empire became for them completely impossible.

Nicholas sought advice and information about his Empire in many different ways. His major source of information, of course, was his ministers, advisers and close friends. But, as we shall see, he also sought to see much for himself. He visited many parts of his Empire to inspect the state of his 'command' and held countless conversations with individuals from all walks of life whom he encountered in the course of his daily walks along the streets and quays of St Petersburg.[37] Probably more than any other Imperial Russian ruler since Peter the Great, Nicholas had a deep respect for the people of Russia and believed that something useful could be learned from them. 'I am a sentry . . . on guard to see all and observe all,' he once remarked.[38] That it was virtually impossible for him to enter into candid conversation with those whom he encountered is, of course, obvious to us, though it was not so to Nicholas. Still that does not detract from the praiseworthiness of his efforts to establish contact with ordinary Russians, or from his pride in being their ruler. As he once wrote to Aleksandra Fedorovna from the town of Kostroma, 'God! What a fine and good people it is! May God keep them so; one is truly proud to belong to them.'[39]

There were three groups of individuals to whom Nicholas turned regularly for advice in governing his vast domain. These were his personal friends, his ministers, and, to a much lesser degree, the members of the Imperial State Council. It is quite true that these men were 'subservient',[40] and saw themselves purely as instruments of their Emperor's will.[41] Nicholas was, after all, an autocrat and, as such, had the power to raise men to great heights or to ruin them if he saw fit. As a result, most of Nicholas's advisers feared to be entirely candid with him. Count Adlerberg who, according to one writer, was 'the only one of his subjects who dared always tell him the truth',[42] was perhaps the most candid. But Adlerberg was far from being a talented adviser and very often shared Nicholas's views on most issues; and although he and Nicholas were very close, he was not appointed to a high government post until 1842, when he became Director of the Empire's Postal Department. Adlerberg was first of all a courtier; he was neither a statesman nor a man inclined to daring opinion. Like Baron Korf, he held the view that it was best 'to tamper neither with the separate [parts] nor with the whole [of the state order]; thus, perhaps, we shall live longer'.[43]

On one occasion or another, most of Nicholas's counsellors are known to have abandoned their 'subservience', but they were so closely tied to the existing order that they could not envisage the vast and fundamental changes which the Empire required. They were either trained for careers in the military, or they were educated in the tradition of the late eighteenth century. In either case, they simply lacked the knowledge, training and expertise to deal with the problems of an increasingly complex and technologically oriented world. General Kiselev, regarded as one of Nicholas's most 'progressive' advisers, was quite candid with his master on occasion. But Kiselev saw questions of reform in Russia only in terms of administrative improvements. For him, the ideal to be attained in Russia was that of a well-ordered, finely tuned machinery of government that would function efficiently and well, guaranteeing the rights of each class or group of individuals within the existing system.

Kiselev once told the Minister of Interior, L. A. Perovskii, in the late 1840s that the two of them (and, indeed, virtually all of Nicholas's ministers as well as Nicholas) were too closely tied to the existing order in Russia to bring about much-needed changes.[44] Much the same was true of Perovskii, who on occasion could also be very open in his comments to his Emperor. But again, Perovskii's criticisms of Russia were directed towards administrative organization and practice. Therefore, while Perovskii could tell Nicholas that 'bureaucratic formalities have reached the point of absurdity'[45] (something which Nicholas already knew only too well because it sometimes took him several months to obtain information from central government offices),[46] he could not argue for fundamental changes in the existing order because he was very much a part of it. Equally important, Nicholas's own emphasis on minor details had developed in these men an outlook which caused them to focus on curing the symptoms of the disease of backwardness which afflicted Russia rather than on seeking remedies.

Truly basic and fundamental criticism of the existing order in Russia thus reached Nicholas only very rarely. One of the truly rare instances when direct and open criticism did reach him occurred in 1841 when General N. Kutuzov wrote to him that 'in the course of my travels through three provinces . . . during the best season of the year, at the time when grain and hay were being harvested, I heard not a single note of happiness, nor anything indicating popular contentment. On the contrary, the seal of dejection and grief was stamped on all faces.'[47] Such a view was very different from that which Nicholas encountered on his own journeys throughout the length and breadth of European Russia, when he could write to his Empress about how the masses had turned out to salute him as he left Nizhni-Novgorod in August 1836, and that 'all together it presented a delightful scene'.[48] But such commentaries as Kutuzov's reached Nicholas far too rarely to offset the many rose-tinted impressions which poured in from all sides.

Nicholas once told Baron Korf that he preferred advisers and counsellors who were 'not wise but service-orientated'.[49] To Nicholas, that was one of the most important virtues a man could possess, for he himself regarded 'all human life as being nothing more than service'.[50] This was why he chose as his ministers men who had devoted their lives to the service of Russia and had long experience in the state service. Count Nesselrode was the only one of Nicholas's ministers who had served for less than twenty years before reaching ministerial rank, and he had been appointed to his position by Alexander I. The remainder of the fifty-two men (not counting members of the Imperial Family) who served Nicholas as ministers all had more than twenty years of service experience before being elevated to ministerial positions, and forty of them had served for more than thirty years. In fact, the average length of these fifty-two ministers' service careers before they became ministers was slightly over thirty-seven years. They were men who had served long and loyally, although they were still in their most productive years when Nicholas appointed them. Only three of Nicholas's ministerial appointees were, in fact, over the age of seventy.[51]

This factor quite possibly accounts for the fact that the first part of Nicholas's reign and the years of the apogee of autocracy in Russia were marked by more energetic state activity than were the years after the mid 1840s. During the first years of his reign, Nicholas had replaced most of Alexander's advisers with younger, more vigorous appointees. This meant that he faced the revolutionary crises of 1830 and 1831 with a group of ministers who were relatively young and energetic, and whose training and experience coincided closely with the world in which they lived. They were men educated in the 1780s and 1790s, not in the 1750s and 1760s, as had been the case with those they replaced. Ten of Nicholas's seventeen ministers at that point were under sixty and, of those, six were under fifty.[52]

But Nicholas tended to keep loyal, service-orientated men in office far beyond their most productive years, and many of his ministers served until death or serious incapacity. Count Nesselrode served as Foreign Minister for the entire thirty years of Nicholas's reign, and he was not an isolated case, though none of Nicholas's other ministers matched his length of ministerial service. Count E. F. Kankrin was Minister of Finance for twenty-one years; Prince A. S. Menshikov was Head of the Russian Admiralty for twenty-seven years; Count D. N. Bludov served alternately as Minister of the Interior, Minister of Justice, and President of the State Council's Department of Laws for twenty-three years under Nicholas and for five more during the reign of Alexander II; Count P. D. Kiselev served as Minister of State Domains under Nicholas for eighteen years; and Prince Paskevich served for twenty-four years as Head of the State Council's Department for the Affairs of the Kingdom of Poland.[53]

These men were at the peak of their powers during the 1830s, but their lengthy terms in office meant that their best years were well behind them as the end of Nicholas's reign approached. When the revolutions of 1848 broke out in Western Europe, only six of Nicholas's ministers were under sixty and their median age had risen to sixty-two years. And, by the outbreak of the Crimean War in 1854, the median age of Nicholas's ministers would have risen to sixty-five; thirteen of his eighteen ministers at that point were over sixty.[54] Such men, sometimes in poor health and educated in the tradition of the late eighteenth century, were neither physically nor intellectually able to deal with the difficult years which Nicholas and Russia would face as the last years of his reign approached.

Further evidence that Nicholas's ministers were very much a part of the existing order in Russia can be seen from the fact that forty-one of his fifty-two ministers were titled aristocrats. Of the eleven who were not, at least ten came from families which possessed hereditary aristocratic status. Equally important, some of those who became members of the titled aristocracy under Nicholas had risen from very humble origins and owed their position to their success in the state service and to Nicholas's favour. For example, Counts Speranskii and Vronchenko were sons of village priests, while Count Kankrin's father had been a mineralogist from Hesse who had entered the Russian service as a director of the Starorusskii salt works in the 1780s. Furthermore, thirty-two of Nicholas's ministers were generals or admirals, and therefore to their loyalty to him as Emperor they added their loyalty to him as their commander-in-chief and their commitment to defend the order he espoused.[55]

Nicholas thus placed extreme value upon loyal service in choosing his ministers; he also had a distinct preference for men who had distinguished themselves in military service, especially by bravery on the battlefield. The fact that he chose ministers in this way indicates that he did not always see the civil service as something which required special training or expertise. If a man could successfully command an army corps or division, then Nicholas assumed he could also 'command' a province or a Ministry. Such an attitude demonstrated Nicholas's critical lack of understanding about civil government, particularly at a time when Russia's ministers were confronting problems for which their education and past experience could not have well prepared them. In the eighteenth century, before Western Europe had entered the Industrial Revolution, the criteria which Nicholas used to choose ministers might have served well enough. But the *ancien régime* world was not the one which now confronted them, especially towards mid-century. Nicholas's emphasis upon loyalty and service experience, especially in the military, thus gave to Russia ministers who could not envisage the broad sorts of changes needed. Instead, their efforts at change and improvement, commitments which Nicholas himself fully shared, would be undertaken strictly within the framework of the old order under which they had matured and to which they were committed by inclination and experience. What was needed in Russia was a revolution from above. Nicholas's ministers could not even determine the sort of revolution that should be.

The men who served on Nicholas's State Council were very similar in experience, background and outlook to those who served as his ministers. With almost no exceptions, Nicholas's ministers also sat on the State Council, together with other senior statesmen and generals. But since Nicholas assigned little importance to the State Council, his closest advisers often were not appointed to it until a number of years after they had risen to positions of influence. Alexander I had called the State Council 'one of the most important state institutions . . . the focal point of all affairs of the central administration'.[56] Nicholas, however, generally regarded it as a body to be consulted only infrequently, for, as he once told Baron Korf, 'the Council exists . . . for the purpose of conscientiously giving me its view on those questions about which I seek such opinions, no more and no less'.[57] The State Council thus played a lesser role in the Nicholas system, and Nicholas often seems to have used appointments to it as rewards for men who had served him well in other capacities.[58] The only exception to this general situation was the council's Department of Laws, to which Nicholas appointed some of the most prominent legal experts in Russia and whom he consulted somewhat more frequently.

Nicholas thus consulted the State Council as a body rarely, and those members who were not ministers infrequently. To his ministers he gave the task of dealing with day-to-day affairs of state, though he insisted upon receiving frequent and regular reports from them and upon overseeing their work closely. His most important sources of advice and counsel, however, were his adjutants and his few close friends, most of whom also held ministerial rank or headed sections of His Majesty's Own Chancery. Nicholas's close personal friends – men such as Benkendorf, Orlov, Adlerberg, Paskevich and, to a slightly lesser degree, Kiselev and Perovskii – were men who played the central role in advising their Emperor during the apogee of his autocracy. When they were in the capital, they saw him on an almost daily basis. They often dined with him and his family, and were, in some ways, an extension of it. Beyond these men in St Petersburg, Nicholas also relied upon his adjutants for information, and, to a lesser degree, advice. It was his regular practice, when he received word of some crisis or catastrophe, to dispatch immediately one of his adjutants to investigate the problem and report to him directly. These were the men whom he sent to observe at first hand epidemics, revolts, famines and other crises, and he relied upon them heavily for information.

But, in the final analysis, Nicholas governed himself, for the ultimate resolution of all important matters (and many lesser problems) rested with him alone. And, in an empire so vast, the extreme form of centralization in decision-making which Nicholas instituted made it impossible for local authorities to respond immediately and effectively to critical problems as they arose. They were the ones who best knew all the facets of individual state problems, yet Nicholas refused them the power to resolve them. This made the rapid transmission of accurate information about Russia to Nicholas himself a problem of vital importance and this emerged as one of the most flawed aspects of the Nicholas system.

3. Nicholas and Russia

One of the most urgent problems in a centralized bureaucracy such as that which Nicholas created in Russia was thus the rapid transference of accurate information to the Emperor. As the French scholar Michel Crozier has shown, decisions in any bureaucracy must be made at the locus of power, and the more extreme the centralization, the higher the point in the bureaucratic structure where the decisions must be made. This, of course, means that the more rigid and centralized a bureaucratic system is, the less possible it will be for the individual (or individuals) with the power to make decisions to obtain first-hand knowledge of the problems they are called upon to deal with. Conversely, in a highly centralized bureaucracy, those on the lower levels, who may have a clearer notion of how to deal with a specific problem, do not have the authority to take any decisive action that might provide workable solutions.[59]

Nicholas insisted that the power, and hence the decision-making authority, should remain in his hands. He believed that he was the first servant of the state, and viewed himself as its 'commander'.[60] He therefore insisted that he have as much information as possible on all aspects of Russian life in order to 'command' effectively. It was for this reason that he required his ministers to provide him with oral and written reports at frequent, regular intervals. This also was why he made a great personal effort to learn more about the condition of the state which he ruled. Yet the system which Nicholas instituted in an effort to be well-informed about his empire had a number of serious deficiencies which, despite the vast quantities of information he received, provided him with a view of conditions in Russia that was far from accurate. Given the vastness of the Empire, and the wretched quality of its communications system, it took a great deal of time for information to reach St Petersburg. Further, because of the incompetence of Russian officials, particularly in the provinces, the information which they submitted to the central administration in St Petersburg was frequently of little value. Local officials were poorly educated and badly trained, often having learned their narrow routines through a crude apprenticeship system. Non-routine requests for information from St Petersburg's chanceries often threw them into panic, and they responded with silence because they feared that the central administration sought the data to do them harm.[61]

The time required to deal with routine paperwork under the Nicholas system made it difficult for provincial officials to reply to requests from the central government for non-routine information, even had they wished to do so. According to a Ministry of the Interior report in 1850, some 31,122,211 official communications were being produced each year in that ministry alone, and 16,697,421 of that number were reports requested by the central administration from provincial offices that were understaffed by inadequately trained clerks.[62] Yet even this output of reports did not suffice to answer all the routine queries sent to provincial offices from the capital. According to one estimate, the total backlog of decrees and requests not acted upon throughout the Russian bureaucracy had exceeded some 3,300,000 by the early 1840s.[63]

Nicholas's ministers and advisers sought to overcome such difficulties by sending specially appointed officials on fact-finding missions to the provinces. But because even these officials were sometimes poorly educated and improperly trained, their reports were frequently so trivial, so inaccurate, and the information in them so undigested, as to make them virtually worthless to the statesmen who had commissioned them. Russian bureaucrats at all levels of Nicholas's 'command' seemed acutely unable to separate the grain from the chaff, and since they could not decide which data were important, they either selected their information poorly or, nearly as bad, simply submitted every fact that they came across.[64]

Perhaps at all levels of administration in Russia, lower officials emphasized the unimportant as a means to obscure the more critical difficulties which the Empire faced. Certainly those men who did not fully understand the problems they encountered, and who, in any case, lacked the authority to resolve them, sought refuge in those aspects of the Nicholas system which they understood best. Form therefore overshadowed content in many government offices, not only because officials understood form better than content, but because Nicholas himself stressed form very strongly. On his inspections of state institutions, such as schools or offices, he placed great emphasis upon seeing to it that everyone wore the proper uniform and that students sat upright with their hands in the proper position.[65] Russia's officials therefore became less concerned about the nature of the problems they faced than with the form in which they submitted the required documents. State officials came to regard all documents as having equal significance, precisely because they considered them as having importance in and of themselves. A report was thus important in Nicholas's Russia, not because of what it contained, but because it was an official document. As M. S. Veselovskii, a young official in the Ministry of the Interior during the 1840s, recalled, 'for the most minute errors in the text, for the unequal spacing of the lines, for faint ink, or some other trivial mishap, a document would be mercilessly rejected and have to be copied over again and again'.[66] But, in many cases, as far as content was concerned, as one official cynically remarked:

... if some irregularity turns up in departmental matters and you are asked for an explanation, never admit your guilt, but write your explanation in as long ... and as confused a manner as possible. No one will read it, but seeing that you have written a great deal, they will consider you to be right.[67]

Of course, this sort of attitude was not confined to minor officials and copy clerks. Even the senior officials saw administration in terms of minor and secondary problems, and, although some of them were perceptive enough to recognize this weakness, and even to criticize it, they were themselves instrumental in perpetuating it. The Minister of the Interior, Perovskii, for example, told Nicholas that, 'bureaucratic formalities have reached the point of absurdity; endless official correspondence absorbs all the attention and energies of those who execute policy'.[68] Yet Perovskii could never find a means to solve the problem and was satisfied with organizing commissions to study ways in which the flood of paperwork might be stemmed, commissions which only aggravated the problem further by proposing additional regulations and procedures in order to make the movement of papers in Russia's chanceries more 'efficient'.[69]

Bureaucratic formalities involved Nicholas's senior advisers in many minor issues. In addition to the purely administrative day-to-day problems, senior Russian statesmen were especially sensitive to any criticism about the manner in which their ministries functioned. All ministers followed the Russian press closely for comments about their agencies, and reacted very sharply to any type of criticism, no matter how mild or constructive. The noted academician P. I. Köppen, one of Russia's handful of truly competent statisticians in the second quarter of the nineteenth century, was severely reprimanded in 1841 because he had commented in the *St Petersburg Gazette* that Russia's postal system was slow;[70] and the Minister of Finance, E. F. Kankrin, was furious about an article which appeared in 1830 and which vaguely criticized an increased tax on silken ribbons.[71] Concern with such minor issues on the part of Nicholas's ministers and advisers was partly the result of their lengthy exposure to the Russian bureaucratic system in either the military or the civil service. Given their long years of service before they rose to ministerial positions, they were so thoroughly steeped in bureaucratic traditions and procedures that, regardless of their political outlooks, they could not help becoming enmeshed in the web of minor issues which became the essence of administration and government in Nicholas's Russia.

Serious as this problem was for Nicholas's advisers, it was even more critical for Nicholas himself because his view of Russia depended heavily upon the information he received. If advisers and ministers were concerned with lesser issues, it was this view that they passed on. And, if he insisted upon knowing the most minor details about a particular problem, it served to focus the attention of his ministers even more upon minor matters. It was a vicious circle which made it virtually impossible for Nicholas and his advisers to spend much time dealing with critical state problems. As A. V. Golovnin, a young official in St Petersburg during the 1840s, and later Minister of Public Instruction (1861–6), remarked in his memoirs, 'from the time when . . . the system developed by which the Emperor would be acquainted with all minor matters, he has been smothered by administrative affairs and does not have the opportunity to give his attention to matters of real significance, to think about them, and to ponder important reports and proposals for new laws'.[72] As a solution, Golovnin proposed that a system be established which would enable the Emperor to deal only with the most important matters in his Empire. Equally important, he argued that the ministers themselves should be given the power to deal with lesser matters either individually or collectively. Such a solution had, in fact, been proposed to Nicholas at the very beginning of his reign by the academician and former professor at the University of Dorpat, Georg Friedrich Parrot, who had from time to time advised Alexander I on state affairs. In 1827, Parrot urged Nicholas to delegate to his ministers responsibility for dealing with lesser problems and to reorganize the Russian administration in a way that would also give his ministers' deputies and department heads a certain degree of power to act independently.[73]

Yet, Nicholas insisted, as an autocrat he must govern personally. His ministers were simply instruments for putting his decisions into effect, and he alone was the commander of Russia. Whenever he took command on the parade ground, he saw in microcosm his awesome power as countless ranks of troops responded instantly to his every command. Quite possibly, this further reinforced his view that Russia could be made to respond directly to his will, just as did his armies on parade. Since Nicholas, in turn, viewed his ministers in much the same way as a military commander regards his adjutants, his minister-adjutants could fulfil specific commissions, or perform routine tasks. But, just as a military commander insists upon holding responsibility for command decisions in his own hands, Nicholas was determined to maintain ultimate control over all policy-making decisions.

While Nicholas relied extensively upon his adjutants – his ministers and advisers – he realized this was not enough. An efficient and capable military commander must himself review the state of his command frequently, and Nicholas thought much the same way. But in his efforts to learn about conditions in Russia, Nicholas faced the same problems that his ministers encountered, only on a much vaster scale. Like his ministers, he resorted to a variety of special fact-finding practices when either central government offices or his advisers themselves could not supply the data he required about specific problems. Realizing that the regular bureaucracy in Russia was not only ponderous and inefficient, but plainly incompetent, Nicholas created special bodies, outside the framework of the regular bureaucracy, which he sought to make directly responsive to his will. These were the new sections added to His Majesty's Own Chancery and secret committees. Under the aegis of the former, Nicholas created, most importantly, the Third Section, which, as we have seen, was intended to serve as a guardian of the Empire's moral and political order and to provide him with accurate knowledge about the state of the Empire at any given moment. He also used sections of His Majesty's Own Chancery as instruments to undertake tasks which the regular bureaucracy had shown itself unable to perform, such as, for example, the compilation of the Russian laws which the Second Section completed under Speranskii's direction in 1833.

Unlike the new sections of His Majesty's Own Chancery, Nicholas did not give any institutional form to the many secret committees which he created. Instead, he used them to amass information about particularly critical problems and to propose solutions. Thus, as we have seen, the Committee of 6 December was empowered to examine the entire fabric of the Russian state order and to propose ways in which it might be improved. It was to another secret committee that Nicholas turned in late 1828 and early 1829, to find solutions to the ineffectual campaign which Russian forces had waged in the Balkans during the summer and autumn of 1828, and to propose ways in which the next year's campaign might be made more effective. There were many other secret committees during the apogee of the autocracy, and, most important, Nicholas created a total of ten such committees between 1826 and 1847 to study the problem of serfdom in Russia and to propose ways in which the condition of the Russian peasants might be improved.[74]

Besides creating these special extra-bureaucratic organs, Nicholas, again like a military commander, sent some of his senior advisers, his adjutants, on special fact-finding assignments. Forty-two special senatorial fact-finding missions were undertaken in the course of his reign, and these included seven of the eleven senatorial studies of the most distant and least-known regions of the Empire that were carried out in the nineteenth century.[75] Further, some of Nicholas's ministers themselves made extensive tours of the areas for which they were responsible.[76]

Nicholas himself also engaged in a continual round of personal inspections. Count Benkendorf has left us a vivid account of his tours, which Nicholas himself considered to be very accurate,[77] and it would appear from Benkendorf's account that these inspection tours nearly always took the same form. Nicholas's inspections in 1830 were quite characteristic of his efforts to learn more about conditions in his Empire, and may serve here as an example. Travelling in a light carriage (*drozhki*), with little advance preparation, he moved from one place to another at top speed. In March 1830, he went to Novgorod to inspect its military settlement. After leaving Novgorod, he ordered his suite to Moscow, commenting to Benkendorf that he had told no one but the Empress of his plans 'in order to keep my route in complete secrecy, all the more to astound Moscow'.[78] After inspecting the administrative offices, schools, hospitals and factories in Moscow, Nicholas returned to St Petersburg in a lightning journey which covered the entire 700 *versty* (approximately 460 miles) in thirty-eight hours. By early May he was in Warsaw to open the *Sejm* and investigate numerous complaints about the conduct of his elder brother as Viceroy. He then returned to St Petersburg by way of a number of smaller towns and cities in the western provinces of the Empire. Then, in July, despite the news of revolutions in Paris, he went on an inspection tour of Finland before returning to St Petersburg in an attempt to deal with the widespread cholera epidemic. Later in the year he went again to Novgorod to investigate a revolt in the military colonies there, at the same time directing Russia's first movements to deal with the Polish revolt which had just broken out in Warsaw.

Yet Nicholas's efforts to obtain the information he required to govern his Empire were far from successful. Benkendorf's account of his visit to Moscow in March 1830 is again instructive for what it reveals about the near-futility of his efforts to discover the true state of conditions in Russia. According to Benkendorf's account, they made the journey from

Novgorod to Moscow in only thirty-four hours, arriving in the Kremlin at two o'clock in the morning so there was no possibility of anyone in Moscow receiving advance warning of their arrival. To be sure, Nicholas's arrival was a total surprise to the servants and the officer on duty at the Kremlin palace, but within six hours a huge crowd had gathered to welcome him, and by the time he had awakened that morning, all of Moscow was buzzing with news of his arrival. Those whose offices and establishments were to be inspected had thus time to cover the most flagrant of their abuses, and, as usual, when Nicholas began his round of inspections that morning, he found everything in good order.

But perhaps such a situation should be expected by a military commander. Certainly anyone who has served in any military establishment is aware of how adept subordinates are at concealing faults from inspecting officers, and Russians made particularly energetic efforts to ensure that when the Emperor himself visited everything would meet with his approval.[79] Therefore, even though Nicholas well knew from the testimony of the Decembrists that his Empire faced serious difficulties, and even though he certainly must have been aware that he was not seeing things as they really were, the information which he obtained from his ministers' and adjutants' reports, and what he saw on his many inspections of his 'command', must have had the cumulative effect of convincing him that the state and social order in his Empire were still basically sound.

Equally important, Nicholas had the impression that effective steps were being taken to curtail many of the abuses about which the Decembrists had complained, and he thought that even the most pressing problems of serfdom could be solved gradually over time. Perhaps one thing which served to mislead him was the impression of widespread activity which he encountered wherever he went. Everyone sought to give the impression of feverish activity at all levels of administration, and since Nicholas saw his own daily labours as serious efforts to govern effectively, he may well have regarded as genuine the seemingly energetic work that he encountered everywhere he went. To be sure, a number of notable accomplishments were made. No one would dispute the importance of M. M. Speranskii's compilation of the Russian laws. Nor would anyone deny that Count E. F. Kankrin's reforms in the Ministry of Finance, or Count Kiselev's reforms in the Ministry of State Domains, were genuine achievements. Beyond this, Nicholas also saw a great deal of impressive construction in St Petersburg itself during his reign. The monumental St Isaac's Cathedral was erected during these years, and the Winter Palace, badly damaged by fire in 1837, was completely rebuilt within a year.

These were genuinely productive labours. Yet much of the activity which Nicholas witnessed was not. A satirical letter written by a senior bureaucrat to a fictional younger colleague during this period exemplifies quite vividly the situation which flourished in the Russian bureaucracy during the apogee of autocracy. 'Always say that you are busy, but do not tell anyone what your work deals with,' the official wrote. 'Let it be assumed that it is a secret matter. That way, people will think that you are occupied continually with important state affairs.'[80] Given the fact that Nicholas insisted upon secrecy in dealing with many important state problems, there was actually no way in which anyone in a given office could tell for certain whether a petty official was working on a secret report or not. Beyond that, agents of the Third Section were not infrequently assigned to pose as minor officials in government bureaux so as to keep senior officials and statesmen under surveillance. As we have seen, even the Grand Duke Konstantin Nikolaevich, Nicholas's second son, became the object of such spying during the 1850s.

But even where the activity of officials was to some positive purpose, and not simply an effort to mislead their superiors or serve as a cover for police surveillance, much of it was simply unproductive. Not only did the bureaucracy manufacture paperwork, but it also created numerous tasks designed to keep track of official documents and to care for them. Each official paper that came into any office had to be registered in a file, as did the action taken, and the reply which was sent. If we recall that, in 1849, 31,122,211 official papers were produced in the Ministry of the Interior alone, we can see that a considerable number of officials had to be employed simply to register them. Most of this work was unproductive in the extreme, as were the many reports central offices required from outside agencies which duplicated the content of reports required by other offices from the same agencies.

Not only Nicholas, but most of his advisers, and the vast majority of civil servants during the second quarter of the nineteenth century, tended to be lulled into the view that activity in and of itself meant accomplishment. All state agencies kept a record of how many official papers were processed each year, and while a few statesmen were perceptive enough to see that increased paperwork hindered effective administration, the majority saw it as an indication of something being accomplished. Further, ministers kept detailed accounts of how many schools were opened, the quantity of trade and similar readily quantifiable data, but all were crudely compiled and gave false impressions. The figure of 125,162 peasant children being enrolled in schools in 1848, for example, which one adviser noted in a report to Nicholas, was a clear case of this sort of deception:[81] these children were not being schooled, but were simply being given practical training in farming.

Yet there were two other factors in Russia which served further to conceal the actual state of the Empire. The first of these was the highly arbitrary nature of the system itself, for the arbitrariness inherent in the Emperor's absolute power was reflected in all levels of Russian society and administration. Possibly the fact that Russia's noblemen (who initially had made up the bulk of the bureaucracy in the eighteenth century) possessed absolute and arbitrary authority over the serfs who tilled their estates had been one important factor in contributing to the growth of arbitrariness in the bureaucracy. Certainly the absence of any updated code of laws in the years between 1649 (the Law Code of Tsar Aleksei Mikhailovich) and 1830 (the compilation of the *Complete Collection of the Laws of the Russian Empire*) was another, for, with no complete collection of the laws to prove them wrong, the gentry-bureaucrats of the eighteenth century could administer the affairs of the Empire as suited their personal caprice.

The Emperor, of course, had the power, at least in theory, to elevate individuals to great heights, or to degrade them, though there were certain boundaries established by tradition which the ruler did not usually violate. Even so, the system in Russia was sufficiently arbitrary to permit an individual to rise high in the state service if he happened, through chance or design, to attract the favourable notice of the sovereign. Among the 148 men who served at one time or another on Nicholas's State Council, individual talent and ability were responsible for the rise of only twenty-eight of them, while birth, military reputations or court connections accounted for the rise of the others.[82]

The vast majority of those who served the Russian state were insulated by distance from both Nicholas's favour and his wrath. What was perhaps more significant was that this arbitrary relationship between Nicholas and his subjects was reproduced throughout the bureaucracy. Superiors had a great deal to do with the futures of their subordinates, and could very effectively advance or impede their careers. The service reports which senior officials submitted about their subordinates played a major role in the award of much-coveted promotions and decorations in the state service.[83] Equally significant, the power of senior officials in the civil service was made even more arbitrary in 1850, when they received the authority to remove at will any subordinate from office without having to specify reasons for doing so. An official who was removed from office, even before 1850, in fact, had little recourse and, even if innocent, often found it difficult to regain his former position. One example of just such a situation was that of A. D. Borovkov, who prepared the summary of the Decembrists' testimony for Nicholas himself, and rose to the position of Senator by the middle of his reign. Yet Count V. N. Panin's accusation that he was guilty of financial misdealings forced Borovkov from office at the height of his career, and despite the fact that his innocence was later proved, he never regained his former service position.[84]

In such a system, where arbitrariness and absolute power flourished everywhere, subordinates were understandably reluctant to report shortcomings and problems to their superiors, especially to Nicholas. At all levels of Russia's administration, officials glossed over problems so as not to endanger their careers, and very little information that reflected badly on any senior official or state policy thus came through the perpetual filtering process to Nicholas at the top. Thus it took a number of months for news of serious famine in some of Russia's provinces to reach high St Petersburg officials in 1840. Officials sent on fact-finding missions tended to report only the information which they thought their superiors wanted to hear, and hence the information which reached ministerial level was far from complete or accurate. Further, because they too were subject to the same arbitrary pressures as their subordinates, Nicholas's ministers almost always sought to put the best possible interpretation on the problems they did learn about.

Most critical in this type of optimistic reporting was the fact that there were no devices to serve as checks on dishonest behaviour. There was no public press which might serve to correct false impressions, and there was not even a free exchange of information among Nicholas's ministers. Many were jealous of the powers and prerogatives of their ministries, and therefore were reluctant to share information.[85] The difficulty was further aggravated because Nicholas himself, in a misdirected effort to obtain more accurate data and to encourage more frank discussion, relied upon secret committees rather than even moderately open discussion of serious state problems.

There were, of course, exceptions to this general scheme of ministerial subservience. For example, Count E. F. Kankrin told Nicholas on numbers of occasions very candidly that state finances could not support some of his favourite projects, and Nicholas kept Kankrin at his post as Minister of Finance for twenty-one years. But even when such isolated voices of criticism did penetrate the web of censorship woven around Nicholas by his advisers, they were so few in number that they could hardly have offset the many glowing reports. For Nicholas had the very human failing of preferring good news over bad. He wanted to believe that his efforts to govern Russia well were succeeding, and he rewarded men who brought him good reports of his success. From the moment of his accession, therefore, he found himself in a situation very similar to that which A. N. Radishchev had described in his *Journey from St Petersburg to Moscow* in 1790.

Radishchev's imaginary traveller saw himself in a dream as a sovereign who had laboured long for the welfare of his subjects. As a result, he was showered with praise from all sides:

One said in a low voice: 'He has subdued our enemies abroad and at home, he has expanded the frontiers of the fatherland, he has subjected thousands of men, of many races, to his power.' Another exclaimed: 'He has enriched the realm, he has expanded internal and foreign commerce, he is a patron of the arts and sciences, he encourages agriculture and industry . . .' Youths, ecstatically raising their hands to heaven, cried: 'He is merciful and just, his law is equal for all, and he considers himself its first servant.'[86]

Such words could have been written about Nicholas, though he was not born until six years after Radishchev published his work. But, unlike Radishchev's imaginary ruler, who was shown that the praise which he heard on all sides was false and that his subjects were, in fact, languishing in want and suffering, the scales were never stripped from Nicholas's eyes.

Apart from the fact that faults were hidden from Nicholas, and that the reports he received were usually neither accurate nor complete, there was still another factor which served to distort his view of Russia. There were careers to be made by providing certain types of information to him and to his advisers, and a number of men took advantage of this situation. If, for example, there was censorship in the Empire, then it stood to reason, in the minds of many officials, that there must be violations of it. Likewise, if there was to be a secret police, then, by definition, there must be evil forces at work. There were careers to be made in both cases, and Nicholas's subordinates were by no means immune to the quite common bureaucratic failing of wanting to expand the agencies under their control. The manner in which the bureaucracy burgeoned throughout the course of Nicholas's reign provides ample evidence. During the last decade of the reign alone, the number of officials in the table of ranks (not counting the petty clerks and copyists not included in the data) increased by almost 40 per cent. In 1847, there were 61,548 officials; by 1850, the numbers had risen to 71,819; and, by 1855, they had risen again to 82,352.[87]

In the sort of situation just outlined, officials both great and small felt called upon to provide information about problems because the nature of the system itself decreed that such problems were supposed to exist or that certain things ought to occur. Obviously, many of Nicholas's officials did not fail to notice that, regardless of how noble their motives may have been, the men who had been instrumental in alerting the Emperor to the Decembrist conspiracy, and those who had played an important part in suppressing it, all saw their careers take a remarkably successful turn after Nicholas became Emperor. Therefore there were numbers of men in Nicholas's service who were more than willing to inform him of new 'conspiracies', the most prominent example of which was that of M. V. Butashevich-Petrashevskii and his circle, so mercilessly suppressed in 1849. For the moment, it is enough to note that, in comparison with the Decembrists, the crime of the *Petrashevtsy* was indeed minor. They were simply a group of idealistic young men who discussed the virtues of the utopian socialist systems of Fourier and Proudhon, and even the extremists among them hardly posed a threat to the security of Nicholas's Empire. Yet, for their crimes, he condemned twenty-one of them to the psychological torture of being condemned to death, and reprieved them only at the moment they had been led out on to the execution square to face a firing squad.

The *Petrashevtsy* provided perhaps the most dramatic example of the search for conspiracies which went on towards the end of the apogee of autocracy. Most of those in Russian state service who sought to justify their existence and advance their careers by providing information did not have the good fortune to uncover such a 'threat' to the Empire. Yet other incidents, especially in the area of censorship, show how very deep Nicholas's officials were willing to probe in their efforts to find the sort of information which they believed their superiors desired. Certainly Counts Benkendorf and Orlov, as Heads of the Third Section, received numerous such reports and took action on many of them. Aleksandr Herzen, in December 1840, was condemned to a second exile, this time in Novgorod, simply because he had repeated a rumour circulating in St Petersburg that a sentry had robbed and murdered a passer-by one night.[88] And there was a scandal, which reached all the way to Nicholas himself, over enthusiastic clapping at the public defence of the historian T. N. Granovskii's dissertation, an event that was blown so out of proportion that it led to a new decree which severely curtailed attendance at such scholarly gatherings.[89]

Of course, it would be inaccurate to give the impression that these sorts of abuses and distorted reporting about events were only the work of men working from purely selfish motives. But the effect of such incidents compounded itself to the point where a number of those close to Nicholas, and even Nicholas himself, began to believe that there was indeed a real menace to the security of the Empire. The end result was that Nicholas had a far from accurate view of conditions in Russia. He was not naïve enough to think that his Empire was a state without difficulties or problems, and he was fully aware that the mass of the bureaucracy was inefficient, often corrupt, and in many cases downright incompetent. Yet he undoubtedly must have thought that he had circumvented at least some difficulties by creating his extra-bureaucratic organs of government.

Equally important, it would have been very difficult for Nicholai not to believe that he knew a very great deal about Russian conditions. His ministers and advisers reported to him at least once a week, sometimes daily. He spent much time, more than any other Russian Emperor, in visiting various parts of his Empire, and when one considers that, until 1851, the only railway in Russia was the twenty-five-kilometre track between St Petersburg and the summer palace at Tsarskoe Selo, we obtain an even more dramatic picture of how monumental Nicholas's efforts to travel the length and breadth of European Russia in a horse-drawn gig really were.

But Nicholas made other efforts to know Russia and the Russians. Hardly a day passed when he was in the capital that he did not venture into the streets on foot, observing as he went, and engaging various passers-by in conversation. Regulations adopted by the police forbade passers-by to approach Nicholas, though this did not prevent him from striking up conversations with them. Certainly his daily strolls gave rise to numerous tales and anecdotes, though it is impossible to know just how much truth there was in such accounts. Most accounts dealt with Nicholas's interest and sympathy for the common man, and, as such, may at least indicate that he was sufficiently generous and concerned about the poorest of his subjects to have caused comment. There is the tale of the drunken serf coachman who told Nicholas that he had become drunk from despair because his master had ordered him to leave St Petersburg and return to the country. Nicholas supposedly purchased for him his freedom and supplied him with a horse and a cab so that he could earn his living on the condition that he stay away from spirits.[90] There was also the episode of the young girl, aged eight or ten, who clutched at Nicholas's sleigh, begging for a ride, whom he took back to the Palace with him, and whom Aleksandra Fedorovna, learning that she was the daughter of a poor official, placed in a finishing school, thereby enabling her to make an advantageous marriage. Nicholas himself, so the story went, provided the girl's dowry.[91] Another time, Nicholas supposedly helped a peasant who did not have the strength to load a huge sack of flour on to his shoulders.[92] And at least one account has it that Minister of the Imperial Household Prince Volkonskii ordered Nicholas's valet not to put money into his master's pockets before he went out because he would give it all away to whatever unfortunate he might encounter.[93] Finally there is the tale which, as one writer has commented, 'seems almost too good to be true', in which an officer of the palace guard had fallen asleep in his room, leaving on the desk before him an open diary in which he had written: 'I am crushed by my debts. Who will pay them for me?' Nicholas supposedly wrote, without awakening the officer, 'I, Nicholas the First.'[94]

Such tales of imperial charity and generosity are, of course, partly legend. Many of them do not come from the most reliable sources, especially those recounted by Paul LaCroix, whose account of Nicholas's reign was commissioned by Count P. D. Kiselev while serving as Russian ambassador to Paris.[95] LaCroix was thus not the most impartial of observers, and much of his material came from papers arranged and collected by Baron Korf, about whom one of his friends once remarked that 'Nicholas Pavlovich was for him almost the ideal Russian ruler'.[96] Still, the fact that a large number of these anecdotes was in circulation in St Petersburg during the apogee of autocracy – a sufficiently large number to have been heard by foreigners – at least gives some indication that they may have a basis in fact, though they do not tell us how much about the state of Russia Nicholas learned from such encounters.

Yet, despite his best efforts, Nicholas's view of Russia remained at best inaccurate. Conversely, he devoted great amounts of energy to problems that were portrayed as important by his advisers, when, in fact they were not. In this connection, we should return for a moment to the problem of serfdom and the problem closely associated with it in Nicholas's mind: that of censorship. When reviewing Nicholas's actions on numerous questions of censorship, it is hard to escape the conclusion that several of them were motivated by his fear that any discussion of Russia's problems which reached the ears of the masses might spark another peasant revolt like the great Pugachev uprising of the 1770s. Nicholas expressed these fears very openly to the Slavophile, Iu. F. Samarin. Samarin had written *Letters from Riga*, a critique of the bureaucracy and its policies in Russia's Baltic provinces, and realizing that it could not be published, had permitted its circulation in manuscript in early 1849. When the Third Section brought the matter to Nicholas's attention, he ordered Samarin to be arrested and summoned for an interview. In the course of their conversation, Nicholas commented:

I know that you did not have this intention. But you have let loose among the masses a dangerous idea, suggesting that Russian tsars from the time of Peter the Great acted only according to the suggestions and under the influence of Germans. If this idea reaches the masses it will produce terrible calamities.[97]

Nicholas's fear of any disquieting materials reaching the masses was to cut him off completely from the one segment of Russian society which could perhaps have proposed effective solutions to Russia's problems. The events of 14 December 1825 had already served to alienate him from the nobility, at least to some degree. The problems of censorship, and the menace of the press that was painted to him in such vivid colours by his advisers, also alienated him from the intelligentsia. As a result, Nicholas was further isolated from Russian reality at a time when, if he were going to deal with the Empire's problems effectively, it was more imperative than ever for him to have ready access to educated public opinion. To argue that Nicholas's alternative to the near-complete suppression of any discussion of Russia's problems in the press was simply to allow free speech to flourish is, of course, to insist upon something that he would never have been able to permit. But some sort of access to public opinion, to a broader range of views than was available at Court and among his senior advisers, was needed. Both the academician Georg Friedrich Parrot in the 1820s, and Nicholas's second son, the Grand Duke Konstantin Nikolaevich in the early 1850s, argued for at least some sort of 'artificial publicity', that is, a limited and structured discussion of certain state problems. In fact, Konstantin Nikolaevich instituted just such a system with some success by allowing naval officers to discuss the coming reform of the Empire's naval regulations in the pages of the journal the *Naval Collection* in the early 1850s.[98]

Nicholas's solution to the problem of his isolation was to rely upon trusted adjutants, ministers and his personal efforts. His solution to Russia's problems was to take more of the burdens of governing upon his own shoulders. This was especially so in matters of reform and change, where even the most minor alteration to the existing order required Nicholas's approval. For, if he sought to hold all decision-making power in his hands in the day-to-day governing of his Empire, he was even more insistent about controlling the winds of change.

4. Nicholas and Reform

The fundamental dilemma which Nicholas and his advisers faced over reform was more complex than any administrative measures could solve and more fundamental even than the absence of legality in Russian society. By taking Europe's eighteenth-century social order as a model, Russia and her rulers in the century after Peter the Great had chosen to emulate a way of life that was already in the process of disintegration in the West. The French Revolution of 1789 and the beginning of the Industrial Revolution in late eighteenth-century Britain changed the nature of European society so that it became far removed from the model that Russia had attempted to follow since the early eighteenth century. Beginning in the post-Napoleonic era, Russia was forced to compete with the West while adopting only those features of the new Western systems that could be fitted into the framework of the eighteenth-century society that the Russian aristocracy, traditionally the pillar of state and autocracy, insisted upon preserving. Thus, most simply stated, the dilemma which confronted Nicholas throughout his reign was that of how the Russian Empire, with its *ancien régime* social order and serf-based economic system, could meet the challenge posed by the industrializing nations of the West as they, following the lead of Britain, began to enter the age of the Industrial Revolution.

This crisis became more acute as Nicholas's reign progressed. Without fundamental changes in its social and economic order, it was impossible for the Russian Empire to meet the Western challenge. A few statistics, imprecise and crude as they are, illustrate the point dramatically. In 1820, France had a population of approximately 30 million, Britain one of about 12 million and Russia one of well over 40 million. Yet, in 1820, Russian pig-iron production was approximately 160,000 metric tons, that of France 113,000 (in 1819), and that of England 364,000. In terms of absolute production, Russia was well behind Britain and a bit ahead of France, although on a *per capita* basis, Russia was already producing significantly less. But, by 1850, the gap had expanded to a phenomenal degree. By that time, France had a population of 35 million, and the population of Britain had risen to about 18 million, while that of Russia stood at approximately 55 million. Yet, by 1850, France was producing 406,000 metric tons of pig iron (nearly a 400 per cent increase), Britain over 2 million tons (an increase of some 540 per cent) and Russia only 227,000 tons (an increase of only 41 per cent over three decades).[99]

This vast disparity in industrial production, and the technological development which accompanied it, was to be a telling factor in Russia's defeat in the Crimean War. It was also significant in terms of the position which Russia occupied in the economic system of the Western world. By the mid 1840s, Russia's foreign trade was about one third that of France and only 18 per cent of Britain's; it comprised only about 5 per cent of the total for the major trading nations of Europe.[100] Equally important, the major items in Russia's export trade continued to be raw materials and foodstuffs. Between 1802 and 1840, exports of flax and hemp increased in value from 5,590,000 silver roubles to 21,427,000 silver roubles (an increase of some 350 per cent). Exports of fat and lard increased in value from 2,752,000 silver roubles to 15,620,000 silver roubles (more than 550 per cent). And exports of grain increased in value from 3,178,000 silver roubles to 14,586,000 silver roubles (approximately 450 per cent). Perhaps most significant was the increase in wheat exports, a commodity produced especially in the south and shipped through the Black Sea ports of Odessa and Kherson. In 1802, Russian wheat exports were valued at 1,158,000 silver roubles, while by 1840 this figure had risen by nearly 1,000 per cent to a value of some 11,174,000 silver roubles.[101] To protect the export of this commodity, the value of which was exceeded only by flax, hemp, fats and lard, it became more vital than ever before for Nicholas to assure access to the Mediterranean for Russian mercantile shipping – a need which will be very important in our considerations of his Near East policies in the following chapter.

Within the framework of Russia's political system, the autocrat alone possessed the power to foster innovation and change. There were both theoretical and practical reasons for this. As M. M. Speranskii, one of the Empire's leading legal experts, explained the nature of the autocrat's power in a series of lectures to Nicholas's eldest son and heir, 'no authority, either within the Empire or outside it, can impose limits upon the supreme authority of the Russian autocrat'.[102] In a more practical sense, Russia was a state and society rife with factionalism, where each social group or class thought only in terms of its own economic interests. Therefore, only the autocrat had the power and, presumably, the interest, to stand above such group concerns and act for the welfare of Russia as a whole. That Nicholas believed in the necessity of acting in such a manner we shall see very clearly. Yet there were severe limits upon his powers to act in the best interests of Russia as a whole. Most important, nearly all of his ministers and advisers were themselves closely tied to the existing order, and thus either could not or, as was more often the case, would not, propose changes which went against their own group interests. Nicholas, as we have seen, sought to circumvent opposition to change and innovation by creating institutions of government which were directly responsive to his will. This was the motivation behind his expansion of His Majesty's Own Chancery, his creation of secret committees to deal with especially critical state problems, and his appointment of military men and Baltic Germans to civil ministerial posts. But even these devices could not serve to negate the economic interests of his advisers and ministers. To be sure, Nicholas succeeded in utilizing the expanded institutions of His Majesty's Own Chancery and secret committees to circumvent the Russian bureaucracy's resistance to change, but he could only do so in areas where the vital economic interests of the Russian aristocracy were not involved. Thus he succeeded in creating a code of laws for the Empire and, in the realm of finances, managed to put the Russian currency on a sound footing for the first time in a half-century. But, most significant, on the question of serfdom, the institution upon which Russia's entire *ancien régime* economy was based, he could not succeed in implementing critically needed alterations so long as he relied upon men whose economic interests were closely tied to the existing order.

Apart from lengthy discussions of serfdom and a number of other economic issues, such as tariff and currency reform, Nicholas and his advisers took only piecemeal steps to promote industrial development in

Russia. At first glance, this may well seem to negate the dilemma which we posed earlier: the need for Russia to compete with the industrializing West. But, in fact, Nicholas saw the competition in terms somewhat different from questions of expanded industrial output. This was the result of his view of Russia's relationship to the West and of the economic views of his chief expert on economic issues, Kankrin.

As we noted earlier, Nicholas had adopted a much more defensive attitude towards the West than had been the case with his elder brother Alexander I. As a result, especially after 1830, he was concerned mainly with erecting a barrier against the threat of revolution from the West and, specifically, against the threat of a revolutionary France. To erect such a barrier, and because of his own predilections for the army, Nicholas saw the competition with the West very much in military terms. Thus it was necessary for Russia to maintain a large standing army capable of defending the existing order in the Empire and in bordering areas. And Nicholas still very much saw the measure of his Empire's strength in terms of men under arms, rather than in economic or technological terms. Even in military terms, this was to prove disastrous in the Crimean War, for while Nicholas had concentrated upon maintaining a large military establishment, the Powers of the West had begun to adopt a number of technological innovations which made their military forces far more formidable than their numbers indicated to Nicholas. While Russia's armies continued to be armed with the weapons they had used in the Napoleonic Wars, the West had begun to adopt faster-firing infantry weapons, more effective rifled cannon, and steam-powered warships – all a measure of their more technologically orientated societies.[103]

Thus Nicholas's defensive policy towards Europe, and his definition of how that defence should be conducted, did not require an active programme of industrialization to compete with the West. And although the real challenge which the West posed to Russia was economic and technological, Nicholas saw it much more in ideological and military terms, and tended to separate the economic and technological challenge from the ideological and military one. Russia would pay dearly for that mistake in 1854–6 in the Crimean War. In the meantime, the government of Nicholas took few steps to foster economic development in Russia and, in an important sense, succeeded in postponing the social crises which faced Europe in the early years of the Industrial Revolution. This was in a large measure due to the economic policies of the Minister of Finance, E. F. Kankrin. Kankrin's views have perhaps been best summarized by Professor Pintner, who once wrote that, 'Kankrin believed that the state had to restrict its activities to the barest minimum: not because of any belief of his in the ideals of *laissez faire* economic theory, which he rejected vigorously, but because of his firm devotion to what he regarded as sound fiscal policy and the need to husband with great care the state's limited supply of money and administrative talent.' For Kankrin was convinced that before the state could (or should) begin an active policy of supporting industrial development, there must be a vast increase in the numbers of trained specialists available in the fields of commerce, industry, technology and agronomy. In short, Kankrin believed 'that "the capital of knowledge" must precede the extension of financial support for industry'.[104] The immediate result of these policies, aside from the fact that state finances were placed on a much more solid base during Kankrin's tenure of office (1824–44), was that Russians felt a sense of stability and security at home as the Empire avoided the social and political upheavals which Europe experienced in 1830 and again in 1848. This enabled one of Nicholas's most significant financial reform measures – that of putting the currency on a stable footing – to succeed, at least temporarily.

As Pintner has commented, 'problems connected with the currency were the most widely discussed economic issues in Russia during the first half of the nineteenth century'.[105] This was particularly the case since there were, in fact, two currencies circulating in Russia: gold and silver roubles, the value of which was determined by the fact that they contained a prescribed amount of precious metals;[106] and paper roubles (assignats), whose value fluctuated considerably during the first four decades of the century. Paper currency was a relatively new phenomenon in Russia, and was first issued only in 1769. But until the end of the eighteenth century, it was issued in relatively small quantities (a total of 213,989,000 roubles in the three decades between 1769 and 1800), and for all practical purposes its value remained nearly at a par with the silver rouble. Only in 1788 did the value of assignats begin to fall, so that by 1800 it required 1·50 paper roubles to buy a silver one. But in the early nineteenth century, the number of assignats issued in Russia increased dramatically, and by 1817 there were a total of 836,000,000 paper roubles in circulation, and in 1813 alone, some 103,440,000 paper roubles were issued.[107] This led to a serious devaluation in Russian assignats to the point where, in 1815, a paper rouble was worth approximately a quarter of a silver one. What these large issues of paper money amounted to in the first two decades of the nineteenth century, of course, was a vast internal loan.

A number of proposals for dealing with Russia's dual currency system were made during the 1820s and early 1830s, but by the middle of the decade the problem was no nearer to being solved.[108] In fact, it became more pressing as a result of the introduction of a very complex system of 'popular exchange rates', 'a peculiar set of discounts and premiums combined with prices set in a hypothetical currency unit'.[109] As a result,

Nicholas, in July 1834, demanded that his advisers, and particularly the Minister of Finance, Kankrin, consider the matter of implementing changes in Russia's currency system.[110]

Throughout his reign, Nicholas displayed a very serious and continuing interest in state finances. He placed great confidence in Kankrin and sought to learn from him. In essence, the first decade or so of Nicholas's reign saw him support Kankrin's conservative fiscal policies and seek to learn more about the intricacies of state economy in his Empire. But, beginning in the late 1830s, Nicholas and his mentor came increasingly into conflict. They had had disagreements before, but their earlier conflicts were the result primarily of Nicholas's demands for the military establishment, and Kankrin's frequent resistance to them since he realized that the state could ill afford such expenses. The disagreements between Emperor and minister which marked the last five years of Kankrin's ministry were more fundamental and far-reaching. While Nicholas saw Russia's relationship with the West more in terms of ideological and military conflict, he was becoming increasingly aware of the changing nature of world economic systems and the technological developments which went with them. And although he usually saw such innovations in terms of their military value, he became increasingly concerned with them as the decade of the 1840s drew near. In fact, in 1838, on the eve of his meeting with the rulers of Austria and Prussia at Teplitz, he contemplated sending experts to the United States to purchase newly perfected steam-ships for testing by the Russian navy.[111] Even more significant, he had sent the young military engineer, Pavel Mel'nikov, to Western Europe for some fifteen months beginning in 1837 to study railway technology; and in 1839 sent Mel'nikov, as well as another engineer, N. O. Kraft, to the United States to study railway development there.[112]

Nicholas thus urged upon his advisers important advances in monetary reform, transport and agriculture, beginning in the mid 1830s. Kankrin resisted them all. As far as the monetary reform was concerned, in 1839, again at Nicholas's urging, the State Council proposed that all financial transactions in Russia be placed upon a silver basis as from 1 January 1840, with the provision that as soon as circumstances permitted, the assignats would be exchanged for silver-based notes. Nicholas himself set the exchange rate between assignats and silver at 3·5 to 1, a measure which favoured those who held bank deposits or assignats, but which worked to the disadvantage of the nobility who owed assignats to state banks for loans. Silver reserves amounting to approximately 20 per cent of the value of the new notes would be set aside as backing.[113] In its straitened state, the Russian treasury could not afford more. On 1 July 1839, therefore, Nicholas issued two decrees which stabilized Russian currency for the first time since 1769, when Catherine II had first begun to issue paper money.[114]

On the matter of railway development, Nicholas was far less assertive and far-seeing, and the lack of a rail network would be one of the most serious disadvantages which Russia would suffer in the Crimean War. Not until 1835, in discussions of proposals made by the Austrian engineer Franz Anton Ritter von Gerstner, did the question of constructing railways first receive serious consideration in high government circles in Russia.[115] Kankrin was totally and stubbornly opposed to railways on the grounds that they were expensive and that they would weaken the moral fibre of Russian society,[116] but Nicholas saw in them a military potential, especially after von Gerstner had discussed the question at considerable length.[117] But Nicholas was cautious. Although he found the military potential of railways intriguing, he did not seem prepared to pay a high price, especially not the exorbitant prices that von Gerstner and his fellow Austrian entrepreneurs were asking.[118] As one scholar has remarked, 'Nicholas was not determined to have them [railways] at any cost. They did not seem to be essential.'[119] The result of Nicholas's caution was that von Gerstner was given the authority to construct a line of some twenty-five kilometres from the Summer Palace in Tsarskoe Selo. It was a small crumb to receive after his hopes for attaining an Empire-wide monopoly over rail construction.[120]

Von Gerstner's venture proved a financial success. Yet most of Nicholas's conservative advisers remained opposed to rail development and would switch over to a pro-rail view only at the very end of the decade. Interestingly enough, Russia's second line, approved in 1838, was a project to connect Warsaw with Vienna, a plan which Nicholas quite possibly approved because it had the enthusiastic support of his 'father-commander' Prince Paskevich and because it appeared to be soundly financed.[121] Only in 1842 did Nicholas approve the construction of the first major railway within Russia itself: a line to connect the Empire's two capitals, St Petersburg and Moscow;[122] and the project was completed only after considerable difficulty and nearly a decade of labour. As a result, because Nicholas did not foster a policy of energetic rail development, the Empire had only approximately 650 miles of track at the outbreak of the Crimean War, while France had more than 2,000 miles,[123] the combined states of Germany over 5,000 miles,[124] Britain more than 7,000 miles,[125] and the North American continent, primarily the United States of America, more than 9,000 miles of track.[126]

Russia's general economic backwardness was one very significant reason for her slowness in developing rail communications during Nicholas's reign. Given the high cost involved (estimates for building the

Moscow–Petersburg line in 1842 were approximately 43,000,000 roubles, more than a quarter of the entire annual state revenues at the time), Nicholas and his advisers could not afford to support much rail construction with state funds. Beyond that, of course, there was traditionally a critical shortage of fluid capital in the private sector of the Russian economy, a factor which hindered not only rail construction but also industrial and agricultural development. And at the root of all these difficulties was Russia's serf economy, which made it impossible for her to compete with the West in economic terms.

The question of serfdom and the need for improvement in the agrarian sector of the Empire's economy was a problem to which Nicholas devoted a great deal of attention during the first two decades of his reign. He was aware of the system's shortcomings, and clearly wished to resolve the many difficulties connected with serfdom. Nicholas perhaps best expressed his attitude towards the entire question during one of his rare appearances before the Imperial Russian State Council in 1842, when he insisted that 'there is no doubt that serfdom, in the form in which we have it now, is clearly and obviously bad for everyone'. But, at the same time, he also stated with equal clarity the dilemma he faced when he insisted that 'to attack it at this point would be even more destructive'. His approach to the problem, therefore, would be a gradual one. As he informed the State Council:

It is impossible to conceal the fact . . . that the present situation cannot continue forever . . . However, if the present situation is such that it cannot continue, and if, as well, a decisive suppression of [serfdom's] methods also is impossible without general upheavals, then it is necessary to at least prepare the way for a very gradual transition to another order of things . . . Everything should be done gradually, and ought not, and, indeed, cannot, be done at once or suddenly.[127]

This would be Nicholas's policy from the very beginning of his reign until 1848 when, in the face of what he perceived to be a broad revolutionary menace from the West, he would cease all efforts to resolve the serf issue and would once again make common cause with the nobility.

Yet two factors hindered and, in the end, paralysed Nicholas's efforts to deal with the serf question. First, he feared that any forced alteration in the existing order would lead to unrest among the nobility. The assassination of his father, and the circumstances of his own accession, had shown him the dangers which could arise from such aristocratic discontent. Perhaps even more important, since Nicholas had proved to himself that he could deal with an aristocratic revolt so long as the army remained loyal, was his fear of a peasant *jacquerie*, such as that which had burst upon Russia in the 1770s under the leadership of the Cossack rebel Pugachev. The 'ghost of Pugachev' haunted Nicholas, and whichever figures are used, it is certain that the numbers of peasant revolts were increasing during the second quarter of the nineteenth century. Probably the best estimates show that, while there were some 148 revolts between 1826 and 1834, the number increased to 216 in the following decade, and that, between 1845 and 1854, there were 348 peasant disturbances.[128] Given his fear of any social or political dissent, Nicholas chose a gradual course which, in fact, achieved very little and which, even by the most generous estimates, could hardly be called measures designed 'to at least prepare the way for a very gradual transition to another order of things'.[129]

Beginning with the Committee of 6 December, Nicholas appointed some ten secret committees to discuss the peasant question in Russia between 1826 and 1847. They all made very little progress towards improving the conditions under which the serfs of the Russian nobility lived.[130] Clearly the fact that their own economic sustenance was directly tied to Russia's serf economy was an important factor in causing the statesmen whom Nicholas assigned to these secret committees to reject any thought of its abolition. Only Nicholas's personal insistence that something be done led to the drafting of two laws designed to enable some few peasants to escape the shackles of serfdom, though neither of these laws went beyond the most innocuous changes in the existing order. In 1842, the government decreed the so-called statute on 'obligated peasants' which enabled landowners to free their serfs from personal bondage and transfer them into a special category known as 'obligated peasants'. Such peasants were to be given the use of a certain amount of land, for which they would be obliged to make a certain mutually agreed-upon payment to their former masters. But this law only provided for voluntary action by the serfowners themselves, and by the end of Nicholas's reign, only 24,708 male serfs had been transferred into the obligated peasant category.[131] A second decree, issued in 1847, permitted peasants to purchase their freedom and the lands they worked if the estate on which they lived was put up for auction, although this law was annulled as part of the reaction of Nicholas's government to the revolutions of 1848.

Perhaps the most significant reform measure taken in regard to the peasantry in Nicholas's Empire applied not to the serfs of the Russian nobility but to those serfs known as 'state peasants'. State peasants were those who were under the control of the state treasury rather than of private individuals, and they comprised slightly more than 50 per cent of the servile population in the Russian Empire. This reform, undertaken directly at Nicholas's request, was mainly the work of one man: General P. D. Kiselev, whom Nicholas made a count in 1839. Under Alexander I,

Kiselev had been a combat commander, was well-known for his bravery under fire, and earned a well-deserved reputation for efficiency and his rare ability to bring about reforms in an establishment which staunchly resisted change.[132] Nicholas himself utilized Kiselev's talents in a number of ways during the first decade of his reign. At first he continued as Chief of Staff of Russia's Second Army in the South. He was given a combat command during the Balkan campaign of 1829, and later that year, Nicholas appointed him Plenipotentiary President of the Divans of Wallachia and Moldavia.[133]

Kiselev's assignment as Plenipotentiary President taxed his abilities to the utmost and forced him to broaden his reform views considerably. For the first time in his career, he had to deal with problems other than military ones, and he found reform in the civil sphere a far different matter from in the army, where one could issue orders with at least some reasonable hope that they would be obeyed. With his work in the Danubian principalities, therefore, Kiselev began his transition from military to civilian reform problems, although at the time when he was relieved of his post in the principalities, the transition was not yet complete. Because the aristocracy was certain to oppose all efforts at reform, Kiselev immediately set out to construct a social base of support for Russian power among the peasantry, something which his nephew, N. A. Miliutin, would attempt on a much broader scale some three decades later in Poland after the rebellion of 1863 had been crushed.[134] Kiselev therefore worked to eradicate the plague and to end the scourge of famine. To eliminate the most offensive abuses which local officials inflicted upon the peasants, he abolished the sale of influence and established an energetic inspectorate to investigate complaints against dishonest officials. He reorganized the system of taxation, and introduced a general head tax. Capital punishment and inquisition by torture were abolished, and a uniform system of justice and court procedure established.[135] He then turned to the most critical problem of all; that of improving the lot of the over-taxed, over-worked, poverty-stricken peasantry.

The peasant problem was not a new one for Kiselev. As early as 1816 he had set down his ideas about serfdom and reform in a memorandum which he had sent to Alexander I.[136] In fact, all of Kiselev's views on the peasant question, at least until 1856, were a series of elaborations on this first proposal. From 1816 onward, Kiselev's views on the peasant reform question held firmly to the principle that the absolute and arbitrary power which the landlords wielded over their serfs must be curtailed by the precise definition of the obligations which lord and peasant had to each other.[137] As Plenipotentiary President, Kiselev had his first opportunity to attempt a practical application of his ideas on peasant reform. His programme had two central features. First, the nobility would be permitted to retain full title to all their lands while the peasants would be free to leave their masters if they wished. Equally important, the new Organic Statute,[138] which was to serve as the law code for the principalities, would clearly define the obligations of the peasants to their landlords, who, in turn, would be barred from breaking their contracts with the peasants so long as the peasants fulfilled their specified obligations.[139] But the result of Kiselev's first efforts to find a practical solution to the complexities of peasant reform fell far short of his expectations. Lacking a clear knowledge of local conditions in the principalities, he allowed the peasants to be burdened with obligations which were far too onerous. Since they could not meet their obligations, the peasants therefore remained very much at the mercy of their masters.

The Petersburg Convention, which Nicholas signed with the Ottoman Empire in mid January 1834, ended Kiselev's work in the principalities as Russian troops withdrew and left Wallachia and Moldavia to be governed by native rulers.[140] Kiselev hastened to St Petersburg once his duties were ended in early April, despite the fact that he needed rest and treatment to restore his health. His long absence from the capital had made him anxious for the security of his future at a court where careers were sometimes made or destroyed by the tongues of those who stood close to the throne. Therefore, despite the trust which Nicholas had placed in him, Kiselev was unwilling to chance a longer absence from the internal politics at Court, for trusted imperial advisers had been brought down before when they had remained aloof from court politics. This need continually to protect oneself against the intrigues which flourished at Court was an added, and extremely important, burden that reformers in nineteenth-century Russia had to bear. Failure to protect his flank had brought down Speranskii in 1812, and would very nearly ruin N. A. Miliutin, a leading figure in the emancipation work, in 1858. Kiselev therefore returned to St Petersburg in the spring of 1834 anxious to learn what future awaited him.

When Kiselev returned to St Petersburg, Nicholas ordered him to make his report without giving him adequate time to prepare the necessary papers. But in response to Kiselev's protestations that he needed more time, Nicholas reportedly replied, 'No, give it to me nevertheless. After all, I am accustomed to reading reports from provincial governors, and there, everything is false. You, however, were accustomed to speak the truth to my late brother.'[141] Kiselev thus gave Nicholas a full account of his work and, during their lengthy interview, Nicholas was particularly impressed by Kiselev's views on serfdom.[142] It appears that it was at that moment that he first began to think of Kiselev as his 'Chief of Staff for Peasant Affairs'.

Indeed, Nicholas was badly in need of a man such as Kiselev. Of the two advisers who had counselled him on the problems of peasant reform at the beginning of his reign, the aged M. M. Speranskii was now obliged to devote most of his time to work on Russian law, and V. P. Kochubei, Nicholas's second adviser on peasant questions, was on his death-bed. During the next two years, while Kiselev spent much time recovering his health at spas in Stettin, Berlin and Karlsbad, Nicholas had several meetings with him and became increasingly convinced that the general was the man he had been seeking to direct the state's efforts to improve living conditions for the Russian peasants. While dining with Kiselev on 17 February 1836, Nicholas once again turned the conversation to a serious discussion of the peasant question. 'Because I know your views on this subject,' he told Kiselev, 'I want to ask you to take over the direction of this entire matter.' He added, 'You will be my Chief of Staff for Peasant Affairs.'[143] After his discussions with Kiselev, Nicholas created the Fifth Section of His Majesty's Own Chancery. Kiselev became the new section's first chief.[144]

By 1835, Nicholas seems to have concluded that there was little hope that secret committees would produce any sort of workable reform proposals relating to the serfs of the Russian nobility. He therefore resolved to concentrate upon improving the conditions under which the state peasants lived in the hope that the government could set an example which would induce the gentry to implement reforms on their estates.[145] This was the task entrusted to Kiselev in February 1836. By May, all of the work on reforms for the state peasants in the Russian Empire had been shifted from secret committees into Kiselev's hands. The truth of the matter was that neither Kiselev, Nicholas nor anyone else had any clear understanding of just what the conditions under which these peasants lived were like. Nor did they have any clear knowledge of just what needed to be reformed, though it was obvious that, while the situation of the state peasants was probably better than that of the average serf, it was still far from ideal or even comfortable. To understand better the problems which faced him, Kiselev personally investigated the living conditions of the state peasants soon after he assumed his duties. For his investigations he chose four provinces: Moscow, Pskov, Kursk and St Petersburg, which he considered to be representative of a broader cross-section of rural economic conditions and peasant life.

Kiselev's feelings led to a complete reversal of the state's attitude towards the peasant commune, the fundamental unit of peasant society and administration in the Empire. During the reign of Alexander I,

reformers such as Speranskii had firmly believed that the peasant commune, with its stagnating effect on agricultural production, should be
abolished in the Russian countryside. Kiselev now turned state policy in
the opposite direction and argued that the commune should be preserved
as an instrument of state administration and control. His initial investigations also led him to the conclusion that a thorough study of peasant life
must be undertaken in all of Russia's provinces, and between 1836 and
1840 he sent investigators into forty-seven of the fifty provinces of the
Empire. As a result, Nicholas's government obtained for the first time a
clear picture of the conditions under which state peasants lived. This in
itself was an important accomplishment. The investigations revealed that
the economic position of state peasants, although generally less onerous
than that of the nobility's serfs, was still much worse than government
officials had imagined. Most peasants had far too little land, and their
tax obligations often exceeded their resources. There were no schools or
public-health facilities in the peasant villages. Drunkenness was rife in
state peasant communities; indeed, the ratio of taverns to peasants was
much higher in these villages than in those of serfs owned by the nobility.
Finally, the peasant local administration was on the brink of disintegration. Petty clerks and officials, often barely literate, were of the most
corrupt variety imaginable. Anything could be arranged for a suitable
price, and nothing was done without some sort of payment. At every level
of administration, whether in village, town or provincial capital, it was
necessary for the peasant to beg, wheedle and bribe every official he
encountered.

Well before the 1836–40 investigations were completed, Kiselev
realized that extensive reforms of the state peasant administration were
urgently needed. He maintained a firm statist view in his approach to
reform and urged that the sought-after goal should be a harmoniously
adjusted, well-tuned state administration. Rationally designed institutions,
he believed, would provide the solution to most of the ills from which
the Russian state suffered. Most important was his insistence upon the
simplification and centralization of administrative functions and responsibility. In holding to this view, Kiselev diverged markedly from the attitude
towards the state and administration which most of the nobility held at
the time. For them, the ideal to be sought in administration was the
opposite: a lessening of the involvement of the central bureaucracy in
provincial and district affairs with responsibility for local administration
being left in the hands of the nobility.[146]

Kiselev therefore viewed reform as primarily an administrative
question and was convinced that improvements in the administration of
the state peasant communities would better their social and economic

position. In Kiselev's opinion, the state should take the initiative in bringing about change. 'The government ought not, and indeed cannot, refuse to deal [with a problem of reform simply] . . . because it is difficult to solve,' he wrote. He added further that 'to leave such a matter to time is useless because in Russia nothing can be undertaken or completed without the leadership of the government'. The main point, he concluded, was to work out 'effective administrative measures'.[147]

Under Kiselev's guidance, and with Nicholas's firm support, eight laws were issued between 1837 and 1840 which dealt with the state peasants.[148] The first of these created the Ministry of State Domains to deal with the administration of the state peasants on a regular and permanent basis. Here Kiselev tried to reconcile Nicholas's desire for an administration which was directly responsive to his will with his own ideal of a finely tuned, well-ordered state administration. The Ministry of State Domains therefore retained some of the features of the Fifth Section which Nicholas most valued. Most important, Kiselev, as Minister of State Domains, continued to be Nicholas's 'Chief of Staff for Peasant Affairs', and the ties between Nicholas and his minister remained extremely close throughout the remainder of his reign. Kiselev often reported to Nicholas daily, was a part of that small and select group which Nicholas sometimes invited to dine with him and his family, and was well-known to other members of the Imperial Family, especially to the Grand Duchess Elena Pavlovna, who acted as the patroness of progressive officials in St Petersburg during the late 1840s and early 1850s.[149]

In seeking to improve the conditions under which the state peasants lived, the guiding principle of Kiselev's reform plan was that the peasants should be given sufficient land to enable them to meet their obligations to the state and provide for their own needs. He insisted further that the taxes the peasants paid must be made to correspond more closely with their economic resources. His fundamental object, then, was not to institute any change in the juridical position of the state peasants, but to define clearly their place within the framework of the existing system and to adjust that system so that it would function far more efficiently. But, as Minister of State Domains, Kiselev did not go beyond administrative improvements in his reform proposals. In no case did he anticipate the emancipation of the state peasants, nor were they to be given any civil rights.[150] The pre-1840 laws thus dealt exclusively with administrative matters. The tax obligations of the peasants were clearly defined and regulated. Further, the peasants were provided with a system of local administration which followed clearly established procedures and fitted into a well-defined hierarchy in which the control of the state bureaucracy over the peasants' affairs was greatly increased. Such an administration, with clear lines of accountability and responsibility, and staffed by reliable civil servants, would, Kiselev believed, free the peasants from the tyranny of the petty provincial bureaucrats who had squeezed them dry through graft and corruption of every conceivable kind.

Kiselev's work on the peasant question, however, was not limited to dealing with state peasants. Throughout the late 1830s and 1840s, he continued to occupy a central place in the government's discussions on measures which could improve the living conditions of the nobility's serfs, and between 1835 and 1848, he served on several secret committees which considered these questions.[151] The emphasis of his arguments was always the same: as a first step in dealing with the serf problem, the arbitrary powers of the nobility over their peasants must be curtailed by clearly defined laws and regulations. Yet in this Kiselev did not succeed. For one thing, the vast majority of sentiment among the Empire's statesmen was against such a course. Perhaps even more important, as his reign wore on and as he became increasingly apprehensive about social and political upheavals as he witnessed new mass movements in Kraków and Galicia in 1846, Nicholas grew increasingly reluctant to approve changes which might, in any way, disturb the social and political equilibrium which his system had imposed upon Russia. Only in the south-western provinces during the mid 1840s, at the insistence of Governor-General D. G. Bibikov, soon to become Minister of the Interior, did Nicholas permit a legal definition of master–serf relations to be introduced in the form of 'inventories' which clearly defined the obligations which serfs had to their masters and which masters had to their serfs.[152]

In terms of improving the conditions under which some 20 million serfs belonging to the Russian nobility lived,[153] Nicholas and his advisers achieved pitifully little. Nicholas had managed to by-pass some of the difficulties surrounding the reform process in Russia, and thus had achieved the financial reform of 1839, the codification of the Russian laws and the reform of state peasant administration. He had done this by going outside the regular bureaucratic structure of the Russian state in the case of codification and the state peasant reform. In the case of the financial reform, he had done much to press the issue to a conclusion himself in the State Council. Where the interests of the nobility were not vitally involved, Nicholas had found the way to reform, and the military men whom he often appointed to civil posts served him well in terms of loyally following his wishes. But in the case of matters which touched directly upon the economic or social situation of the nobility, even Nicholas's loyal servants could (or, in some cases, would) do nothing to bring about reform and change.

The will of the autocrat was thus not enough to bring about reform in Russia. Although Nicholas's power was in theory absolute, it was not so in practice. As a result, his desire to resolve the serf issue was tempered by his apprehensions about possible unrest among the Empire's aristocracy and by fears of revolt among Russia's peasant masses. Equally important, when Nicholas sought to initiate reform in an area where the vital economic interests of the aristocracy were threatened, he found that even his most loyal advisers – Baltic Germans and army generals – would not go against the interests of their class. Even Kiselev, usually regarded as one of Nicholas's most progressive ministers, sought to deal with the peasant problem only within the framework of the serf system during Nicholas's reign.[154] For the fundamental socio-economic reforms which the Empire required, two elements in addition to efficient civil servants were therefore necessary, and Nicholas could provide neither of them. First, there had to be a firm commitment by the autocrat himself to such reforms. Secondly, there had to be found men whose economic interests would not be challenged by such alterations in the existing order.

Only Russia's crushing defeat in the Crimean War would provide the first of these requirements. The second, however, was developing during the latter half of Nicholas's reign in the form of a group of 'enlightened' bureaucrats, especially in the Ministries of the Interior and State Domains; and, towards the very end of the reign, in the Admiralty. These were officials who believed not only in progress, but who also shared the social conscience of the intelligentsia. As one of their number described them:

Their ideal was the introduction of legality into all spheres of life ... Along the path to attaining this ideal, they had two guideposts: work and a sense of duty. In work they saw not only the means without which it is impossible to improve one's position legitimately ... but also a necessary requirement for the full enjoyment of life. In the fulfilment of their duty, they saw a basic law of morality.[155]

But in the 1840s, these men were still submerged in the mass of the bureaucracy, usually occupying positions no higher than those of section chiefs or department heads. Only towards the end of Nicholas's reign would they reach positions in the bureaucracy sufficiently high to enable them to influence affairs of state. These were men who would be called upon to draft the Great Reforms in the following reign, and it was their unique background, training and outlook that would enable them to do so.[156]

6

Europe's Gendarme Emerges

'[Nicholas I] is stern and severe – with fixed
principles of duty which nothing
on earth will make him change; very clever I do
not think him, and his mind is an
uncivilized one; his education has been neglected;
politics and military concerns are the
only things he takes great interest in; the arts and
all softer occupations he is insensible
to, but he is sincere, I am certain, sincere even in
his most despotic acts, from a
sense that that is the only way to govern'

QUEEN VICTORIA, TO LEOPOLD,
KING OF THE BELGIANS, JUNE 1844

The agreements which Nicholas concluded with Austria and Prussia in the early autumn of 1833 at Münchengrätz and Berlin formalized a new European order. The notion of a pan-European community, implicit in the agreements signed by the victors over Napoleon in 1814 and 1815, gave way to a less exalted, but perhaps more realistic, view of European politics, which balanced the two constitutional states of the West – France and Britain – against the three absolute monarchies of the East – Austria, Prussia and Russia. Although the balance would waver from time to time, and be at one point, in the early 1850s, almost destroyed, this order would survive into the last third of the century. Not until the emergence of a united Italy and a unified Germany under the aegis of Prussia would the edifice constructed by Nicholas and Metternich begin to crumble, so that the early twentieth century would find Germany, Austria and Italy arrayed against what, in the 1830s, would have seemed the very improbable union of France, Britain and Russia.

Each of the three Eastern powers entered into the union cemented by

Metternich and Nicholas at Münchengrätz for different reasons, the one thing they shared being fear of revolution and a desire to construct a barrier which revolutionary attacks such as they had witnessed in 1830 and 1831 could not penetrate. During those years all three monarchs had felt the tremors of revolution in portions of their domains. The Habsburg monarchy, by that time an unwieldy conglomerate of diverse and antagonistic nationalities subject to the seductive call of their respective national pasts, was perhaps most vulnerable of all to revolutionary attack. But Prussia, too, had felt the rumbles of revolution in Germany during 1830, and all three states had been threatened by the revolutionary events in Poland. The menace seemed very real, even though they perhaps saw it as more threatening than it was. All three powers thus perceived the need for unity in the face of the revolutionary threat and, especially, the personification of that menace, the France of Louis-Philippe.

Yet this union of the so-called 'Northern Courts' was a very unequal partnership, for in terms of natural resources and raw military power, Russia was vastly superior to Austria or Prussia. To be sure, in comparison with the West, Russia may have appeared undeveloped in terms of her industry and economy. And, in cultural terms, she had only very recently emerged from the stage where the culture of her upper classes was nothing more than an imitation of the West. There were many in the West who still regarded Russia as barbarous, Oriental or backwards, or some combination of all three. But upon one thing all observers in the 1830s agreed: Russia was a mighty military power – the possessor of vast resources and manpower reserves which enabled her to maintain the largest war machine in all of Europe. And it had been the presence of that army at the gates of Berlin in 1761, and on the Champs-Elysées in 1814 and 1815, that had maintained for Russia the status of a great European power which Peter the Great had won for her at Poltava in 1709.

The Russia of Nicholas was thus by far the dominant member of the entente which emerged in the wake of the revolutions of 1830 and 1831. During the remainder of the 1830s and 1840s, as Friedrich Wilhelm IV replaced his father on the Prussian throne, as first Ferdinand and then Franz Josef replaced the Austrian Emperor Franz, and, most of all, as the influence of Metternich began to weaken during the last years of this period, Nicholas's position in Eastern and Central Europe became even stronger. He emerged as the senior statesman by the mid 1840s. Perhaps even more important, both Prussia and Austria knew that it must be Nicholas to whom they must turn to save them from the attacks of revolution should the need arise, and indeed, that was precisely what happened in 1849 when Austria's young Emperor Franz Josef had to seek Nicholas's aid to suppress revolution in his Hungarian domains.

Backed by the might of his million-man army, Nicholas emerged as the gendarme of Europe on the eve of 1848, especially in the lands east of the Rhine. For, unlike Austria and Germany, revolution would not touch his Empire. As the 1840s drew to a close, Nicholas's domains would be looked to as the one haven in Europe that was safe from revolution. While the rest of Europe was shaken by revolutions in 1848, not even Nicholas's Polish domains would stir.

The alliance of Prussia, Austria and Russia thus seemed the most natural of unions in the 1830s. As the Austrian ambassador to St Petersburg, the Comte de Ficquelmont, wrote to Metternich, 'People say that the union of the three Courts is like a legal marriage which brings order and happiness whilst the alliance of the two maritime Powers is like the liaison of two libertines, which only brings corruption and disorder.'[1] Yet while the three Courts were at one in their fear of revolution and their desire to defend their domains against it, they were perhaps less united on the other major issue of the day – the question of the future of the Ottoman Empire and the Eastern Question in general. The Eastern Question, wrote the Austrian diplomat Count Anton Prokesch von Osten, was indeed 'a question between Russia and the rest of Europe'.[2]

While the issue of the Ottoman Empire's future was of little concern to Prussia, it was of great significance to Austria and to Metternich, who considered Austria to have vital interests in the Balkans. Metternich had been especially firm in his opposition to Nicholas's efforts to resolve the Greek Question in the 1820s, had opposed his war against the Sultan in 1828 and 1829. It was quite probably Metternich's opposition which had led Nicholas to make common cause with Britain and France in the 1820s in the Near East. Russia's victory over the Turks in 1829 and the Peace of Adrianople, in which Nicholas gave evidence once again that he did not 'want a single inch of Turkish soil', perhaps set some of Metternich's fears to rest. Certainly, by early 1853, he could write to Baron Neumann in London that 'the Emperor of Russia follows a very enlightened policy in that he understands very well the needs of his own Empire as well as the situation in Europe'.[3] Equally important, the events of the half-decade following the Peace of Adrianople would leave Metternich with little alternative but to seek an accommodation with Nicholas and Nesselrode on the Eastern Question as Russia's influence in the Ottoman Empire strengthened even further. If a fear of revolution was the long-range factor which brought Nicholas and Metternich together in 1833 at Münchengrätz, Nicholas's diplomatic successes in the Ottoman Empire in early 1833 perhaps provided the final catalyst for their union. Long before he became known as the 'gendarme of Europe', Nicholas had assumed the role of gendarme of the Balkans and the Near

East. For his entire policy in Europe after 1830 would be one of 'gendarmism': to protect the established order in the Ottoman Empire; to guard the integrity of the newly established governments in the Danubian principalities of Wallachia and Moldavia; to prevent the infiltration into Russia of dangerous ideas from the West; and to preserve order and tranquillity in Poland.

1. Unkiar-Skelessi

As Baron F. I. Brunnov, for many years Nicholas's ambassador to London, once wrote, 'The Eastern Question occupied the attention of the Emperor [Nicholas] from the very first days of his reign and never ceased to demand his most serious attention.'[4] Indeed, the Eastern Question became the dominant international object of contention between the European powers during most of Nicholas's reign. Once Nicholas had dealt with the menace of revolution in 1830 and 1831, and once the union of Austria, Prussia and Russia had been cemented at Münchengrätz and Berlin, the Eastern Question, involving as it did not only the question of access to the Straits, but also the issues of Egypt, Greece and the remainder of the Balkans, became the major factor in Nicholas's relations with Europe. France's support of the Sultan's rebellious vassal Mehemet Ali in Egypt, Britain's misunderstanding about Nicholas's attitude towards the preservation of the Ottoman Empire, and deep-seated Austrian apprehensions that if, despite their best efforts, the Ottoman Empire should collapse, Nicholas would challenge their interests in the Balkans, were all major forces in disrupting the European political scene in the two decades before the Crimean War. It was a double tragedy for Europe, first, because the periodic outbreaks of tension in the Near East were usually something over which the major powers had little control. During most of this period, European statesmen found themselves reacting to crises brought on by the nationalist aspirations of the Balkan peoples, or by the ambitious schemes of Mehemet Ali and his son, the brilliant general Ibrahim. Equally important, the Eastern Question posed a tragedy for Europe because Russia and Britain, the two major powers with perhaps the most vital stake in resolving the issue, regarded each other with such suspicion that they failed to realize that they shared the common goal of seeking to preserve the Ottoman Empire from collapse. This was especially true in the case of Britain, whose statesmen could never be convinced that Nicholas did not want to seize the Straits and Constantinople, but instead sincerely hoped to avert a major European crisis by shoring up that crumbling edifice that was the Ottoman Empire.

Certainly the question of Russia's relations with the Ottoman Empire was one of the first foreign-policy matters with which Nicholas had to contend. To Europe he proclaimed that it was a question of forcing the Sultan to honour the treaties which his Empire had concluded with Russia during the course of more than a half-century.[5] In fact, it was a far more serious problem – and one which directly involved the economic well-being of Nicholas's Empire. Ever since the opening of the port of Odessa on the northern shore of the Black Sea in the late eighteenth century, access to the Straits, and hence to the Mediterranean, had become a question of vital importance for the Russian Empire. Increased exports of grain from Russia to meet growing demand in the West comprised a major item in the Empire's foreign trade. More than that, it formed a vital part of the economic life of the Russian nobility, who purchased the Western luxury goods to which they had become accustomed in the course of the eighteenth century by the sale of produce from their estates. With the increased development of large-scale agriculture in southern and south-western Russia in the late eighteenth and early nineteenth centuries, trade from Russia's southern ports to Western Europe via the Straits and the Black Sea increased significantly. By the mid nineteenth century, in fact, nearly one third of all Russian exports were shipped from Black Sea ports, while a half-century earlier, less than 3 per cent of the Empire's sea-borne trade had been concentrated in that area.[6]

Nicholas recognized that this export trade must be protected and fostered and that it was essential to ensure access of Russian merchant vessels to the Straits and hence to the Mediterranean. Should the Straits be closed, as the Sultan had done in 1828, Russia's already fragile economy would be further weakened. Herein lay one of the major misunderstandings about Nicholas's aims on the part of Western statesmen. From at least the mid eighteenth century, Western diplomats had seen Russia's interest in the Ottoman Empire as being connected with a vast scheme of imperialist expansion centred around a Russian desire to seize Constantinople and thus replace the Sultan's dominion over the Balkans and the Near East with Russian sovereignty. Such fears were, of course, given added substance by Catherine II's fanciful schemes, set forth late in her reign, for establishing her second grandson, the Grand Duke Konstantin Pavlovich, as ruler in Constantinople. But, for Nicholas, the issue was not one of seizing the Sultan's throne. His repeated protestations that he 'did not want a single inch of Turkish soil' so long as no one else took any, were true. And the fact that when the road to Constantinople lay open before his armies in 1829, Nicholas did not seek territorial gains in Europe from the Sultan, gives added weight to his protestations. To be sure, outright seizure of the Straits by Russia would very probably have confronted Nicholas with a European coalition, something which Russia certainly could not have withstood. But there was also much truth in Nicholas's statement to the Count Saint-Priest in early 1826 that, 'I do not want, do not desire, and do not plan to add a single inch of territory [in the Near East] to the holdings of Russia which is already large enough as it is.'[7] In fact, Nicholas formally adopted this policy of preserving the Ottoman Empire in the Balkans and the Near East in September 1829. After some extended discussions with several of his close advisers, whom he had formed into a special committee for the purpose of studying the question of Russia's future relationship to the Ottoman Empire, Nicholas concluded that the collapse of the Ottoman Empire 'would be contrary to the best interests of Russia'.[8] This decision, which was in opposition to earlier Russian grand schemes to seize control of Constantinople, would determine the general lines of Russian policy in the Near East for the remainder of the imperial period of Russian history.

It thus was Russian mercantile shipping interests and their protection from attack by the West in the Black Sea, or by the Ottoman Empire in the Straits, that dominated Nicholas's dealings with the Sultan during the 1830s. He required assurance that trade from Russia's southern ports would be protected and that it would be free to continue and to expand. Nicholas's first step in this programme, as we have already seen, was taken in the Peace of Adrianople, which gave neutral ships free access to the Black Sea and the Danube and, most important, placed Russian merchants in the Ottoman domains under the control of Russian consuls rather than Turkish authorities.[9] But the position of Russian shipping in the Straits and in the Mediterranean was still far from secure, especially in view of the growing power of Mehemet Ali, the Pasha of Egypt.

Although nominally the Sultan's vassal, Mehemet Ali had embarked upon a number of independent campaigns of conquest since Nicholas had ascended the throne. Until 1824, he had concentrated his military energies upon the African continent, against the Wahhabites of Arabia, the natives of the upper Nile and the Sudan.[10] But in 1824, Mehemet Ali and, especially, his son Ibrahim, a brilliant general thoroughly trained in modern warfare, had turned their attention to Europe, most notably towards Greece. But by the time that the Allies had intervened in Greece, and Nicholas had concluded peace at Adrianople, all that Mehemet Ali had gained from the Sultan as a reward for his efforts to defend his master's domains against the West was the island of Crete.[11] Bitter at the Sultan's refusal to grant him further territories, and determined to extend his domains, Mehemet Ali turned towards Syria in late 1831. By mid 1832, Ibrahim had seized Jaffa, Gaza, Jerusalem, Acre and, finally, Damascus.[12] Thoroughly alarmed by Mehemet Ali's advances, the Sultan Mahmud II declared him and his son outlaws and sent an army under Hussein Pasha against him. But, by late July, Ibrahim had already defeated the Sultan's forces. By the end of 1832, he had crushed the Sultan's second army under Reshid Pasha as well. It appeared that nothing could keep him from Constantinople itself should he determine to march against it.[13]

It was in this crisis that Mahmud II first appealed to the Western Powers for aid in the summer of 1832 since his antiquated forces could in no way match the modernized armies, trained in Western tactics and armed with modern weapons, that Ibrahim threw against him. At first he found little active support for his cause among the Western Powers. Britain in 1832 had just weathered the crisis of the Reform Bill, and Palmerston was still preoccupied by the question of who would rule Belgium.[14] Further, the British had just begun naval operations in the North Sea, off the coast of Holland, and were still maintaining a fleet off the coast of Portugal. They had small resources at the moment to send to the Near East. France, on the other hand, had maintained close cultural and economic ties with Egypt ever since Napoleon's invasion in 1798. Equally important, as one historian has remarked, in France 'there had sprung up a curious but undeniable cult for Mehemet Ali, particularly among the Bonapartists, who regarded him as the disciple of Napoleon, almost as his apostolic successor in Egypt'.[15] Austria sought not to aid the Sultan against his enemy, but to act as mediator between the two. And, most important, Metternich did not propose military force as an alternative should his proposed mediations fail.[16] There thus remained only Russia to whom the Sultan could turn for aid in driving back his rebellious vassal, although he resisted that alternative for as long as possible because he realized that Russian aid would bring with it even more Russian influence in Balkan and Near Eastern affairs.

Nicholas was more than willing to oblige the Sultan, and for several important reasons, none of which were connected with any schemes to seize Constantinople or to aid Russia's co-religionists in the Near East. Perhaps most important, Nicholas saw the irresistible advance of Ibrahim's armies as a major threat to the accord which Russia had reached with the Ottoman Empire only three years before. 'With Mehemet Ali [ensconced in Constantinople], Russia would exchange a weak and defeated neighbour for a strong and victorious one,' Nesselrode warned. A weak Ottoman Empire controlling the Straits would enable Nicholas to continue his protection of Russian shipping. But a new and dynamic ruler such as Mehemet Ali could easily undo the carefully wrought system which Nicholas and Nesselrode had established. As Nesselrode wrote in November 1832, 'The success of Mehemet Ali would prepare a fatal catastrophe for the Ottoman Empire . . . The direct advantages which Russia owes to the Treaty of Adrianople might thus be brought into question.'[17]

Coupled with this threat to Russia's economic interests was Nicholas's fear of allowing the revolutionary poison of the West to approach so close to Russia's frontiers and, in particular, to give the Polish revolutionaries, who had taken refuge in France, a possible haven so close to their Slavic brethren. Again, as Nesselrode noted, 'With the victory of Mehemet Ali, French influence would increase in Constantinople, which would very soon become a hot-bed where all those without principles and without a country, who conspire against Russia, would gather.'[18] Nicholas put the matter more bluntly to General N. N. Murav'ev, his special emissary to the Sultan:

This entire war [between Mehemet Ali and Mahmud II] is nothing other than a consequence of the subversive spirit reigning at the moment in Europe and, especially in France . . . With the conquest of Tsargrad [Constantinople], we will have right in our own back yard a nest of all those homeless individuals, men without a country, who have been banished from all well-ordered societies.[19]

What happened in Egypt, North Africa or even in Syria was ultimately of far less concern to Nicholas than the question of who held sway in Constantinople and controlled the Straits. And, while he was willing to make gestures against Mehemet Ali's violations of the principles of legitimacy and legality, even to the point of withdrawing the Russian consul from Alexandria,[20] he would in the end have been willing to set his scruples aside to preserve a greatly weakened Turkish state on the Bosphorus rather than have it fall to Ibrahim's armies. And, were he faced with the choice of seizing Constantinople himself or allowing Mehemet Ali to rule a large portion of the Sultan's domains, he was clearly in favour of the latter course. Nesselrode wrote to Prince Lieven in London:

The thought of chasing the Turks out of Europe and of re-establishing the worship of the true God in St Sophia is certainly very fine, but what would Russia gain from it? Glory, undoubtedly, but at the same time the loss of all the positive advantages offered by the proximity of a state weakened by a succession of wars.[21]

In the face of a serious threat to Russia's newly won advantages in terms of protecting her Black Sea commerce, and fearing a resurgence of the revolutionary upheavals of 1830 on his southern borders, Nicholas thus moved to preserve the Sultan in Constantinople by any possible means, even to the point of dividing the Ottoman Empire between

Mehemet Ali and the Sultan if necessary. 'Perhaps the time has come to divide the Turkish Empire into two kingdoms,' he told General Murav'ev. 'It makes no difference to me whatsoever even if they let the Egyptian Pasha have all of Syria.'[22]

Carrying Nicholas's offer of aid, mediation or intervention, General Murav'ev left St Petersburg on 5 November 1832. Just more than a month later, on 9 December, he reached Constantinople aboard the Russian frigate *Standart*, and on the very day of his arrival, Mahmud's position took a decided turn for the worse. Indeed, his situation seemed nearly hopeless for, on that day, Ibrahim had defeated the remaining Turkish army under Reshid Pasha at Konieh.[23] Murav'ev thus offered Mahmud a Russian naval squadron to protect his capital. Yet the Sultan still hesitated to accept an offer of aid which would have brought Russian forces to the very gates of Constantinople, and Murav'ev sailed for Alexandria in an effort to persuade Mehemet Ali to order Ibrahim's armies to cease their advance. Arriving in Alexandria on 23 December, Murav'ev succeeded in convincing Mehemet Ali to halt his army's advance upon Constantinople.[24] But before word from his father reached him, Ibrahim had already led his armies closer to Constantinople and was, in fact, poised to attack Brusa. It was at that point that the Sultan decided to ask for direct Russian aid.

The aid which Mahmud requested through A. P. Butenev, the Russian ambassador at Constantinople, included one naval squadron and an army corps of some 30,000 men.[25] In anticipation of such a request, Nicholas had already ordered his forces on to the alert, and by 8 February 1833 a squadron including four ships of the line and one brig under the command of Rear-Admiral Lazarev had entered the Bosphorus and anchored beneath the walls of Constantinople itself.[26] Just over six weeks later, 5,000 Russian marines landed and camped in the valley of Unkiar-Skelessi.[27] In less than a month, another contingent of troops arrived with orders from Nicholas to remain until Mehemet Ali had signed an agreement with the Sultan, and Ibrahim had withdrawn his armies to a position behind the Taurus Mountains.

Nicholas had taken care to tell Metternich and Friedrich Wilhelm of his plans in advance, and had received their agreement to the course which he proposed. As Metternich had written to Count Prokesch von Osten at the beginning of February. 'There is absolutely no difference of opinion between the views of His Imperial Majesty of All the Russias and those of our August Master on their view of the Turko–Egyptian question;[28] Prussia had once again followed the lead of Metternich on the issue. But Nicholas's decisive action in the Near East caught both Britain and France by surprise, for neither had been forewarned; in fact, considerable pains had been taken to conceal Russia's plans from the French.[29] Both governments had refused the Sultan aid when he had appealed to them in 1832, but, upon learning of the arrival of a Russian fleet and marines at Constantinople, they immediately dispatched fleets of their own to the Dardanelles, thereby creating a situation which Nicholas would later describe to Lord Aberdeen as 'so many powder barrels close to the fire, how shall one prevent the sparks from catching?'[30] At the last moment, however, a confrontation was averted. Britain's fleet was prevented from entering the Dardanelles by the British ambassador to the Porte, Lord Ponsonby, while the French fleet remained in the Mediterranean because Nicholas had informed the French government that the appearance of French warships in the Straits themselves would be considered an act of war.[31]

But Butenev was perhaps too unassertive and modest to carry out the delicate diplomatic manoeuvres demanded by such a tense situation. Nicholas therefore sent Count A. F. Orlov, one of his most trusted adjutants, to the Porte as his ambassador extraordinary.[32] He gave to Orlov very broad powers and a great deal of freedom to negotiate with the Sultan within the general framework of protecting Russia's interests in the Straits, preserving the Ottoman Empire from dissolution, combating the influence of French representatives at the Porte and, perhaps above all, convincing the Sultan and his advisers 'that their salvation depends solely upon the generous support of the [Russian] Emperor'.[33]

Orlov arrived in Constantinople in late April 1833,[34] just before word reached the city that Mehemet Ali had signed the Treaty of Kutahiya by which the Sultan had conceded to the Egyptian Pasha full authority over all Egypt and Syria, and had given Ibrahim the right to rule the district of Adana. In return, Mehemet Ali agreed to remain formally a vassal of the Sultan.[35] This removed for the moment the menace of Ibrahim and Mehemet Ali to Constantinople, but the situation was still potentially very explosive, especially because of the presence of the French fleet in the eastern Mediterranean. As Orlov wrote to Nesselrode in mid May, 'If foreign forces arrive, that will mark the beginning of the end . . . for, in the collision of these different interests and rivalries . . . God only knows what will happen.'[36]

It thus was Orlov's task, in keeping with the policy of his master, to arrange an agreement with the Ottoman Empire which would protect Russia's interests and, at the same time, neutralize the very explosive situation in the eastern Mediterranean. Orlov succeeded brilliantly. At their first meeting, on 30 April, the Sultan had expressed to him a wish to conclude a closer alliance with Russia, the very thing which, according to Brunnov, Nicholas had begun to consider seriously a few months earlier,[37] and which was probably behind his instruction to Orlov that he should try to convince the Sultan that his 'salvation depends solely upon the generous support of the [Russian] Emperor'.[38]

As a result of his careful negotiations, Orlov signed with the Sultan the Treaty of Unkiar-Skelessi on 26 June 1833. The treaty was the product of much careful labour and consideration by Nicholas and Nesselrode, and its proposed text had been sent to Orlov on 8 May. Nicholas regarded it as a means 'to legitimize, by means of a defensive alliance, the direct interest which we have in protecting European Turkey against all aggression and thereby to ensure that a strong and daring enemy will not replace a weak neighbour on our frontiers'. Most important, Nicholas proposed a secret clause to the treaty which 'would secure for us a guarantee that would make the southern provinces of the [Russian] Empire along the Black Sea safe from attack'. What Nicholas demanded was that the Sultan agree 'to forbid entry into the Dardanelles to foreign warships', a formal statement 'of principle which [the Porte] has always held to firmly'.[39] To this the Sultan agreed, and on 28 June 1833, Russia's warships and troops left Constantinople to retire behind their own frontiers.

The Treaty of Unkiar-Skelessi provoked considerable outcry in the West, especially in France. The statesman and politician François Guizot would later comment that 'the cabinet of St Petersburg, converting the fact of its predominance in Constantinople into written law, made Turkey its official client and the Black Sea into a Russian lake, the entry to which was guarded by this client against all possible enemies of Russia'.[40] Both Britain and France presented notes of protest in St Petersburg, declaring that they 'would act as if the Treaty were not in existence'.[41] In fact, there seems to have been some confusion, even in Nicholas's mind, as to what was permitted and what was denied to Russia by the secret article about the Straits. The defensive purpose of the alliance – to protect Russia's merchant shipping and Black Sea provinces from attack by the Western Powers, especially France and Britain, in event of war, and to guarantee to Russian commercial vessels access to the Bosphorus, the Dardanelles and the Mediterranean – was clear; as was Nicholas's commitment to protect the Sultan from further attacks and thus guarantee the preservation of the Ottoman Empire in its weakened state. But there is evidence that Nicholas also had the impression that, while the Sultan guaranteed to close the Straits to Western warships, he would permit their use by the Russian navy. Exactly what significance this had, since Russia was certainly disinclined to use her Black Sea fleet in the Mediterranean in the 1830s, is not clear. But in 1838, when the Eastern Question was once again beginning to boil, Nicholas proposed to send two ships of the line from his Baltic fleet into the Mediterranean through the Straits, evidently to assert rights which he believed to be his by the Unkiar-Skelessi treaty.[42] Only when Nesselrode explained in a lengthy memorandum to Nicholas the precise nature of the agreements arrived at in 1833 did it become completely clear what the true nature of the treaty was:

The treaties oblige that power [Turkey] *to close* entry to the Dardanelles to any foreign flag of war, but these transactions in no way oblige it *to open* them to us. The treaty of Adrianople, confirmed by that of Constantinople, stipulates explicitly in our favour only free passage of *merchant* ships; but no stipulation authorizes us to demand entrance to the Bosphorus of our *warships*.[43]

The Unkiar-Skelessi treaty was thus defensive rather than offensive or aggressive in nature. In a very important sense, however, it established Nicholas as the gendarme of the Near East. Nicholas had become the gendarme of the Danubian principalities in 1829 by the Treaty of Adrianople, whereby he had undertaken to protect the independent national governments in those areas which remained nominally under Turkish suzerainty. He now took upon himself the responsibility of protecting all the Sultan's 'European domains' against attack from any foreign power. But Nicholas was not yet ready to assume the role of gendarme of the Balkans and the Near East by himself, and this was one of the fundamental precepts agreed upon at Münchengrätz – that Austria and Prussia would commit themselves jointly to that principle which Nicholas and his advisers had formally agreed to in 1829: that the Ottoman Empire should be preserved intact. Yet there could be little doubt about which power would have to undertake the military measures to defend the Sultan should he request aid. In time of crisis, Austria's forces were needed to protect her increasingly tenuous grasp on Hungary and her provinces in Italy. In military terms, then, Nicholas had in fact become the gendarme of the Balkans and the Near East, as well as of the Danubian principalities and Eastern Europe by the end of 1833. In less than two decades, he would have become the gendarme of Central Europe as well.

2. *From Unkiar-Skelessi to London*

Nicholas's conclusion of the Unkiar-Skelessi treaty with the Sultan in late June 1833, and Austria's agreement to a joint policy of seeking to preserve the Ottoman Empire, marked the high point of Russia's influence in the Near East. It also spread wider the gap which separated Russia from the two maritime and constitutional powers of the West. Nicholas's antipathy to the régime of Louis Philippe was well known, and, in any case, his efforts to conceal his plans and policies towards the Ottoman Empire from the French were hardly calculated to improve the already strained relations between the two powers. But his efforts to keep the French government in ignorance about his plans towards the Ottoman Empire had not been without good reason. While there is evidence that Louis Philippe's ministers were willing to reach an agreement with Russia on a common policy for the Eastern Question, the attitude of the king himself had seemed so capricious that Nicholas's ambassador, Count Pozzo di Borgo, feared to become involved with him in dealing with the Sultan. As he reported back to Nesselrode and Nicholas, the final determination of France's policy lay in the hands of Louis Philippe himself, who inspired 'neither confidence nor respect' and who 'ruled his ministers according to his whim and his kingdom according to his feelings at any given moment'. Indeed, the Russian ambassador found the French king's attitudes perplexing in the extreme. At one diplomatic reception, he told Louis Philippe that Russia and France were in complete agreement about the need to preserve peace in the Near East and to bring about a reconciliation between the Sultan and Mehemet Ali. Louis Philippe's reply was that Nicholas 'must be made to realize that Europe would never allow him to establish' Russian military forces in Constantinople, a step which di Borgo had just told him that Russia would never undertake so long as the Ottoman Empire remained in existence. Confronted by this and other threats from the French king, di Borgo had urged upon Nicholas a policy of remaining apart from the French in matters relating to the Eastern Question.[44]

In the case of Britain, however, the increased suspicion and antipathy towards Russia which news of the Unkiar-Skelessi treaty produced was unfortunate, especially since much of it resulted from a misunderstanding of Nicholas's policies in the Near East. While Nicholas had firmly adopted the position that the collapse of the Ottoman Empire 'would be contrary to the best interests of Russia', and that 'the advantages of maintaining the Ottoman Empire in Europe outweigh the disadvantages',[45] as early as 1829, and even though he had stated repeatedly that he had no territorial designs upon Turkey's European domains, Palmerston insisted upon believing otherwise. While Count Orlov was at work negotiating the Treaty of Unkiar-Skelessi to protect Russian shipping and her southern sea-coast, Palmerston declared that 'the [British] Government would feel it to be their duty to resist to the utmost any attempt on the part of Russia to partition the Turkish Empire'. 'The integrity and independence of the Ottoman Empire,' he added, 'are necessary to the maintenance of the tranquillity, the liberty, and the balance of power in the rest of

Europe.'[46] It would be the tragedy of the next two decades in Europe that Nicholas and Britain both sought to preserve the Sultan's dominion in the Near East, but that, despite the repeated assurances of Nesselrode, the ambassadors Count Lieven and Baron Brunnov, and, in mid 1844, even the personal assurances of Nicholas himself, the British government could not set aside its conviction that, at root, Nicholas wished to dismember the Ottoman Empire and seize Constantinople and the Straits for Russia. Unkiar-Skelessi was, as one noted scholar has commented:

a true turning-point in the attitude of English statesmen towards Russia. It bred in Palmerston a fatal hostility to Russia . . . The conversion of Stratford Canning [for many years the British ambassador to Constantinople] had preceded that of Palmerston, and the anti-Russian feeling of these two men was one profound cause of the Crimean War.[47]

Much effort on the part of Nicholas and his ministers in the two decades after Unkiar-Skelessi would thus be directed towards seeking an accommodation with Britain on the most pressing issue of the day, the Eastern Question. It is true that Nicholas never sought to achieve the sort of accommodation in his relations with Britain that he had reached with Austria and Prussia. But in the years after Unkiar-Skelessi he would seek an understanding with his British antagonists – even make concessions to them – in an effort to attain his major goal in the Near East: the protection of Russia's merchant shipping and the lessening of political tensions by preserving the Ottoman Empire. But anti-Russian feeling in Britain ran high. Especially in the years just after Unkiar-Skelessi, both the Foreign Secretary, Palmerston, and Britain's ambassador to Constantinople, Lord Ponsonby, became notorious for their anti-Russian sentiments, and their attitudes doomed any effort at conciliation on Russia's part.

Palmerston 'recovered his balance by 1836', one historian noted.[48] But his hostility towards Russia and, especially, towards Nicholas's policy in the Near East was intense while it lasted. Russia was in his view 'still more ambitious than strong and not less wily than ambitious, profiting by the weak compliances of its allies to strengthen itself daily at their expense and to their future detriment'.[49] But, if Palmerston's fear of Nicholas's aims in the Near East was only momentary, that of Lord Ponsonby, Britain's ambassador to the Porte, was far more durable. Ponsonby was possessed of a deep-seated hatred for Russia which coloured all of his decisions. He freely admitted that 'I have always treated as wholly erroneous the belief entertained by some that Russia could act with what people call moderation in these matters or cease for one moment to aim at the subjugation of Turkey.' Ponsonby would go so far as to urge that English warships be sent to the Black Sea and that Britain aid the natives of the Caucasus in their perennial struggles against Russia's efforts to subjugate them. In fact, in March 1834, Ponsonby succeeded in obtaining from the still russophobic Palmerston a 'discretionary order' which gave him the necessary authority to order British warships into the Straits and the Black Sea if he deemed it necessary. For eight months, until the Duke of Wellington succeeded in cancelling the order in November, the peace of the Near East, and perhaps of Europe, lay in the hands of a single ambassador about whom Lord Melbourne once remarked that his 'ridiculous russophobia . . . leads him to shut his eyes to everything else'.

In this situation, Nicholas's first effort to reduce tensions after the treaty of Unkiar-Skelessi came to nothing. In January 1834, he and the Turkish representative in St Petersburg, Akhmet-Pasha, concluded a convention which provided for the immediate withdrawal of Russian forces from the Danubian principalities; for full recognition by the Sultan of the Organic Statute, which recognized the establishment of native governments in that area under the nominal suzerainty of Turkey but under the guarantee of Russia; and for a sizeable reduction in the indemnity payments still owed by the Porte to Russia in consequence of the 1828–9 war.[50] Nicholas thus once again gave evidence of desiring no territorial acquisitions at the expense of the Ottoman Empire in Europe. But Palmerston was again suspicious because the convention had provided that a Russian garrison would remain in the fortress of Silestria for eight more years until the indemnity was fully paid, and because it allowed for a small frontier adjustment in the East which 'brought Russia closer to Kars and to the caravan route between Persia and the Black Sea coast'.[51] Palmerston proclaimed that the frontier adjustment 'would open a free passage for Russian troops in the direction of Bagdad', and regarded the continued presence of Russian forces in Silestria as part of the 'general desire we know to exist in the Russian government to establish a predominant influence in Greece . . . to make the policy of that country subservient to Russian objects'.[52]

Palmerston thus answered Nicholas's proclamation that he was withdrawing nearly all Russian troops from the Balkans by sending the notorious 'discretionary order' to Lord Ponsonby in Constantinople. At that point there seemed no end to his suspicions of Nicholas and of Russia. As he wrote to Sir William Temple:

Russia follows a system of attacking indiscriminately, on all sides, in part because of the personal character of the Emperor and, in part, as a consequence of her . . . system of government. She is erecting on the Åland Islands, not thirty miles' distance from Stockholm, a fortified camp with quarters for some 20,000 men . . . She is constructing fortresses along the Vistula, evidently for the purpose of threatening Austria and Prussia; she intrigues in order to hold some fortresses along the Danube . . . All these German conferences and measures seem to me as much Russian as Austrian.[53]

William IV turned Palmerston out of office in 1834, and temporarily replaced him with the Duke of Wellington, who sought immediately to cool Ponsonby's ardour for an anti-Russian policy in Constantinople and elsewhere. For nearly half a decade, the Eastern Question remained in the wings of the international political stage. But during these years, major changes occurred in the alignments of European courts which would have an impact upon the resolution of the Eastern Question when it again burst into flame following Mahmud's declaration of war on Mehemet Ali in 1839. For one thing, although Metternich was more than pleased with the entente of the three Northern Courts forged at Münchengrätz, he was far from satisfied to have Europe rigidly divided into two camps, France and Britain on one side, and Russia, Austria and Prussia on the other. As had always been his way, he tried to mediate, to negotiate, 'to act', as one scholar noted, 'as the umpire and balance between the two opposing forces'.[54] This was especially the case in regard to the Near East, an area in which he preferred not to see Austria become involved militarily. Metternich therefore sought to balance the Anglo-French entente against Russia. He even sought to expand the Münchengrätz agreement made between Russia and Austria on the Ottoman Empire to include Britain and France.[55] In 1834, however, the lines of conflict between East and West were too sharply drawn: British hostility towards Russia was too intense and Russian suspicion of Louis Philippe was too deep-seated for the East–West chasm to be bridged. The situation would be different, however, a half-decade later when war broke out between Mahmud II and Mehemet Ali.

During the years between 1833 and 1839, the entente between France and Britain, which had emerged in the wake of the upheavals of 1830, ran into rocky seas. They came into conflict in Greece over Palmerston's pressure for King Otto to grant a constitution to his subjects; they supported different factions in Spain; they had sharp differences of opinion about the final settlement between Holland and Belgium in 1838 and 1839; and finally, the French were as always wary about having to face alone British seapower in the Mediterranean.[56] At the same time, the French were beginning to see that they shared certain interests in common with Russia. Russia, after all, was in the end willing to see Mehemet Ali become independent of the Sultan. As Nicholas had said in 1833, 'it makes no difference to me whatsoever even if they let the

Egyptian Pasha have all of Syria'.[57] And, in 1839, Palmerston had come to realize that, where their interests did coincide, as in the Belgium issue, Russia and Britain could work together.[58] He had also come to realize that a Franco-Russian agreement was a dangerous possibility. As he wrote to Granville in June 1838, 'one great danger to Europe is a possibility of a combination between France and Russia'.[59]

For our purposes here, it will be sufficient to sketch in briefly the part Nicholas himself played in the Near Eastern crisis of 1838–41.[60] During the half-decade after the peace of Unkiar-Skelessi, the Sultan Mahmud II, anxious to avenge himself upon Mehemet Ali, had undertaken to modernize his armed forces with the aid of Prussia. The Prussian king had sent him a young officer, Helmuth von Moltke, who later won fame as the conqueror of France and Austria.[61] At the same time, Mehemet Ali, chafing to declare his complete independence from the Sultan, was restrained from doing so only by very direct pressure from the Great Powers.[62]

It was Mahmud II who broke the restraints imposed by the Great Powers, and in the spring of 1839 his troops invaded Syria despite von Moltke's warnings that his army was not yet ready for war. The Turkish armies thus crossed the Euphrates in April. By the end of June, over 10,000 were Ibrahim's prisoners, and nearly all of the Turkish artillery was in his hands.[63] At about the same time, the Turkish fleet sailed from the Straits to Alexandria and surrendered unconditionally to Mehemet Ali.[64] But fate spared Mahmud the shame of knowing total defeat at the hands of his hated foe, for he died on 30 June (NS) 1839, just before news of Ibrahim's victories reached Constantinople. His son, the sixteen-year-old Abdul Mejid, his fleet and army both in the hands of the enemy, immediately sought to open negotiations with the Egyptian Pasha to end the war.[65]

Ibrahim's swift and total victory over the Turkish forces presented the Great Powers with a dilemma which demanded immediate solution, for none, except perhaps France, wanted to see Mehemet Ali installed in Constantinople. It was a crisis which they had foreseen for some time, however, and for which they had earlier sought solutions. Nicholas's major concern, as always, was to ensure access to the Straits for his Empire's mercantile shipping, and to preserve a weak power on his southern flank. As a result, when Mehemet Ali had first threatened to declare his independence from the Sultan in 1838, Nicholas was well-prepared to meet this challenge to the stability which he had imposed upon the Near East five years earlier. His Black Sea fleet was ready to move at a moment's notice, and three infantry corps stood poised to descend upon the Bosphorus from their headquarters at Sevastopol and

Kherson in southern Russia.[66] Equally important, Nicholas had reassured himself of the diplomatic support of Austria. Metternich, as we have seen, had sought to expand the joint Austro-Russian guarantee of the Ottoman Empire into a Europeanwide agreement by proposing that France and Britain be invited to join in the resolutions reached at Münchengrätz, something which Nicholas and Nesselrode had studiously avoided. Therefore, Nicholas's meeting with Metternich at Teplitz in July 1838 was especially significant in enabling him to face the crises created by Ibrahim's victories over the Turkish armies a year later.

The meeting at Teplitz was one of a series of gatherings between the rulers of Russia, Prussia and Austria, and their ministers, which had occurred regularly since 1833. Although this meeting lasted for several days, probably its most significant moment was on 22 July, when Nicholas and Metternich were closeted for nearly three hours to agree on principles regarding the crisis in the Near East. 'Everything . . . is clear; everything is uniform in terms of principles,' Metternich wrote.[67] Indeed, there was a familiar stability at Teplitz in which they could all take comfort at a time of pressing problems elsewhere. 'Everything turns and alters except these people, including myself, who holds a place in this framework of immobility,' Metternich wrote to his wife at the time.[68]

But the agreement which Nicholas reached with Metternich at Teplitz was not designed to exclude France and Britain from a commonly arrived at settlement of the Eastern Question. Although he remained suspicious of the two maritime powers, he was nevertheless prepared to reach an accommodation with them. He was not, however, willing to submit the position which Russia had gained by the Unkiar-Skelessi treaty to general European discussion. Nor was he willing to allow European powers to limit the action he considered called for on Russia's part in the Near East. The Russian policy which emerged from the Teplitz meeting thus took the form of a declaration to be made first to Britain, and then, after Nicholas's ambassador to the Court of St James's had evaluated its impact in London, it would be made to France. Nicholas thus reasserted, to Britain and France, the position which Russia had won at Unkiar-Skelessi, urged them to seek a resolution of the Eastern Question which would prevent Mehemet Ali from declaring his independence of the Sultan, and warned that Russia would not hesitate to intervene, as she had done in 1833, should the continued existence of the Ottoman Empire be threatened.[69]

To Palmerston, Nicholas's declaration seemed a direct challenge. Still smarting from the diplomatic hand-slapping that he had suffered in

1836 as a result of Russia's seizure of the *Vixen*, a British merchant ship loaded with contraband munitions for the Circassian natives,[70] he sought to open a European conference where Nicholas might be forced to subordinate his Near Eastern policy to the joint decisions of the major powers. And, when he failed, he sought to deceive Nicholas's ambassador, Count Pozzo di Borgo, into attending a meeting of the European powers at his residence at 10 Downing Street. Thus, in September 1838, when di Borgo arrived for a scheduled private interview with Palmerston, he found the ministers of Austria, Prussia and France there as well. Palmerston then urged that they discuss how best to resolve the Near East crisis, a suggestion which di Borgo met with stony silence. Similar reactions by the Austrian and Prussian ambassadors destroyed Palmerston's efforts to hold an impromptu conference even before it could begin.[71] Nicholas and his crafty ambassador had succeeded once again in avoiding a European discussion of Russia's favoured position in the Near East as self-appointed protector of the Ottoman Empire. As Nesselrode wrote, 'In international politics, nothing is more dangerous than the desire to discuss eventualities, more or less remote, which perhaps may never come to pass in the first place.' The Russian government, he added, did not see the necessity, 'either in principle or in practice', for a European conference on the Eastern Question at that point, since, by that time, Mehemet Ali had been restrained from declaring independence.[72]

France's reaction to Russia's declaration of principles, despite the fact that, as one scholar has noted, it was 'communicated with offensive delay to the Paris cabinet',[73] was much more positive than had been the case with Palmerston. In early June (NS), even before the Teplitz conference, Louis Philippe had indicated that Russia and France could cooperate on the Eastern Question and promised to use his influence to restrain Mehemet Ali.[74] And while the French were by no means willing to break away completely from the British on the Eastern Question, Louis Philippe's prime minister, Count Molé, had a very open and candid discussion with the Russian ambassador in August, pointing out that 'in the affairs of the Orient we cannot attach the same importance as does England to combating your supremacy'.[75] It thus appeared that there might be some ground for agreement between Russia and France on the Near East in mid 1838. Certainly that was the course which di Borgo urged upon Nicholas and Nesselrode. But Nicholas appears to have been unable to set aside his still-festering dislike of Louis Philippe's régime. More important, he did not believe in its stability, a conviction that would be justified in 1848. And he did not consider that the French government, with its frequent changes of ministers and led by what he considered to be a capricious ruler, could carry out an independent and assertive foreign policy. On the other hand, despite their many differences, Nicholas did believe that Palmerston could do so. As Brunnov summed up his Emperor's attitudes to Lord Palmerston, he established 'an invariable distinction between France and England. The former is not a regular power upon which one can rely; the latter is a power with which one can negotiate because, since it is founded on lawful bases, it will always fulfil and respect the agreements which it makes.' 'These are my very words,' Nicholas later commented in the margin of Brunnov's report.[76] In 1839, Nicholas therefore turned to Britain and not to France in his search for entente.

As a result, in May 1839, Nicholas's eldest son and heir, the Grand Duke Aleksandr Nikolaevich, visited England. His visit left a favourable impression upon his hosts and improved the atmosphere between the two powers. 'I was filled with admiration for his bearing, his reserve, his easy manner and, at the same time, his kindness, which proclaimed itself in every word and in all of his manners,' wrote di Borgo.[77] At the same time, the gracious nature of the Grand Duke's English hosts led them to cease all attacks against Russia and Russian policy in the press during his visit.[78] It was in this atmosphere of momentarily lessened tensions that Nicholas chose to send one of his most capable diplomats, Baron Brunnov, to London for direct discussions of the new crisis which had arisen in the Near East as a result of the defeat which Ibrahim had inflicted upon the Sultan's armies in Syria. Nicholas seems to have concluded that, since neither Russia nor Britain had succeeded in dominating the Ottoman Empire completely, it perhaps would be better to seek a means for cooperation in the Near East.[79]

Nicholas thus instructed Brunnov 'to invite the British government to tell us candidly what it thinks, what it wants, and where it wishes to go'.[80] Brunnov carried with him a number of concessions which, Nicholas hoped, would clear the atmosphere, and perhaps pave the way for Anglo-Russian cooperation in solving the Eastern Question. In fact, Nicholas had instructed Brunnov to tell Palmerston very frankly that the Russian government would be willing to establish an entente on the basis of the maritime powers renouncing the idea of proclaiming the inviolability of all possessions of the Ottoman Empire; agreeing to the closure of the Dardanelles and the Bosphorus to warships at all times as a principle of the international law of Europe, binding upon all powers without exception; and renouncing the intention of sending French and British warships into the Sea of Marmora to protect Constantinople.[81] Should Palmerston be willing to consider such proposals, Nicholas instructed Brunnov to tell him that Russia would in return guarantee collectively, with all powers, the arrangement concluded between Turkey and

Mehemet Ali; would promise not to renew the treaty of Unkiar-Skelessi when it expired in 1841; and if she considered it necessary to send military forces through the Bosphorus to defend the Ottoman Empire, would do so only on the basis of a mandate from all Europe, in the name of all the major powers.

When Baron Brunnov arrived in London on 3 (15) September 1839, he found Palmerston in a more agreeable mood. But the Russian proposals took Britain's Foreign Secretary completely by surprise. 'I cannot describe to you the sensation which these words [Nicholas's proposals] produced upon Lord Palmerston,' Brunnov wrote to Nesselrode a few days after his arrival, adding that 'everything about him betrayed both surprise and admiration'.[82] Not only Palmerston, but the entire British Cabinet, was thrown into a turmoil by the proposals. Britain was in the throes of an economic crisis which occupied their most immediate attention. Beyond that, however, it seemed to Brunnov that the British ministers had no clear-cut plan for settling the Turko-Egyptian conflict, and he was convinced that 'for the moment the English neither can, nor even wish to, do anything' concerning the Near East crisis.[83] Still, Brunnov's overall impression of the British attitude was favourable and, by the end of September, the prospects for an agreement looked more promising. At that point, he reported that 'England is not yet with us, but she is no longer entirely with France either'.[84] Brunnov's convictions were further strengthened the following month by conversations with the Duke of Wellington in which the duke referred to the Anglo-French entente as 'a *papier-mâché* alliance which draws near its end'.[85]

Part of Brunnov's limited success in September 1839 was the result of his own considerable talents as a diplomat and the fact that Palmerston and Melbourne seemed ready at least to consider alternatives to an Anglo-French entente in the Near East. Brunnov's success was also in some measure the result of efforts by Lord Durham, former ambassador to St Petersburg, and Lord Clanricarde, Britain's current representative at the Winter Palace. Both admitted to having fallen victim, in some degree, to the considerable charm which Nicholas exercised upon foreign ambassadors,[86] and Durham, who had gone to St Petersburg a convinced opponent of Russia and of Nicholas, had become something of a russophile by the time of his return.[87] 'All the Durhams have become Russian,' Brunnov reported to Nesselrode.[88]

By the end of September (early October NS), the combination of these factors led the British Cabinet to agree to some of the proposals which Brunnov had brought to London. Palmerston declared that Britain would be willing to act in concert with the other European Powers, and especially with Russia, in an effort to resolve the Turko-Egyptian conflict.

Further, Britain recognized Russia's right to send troops to aid the Sultan should Mehemet Ali threaten Constantinople. But Palmerston insisted that Britain must reserve the right to take part in such measures as Russia might undertake to aid the Porte. Specifically, should Russian warships and troops enter the Bosphorus, some English ships must enter the Dardanelles. Otherwise, Palmerston warned, it would surely mean the fall of the Whig Cabinet should his government agree to the exclusion of Britain from such an enterprise.[89] This was the issue which remained to be resolved.

Brunnov's response to Palmerston is worth noting at some length because it embodied a very precise statement of Nicholas's policy towards the Near East. He told Palmerston:

Suppose that the geographical position of England were similar to our own, and that your trading fleet was forced to pass through a narrow canal in order to maintain its relations with the rest of the world. And imagine to yourself that Russian warships would be stationed at the entrance to this canal. I leave it to you to imagine what your merchants would say! Do you, or do you not, wish to preserve the Ottoman Empire? If you value its existence, then leave Russia in peace, respect the closure of the Dardanelles, and do not force our Emperor to seize them. For, mark my words well, on the very day that you force a passage through the Straits, Russia will set her armies in motion and the final hour of the Ottoman Empire will have struck.[90]

Nicholas had repeated these words in person or through his ambassadors to every monarch in Europe, almost from the day of his accession. He would repeat them again himself, almost verbatim, to his English hosts when he visited London and Windsor in 1844.[91] A decade later, Western Europe would learn that he had meant exactly what he said.

Unable to reach a full agreement with Palmerston, and convinced that the Melbourne cabinet was on the point of collapse, Brunnov left the English 'to sink up to their necks in their own muck', and returned to his post as Russian ambassador in Stuttgart. When Nicholas sent Brunnov back to London in mid December to continue the negotiations, the nature of the discussions had been altered so as to invite the participation of Austria, Prussia and France.[92] Brunnov had discussed the Russian and British proposals with Metternich in the interval between his first and second journey to London,[93] with the result that Austria sent Baron Neumann as Plenipotentiary to London.[94] In conjunction with the Prussian representative Bülow, Brunnov and Neumann hoped to produce a convention on the Eastern Question to which all parties could agree.

Negotiations extended over a period of several months and progressed much more slowly than Nicholas had hoped. By May 1840, agreement still had not been reached, and Nicholas, accustomed to the more direct sort of negotiations which he had conducted in the past with Prussia and Austria, gave some indication of his frustration at dealing with a parliamentary government by noting in the margin of one of Brunnov's reports that 'all this is wretched and I see absolutely no end to all this chatter. I am losing patience and, if everything is not finished within a month, then I will think of other measures for the decision of this matter in accordance with our dignity.'[95]

But Nicholas could not hasten the pace of negotiations, and preferring not to be the one to destroy the possibility of a settlement of the Near East crisis, he encouraged Brunnov to persist. Finally, on 3 (15) July 1840, the first London Convention was signed by representatives of Austria, Britain, Prussia, Russia and Turkey. By the first London Convention, Mahmud's successor agreed to offer Mehemet Ali hereditary title to Egypt, along with life-long title to Acre and Syria. Beyond that, Russia, Prussia, Austria and Britain agreed among themselves that, should Mehemet Ali refuse their offer, then they would force it upon him, cut sea communications between Syria and Egypt, and act to defend Constantinople and the integrity of the Ottoman Empire.[96] Most important, the treaty of Unkiar-Skelessi was dead. It would not be renewed when it expired in 1841.

The unknown factor in the diplomatic equation in mid 1840, of course, was France, which had not signed the convention and was not even aware that it was being signed until later in July. France had been offered opportunities to join the discussions in London earlier in the year, but Guizot, her ambassador to St James's, and the new Prime Minister, Thiers, had remained aloof, largely because, as Mehemet Ali's strongest supporter among the European powers, France would not agree to any coercion of the Egyptian Pasha once he had called a halt to hostilities in Syria in July 1839, under pressure from the five European Powers. When the French were told of what had transpired in London, there was, at first, much talk of war. Thiers and Louis Philippe determined to follow a policy of isolation from the rest of Europe and to carry on extensive preparations for an outbreak of hostilities.[97] Thus, the four powers were still faced with a serious dilemma once they had signed the Convention: they needed to put the pact of July 1840 into effect and, at the same time, to neutralize the bellicose attitudes of a French government deeply insulted by the conclusion of a pact without her signature. But the winds of opinion shifted quickly in France. Brunnov's ironic characterization of French policy in regard to the Eastern Question was that it consisted of '*evading* – under the [first] ministry of Soult; of *threatening* – under Thiers; of *begging* – under the present ministry [that of Guizot who had just succeeded Thiers]; that is how France has thought to direct the great affairs of the Near East'.[98] France thus took an active part in the discussions the next year in London which led to the conclusion of the second London Convention on 1 (13) July 1841.

During the year which separated the first and second London Conventions, the issue of Mehemet Ali's relationship to the Sultan had finally been resolved. Confident of the full support of France (which, in the end, he did not receive), the Egyptian Pasha had refused the conditions offered him by the London Convention in 1840. But this time, Mehemet Ali and his son had to face the guns of British and Austrian men-of-war, not those of the Sultan's armies. On land, as one historian noted, 'the first of oriental generals, who had hitherto been invincible, was vanquished by a handful of British marines, a few thousand Turkish soldiers, and some bands of hastily armed mountaineers'.[99] By 16 January 1841 (NS), Mehemet Ali had submitted unconditionally to the Sultan. The conflict between the two was ended.

Mehemet Ali had come to grief because, when the moment of truth arrived, the French would not risk a war with other European powers on his behalf. It now remained for all of Europe to settle the Eastern Question with the participation of France. The last half of 1840 was thus spent in bringing France back into the European concert. By mid 1841, after considerable discussion and wrangling in London and Constantinople, the powers had produced an acceptable draft of what would become the second London Convention. The Sultan recovered Syria, Crete and Arabia, while Mehemet Ali's only gain was confirmation of his hereditary status as Pasha of Egypt. The conflict between the Sultan and his rebellious vassal was over. Perhaps even more important in the eyes of France and Britain, Nicholas had repudiated his claim to a protectorate over the Ottoman Empire and had torn up the Treaty of Unkiar-Skelessi. Most important of all, the Bosphorus and the Dardanelles were closed to all foreign warships in time of peace.[100] As Professor Marriott remarked many years ago, 'Turkey was rescued both from the hostility of Mehemet Ali and from the friendship of Russia.'[101] Nicholas had thus forfeited the privileged position in the Ottoman Empire that he had gained in 1833, though he had preserved all other privileges which Russia had won in earlier agreements with the Porte. But he had, in his view at least, substituted for the Treaty of Unkiar-Skelessi a European guarantee that would defend Russia's southern coast and her mercantile fleet from attack and assure her vessels of access to Western ports. Nicholas had 'the full conviction that the Porte, as the guardian of the two Straits, would not fail to fulfil its engagements in regard to Russia to the letter'.[102]

The first and second Conventions of London thus resolved for the moment the conflict between the Great Powers in the Near East and for a decade the issue would lie dormant. The question of Nicholas's relations with Britain and France was not resolved, however, and there still lingered a suspicion of him in the West. Where France was concerned, Nicholas remained aloof from Louis Philippe's government as long as it existed. In the case of Britain, however, Nicholas continued his efforts to improve relations and sought to come to some agreement about the conflicts in the Near East, Central Asia and elsewhere. For this reason, he went to London himself in June 1844.

We do not know for certain whether it was the Russians or the British who took the initiative in proposing the visit. If we accept the accounts of Bloomfield, Britain's ambassador to St Petersburg, and of Baron Brunnov, by then Russia's ambassador to the Court of St James's, we encounter the remarkable coincidence that overtures for the visit were made simultaneously, and somewhat casually, in both capitals on 11 (23) January 1844. On that evening, according to Bloomfield's account, he attended a ball at the Winter Palace where Nicholas reportedly mentioned that he would like to visit England again as he had not been there since 1817. Baron Brunnov, however, would have us believe that the initiative for the visit came from the British. According to his version, on 11 (23) January, he dined at Lord Aberdeen's in London and, during the course of the dinner conversation, Sir Robert Peel mentioned that he hoped Russia's Emperor would soon visit England.[103]

Regardless of who made the first overtures, it is clear that a few weeks later it was Sir Robert Peel who took a further step in preparing the way. On the evening of 2 March (NS), Peel and Baron Brunnov attended the annual dinner of the Russian Trading Company at the London Tavern, where, after proposing toasts to Britain's Queen, the Russian representative presiding at the gathering again ventured the hope that his Emperor would visit England in the foreseeable future. In reply, Peel rose to propose a toast 'to eternal friendship between Great Britain and Russia'. Peel's words created a great deal of speculation when they were reported in the British press. Although he may have spoken without first consulting Britain's Foreign Secretary, it seems evident that Lord Aberdeen shared Peel's view on the need for improved relations with Russia. When Baron Brunnov raised the matter with him the next day, Lord Aberdeen agreed enthusiastically with Peel's statement and set forth his views in quite outspoken terms: 'Nothing could be better than Peel's words. I am delighted that he spoke so positively about our "cordial agreement" with Russia.'[104]

Once Britain's ministers had made public their support for Nicholas's proposed visit, an official invitation soon followed, and despite the fact, as she later wrote to her uncle, that she was at first 'extremely against the visit',[105] Queen Victoria agreed to receive Nicholas in late May or early June. Nicholas accepted the invitation in early April, but gave no indication as to when he intended to arrive in London. By the time Bloomfield received word from Count Nesselrode on 12 May that the Emperor had left St Petersburg, Nicholas had already been on his way for some twelve hours. Thus, it was Nicholas's courier who brought word to the British that he was *en route* for England. Nicholas had arranged it so that the British had just less than forty-eight hours in which to prepare for his arrival.[106]

At a time when such state visits were often planned with meticulous care, it may perhaps seem strange that Nicholas took such pains to ensure that his hosts would have the minimum time to make preparations. His sudden departure from St Petersburg, however, and his plan to give the British only the most brief advance notice, were much in keeping with his personality and manner of conducting state affairs. Accustomed as he was to setting off on hurried and sometimes unannounced tours of Empire, Nicholas, on occasion, planned state visits to neighbouring monarchs in the same way.

Yet habit was quite probably not the only reason for the secretive manner in which he sometimes planned journeys to foreign courts. Ever since the Polish Insurrection of 1830–31, he had lived in apprehension of being assassinated by Polish nationalists. Count Benkendorf recounts an episode when Nicholas gave his suite notice one evening in October 1834 that they were to be ready to leave with him for Berlin in exactly an hour. Travelling incognito on that occasion, Nicholas arrived at the Prussian Court unannounced and totally unexpected.[107] A year later, his apprehension about possible assassination had reached such a point that, before leaving for an announced meeting with the Prussian king, he wrote for his son and heir a testament filled with advice on how to rule Russia in the event of his death.[108] By 1844, Nicholas may have lost some of this apprehension, but traces of it remained and certainly may account for the secrecy with which he surrounded his departure for Britain.

Nicholas thus arrived at Woolwich on 1 June (NS), travelling incognito as 'Count Orlov'. Not even Baron Brunnov knew the full details of his arrival plans, and as a result spent an entire day in Woolwich awaiting his master's arrival. It was not until ten o'clock on a clear, moonlit night that Nicholas, wearing the pale-grey travelling cloak he habitually wore ever since the Turkish campaign of 1828, disembarked from the Dutch steamer *Cyclops*.[109] Within an hour of setting foot on British soil, he was in London. Once in England's capital, he did not go to Buckingham Palace, where Queen Victoria had prepared rooms for him, but went immediately to the Russian Embassy at Ashburnham House. Although it was already well past midnight by the time he settled in his rooms, Nicholas, in his characteristically direct manner, requested pen and paper and immediately dispatched a note to the Prince Consort saying that he wished to meet the Queen at her earliest convenience.[110] For even a visiting monarch to awaken the Prince Consort in the early-morning hours may well appear both inconsiderate and rude, as, in fact, it was. But questions of time and place had little significance for Nicholas. He often worked into the early hours and rarely arose later than 7 a.m. Indeed, he even made rather a point of his spartan life on his journeys, carrying a straw-filled leather pallet upon which he slept. Despite the luxurious accommodations which Brunnov offered him at Ashburnham House, he once again insisted that a cot with his pallet be set up before he slept that night. He would astonish the Queen's servants at Windsor Castle two days later by repeating the same ritual there.

Nicholas remained in England until 9 June (NS). During that time, he had a number of conversations with the Queen and Prince Albert, and Sir Robert Peel and Lord Aberdeen, as well as with the leaders of the opposition, Palmerston and Melbourne. As we noted earlier, the main purpose of his visit was clearly political: to explore the possibilities for improving Russia's relations with Britain, and, most of all, to discuss the problem ever-present in his mind: the future of the Ottoman Empire. Believing that there was no real basis for friendship between the British and the French because of England's growing concern about the foreign policy of the July Monarchy, Nicholas appears to have hoped to improve Russia's relations with Britain at the expense of Louis Philippe's government. Certainly he made this point clearly enough in one of his conversations at Windsor when he commented that, 'I highly prize England; but for what the French choose to say about me, I care not at all – I spit upon it.'[111]

Nicholas seems to have lost no opportunity to engage in frank discussions with his British hosts, particularly during the days from 3 to 7 June (NS) that he spent at Windsor Castle. On one occasion, he spoke so loudly and freely with Peel near some open windows at Windsor Castle that those outside could hear all that was said. According to one account, Peel was obliged to ask him to move to the other side of the room before continuing their conversation.[112] The essence of Nicholas's concern was his fear that the Ottoman Empire might collapse despite everyone's efforts to preserve it. As he told Aberdeen,

Turkey is a dying man. We may endeavour to keep him alive, but we shall not succeed. He will, he must, die. That will be a critical moment. I foresee that I shall have to put my armies into motion and Austria must do the same . . . In such a case, must not England be on the spot with the whole of her maritime forces? Thus, a Russian army, an Austrian army, a great English fleet, all congregated in those parts. So many powder barrels close to the fire, how shall one prevent the sparks from catching . . . ? I do not claim one inch of Turkish soil, but neither will I allow that any other shall have an inch of it . . . We cannot now stipulate as to what shall be done with Turkey when she is dead. Such stipulations would only hasten her death. I shall therefore do all in my power to maintain the *status quo*. But, nevertheless, we should keep the possible and eventual case of her collapse honestly and reasonably before our eyes. We ought to deliberate reasonably, and endeavour to come to a straightforward and honest understanding on the subject.[113]

In the course of his discussions with his British hosts, Nicholas's efforts were mainly directed towards reaching just such a 'straightforward and honest understanding'. As Queen Victoria recorded, Nicholas did not want to develop friendly ties with England 'to the exclusion of others',[114] but he nevertheless seems to have sought a more binding agreement than the British were prepared to give. It was to be a tragedy for Europe that Nicholas and his advisers evidently regarded the conversations held in London to be formal statements of policy, while the British appear to have regarded them as simply an exchange of views on questions of mutual interest and not as something binding in any formal sense.[115] Thus, if Nicholas left Britain on the evening of 9 June (NS) with the idea that he had made a great and staunch friend of the young British Queen, or that he had dispelled fully the many suspicions which the British still harboured about the Russian colossus, he was sorely mistaken. Certainly Queen Victoria found him impressive. As she wrote to her uncle, Leopold, King of the Belgians:

He is stern and severe – with fixed principles of *duty* which *nothing* on earth will make him change; very *clever* I do *not* think him, and his mind is an un-civilized one; his education has been neglected; politics and military concerns are the only things he takes great interest in; the arts and all softer occupations he is insensible to, but he is sincere, I am certain, *sincere* even in his most despotic acts, from a sense that that *is* the *only* way to govern.[116]

Nicholas's British hosts had generally found him far more civil and charming than they had expected, and he received an unmistakably warm welcome. But since he and the British did not enter into any formal agreements, his visit and his miscalculation of the extent to which the British were willing to commit themselves to giving formal assurances about the future actually laid the bases for future conflicts. Just how serious these misunderstandings and conflicts were became very evident just a decade later. Within ten years of his warm farewell to the Prince Consort on the Woolwich dock, Nicholas would indeed put his armies in southern Russia 'into motion', as he had warned Aberdeen, and the British and Russians would meet as enemies on the blood-soaked fields of the Crimea.

3 . The Fruits of Entente in Eastern and Central Europe

Conflicts with the maritime powers of the West marked much of Nicholas's reign. Although he reached a brief accommodation with France during his first years on the throne, and, intermittently, with Britain during the 1840s, the causes for dispute far outnumbered the bases for agreement. For nearly two decades, from 1830 until 1848, Nicholas rejected the July Monarchy as illegitimate, and his relations with Napoleon III were scarcely better. Equally important, though he respected England and personally had many English tastes, Nicholas always harboured a fundamental distrust of the British constitutional system. His was a personal type of diplomacy, one of agreements worked out in direct discussions with other rulers, and he could never really negotiate with, or even truly comprehend, a government which depended upon approval for its decisions by an elected parliament. Further, Russia and Britain simply came into conflict in too many areas of the globe for them to work out any sort of long-standing accord. British statesmen continually perceived a challenge to their ventures in India from Nicholas's policies in Central Asia, and neither power could fully trust the other in the Mediterranean and the Near East.

Nicholas's relations with Prussia and Austria, however, were far closer. Austria and Russia had conflicting aspirations in the Balkans, to be sure, and by the end of Nicholas's reign, these would lead Austria to deny Russia her support in the Crimean War. But the common interests of the three 'Northern Courts', as they were often known, far outnumbered the causes for conflict, especially in the 1830s and 1840s. Nicholas was closely tied to Prussia by sentiment and by his marriage to a Prussian princess, as well as by the marriages of others in his family to Germans. He found Prussian militarism to his liking and felt completely at ease and at home in the Prussian Court. All three powers were further united after 1830 by their fear of revolutions in the West and their desire to make common cause in a defence against them. And, after 1831, they were joined by their common need to suppress revolutionary sentiments in their Polish domains.

In 1833, the Münchengrätz agreements signalled the consummation of the closer union that all three powers would be at pains to preserve throughout the next two decades. Fear of revolution quite probably held them together most closely of all; both Austria and Prussia had to maintain sizeable forces facing the West, for both feared a revolutionary France, having suffered the attacks of Napoleon at the turn of the century. In addition, Austria had continually to be on guard against upheavals in her Italian domains. Thus, should revolution attack from the East – from Poland in the case of Prussia, or from Galicia or Hungary in the case of Austria – it would be Nicholas's armies which would be needed to stem the revolutionary tide.

But although the entente of the three Northern Courts had definite political and diplomatic advantages for Austria and Prussia, its preservation was especially close to Nicholas's heart. Perhaps more than any other statesman in Eastern or Central Europe, he remained faithful to it and to its principles. The entente with Austria and Prussia was for Nicholas a bulwark against the revolutionary menace of Europe, and assured him of much-needed allies in his conflicts with the maritime powers in the Near East. As he once commented to the Comte de Ficquelmont, the Austrian ambassador to St Petersburg, 'the union and the steadfastness of the three allies will always serve as the sole fulcrum of the social order and as the last anchor of safety for the monarchical cause'.[117] Nicholas's relations with Austria and Prussia during the years between Münchengrätz and the revolutions of 1848 were thus concerned more with maintaining a close relationship between their Courts than with resolving serious conflicts (as was the case in his relations with Britain), or maintaining an uneasy peace in the midst of many diplomatic tensions (as was the case with France). The three Northern Courts remained loyal allies, and although there was continuing sentiment in Vienna in favour of renewing Austria's traditional alliance with England during these years,[118] preservation of the alliance with Russia continued to receive first priority in the minds of Austrian statesmen. As far as the Prussian government was concerned, the entente between Russia and Austria, which Prussia had joined at Berlin in late 1833, was 'the basis of peace and of world civilization'.[119]

A close union with Austria and Prussia was undoubtedly of considerable value to Nicholas in his conflicts with France and Britain over the future of the Ottoman Empire and his self-appointed role as the Sultan's protector in the 1830s. At the same time, Nicholas expressed a willingness to assume something of a similar role in defending Austria and Prussia against the threats of revolution. The declarations at Münchengrätz and Berlin had made the three powers' mutual interest in erecting a barrier against revolution quite explicit, and conversations between the three monarchs had even specified the areas which each was to defend, although such commitments were not written into the declarations. Austria was to mount a vigilant watch against revolutionary attacks in Italy, Switzerland,

Spain and Portugal, and thus would have the major voice in determining a mutual policy in those areas. Prussia's responsibilities were to guard against revolution in Northern Germany and Holland, while Russia was to serve as the reserve force of the entente in guarding against revolution in Western Europe, and at the same time agreed to assume the heavy responsibility of defending Poland, Hungary and the Balkans, 'from the Pruth and the Danube to the Bosphorus', against revolutionary attacks.[120]

Such commitments were burdensome ones, but Nicholas was also willing to assume further obligations. In particular, by the end of 1833, he had announced to the Prussian Court that he was ready 'at the first request of the Prussian government, to fly to its aid in a struggle against insurgents'.[121] Perhaps most important, Nicholas and his advisers saw one of the 'most criminal' aspirations among liberal forces in Germany as being 'to succeed in the unification of Germany'.[122] It was with this in mind that Nicholas ordered his ambassadors and consular officials in Germany to report in considerable detail on the activities of student corporations (*Burschenschaften*) in various parts of Germany. Equally important, he made nearly as explicit a commitment to Austria in early 1835 when, on the death of the Emperor Franz and the accession of the new Emperor Ferdinand, he promised 'to consider in the future the conservation and the internal tranquillity of the two Empires [Russia and Austria], as well as their external security, a question of mutual interest', and committed to this goal 'all the resources and all the power with which Providence had endowed him'.[123] Two years later, he made the commitment even more explicit when he ordered his ambassador in Vienna, Tatishchev, to state 'that *in any eventuality*, Austria can count on Russia, for the Emperor will never forget that which he promised at München-grätz'.[124]

But although all three rulers feared revolution and sought to guard against it, neither Friedrich Wilhelm III, his son Friedrich Wilhelm IV nor the Austrian Emperor Ferdinand were as rigid in their opposition to revolution or as vigilant in their watch for its earliest signs as was Nicholas. Nicholas even instructed his ambassadors in the West to be continually on the watch for even the slightest signs of revolutionary disturbances and to include comments on the 'revolutionary movement' in their dispatches.[125] For Nicholas's attitudes towards revolution allowed no murmur of dissent to be heard in areas where he feared that revolution might appear. Nowhere, perhaps, were his paternal and firm sentiments against dissent more evident than in his speeches to the Poles. In the autumn of 1835, Nicholas visited Warsaw and received a delegation of Polish citizens with the comment, 'I know, gentlemen, that you want to

present a speech to me; I even know its contents and, in order to save
you from the necessity of being false, I desire that your speech not be
given in my presence . . . I know that your feelings are not such as you
would like to have me believe.' Nicholas then continued:

At my command a citadel is being erected here and I declare to you that in the
event of the slightest disturbance I will order the destruction of your city; I
shall demolish Warsaw and, of course, I will not rebuild it. Believe me, gentlemen [he concluded], to belong to Russia and to be under her patronage is true
happiness. If you will conduct yourselves properly, if you will fulfil all your
obligations, then my fatherly solicitousness will extend to all and, in spite of
everything that has happened, my government will always be concerned about
your welfare.[126]

To reassure his allies of his high regard for their close relations with
Russia, Nicholas travelled on a number of occasions to Prussia and
Austria to exercise that personal diplomacy upon which he relied so
extensively. In late October 1834, he visited Berlin incognito, giving his
suite only one hour's notice of his planned departure,[127] to spend almost
two weeks at the Prussian Court where Aleksandra Fedorovna was
visiting her relatives.[128] If we are to believe Count Benkendorf, there was
another factor in Nicholas's concern to visit the courts and capitals of
his allies at various intervals, and this was a desire to offset negative
portrayals in the press. For, in his view, and in the opinion of his advisers,
the Prussian press had assumed a particularly hostile attitude towards
him in 1834, a view which Benkendorf, at least, believed to be the result
of the 'malice and spite of the liberals'.[129]

Nicholas did much the same thing in Austria the next year, following
a number of requests by Metternich and the new Emperor Ferdinand
for reassurance about Russia's commitments. As a result, after a meeting
of the three monarchs at Teplitz, Nicholas suddenly announced to
Metternich that he would visit Vienna. 'Write to your wife,' Nicholas
told the Austrian chancellor, and 'I shall be the carrier of your letter'.[130]
Nicholas then left for Vienna, where he spent the weekend paying visits to
the Dowager Empress, to Metternich's wife the Princess Melanie and a
number of others. He was cheered by the crowds of Vienna,[131] and
according to the Princess Melanie he showed to all 'the most exquisite
tact and most perfect propriety'.[132]

Nicholas's relations with the other two absolute monarchies of Europe
were thus very close during the years between Münchengrätz and the
revolutions of 1848. With Austria, there were periodic conflicts as both
Nicholas and Metternich sought to play the dominant role in European
politics, and as Metternich's efforts to serve as the mediator between

Britain and Russia on occasion produced moments of tension. With Prussia, however, as a result of the monarch's personal friendship and their common love of the army, Nicholas's relations were so close that, in 1834, Prussian and Russian troops held a joint military review at Kalish on the border of Prussia. So intimate were the relations between the two powers at the time that a sizeable portion of the Guards regiments brought from St Petersburg for the occasion were sent by sea to Danzig and then marched to Kalish through Prussian territory.[133]

During the 1840s, the pressures which had helped to bring the three Northern Courts together became more threatening and their desire to mount a common defence against the threat of revolution perhaps served even to intensify revolutionary sentiment. Progressive and radical sentiments in Prussia and in Germany could not be suppressed; in Austria's Italian and Hungarian domains, demands of nationalist groups seeking autonomy or independence intensified. Poles at the Hôtel Lambert in Paris continued their verbal attacks against Nicholas, as well as making one attempt on his life in Poznań in 1843 and another possible one at Windsor Castle in 1844.[134] And, in Spain and Portugal, conflicts between the forces of left and right continued.

In this atmosphere, Austria and Prussia were forced to rely upon Russia more than ever, for there was a stability and apparent tranquillity about Nicholas's Russia that other states appeared to have lost. Further, there was the matter of Russia's vast military strength in Eastern Europe, and even as early as 1834 there were observers in Europe who believed that Prussia had participated in the Kalish manoeuvres not because the king wished it so, but because he could not refuse.[135] Relations between Russia and Austria cooled for a time in the late 1830s and early 1840s (though never so much as to threaten the existence of the entente produced at Münchengrätz), but with the revolts of 1846 in Galicia and in Kraków, they became closer than ever. Both Austria and Prussia had come to rely upon Nicholas and his armies as a vital defence against revolution, a force which they could call upon in the final moment of crisis to shift the balance in their favour should it be necessary. Even in the 1830s, the Prussian government had begun to send to St Petersburg reports about the revolutionary movements in Germany and measures taken to repress them.[136] And, throughout the 1840s, the dependence seems to have become more pronounced, especially after the accession of Friedrich Wilhelm IV, Nicholas's brother-in-law and close friend 'Fritz', to the Prussian throne in 1840. While Nicholas had always been at some pains to give the impression that he regarded Friedrich Wilhelm III as a 'father' and a mentor, the roles were reversed for a time after 1840. 'Fritz' wrote to Nicholas in great detail of his plans, informed him of internal measures with which he proposed to stem the tide of revolution, and respectfully listened to his brother-in-law's sharp criticisms and admonitions when he proposed to summon a national consultative assembly in 1846.[137]

In Vienna much the same sort of dependence developed during the mid 1840s. The Emperor Ferdinand was far from competent, and his ministers were aged and unable to cope with the new demands which events imposed upon them. As Nicholas wrote to Aleksandra Fedorovna during his visit to Vienna in late 1845:

I must tell you that everything goes badly here. Metternich is only a shade of his former self; Kolowrat is also old; the Archduke Louis is more irresolute than ever, and the Archduke Franz, the heir to the throne, is blasé and dissatisfied. That is the government. Hungary is sullen [and] Galicia is on the point of breaking into flame.[138]

In 1846, Nicholas's dire predictions came to pass. When disorders broke out in Kraków, both Russian and Austrian troops occupied the city. It was Nicholas who mediated a change in the order of Eastern Europe by approving the incorporation of Kraków into the Habsburg domains, and who undertook to convince Friedrich Wilhelm of the need for approving such a course.[139]

Even before the revolutionary tide of 1848, Nicholas had therefore come to occupy the dominant position in Eastern and Central Europe. By the provisions of the Adrianople Treaty he had assumed a role as gendarme of the Danubian principalities as early as 1829. Four years later, he had taken on a similar task in relationship to the Ottoman Empire itself. And, also in 1833, he had become the gendarme of Poland as a result of the meetings at Münchengrätz. More than that, in the mid 1830s, he made commitments to Prussia and Austria by which he began to assume responsibilities of defending their territories against revolution as well. By the end of 1833, he had pledged that, 'at the first request of the Prussian government', he would 'fly to its aid in a struggle against insurgents'; and, by 1837, he had made very similar commitments to Austria.[140] Nicholas had, of course, relinquished his position as gendarme of the Ottoman Empire as a result of the London Conventions of 1840 and 1841, which substituted for the Treaty of Unkiar-Skelessi a European guarantee of the Sultan's domains. But this still left standing his commitments to defend the integrity of the Balkans,[141] as well as Prussia, the Habsburg Empire and Poland against revolutionary attacks. In 1849, Nicholas would be called upon to fulfil one of these commitments when the Austrian Emperor requested his aid in crushing Lajos Kossuth's rebels in Hungary. The redoubtable Prince Paskevich would add Hungary to the list of conquests which he laid at his Emperor's feet, and Nicholas would then be called the gendarme of Europe.

But Nicholas was the gendarme long before the revolutionary conflagrations of 1848. While his foreign policy was a defensive one, the duties he had assumed were far beyond the limit of Russia's resources. Vast portions of the state budget in Nicholas's Empire went to meet the needs of Russia's military forces. These needs were larger than they should have been because of widespread corruption in the army,[142] and very little was left over for the expenses of governing Russia itself. As a result, in comparison with the West, Russia lacked railways, industrial development and efficient administration. Additional state expenditures in those areas would not have solved the problem alone. But in the case of developing railways and industry, increased state support was essential in a land where liquid capital was scarce in the private sector of the economy. And, in an Empire where their salaries were not adequate to provide even the necessities of life,[143] increased payments to officials were certainly a prerequisite for bringing more talented officials into the bureaucracy. In the years after 1848, even the army would suffer. For a state with limited financial resources to bear the cost of maintaining an army which, in the early 1850s, numbered 938,731 regular troops as well as some 245,850 irregulars (mainly Cossack detachments), was ruinous, all the more so since the death rate from disease was so high that new recruits had to be added in large numbers to keep the army up to its authorized strength. During the first quarter-century of Nicholas's reign, it has been estimated that 1,028,650 men in the army perished from disease alone.[144]

Unable to bear the cost of maintaining a million-man army to meet Nicholas's defensive commitments as 'gendarme', his advisers imposed economies which would appear ludicrous had they not been fatal to the army's fighting efficiency. Since the emphasis was upon parade-ground performance, expenses for uniforms could not be reduced, but expenditures for such combat necessities as powder and ball could. Innovations such as the breech-loading rifle were rejected out of hand because, as one general remarked in 1834, the Russian infantry already fired too many cartridges in combat and the introduction of faster-firing weapons would only induce them to fire more rather than use their bayonets. Even worse, many line regiments were issued only three ball cartridges each year for target practice.[145] And more attention was paid to training the infantry in a manner so as 'to ensure that at the command "fire!" they should pull the triggers at the same time',[146] than to teaching them to achieve even the minimal accuracy of which their smooth-bore muskets were capable. The result of these sorts of misplaced economies, the financial burdens of Nicholas's gendarme duties, the lack of industry and rail development, would all become painfully evident in a very few years. For, if Nicholas was regarded as the gendarme of Europe in 1848, and if his Empire stood as a bastion of order and tranquillity, this was only a façade which would soon be stripped away by the victories of the Allied armies in the Crimea.

Part Four

The Attack
Begins

'For a long time, only two real forces have
existed in Europe – Revolution and
Russia . . . No transactions, no treaties,
are possible between them; the
existence of one is the death of the other'

F. I. TIUTCHEV, APRIL 1848

7

Nicholas and Russia's Intellectuals

*'To be sure, there is no country in all of Europe
which can pride itself on possessing such a
harmonious political existence as our own
motherland. Almost everywhere in the West,
wrangling over principles has been recognized
as a law of life, and the entire existence of peoples
is consumed by grievous struggle. Only among
us does Tsar and people comprise one indissoluble
entity'*

PROFESSOR S. P. SHEVYREV

*'It is oppressive and vile to live in Russia.
That is the truth'*

ALEKSANDR HERZEN

The three decades of Nicholas's reign have often been portrayed as a time of intense reaction and obscurantism in the life of Russia's intellectuals. The reign opened in an atmosphere of oppression and bloodshed; the severe punishment which Nicholas inflicted upon the Decembrists was soon identified with the repression of foreign ideas in Russia. Indeed, Nicholas's suppression of the revolt was sufficiently rigorous as to prevent Russia's intellectuals from challenging his authority for nearly two decades. And, even though some of the intelligentsia would begin to challenge the Nicholas system later in his reign, none of them would pose political alternatives to autocracy during Nicholas's lifetime. Even at the time of Nicholas's death in 1855, a number of progressive Russians had no greater expectation than that repression might be lessened under his successor. Certainly, they proposed no political alternatives to autocracy in the immediate future. Such was the view of the jurist, historian and publicist K. D. Kavelin, for example, when he wrote to his friend and former colleague at Moscow University, the historian T. N. Granovskii, in early March 1855, that 'if the voice of public opinion will reach him [the new Emperor] even in the most limited way, that in itself, with no reforms or transformations, will be sufficient for ten or fifteen years'.[1]

The atmosphere of intellectual repression which Nicholas and his advisers created by their suppression of the Decembrist revolt was further fostered during the early years by the measures they took to strengthen the state's censorship apparatus and to curtail the access of non-noble youths to the Empire's institutions of higher education. At the beginning of Nicholas's reign, the major responsibility for overseeing censorship in Russia lay with the Minister of Public Instruction, Admiral A. S. Shishkov, a man who had served his ruler faithfully since he had entered the Russian navy in 1772, and who was, at the time of the accession, over seventy years of age. Shishkov blamed the spread of the ideas which had produced the Decembrist movement upon the censors' carelessness, and also upon deficiencies in the Empire's censorship law. He therefore determined that a more comprehensive censorship law was needed, and in 1826 he set about preparing one. Because of his poor health, however, he turned much of the work over to the far less able director of his personal chancery, Prince Shikhmatov.[2]

The efforts of Shishkov and Prince Shikhmatov produced the so-called 'cast-iron statute' on censorship in June 1826. As one of the leading specialists on the Third Section during Nicholas's reign has described it, the 'cast-iron statute' departed from earlier laws on censorship in four important respects:

. . . publishers remained responsible for what they printed, even after the censor's approval; ambiguous passages were not permitted, or were at least to be interpreted by the censor in their most unfavourable sense; purity of language (Shishkov's great obsession) was to be enforced, grammatically, syntactically, and philologically; and minor changes and deletions in manuscript were permitted the censor without the author's consent.[3]

Russia's periodical press was still in its infancy, and at the time of Nicholas's accession there were being printed in all of the Russian Empire only twenty-six periodical publications, including scholarly journals, official government publications, literary journals and children's magazines.[4] Shishkov's 'cast-iron statute' helped to prevent further development by establishing vague and undefined requirements for the founding of new journals. According to Article 129 of the statute, permission to begin a new periodical would be given only 'to a man of good morals, already well-known in the realm of native letters, who has demonstrated a beneficent mode of thought as well as his loyalty in his works, a man capable of guiding public opinion to a useful goal'.[5]

Shishkov's statute also forbade the publication of anything regarded as prejudicial to the Russian government or to the Emperor, and this prohibition was cast in very broad and vague terms.

Not only that which opposes the government and the powers ordained by it is forbidden, but anything which may tend to weaken the respect which is its due . . . Anything is forbidden that in any way reveals in author, translator, or artist a person who violated the obligations incumbent on a loyal subject to the holy person of the Sovereign Emperor.[6]

Thus, depending on the manner in which the Minister of Public Instruction and his censors chose to apply these provisions, the 'cast-iron statute' could be very oppressive or could, on the other hand, be quite lenient. As one censor commented, 'even the Lord's Prayer could be interpreted as a Jacobin speech' under the broad and amorphous provisions of the law.[7]

The need to interpret Shishkov's 1826 statute raised difficulties from the outset. Certainly Nicholas himself did not see the function of censorship as being oppressive at the time, and in fact regarded the question of censorship in much the same way as he had viewed the creation of the Third Section. Both were to be paternalistic and were to play a positive role in Russian life by guiding individuals along the correct path, by punishing those who were evil, thoughtless or straying, and by rewarding those who were virtuous. Shishkov himself expressed this view quite clearly in his first report to Nicholas in which he pointed out the need for detailed and clear-cut rules to guide censors so that 'not only would the freedom to write and appraise not be removed from writers, but they would be encouraged . . . to write'.[8] But Shishkov and Shikhmatov had done very little to provide the censor with any sort of positive role. Only the first of the 230 articles dealt with that question,[9] and that one stated only in the most vague and general terms that the censor should carry out his tasks in such a manner that the arts and letters in Russia 'should be given a direction which is important, or at least harmless, for the well-being of the fatherland'.[10]

In an effort to develop more fully what he regarded as the positive role of censorship, Nicholas soon had Shishkov's statute replaced by a new law in 1828, and Shishkov himself was replaced as Minister of Public Instruction by Prince A. K. Lieven, formerly rector of the University of Dorpat. Lieven has been described as a man who was unusually firm and independent.[11] And, as a greater moralist than Shishkov, he was much more convinced that censorship should direct authors along useful paths.[12] The new law which Lieven was to administer was far more lenient than Shishkov's 'cast-iron statute', and, as one historian has commented, 'the role of the censor was conceived as that of an amiable legal guardian of letters, a foster father of the arts and sciences. The prevailing moral order . . . could not be assailed, but in terms of the new law it could be interpreted with a wider degree of latitude.'[13] Indeed, many educated individuals in Russia regarded the protective aspects of censorship as a necessity, and very few seem to have been opposed to censorship as a matter of principle, including the famous poet Pushkin, who wrote that 'what is right for London is early for Moscow. Be strict, but be intelligent.'[14]

All this is not to say that the system of censorship which Nicholas developed during the first half-decade of his reign would not eventually become oppressive, even reactionary, as over-zealous censors and men seeking to make careers by discovering threats to the established order, probed deeper into the underlying meanings of what was printed in Russia. But to portray the Nicholas era as a time of oppression and intellectual sterility is to tell only the side of the story that has been told often and dramatically by such alienated intellectual figures as Aleksandr Herzen, Vissarion Belinskii and I. I. Panaev, the editor of the journal the *Contemporary* which suffered especially from the censor's pen. Nicholas's reign was, after all, the Golden Age of Russian literature; it saw the emergence of some of Russia's first major composers; and it marked the development of the Russian theatre to a point where it assumed a complete identity of its own and was no longer a mere copy of the West as it had been during much of the eighteenth century. It also saw the beginnings of Russian science on a broader scale, as well as significant research in other fields. For the first time, jurists were trained in Russia, and the men trained in the Imperial School of Jurisprudence, which Nicholas himself founded in 1835, would provide the expertise for making the Judicial Reform of 1864 a reality and possibly the most successful of the Great Reforms. Statistics began their development as a science in Russia under Nicholas,[15] and a number of important geographical explorations were undertaken in Central Asia, the Far East and the Caucasus.[16]

The fact that so much intellectual and scholarly endeavour flourished under the Nicholas system is evidence of a phenomenon frequently over-looked in studies of Russian history. Though much of Russian educated society would ultimately find the Nicholas system repressive, especially after 1848, it never became alienated from the state or the autocrat during Nicholas's reign to the same degree as would be the case in the 1860s and 1870s. Disappointment with the Great Reforms of the 1860s, and bitterness at what radical intellectuals regarded as Alexander II's betrayal of their hopes, were the major factors which led to the emergence of a revolutionary intelligentsia in Russia,[17] not the restraints which Nicholas and his ministers imposed upon a few dissident intellectuals. Even Aleksandr Herzen, and such radicals as N. G. Chernyshevskii, continued to look to the autocrat as Russia's major reforming force until several years after Nicholas's death. Most educated Russians were able to reconcile themselves to the limits imposed by the Nicholas system, and found it possible to work successfully and creatively within the framework of Official Nationality, at least until the last few years of Nicholas's life, when his régime retrenched in the face of what he regarded as attacks by intellectuals at home and the fears inspired by revolts in Austrian Poland in 1846 and the revolutions of 1848.

Official Nationality was thus by no means a purely obscurantist and repressive system during much of Nicholas's reign, and it certainly was not intended as such by its creater, S. S. Uvarov, the Minister of Public Instruction. Uvarov was, in fact, an extremely cosmopolitan nobleman, well-educated in the best tradition of the Enlightenment. He was a classical scholar of considerable talent who placed a high value upon learning and knowledge. But, as we shall see, there were elements in Uvarov's outlook and in the Nicholas system itself which ultimately led to a perversion of his aim to construct an enlightened conservative society in Russia. As a result, Official Nationality came to be reactionary, even obscurantist in nature, and caused the Nicholas system to be remembered for many decades as the epitome of intellectual and cultural repression.

1. Official Nationality:
The Ideology of the Nicholas System

For Nicholas personally, the theory of Official Nationality[18] was inextricably bound up with his own personality, world view and daily life. From his earliest childhood, the spirit of Orthodoxy, Autocracy and Nationality – which his Minister of Public Instruction, Uvarov, articulated as the trinity of Official Nationality in 1833 – comprised the very essence of his training, education and experience. It could not have been otherwise, for these elements had comprised the essence of Russian kingship since at least the sixteenth century. Ivan IV had expressed these attitudes quite forcefully in the dramatic first paragraph of his letter to Prince Kurbskii in mid 1564, when he wrote that 'the autocracy of this Russian kingdom of veritable Orthodoxy, by the will of God, [has its] beginning from the great Tsar Vladimir . . . and has come down even to us'.[19] This theme was defended and elaborated by Russian rulers over the nearly three centuries which separated Ivan IV from Nicholas I. Thus, Nicholas never considered it necessary to formulate an ideological justification for his system; to his mind, it was one of those self-evident truths which required neither explanation nor defence. In his view, the Russian Empire, the Orthodox faith and the undivided power of autocracy were all joined and personified in the ruler of the Russian state. As the historian A. E. Presniakov summarized Nicholas's outlook:

Far from that intense intellectual effort which compelled Catherine [II] to seek theoretical justifications for this [autocratic] power, and impelled his brother Alexander [I] to seek to reconcile it with contemporary political ideas and requirements, he [Nicholas] held to it as a self-sufficient value which required absolutely no justification or explanation. Autocracy was for him an unshakeable dogma.[20]

The situation was neither so clear-cut nor so lacking in complexity for Nicholas's advisers and supporters, however. Nicholas had seen the Decembrist revolt as a political attack upon legitimacy, impelled in particular by examples which young army officers had observed in the West. Certainly he was not inclined to view the Decembrist movement, or any other events, in intellectual terms, and neither were some of his closest advisers: men such as Generals Benkendorf, Chernyshev and Vasil'chikov. But some of Nicholas's advisers were inclined to see the Decembrists' ideas as an ideological threat to the official order in Russia which had not yet received its full formulation. For, although the institution of autocracy was approaching its fullest evolution at the time of Nicholas's accession, its ideological justification was only just beginning. The Empress Catherine II had taken some very rudimentary steps in this direction near the end of her reign with the manner in which she had fostered a renewed interest in Russia's national past,[21] and during the first quarter of the nineteenth century the court historian N. M. Karamzin had gone much further in his glorification of Russia's past, and especially the institution of autocracy. Karamzin's defence and glorification of autocracy in his monumental *History of the Russian State* was, of course, to some extent a part of a much broader European movement to revert to tradition in the face of the excesses of the French Revolution. Within Russia itself, however, Karamzin's articulation of an integrated and comprehensive conservative outlook and its corresponding defence of autocracy, emerged as the product of the union between aristocracy and the autocrat which had evolved during the eighteenth century.[22]

It was this growing conservative movement in Russia, and its increasing demand for an ideological articulation of its position and attitudes, which was instrumental in the development of the theories of Official Nationality.

Faced by a Europe in which many cherished institutions seemed to be crumbling and where old values were coming increasingly under attack, many Russians sought an ideology which could serve as a bulwark against the challenge which Western ideas posed to the established order. This was particularly significant in a country such as Russia where the vast majority of educated opinion in the 1820s and 1830s was part of an aristocracy which had consciously patterned its life and values upon the Western example for nearly a century. Their model had been the society of *ancien régime* France. But, just as they had succeeded in creating the framework for such a society in Russia during the latter third of the eighteenth century, they had seen their cherished model society in the West fall into the final stages of decline. The newest Western ideas, to which they themselves had paid lip-service in the eighteenth century, turned to destroy the society which they aspired to achieve. They thus demanded an ideological defence of their society in Russia which could parry attacks from the West.

S. S. Uvarov, Russia's Minister of Public Instruction from 1833 to 1849, recognized the need for such an ideology by educated society and the state very explicitly in 1843, a decade after he had assumed office. In summarizing the first decade of his work as minister, Uvarov wrote:

In the midst of rapid collapse in Europe of religious and civil institutions, at the time of a general spread of destructive ideas, at the sight of grievous phenomena surrounding us on all sides, it was necessary to establish our fatherland on firm foundations upon which is based the well-being, strength and life of a people; it was necessary to find the principles which form the distinctive character of Russia, and which belong only to Russia; it was necessary to gather into one whole the sacred remnants of Russian nationality and to fasten them to the anchor of our salvation.[23]

These principles, around which the ideological defence of the Nicholas system would be constructed, were, in Uvarov's words, 'Orthodoxy, Autocracy, and Nationality'. As he wrote in March 1833, 'Our common duty is to see to it that, in accordance with the Supreme intention of our August Monarch, the education of the people is carried out in the united spirit of Orthodoxy, Autocracy, and Nationality.'[24] As Uvarov elaborated upon this theme a decade later,

A Russian, devoted to his fatherland, will agree as little to the loss of a single dogma of our *Orthodoxy* as to the theft of a single pearl from the tsar's crown. *Autocracy* constitutes the main condition of the political existence of Russia. The Russian giant stands on it as on the cornerstone of his greatness . . . The saving condition that Russia lives and is protected by the spirit of a strong, humane, and enlightened autocracy must permeate popular education and must develop with it. Together with these two national principles there is a third, no less powerful: *Nationality*.[25]

It is significant that Uvarov's articulation of the formula 'Orthodoxy, Autocracy, and Nationality' coincided almost exactly with the full emergence of the Nicholas system at home and abroad. It is equally important to emphasize that this formula was not one which had to be forced upon most Russians. Much of educated Russian opinion favoured such a concept, and there can be no doubt that the Russian peasantry, though far from satisfied with their wretched economic plight, revered the autocrat and autocracy. At no time before the early twentieth century did the Russian masses propose an alternative to autocracy, and even those who participated in such monumental revolts as that of Pugachev in the 1770s sought nothing more than to replace a ruler whom they regarded as illegitimate with one who favoured the peasants' interests and hence, by definition, was legitimate. To the Russian peasantry, the autocrat was their 'little father' and the wretched quality of their lives was the fault of their aristocratic masters, not the ruler. It was not until the tragedy of Bloody Sunday, when hundreds of peaceful Russian peasants and workers were shot down while seeking to present petitions to the Emperor Nicholas II on 9 January 1905, that the Russian masses became convinced that the Emperor was not their 'little father' but, in fact, the greatest nobleman of them all.

Thus Uvarov's trilogy of Orthodoxy, Autocracy and Nationality expressed sentiments which appealed to the majority of Russians and which, in fact, formed an integral part of their lives and outlook. Numerous Russian writers seized upon the formula and elaborated it in their works, and more than a score of periodicals extolled its principles during the 1830s and 1840s. To be sure there was an element of self-interest involved in the actions of many, since enthusiastic support for state policies and principles could bring rewards and Uvarov himself was made a count for his dedication to his formula. But the tribute which so many Russians paid to the ideological defence of the Nicholas system was motivated by considerably more than self-interest, for by the early 1830s they had reached a point where all but a handful regarded their state and ruler with a great deal of satisfaction and admiration. The West had suffered the violence of the French Revolution of 1789, the tyranny of Napoleon, a number of small revolutionary outbreaks in the 1820s and, finally, the widespread revolutionary upheavals of 1830–31. This last revolutionary wave had, it is true, included a serious revolt in Poland, but within the Russian land itself revolution had not appeared except for that brief moment in 1825, only to be crushed immediately by Nicholas's resolute actions. This, of course, is not to deny that many Russians felt a great deal of sympathy for the Decembrists, but compassion and charity for those sentenced to exile had for many decades been an element of the Russian outlook.

For the vast majority of Russians, the fact that revolution had been kept away from their lives was something for which they were extremely grateful, and they attributed this good fortune to the nature of the state and society in which they lived. As one writer put it, 'in Russia there exists everything necessary for national welfare'.[26] And, as a professor at the University of Moscow, S. P. Shevyrev, remarked in the first issue of the *Muscovite* in 1841:

Although we suffered some inevitable faults from our contacts with the West, we still have preserved within ourselves, in their purity, three essential sentiments [Orthodoxy, Autocracy and Nationality] in which lie the seed and the security for our future development. To be sure [he added], there is no country in all of Europe which can pride itself on possessing such a harmonious political existence as our own motherland. Almost everywhere in the West, wrangling over principles has been recognized as a law of life, and the entire existence of peoples is consumed by grievous struggle. Only among us does Tsar and people comprise one indissoluble entity.[27]

To Nicholas personally, Orthodoxy, the first article of Uvarov's trilogy, had a deep significance which sustained him even during the deepest political and personal crises: during war, famine, plague and revolution. As one noted scholar has summarized this factor in his life:

It was his firm faith in God, Christ, the Divine Will, as revealed in the teachings of the Orthodox Church, that sustained the disappointed and at times even desperate Emperor in all the trials and tribulations of his hard life. Only Christ, only Orthodoxy, represented for the Russian monarch light, guidance, and salvation in this vale of sorrow and strife.[28]

Such a view of God and Orthodoxy were very characteristic of Nicholas, especially during the bitter trials of the Crimean War. By that time he was exhausted, ill, nearly at the end of his resources, and his powerful organism was beginning to crumble under the strain of more than a quarter-century as Russia's supreme commander. It was at that point that his utterances began to assume a much deeper tone of fatalism as he declared that 'I shall carry my cross until my strength is exhausted',[29] and that 'nothing is left for me but my duty so long as it shall please God to leave me at the head of Russia'.[30]

But this deeply personal quality of Nicholas's relationship to God was highly characteristic of him throughout his reign. He saw himself as the supreme force in the daily lives of his subjects, and saw himself in turn as answerable directly to God, to 'the Russian God', as he sometimes said,[31] for their welfare. As he once prayed aloud at a great military review in the autumn of 1837, 'O God, I thank Thee for having made me so powerful, and I beg Thee to give me strength never to abuse this might.'[32] Thus, as Emperor, he held a power that was truly awesome in the eyes of all men; but, in relation to God, he stood in the same position as his subjects did to him. He served Russia with a devotion matched in Imperial Russian history only by Peter the Great, since he regarded 'all human life as being nothing more than service',[33] and because he regarded it as a sacred duty. And, as he wrote to his wife at the time of the Hungarian campaign in 1849, 'Duty! . . . That is my watchword . . . I suffer more from it than I can say – but I have been created to suffer.'[34] But, in the final analysis, Nicholas believed that the outcome of his labours lay in the hands of God. As he once wrote to Prince Paskevich, 'His will be done!'[35]

That virtually all of Nicholas's subjects, from the greatest to the smallest, saw themselves in a similarly humble relation to God in the context of Orthodoxy goes without saying, and there was a considerable amount written during his reign which more than proves the point.[36] Any review of this rather considerable body of literature, however, would take us too far from Nicholas himself, our main subject of concern. But perhaps even more interesting than what may appear as crude and naïve statements in these works about God 'as the ultimate answer to man's quest, the beginning and end of human wisdom',[37] is that Nicholas's relation to his subjects and to God was reproduced throughout Russian society on many different levels in the relationship between masters and serfs. The often misunderstood novelist, N. V. Gogol', summarized this relationship in his controversial work, *Select Passages from Correspondence with Friends*, when he advised Russian landlords:

First of all, gather the peasants together and explain to them what you and what they are; that you are their master not because you wanted to command and be a landlord, but because you are already a landlord because you were born a landlord, and that God will call you to account if you should change this calling for another; because every man must serve God in his place and not in some other, precisely as they, having been born in a subservient condition, must submit to that power to which they are subject, because there is no power that is not from God.[38]

That Gogol's was not an isolated or unique view of social relations in Russia during Nicholas's reign becomes especially obvious from a comment provided by the Baron von Haxthausen-Abbenberg, a German traveller to Russia in the 1840s. According to Haxthausen's account, he once heard a nobleman address his peasants in the following manner:

I am your master, and my master is the Emperor. The Emperor can issue his commands to me and I must obey him; but he issues no commands to you. I am the Emperor on my estate; I am your God in this world and I have to answer for you to the God above.[39]

Such a comment clearly stated the relationship which Nicholas's aristocratic subjects had with the Emperor and with God. Equally important, perhaps, it also indicated a basic dilemma of power which Russian rulers faced from the mid eighteenth to the mid nineteenth century: that the power of the Emperor and the state was diluted by the need to rely upon the nobility to carry out the imperial will in the provinces of the Empire. Faced by an aristocracy which opposed any fundamental alteration in Russia's social order, Nicholas and his advisers could not rely on local authorities to carry out decrees that conflicted with their class interests. Haxthausen's nobleman may have said that, 'the Emperor can issue his commands to me and I must obey him', but many nobles were prepared to take the sin of disobedience upon their consciences if it meant protecting their economic position. Far more significant in Haxthausen's account was the fact that his nobleman insisted to his peasants that 'I am the Emperor on my estate' and that the Emperor 'issues no commands to you'.

While the matter of Orthodoxy held the key to salvation in the minds of Nicholas and his subjects, the question of personal and political power had a far more direct impact upon their daily lives. Orthodoxy related to the hereafter, while the much more immediate phenomenon of autocracy was very much tied to the present. The nature of autocracy and its place in Russian life was made very clear in the Fundamental Laws of the Russian Empire themselves. 'The Russian Emperor is an Autocratic and absolute Monarch. Submission to his supreme authority must come not from fear alone, but also as a matter of conscience, as God himself decrees,' these laws proclaimed.[40] And the relationship of this autocratic power to society was made explicitly clear in the laws as well, for it was stated that 'the Russian Empire is governed on the firm bases of absolute laws, regulations, and statutes which originate with the Autocratic Power'.[41] Thus the Emperor alone was the only source of law in the Russian Empire.

The *Digest of the Russian Laws* implied that laws once issued had an independent existence ('the Russian Empire is governed on the firm bases of absolute laws'), but in fact the concept of law was a very personal one during Nicholas's reign. Ideally, the state was to be governed on the basis of law, with the rights and privileges of each class in society clearly set forth and defended, but this never came into being under the Nicholas system and was always tempered by the fact that Nicholas was an 'absolute and autocratic monarch' from whose person all law originated. Nicholas thus dispensed justice, laws, mercy and many types of privileges, just as the Tsar had done during the Muscovite period of Russia's history, and by winning his favour, as we noted earlier, an individual could achieve great success. That the autocrat could in theory circumvent the law, or even act contrary to it, is obvious. But this in itself could not be defined as illegal since it was the Emperor who was responsible to God for all of his actions and for the behaviour of his subjects.

The absolute nature of Nicholas's power was thus very closely linked with God himself, for his power, absolute and arbitrary as it was, came directly from God. As the poet V. A. Zhukovskii, tutor to the Empress and her sons, commented at one point, 'in the Christian world autocracy is the highest level of power; it is the last link between the power of man and the power of God' . . . 'Human law,' he added, 'becomes *divine truth*, for it derives from an authority permeated by divine truth.'[42] Thus the autocrat answered to no man, and stood above them all; yet before God, he was as the humblest of his subjects, bearing all the responsibility for their transgressions and his own. As Gogol' described it: 'That one among men [the autocrat] upon whose shoulders rests the fate of millions of his fellows . . . is freed from all responsibility before men as a result of his terrible responsibility for them before God.'[43] The fact that the autocrat could act contrary to the law was thus elevated to a virtue. As Gogol' wrote, in enthusiastically agreeing with what he erroneously deemed to be the poet Pushkin's view of autocracy:

Why is it necessary . . . for one of us to be above everything and even above the law? Because the law is like wood; you will not get far by only fulfilling the letter of the law; of course, no one of us ought to break the law or not fulfil it; however, you need a superior mercy so as to soften the law, and this can only come to us in the form of absolute monarchy. Without an absolute monarch, a state is an automaton . . . A state without an absolute ruler is like an orchestra without a conductor.[44]

Gogol' could not have summarized Nicholas's own view of his power and his obligations as ruler more accurately, for Nicholas acted in precisely this manner from the moment he came to the throne. To some Decembrists, he appeared stern but fatherly; to others, he was like the God of the Old Testament, vengeful, wrathful and unforgiving; and to others he was like a priest, hearing their confessions yet insisting that proper penance must be done. And throughout the three decades of his reign, Nicholas's behaviour remained consistent. As Baron Korf described him during the 1840s, he was stern, yet charitable and forgiving, a ruler acting in what he considered to be the best interests of his subjects and Empire, who disciplined those who strayed from the path of virtue in the manner which he considered best for them. Thus, for example, in 1841 Nicholas had to deal with the case of a young nobleman, a member of the highest social circles, who had become so disillusioned with life in Russia that he believed it was necessary to assassinate his Emperor 'for the general good'. Count Benkendorf showed the incriminating letters to Nicholas and, according to Korf, Nicholas replied: 'Return the letters to this young man and tell him that *I have read them.*' Once again, Nicholas, as mediator between God and his subjects, dealt with the problem in the way which his paternalistic judgement deemed most appropriate.[45]

Such examples of Nicholas's behaviour are numerous and have been often quoted, and to recount additional tales would add little to our understanding of his view of himself as autocrat. Yet another side of his conception of his role as autocrat, who had received his power from God and was answerable to Him for the manner in which he used it, can be seen in Nicholas's open-handed charity to the poorest of his subjects whom he encountered during his daily strolls through the streets of Russia's capital. As we noted earlier,[46] many stories circulated in the capital about Nicholas's generosity to those in need whom he encountered on the capital's streets, and while there is no way of ascertaining the veracity of such anecdotes, the fact that they existed, and most probably had some basis in fact, adds to the image of Nicholas as God's chosen representative on earth.

Within the context of autocracy, then, Nicholas served as God's agent in Russia and as 'the Christian conscience of Russia'.[47] Such a view found widespread acceptance, especially in a state where the vast majority of its inhabitants, themselves of a superstitious and mystical turn of mind, were regarded by their noble masters as child-like and in need of paternal guidance at every step. The notion that man, in general, was weak, perverse and inclined to evil actions, and thus requiring 'to be driven by a benevolent supreme authority in order to achieve desirable social ends',[48] found expression frequently and at many levels of society. For, if all accepted him as the Christian conscience of Russia, his main servitors, the nobles, regarded themselves as the Christian conscience of their peasants on their estates. As Haxthausen's nobleman said to his peasants, 'I am your God in this world and I have to answer for you to the God above.'[49] Such a view was echoed by Nicholas's ministers and the ideologists of Official Nationality. M. P. Pogodin, whose writings on orthodoxy and autocracy comprised a fundamental part of the literature espousing the doctrines of Official Nationality, observed as early as 1826 that 'the Russian people is marvellous, but marvellous so far only in potentiality.

In actuality, it is low, horrid, and beastly . . . [and] will not become human beings until they are forced into it.'[50]

Such a view of mankind also dominated the outlook of some of Nicholas's ministers. The Minister of Public Instruction who was responsible for the more liberal censorship law of 1828, Prince A. K. Lieven, was just such a man. In his first circular as Minister of Public Instruction, in 1828, Lieven wrote: 'From his very birth, man carries within himself an aspiration towards evil; evil inclinations develop in him with age; tempting examples foster them and experience strengthens them.'[51] Men with an inborn propensity for evil required careful training and guidance to mould them into beings who would serve the best interests of the state and humanity. In this undertaking, the supreme power and morality of the Emperor (and, by extension, his agents, his ministers) was destined to play a critical part in enabling Russia to fulfil the role ordained by God. Thus, as Nicholas once commented, 'the best theory of law is good morality and it ought to be in one's heart independent of . . . abstractions and should have as its basis religion'.[52] Put into practical terms by Nicholas's advisers, these ideas demanded that the state power, personified by the Emperor, should become the highest authority in all social relationships. Ia. I. Rostovtsev, the young army officer who had warned Nicholas about the Decembrists' plans and who would preside over the drafting of the Emancipation of 1861 under Alexander II, stated this view with particular clarity in his 'Instructions for the Education of Students in Military Schools'. Rostovtsev wrote: 'The supreme power is the "social conscience". For the actions of man it ought to have that same significance as his personal conscience has for his inner motives.'[53] Nicholas's decisions therefore were to have the same moral imperatives for each of his subjects as their own consciences had in their private lives.

To fulfil such a function in the lives of his subjects, Nicholas insisted that each of them observe all the restraints which the precepts of Orthodoxy and Autocracy should impose upon them. To do so, Nicholas and his ideologists insisted that civil order be maintained at all costs, for, as Faddei Bulgarin, one of the proponents of Official Nationality wrote in his memoirs, 'it is better to unchain a hungry tiger or a hyena than to take off the people the bridle of obedience to authorities and laws'.[54] Such a negative view of mankind caused Nicholas's advisers to fear the masses, an apprehension which Nicholas himself fully shared. Indeed, fear of the masses was a major factor behind many of his internal policies. He created the Third Section partly in an effort to gauge mass opinion; and the whole apparatus of censorship, both in the Ministry of Public Instruction and the Third Section, was devoted especially to preventing disquieting works from reaching the masses. As a result, some books (especially those from abroad) were censored for mass distribution, but were permitted to certain of the upper classes,[55] and it was for similar reasons that Nicholas and his censors permitted writers to criticize 'Servility to the Aristocracy' (1830), but refused to allow such things as an article 'On the Peasantry' (1830) to appear in print.[56]

Nicholas seems to have been relatively confident that he could deal with unrest among the educated minority in Russia should it occur. Of course, he could not tolerate or permit dissent, given the moral imperatives which Orthodoxy and Autocracy imposed upon Russian society, and especially upon himself. But such dissent, Nicholas seemed confident, could be dealt with by the state organs at hand. He therefore punished intellectuals who wrote pieces considered to be dangerous or immoral, not so much because he feared them, but because the dictates of Orthodoxy and Autocracy required that he do so. As far as the masses were concerned, however, it was another matter entirely. Nicholas could deal with another Decembrist revolt. But another *pugachevshchina* – an elemental peasant upheaval such as that led by the Cossack Emelian Pugachev in the 1770s – was something he feared and sought to prevent at all costs.

Nicholas made this fear of the masses very clear to the Slavophile Iuri Samarin in the interview already quoted in which he told him that he had 'let loose among the masses a dangerous idea, suggesting that Russian tsars from the time of Peter the Great acted only according to the suggestions and under the influence of Germans'. Should that idea reach the masses, Nicholas told Samarin, 'it will produce terrible calamities'.[57] He made this point even more specifically in addressing the representatives of the St Petersburg nobility on 21 March 1848:

Among us there exists a class of very foolish people and I ask you to pay particular attention to them. These are the household servants [*dvorovye liudi*] . . . These people generally are demoralized and are a threat both to society and to their own masters. I ask you to be extremely cautious in your relations with them. Frequently, at table or in evening conversation, you discuss political, governmental, or other affairs, forgetting that these people listen to you and, because of their ignorance and stupidity, misinterpret your opinions in their own way. Furthermore, these conversations, harmless among educated people, often inspire in your servants thoughts that would never have occurred to them on their own. This is very dangerous![58]

Nicholas thus regarded the masses as his most dangerous enemy, both at home and abroad. A *coup d'état*, such as the revolution which drove Charles X from the French throne in 1830 appeared at first report, was something which Nicholas opposed in principle. But a mass movement, a revolution, was something he feared much more, and his strong objection to Louis Philippe as Charles X's successor was only partly because he had violated the order of succession and therefore was 'illegitimate'. Perhaps even more objectionable in Nicholas's view was the fact that Louis Philippe was elevated to the throne by the Parisian crowd; he was King of the French, not the King of France.

Yet Orthodoxy and Autocracy did not comprise the whole doctrine of Official Nationality, though they were the two most easily definable elements. What made Orthodoxy and Autocracy unique in the context of world politics and civilization was the fact that they were Russian and held sway in Russia. Thus 'Nationality', at once a romantic myth, a dynastic justification and a messianic outlook of complex, difficult to define and even contradictory elements, comprised the third element in Uvarov's trilogy. As one scholar has defined it, it was an 'affirmation that the Russian people were docile and obedient subjects to their tsar and their landlords', while 'on the romantic plane "Russia" and "the Russian people" acquired a supreme metaphysical, even mystical, importance, leading to belief in such doctrines as Pan-Slavism and such practices as Russification'.[59] Russians were thus in a special sense unique, and this uniqueness was tied, in a mystical and mysterious manner, to Orthodoxy, to Autocracy (or, more properly, the person of the Tsar), and to the fact of Russia's existence itself.

Such a view was an integral part of Nicholas's outlook, and as such it differed sharply from the cosmopolitan views of his elder brother Alexander I. Alexander, and his grandmother Catherine II before him, had seen Russia as very much a part of Europe. As Catherine had written at the beginning of the first chapter of her famous 'Instructions' to the Legislative Commission of 1767, 'Russia is a European power.'[60] But Nicholas regarded 'Russia' and 'Europe' as two distinct entities. 'Europe' was evil; 'Russia' was virtuous – a distinction which he made clear in his manifesto announcing the execution of the Decembrists on 13 July 1826. The blood of those who died or suffered injury defending the throne, he announced, was 'Russian blood poured forth . . . for its faith, its Tsar, and its country'.[61] In describing the uprising, Nicholas saw it as a 'thundercloud of revolt' which 'was in harmony with neither the character nor the feelings of the Russian nation'. It involved sentiments and ideas taken from the West, 'entertained by a handful of vile criminals . . . but in the course of ten years of criminal efforts it never penetrated, it could never penetrate, any farther. The heart of Russia has ever been, and will ever be, inaccessible to its poison.'[62] So long as the Tsar, their father, treated them firmly, showed them the way to obedience, and guided their steps by his example and his concern for their spiritual and moral welfare, the Russian people, in Nicholas's view, would never become infected with the evils which ran rife in Europe. As he once wrote from the banks of the Volga to his Empress, 'God, what fine and good people these are! May God keep them so; one is truly proud to belong to them.'[63]

By nature, even by definition, Russians were considered better and more virtuous than other peoples, a theme which Nicholas and all those who supported his system never tired of emphasizing. 'The drama of contemporary history is expressed by two words, one of which sounds sweet to our heart! The West and Russia, Russia and the West – here is the result flowing from the entire past; here is the last word of history; here are the two basic facts for the future,' wrote Shevyrev as one who wholeheartedly supported the Nicholas system.[64] 'The East is not the the West,' proclaimed M. P. Pogodin, another of the ideologists of Official Nationality. 'We have a different climate from the West . . . a different temperament, character, different blood, a different physiognomy, a different outlook, a different cast of mind, different beliefs, hopes, desires . . . [We have] different conditions, a different history. Everything is different.'[65] 'Suspicion and fear reign in the West, while among us there is only trust,' he added. 'Our speech is broad, sweeping, as is our national character,' Shevyrev insisted.[66] And, perhaps most crucial of all, as the poet Tiutchev wrote in April 1848, 'for a long time only two real forces have existed in Europe – Revolution and Russia . . . No transactions, no treaties, are possible between them; the existence of one is the death of the other!'[67]

Perhaps Nicholas would not have posed the conflict in such stark terms during most of his reign, but, in 1848, he too saw it as a struggle between good and evil, between the sacred and the profane, between Russia and revolution. In March 1848, as revolution spread from Paris to Germany and to the Habsburg Empire, Nicholas proclaimed:

At this moment, this [revolutionary] insolence, knowing no limits, threatens in its madness even Our Russia entrusted to Us by God. But it will not succeed! Following the example of Our Orthodox ancestors, and invoking the help of Almighty God, We are ready to meet Our enemies.[68]

No power in Europe threatened Russia's borders at the time. But, to Nicholas, the threat was no less real. For the threat was from the dark, evil and not always readily identifiable forces of revolution which might strike anywhere at any time, even in Holy Russia.

This, then, was the Russia which Nicholas, his advisers and defenders saw. It was of vast size, of monumental proportions, an Empire of some 60 million all joined together as one family under the patrimonial authority and fatherly care of their Emperor. Nicholas himself emphasized this relationship in December 1850, when he addressed the Preobrazhenskii Guards on the twenty-fifth anniversary of the Decembrist revolt in which they had played an important role in defending the throne. 'We form one joint family,' he proclaimed to them, 'and my family belongs to you, just as you belong to me.'[69] And, as such a father, he ruled Russia in all of its vastness. As Pogodin wrote:

Russia, a distance of ten thousand *versts* [a verst is about two thirds of a mile] in length on a straight line from the nearly central river of Europe across all of Asia and the Eastern Ocean, to the far-distant American lands . . . ! What state compares with it? With its half? How many states can equal its twentieth, its fiftieth part?[70]

It was this vastness, which encompassed the Russian land, the Russian God, the Russian Tsar and the Russian People. And it was this which comprised Uvarov's trilogy: Orthodoxy, Autocracy, and Nationality, which many regarded as 'the past, the present, and the future of Russia, Russian tradition as well as Russian mission, Russian culture as much as Russian politics'.[71]

Who would challenge it? To Nicholas and those around him, any challenge was almost unthinkable. Official Nationality and the Nicholas system represented the culmination of Russia's entire religious, historical and political experience, an experience the validity of which had been proved time and again in comparison with the West. For the West fell victim again and again to the attacks of revolution, while Russia remained a bastion of peace, tranquillity and order. Yet the challenge would come – and soon. While Nicholas, Uvarov and the proponents of Official Nationality sought to control all aspects of Russian life and direct Russians along the course which they regarded as virtuous and desirable, there were others who saw different paths as more desirable and virtuous, men who would question the official versions of Russia, the West and Russia's future. Some would turn to Russia's past; others would turn to the West for their models. But all would envisage a Russia of the future that would be far different from the Russia of Nicholas and the Nicholas system.

2. The First Challenges

That the Nicholas system was first challenged by educated Russians, most of whom were nobles, is not surprising. Certainly, given the rigid system of control which Nicholas sought to impose upon Russia, and because the Cossacks, traditionally the most explosive social element in the seventeenth and eighteenth centuries, had been coopted into the state military apparatus by the early nineteenth century, the challenge could hardly have come from any other quarter. The challenge had its roots in the experience of certain noble youths during the 1830s, most of them young men who had attended the University of Moscow, away from the constricting and more rigidly regulated atmosphere of St Petersburg. Most of these were still children or adolescents when Nicholas ascended the throne, and the Decembrist revolt, for many of them a romantic and heroic event, made a lasting impression. Among a number of them a 'cult of the Decembrists' emerged as they moved from their adolescent world of private tutors to life in the university.

A discussion of the intellectual odysseys upon which these aristocratic youths embarked, their experiences in the university and their efforts to come to terms with various Western (and particularly German) philosophical systems ranging from the Romantic writings of Schiller to the more complex philosophical systems of Schelling, Fichte and Hegel, is far outside the scope of our study of Nicholas I.[72] What concerns us here especially is the reaction of these young men to the Nicholas system as it flowered and matured in Russia, and even more important, the sorts of challenges they posed to it, especially as the system closed in upon them, causing some to suffer imprisonment or exile, and all of them to feel the oppression of an increasingly rigid censorship. All told, their numbers most probably totalled less than a hundred, and there were many other youths who attended Russia's universities and élite secondary schools during the 1830s and 1840s who did not follow their path. Yet the impact which these men who first challenged the Nicholas system had upon Russia's future course was out of all proportion to their very limited numbers.

That these young men found oppressive the limitations imposed upon them by the Nicholas system goes without saying. What is more crucial for our purposes is why they found themselves at times so bitterly at odds with it, for their experiences, in an important sense, were the rare exceptions rather than the rule in Nicholas's Russia. Most of these young men were of noble origin. Most significant, however, the great majority of them came from the old Moscow aristocracy rather than from the nobility of St Petersburg, with its service orientation, regimentation and century-long tradition of close ties to the Court and the throne. The St Petersburg aristocracy was in a very real sense the creation of Peter the Great and his successors. They owed their position, wealth, success and even their noble rank to the Petrine system of state service. Equally important, as a result of their experiences in the eighteenth century, they were accustomed to follow the example of the ruler and the Court in cultural, social and political matters.

On the other hand, the Moscow nobility had remained apart, at least to some degree, from court society and culture during the eighteenth and the first part of the nineteenth century, and had developed their own (often more balanced) relationship to the ideas and culture of the West. This is not to say that Moscow aristocrats held to the old Russian, Muscovite ways and remained isolated from the ideas and culture of the West during the century after Peter. But they dealt with the culture of the West on different terms, and were less inclined to follow the cultural, social or intellectual fads which were so much a part of daily life among St Petersburg's *haute société*. In intellectual terms, at least, this Moscow aristocracy perhaps had earlier ties with the ideas and culture of the West than had the Court-centred nobility of St Petersburg. As early as the 1730s and 1740s, when the Court aristocracy in Russia's new capital had assimilated only the thinnest veneer of Western culture, their counterparts in Moscow were already discussing sophisticated Western political and philosophical ideas in a more serious and thoughtful manner.[73] But, in doing so, they remained less isolated from Russia's past, and the fact that the Court aristocracy of St Petersburg had turned away from their Russian roots was an accusation which Moscow aristocrats continually levelled against them. In 1787, for example, Prince M. M. Shcherbatov, a man who served the Russian state as well as being a man of letters and one of Russia's first historians, made the accusation very emphatically in his tale about an imaginary *Journey to the Land of Ofir*.

Shcherbatov, of course, wrote of Russia's eighteenth-century experience in allegorical terms. He spoke of the ruler Pereg (Peter the Great) who had founded a new capital, Peregab (St Petersburg), remote from the centre of the country, in which the nation's rulers lost the close, paternalistic touch with their land and their subjects which had characterized them earlier. Shcherbatov did not regard much of what the ruler Pereg had brought from the West as evil, however. He praised him for bringing the arts and sciences, modern technology, modern industry and administration to his backward country. But he considered it a tragedy that, in the new capital of Peregab, there had emerged, in the course of the eighteenth century, a new élite, a Court aristocracy, which looked only to the new westernized Court and which had turned away from its country in favour of the tastes and life at Court.[74] Shcherbatov looked to Moscow as the true centre of Russian life, and he regarded the Moscow aristocracy as the true Russian aristocracy while that of St Petersburg was little more than a foreign transplant with no understanding of Russia and with little concern for her best interests or welfare.

Perhaps even more important was the fact that the Moscow aristocracy was less service-orientated than their Petersburg counterparts. Where the St Petersburg aristocracy owed everything, even their noble status, to the service system created by Peter the Great, the Moscow nobility had received their titles long before Peter came to the throne. Many of them traced their noble status to the sixteenth century and earlier. They thus owed far less to state service than did their St Petersburg counterparts, and as a result their lives tended to be less taken up with concerns of the state service.

This is not to say that the Moscow aristocracy regarded state service in entirely negative terms, but state service was considerably less a part of their lives than was the case with the nobility of St Petersburg, and their different view of service became a critical element of their outlook and attitude towards the Nicholas system. Because they were less concerned about service, and because their aristocratic status had its roots in old Russia rather than in the more regulated, service-orientated St Petersburg, they fit less easily into the rigid mould which Nicholas sought to impose upon military and civil servants alike. In a word, the Moscow nobility was less accustomed to regimentation and was unused to efforts to limit or direct their contact with Western ideas. They were, moreover, perhaps less accustomed to censorship, especially the rigid sort of censorship which Nicholas and his ministers sought to impose. For such censorship, aimed at limiting contact with Western ideas, was a relatively recent phenomenon. During most of the eighteenth century, the autocrat had been in the unique position of urging more Western culture, ideas and technology upon Russians rather than seeking to prevent access to it.[75]

Given the fact that the Russian ruler and the Court of St Petersburg were the foremost proponents and devotees of Western culture during most of the eighteenth century, one might expect that the St Petersburg aristocracy would be even more involved with Western ideas than that of Moscow in the early nineteenth century. The reverse was the case because the St Petersburg nobles' interest in Western ideas was very superficial. While the cult of Voltaire (the *voltarianstvo*) had arisen under Catherine II in the 1760s and 1770s, among the nobility it had been much more a matter of style, of being in vogue, than of conviction. A passing acquaintance with the ideas of the Enlightenment was a necessary attribute for life in polite society, but no more was needed. And, as a result, many Petersburg noblemen changed their intellectual loyalties just as they changed their clothing styles.[76] Because they found it a relatively simple matter to change from one fashion of thought to another, one may assume that the St Petersburg aristocracy found censorship not very burdensome. For nearly a century before Admiral Shishkov had drafted the 'cast-iron statute', they had been accustomed to accepting or rejecting Western ideas as the taste of the ruler and Court changed. Therefore, one might argue, censorship only institutionalized a phenomenon which had always been very much a part of their lives. As such, it presented them with no great moral or intellectual dilemmas.

In Moscow, on the other hand educated society took Western ideas more seriously. They were not simply discussed in polite conversation, but were grappled with, picked apart, analysed and, when accepted, were adopted as the result of deep intellectual conviction. Such a process was certainly evident in the experience of the Moscow freemasons in the 1770s and 1780s when men such as Ivan Lopukhin and Nikolai Novikov rejected the ideas of the Enlightenment after a deep intellectual and moral struggle because they could not reconcile them with their own intellectual heritages, experiences and values.[77] The Moscow freemasons sought a system of thought that would satisfy the shortcomings which they perceived in their intellectual heritage without forcing them to abandon it entirely, a system of thought which they found in the theories of Berlin's Rosicrucians.[78] What intellectual dissent from the ideas and culture of the St Petersburg Court there was in Russia during the eighteenth century thus was centred largely in Moscow, and it was perhaps no accident that Aleksandr Radishchev, sometimes referred to as the 'first Russian radical', cast his fictitious journey in terms of travelling from St Petersburg to Moscow rather than the reverse, and that he concluded the account of his imaginary journey with the joyous cry: 'Moscow! Moscow! ! !'[79]

Educated opinion in Moscow thus quite probably took Western ideas more seriously than was the case in St Petersburg, not only for the reasons we have already suggested, but also because Moscow was the home of Russia's greatest university. The Imperial Russian Academy of Sciences was housed in St Petersburg, but was much more court-centred than was the University of Moscow. And, certainly, the first introductions into Russia of German Romanticism and idealism, out of which would evolve the first challenges to the Nicholas system, occurred in Moscow (and, to a lesser degree, in Kazan) rather than in St Petersburg.

It was in this atmosphere that the young men of the 1830s and 1840s, those who would offer the first challenges to the Nicholas system, matured. They shared a serious concern for the welfare of Russia, a deep respect for Russian tradition and a commitment to serious intellectual inquiry. They came from a social group which, while it served the state and regarded service as honourable, did not owe everything to achievements in the state service. And they were unaccustomed to the rigid sorts of restraint which had first entered St Petersburg society with the reign of Paul I in the very late eighteenth century. The militarism of Paul I, carried on by Alexander I and raised to an even more pervasive level under Nicholas I, was far less a part of the Moscow nobleman's experience than was the case in St Petersburg. As a result, the young nobleman who reached maturity in Moscow in the 1830s and 1840s found it difficult, sometimes impossible, to fit himself into the rigid service mould which Nicholas required of all who served the Russian state.

Peter III had emancipated the Russian nobility from compulsory state service in 1762, and so one might well point out that, since these young men could not fit into the service framework of Nicholas's Russia, there was nothing impelling them to enter the service or to remain in the service once they had entered. But this was the time when the 'superfluous nobleman' was becoming very much a phenomenon in Russia, certainly among the Moscow nobility. Being an aristocrat and living from the labour of one's serfs was not enough to satisfy the self-image of such men. It was necessary to fulfil some worthwhile function in society for them to justify their existence to themselves and to their associates.

But in Nicholas's Russia, the values of Russian society were more than ever focused upon state service since the Emperor himself insisted that it must be so. And, as we have noted, these young men found life in the service difficult, sometimes impossible, to bear. They could not always forsake their own ideas and values, and abandon their more free life at the university and in Moscow society for the uniform of a civil servant or army officer. And they could not set aside their very real concerns about such cosmic questions as the nature of beauty, love, truth and right in favour of the mundane concerns of state servitors which centred upon rewards, decorations and promotions. These young men were concerned with learning, with literature and with ideas. As one of their number, a rare commoner in their midst, the critic V. G. Belinskii, would write later in 1847, 'among us the title of poet and writer has long since eclipsed the tinsel of epaulettes and gaudy uniforms'.[80] But they faced the very frustrating dilemma of living in a society which generally provided no justification for intellectuals *per se*. For it was not enough to be a thinker in terms of the values held by much of Russian society at the time. As we have seen, it was also necessary to serve in order to be considered worthwhile in the Russia of Nicholas, and so professors in the university served the state (holding civil service rank), and many writers of belles-lettres and criticism served in the bureaucracy at some point in their careers.

The fact that society provided them with no justification for their existence, and that they could not, or would not, serve the state in the accepted manner, caused these young men to become increasingly alienated from Russian reality. And the fact that they fell under suspicion of Nicholas's Third Section and censors because they were seriously concerned with ideas, alienated them even more. Thus these young men, unlike their immediate predecessors, the Decembrists, were not simply critical of Russian reality but alienated from it. And because they did not share the cosmopolitanism which had caused the Decembrists to think it possible to apply the political ferment and ideas of post-Napoleonic Europe to Russian conditions, and to seek solutions similar to those which their counterparts had sought in the West or in America, the young men at the University of Moscow in the 1830s at first turned inward to the more contemplative doctrines of German Romanticism and idealism rather than to the more active path of the Decembrists.

As one writer has noted recently, 'In Russia, as elsewhere, the principal consequence of Idealism was greatly to enhance the creative role of the human mind.'[81] In its earliest Russian form, this concern with the creative role of the human mind took the form of a cult of Schiller and a glorification of his Romantic theme that focused upon the self-fulfilment of the individual as the means by which the individual could attain true freedom. For the young nobleman of Moscow in the late 1820s and early 1830s, this emphasis upon the self-fulfilment of the individual was especially significant since Schiller had seen it as taking place outside the framework of social or political life. As Schiller had argued:

[It was] only in the inner world of the spirit, in the development of a beautiful soul – *die schöne Seele* – that man is free and fully realizes himself . . . Art, friendship, and love, all three grounded in sentiment, are the ultimate values for Schiller and the only path to true liberty . . . The ego is immeasurably exalted, but it is placed in isolation where it can express itself only in fantasy.[82]

For young men who found the Russia of Nicholas spiritually deadening, but were forced to live in the alien world which it had created, such a glorification of the ego, of the self, in an internalized world free from all political and service demands, offered an ideal means of escape. It served as a compensation for the freedom which life in the real world denied them, and in their dreams and fantasies these youths could give free reign to their aspirations and identify with the greatest heroes of man's past. It provided more: a justification, even glorification, of their retreat from the real world into an ideal world from which all distasteful and oppressive reality could be banished by philosophical construct. Schiller's aesthetics, his cult of love, art and friendship, supplied the basis for their self-imposed isolation, and this isolation served as the cement which bound them together during their university years in the 1830s.

While the intellectual development of the Decembrists, the young men who reached maturity during the Napoleonic wars, took place in the salons of St Petersburg and Western Europe, that of the young men of the 1830s and 1840s, who would pose the first challenges to the Nicholas system, began in the salons of Moscow. There was an important difference between the two types of experience. In the salons of St Petersburg and the West, the Decembrists had encountered a wide range of ideas stemming mainly from the eighteenth-century Enlightenment. The salons where they encountered these ideas, however, were the salons of polite St Petersburg society where a passing acquaintance with such ideas was essential, but where it was regarded as being in rather poor taste to probe too deeply into such matters in polite conversation. The result was that the Decembrists' outlook was very eclectic and superficial and, above all European. The Decembrists felt so at ease in the West that they simply assumed that their Western ideas could be applied to Russia. On the other hand, the intellectual life of the Moscow salons was quite different. Although attended by polite society, there were some salons where serious intellectual discourse predominated. On Thursday evenings, leading writers, scholars and others concerned with philosophical, literary and cultural questions gathered at the home of the Moscow university professor Pavlov; on Fridays, they met at the salon of the Sverbeevs, and on Sundays, there were gatherings at the home of Madame Elagina, the mother of two Slavophiles, Ivan and Petr Kireevskii.[83] It was in such salons that many future Westerners and Slavophiles would have their first encounters with the Romantic and idealist literary and philosophical systems which would provide the structural framework for the theoretical edifices they began to erect in the 1830s and would complete in the 1840s. It was there that young men such as the Kireevskii brothers, Konstantin Aksakov, Nikolai Stankevich, V. G. Belinskii, Mikhail Bakunin, V. P. Botkin, Aleksandr Herzen, Nikolai Ogarev, Timofei Granovskii and a number of others would begin the intellectual odyssey which, between 1826 and 1840, would lead them from the philosophical systems of Schelling and Hegel to the utopian socialist ideas of Fourier and Saint-Simon. As V. G. Belinskii wrote, 'during this decade [beginning in 1826], we experienced, thought through, and lived through the entire intellectual life of Europe'.[84]

The young men who began their discussions of German Romantic and idealist systems in the Moscow salons developed their views further at Moscow University during the early and mid 1830s. But the lectures they heard, and their relationships with the university's professors, comprised only a part of their intellectual experience. There was no forum for their views in Moscow, or even in Russia. Not a single periodical or journal shared their concerns, enthusiasms or infatuations with the works of their German masters. They were alone. Isolated, they felt themselves adrift in an alien world, and it was quite probably the failure of the Russian environment to nourish their aspirations which led them to band together in 'circles' (*kruzhki*) of like-minded youths to discuss and test their ideas.

It would be difficult to over-estimate the importance which the 'circle' had in the lives of these young men. It was more than a debating society, and more than a fraternity in either the nineteenth- or twentieth-century meaning of the term. It was, in an intellectual and emotional sense, a close-knit brotherhood where young men were held together in the closest of bonds by common aspirations and by shared commitments to certain ideas. To them, the 'circle' was of supreme importance in their lives and in their intellectual development. In a very important sense, the 'circle' would alter the lives of many of them. The critic V. G. Belinskii described the meaning of these 'circles' and underlined their importance in a letter to V. P. Botkin, one of his close friends and a fellow Westerner, in mid 1840. As he wrote to Botkin: 'Our upbringing deprived us of religion; the circumstance of life (the cause for which was in the condition of society) did not provide us with a favourable education and deprived us of any opportunity to master knowledge; we were in conflict with reality and, to be honest, we loathe and despise it just as it quite frankly loathes and despises us.'[85]

These 'circles' were more closely knit than were salons, although one did not replace or supersede the other, and the young men at the university who, during the 1840s, would become bitter enemies as their ranks split into Westerner and Slavophile camps, could be found at both, discussing the ideas of their German masters. Equally important, not all circles at Moscow University consisted of young men devoted to German idealism who were simultaneously alienated from their surroundings. For our purposes, however, two circles were crucial in the intellectual development of the men who would first challenge the Nicholas system. One was that of Aleksandr Herzen and Nikolai Ogarev; the other was the circle of Nikolai Stankevich. These two circles, as one historian has written, 'produced most of the philosophical- and political-minded talent of the thirties and forties, and they dominated the intellectual life of Moscow, and, indeed, of Russia, for the bulk of the reign of Nicholas'.[86]

Although their members would later share many of the same views, there were sharp differences between the circles of Herzen and Stankevich during the early 1830s. As Herzen himself later characterized them, 'They did not agree with our almost exclusively political orientation and we did not adhere to their almost exclusively speculative outlook. They considered us to be *frondeurs* and francophiles; we considered them senti- mentalists and germanophiles.'[87] Herzen's and Ogarev's circle was forced to be more secretive because of its political interests, and as a result it had a far narrower influence upon the Moscow youth than did that of Stankevich. Indeed, even before the middle of the decade, nearly all of its members, including Herzen and Ogarev, had been arrested and sent into exile. As a result, it was the circle of Stankevich which, in the 1830s, played a major role in the intellectual development of those who were to become Slavophiles and Westerners in the following decade.

The Stankevich circle, like that of Herzen and Ogarev, had no formal organization, as had been the case with the circles of the Decembrists or those of the 1820s, such as the Lovers of Wisdom. The circle was held together exclusively by the common ideals which its members shared, and most important by the magnetic personality of Stankevich himself. Stankevich himself lived only briefly. He was born in 1813, the year after Herzen, and in April 1840, at the age of twenty-seven, he was already dead, a victim of tuberculosis. Yet, in his few short years of life, Stankevich achieved a great deal and became a legendary figure in the circles of Russia's infant intelligentsia. He came to Moscow in 1830 at the age of seventeen and studied music under the German composer, F. K. Gebel. He became an accomplished pianist, a poet of some significance, and a frequent contributor to literary magazines. Philosophy and history, however, became his burning passions. He translated numbers of articles on Western philosophy, and even produced a dissertation 'On the Causes of the Gradual Rise of Moscow to Pre-eminence during the Period up to the Death of Ivan III'.[88]

Stankevich possessed a brilliant and magnetic personality besides his many intellectual and artistic accomplishments. And it was his personality, as well as his learning, which drew to him a number of kindred spirits. Mikhail Bakunin, later to become known throughout Europe as an anarchist and an opponent of Marx, was perhaps the leading member of the circle, and by mid-decade his influence grew to rival that of Stankevich himself. But there were also several others: V. G. Belinskii, one of the rare commoners among the Russian intelligentsia of the 1830s, who would later become one of Russia's greatest literary critics; Timofei Granovskii, an important historian; Mikhail Katkov, later a famous conservative literary critic and publisher of an important Moscow journal; Konstantin Aksakov, a famous Slavophile; V. P. Botkin, a traveller, writer and one of the leading Westerners in the 1840s – these, and some lesser figures, made up the circle during the 1830s. The aesthetics of Schelling were the corner-stone from which the circle constructed its *Weltanschauung* in the early 1830s. From that point, they progressed to the ethics of Fichte and, finally, to the logic of Hegel.[89] Stankevich and his followers were concerned not with reality, but with the abstract and ideal world into which the aesthetics of Schelling had led them as a reaction to the reality which they found alien and oppressive. But for some, in fact most of them, their efforts to grapple with questions of beauty, right and truth in a vacuum, in an ideal world from which the real world was excluded, became a tortuous and painful experience. For the world from which they sought to isolate themselves was too obvious and too real to be ignored or banished by philosophical construct, and nearly all of them, as the decade came to an end, would make some effort at reconciliation with reality.

This inner need for an affirmation of reality was especially evident in the ideological development of Belinskii. Unlike his aristocratic fellows in the Stankevich circle, Belinskii was desperately poor, and thus, to the oppression of a reality which could not nurture his intellectual life, was added the crushing burden of poverty. By the late 1830s, his spirit exhausted by abstractions, Belinskii began to think that he could serve society as he was, and in doing so began the process of self-affirmation that would take him first to Right Hegelianism and then to Left Hegelianism. Belinskii thus questioned the romantic idealistic withdrawal from reality which had characterized the Moscow youth of the 1830s, and by the end of the decade rejected it in favour of a complete acceptance of the concrete world in which everything that was real was a phenomenological manifestation of the absolute.[90]

Together with Bakunin, Belinskii embarked upon an acceptance of Russian reality and, throughout 1838 and 1839, they sought to apply their crudely formulated understanding of Hegel's dictum that 'the real is the rational and the rational is the real' by glorifying autocracy, serfdom and the doctrines of Official Nationality. Indeed, they glorified the entire Nicholas system. Such an acceptance of all that he regarded as evil and unjust, of what appeared to him as a negation of the privations he had suffered in exile, infuriated Herzen, who had just returned from four years of exile in Viatka and Vladimir. For a year, the conflict between him and Belinskii raged at fever pitch. In April 1848, Belinskii would write to Botkin that, as far as Herzen was concerned, 'I spit on him.'[91] But, by the end of the year, the conflict had been resolved. Both had reached a point of agreement in their acceptance of the doctrines of Left Hegelianism, and Belinskii could write of Herzen:

I like this man more and more. It is true that he is the best of all . . . He evidently is changing for the best in his understanding. I feel free and at ease with him. That he cursed me in Moscow for my absolutist articles – this is a new claim on his part to my respect and my liking for him.[92]

Belinskii's affirmation of his own experience as a new ideal had led him and others to accept the Nicholas system in its entirety. But they were thinking, passionate men, accustomed to critical thought, and their affirmation of a reality that was so alien to their inner beings could not but have been of short duration. Thus, as a result of Herzen's preachings during 1840,[93] Belinskii was led to a dynamic affirmation of the necessity to challenge reality rather than accept it passively. By 1841, Belinskii had become a Left Hegelian, passionately believing and arguing that the human personality could only have meaning in a struggle against the oppressions of the external world.[94] He thus challenged the Nicholas system by proclaiming that the artist must be the conscience of his time and of his society. He insisted that the artist was the only effective moral agent to combat an immoral world.

3. *Westerners and Slavophiles*

The change in the outlooks of Belinskii, Herzen and their comrades was accompanied by a shift of ideological loyalties from Germany to France, from the world of idealism to the world of utopian socialism. And, at that point, the two currents of the 1830s – the circle of Stankevich and the circle of Herzen and Ogarev – merged into the movement of the Westerners of the 1840s. Their new philosophy was 'social metaphysics' – abstract solutions to concrete social problems – and Herzen, Belinskii and their friends abandoned themselves to an orgy of reading the works of the French utopian socialists: Proudhon, Saint-Simon and Fourier in particular, along with Louis Blanc's *Histoire des dix ans* and *Organisation du travail*, as well as Thiers's *History of the French Revolution*.[95]

But the Westerners represented only one product of the Moscow salons and 'circles' of the 1830s. Equally important, the many evenings spent in debate among friends had produced another group – the Slavophiles – who would become the bitter rivals of the Westerners during the 1840s. The Slavophiles had shared many experiences with the Westerners during their years in Moscow. A number of future Slavophiles had been an integral segment of Stankevich's circle, and a number of Westerners, especially Herzen, had been regular visitors to Madame Elagina's salon on Sundays. All of them had shared a burning interest in German Romantic and idealist works, and they had discussed much of this body of knowledge in the course of many evenings together. Most important of all, as Herzen himself later emphasized, both groups shared 'a boundless feeling which encompassed our entire existence – a love for the Russian masses, the Russian way of life, and the Russian cast of mind'.[96]

Yet, although they shared a number of experiences in the 1830s, the Slavophiles were unlike the Westerners in a number of important ways. Although their founding fathers, Ivan Kireevskii and A. S. Khomiakov, had been educated in the European tradition, their backgrounds were in some sense unique. The men who became Slavophiles were bound together not only by their common commitment to certain ideas, but by

ties of marriage and very similar social and economic backgrounds. Both
Westerners and Slavophiles came from the Russian aristocracy with very
few exceptions. But the Slavophiles came from a much narrower group,
what we might call the middle gentry, not vastly wealthy, but very
comfortably well off.

Although future Slavophiles and future Westerners continued to be
close socially during much of the 1830s, there were elements introduced
into their lives which played a very important part in driving them apart
in the 1840s. Perhaps most important of these was religion. Interestingly
enough, the coming Westerner-Slavophile conflict was first played out in
the childhood environment of the future Slavophiles, for most came from
families in which one parent was strongly Westernized while the other
was much more deeply committed to Russian culture and the Orthodox
faith. In the cases of both Kireevskii and Khomiakov, however, both took
the Westernized path at first. But they were driven back to the path of
Russian culture and, particularly, Russian Orthodoxy, by their marriages
to women who were intensely religious and who actively sought to involve
their husbands in doctrinals.[97] As the decade of the 1830s drew to an end,
therefore, both Kireevskii brothers and Khomiakov turned more to
Orthodoxy, while Herzen, Belinskii and the other Westerners turned
further from religion. Indeed, it was religion and philosophy which comprised their basic differences until the early 1840s, when the differences
would take on political overtones[98] and become concerned with the
historic mission of Russia – Russia's role in universal civilization.

The spark which ignited the conflagration between Slavophiles and
Westerners, which would rage among the intelligentsia for nearly two
decades, was struck by Petr Chaadaev. Chaadaev was older, more a part
of the intellectual generation of the Decembrists, than the men whom we
have been discussing, and he remained at a certain distance from all of
them, striking an 'eternal pose' in their company.[99] Chaadaev was deeply
influenced by Roman Catholicism, which he saw as the crucial factor in
the experience of Western Europe. To him, Catholicism was the major
cause of the unity and sequence of Western history; it was of critical
importance in enabling the West to outstrip Russia in the eighteenth
and early nineteenth centuries. Roman Catholicism well may have had
for him the same psychological function as Schelling's philosophy for
Stankevich and his circle; it was a refuge from the alien reality which had
sent many of his Decembrist friends to exile or death. Perhaps equally
important, Chaadaev's idealization of medieval Catholic unity enabled
him to preserve that cosmopolitanism which was so much a part of the
Decembrists' outlook by moving it back in time to an earlier period when,
he believed, there had been a harmonious civilization of nations in the

West, nations free from national prejudice yet able to maintain an individual national consciousness while acknowledging the broader interests of mankind.[100]

Chaadaev set forth his views on Russia's past, present and future in a series of 'Letters on the Philosophy of History' which he wrote between 1829 and 1831, but which he published (only in part) in 1836. They were written in French, translated into Russian by Belinskii, and the first of them was published anonymously in the journal *Telescope* in 1836.[101] The 'Letters' were written from 'Necropolis' (the city of the dead), and they were an extreme response to the disintegration of the naïve cosmopolitan aspirations of the Decembrists.[102] Russia, he insisted, was a country without a history which had itself contributed nothing to civilization. As he wrote in the letter which appeared in *Telescope* (the rest were suppressed), 'We live entirely within the narrowest confines of the present, without a past or a future, in the midst of a dead calm.'[103] And Russia's stagnation, her inability even to respond to stimuli to progress, was to be explained by the fact that she had drawn her Christianity from the tainted source of Byzantium, thereby cutting herself off from the true source of spiritual life which issued from Rome.

Chaadaev's letter rang out 'like a pistol shot in the night'.[104] He was officially declared insane, and *Telescope*'s editor, N. I. Nadezhdin, was exiled to Siberia. Nicholas and his censors found Chaadaev's letter offensive because he had attacked one of the fundamental tenets of Official Nationality: Orthodoxy. To the men who were soon to be identified as Slavophiles – the Kireevskii brothers, Khomiakov, Konstantin Aksakov and several others – the letter was equally alarming. For, while they believed in progress in Russia, they wanted it to come about within the framework of Russian tradition. Chaadaev's totally negative assessment of Russia's past, present and future was thus offensive to Slavophile and Westerner alike. In the face of his challenge, both groups began to articulate their views more precisely, and it would be this clarification which, in the mid 1840s, would lead to the bitter break between them.

The Slavophiles began to clarify their views first, since the Westerners were still engaged in conflict among themselves over the nature of Hegel's philosophy, and some of them, Herzen and Ogarev in particular, were still in exile. For the Slavophiles, 'The cardinal point of their creed was that human reason was a shaky reed, and that the only rock of truth was religious faith.'[105] The rationalism of the West was the single poisonous seed from which all of the evils from which the West suffered had sprung. And rationalism itself was the result of the West's connection with Rome. Only Russian Orthodoxy and the communal spirit (*sobornost'*) which it fostered, had remained faithful to true Christian ideals, and it was this quality of *sobornost'* which was the unique feature of the Russian national character and would comprise Russia's greatest contribution to the future development of universal culture. Thus, the Russian family was patriarchal, while the family in the West was individualistic. In Russia, property was held communally; in the West, there was private ownership. True civilization – Old Russian, pre-Petrine civilization – was based on the land; in the West, civilization was based in the towns and cities. And it was these differences between Russia and the West which had caused those Russians who had followed the Western path to become alienated from their past and their civilization. The solution to the alienation from which the intelligentsia suffered, the Slavophiles argued, was once again to submerge themselves in the community, once again to become at one with *sobornost'* and to return to their true faith. Nowhere in Russia were these unique Russian attributes more evident or to be found in a more pure form than in the commune (*mir*). In the Slavophiles' view, the *mir* embodied all of the unique Russian virtues and had preserved them from the corrosive path upon which Russia had been forced by Peter the Great. The *mir*, a unique Russian institution, would lead Russia back to the true path of civilization.[106]

The Westerners clarified their views somewhat later, and only after they had jointly accepted the notions of Left Hegelianism and completed their shift of ideological loyalties from Germany to France. They were extremely critical of Russia's past and present, and were unanimous in rejecting the Slavophiles' idealized version of the differences between the historical development of Russia and the West. Equally important, they rejected as superstitious and dangerous the Slavophiles' emphasis on religion in Russia's development and saw little merit in their deep Orthodox religiosity. As Belinskii wrote to Gogol in 1847:

Russia sees her salvation not in mysticism, not in asceticism, not in pietism, but in the successes of civilization, in enlightenment, and in humanity. She needs not sermons (she has heard enough of them already!) nor prayers (she has repeated them too often!), but the awakening in the masses of a sense of their human dignity, lost for so many centuries amidst filth and refuse. She needs rights and laws not in conformity with the teachings of the Church, but in conformity with common sense and justice in its strictest sense.[107]

And, as Belinskii noted further, 'The Church became a hierarchy and a champion of inequality, a flatterer of authority and an enemy and persecutor of brotherhood among men – and so it continues to be to this very moment.'[108]

The final split between the two groups came in 1844 when, in a series of public lectures, which became one of the major events of the Moscow

season, the Westerner historian, T. N. Granovskii, dealt with the history
of the medieval West in Hegelian terms. Although he concluded his
lectures with a glowing account of Russia's future, and although the two
groups were momentarily reconciled as a result, the debate broke out
with renewed force within a few weeks. The rift widened even more in
the next decade, especially in the mid 1850s, when a young Westerner
historian, B. N. Chicherin, argued that the peasant commune, as it
existed in Russia at the time, was of relatively recent origin, that it was
not the product of indigenous peasant values, but that it had been brought
into being by a clear-cut state policy designed to ensure the collection of
taxes in the eighteenth century.[109] As a result, by the time of Nicholas's
death, the Westerners and the Slavophiles appeared to have become
irreconcilable enemies.

Although the Westerners were at one in their opposition to the Slavophiles' views, they were far from united on the question of Russia's
future. Certainly they seemed to have no ideology in common. Some
were liberal or, more accurately, moderate; others were radical, even
revolutionary. But their views, taken as a whole, were a shifting quick-
sand of ideological devotions to socialism and liberalism, to evolution and
revolution, to the glorification of the masses and to a reliance upon an
élite. Indeed, towards the end of his life, Belinskii would suddenly shift
his position to argue that 'what Russia needed was not socialism but a
bourgeoisie',[110] and Herzen would, at the very end of his life, reject
revolution as well. But even at the height of their unity against Slavophiles,
the Westerners' ranks were breaking apart over the question of evolution
as opposed to revolution and liberalism as opposed to socialism. By late
1846, the Westerners had split and the rift became so bitter that Herzen
found himself almost totally isolated; even Belinskii was having doubts
about the socialism which Herzen so passionately espoused.[111] As a
result, in January 1847, Herzen left Russia never to return.

There remained behind a much more moderate group. Herzen and
Ogarev had gone to the West; Belinskii, alone in St Petersburg, was
turning away from socialism; and those who remained in Moscow,
headed by the magnetic but gentle Timofei Granovskii, were convinced
of the virtue of the evolutionary path to improvement. But even in the
Moscow circle there was no final agreement nor anything resembling an
ideological unity, for they were, in truth, not ideologues but critics.
Criticism of Russia's past and present best characterized their attitudes,
and it is perhaps symbolic that probably the leading exponent of
Westerner views – V. G. Belinskii – was above all a literary critic. From
St Petersburg and his forum in the journals *Notes of the Fatherland* and
the *Contemporary*, Belinskii, until his death in 1848, thundered against

those who refused to agree that literature must deal with critical social issues. And ultimately that is what the Westerner movement was – a thundering of alienated men against the injustices which the Nicholas system had heaped upon them – a new conscience of a society which refused them the opportunity to use their broad talents for the country they loved.

The debates among the Slavophiles and Westerners about the nature of Russia's past, present and future seem far too minor in retrospect to have caused such an outpouring of animosities. But their bitterness was in a great measure the result of the fact that the Nicholas system denied them the positive role that they craved in society. They threw themselves into the debates of the 1840s with a passion which consumed all their energies, and their bitterness was especially deep because they were discussing questions of how to structure the future so that they would be provided with a role in society that would be commensurate with their abilities. The importance of their need for a positive social and political role becomes evident if one looks ahead to the emancipation work of the late 1850s where those Westerners and Slavophiles who were invited to participate quickly buried their differences and reconciled themselves to society and the state. Only among those who were given no part to play in the emancipation work did the debate continue.

But, as far as the debates of the 1840s were concerned, they were soon interrupted by other events. Most of all, the year 1848, while it initially promised a realization of the Westerners' dreams in the West, soon led to bitter disillusionment as the revolutions followed other paths. Yet the disillusionment with 1848 had hardly begun when the Westerners suffered an even more tragic blow. In May 1848, tuberculosis, that scourge of Petersburg in the nineteenth century, claimed Belinskii's life. On the heels of his death came the rigid censorship of the last years of Nicholas's reign, when it became difficult to publish anything about history, literature, philosophy or politics in Russia. By the end of the year it was clear to all that the 'marvellous decade'[112] had ended. For those who remained, there would begin a time of waiting, of withdrawal, of retreat in the face of growing oppression.[113] Their ranks would be broken by exile, and many could no longer discuss their views in print. For these men, the last years of Nicholas would be a long purgatory. And, when Russia's defeat in the Crimean War made it possible to discuss Russian life once again, they would have to contend with different problems.

8

The Year 1848

*'The people need potatoes, but not a constitution in
the least; that is wanted by the educated
urban classes, who are incapable of doing anything'*

V. G. BELINSKII

*'Our main defence . . . against a mass . . . revolution
lies in the fact that among us there are
neither the elements nor the instruments for it . . .
There are no elements [for revolution]
because freedom of the press, popular representation,
national guards, and things of that
nature . . . are complete nonsense to nine tenths of the
Russian population'*

BARON M. A. KORF

At the beginning of 1848, most of Russian educated society looked forward to a continuation of the orderly life that they had enjoyed ever since Nicholas had ascended the throne. As we have seen, many Russians regarded those years as good ones, as a time of prosperity and promise. Gone were the uncertainties of the days of Alexander I, when talk of constitutions and emancipating the serfs periodically disturbed the comfortable lives of the aristocracy. Gone, too, were the devastations which Russia had suffered during Napoleon's invasion; gone were the wars which, between 1805 and 1815, had been so costly in terms of Russian blood and treasure. The first two decades of Nicholas's reign saw Russian soldiers in combat against Persia, against the Turks, in the 1831 invasion of Poland and in the annual campaigns against the natives of the Caucasus. But these conflicts were distant rumblings which few heard and in which fewer participated. Not until 1853 would Russian society be mobilized for war as it had been under Alexander I during the Napoleonic campaigns. Only with the periodic announcement of glorious victories did the awareness of war intrude upon the consciousness of most Russians. In Europe and in Asia, Russian arms seemed invincible, and more than three decades had passed since an enemy soldier had set foot on Russian soil.

Life was comfortable and far more predictable than for some time past, though the burdens of labour, taxation and military service weighed heavily upon the enserfed peasantry; more so, in fact, than ever before. There was also that small number of aristocratic intellectuals, increasingly alienated from the mainstream of Russian life, who bitterly criticized Nicholas's government and who, for a brief moment, dreamed of revolution as an antidote to the poisons which, they were convinced, had been injected into the veins of their motherland by the growing abuses of the Nicholas system. Belinskii had summed up the views of both masses and dissident intellectuals quite well in 1846 when he had written to some of his friends that 'the people need potatoes, but not a constitution in the least; that is wanted by the educated urban classes, who are incapable of doing anything'.[1] But the masses presented no real threat of upheaval in 1848, and the critical intelligentsia, as Belinskii had said, were 'incapable of doing anything'.

To many of the Russians in the main streets of St Petersburg in 1848, life thus was far from unattractive. Certainly, for the aristocracy of the capital, it was a comfortable time. For the merchants it was an era of prosperity and rising prices, and even for the petty clerk in the warrens of the capital's dark chanceries, the opportunity to participate, albeit vicariously, in the glittering and magnificent life of Russia's capital was a chance not to be missed. For St Petersburg held a magical fascination for provincials and inhabitants of the city alike. As the novelist M. E. Saltykov-Shchedrin would describe it some years later in his tale, *Diary of a Provincial in Petersburg*: 'We provincials somehow turn our steps towards Petersburg instinctively . . . It is as if Petersburg all by itself, with its name, its streets, its fog, rain, and snow, could resolve something or shed light on something.'[2] St Petersburg personified the Russia of Nicholas in many ways. It was a city where order and regularity reigned supreme.[3] 'No dissonances marred the general harmony, for there was a conservative monarchical sentiment in all strata [of society] and there seemed to be no possibility of any other,'[4] was how one observer in the 1840s summed up his impressions.

It was, then, a time of prosperity. The Empire's currency had been fully stabilized by 1843,[5] and with the exception of the iron industry, there had been considerable industrial expansion in Russia under the Nicholas system. Raw cotton imports (an indication that the Russian textile industry was producing more of its own thread) rose from an average of 5,400,000 pounds in 1831 to an average of 40,400,000 pounds in 1848.[6] And the production of beet sugar had risen from 540,000 pounds in 1825 to 38,286,000 pounds in 1850.[7] Likewise, the number of factories and manufactories had increased from 5,261 in 1825 to 8,929 in 1848, and most importantly, the number of industrial workers had more than doubled in the same period from 210,568 to 483,542.[8] Finally, the export of grain, one of Russia's most important foreign trade commodities, had risen in value from 7,100,000 silver roubles in 1820 to 11,074,000 in 1840, and was in the process of beginning a rapid take-off, caused by the repeal of the Corn Laws in England, which would lead grain exports to reach the value of 37,508,000 silver roubles by 1860.[9]

But 1848 would be the most difficult year Nicholas had faced since his accession. Russia would suffer an almost universally bad harvest and would have to face the ravages of famine in many provinces. The famine of 1848 was the most extensive to occur during the entire second quarter of the nineteenth century, and according to figures compiled by the Ministry of the Interior, the average harvest for the year was 'in general not more than half the amount planted'.[10] Equally serious would be a cholera epidemic, far more widespread than usual, which would touch every corner of European Russia and even some parts of Siberia. It was a dread disease, killing a large proportion of its victims, and no one at the time understood how it spread or how to treat it effectively. The cholera struck Russia unseasonably early in January 1848. Once the spring thaws had come and gone, and river traffic had opened in the spring, the disease spread everywhere, carrying terror and death throughout the Empire.

Yet another catastrophe appeared outside Russia's borders at the beginning of the year: the revolutions of 1848 in Western and Central Europe. These caused Nicholas and his advisers to become increasingly oppressive in their policies and to suppress ruthlessly even the most innocent signs of dissatisfaction. Nicholas ordered reinforcements into the Russian-held provinces of Poland, sent an army into Hungary to suppress Lajos Kossuth's rebels, and instituted measures designed to stamp out all sparks of revolution that might fall into the Empire itself. Baron Korf, as one of the officials most closely involved with spreading a tighter net of censorship over Russia after mid 1848, noted in his diary:

Our main defence . . . against a mass . . . revolution lies in the fact that among us there are neither the elements nor the instruments for it . . . There are no elements [for revolution] because freedom of the press, popular representation, national guards, and things of that nature . . . are complete nonsense to nine tenths of the Russian population. There are no instruments [for revolution] because there are no elements [for it].[11]

There would be only one extremely timid stirring of revolutionary sentiment in Russia itself – the circle of M. V. Butashevich-Petrashevskii in 1849. The Third Section and other police officials, urged on by Nicholas, would crush them ruthlessly to make certain that neither the elements nor the instruments of revolution could take root.

1. Crises from Within

Even before 1848, Nicholas had begun to show signs of age; strong and powerful though his constitution was, the strain of ruling had taken its toll. As the Austrian ambassador reported to Metternich in 1846:

He has to make an effort to conquer fatigue, to do what seemed easy to him until now. He has become silent, he avoids assemblies; he says that society, balls, and fêtes, have become a drudgery and that he prefers to live like a bourgeois ... The conviction is gaining more and more ground that the Emperor, in spite of his constant work and his energy, will not succeed in doing the good he wants to do, nor in destroying the evil he sees.[12]

Nicholas was no longer the self-possessed young paladin who had returned to the arms of his Empress on the night of 14 December 1825 after crushing the Decembrists. Nor was he the dynamic conqueror who had strode through the palace halls at Münchengrätz some fifteen years earlier. Nicholas, like his two brothers before him, had aged quickly once he neared the age of fifty. As with Alexander I and Konstantin Pavlovich, a sense of frustration at what had not been accomplished, tinged with vague feelings of defeat and a certain fatalism, set in. Early in 1847, he suffered a serious abdominal inflammation and thought he was dying. A few months later, another illness had struck, lingered briefly, and strengthened further his awareness of his own mortality.[13]

The ever-presence of death must have occupied Nicholas increasingly as he passed the age of fifty. The Grand Duchess Aleksandra Nikolaevna, his youngest daughter whom he loved as the image of her mother, had died even before he reached his fiftieth birthday. Even more depressing for him, the health of his beloved Empress got no better, and from the mid 1840s until the end of his reign there were times when she seemed at death's door.[14] Death also began to claim Nicholas's closest advisers. Benkendorf, perhaps his closest companion and a comrade-in-arms for more than two decades, was the first victim in 1844. Kankrin died the following year, Vasil'chikov in 1847, and Levashov in 1848. Nicholas's only remaining brother, Mikhail Pavlovich, would soon follow in 1849. By 1848, then, nearly all of Nicholas's closest confidants, the men with whom he had shaped the Nicholas system, were dead.

Nicholas, the military commander who saw 'each one of his days . . . [as] a day of battle',[15] thus faced the many crises of 1848 with weakened reserves. He was beginning to look old and, more important, to feel old; he had not the strength of body and soul with which he had faced the crises of 1830–31. His Empress, the fragile and beautiful princess he had begun to love in that Prussian autumn so long ago, his faithful 'Mouffy' with whom he had always found 'happiness and repose' from the cares of ruling,[16] had become worn and gaunt, aged well before her time, a woman 'to whom one would give sixty years . . . [when] she had only passed her fortieth'.[17] Gone forever were the intimate gatherings at the Winter Palace where Nicholas had met in the late afternoons and evenings, often over dinner, with energetic counsellors, to deal with the crises which confronted them.

All of the crises of 1848 burst upon Nicholas at once, early in the year. In January, the cholera broke out in the south-eastern provinces of Kazan and Orenburg, as well as in the south-western grain-growing provinces of Poltava and Chernigov. It reached the trading centre of Nizhnii-Novgorod, the site of Russia's largest annual fair, by February, and in mid March it reached Moscow. By late spring the disease was raging throughout the European portions of the Empire, and by July it had crossed the Ural Mountains into Siberia where it had never penetrated before.[18] According to official statistics of 1848, the epidemic in St Petersburg alone infected more than 22,000 and killed some 12,228, a figure which may have been lower than the actual number of cases and deaths, since at least one contemporary observer placed the number of deaths in mid July at over 15,000.[19] But even according to the official statistics, one in thirty-six Petersburgers died from the disease, and one in twenty fell ill.

Cholera brought panic in its wake. No one knew how to prevent its spread, and there was no effective cure. As one observer remarked:

It spared no one, but it seized especially many victims from among the poor. The slightest carelessness in food, the slightest cold, was enough to bring it on; after four or five hours, a person would be no more. Terror reigned everywhere throughout the entire summer.[20]

St Petersburg, a city of about half a million inhabitants, became a ghost city within a few weeks. V. P. Bykova, a young woman attending the Smolnyi Institute, a prestigious finishing school for young ladies of good family, wrote in her diary on 4 July 1848:

During the past two weeks about 100,000 inhabitants have left St Petersburg. The common people also are dispersing to their villages . . . There are almost no hackney drivers. The city is empty; in the Gostinyi Dvor [a building which housed small shopkeepers' stalls], many shops have barred their doors – trade has ceased completely.[21]

Outside the capital, the situation, in some places, was even worse. Out of a total population of 46,867,701 in the portions of the Empire where cholera appeared, 1,671,324 contracted the disease and 660,877 died from it. Cholera thus struck one in twenty-eight Russians on average, and was fatal to one in seventy. In several areas, the ratio of deaths to total population was one in fifteen, and in the city of Novgorod, it reached true plague dimensions: one in every nine died. Official statistics themselves, however, can hardly transmit the full horror of the disease's progress. In the province of Riazan, for example, official statistics listed a total of only 27,878 cases and 13,036 deaths out of a population of 1,267,833, but the impact in some areas was far more deadly.[22] A. V. Golovnin, later to become Minister of Public Instruction during the reign of Alexander II, and in 1848 a young man of twenty-seven, described the path of the cholera in Riazan province in a letter to a friend:

My journey from the time of my departure from Moscow was confined to various districts of Riazan province and resembled more a wandering through a graveyard than a journey through the countryside . . . There were groups of peasant huts in which the only ones alive were small children; there were fields filled with grain and no one to harvest them . . . The common people are gripped by deep depression and in places there is talk of mass evacuations.[23]

And to the terror of cholera was added a dramatic increase in the numbers of fires in many Russian towns and cities that left many homeless and aggravated the conditions which enabled the disease to spread. The summer of 1848 was unusually dry and fires increased in comparison with the previous year by some 25 per cent. The provincial capital city of Orël was on 26 April almost destroyed by a fire in which 1,241 buildings burned; Kazan, a major city and trading centre in the south-east, had 586 buildings destroyed by fire on 14 August; and in more than 550 other instances there were fires which destroyed twenty-five or more buildings.[24]

Nicholas himself knew well the strength of the disease and the terror it brought with it. It had killed his elder brother, Konstantin Pavlovich, as well as the commander of his forces in Poland, Count Dibich, in 1831. In 1831, too, St Petersburg had suffered a similar epidemic, and during that terrible summer, when some 600 Petersburgers were dying each day, the common people had rioted in the Haymarket. Nicholas had himself gone to calm them on 23 June; he had seen the terror in their eyes, and had learned at first hand the irrational madness of a crowd.[25] Only the force of his personality had brought the riot under control. Standing in the midst of the terror-stricken masses, with no guards and only two trusted adjutants, he had ordered the assembled thousands to their knees and had calmed them with the words:

I have come to ask God's mercy for your sins . . . You have offended Him deeply . . . You have forgotten your duty of obedience to me . . . and I must answer to God for your behaviour . . . I order you to disperse immediately, go to your homes, and pay attention to everything that I order to be done for your welfare.[26]

There was pitifully little that Nicholas could do for his subjects' welfare in 1831; he could do no more in 1848, for Russia's medical facilities were so inadequate as to be virtually non-existent. For a population of some 68 million there was a total of 7,954 doctors, mostly poorly trained *feldshers*, or an average of one doctor for each 8,550 inhabitants.[27] Most doctors with any real medical skill, however, practised in the large cities, and the common people could not afford their fees. As a result, the urban masses were without medical care except for the few who could gain entrance to one of the charity hospitals where a large percentage of the patients died from unsanitary conditions. And, in the villages and hamlets, where the disease struck the hardest in 1848, there were simply no doctors at all. Even under normal conditions, the vast majority of peasants lived out their lives without seeing a doctor. Thus there was little that Nicholas or anyone else could do to lessen the impact of cholera except to wait for the approach of winter which usually drove out the disease.

If Nicholas was powerless to deal with cholera, he could not do much more to combat the other natural catastrophe which struck at nearly the same time. In 1848 Russia suffered a famine which has been described as 'the most extensive of any in the second quarter of the nineteenth century'.[28] Famine was a scourge which the Empire faced almost every year in some area, and the Emperor and his advisers had never succeeded in developing the means to deal with it effectively. For one thing, there was no efficient method for moving grain great distances from one area to another. In summer, transportation centred upon the rivers, which mainly flowed north and south, but there was no adequate network of east–west canals to connect them. The roads, inadequate to begin with, could be used only in winter and summer, in spring and autumn they became seas of impassable mud.

Famine relief was made even more difficult because the crop yields were so very low to begin with. A yield of three bushels of wheat or rye for every one planted, far below the normal yield in Western Europe, was considered average. Such yields were the result of primitive agricultural techniques employed by the Russian peasant, and given their inborn resistance to change, partly as a result of serfdom and partly as a result of the conservatism common to all peasants, there was little hope for immediate improvement. Yet, even had the peasant been more receptive to such agricultural innovations as introducing new crops, crop rotation and more modern implements, there were few landlords with the necessary capital to finance such improvements. Landlord indebtedness was a major impediment to agricultural modernization throughout the first half of the nineteenth century as the nobility continued to sink further into debt.

This combination of problems – transportation difficulties, low yields and lack of capital for agricultural modernization – all led to a fluctuation in grain prices which was extreme by comparison with Western Europe. In France, for example, the prices for grain in 1838 fluctuated between a high of 25 francs 89 centimes per hectolitre and a low of 14 francs 50 centimes per hectolitre, and in Prussia the differential was very much the same, though it was lower in Poznań. In no case was the maximum more than twice the minimum.[29] In Russia, by contrast, the entire first half of the nineteenth century was characterized by wild price fluctuations. In 1804, the fluctuation between minimum and maximum prices for grain was 650 per cent. In 1843, there was more than a 500 per cent variance between the two figures. The fluctuations were even greater from one part of the Empire to another. In January 1845, one *kul'* (325 pounds) of rye flour cost 7 roubles 50 kopeks in Pskov while it cost only one rouble (a difference of 750 per cent) in Tambov and Kharkov. And, even in the same province, prices fluctuated greatly from one year to the next. In Kursk, for example, a *kul'* of rye flour in 1829 cost 3 roubles; in October 1833, 23 roubles, and in 1836, 4 roubles.[30]

Rapidly fluctuating grain prices in addition to transportation problems meant that it was almost impossible for the government to purchase grain in one area of the Empire and ship it to provinces suffering from famine. That had been attempted without much success in 1840, for example, when there had been a far less serious famine in the area between St Petersburg and Moscow. By the autumn of 1841, grain prices had fallen significantly in the famine provinces, though that often occurred without government aid when a relatively bountiful harvest followed a poor one. But state officials had been so incompetent and dishonest in purchasing grain for the famine areas that, when the final shipments of state-purchased grain reached some of the provincial towns in the spring of 1841, their wholesale cost was well above local grain prices.[31]

While the government might be able to afford famine relief in small areas of the country, it could not afford it in an Empire-wide famine like the one of 1848. And, even had the resources been available, the problem of transportation would have been insurmountable. The harvests in Penza and Taurida provinces provided only enough grain for the next year's planting, while in Ekaterinoslav province, one of the major grain-growing areas, the harvest yielded only one third of the amount planted the previous spring. In Saratov province (another major grain-growing area) the harvest produced only seven tenths of the amount needed for planting, while in seven other provinces, the harvest yields ranged from between 140 and 190 per cent of the amount of seed planted. Only in a few grain-growing provinces did the harvest produce more than twice what had been planted, and even there the yields were scarcely above the 200 per cent figure.[32]

Such a catastrophic harvest as that of 1848 naturally had far-reaching consequences for the economy of a country where well over 90 per cent of the work force was engaged in agriculture. As provincial governors made clear with dramatic similarity in their annual reports, livestock had to be killed because there was nothing to feed them on during the winter months; the planting of winter wheat could not be undertaken; and untold numbers of peasants, the producers of Russia's major export commodities, were dying from starvation after thousands had already died from cholera.[33] As a result, even setting humanitarian considerations aside, Russia's most valuable resource (human labour) and her major export commodities (agricultural products) were depleted to an alarming degree. Moscow's governor made very clear the impact of these losses upon the economy as a whole in his annual report for 1848:

As a result of the epidemic raging throughout the Empire, the fires in many cities, and what in the autumn turned out to be a famine, the trade of Moscow, and its surrounding provinces, for the year 1848 was significantly reduced in comparison to that of previous years . . . Furthermore, the course of commercial affairs in the most important fairs in the Empire not only failed to improve the merchants' trade, but, on the contrary, reduced it even more . . . Our local merchants are in the most difficult straits imaginable.[34]

Foreign trade was in no better condition. According to one estimate, exports of grain, forest products, and leather goods to Western Europe in 1848 were just over one third of what they had been the previous year. Most dramatic of all, of course, was the decline of grain exports themselves. While in 1847 St Petersburg had exported a total of 14,155,050 bushels of grain, in 1848 the figure was down some 700 per cent to a meagre 2,034,900 bushels. While not quite as catastrophic, the situation was not very encouraging in the major southern grain-exporting centre, Odessa, where 19,282,664 bushels had been exported in 1847, while in 1848, the total was only 12,123,682. In all, the value of total grain exports was less than 30 per cent of what they had been in 1847. The entire economy was in turmoil and in a catastrophic decline.[35]

2. *Nicholas and the Revolutions of 1848*

In the course of 1848, Nicholas would see one in seventy of his subjects die from cholera in European Russia; he would see untold thousands more perish from famine, and portions of some of the Empire's major towns and cities ravished by fire. At the same time, he faced what he regarded as the greatest threat he had yet encountered from the West, for the revolutions of 1848 threatened the very fabric of his foreign policy system and, for a time, raised the possibility that his many commitments to protect Eastern and Central Europe against the onslaught of revolution would all have to be met at once. For a few months in mid 1848, he faced the prospect of reconsidering his role as the defender of the established order, or leading Russia into a European war. That he managed to find a middle course between these two extremes shows that he and his system still retained a remarkable resilience.

Warnings of the impending revolutionary tide about to engulf much of continental Europe in 1848 reached Nicholas at the very beginning of the year. In early January, N. D. Kiselev, his representative in Paris, wrote that the growing opposition to Louis Philippe's régime 'convinces me of [the possibility of] a revolution in 1848'.[36] Almost at the same time, Metternich spoke of the danger of revolution in Italy, and warned Nicholas that 'the South of Europe is gripped by revolutionary forces and, in Italy, a crisis inevitably arises which the efforts of Central Europe cannot prevent'.[37] Metternich's predictions came to pass before those of Kiselev, but the objects of both of their warnings were realized within six weeks. The first revolutionary spark to burst into flame was struck in Palermo on 12 January when the populace clashed with Austrian troops following the so-called 'tobacco-riots' in Milan a few days before.[38]

News of the outbreak of revolution in Paris did not reach St Petersburg until 20 February, some ten days after the first demonstrations on the Place de la Madeleine.* Nicholas first received the news at a court ball, and, heard only that the Paris masses had thrown up barricades in the streets and that a group had gone to the Chamber of Deputies but had

* The first demonstrations in Paris occurred on 8 February on the Russian calendar, that is, on 20 February according to the Gregorian calendar in use in Western Europe.

been successfully turned back by the police. At the time, Nicholas and his Court were unaware that Louis Philippe had abdicated. Only on the following day did they learn that the July Monarchy had fallen. During that morning, Nicholas had been discussing some routine foreign policy matters with his Foreign Minister, Count Nesselrode, when he received word of Louis Philippe's abdication. Perhaps the most vivid description of the arrival of the official news at Court was recorded in his diary by Nicholas's second son, the Grand Duke Konstantin Nikolaevich, who was then just twenty years old:

We all were thunderstruck and the dispatch fell from Nesselrode's hands. What will happen now only God knows, but for us only blood is visible on the horizon. Papa sent me to read this dispatch to Mama. She too was frightened . . . Louis Philippe . . . ruled for eighteen years and . . . [everyone thought] he was powerful and firmly seated upon the throne; yet after only two days [of revolt] he is no more! O Lord, preserve your Holy Russia, so that she can always remain faithful to you![39]

Because telegraph communications had been disrupted by the disorders in Paris, and because Central and Eastern Europe was blanketed by fog and rain, news that a republic had been declared in France did not reach the Russian Court until Sunday, 22 February. Again, Konstantin Nikolaevich's diary provides us with an account of how the news was received:

After Mass there was a review and, after the review, Sasha [the heir to the throne, the future Alexander II] gave a dinner dance. During the mazurka, Papa arrived with new dispatches from Paris. In France there is a *Republic*, the royal family has fled to an unknown destination. France is governed by a National Assembly and a council made up of the following: *Arago, Lamartine, Armand Marrast, Flocon* (the last two are the publishers of the journal *Le National* and *Le Constitutionnel*), and *Albert*, a WORKER . . . ! This is what we have come to! A repetition of the terrible events at the end of the last century.[40]

When word that the French had declared a republic reached Court, there was enthusiastic speculation that the Russian army would attack the revolution in the West, and, as Konstantin Nikolaevich noted in his diary that day, 'the young officers rejoiced because there is hope of war'.[41] Within the week, Nicholas himself added further substance to these rumours when he called for a partial mobilization of the Russian army on the Empire's western borders, stating that 'the friendly treaties and agreements, binding Russia with neighbouring powers, place upon us the sacred obligation to institute timely measures for mobilizing certain portions of our army in order to establish an effective line of defence against the pernicious rising [force] of anarchy if the situation so demands'.[42] Furthermore, on 29 February, just one week after he had learned that a republic had been declared in France, Nicholas wrote to his brother-in-law Friedrich Wilhelm IV and emphasized that 'by the month of July, I will be able to enter the field with 350,000 effectives and two reserves of 150,000 and 100,000 men'.[43]

Statements such as these led many in 1848 and afterwards to conclude that Nicholas was prepared to march against revolution wherever it might be, and to use all of Russia's might to crush it. Once again the eyes of European statesmen turned to the East, filled with the spectre of Russia's vast hordes descending upon them. But Nicholas was too astute a politician and too prudent a statesman to act in such a precipitous manner. As we have seen, he weighed alternatives carefully before committing himself in European affairs. His commitments to defend legitimacy and order in Europe had increased during the 1830s and 1840s, but this was more the result of Austria's growing weakness and Prussia's increasingly indecisive policies. In the eyes of Austrian and Prussian statesmen, Nicholas ruled a mighty military power but had, at the same time, kept his Empire free from the revolutionary contamination of 1830. As a result, they had sought more commitments from him, and he, in his glorification of legitimacy and his commitment to the established order, had given them. But Nicholas still had a clearly delineated conception of where Russia's interests lay, and he would not move beyond it. He believed that he had an irrevocable commitment to protect legitimacy and order in Eastern and Central Europe, including the holdings of the Habsburgs and Prussia. But he firmly believed that Russia should serve only as the last line of defence for Austria and Prussia in their eastern domains. As he wrote to his brother-in-law the week after he had learned that a republic had been declared in Paris:

I will not stir without the call of necessity . . . It is indispensable to check instantaneously these . . . demonstrations by force. Dear friend, be the deliverer of Germany . . . Do not draw back from the task which Providence has given you.[44]

Still, Nicholas did not define publicly what he meant by 'necessity', nor did he specify the location of 'the pernicious rising [force] of anarchy' that he was prepared to march against. These vagaries in his official statements, coupled with the manifesto which he issued on 14 March, thus left room for speculation as to what his real intentions were in late February and early March. Yet, in some of his more private statements, Nicholas was very specific. 'I give you my word that not one single drop of Russian blood will be spilt on account of these worthless Frenchmen,' he told the assembled commanders of his Imperial Guards on the day after he learned that a republic had been declared in France.[45] He was equally specific to Metternich in January on the subject of Russian military aid for Austria in dealing with revolts in her Italian provinces. 'I will never agree to send my troops to such a distant country,' he warned.[46] But Central and Eastern Europe were entirely another matter. As Nesselrode made clear in a letter to Metternich in early February, Russia would keep her forces in reserve in case of a revolutionary outbreak in Poland or in Germany. Should France or Britain intervene in Austria's struggle to hold her Italian possessions, then Nesselrode made it very clear to Metternich that Russia would consider such an attack as 'an attack against Russia' and that Nicholas's armies would intervene.[47] Otherwise, Austria would have to rely upon her own resources to contain the revolutionary menace in Italy, for that was to be Austria's sole responsibility in containing the revolutionary threat. 'Her [Austria's] role,' Nicholas wrote to Friedrich Wilhelm IV on 24 February, 'is to defend Italy and our left flank; in her present wretched condition that is enough for her to do.'[48] But although Eastern Europe (especially Poland) was an area in which Nicholas would permit no revolutionary developments at all, he would not move to suppress revolution in Central Europe unless asked to do so. As he wrote to Friedrich Wilhelm IV, 'In three months I will be able to follow you [into combat against revolution in Germany] with 300,000 men, ready *at your call*.'[49]

In fact, Nicholas was not at first over concerned about the revolution in Paris itself, never having had any great liking for Louis Philippe and regarding him as an usurper. In discussing the broader lines of policy which should be followed in dealing with the new revolutionary threat, Nicholas wrote to Friedrich Wilhelm IV: 'I would like to leave the French to fight each other as much as they wish. We ought to confine ourselves to preventing them from disentangling themselves and suppress at the same time all attempts at revolution in Germany.'[50] Certainly he had no intention of marching on Paris, and there is no doubt but that the tale that Nicholas proclaimed: 'Gentlemen, saddle your horses. A republic has been declared in France!' is apocryphal. He was indeed fully willing 'to leave the French to fight each other as much as they wish'; but what he feared was a recurrence of 1789. 'This is what we have come to! A repetition of the terrible events at the end of the last century,' his son had written in his diary. The words could have been spoken by Nicholas in 1830, and again in 1848. Certainly, they summed up his worst fears.

But if Nicholas had no intention of taking any measures against revolution in Paris, his actions at home were another matter. On the very day he learned that a republic had been declared in France, Nicholas òrdered the head of the Third Section, Count Orlov, to warn all French citizens in the capital that they could continue their residence in St Petersburg or were free to leave immediately. Should they choose to remain in Russia's capital, however, Nicholas insisted through Orlov that they must give firm guarantees that they would in no way seek to fan revolution in Russia.[51] Moreover, Nicholas and his advisers at first sought to prevent news of the revolution in Paris from spreading in Russia, although foreign newspapers, which were easily obtainable in the capital, had begun to feature reports about it. At first glance it would seem that Nicholas's failure to prevent the importation of foreign newspapers, while at the same time seeking to keep all word of the revolution out of the Russian press, was a serious oversight. But once again it was a question not simply of the existence of the news itself, but of who read the news. As always, Nicholas's major fear was the masses. If Petersburg society knew of the revolution, he could deal with them should they be inspired to start a revolution in Russia. But, should the masses learn of it and begin a revolt, Nicholas could not predict the outcome. For Petersburg educated society to read about the revolution was no crime; but to speak of it, especially so that the masses might learn of it, was a very serious matter. 'Frequently you discuss political, governmental, or other affairs,' Nicholas told the Petersburg nobility in March 1848. 'These conversations, harmless among educated people, often inspire in your servants thoughts that would never have occurred to them on their own. This is very dangerous,' he added.[52]

Just how dangerous such conversations were regarded became evident in the measures which Nicholas and his advisers ordered to be put into effect in the capital. V. R. Zotov, a young official in the War Ministry, recalled the situation in March 1848, in his memoirs:

When printed word of the events arrived from abroad, I decided to raise the question [of revolution in Paris] with the chief of police Trubacheev, a very good and responsible man, who was always extremely attentive to journalists and theatregoers and was sitting next to me at the theatre . . . Trubacheev changed his expression perceptibly and answered almost in a whisper: 'I beg you not to speak a word of this either to me or to any of your acquaintances unless you can trust them completely . . . The police has the order to notify the Third Section of those who speak of revolution. They are even ordered to arrest those who speak of it in detail.'[53]

The crime thus was not in learning of the revolution from the Western press, but discussing it with others. In Nicholas's view, the danger was in those who discussed it where the common people might hear; translated into action by his over-zealous adjutants in the Third Section, Nicholas's own apprehensions were broadened to include all who might speak of the revolution in Paris to anyone, even if none of the lower classes were within hearing.

It is quite probable that there were other reasons than simply over-zealous attention to duty which caused the Third Section and the Petersburg police to limit discussion of the revolutions in France. Indeed, they witnessed all around them in Petersburg the unique phenomenon of the Empire's upper classes displaying an intense interest in the revolution in Paris. This was an interest in distant revolutionary events; it was not a manifestation of any desire to have such a revolution in Russia. General A. E. Tsimmerman, at the time a young army officer, recalled later that 'what appealed to me in the revolution [in Paris] was the free play of human passions and the great tragic element of events. As an enthusiast for theatrical spectacles, the dramatic grandiose effects, the . . . solemn proclamations of freedom and republics, fascinated me.'[54] Tsimmerman's reaction was no doubt common to many in St Petersburg, but the enthusiasm of the capital's upper classes made the police appre-hensive. Indeed, a few days after foreign newspapers reached the capital with the news, the new republic in France was the topic of the day. Baron Korf left a lengthy and detailed account of the first days after the news had arrived in St Petersburg:

In general, the passage of the Lenten season . . . went almost completely un-noticed. Public attention was so concentrated on the events in Paris, everyone was so occupied with higher thoughts, and so longed for the dénouement of this thunderous drama, that there was almost no place either for other conversations or other thoughts and everyone very easily and quickly forgot about plays, dances . . . and balls. During the first days of Lent the entire city was buzzing, so to speak; everyone flitted from house to house with the latest news, besieged the newspaper offices, and were all the more perplexed and alarmed because the newspapers themselves, which they awaited with such impatient eagerness, contained only contradictions, omissions, or news of dubious validity.[55]

In St Petersburg there was such a clamour for news of events in the West that the demand for daily and weekly newspapers far exceeded the supply, and they were bought up as soon as they appeared for sale. Coffee houses in the capital took on a particular significance. Since only Russia's most conservative newspapers and journals were permitted to print news of political events in the West, and since they were slow in reporting the revolution in Paris (news of the fall of Louis Philippe was not reported in St Petersburg until 25 February), more extensive re-porting about political events in Western Europe could at first be obtained only from foreign newspapers. And during the days of February and March 1848, those who could read Western languages congregated at

Petersburg's coffee houses to read the copies of foreign newspapers provided for public use.

But discussion of the revolution in France was by no means unrestrained in such places. 'I beg you not to speak a word of this [the February revolution] either to me or to any of your acquaintances unless you can trust them completely,' the police chief Trubacheev had told the young official Zotov. Agents of the secret police were indeed often present at public gatherings, and their activities were not limited to eavesdropping. Tsimmerman described in his memoirs a particular type of police agent, the *agent provocateur*, who was frequently found in such public places as coffee houses:

His conversation seemed particularly strange to me for, while he spoke very freely and abused the government, it was evident that he possessed not even the most elementary information about history and politics. Once, when leaving the shop with me and walking with me past the palace of the Grand Duchess Mariia Nikolaevna, he began to rail against her so rudely and cynically that I stopped him from speaking further on the subject . . . This man was an *agent provocateur*, though not a very clever one.[56]

Much of Petersburg aristocratic society paid a great deal of attention to the revolutionary events in Paris, and at least a segment of educated public opinion even displayed a certain romantic interest. Such attitudes changed dramatically, however, after the tide of revolution began to flood into Germany and the Habsburg Empire, and a variety of factors played a part in bringing about this change. For one thing, Russia's newspapers had begun to report on the events in Western Europe in some detail. At the outbreak of the revolutions in the West, the Russian press had been restrained from printing news. But once it became clear that the overthrow of the French monarchy had been accomplished, and that it was impossible to restrain public interest in it, Russian newspapers and journals were allowed to give more systematic coverage. Between late February and early April, the Petersburg press published extensive reports about revolts in Marseille, in Amiens, in Lille, in Baden, in Cologne, in Naples, in Venice and in Madrid, to mention a few from a rather lengthy list. Clearly the revolution was becoming far more widespread than it had originally seemed, and even more important, it appeared to be moving closer to Russia's borders. As the revolutionary upheavals spread to Central Europe, and the conservative system of Metternich began to totter in the face of onslaughts from the crowds in Prague and Vienna, many educated and upper-class Russians, who had hitherto viewed the events in Paris with a certain sympathy or romantic interest, became increasingly apprehensive.

Russian society's fears were not restricted to the political consequences of the revolutions which had overthrown the monarchy in France. As the depth of press coverage increased, many came to view the revolutions in the West as being social as well as political in nature. During the first week of March, a leading Petersburg newspaper, *Russkii invalid*, a semi-official mouthpiece for the government, reported that the 'demand to satisfy the proletariat most of all occupies the provisional government [in France]', and then went on to explain that the government had created a special commission to improve the workers' lot, that national workshops were to be created and that the Minister of Public Works had decreed that royal residences be sold and the proceeds used for aiding the lower-class victims of the revolution. *Russkii invalid* further stated that 'the masses concern themselves very little with the form of government and all their demands can be defined by two phrases: how to get higher wages and how to work less . . . Everything belongs to the masses and they can seize everything whenever they wish.'[57] Just over a week later, the Prussian correspondent for *Russkii invalid* reported as follows:

I was also in Paris in 1830, but the present revolution is vastly different from that one. The upper and middle classes – men of moderate views and inveterate opponents of Louis Philippe – are all unified now by a feeling of fear instilled in them by the lower classes. Almost all of them say to each other: 'Let us stand unified for the preservation of the present government so that we will not end up with something worse.'[58]

Such observations about the social revolutionary character of events in the West caused the majority of educated and aristocratic opinion in Russia to grow far less sympathetic. Nicholas, too, became much more alarmed, for his worst fears seemed about to be realized as the revolution spread from France into Central Europe. The French could 'fight each other as much as they wish' as far as he was concerned, but when revolution began to spread outside France's boundaries, he saw the spectre of 1789 looming. The spread of revolution thus threatened the stability in Central and Eastern Europe which he was sworn to defend. Still, while seriously considering the need to send troops to Central Europe, should he be summoned there by the Prussian or Austrian monarchs, Nicholas preferred that the issue be settled by the Central European rulers themselves. Austria, in his opinion, was weak, far weaker than ever before. He had become convinced of that in 1845 when he had written to his Empress from Vienna that 'everything goes badly here. Metternich is only a shade of his former self . . . Hungary is sullen [and] Galicia is on the point of breaking into flame.'[59] He thus looked to his brother-in-law in Prussia to lead the assault against the forces of revolution. 'Dear

Friend, be the deliverer of Germany . . . Do not draw back from the task which Providence has given you,' he had written in late February.[60]

'In these times, governments which lose courage and make concessions when the masses are in the streets will most certainly fall,' Baron Peter Meiendorf, Russia's ambassador to Berlin, had noted in one of his reports in early 1848.[61] 'That is absolutely certain,' Nicholas had commented in the margin of the dispatch.[62] But Nicholas was by no means convinced that Friedrich Wilhelm IV possessed sufficient resolution or strength of character to deal with the revolutionary menace. In his view, any concessions which revealed even the smallest flaw in the armour of absolutism could be potentially fatal, as Russia's experience in Poland between 1815 and 1830 had shown. 'We paid for our mistake with our blood, and this problem was resolved only on the ramparts of Wola [a suburb of Warsaw] in 1831,' Nicholas warned the Prussian king.[63] And when his brother-in-law persisted in summoning the united Landtag, he sadly concluded, despite Friedrich Wilhelm's protestations to the contrary, that 'Prussia has entered into a completely new era'.[64]

By mid March, Nicholas could no longer hope that the revolutionary upheaval in the West would be contained in France. Revolution had struck Berlin early in the month, and Baron Meiendorf had reported from the city that 'the king is in the power of the bourgeoisie'.[65] In the Habsburg domains, the situation was equally dismal. In early March (still February in Russia), Lajos Kossuth had made a passionate speech in the Hungarian Diet in which he declared that 'the time had come to put an end to absolutism, to centralized bureaucratic government and indeed to all the repressive measures of the "Metternich System" '.[66] By the middle of the month, faced by hostile crowds in the streets of Vienna, the Austrian government agreed to recognize civil rights and promised a constitution.[67] The march of revolution eastwards across Europe seemed irresistible – and both Prussians and Austrians had failed to stem the tide. At least, that was how it appeared to many Russians and to Nicholas in St Petersburg. 'The triumph of revolution in Vienna, where Metternich, the patriarch of the conservatives, presided . . . seemed an inexplicable event,' recalled one Russian memoirist. 'The turmoil of revolution continued, it seemed, with unrestrained force.'[68]

In the face of these new revolutionary outbreaks, Nicholas knew that he must act, but he was not entirely certain as to how he should proceed. He could not intervene directly in Prussia or Austria except at their request. To do otherwise would be an invasion of a friendly power, and neither had yet issued a call for Russian troops. Indeed, from Berlin, the Ambassador, Baron Meiendorf, warned Nicholas that 'any military demonstration on our part would be dangerous at this moment and would lead to a republic. It is necessary to make public the fact that we will not attack, but that we will only defend ourselves.'[69] At the same time, the possibility of revolution entering Poland, where Nicholas was free to act unilaterally to crush it, seemed very real. 'Adam Czartoryski [one of the leading figures in the Polish revolution of 1830–31] is here [in Berlin],' Meiendorf warned. 'The force of events could lead to war.'[70] Nicholas thus faced the need to issue a stern warning that there was a barrier beyond which he would not permit revolution to pass while avoiding any decisive action which might provoke even more radical outbreaks in Central Europe. Equally important, all Russians must be put on notice that the European revolutions posed a threat to their motherland and that they must be prepared to fight to defend the faith, the Tsar and the Russian land. Nicholas thus sought to mobilize Russian public opinion in defence of Orthodoxy, Autocracy and Nationality.

To meet these several needs, Nicholas issued an imperial manifesto on 14 March 1848:

After a blessed peace of many years, the western part of Europe suddenly has been disturbed by the present troubles, threatening the overthrow of legitimate powers and the entire social order. At this very moment, this insolence, knowing no limits, threatens in its madness even Our Russia, entrusted to Us by God. But it will not succeed! Following the example of Our Orthodox ancestors, and invoking the help of Almighty God, We are ready to meet Our enemies . . . [and] We shall, in indissoluble union with Our Holy Russia, defend the honour of the Russian name and the inviolability of Our frontiers. We are certain that every Russian, each of Our faithful subjects, will answer with joy the call of his Emperor and that our ancient cry: 'For the Faith, the Tsar, and the Motherland', will now show us the way to victory and . . . we all as one will cry out: 'God is with us! Take heed, O nations and submit, for God is with us!'[71]

Such a ringing cry, expressed in archaic language and seeming to call Russians to a Holy War when no attack had yet been launched against her frontiers, may well strike the Western reader as strange. Indeed, it was widely misunderstood at the time, and interpreted to mean that Russia was preparing to launch an attack upon Europe. But the language which Nicholas employed in his manifesto was very much in keeping with the language of Official Nationality, the values which Russian society adhered to throughout his reign, and, as such, was calculated to strike a responsive chord in the hearts of Russians. Within the context of Official Nationality, the language of the manifesto was perfectly clear. In a word, Russia was ready to meet her enemies and to 'defend the honour of the Russian name and the inviolability of Our frontiers'. This point was made even more forcefully by Count Nesselrode in an official statement in which he insisted that 'our attitude will be entirely defensive:

the manifesto has no other meaning . . . Let the other countries manage as they can, we shall let them alone as long as they do not touch us.'[72]

If Russia's only stance in facing the revolutions of 1848 was to be purely defensive, then one might well ask why Nicholas issued such a manifesto when the revolution had moved no further east than Vienna and Berlin. There are at least two possible explanations. First, the tide of revolution in the first half of March 1848 seemed to some Russians irresistible. Even more important, by early March there were signs that the revolution was spreading into the Empire itself in the form of unrest among some of the national minorities, especially in Poland, and in the Baltic and Western provinces. News of the revolutions in the West reached these areas more rapidly, and, in comparison to the rest of the Empire, in proportionately much larger quantities except for St Petersburg and Moscow. During 1848, some 375,000 letters entered Russia from abroad through the Russian post office, not including those carried by private individuals. Of that number, 148,000 went to St Petersburg and 31,000 to Moscow. Most significant, perhaps, for possibly spreading unrest among the national minorities, 23,500 letters from the West were sent to the three Baltic provinces; 25,500 were sent to the six so-called 'western' provinces along the Polish border; and 24,500 went to the three south-western provinces of the Ukraine. And, of all the mail sent to Russia from Western Europe during 1848, 90 per cent of it came from countries with serious revolutionary disturbances.[73] Moreover, these provinces of the Russian Empire were the closest to Poland, where there was a growing movement in 1848 to call upon the Russian masses to forget past differences and to join together in a united front to overthrow Nicholas, as was the case with the authors of the inflammatory verses 'To Our Russian Brothers', written in Lwow in mid April, and sent into Russia's south-western province of Podolsk in early May.[74]

Evidence of such revolutionary sentiments began to appear among national minorities in Nicholas's Empire very early in 1848. As early as the morning of 3 March, notices which proclaimed 'Long Live the Livonian Republic! Down With the Emperor!' were pasted upon the cathedral doors in Riga,[75] and by the beginning of the summer revolutionary pamphlets also appeared. Of all the border areas, revolutionary sentiment was especially strong in the western and south-western provinces where an overwhelmingly White Russian and Ukrainian population was ruled by a Polonized aristocracy, for it was in these areas where Nicholas and his advisers had implemented their most thoroughgoing programme of russification. As a result, the population held anti-Russian sentiments even more than in Poland proper where russification policies had not yet been implemented. In contrast to the Baltic provinces, where an indigenous (and anti-Russian) peasantry was ruled by largely pro-Russian Baltic German nobles who had made their way in the Russian state service, noble and peasant alike tended to be anti-Russian.

The vast majority of the inflammatory leaflets which called the population in these areas to revolution were actually printed in the West. Most appealed directly to specific national minority groups in the area, but in some cases they urged the Russian masses to seek their freedom and not to threaten the victory of revolution in the West by marching with Nicholas's armies should they be ordered abroad. Perhaps one of the most dramatic in this last respect was a manifesto printed in Germany which appeared in the south-western Russian province of Kiev in March.

Awaken from your slumber, O Russian people [it urged]. Your brothers: Germans, French, Italians, Austrians, and some Danes and Belgians, have already blazed the trail for you. Especially in Berlin . . . many have shed their blood for freedom. We are free, follow us; think of yourselves as human beings, that the poorest of you is also a man. Abandon the knout* and turn it only against the high and mighty . . . Beware of standing in the way, Russians . . . Throw down your arms and do not shed your blood uselessly against your European brothers who should be free . . . In Germany, not only every soldier, but every citizen, townsman, and peasant are armed. Kings ought not to do whatever they desire, but they ought to do that which the common people demand, for they stand lower than the common people. Soldiers ought to take up their weapons only when the common people, or citizens, order it.[76]

The native population of the Baltic provinces, Poles, White Russians, and, especially, Ukrainians, thus tended to be receptive to anti-Russian revolutionary propaganda in the spring and summer of 1848. But the most oppressed minority of all, the Jews, remained largely passive. It is one of the ironies of Russian history that a minority group, so incessantly persecuted and so unjustly treated by imperial officials, remained basically loyal to the imperial government until late in the nineteenth century. Even during so major an upheaval as the Napoleonic invasion of 1812, the Jews remained loyal, a fact that Nicholas himself had noted with some amazement in his travel diary in 1816.[77] Nevertheless, such loyalty on the part of the Empire's Jews brought them no thanks or reward. Another passage in Nicholas's travel diary marked his attitude towards them very clearly. In commenting on the depressed economic state of the western provinces, Nicholas wrote: 'The general ruin of the peasants of these provinces are the *zhids* [a pejorative term for Jew in Russian] . . . They are absolute leeches, fastening themselves everywhere and completely exhausting these unfortunate provinces.'[78] As a result of his anti-semitic views, Nicholas instituted forced conscription of Jews into Russian

* A knout was a type of Russian whip, incorporating a lash with weighted ends.

military service, taking some of them as early as the age of twelve years in an effort to convert them to Orthodoxy before they would be old enough to enter active service.[79] And, because Nicholas considered all Jews to be cowards, he urged that they be forced to serve in the navy where they would have fewer opportunities to desert.[80] Equally oppressive, Nicholas insisted that all Jewish schools be brought under the jurisdiction of the Ministry of Public Instruction, and dissolved autonomous Jewish communities (*kahals*) in the western provinces.[81]

Yet, even though other minorities appeared more susceptible to revolutionary propaganda, there was never any serious threat of revolution within the Russian Empire. In 1848, Nicholas was fully capable of dealing with any outbreak of revolutionary violence in the western borderlands. Soon after he issued his manifesto in March, he moved a large number of troops into the western provinces. These military units, in the words of the Soviet historian Nifontov, 'formed a solid cordon from the shores of the Baltic to the Black Sea and could be moved to suppress the revolutionary movement in the border provinces and . . . the revolution in "neighbouring friendly states" '.[82] Thus, by the summer of 1848, Nicholas and his government had come to grips with the situation in their western provinces, and switched their attention back to events in the West. As the centre of the revolutionary movement shifted from Western Europe into Hungary, and as the internal situation in Russia became further stabilized, Nicholas once again turned to defend Russia from further revolutionary onslaughts. As he wrote to his 'father-commander' Prince Paskevich in early December 1848:

At this moment, both Vienna and Berlin confront a difficult situation: to destroy the name of anarchy. Will they know how to do it? If they do not decide to tear out revolution by its very roots but, instead, are satisfied only with the restoration of outward order, then things will soon be worse than before. Radical treatment, or the extirpation, of this evil is needed, not half-measures. It is necessary to recognize one's errors and to return to that order which has been sanctified by centuries.[83]

Very soon the opportunity came to fight revolution head-on. On 8 May 1849, after a formal request from the Habsburg government, Nicholas ordered his armies into Hungary, and on 6 June Russian troops poured into Galicia, Hungary and Transylvania. The Nicholas system had now moved to defend itself actively against threats from the West. Soon it would move to eradicate all potential threats at home as well.

Part Five

―――

Dénouement

―――

'The Emperor Nicholas has within himself the
qualities of Peter the Great, Paul I,
and a medieval knight. But, as the years have
passed, it is now the qualities of Paul I
which rise more and more to the fore'

MARQUIS DE CASTELBAJAC,
FRENCH AMBASSADOR TO RUSSIA

―――

9

The Last Years
of the
Nicholas System

*'How strange is my fate! They tell me that I am
one of the mightiest Princes on earth. And, one
must admit that anything – that is, anything which
is permissible – ought to be possible for me, and
that, in fact, I could be anywhere and do anything
that I wished. But, for myself in particular,
however, just the reverse is in fact true.*
*And, should I be asked the reason for this anomaly,
there is but one possible reply: Duty! Yes, that is
not a meaningless word for one who from childhood
was taught to understand it as I was. This word has
for me a sacred meaning before which every
personal impulse must give way. All must . . . yield
to it until one vanishes into the grave. Such is
my watchword'*

NICHOLAS I

That there were few revolutionary stirrings and no serious revolutionary
threats in the Russian Empire showed that the Nicholas system still
possessed remarkable strength in 1848. The Kingdom of Poland remained quiet under the firm hand of Prince Paskevich, Nicholas's faithful
lieutenant in Warsaw. The behaviour of educated Russian opinion in 1848
showed that the system still commanded considerable support at home.
There were few who would have agreed with Baron Korf that Nicholas
was 'almost the ideal Russian ruler',[1] but there were even fewer who in
1848 regarded the Nicholas system as hopelessly ineffective, over oppressive or anachronistic in any significant sense. Most believed, with A. E.

Tsimmerman, that 'our common people love to see in their ruler a powerful and stern sovereign', and asked, 'Why change that political system which made her [Russia] a first-class power in the world?'[2] Like Tsimmerman, the vast majority of educated opinion in Russia believed that 'it is possible to improve this system, but to undermine its foundations, everything that constitutes its strength and essence, is ill-advised and dangerous'.[3] Thus, any shortcomings in the Nicholas system could still be remedied within the framework of the existing order. Incompetent ministers could be replaced; corruption could be eradicated; and malpractices in administration could be eliminated by changes in procedure. In mid 1848, therefore, most in Russia still regarded the Nicholas system as basically sound. That it would collapse in less than a decade was a possibility that occurred to few.

Yet Nicholas faced the crises of 1848 with depleted resources and seriously weakened reserves. The Emperor was older, as were his ministers and close advisers.[4] For the most part, they had reached adulthood at the turn of the century. At best, as with Uvarov and Kiselev, they had been educated in the tradition of the eighteenth-century Enlightenment. More often, however, they shared the militaristic values of Nicholas himself, but had little of his broader view of state affairs. In an unfortunately large number of cases, they were more like Nicholas's younger brother, the Grand Duke Mikhail Pavlovich: men with narrowly militaristic training and outlooks. Virtually none of them, as we have said, had the education or experience to enable them to cope with the world of mid nineteenth century Europe in which they were obliged to function as diplomats and policy-makers.

By 1848, the Nicholas system had begun to produce its inevitable negative results. Nicholas preferred advisers and counsellors who were, as he said, 'not so much wise as service-orientated'.[5] Such men were deeply loyal to their Emperor, but many were not over talented, their greatest claims to prominence being their long records of loyal service. Schooled for decades in a service milieu where talent was in critically short supply, and jealous of their own power and positions, such men mostly adhered to the fundamental bureaucratic principle that it was unwise to advance talented subordinates to positions from which they might challenge the position of a less able superior. As a result, when age, ill-health and death began to thin their ranks, those who followed were often less capable. Prince Shirinskii-Shikhmatov, who replaced Count Uvarov as Minister of Public Instruction in 1849, and who once stated that 'I have neither my own thought or will; I am only the blind tool of the Sovereign's will',[6] was not even a pale shade of his predecessor. Much the same can be said of Count Vronchenko, who replaced Count

Kankrin as Minister of Finance in 1844, and of P. F. Brok, who replaced Vronchenko in 1851. As one observer remarked in his diary:

Why is it that we have so very few able statesmen? Because only one thing is demanded from every one of them – not skill in fulfilling their tasks but obedience and so-called energetic measures so that all subordinates will obey as well. Can such an unwise system train and educate statesmen? Each official, when taking on some important responsibility, thinks only about one thing: how to personally satisfy that particular request, and his intellectual horizon involuntarily shrinks to the narrowest possible framework. Here nothing must be discussed or considered; one only swims with the current.[7]

Only in the Ministries of State Domains and the Interior were there notable exceptions to the general decline in talent and ability of ministerial personnel during the last years of the Nicholas system.

1. The Reaction Begins

The contrast between the internal policies which Nicholas adopted after the revolutionary crises of 1830 and those which he followed after the revolutions of 1848 could not have been more striking. The former were followed by the final formulation of the Nicholas system, while the latter heralded its demise. The years immediately after 1830 saw the publication of Russia's first compilation of laws since 1649, and a number of efforts to reform the Russian economy and state order. Under the guidance of Nicholas and his 'Chief of Staff for Peasant Affairs', P. D. Kiselev, serious efforts were made even to improve the condition of the state peasants in the Empire. At the same time, the 1830s and the first half of the 1840s saw no appreciable intensification of state censorship and marked the beginning of the Golden Age of Russian literature. The poet Pushkin reached the zenith of his career at that time, as did the writers Lermontov and Gogol'. Towards the end of those years, Turgenev and Dostoevskii published their early works, Nekrasov began to write, and so did a number of others. In the pages of the 'thick journals', the essays of the critic Belinskii held the attention of Russia's youth and educated society. It was a time that much of Russian educated society would recall with fondness, even longing, during the trying years of the 1860s and 1870s, when Russia had to face the traumatic adjustments demanded by the Great Reforms and, at the same time, to cope with the rising threat of revolutionary terror and violence.

The last years of Nicholas's reign, between mid 1848 and his death in February 1855, left a vastly different impression, however. The grip of censorship had begun to tighten significantly as early as 1846, largely as a result of Nicholas's fears that the peasant revolts in Austrian Galicia might spread to the Polish kingdom or to Russia's western provinces. But initially the increased oppression of censorship had been felt mainly by dissident intellectuals. However, almost from the moment that news of the February revolution in Paris reached St Petersburg, the weight of an almost paranoid censorship began to settle upon a much broader segment of educated society as the Empire entered what one writer has called the 'epoch of censorship terror'.[8] During these years, no one was safe from suspicion, and even such staunch defenders of the Nicholas system and Official Nationality as Faddei Bulgarin felt the prick of the censors' ever-ready pens.[9]

The worst thing about the type of censorship which became so much a part of Russian life after 1848 was its arbitrariness, which reached into every area. Arbitrariness, of course, had always been a fundamental aspect of the autocratic régime in Russia and of the Nicholas system in particular. All in Russia were subject to the unlimited power of the Emperor, and in practice the peasants were subject to the unlimited power of their masters. But, before 1848, tradition, regulations, even certain laws, had limited the capricious exercise of absolute power. After 1848, however, arbitrariness was given much freer rein, and was per-mitted, even encouraged, by the regulations which Nicholas's advisers implemented. In the realm of censorship, this meant probing into the 'inner meanings' of published work and manuscripts.[10] Elsewhere this institutionalized arbitrariness took such forms as the regulation which declared, in late 1850, that a superior could remove his subordinate from office for 'faults or misdemeanours which cannot be proved' and that no explanation for such dismissals need be given.[11] As a result, Russia's entire official world was deprived of any protection of the laws by a single stroke of Nicholas's pen.

The crucial question that one must ask, of course, is why Nicholas, who believed that an autocrat should be 'gentle, courteous, and *just*',[12] and that 'the best theory of law is good morality',[13] should condone arbitrary and despotic behaviour on such a scale. There can be no doubt that he over-reacted to the revolutionary events of 1848. He certainly had some reason to see revolutions in the West as a threat to the system he had so carefully and laboriously constructed as a bulwark against revolution in Central and Eastern Europe. But within Russia itself, Nicholas very genuinely saw the appearance of every printed revolutionary pamphlet as a real threat to Russia's internal security and was determined to deal severely with each such challenge. To Paskevich he wrote at the end of March 1848, 'In general one cannot foresee anything; only God alone can save us from general ruin!'[14] Yet a few inflammatory pamphlets, almost always printed abroad and smuggled in small numbers into Russia, were the most visible revolutionary disturbances which Nicholas faced within his domains in 1848, while in 1830–31 he had been forced to wage a full-scale war for more than nine months to put down revolution in the Polish kingdom.

In the final analysis one cannot say decisively why Nicholas saw the events of 1848 as such a threat to internal security, but certainly his growing sense of isolation from political and economic realities in Russia was an important factor. Nicholas had few doubts about the loyalty of his ministers and advisers in 1848, for their lengthy records of service were unblemished. But the men who served him after 1848 were not the comrades-in-arms with whom he had served during the first two decades of his reign. There was not that deep sense of trust, that close personal bond, which was such a vital ingredient in the Nicholas system. Nicholas and his earlier ministers and advisers had been bound together by an indestructible union born of their common experiences in suppressing the Decembrists, or by their service with the Russian army in the West at the time of Napoleon's defeat. By 1848, however, those men were dead and the experiences which had bound them together were part of another age.

All of these factors combined to isolate Nicholas from Russian reality more than ever before. Senior officials and advisers, anxious to advance their careers and to win the approval of their sovereign, surrounded him with a web of censorship that was virtually impenetrable and which he succeeded in pulling aside only on rare occasions. It was the ultimate irony that Nicholas, who had sought to guide his subjects along the path of virtuous behaviour by protecting them from the contamination of moral or intellectual evils, found his own actions being conditioned by the very system he had created. No longer served by men whose personal friendship would lead them to tell him the truth, at least on occasion, and too worn by the strain of ruling Russia for nearly a quarter of a century to continue his inspection tours, Nicholas saw Russia more and more through the eyes of his senior officials. Especially after 1848, Nicholas saw Russia as his officials wanted him to see it.

Certainly the Emperor was aware of the isolation that separated him from Russian reality. But he was uncertain as to how to break out of it. He was no longer the dynamic young monarch who raced from St Petersburg to Novgorod to Moscow and back to his capital in the space of a few days, as he had done during the early years of his reign. Indeed, his growing sense of isolation may well have been a factor in the increasingly fatalistic attitude expressed in such statements as, 'I shall carry my cross until my strength is exhausted.'[15] 'I am astonished that you have so many friends,' he told the Slavophile Iuri Samarin in 1848. 'I have lived longer than you and have not found more than three to whom I can speak freely from my soul.'[16] Of these three, Benkendorf was dead. A second, Nicholas's 'father-commander' Prince Paskevich, was far away in Warsaw and could not be spared from the tasks there. The third was either Nicholas's brother Mikhail or his Empress. Mikhail Pavlovich would be dead within a year; the Empress was too worn and ill to offer that solace, that 'happiness, joy and repose',[17] that he had found in her company for so many years.

Nicholas's isolation could not have come at a more critical time. He was faced with a difficult situation in the West; for a few months in mid 1848, he faced the prospect of either vastly altering his role as defender of the established order in Central and Eastern Europe, or of leading Russia into a European war. He therefore had to be assured, above all else, that Russia herself would remain totally untouched by the revolutionary menace, so that he would be free to commit if need be all of his already dwindled reserves to combat the onslaught of revolution in Central and Eastern Europe.[18] By the spring of 1848, Nicholas therefore took measures to ensure that Russia would remain absolutely unruffled by revolutionary events in the West. And because his over-zealous advisers, often seeking to advance their careers by attacking a non-existent menace, painted for him an inaccurate view of the situation in Russia, Nicholas imposed far more restrictions than were necessary. His programme of paternal guidance for all Russian society therefore degenerated into a system of obscurantism which suppressed even the most innocuous expressions of independent views, and made it impossible to discuss even remotely progressive ideas in print.

Nicholas's internal policies in the spring and summer of 1848 focused upon four broad areas, all closely interrelated. First, he permitted no further discussions of change and reform, either within the central state agencies or in private discussions. Secondly, police surveillance, especially over various groups of educated society, was increased. Thirdly, the apparatus of censorship was greatly expanded to ensure that no objectionable opinions, especially views which might stir the masses to revolt, would appear in print. Finally, Nicholas sought a reconciliation with the Empire's aristocracy, whose position he had previously sought to weaken, in an effort to re-create the social base of support upon which the autocracy had relied in the past.

Nicholas's prohibitions of any further discussion about change in Russia came at a particularly critical juncture, when state agencies had been discussing the serf question with considerable attention and regularity. Complete abolition of serfdom, of course, had never been seriously proposed at any time during Nicholas's reign, but the fact remained that all efforts to improve the condition of the serfs in the Empire had come to naught, largely because the nobles who advised Nicholas could not go directly against the economic interests of their class, no matter how loyal they might be to their sovereign. Then, during the 1840s, a new approach to the serf question was designed clearly to establish (and thus limit) the obligations which serfs had to their masters and, at the same time, to define the obligations which masters had to their serfs.

These limitations of serfs' obligations and definitions of their masters' obligations were known as inventories. They had first been proposed by Count Kiselev as early as 1816.[19] Throughout Nicholas's reign, Kiselev had continued to insist that the absolute and arbitrary power which landlords wielded over their serfs must be curtailed by the precise definition of their mutual obligations.[20] But only in the 1840s did Kiselev's ideas begin to be implemented by D. G. Bibikov, Governor-General of the provinces of Kiev, Podolia and Volynia. Bibikov had first considered the possibility of introducing inventories in Russia's south-western provinces in 1844, though at that time he had considered that the best means for doing so would be through proposals worked out by local committees of the nobility.[21] Two years later, Bibikov had concluded that it was impossible to rely upon the nobility to undertake such work and had urged that such inventories should be introduced directly by the Governor-General. Early in 1848, Nicholas had given his approval for Bibikov to proceed.[22] Equally important, in late 1847, Nicholas had approved a decree by which serfs could buy their freedom and the land which they tilled if their estate was put up for public auction.[23]

Thus, on the eve of the revolutions of 1848, Nicholas had approved two decrees which had significant and far-reaching implications for the future of serfdom in Russia. But then, in his efforts to remove all possibility of social upheaval in the Empire, he implemented new measures in mid 1848 which in effect negated the law of 8 November 1847.[24] At the same time, he allowed no further introduction of inventories in the western provinces.[25] Nicholas's last serious efforts to deal with the serf question had thus fallen foul of the tensions and apprehensions created by the revolutionary movement in the West. He would make no other efforts to improve the conditions under which the serfs lived except for periodic exhortations to the nobility, as in March 1848, when he told them that 'turning to the condition of the serfs, I must tell you that it is essential to pay particular attention to their welfare'.[26]

If Nicholas and his advisers were to be confident of the tranquillity of the Empire, it was necessary, in their view, to increase police surveillance to a significant degree. Considerable numbers of Third Section officers shed their sky-blue uniforms for civilian dress so as to circulate inconspicuously in Russian society.[27] But alert Third Section officers throughout the Empire's major cities were not in themselves sufficient to satisfy their superiors' unquenchable thirst for information, and they began to employ spies and secret agents on a much broader scale. Given the emphasis upon secrecy which characterized the Nicholas system, large numbers of state officials were given secret missions at one time or another,[28] but a number began to make a profession out of the unsavoury trade of pandering information which they believed their superiors wished to obtain. Most notorious of all was the agent I. P. Liprandi, who during the mid and late 1840s undertook more than a hundred secret assignments, the nost notable of which was that of spying upon the circle of M. V. Butashevich-Petrashevskii and supplying information which led to their apprehension in 1849.[29]

Beyond this increased surveillance of Russians at home, Nicholas's agents paid more attention to Russians abroad and to foreigners, including diplomats, within Russia itself. In the case of Russians living abroad, any refusal to comply immediately with Nicholas's orders to return from the revolution-ridden West drew suspicions of disloyalty. Even V. A. Zhukovskii, tutor to the Empress and her sons, came under suspicion briefly because he was unable to return instantly to Russia after revolution struck Germany. Those Russians who remained abroad were the objects of surveillance by members of the Russian diplomatic corps, and in 1849 alone the collected files on such individuals comprised nearly five hundred manuscript sheets. Foreigners in Russia were subjected to far more intense surveillance, and were even held responsible for what they wrote about the revolutions in the West in their private correspondence; by Nicholas's own decision, over thirty of them were expelled from Russia during 1848 alone for comments they made in letters to friends about the Western revolutionary movement.[30]

Such activities reflected a decided change in the character of the Third Section and in Nicholas's personal view of it. No longer was it regarded as a positive moral force, whose major responsibilities included being 'the moral physician of the people'.[31] By mid 1848 the section had become an active counter-revolutionary force, seeking to rout out all possible sources of discontent in the Empire, and its arsenal had come to include such standard secret police weapons as *agents provocateurs*, although it was not very skilled in their training or use.[32] Most important, by mid 1848 the Third Section had withdrawn much of its energies from the tasks of censorship, leaving those responsibilities to committees created especially for the task so as to have the major portion of its man-power available for secret police work.[33]

The grip of censorship meanwhile strengthened markedly. One of

Nicholas's first reactions to the spread of revolution was to approve a series of special censorship committees proposed to him by the opportunistic Baron Korf. Korf certainly had no sympathy for revolution. Indeed, he regarded it as totally evil, for, in his view, it destroyed 'respect for government, for authority, for laws, and for all bases and conditions of political and moral existence: for religion, for family ties, and for property'.[34] But, as we have seen, Korf was confident that revolution posed no threat to Russia since there were 'neither the elements nor the instruments for it' and because 'freedom of the press, popular representation, national guards, and things of that nature . . . are complete nonsense to nine tenths of the Russian population'.[35] However, Korf stressed the danger of revolution very strongly in his reports to Nicholas and urged upon him the need for greatly increased censorship. His actions were a classic instance of a senior official seeking to advance his own interests by reporting conditions inaccurately in the hope that his reports would reflect badly upon a service rival. In this particular case, Korf hoped to replace Uvarov as Minister of Public Instruction, and stressed the need for further censorship in an effort to convince Nicholas that Uvarov had been irresponsible in the performance of his ministerial duties by failing to be sufficiently vigilant in watching the press in Russia.

Korf failed to obtain Uvarov's post for himself, but his efforts did lead to the creation of the Menshikov and Buturlin Committees, whose extreme demands for broader censorship soon drove Uvarov from office. Uvarov's replacement was the dull, but absolutely loyal, Prince Shirinskii-Shikhmatov, the same official who, as a much younger man, had helped Admiral A. S. Shishkov to draft the 'cast-iron statute' of 1826. As a result, not only did it become virtually impossible to publish opinions about religion, philosophy or politics, but even the earlier writings of N. M. Karamzin, court historian in the early nineteenth century, and a very close confidant of Nicholas's during the difficult days following the Decembrist revolt, were suppressed, as were the works of Plato and Tacitus.[36]

Increased police surveillance, broadened censorship and the suppression of all discussion of reform and change were, in Nicholas's view, the consequences of his deep paternal concern for Russia's welfare. Very soon after revolutions broke out in Western Europe, he appealed to the Empire's nobility to adopt a similarly paternalistic view towards the lower elements of society. In a word, Nicholas sought to re-create the sociopolitical base of support upon which autocracy had rested in the past. In doing so, he negated, in an important sense, nearly a half-century of efforts on the part of the Empire's rulers and their reformist advisers to modernize Russian life, for he now sought firmly to re-establish the *ancien régime* social and political order which had emerged in Russia during the late eighteenth century.

Ever since the Revolution of 1789 had brought down the old order in France, Russian rulers had been faced with the need to compete with a modernizing West, while preserving a social order rapidly becoming antiquated. Their solution had been to permit the aristocracy to remain as the Empire's élite social class while weakening the aristocracy's political role by means of creating a bureaucracy that in social and economic terms, was increasingly independent of the aristocracy.[37] At the same time as the bureaucracy's growing power made it possible for Nicholas to see at least a possible alternative to the serf-owning nobility as the socio-political base of support for the autocracy, he had begun to propose limitations upon their absolute and arbitrary power over their serfs. Coupled with this, he had sought to strengthen the ties between bureaucratic service and elective gentry offices in the provinces by adorning such offices with a number of important civil service perquisites: those nobles who held higher-level elective posts in the provinces were given civil-service rank, awards, decorations and, in some cases, pensions.[38] But the revolutionary threat had come before the bureaucracy or any other group had grown strong enough to pose a reasonably viable alternative to the aristocracy as the social and political base of autocratic power. As a result, in 1848, Nicholas sought to re-create that ethos which had been so characteristic of the Golden Age of the Russian nobility under Catherine II in the late eighteenth century.

Nicholas set the tone for a full reconciliation with the nobility of the Empire when he addressed the assembled St Petersburg aristocracy on 21 March 1848. He urged them to join him in assuring order in Russia:

Each of you is my steward and for the tranquillity of the state you ought to bring to my attention all evil acts and occurrences . . . If you perceive abuses or disorders in my domains, then I urgently beg you to spare no one and to report them to me immediately . . . We shall act together with one accord and we shall be invincible.[39]

And, for such support from the nobility of the Empire, Nicholas was prepared to give them important assurances for the future. Only three days later, on 24 March, the Minister of the Interior, L. A. Perovskii, informed provincial governors and marshals of the nobility that Nicholas had instructed him to assure them that the 'unalterable will of His Imperial Majesty is to preserve the unshakeable power and right of the serf-owners over their serfs through the defence of the legal and just relations of serf-owners with their peasants'.[40] Nicholas thus proclaimed to Russia's nobility that he would in no way challenge further their position as serf-owners and as the Empire's élite privileged class. Further discussion of altering the nature of serfdom in the Russian Empire during Nicholas's reign was out of the question. To ensure the complete tranquillity of his Empire, Nicholas was willing to pay the price of no further discussions of change.

2. A Last Challenge: The Petrashevtsy

Yet before Nicholas was free to turn his entire attention to the revolutionary threat abroad, he had to face one final challenge at home. Not since 14 December 1825 had the Russian authorities felt themselves confronted by a political case of such magnitude as that which came to light in April 1849. Acting on evidence obtained by two undercover agents, the St Petersburg police and agents of the Third Section arrested Mikhail Vasil'evich Butashevich-Petrashevskii on the night of 23 April. Petrashevskii was a young official in the Ministry of Foreign Affairs, and the police regarded him as the chief figure in what they believed to be a widespread conspiracy to overthrow the Russian state and to introduce a society based upon the principles of the French utopian socialist, Charles Fourier. Spurred on by the revolutions in the West, and knowing that Nicholas would tolerate no such outbreaks in his Empire, the imperial authorities proceeded to question 252 individuals, sent fifty-one of them into administrative exile, and condemned to death twenty-one young men, including the young novelist F. M. Dostoevskii.

M. V. Butashevich-Petrashevskii, the central figure in this so-called conspiracy, was the son of a prominent army physician. He had been educated at the élite Imperial Lyceum at Tsarskoe Selo. At the lyceum, he was regarded as enough of a troublemaker for him to be given the lowest rank in the table of ranks when he graduated in 1839, a rare occurrence for a graduate of that prestigious institution. When Petrashevskii became a low-ranking civil servant in the Ministry of Foreign Affairs in early 1840, he entered a world that was far more uncongenial than had been the lyceum. At Tsarskoe Selo, Petrashevskii's inability to become a part of the society of his school-mates was the result of his own peculiar personality, for most graduates found the atmosphere congenial and began life-long friendships there.[41] The St Petersburg service and social milieu, on the other hand, was notorious for its coldness and impersonality. Indeed, many young men who entered this world suffered a serious psychological shock as a result of their first encounters in the capital, and there is at least some evidence to indicate that their initial encounters with life in St Petersburg were instrumental in shaping their attitudes towards Russia and the problems of change which confronted them.[42]

The impact of their initial experiences in the capital as a factor in shaping the attitudes of these young officials and intellectuals is a highly complex, though extremely important, aspect of Russian intellectual and social history which has yet to be investigated with any degree of thoroughness. It would seem that very many of these young men often floundered around in the capital for several years until their future course of action was determined by some chance event. For some, such an event was an unlooked-for opportunity to engage in work in the civil service which they considered constructive or useful. For others, it was a chance encounter with radical ideals. Particularly later in the decade, some of these young men became so alienated from the world in which they found themselves that they consciously took up a radical course in which they sought to construct a new society that would provide some justification for their existence as intellectuals. All of these young men were confronted, too, by the fact that their service responsibilities called for little talent and frequently discouraged initiative of any sort.[43] They thus often had to reconcile the romantic idealism of their school years with the hard realities of their early service experience.

A further problem for some of these young men was posed by the vast number of leisure hours which they had to fill. For many, their service duties were of such a mechanistic nature that they required little or no effort.[44] Yet, at the same time, they often found it difficult to gain entry to the social life of the capital because they knew few people, and the society was extremely formal and structured.[45] Some of these young men turned to the University of St Petersburg to fill their leisure hours, enrolling in lectures then fashionable in intellectual circles. Petrashevskii followed this course in the autumn of 1840 when he began to attend the lectures of V. S. Poroshin, a young professor of political economy and statistics who was a proponent of the theories of Fourier. Indeed, Petrashevskii was not the only student upon whom Poroshin's brilliant lectures left a mark. In the midst of an often pedantic faculty, who generally treated the new thinkers of Western Europe with contempt, Poroshin stood out as one well-acquainted with the most recent European theoretical works in political economy. Seeking a system of thought and a plan for social and political action which would fill their psychological and intellectual needs, the intense young Russian university students of the 1840s flocked to his lectures.

Poroshin opened to his students the world of French utopian socialism in which the dignity of the individual was sacred above all else, and where the well-being of all members of society, not the interests of a privileged few, was of paramount importance. Fascinated by the world to which Poroshin introduced him, Petrashevskii began an earnest study of the writings of Proudhon, Fourier and, later, Louis Blanc. Almost from the beginning, he accepted two basic principles which were to become the guideposts for his thoughts and actions throughout the rest of his life. He was convinced, at least in theory, of the immorality of private property and of the inviolable dignity of every individual regardless of political opinion, social status or wealth.[46]

Like the majority of the Russian intelligentsia of the 1840s, Petrashevskii tended to regard his new ideals as absolute, as something to be applied at full strength and undiluted by common sense or any notion of historical relativism. Indeed, there was always something of the romantic revolutionary in Petrashevskii's world view. Even after his arrest in April 1849, when he was taken before the special investigating commission organized to investigate his conspiracy, he spoke candidly about his initial reaction to Fourier's ideas: 'When I read his works for the first time, I was, so to speak, re-born, and I stood in awe before the greatness of his genius . . . I rejected all of my other deities and made him my one and only idol.'[47] His new master's works became for him a Bible which served as a major source of inspiration in his continued search for a solution to Russia's economic and social ills.

A firm conviction about the justness of his new Fourierist ideals led Petrashevskii to proselytize his beliefs, particularly among the intelligentsia of St Petersburg. He attempted to obtain a teaching position, which would have afforded him an opportunity to preach regularly about his ideals, and in the summer of 1844 he applied to teach Russian and foreign languages at the lyceum. Because of the many difficulties he had encountered with the authorities during his school years, he was refused the appointment, but, despite his failure, it appears that he continued to make contacts among students in Petersburg and at Tsarskoe Selo.[48] Indeed, many of the young men who eventually attended his Friday gatherings were lyceum graduates.

Unlike the situation in Moscow, where the intelligentsia had sharply polarized into the two opposing camps of the Westerners and the Slavophiles, the intellectual atmosphere in St Petersburg was much more fluid. There was an incredibly rich banquet of ideas and systems, the entire spectrum of the political, social and economic thought produced in France and Germany during the previous two decades, which was greedily sampled by the capital's intelligentsia. Intellectual lines of conflict were not yet clearly drawn, and many who shared the feeling that there must be some sort of change in Russian conditions were at home in the aura of utopian-romantic-idealistic enthusiasm which surrounded Petrashevskii and his associates. His Friday gatherings were attended by writers (F. M. Dostoevskii and M. E. Saltykov-Shchedrin were the most prominent), university students and young lecturers, and a sizeable number of lesser civil servants as well as a few Imperial Guards officers.

It is not clear precisely when Petrashevskii's 'Fridays' began. In his testimony to the special investigating commission, he dated their beginning in early 1846, but from the evidence provided by the testimony of other members, it appears that the meetings may have begun as much as a year earlier. It is certain that, in 1845, Petrashevskii organized a library of foreign books, numbers of which he evidently obtained from foreigners with whom he dealt in the course of his work in the Ministry of Foreign Affairs.[49] Many of these foreign books were forbidden to Russians by the authorities, but Petrashevskii made them available to the young men who frequented his house. The capital needed to finance the venture was provided by several acquaintances sympathetic to his views.[50]

Between 1845–6 and 1848, Petrashevskii's 'Fridays' were markedly informal so far as their membership and topics of conversation were concerned. Unlike the gatherings of the Westerners and Slavophiles in Moscow, they did not constitute a 'circle' in the usual sense. While Slavophiles and Westerners seriously grappled with the questions of Russia's past, present and future, and made or broke friendships on the basis of their views about these problems, the young men in St Petersburg attended Petrashevskii's 'Fridays' for a variety of reasons. Some came because they were seriously seeking solutions to Russia's many problems; others appeared because they enjoyed the company that they found; and still others came, as one observer noted, because Petrashevskii provided a plentiful supply of food and drink.[51]

In examining the motives for attending Petrashevskii's weekly gatherings, the need to feel a part of some group must not be overlooked for, as we noted earlier, some of these young men felt bitterly alone in Russia's glittering but old northern capital. Many of them had been uprooted from the security of their provincial environments and thrown headlong into the overwhelming impersonality of the civil service in the capital. Others (though their numbers were far fewer than those craving the society of friends) lived a lonely and poor existence as university students or young lecturers, living sometimes from one day to the next in what seemed to them to be an environment which had no place for them and could not nourish their talents and dreams. These young men were far more prone to become alienated from the Russian state and society, and like N. G. Chernyshevskii (the radical publicist and critic who knew many of those who attended Petrashevskii's 'Fridays', although he had not yet joined their group at the time of their arrests), they became the angry men of the 1850s and 1860s, more willing than their predecessors to destroy what they found in Russia so as to rebuild a society which would be more hospitable to them as intellectuals.

D. D. Akhsharumov, one of the young men who attended Petra-shevskii's 'Fridays' quite regularly, has left us what is perhaps the best general characterization of the gatherings. In his memoirs he wrote:

We did not have any sort of organized society or general plan of activity, but once each week at Petrashevskii's there was a gathering . . . and it was always possible to meet new people there . . . The city's news was brought there and everyone spoke loudly about everything, without any reservations whatsoever . . . At these gatherings, no specific projects or proposals were worked out, but judgements about the existing order were expressed, jokes were often told, and complaints about our present condition were voiced . . . Our small circle, centred around Petrashevskii at the end of the 1840s, carried within it the seeds of all the reforms of the 1860s.[52]

Petrashevskii's gatherings continued unhindered by the police or the Third Section until 1848, and it was only when he tried to raise the serf question publicly that they attracted police attention.

Of all the reform issues which Russia's intellectuals considered during the 1840s, the peasant question was the one on which the government was most sensitive. Committed to a policy of total secrecy and extreme caution in approaching the serf issue, Nicholas and his advisers were highly sensitive to having it raised publicly. Therefore, in February 1848, when Petrashevskii publicly distributed to his fellow nobles in the Petersburg provincial assembly of the nobility a lithographed brochure entitled 'On the Means for Increasing the Value of Populated Estates', Nicholas's anger and that of his advisers was aroused.[53]

Petrashevskii had focused attention on a problem that was indeed sensitive. In those portions of the Empire where gentry estates were over-populated and all working hands could not be put to profitable use, lands with serfs living on them were of less value than were those without them, because the latter could be farmed at a higher profit with serfs rented from other landowners. To alleviate this problem, Petrashevskii proposed several measures which struck directly at the jealously guarded privileges of the nobility. He argued, moreover, that merchants should be allowed to purchase estates from impoverished nobles at a time when only the nobility was permitted to own populated estates. This was to be done on the condition that they free the serfs in accordance with the Law on Obligated Peasants of 2 April 1842, which allowed landowners to free their peasants from personal bondage provided that they were given use of a portion of land in return for payment of a fixed annual rent in cash or labour services.[54]

If Petrashevskii's plan to allow merchants to purchase gentry estates shocked his fellow nobles, his proposal that the new merchant-landowners be given equal status in the provincial assemblies of the nobility angered them even more, for they considered membership in these bodies to be a sacred and inviolable aristocratic class privilege. Therefore the immediate reaction to Petrashevskii's brochure in the capital was one of anger, not only from the authorities, but also from the nobility. Nicholas's first reaction was to instruct the Petersburg marshal of the nobility to tell Petrashevskii that 'there [would] be no further discussion about this matter'. At the same time, the Minister of the Interior, L. A. Perovskii, assigned I. P. Liprandi, his most clever and trusted agent of special commissions, to investigate Petrashevskii's activities in secret.[55]

It was unfortunate that at precisely the time when the imperial authorities began to investigate Petrashevskii's 'Fridays', the gatherings themselves took on a more formal and, from the point of view of the investigators, more objectionable, character. According to the testimony which Petrashevskii himself gave to the investigating commission, 'In May 1848, I suggested that loose discussions [at my gatherings] be discontinued so that everyone could speak about the things that he knew best'. Because he spent the summer of 1848 in the provinces, Petrashevskii's idea was not put into practice until the autumn. 'Beginning in November 1848,' he testified, 'I usually endeavoured to have someone at my Friday gatherings to speak on some particular subject.'[56] By late 1848, criticism of the conditions in Russia, and discussion of the ideas of the French utopian socialists, had become central topics of debate. As Akhsharumov, by that time a regular Friday visitor, testified after his arrest:

Although . . . people spoke about everything – about religion, philosophy, and literature – they were primarily concerned with questions about the present condition of things and about the government. Their aim was to produce a change in social opinion: to achieve by means of a general and widespread demand, freedom of the press and public trial procedures. Their final goal was the introduction into Russia of a social life [the realization of a socialist order].[57]

Petrashevskii's efforts to introduce a measure of formality into his Friday discussions also led to a fragmenting of the group which attended them. Some of the visitors, becoming apprehensive about the increasingly sharp anti-government sentiment voiced in the discussions, began to attend only at very irregular intervals or stayed away altogether. More serious, the formal discussions made the diversity of views that had always existed at Petrashevskii's evening gatherings more evident. Before the autumn of 1848, the gatherings had tended to break up into small groups where people of like views shared their opinions, but rarely did proponents of conflicting positions clash openly. Now the diversity of opinion became much more evident. The central core of the circle remained Fourierist in outlook, and Petrashevskii continued to be its most dominant personality. But others had begun to follow different paths. N. A. Speshnev, a rich landowner from Kursk province, a man of broad education and a radical turn of mind who had lived abroad for several years, embraced not Fourierism, but communism. Unlike Petrashevskii, Speshnev argued the need for a conspiracy in which he and his followers would seize power and implement a revolution from above by means of a revolutionary dictatorship.[58] At the same time, while Speshnev and Petrashevskii clashed over the former's extreme leftist orientation, others, most notably the brothers I. M. and K. M. Desbout, began to interpret Fourier in a more Populist sense and tried to reconcile his Phalanstery ideal with the Russian peasant commune.[59]

The comfortably amorphous quality of the intellectual atmosphere at Petrashevskii's 'Fridays' therefore began to break down under the impact of the more formal debates which took place during the winter of 1848–9. It appears somewhat doubtful whether the circle could have held together much longer under the ideological strains to which it was subjected. Speshnev had already formed his own circle of men who shared his more radical ideals, and several other regular visitors at Petrashevskii's evenings had done the same.[60] In the end, it was not ideological conflicts which destroyed the Petrashevskii circle. The debate which raged at his Friday gatherings was witnessed directly by an undercover agent of the Petersburg police and soon led to the arrest of the Petrashevskii circle.

Soon after he began his investigations in mid 1848, Liprandi found someone sufficiently well-acquainted with the advanced thought of Western Europe to be able to enter Petrashevskii's circle without attracting suspicion. This was P. D. Antonelli, like Liprandi a Near Eastern scholar willing to undertake the odious task of becoming a police informer. In mid 1848, Antonelli was assigned to the same office as Petrashevskii in the Ministry of Foreign Affairs, and he immediately began to woo Petrashevskii's confidence. Although the two soon became quite friendly, Petrashevskii continued to avoid inviting Antonelli to his Friday discussions. Antonelli's superiors must have insisted that he penetrate the circle itself, for eventually, on 11 March 1849, he took the initiative and went uninvited to one of Petrashevskii's evening meetings. Somewhat to his surprise, he was warmly received, and from that date Antonelli became a regular visitor, observing everything that occurred, noting who attended and reporting the views expressed.[61]

In mid April 1849, the authorities concluded that the evidence was sufficient for their purposes, and on the night of 23 April agents of the Petersburg police and the Third Section arrested Petrashevskii and several others. The prisoners were immediately transported to the Peter-Paul Fortress, an austere, forbidding, political prison on a small island in the Neva River, opposite Nicholas's Winter Palace which, during the last century of the Russian Empire, became well-known to so many of Russia's revolutionary youth. Almost immediately, Nicholas convened a special investigating commission to interrogate the prisoners, and by the middle of December their fate had been decided. Twenty-one young men, including Petrashevskii and Speshnev, as well as the novelist Dostoevskii, were condemned to death, and fifty-one others were sentenced to administrative exile or to life as private soldiers.

Nicholas wrought one final piece of vengeance on the young men who had seen fit to criticize him and his Empire and who, he believed, had threatened the tranquillity of Russia at the critical moment when he needed all his resources for confronting the revolutionary threat abroad. The condemned men, he decided, should be made to suffer all the psychological agonies of facing death, and only at the last moment would they be spared. In the cold, grey dawn of 22 December 1849, the twenty-one prisoners were led out to the Semenovskii Square to what they believed was their execution. The scene was vividly described by Dostoevskii in a letter to his brother:

Today, December 22nd, we were all taken to the Semenovskii Square. There the sentence of death was read to us, we all were made to kiss the cross, a sword was broken over our heads, and we were told to don our white execution shirts. Then three of us were tied to the stakes in order to be shot . . . For me, only one minute of life remained . . . Then the drums sounded retreat . . . and an order from His Imperial Majesty was read which granted us our lives.[62]

For most of the intelligentsia, the arrest and punishment of the Petrashevskii circle signalled the start of a period of repression and silence, the final in a series of events which decisively altered the intellectual climate in St Petersburg for the remainder of Nicholas's reign. The first two decades of the reign had seen the intelligentsia retreat from the problems of real life into the egocentric philosophical systems of the German Romantic philosophers. Not until the 1840s had they begun to emerge from these ivory towers of philosophical speculation and made an attempt to deal with the real problems of life in Russia. Having failed to find the solace they craved in the philosophical systems of Schelling, Fichte and Hegel, they turned to a more radical interpretation of Hegel's theories and argued that life in Russia must be altered to provide them with the role in society they desired. This had led them to consider once again questions of change, though admittedly in ideal rather than practical terms. The first blow to their new interests in questions of change and reform had come with the death of Belinskii in 1848,[63] which seems to have left the St Petersburg intelligentsia momentarily stunned and with no sense of direction. Following closely upon the heels of Belinskii's death came the revolutions of 1848 in Western Europe and the harsh reaction of Nicholas of which Petrashevskii and his circle were the most prominent victims.

The arrest and punishment of the Petrashevskii circle was the final blow to the intelligentsia's newly emerged interest in questions of change.[64] The more timid ceased discussing questions of change altogether. The more radical intellectuals, such as the Westerner Aleksandr Herzen, continued to level barrages against Nicholas and his Russia, but from the security of exile in Western Europe. Many who remained in Russia withdrew further into the ivory towers of their private discussion groups where the emphasis shifted again to theoretical questions about Russia's past and future. All of these reactions shared one element: they rejected discussions of practical reform measures in favour of more idealistic goals. Only among certain elements of the progressive bureaucracy and moderate intelligentsia, particularly those who had the patronage (and hence protection) of the Grand Duchess Elena Pavlovna, did discussion about questions of reform and change continue,[65] and here it was done on a vastly reduced scale. It was from this group, which had been only on the outer fringes of Petrashevskii's circle, that the major ideas for the reforms of the 1860s would come.

3. The Hungarian Campaign

Once Nicholas had ensured absolute order and tranquillity in Russia, he turned to reach a resolution of the revolutionary threat in Eastern and Central Europe. During the summer and autumn of 1848, Nicholas had not been obliged to honour his commitments to defend Austria or the German states from revolution, mainly because they had not invited his intervention and he could not invade the territory of a friendly power. Then as 1848 wore on, the forces of revolution suffered serious defeats in Paris, Vienna, Berlin and Italy. In late June, General Cavaignac, using the tough and well-trained Garde Mobile, and aided by artillery, smashed the insurgent barricades erected during the June Days in Paris. By early July, the last centre of resistance in the Faubourg Saint-Antoine had been destroyed. Thousands of Communards were hunted down and slain[66] in a manner so brutal that the Russian radical Aleksandr Herzen, who witnessed the events, commented that 'Cossacks . . . were meek as lambs' compared to the brutal French forces.[67] By late autumn, order had been restored in Vienna and Berlin as well, as Prince von Windischgrätz and General von Wrangel seized control of the Austrian and Prussian capitals.[68] By late March 1849, after the Austrian Field-Marshal Radetzky's victory over the Italians at Novara, the tide of revolution had been turned aside in Italy as well.[69] By early 1849, the only revolutionary force remaining in Europe was in Hungary.

The revolutionary movement in Hungary, under the command of Lajos Kossuth and General Görgei, posed what Nicholas regarded as the most serious threat to the system in Eastern and Central Europe. First of all, the threat was centred in Habsburg territory, and Nicholas regarded the Habsburg monarchy as the weakest link in his defence against revolution, at best only able to fight revolution in Italy. 'In her present wretched condition, that is enough for her to do,' he had written to the Prussian king in late February 1848.[70] Therefore, when war between the Hungarian rebel forces and those of the Habsburg Empire broke out in September 1848, Nicholas was deeply concerned. He was particularly fearful that those portions of the Hungarian forces commanded by the Polish General Josef Bem might, if successful against the Austrians, invade Galicia. General Bem had been one of the leaders of the Polish revolution of 1830–31, and Nicholas feared that his invasion of Galicia might incite patriots in Russian Poland to revolt.[71]

To protect Russian Poland and the Empire's western provinces from revolutionary attacks, Nicholas ordered large numbers of troops into those areas, beginning in mid March 1848, and told Prince Paskevich 'to order the army [in Russian Poland] on to a full military footing immediately'.[72] According to Nicholas's plans, Paskevich would have the Second and Third Russian Army Corps, in addition to assorted brigades, in Poland. The First Army Corps would be stationed in Lithuania, and the Fourth Corps in the south-western Russian province of Volynia. By the summer, Paskevich had some 250,000 troops under his command,[73] and according to the claims which he made to Friedrich Wilhelm IV, Nicholas had 420,000 battle-ready troops, plus some 100,000 reserves, in Poland and the western provinces of his Empire by mid July.

The mission of this army [Nicholas wrote] is to defend the integrity of our frontiers and to thwart any wretches or madmen who dream of the possibility of restoring a Poland other than that which Russian arms so gloriously gained for the Empire. *I will not lay a finger on anyone, but woe to him who dares to touch us!*[74]

Although Nicholas continued to strengthen his forces throughout 1848, and even ordered a special recruit levy of ten recruits from each 1,000 male peasants in the western provinces,[75] he did not use them against the revolutionary threat except for those 45,000 troops which he sent into Moldavia and Wallachia in July and August to put an end to revolutionary agitation there.[76] Only in the early spring of 1849 did it become clear to Nicholas that he might soon be called upon to use his armies in Hungary and it would seem that he was not fully prepared for a call for aid from that quarter. While the Austrian Archduchess Sophia had begged Nicholas to support her son, the young Emperor Franz Josef, in December 1848,[77] it would seem that he had continued to look for the major revolutionary attack, if it came, to be launched from Galicia or Russian Poland. Certainly he did not begin to plan for a campaign in Hungary before March 1849.[78]

The Austrian government seriously began to consider calling for Russian military aid in that month. Their initial tactics, however, were directed towards trying to incite the Russians to intervene spontaneously and thus spare themselves the humiliation of formally requesting intervention.[79] By April, the Austrian position in Hungary had become truly desperate as the rebel generals Görgei and Bem won a number of impressive victories. On 14 April (NS), Kossuth proclaimed Hungary independent of the Habsburg Empire and the Habsburg dynasty deposed.[80] The young Emperor Franz-Josef, desperate for Russian aid, had no choice but to comply with Nicholas's terms: the Russian army under Russian generals must be free to act independently in Hungary. 'Now Austria leaves the mode and scale of aid completely up to me,' Nicholas wrote to his 'father-commander' Field-Marshal Paskevich on 13 April. 'In case the Austrians repeat their request to intervene, calling upon God for aid, I shall permit you to advance.'[81] The request came almost immediately. Franz Josef wrote to Nicholas:

From my childhood, I have been accustomed to see in Your Majesty the firmest supporter of the monarchical principle and the sincerest, most faithful friend of my family. It is enough for me to be convinced that Your Majesty, with the great wisdom that distinguishes him, has realized the true character of the struggle, of which Hungary is the blood-stained arena, to be sure of the help of his powerful arm.[82]

The die was cast. On 26 April Nicholas issued a manifesto announcing Russian intervention, proclaiming that:

The Emperor of Austria has requested Our cooperation against Our common enemy. We shall not refuse him. We have ordered Our various armies to advance in order to quell the revolt and to annihilate the audacious criminals who are attempting to destroy Our peace and Our lands.[83]

On 21 May (NS), the young Austrian Emperor came himself to plead Austria's cause in Warsaw. Conscious of his ally's humiliation at being forced to seek foreign aid, Nicholas 'paid the Austrian Monarch the customary military Honours rendered to a Superior'.[84] Franz-Josef's visit to Warsaw was an act of submission which Nicholas required, however, and the young Habsburg monarch would remember it well when Nicholas faced France and Britain alone in the Crimean War only a few years later. The formal Convention between the two powers was signed on 29 May (10 June) 1849.[85] A week later, on 6 (18) June, Russian troops entered the Habsburg domains in force.

When Nicholas's armies entered the field, the Habsburg forces were both out-generalled and out-numbered by the Hungarian rebels. Even the most modest estimates place the total number of troops in the field under Generals Bem and Görgei at approximately 170,000, while Austria had some 120,000.[86] The balance was dramatically altered by Russia's entry. The main Russian force, led by Paskevich, numbered just over 100,000 and attacked from the north through Galicia and across the Carpathians. At the same time, a second Russian force of some 40,000, led by General A. N. Lüders, attacked from Transylvania in the east.[87] During the course of the summer, these forces were further increased; by the end of the campaign, the Russians had sent more than 350,000 men into Hungary.[88] Such an overwhelming preponderance of numbers on the Austro-Russian side meant that it was only a matter of time before the Hungarians must yield. That General Görgei managed to postpone his final surrender until August was a tribute to his brilliant generalship, to the ineptitude of the Austrian commander, General von Haynau, and to the slowness of Paskevich's advance as a result of supply problems and a serious outbreak of cholera.

Indeed, Paskevich's forces were plagued by problems of supply from the outset. He had crossed the Carpathians into Hungary with nearly three weeks' reserve of provisions and with much larger stores awaiting transport from Galicia. His chief difficulty lay in obtaining the necessary wagons and draught animals to carry supplies through the mountain passes into Hungary.[89] By mid July, the supply problem had to some extent been solved, the cholera epidemic among the Russian troops was dying out, and Paskevich moved to the offensive in an effort to conclude the campaign. He had missed a superb opportunity to destroy General Görgei's main force in early July,[90] and his slow pursuit of the main Hungarian force was a source of deep frustration, even irritation, to Nicholas, especially in view of the brilliant advance which General Lüders had made through Transylvania. In a campaign of only two months, Lüders's forces had fought more than two dozen battles and had engaged in some fourteen skirmishes; they had routed General Bem's Hungarian forces, and by the end of July the fighting in Transylvania was over.[91]

By late July, Nicholas, with some irritation, began to press Paskevich to finish with the Hungarians.

I regret very much indeed that Görgei, with his entire army, escaped you, and I will only be able to understand it completely when you personally explain to me that which can scarcely be understood by anyone here . . . Now one must hope that military operations can be pursued more quickly and decisively in order to conclude them before the onset of foul weather and bad roads.[92]

Nicholas and Paskevich did not have long to wait. Even before his Emperor's letter reached him, the Russian field-marshal received the request to surrender which General Görgei had written on 30 July (NS).[93] With Bem's Transylvania army gone, and after General von Haynau's long-sought victory over the Hungarian forces at Temesvar, Görgei had no further hope of success in the field. He thus hastened to surrender to Paskevich and the Russian General Rüdiger so as to be spared the necessity of surrendering directly to General von Haynau and his Austrians.[94] Once again, for the third time in his career, Paskevich laid a conquered land before his master. 'Hungary lies at the feet of Your Imperial Majesty,' he reported.[95]

Görgei had made a wise decision in choosing to surrender to the Russians. Events would soon prove that the Austrians were bent on a vicious revenge. Not long after Görgei's surrender, von Haynau executed thirteen Hungarian generals at the fortress of Arad. These officers had surrendered their swords to Paskevich, but had then fallen into Austrian hands. Nicholas was appalled, his sense of honour deeply outraged. 'The punishment . . . upon those who surrendered to our army is infamous, and an insult to us. I am deeply wounded by it,' he wrote in a report to Nesselrode in mid October.[96] Many Russians shared Nicholas's indignation towards the Austrians, for the Russian victors and their Hungarian foes shared a deep mutual respect, while neither had much fondness for the Austrians. Paskevich and Rüdiger continually urged a policy of leniency towards their conquered opponents,[97] and Russian magnanimity towards their fallen foe was a source of wonderment to the Hungarians. As General Görgei wrote to the commandant of the fortress at Arad in early August, 'They are treating us in such a fashion that we marvel at it and are almost ashamed, for if we were in the reverse position, I could not, it seems, guarantee such kind and magnanimous treatment on the part of our officers towards enemy prisoners of war.'[98]

By the autumn the campaign was over. Nicholas tried desperately to portray it as another glorious and heroic victory of which Russians could justly be proud. In Warsaw and in St Petersburg, he ordered triumphal artillery salutes and displays of fireworks,[99] and he heaped lavish rewards and decorations upon officers who had fought in the Hungarian campaign. Upon Paskevich Nicholas bestowed the supreme honour of being received with the same military honours as the Emperor himself.[100] 'Ivan Fedorovich!' he proclaimed a year later. 'Thou art the glory of my twenty-five year reign – Thou art the history of the reign of Nicholas!'[101] And so he was. On parade, Paskevich's armies were perfect. In the field he moved cautiously, doing everything according to regulations. But, like Nicholas, he now belonged to another and earlier age.

Despite Nicholas's persuasions, the glory of the Russian victory was tarnished by the timidity and pedantry of Paskevich's generalship. His tactics were long-outdated and his armies fought with weapons that were sorely antiquated. Nicholas had begun to recognize that Russia's military technology was backward in comparison with that of the West even before the Hungarian campaign. Flintlock muskets, he knew, were less effective than the more accurate, reliable and rapid-firing percussion-type weapons being used by Western armies, and he said as much to Paskevich in mid 1848. But Nicholas realized that 'we cannot change weapons immediately'[102] and he was satisfied to substitute conical bullets for the ball ammunition that the Russian infantry used previously to increase somewhat the range and accuracy of their 1812-vintage weapons.[103]

Timid generalship and antiquated weapons in the 1849 campaign had been offset by Russia's vast numerical superiority, and by the weapon which Russian commanders believed in above all others: the bayonet. That the Russian soldier was, when well-led, an enemy to be seriously reckoned with, despite his outdated weapons, was amply demonstrated by General Lüders's campaign in Transylvania. A half-decade later, however, Russia would be plagued by all of the faults and shortcomings of the 1849 campaign, but would have few of the assets. Poor strategy, antiquated weapons, out-moded tactics, wretched supply systems and widespread incompetence would exact a terrible toll from Nicholas's armies in the Crimea as they faced the technologically superior forces of the Western Allies. The bloody battles of the Crimean War would demonstrate all too clearly how little Nicholas and his generals learned from their experiences in Hungary in 1849.

4. The Era of Censorship Terror

'The Emperor Nicholas, until that time filled with youthful energy, returned from the Warsaw celebrations, which followed the pacification of Hungary . . . very much aged,' wrote the Bavarian diplomat Count Otto von Bray-Steinberg. 'The Emperor returned to St Petersburg in late autumn, 1849, grey-haired . . . and was firmly convinced of the need to strengthen repressive measures so as to preserve the present order.'[104] Even before 1848, observers had commented that Nicholas had begun to age noticeably, but there can be little doubt that the events of 1848-9 affected him markedly. Despite the rewards which he heaped upon Paskevich and his officers to celebrate the victory in Hungary, the Russian army's mediocre performance in the field had not escaped his notice.

It would have been difficult for Nicholas not to draw the conclusion after 1849 that he had created a technologically inferior military colossus, but there was no way in which he could reverse the process. For one thing, the cost of rearming the Russian army with modern weapons was prohibitive, especially since Russia did not possess the industrial capacity to produce them. Even when defeats in the Crimea in 1854 made it clear that Russia must obtain large numbers of newer, faster-firing, more accurate, long-range weapons like those the Western infantry possessed, most of the orders had to be placed abroad.[105] And apart from the problem of re-equipping Russia's huge army, Nicholas's senior officers very much opposed the introduction of technological improvements and tactical innovations. There was nearly universal opposition among senior officers to the introduction of faster-firing weapons before the Crimean War, and even in 1855, after many Russian officers had witnessed the effectiveness of the Western Allies' superior infantry weapons in the Crimea, experts still insisted that a major objection to breech-loading rifles was that 'the rifleman, in the confusion of battle, has the possibility of firing all his cartridges in an instant and will be defenceless'.[106] In terms of combat tactics, Russian senior officers still held to the Napoleonic concept of large, massed formations when Western European military planners had long rejected them in favour of more manoeuvrable and smaller tactical units. In this, Nicholas himself shared a large portion of blame because of his insistence that, above all else, Russia's armies must be trained to perform to perfection on the parade ground. However, even Nicholas had, on occasion, urged greater and more effective combat training for particular army units.[107] His senior commanders, however, did not share his concern. Anxious to impress their sovereign with the precise order of their parade-ground formations, they continued to insist upon strict adherence to the precise letter of the military regulations.

Precisely how aware Nicholas was of the serious shortcomings in the Russian army after the Hungarian campaign is difficult to say. He knew that the army had not done as well as he had expected, and he realized that both the infantry and cavalry required more effective combat training.[108] But his senior officers and advisers continued to oppose innovations and he certainly made no serious effort to replace them with more innovative junior officers. His officers, of course, made every effort to conceal from their Emperor any shortcomings in the military establishment. It would be hard to imagine that Nicholas returned from the celebrations in Warsaw following the victories in Hungary without some sense of uneasiness, even foreboding for Russia's military future. His answer was an attempt to further strengthen the centralization of the Russian state and military establishment so as to take more and more decisions into his own hands. As Colonel D. A. Miliutin, a special consultant to the Minister of War, Prince V. A. Dolgorukov, remarked, 'all commands, to the most minute, had to flow from the centre – from the Ministry [of War] or, more accurately speaking – from the Winter Palace . . . The War Minister, in the literal sense of the word, was only a secretary for military affairs to the Tsar.'[109] This would lead to further difficulties very quickly. Recalling the opening days of war in the Crimea in 1854, Miliutin commented that, 'Imperial approval or confirmation was sought for the smallest details. It was hardly possible for the military administration to progress to more absolute centralization'.[110]

Perhaps sensing how difficult any further military confrontation with the West might be, Nicholas, as Count von Bray-Steinberg remarked, sought to further ensure absolute order within Russia itself. Nowhere were his efforts more evident than in the limits which he and his ministers sought to impose upon the exchange of ideas and knowledge among Russia's educated public in what became known as the 'era of censorship terror'. As we have noted, censorship had been a part of Russian life from the moment of Nicholas's accession. It had grown increasingly rigid as a reaction to the peasant revolts in Austrian Galicia in 1846, but reached its peak following the outbreak of the February revolution in Paris in 1848. Indeed, almost from the moment that word of the Western European revolutions reached St Petersburg, a wave of anti-revolutionary hysteria broke out among state officials. The historian S. M. Solov'ev recalled in his memoirs that 'the Petersburg government was given a great fright . . . and they thought that revolution would immediately burst into flame in Russia'.[111] P. A. Valuev, as governor of the Baltic province of Courland, described the fear even more vividly in his diary in mid March:

Our pseudo-statesmen do not know what to make of it all . . . Yesterday they were convinced that Tiflis and Warsaw had burst into flame . . . Among our high officials and political figures, some are in silent fear . . . while others in bitterness think only of the means to crush everything.[112]

The fears of such men took a unique and specific form: anticommunism. As early as 1846, Faddei Bulgarin, one of the leading proponents of the doctrines of Official Nationality, had sent to the Third Section a report entitled 'Socialism, Communism, and Pantheism in Russia in the Past Quarter-Century'.[113] Bulgarin obviously knew little about communism, but his efforts to link a whole variety of radical movements together into one all-encompassing threat shows the roots of the anti-communist hysteria which broke out in Russia in 1848. 'Socialism and Communism are two types of one and the same idea which gave birth to Jacobinism, sans-culottism, carbonarism and, in general, all sects and societies aspiring and having aspired to overthrow monarchy and every sort of civil order,' Bulgarin wrote.[114] This was an outlook, he argued further, which appealed to a wide audience in Russia. 'The ruined and depraved segments of the aristocracy, foolhardy youth, and a huge class of people who multiply daily, people who have nothing to lose and, in a revolution, hope to gain everything' – such, in Bulgarin's view, was the broad group in Russia to whom such ideas appealed.[115]

Bulgarin in 1846 was seeking to stir up powerful sentiments against the journal *Notes of the Fatherland*, which so threatened the success of his own publication, the *Northern Bee*, but in 1846 he found little sympathy for his views or interest in his accusations, even in the Third Section itself.[116] Two years later, it was entirely another matter. On 6 March 1848, Bulgarin sent another memorandum to the authorities in which he insisted that Russia's most progressive journal, the *Contemporary*, was edited by a man 'whom the party of Communists selected' to fill the post.[117] This time, Bulgarin was not alone in his accusations. In early February the Third Section had received several anonymous denunciations that the *Contemporary* and *Notes of the Fatherland* published works in which there was 'something very much like Communism and that from such materials the younger generation could become fully Communistic'.[118] Such warnings had reached Nicholas himself on 23 February, when he summoned Count Orlov, Head of the Third Section, and asked for a report on the periodical press in Russia. Orlov repeated these accusations and concluded that the progressive periodical press 'could instil in the younger generation ideas about political questions in the West and about Communism'.[119] Orlov recommended that the press be more rigidly controlled. At almost the same time, Nicholas received similar urgings from his eldest son's tutor, Baron Korf, who, as we noted earlier, was not particularly fearful that revolution might actually penetrate into Russia, but was perfectly willing to play upon Nicholas's fears to undermine the position of Minister of Public Instruction, Count S. S. Uvarov, whose post he coveted. By the evening of 23 February, the very day that Nicholas had discussed the question of censorship with Orlov, Korf had written a memorandum urging stricter censorship and sent it to Nicholas through the Heir Apparent, the Grand Duke Aleksandr Nikolaevich.[120]

Faced by his ministers' urgings to strengthen the bonds of censorship, and himself fearful of the revolutionary menace, Nicholas acted quickly to create the so-called Menshikov Committee on 27 February to oversee both the journals and the censors.[121] Only advocates of the strictest sort of censorship were included: Prince A. S. Menshikov, Baron Korf, Count A. S. Stroganov, D. P. Buturlin, General Dubbelt of the Third Section and P. I. Degai.[122] Korf, Buturlin and Degai especially spared no efforts to uncover any even remotely dangerous materials in the periodical press. K. S. Veselovskii, a statistical expert in the Ministry of the Interior, later to become a prominent academician, quite probably turned his attention from municipal problems to studies of climatology and meteorology because the Menshikov Committee found an article which he had written on housing for workers to be 'dangerous to the civil order'.[123] Likewise, M. E. Saltykov, another official in the Ministry of the Interior, who later achieved considerable fame as a novelist, was exiled to the small provincial town of Viatka for publishing his novel, *A Tangled Affair*. So anxious were some of the Menshikov Committee members to find seditious works in the Russian press that Degai reportedly exclaimed: 'Eureka! Eureka!' when he first discovered Saltykov's novel in the pages of *Notes of the Fatherland*, soon after the committee had begun its sessions.[124]

But the Menshikov Committee was only a stop-gap measure, and oppressive as its activities were, worse was to come. On 2 April 1848, less than a month after the committee had begun to meet, Nicholas replaced it with a permanent body presided over by Buturlin, with Degai and Korf as members. Buturlin himself has been remembered by contemporaries as an intelligent man, and a charming dinner companion, but one who was somewhat strange and despotic.[125] Korf, as we have seen, was something of an opportunist, seeking to use his position on the committee to settle old grudges. Degai was simply a narrow-minded civil servant of minimal talents who had made a successful career by doing his superiors' bidding.

The creation of the Buturlin Committee marked the capping of the edifice of a censorship that was obscurantist in outlook and all-pervasive in nature. By 1850, there were twelve different agencies to deal with censorship, and according to one contemporary estimate, the number of individuals working in the state censorship apparatus actually exceeded the number of books published by mid century.[126] Russia was truly gripped by censorship terror or, as one observer remarked, 'a Holy War against scholarship and knowledge'.[127] The Buturlin Committee in particular saw threats on all sides. An article relating to medieval Russian history on 'The Condition of Russia in the Reign of Vasilii Ivanovich

Shuiskii' was considered dangerous because the author noted that Dmitrii the Pretender had told the Russian peasants they were free. While accurate and acceptable for publication in a specialized historical journal, the committee decided that such a statement should never have been allowed to appear in the *Contemporary*, 'a journal which has a large circulation among all classes of people'.[128] Other publications, such as I. I. Davydov's study, 'On the Significance of Russian Universities', an article commissioned by Count Uvarov himself, was found dangerous despite the fact that, on the surface at least, it contained nothing objectionable. However, the Buturlin Committee censored the article and its author because of its 'inner meaning',[129] and, despite Uvarov's spirited defence, Nicholas himself settled the matter with the statement that, 'I absolutely *forbid* all similar articles in journals, regardless of whether they are *for* or *against* universities.'[130]

Censors were not satisfied to focus their energies only on new works, however. The censor A. I. Mekhelin devoted a considerable effort to removing all references to the words 'republic' and 'republicanism' from earlier studies on Ancient Greece and Rome.[131] Perhaps even more ludicrous, the censor N. Rodzianko urged that Shakespeare's *Richard III* not be republished or performed on the stage any longer because it dealt with themes which were 'dangerous in a moral sense'.[132] Fables and other works of the eighteenth-century authors Kantemir and Khemnitser could not be republished because, especially in the case of Kantemir, the censor decreed that 'he only belongs on the rear shelf of the library'.[133] Some of the writings of N. M. Karamzin, court historian under Alexander I, and a close confidant of Nicholas during his early days, were suppressed, as were the works of Tacitus and Plato.[134] Even the letters of Catherine the Great to Voltaire and other prominent figures of the Enlightenment, which had appeared in a small edition in 1802, could not be reprinted in 1850.[135] It was always the fear of the masses which lay behind these actions. Over and over again it was insisted that certain things were acceptable and appropriate for limited audiences but not for broader circulation.[136]

The work of the Buturlin Committee and other censorship organs during the era of censorship terror focused upon the persons of Russian writers as much as upon the things they wrote, for it was not enough that the works themselves should be censored; the authors themselves must be punished, and, preferably, kept from writing in the future. The gentle and (virtually) apolitical philologist, V. I. Dal', was accused of communist leanings, and at the insistence of Nicholas and Buturlin was told by the Minister of the Interior, Perovskii, that if he wished to keep his post in the civil service (an economic necessity) he must stop writing.[137] 'Give this

writer a stern reprimand, all the more so because he is in state service,'
Nicholas had decreed. Even the loyal servant of Official Nationality,
Faddei Bulgarin, received a reprimand for writing in the *Northern Bee*
that hackney drivers in St Petersburg charged exorbitant and arbitrary
fees in bad weather.[138] 'No criticism whatsoever of the activities or
administration of the government and the established authority [who
were supposed to see to it that hackney drivers' fees were carefully
regulated], even though it be indirect, will be allowed in print,' the
Buturlin Committee concluded after dealing with Bulgarin's case.[139]
Police surveillance and brief arrests became part of the lives of writers
under the committee's oppressive hand. Between 1848 and 1855, nearly
every major Russian writer fell foul of the authorities. The playwright
A. N. Ostrovskii, and the Slavophile writers Ivan and Konstantin
Aksakov, A. S. Khomiakov, Ivan Kireevskii and Prince V. A. Cherkasskii
were all placed under police surveillance.[140] The Slavophiles Iurii
Samarin and Ivan Aksakov were arrested for brief periods at Nicholas's
express order, and the novelist Ivan Turgenev was sent into exile on his
estate for more than a year for writing an obituary on Gogol.[141]

Such arrests, exiles and surveillances comprise only a few of many
examples. To discuss further cases would only reinforce the point how
oppressive the censorship, and especially the Buturlin Committee, were
for most Russian writers during the era of censorship terror. Most
significantly, such capricious and oppressive acts of censorship forced
many thinking Russians to cease discussing questions of change in the
context of modernizing their country to make Russia better able to
compete with the West. Writers turned increasingly to 'safe' subjects such
as bibliography, and the Empire's progressive journals, which, during the
mid 1840s, had published an array of thoughtful and perceptive discussions of social problems, as well as some of Russia's greatest literature,
now filled their pages with bibliographical works. As the radical critic
N. G. Chernyshevskii wrote to the Ukrainian historian N. I. Kostomarov
in 1853:

Apathy in Petersburg has reached an extremely high level of development; it is
impossible to recognize those people whom I knew two years ago . . . The place
of Belinskii is now occupied by [the bibliographers] Gennadii and Tikhonravov
. . . I recognize the importance of bibliography as an auxiliary science for the
history of literature. But to place [it] above all else in the world . . . seems to me
to be pure pedantry.[142]

Chernyshevskii was not alone in this opinion. Just a few years later,
the man who would become his associate and fellow critic, the radical
publicist N. A. Dobroliubov, commented:

Nowadays people place great value on every tiny fact of biography and bibliography: to whom does the signature 'A' or 'B' belong . . . What house did a certain famous writer visit; with whom did he meet; what sort of tobacco did he smoke; what sort of boots did he wear? These are their favourite subjects of research, discussion and thought. [143]

This sort of obscurantist oppression deadened Russia's intellectual life almost totally during the last years of Nicholas's reign. As the historian T. N. Granovskii, a moderate Westerner, wrote to a friend in 1854:

Can I speak frankly to you? Formerly, I loved Ketcher [a mutual friend], but now I scarcely speak with him once or twice in the course of a year . . . He has become intellectually paralysed . . . and, in many ways, has gone backwards.[144]

But the impact upon Russia's intellectuals was more than oppressive and deadening; it filled them with such a sense of total frustration that it nearly destroyed a number of them physically, morally and intellectually. Some began to drink heavily; others, the writer N. A. Nekrasov, for example, became almost incurably addicted to cards.[145] Beyond this, erotic – sometimes simply pornographic – literature enjoyed a surge of popularity during the late 1840s and early 1850s among the intelligentsia. The novelist Ivan Turgenev, who lived in St Petersburg during these years, attributed this directly to the repression which Nicholas and his advisers had imposed. In discussing Boccaccio's *Decameron*, and the manner in which noble men and elegant women tried to forget the terrible plagues around them by amusing each other with bawdy, sometimes obscene tales, Turgenev posed the question to his friends: 'And, really, wasn't the Nicholas oppression its own type of plague for educated society?'[146] Turgenev had a point. Men who had been (and would again become) some of Russia's most creative and sensitive writers, abandoned their nightly discussions of social problems relating to Russia's past, present and future, and instead devoted the evenings to reading and writing erotic verse, to drinking, cards and prostitutes.[147] For all of them, the loss during these years would be tragic. For some, it would be fatal: V. A. Miliutin, a brilliant and promising political economist, who was close to this circle, contracted syphilis, most probably at one of these gatherings, and died from it before he reached the age of thirty.[148]

Such men would remember the last years of the Nicholas system with bitterness and thinly veiled hatred. A few days after Nicholas's death in 1855, the jurist, publicist and historian K. D. Kavelin wrote to a friend that, 'Russia, exhausted, ravaged, crushed, pillaged, degraded, has been deceived and benumbed by a thirty-year tyranny.'[149] And, later in the year, the censor A. V. Nikitenko would write in his diary:

It is now only beginning to become evident how terrible the past twenty-nine years were for Russia. Administration is in a chaos; moral feeling has been trampled upon; intellectual development has been stopped . . . All this is fruit of a scorn for the truth and a blind and barbaric faith in material force alone.[150]

The last years of the Nicholas system were a far cry from the earthly paradise which the proponents of Official Nationality continued to applaud in poetry, belles-lettres, even official reports. The High State Counsellor Aleksandr Kamenskii, for example, proclaimed:

Under the sacred, beneficial protection of autocracy, this fortunate land of Russia blossoms . . . Foreigners gaze upon her prosperity with intense regret. To them it is evident that . . . this awe-inspiring colossus towers above them.[151]

But the 'awe-inspiring colossus' of the north would not continue to tower above foreign powers for much longer. The Nicholas system was soon to face its most trying hour in a crisis and military defeat which would lead to its destruction. The successful defeat of the Hungarian rebels and the re-establishment of order in the West had led to very important changes in the political temper of Europe. Western statesmen had not missed the lessons to be learned from Russia's difficulties in the campaign of 1849. The image of the military colossus of the East was considerably tarnished, and before long the West and Russia would be locked in what would be for Nicholas the last test of strength. The final act of the drama would be played out on the blood-soaked plains of the Crimea; the opening scene, however, would be laid in Central Europe.

10

The Last Act:
The Crimean War

*'A terrible struggle has burst upon us. Monumental
and contradictory forces are on a collision course:
the East and West; the Slavic world and the Latin
world . . . What will be the outcome of this
struggle between two worlds? There can be no doubt.
We, Russia, are on the side of truth and ideals:
Russia fights not for material gain and worldly
interests, but for eternal ideas'*

A. F. TIUTCHEVA, A MAID-OF-HONOUR
AT THE RUSSIAN COURT

Throughout 1848 and 1849, Nicholas and his advisers had faced the
spectre of revolutions in Europe, but by the late summer of 1849, all the
revolutionary movements had died out or been crushed. Order had been
restored in France, and the new president of the French Republic, Louis
Napoleon, was already laying the groundwork for the *coup d'état* which,
in December 1852, would enable him to become Emperor. In Central
Europe, revolutions in Vienna, Prague, Berlin and Hungary had all been
put down, and a conservative order was being restored. But the crushing
of these revolutions had given birth to an equally ominous menace from
Nicholas's point of view, and one that would have a lasting and far-
reaching impact upon the Russian state during the last seven decades of
Romanov rule. For, with the momentary triumph of liberal forces in 1848
had arisen the spectre of German unity, and a united Germany, as
Nicholas and his advisers well knew, would alter dramatically the political
balance along Russia's western frontiers. There was much to be feared,
as Count Nesselrode remarked in 1848, from a Germany that was
'federated, united, democratic, aggressive, [and] avid of supremacy and
territorial gains'.[1]

The question of German unification had been discussed at length even before the revolutions of 1848, and it was one of the most pressing issues which the Frankfurt Parliament faced once it began to meet in May 1848. All were in general agreement that a unified German state was desirable; far more debatable was the question of what territories should be part of the new German Empire.[2] When, in the first months of revolutionary upheaval, it had seemed that the Habsburg Monarchy was doomed to extinction, it had appeared certain that Austrian Germans would be included in the new German state. But, in the face of Prince Windischgrätz's victory over revolution in Prague, and the failure of revolution in Vienna, the majority of the Frankfurt Parliament had concluded, by the autumn of 1848, that it would be wiser to seek a united Germany which did not include Austrian German lands.[3]

Prince Schwarzenberg's insistence that the Habsburg Empire be preserved as a unified state in late 1848 had caused the resignation of Count Anton von Schmerling's Frankfurt cabinet and had led to the rise of Heinrich von Gagern, a liberal Hessian aristocrat who urged a unified Germany under the leadership of Prussia.[4] The Frankfurt Parliament thus offered the imperial crown of a united 'lesser' Germany to the Prussian king Friedrich Wilhelm IV in early April 1849. But, although he favoured German unification, Friedrich Wilhelm refused the crown offered him by 'bakers and butchers, and reeking with the stench of revolution'. Such German unification as he envisaged must come according to his own plan, a more traditional programme drafted by his friend and adviser Josef von Radowitz, who was convinced that 'German unity was the best antidote to revolution'.[5]

Friedrich Wilhelm's refusal to accept the imperial crown doomed the Frankfurt Parliament, but it by no means ended the debate over German unity. Once the rump of the Frankfurt Parliament had been dispersed by local troops at Stuttgart on 18 June 1849, the centre of controversy shifted to Prussia and Austria, the two most powerful states within the 'greater' German realm. Conflicts between them during the next eighteen months would force Nicholas into the diplomatic arena by the autumn of 1850.

1. Storm Clouds Gather

The immediate conflict between Austria and Prussia focused upon the latter's efforts to create within Central Europe a well-integrated inner German Empire under Prussian leadership, while proposing that this be a part of a larger (and looser) Central European federation of which the entire Habsburg Empire would be a part.[6] Austria's need to call upon Nicholas for aid against the Hungarians had certainly not improved her diplomatic position and prestige in Central Europe, and in the summer of 1849 she could do little more than fight a diplomatic holding action, for all of her energies and resources were directed towards crushing the Hungarian rebels. As soon as that problem had been dealt with in the autumn of 1849, however, Prince Schwarzenberg turned to deal more decisively with the Prussian menace in Central Europe, though not before some twenty-eight lesser German states had agreed to follow Prussia's programme. By early 1850, Schwarzenberg was prepared to offer as a counter-proposal to Prussia's programme a plan which would provide for a middle European customs union, drafted by his Minister of Commerce, Karl Ludwig von Bruck.[7]

The diplomatic struggles between Prussia and Austria during 1849 and 1850 need not concern us except to note that the two powers reached a stalemate by mid 1850, not only because of their disagreement on the matter of German unification, but also because of tension over Prussian policy in the Schleswig-Holstein affair. War seemed very near, and, as Count Peter von Meiendorf, the Russian ambassador to Berlin, wrote to Nicholas and Nesselrode at the end of 1849, 'Prussia will pay dearly for this experimental course upon which Radowitz [Prussia's Foreign Minister] has placed her.'[8] Indeed, he regarded Radowitz as 'the most odious man in the entire nation', a man of 'unconquerable vanity'.[9] Meiendorf insisted that Russia should stand openly on the side of Austria because her policies were formulated 'upon the basis of treaties, while Prussia takes her stand upon revolution'.[10]

Nicholas could not have agreed more with Meiendorf's views. He had no desire to see a strong and united Germany on Russia's western frontier, and throughout 1849 and 1850 insisted to Friedrich Wilhelm that he would recognize 'no legal basis for an European order other than that which has been ratified by the treaties of 1815'.[11] But the conflict between Austria and Prussia had to be resolved by either war or diplomacy, and in an effort to mediate their differences, Nicholas arranged to preside over a meeting at Warsaw between Baron Otto von Manteuffel (soon to become Prussian Foreign Minister), the Prussian Crown Prince Wilhelm, Austria's minister president Prince Felix Schwarzenberg, and Baron Meiendorf (about to be transferred to Vienna), in an effort to lessen their conflicts and, at the same time, head off the Prussian unification scheme.[12]

Although at first it seemed to cool the tempers of Austria and Prussia, the Warsaw meeting did not resolve the tensions in Central Europe. Prince Schwarzenberg had been notably conciliatory, and to Meiendorf at least it also seemed that Prussia had come to realize 'that the true interests of Prussia compel her to seek an alliance with Russia'.[13] But,

within a month, the Prussian king was accusing Schwarzenberg of treason
and insisting that 'on his return from Warsaw he seems to have forgotten
completely that which he promised there'.[14] Schwarzenberg had ordered
some 130,000 Austrian troops to be massed in Bohemia on the frontiers
of Prussia and Saxony, and in early November Prussia responded by
ordering a full mobilization. On 8 November, Prussian and Bavarian
troops clashed in Hesse[15] and war seemed inevitable. All feared that
Prussia would be the loser in an armed struggle with the Habsburg
Empire, and some Middle German States were already looking forward
to being freed from the threat of Prussian domination in a united 'lesser'
Germany by an Austrian victory.[16]

While Nicholas regarded a Germany firmly united under Prussian
control as a threat to Russia's position, he did not wish to see Austria
emerge as undisputed victor in a central European conflict. He had therefore urged his ambassadors in Berlin and in Vienna to seek a conciliatory
path throughout the autumn of 1850 and pressed for a peaceful resolution
by threatening both Prussia and Austria that he would throw all his
resources on the side of the other if war began. Friedrich Wilhelm was
unwilling to chance the possibility of a German civil war, and the majority
of his cabinet was openly fearful that a test of strength might prove
disastrous. As a result, Radowitz, the foremost proponent of a Prussian
unification of Germany, was forced to resign as Foreign Minister, and
Prussia's scheme for a German Union was, for the moment, dead.[17]

Yet the questions of Schleswig-Holstein and Hesse (occupied by both
Prussian and Bavarian troops) still remained very much at issue, and
Schwarzenberg pressed for immediate settlement. On 24 November he
sent Friedrich Wilhelm an ultimatum demanding that his troops evacuate
the Hessian fortress of Cassel within forty-eight hours. The Prussian king,
uncertain of Nicholas's position in the event of a confrontation, moved to
seek a peaceful solution.[18] Baron Manteuffel, Prussia's new Foreign
Minister, thus proposed to Prince Schwarzenberg that they meet to
resolve the crisis, and on 28 November the two ministers and Baron
Meiendorf (now Russian ambassador to Vienna) met at Olmütz.[19] With
Meiendorf serving as something of a mediator, Prince Schwarzenberg and
Baron Manteuffel settled their differences on 29 November by signing the
Convention of Olmütz. Schwarzenberg no longer insisted that the Prussian
army evacuate Hesse completely; the two ministers agreed that Austrian
and Prussian forces would jointly occupy the fortress of Cassel; Prussia
would abandon Radowitz's plan for a German Union; and it was agreed
that the foreign ministers of all German states would meet at Dresden to
study the question of German unification further.[20]

For the moment, the danger of an armed confrontation between

Prussia and Austria had been averted, and Nicholas was regarded as having played a major role. Certainly he had pressed for a peaceful resolution of the crisis, and there is no doubt that both Baron Meiendorf and Nicholas's Foreign Minister, Count Nesselrode, had strongly favoured Austria. On receiving news of the Olmütz Convention Nicholas reportedly spoke of the 'noble moderation' of the Habsburg Emperor, and Nesselrode referred throughout November to the 'very moderate proposals of Austria'.[21] The degree of pressure which Meiendorf imposed upon Schwarzenberg and Manteuffel, however, is less clear, and the best estimates are that, while the threat of Russian interference lay in the back of both statesmen's minds and seemed especially threatening to the Prussians, the two ministers reached an accord at Olmütz on their own.[22]

For the Prussians, however, Olmütz was a humiliation because they had been forced to yield both on the question of German unification and on the Hesse and Holstein issues. Friedrich Wilhelm and his ministers had accepted the convention since they had little choice in the matter, although the Prussian Parliament had come close to rejecting it despite a brilliant defence of the king's policy by a rising young statesman, Otto von Bismarck.[23] Prussian statesmen and the king and queen themselves had made the appropriate gestures of thanking Nicholas for his intervention, and Friedrich Wilhelm even reportedly remarked that he 'was happy to be free of the influence of his dangerous adviser Radowitz'.[24] But a deep bitterness remained, and Prussia would not soon forget that Nicholas had failed to support her in her hour of need. As the famous philologist Max Müller wrote to a friend, 'Have thousands of men in the past sacrificed their lives and well-being to see Germany today governed by the grace of Russia?'[25]

By the end of 1850, Nicholas's power in Europe was thus as awesome as ever, perhaps more so. As Nesselrode wrote to him on the twenty-fifth anniversary of his accession: 'In the wake of . . . revolutions, [Your Majesty] has become for the world the representative of the monarchical ideal, the mainstay of the principles of order and the impartial defender of European equilibrium.'[26] And, indeed, much of Europe agreed with these sentiments, though while they inspired admiration in some, they evoked fear in others. 'No one,' wrote one diplomatic observer, 'has been more the master of Europe, except perhaps Napoleon I. No one has inspired so much sympathy, anger, or hatred!' 'The Emperor Nicholas is master of Europe,' concluded Prince Albert, the consort of Queen Victoria.[27]

In looking back over his twenty-five years on the Russian throne, it would have been difficult for Nicholas to think otherwise. He had fought revolution in St Petersburg, France, Prussia, Austria and Hungary, and had always emerged victorious. He had imposed his will upon Central Europe, first at Münchengrätz and then at Olmütz. During his reign, three defeated nations – Persia, Poland and Hungary – had been placed at his feet by his faithful 'father-commander' Prince Paskevich. Everywhere his armies had been victorious, and always his domain had been a bastion of peace, order and stability. But the destructive termites of change were gnawing at the underpinnings of the Nicholas system; despite its powerful and imposing exterior, its inner structure was eroding. Should Russia be forced to face Europe, it would be with an economic and social order which, by comparison to the West, was backward and antiquated, and an army whose technological inferiority had been demonstrated in the Hungarian campaign. For the tempests of change, blown by the French Revolution of 1789, the revolutions of 1830 and 1848, and the Industrial Revolution in the West, were as yet not even gentle breezes upon the Russian horizon.

In his relations with the Western Powers, Nicholas had built up a deep reservoir of resentment which would one day overflow. Austria was an embarrassed debtor, resentful at having had to beg directly for Russian aid in Hungary, and insulted by the friendly conduct of Nicholas's armies towards their Hungarian foes. Prussia would not soon forget her humiliation at Olmütz. Nicholas had never maintained close relations with France, at least not since the revolution of 1830. And, with Britain Nicholas had never succeeded in establishing that personal amity with Queen Victoria and her ministers that he had courted assiduously in 1844.

In this atmosphere of tension, resentment, hostility and misunderstanding, with Western Powers fearing Nicholas's strength as a threat to European equilibrium, the focus of Europe's diplomatic concerns shifted once again to the 'Sick Man', the Ottoman Empire.

2. The Approach of War

Nicholas's manner of conducting diplomatic relations with the West came from a bygone age. Personal diplomacy was for him the key to the successful resolution of international issues, and as the nineteenth century passed its mid-point, he continued to rely far too heavily upon his personal charm in dealing with foreign powers. In his relations with Central Europe, Nicholas had seen his personal diplomacy succeed time and again: at Münchengrätz, at Teplitz and at Olmütz. But in these cases he had failed to see that his personal charm worked upon his Austrian and Prussian allies either because their interests coincided with his (like Nicholas, they sought to erect a barrier against revolution in Central Europe at Münchengrätz and Teplitz), or because they had not the strength and resources to oppose so powerful a neighbour (as had been the case at Olmütz). With France, Nicholas's personal diplomacy had been restricted before 1830 to charming old comrades-in-arms or *ancien régime* aristocrats like Count de la Ferronnays and Baron Bourgoing, and General Castelbajac after 1848. Between 1830 and 1848, his relations with France had been cool, often openly hostile and, despite the sometimes brilliant efforts of Brunnov and Kiselev, his ambassadors in Paris, Nicholas had few friends in the French capital.

With Britain, Nicholas's relations were perhaps the most confusing of all. He was something of an anglophile and loved the life of an English country gentleman. But he did not comprehend the political system within which British diplomats were obliged to work, and he found the institution of Parliament and its political debates incomprehensible. Most of all, he simply did not understand the way in which British statesmen negotiated, and he completely failed to perceive the nature of England's world-wide concerns in the Far East, in Central Asia and, especially, in the Near East and the Eastern Mediterranean. As an autocrat, Nicholas was accustomed to speak his mind. He was candid and straightforward, and expected others to be the same. British statesmen considered him ambitious but honest, and above all a gentleman.[28] But Nicholas could never understand that his British counterparts, who were not autocrats and had to answer to Parliament, could not afford the same candour he could permit himself. Nicholas had left England in June 1844, convinced that his personal charm had worked its spell upon Queen Victoria and her ministers. He never fully realized that personal friendship could not alone determine British policy, and that British statesmen would not tie their hands by long-range commitments. As Nesselrode once warned him, 'The fundamental condition of her [England's] policy has always been never to make commitments for a more or less uncertain future, but to wait for the event in order to decide what course to adopt.'[29]

The tragedy of Nicholas's relations with Britain in the decade after 1844 was that, while he sought through personal charm and candour to dispel British apprehensions about his designs upon the Ottoman Empire, he only succeeded in instilling greater fears. His repeated references to the 'Sick Man's' approaching demise, and the need for Russia and Britain to be prepared for that event, only convinced British diplomats that he was preparing to seize portions of the Empire, especially the Straits, for himself. Nicholas insisted that 'the bear [Turkey] is dying',[30] while the British and his own more cautious foreign minister, Count Nesselrode, hoped to preserve the Ottoman Empire as long as possible. Sir George Seymour, the British Ambassador to St Petersburg, reflecting the views of the British Prime Minister Aberdeen, 'advocated a physician, not a surgeon' to treat Turkey's ills;[31] and Nesselrode once confessed to Seymour that 'the Emperor . . . occupied himself too much with what might happen on the fall of the Ottoman Empire. Perhaps its existence is precarious, but above all let us occupy ourselves with prolonging it as long as possible.'[32]

The suspicions which Nicholas's comments about the coming demise of the Ottoman Empire engendered in the minds of British statesmen were given added substance by a series of conversations which he had with Seymour during January and February 1853. During them Nicholas spoke repeatedly of the need for Britain and Russia to agree upon a course of action in the event of the break-up of the Ottoman Empire. He insisted that he had abandoned Catherine the Great's schemes to seize Constantinople or to re-create a modern Greek Empire under Russian control. But his statements that Russia might be forced to occupy Constantinople temporarily, 'if no previous provision were made, if everything were left to chance',[33] engendered deep distrust in Seymour's mind, and he passed it on to the Foreign Office. British suspicions were quite probably also aroused by several other factors. First, it must have been difficult for them to believe that Nicholas had no plan to resurrect the Empress Catherine's imperial designs upon the Balkans when he proposed that Wallachia, Moldavia, Serbia and Bulgaria should be independent princely domains under Russian protection.[34] Equally important, Aberdeen had heard Nicholas express similar views and had reacted to them with like scepticism during the Emperor's visit to England in June 1844. Finally, until early 1853, Seymour had been isolated in St Petersburg, and as late as December 1852 had complained to the Earl of Malmsbury that 'I have had an opportunity of conversing freely with the Emperor upon public affairs – once – and only once – during the fourteen months that I have passed in Russia . . . The Prussian Envoy sees the Emperor as often in the course of each day as the English Minister does in the course of a year.'[35] Certainly one may expect that Seymour felt somewhat suspicious when, after speaking to him about diplomatic matters only once in the course of fourteen months, Nicholas summoned him for private conversations on four different occasions during January and February 1853.

British suspicions of Nicholas's claim that he did not wish to seize Constantinople, the Straits or any territory for Russia, were particularly unfortunate, for in his conversations with Seymour he was being quite honest. From his own memoranda, written after he had discussed the Turkish question with Prince Paskevich in late January, we know that in the event of the Ottoman Empire collapsing he envisaged Constantinople becoming a free port, Serbia and most of Bulgaria becoming independent, Russia garrisoning the Bosphorus and Austria garrisoning the Dardanelles, Britain receiving Egypt together with Cyprus or Rhodes, and France receiving Crete. Nicholas did not mention to Seymour that the Danubian principalities (Wallachia and Moldavia) would be 'Russian'. Even so, except for this one sphere of influence, which hardly seemed unreasonable in view of the fact that France, Austria and Britain actually stood to gain important territories, Nicholas's personal views about the allocation of Ottoman domains were precisely what he told Seymour.[36]

He did, however, remain blissfully and dangerously ignorant of British suspicions. The British had not openly committed themselves to any firm course of action, and Lord Russell had even implied to Nicholas in early February that 'no man and no engagement could guarantee the future'.[37] Nicholas misunderstood completely. To him, Lord Russell's warning, issued in veiled terms as it was, seemed a guarantee that Russia and Britain shared a common view of the Eastern Question. 'I am very appreciative, for I see [in all this] the guarantee against the future which I fear,' Nicholas had written in the margin of Russell's letter.[38] Thus, in March 1853, as Nicholas prepared to send Prince Menshikov on a delicate mission to Constantinople in an effort to settle disputes between Roman Catholics and Orthodox about who would control the Holy Places, he was operating upon a set of assumptions which were dangerously flawed. He believed guarantees existed where none had been given, and he thought that the British understood his views on the Eastern Question when, in fact, they did not.

Although France, Britain, Austria and Russia had been embroiled in disputes relating to territory or political events in the Ottoman Empire on a number of occasions during Nicholas's reign, nothing proved so inflammatory an issue, or so clouded the reason of rulers and diplomats, as the dispute between France and Russia over the Christian shrines in Palestine. Control of the Holy Places within the Ottoman Empire had been a subject of controversy among Roman Catholic and Orthodox Churches for several centuries, but during the eighteenth century the Orthodox had gained the upper hand. This was partly by design (the Orthodox had succeeded in having the Roman Catholics excluded from control of the shrines in 1757) and partly by default, because very few Roman Catholic pilgrims visited the Holy Lands during the eighteenth and first half of the nineteenth centuries. A French monk, visiting Jerusalem on Christmas Day 1831, found only four pilgrims out of some 4,000 who were Roman Catholics, and was told that at Easter there were perhaps twenty Roman Catholics out of 10,000 pilgrims in the city.[39]

There is no doubt that Orthodox interest, and, above all, Orthodox (mainly Russian) gold, maintained the Christian shrines in the Ottoman Empire during the eighteenth and first half of the nineteenth centuries. For Russians, the holy shrines of Palestine were objects of intense and passionate devotion. Many made the long, arduous and dangerous journey to the Holy Land, and for many it was a pilgrimage from which they did not return, so fraught with peril was the long trek across Russia, through the Caucasus, or through Syria and Asia Minor. So important were the sacred shrines of Palestine to Russians, that in popular mythology many even came to believe that Nicholas's elder brother Alexander I – upon whom the Holy Synod, the State Council and the Senate of the Russian Empire bestowed the title of Alexander the Blessed in 1814 – had not died in Taganrog in November 1825, but had gone as a pilgrim to the Holy Land before spending the remainder of his life as a holy wanderer in Siberia.[40]

By contrast, as one historian so aptly put it, 'The Holy Places were objects of sentiment rather than of devotion in France, and a pilgrimage was a mode rather than a passion.'[41] The French had in fact turned away from religious matters under the impact of the Enlightenment and the French Revolution, and not until 1843 was the first French consul established in Jerusalem. As such, he and his government had challenged Russia's long-standing informal protectorate of the shrines, creating further dissension between the two powers. 'Jerusalem is now a central point of interest to France and Russia,' reported the British consul in 1844.[42] More potent political forces thus entered upon the scene where previously clerics and pilgrims had engaged in rivalries and conflicts.

In 1851, seeking support from the Roman Catholics whom he knew he would need to declare himself Emperor of France, the Prince-President Louis Napoleon began to press the Porte to grant the Roman Church a greater role in dealing with the Christian shrines of the Holy Land. 'It has become necessary to seek a compromise which will put an end to these deplorable and too-frequent quarrels about the possession of the Holy Places,' he declared.[43] Louis Napoleon's first efforts to deal with the question of the Holy Places were indeed quite conciliatory. As his ambassador to Constantinople he replaced General Aupick with the Marquis de Lavalette, who was more moderate in his demands, and Lavalette sought a middle ground for a solution. About to launch his *coup d'état*, in which he would tear up the French Constitution and dismiss the French parliament, Louis Napoleon certainly needed Catholic support. But beyond that he was hardly in a position to face foreign difficulties while he sat so uneasily in his new position at home. Napoleon thus apparently disavowed to Nicholas the threats which his ambassadors had made earlier in Constantinople.[44] As one observer put it, he needed only 'some little concession . . . [over the Holy Places] to enable him to retire with honour'.[45]

By mid 1852, however, Nicholas and Louis Napoleon were no closer to settling these disputes than they had been a year earlier. Both wished to resolve the issue, but Nicholas could in no way relinquish the role as protector of all Orthodox Christians in the Ottoman domains, which Russian Emperors had assumed for more than a century. Likewise, Louis Napoleon, who would have been satisfied with only 'some little concession . . . to enable him to retire with honour', could not risk a diplomatic defeat over the religious issues at a time when he badly needed Catholic support at home. And the Turks, in an effort to free themselves from the pressure of both powers, had cleverly succeeded in intensifying the diplomatic tensions between them. The rest of the year saw threats by the French, counter-threats by the Russians, and ended with the French violating the London Convention of 1841 by sending a ninety-gun warship through the Dardanelles.

Most important, the growing strength and belligerency of France raised new fears in Britain which drove the new Aberdeen cabinet closer to Russia than it had been for several years. Just before he became Prime Minister again at the end of 1852, Aberdeen confided to Russia's ambassador, Baron Brunnov, that he feared a French invasion.[46] Nicholas thought the British government weak and cowardly,[47] but he thought that he might use their fear of Napoleon to unite with them against France. There was also perhaps a possibility for Russia to wrest from Turkey her only European ally. Certainly, Aberdeen's dislike of the Turks was well-known. 'I despise the Turks,' he had once remarked, 'for I consider their government the most evil and the most oppressive in all the world.'[48] It was at that point that Nicholas began his conversation with the ambassador, Seymour, in St Petersburg. Most of all, he was convinced that Aberdeen would prevent Britain from going to war,[49] and this was one of his two most fatal misjudgements. The other was that he seriously under-estimated the importance of France's considerable mercantile and financial interests in the Ottoman Empire, and the resolution of the French to protect those interests.[50]

Nicholas's false hopes for an alliance with Britain, and his inability to accept the affronts which the Ottoman Empire, by favouring the French, had given to those Orthodox Christians under his protection, led him to mobilize the Fourth and Fifth Armies in southern Russia. 'Russia cannot swallow the insult which she has received from the Porte,' Nesselrode declared. '*Si vis pacem, para bellum!*'[51] As in 1828, Russia approached the Ottoman Empire with a small olive branch in one hand and a very large sword in the other, for to Nicholas and his advisers it was simply a matter of raw military power. 'Russia is strong; Turkey is weak. That is the preamble to all our treaties . . . This epitaph is already inscribed upon the grave of the Ottoman Empire,' was the way in which Brunnov summed up the situation.[52] But Turkey had not given way in 1828, and she would not do so in 1853; Nicholas would once again be forced into a war that he thought would never come.

Nicholas took one further step along this road in late January 1853, when he sent a special ambassador to Constantinople in an effort to force the Turks to recognize all of the traditional privileges of Orthodox Christians in the Holy Places and to reassert Russia's right to protect them.[53] Nesselrode had hoped that Orlov, the masterful diplomat who had negotiated the Treaty of Unkiar-Skelessi in 1853, or Kiselev, who had dealt so adroitly with problems of reform in Wallachia and Moldavia after 1828, would be chosen for so delicate a mission.[54] Instead, Nicholas chose Prince A. S. Menshikov, a devoted servant, but a man who lacked Orlov's great tact; and he gave Menshikov instructions which so limited his freedom of action that he had little hope of succeeding should the Porte decline to make an abject surrender to the Russians.[55]

Menshikov himself knew he did not have the finely honed diplomatic skills needed for such a task. A quarter-century as Chief of the Russian Navy had conditioned him far too much for command and far too little for negotiation. Beyond that, Menshikov was well over sixty and longed for retirement. As he wrote to a friend, 'I have great hopes that this [mission] will be for me the last official action in my . . . life, which now demands repose.'[56] This, then, was the man to whom Nicholas entrusted the delicate task of negotiating a final settlement with the Turks; a man who, throughout his career, had been accustomed to giving orders and having them obeyed, a man who was ageing, worn and longing for rest. It was a poor choice indeed.

Menshikov arrived in Constantinople on 16 (28) February 1853, on board the Russian warship *Thunderer* in the company of several imperial adjutants, generals and admirals.[57] But although he had filled the entire ship's hold with personal baggage, he had forgotten the maps of the Ottoman Empire which he needed to determine precisely the boundaries of the areas he was dealing with, and he therefore had to delay his negotiations for three weeks while he sent to his close friend, the Austrian Chief of Staff, General Baron Hess, for them.[58] Menshikov had, in fact, arrived in Constantinople at an ideal time to negotiate with the Sultan, for Britain's ambassador, Viscount Redcliffe (formerly Sir Stratford Canning), had not yet returned to his post from London, and the British were represented by a far lesser man, the *chargé d'affaires* Colonel Hugh Rose. Rose and the French *chargé d'affaires*, M. Benedetti, were no match for

Menshikov, and for a moment he had the upper hand. But, by the time his maps reached him and he was ready for serious discussions, Lord Redcliffe had arrived. And Redcliffe, as one contemporary remarked, 'had more pluck in his little finger than the whole *Divan*.'[59] As soon as the British ambassador had reached Constantinople on 5 April, Menshikov lost a critical advantage. It was no longer a matter of negotiating only with the Turks; the outcome of his mission now depended upon other factors.[60]

Turkey's new Foreign Minister, Rifaat Pasha, counselled Menshikov to be moderate in his demands. He urged him not to demand a formal treaty as a guarantee of Russia's rights to protect Orthodox Christians in the Ottoman Empire and commented to an intermediary that Russia need only 'desist from the idea of a treaty and all would be arranged'.[61] At least to some extent, Menshikov agreed with that opinion, and he decided to postpone a final confrontation until he received new instructions from his master in St Petersburg. Nicholas would have none of it, however. 'Without a crisis of compulsion,' he wrote, 'it would be difficult for the Imperial [Russian] Legation to regain the influence it formerly exercised over the *Divan*.'[62] Compromise and moderation was not a path which Nicholas was willing to follow, and that was how things stood at the beginning of May when Menshikov presented his final demands at the Porte.

Menshikov had waited to present his final ultimatum until he received further instructions and 'until our military preparations are nearly complete'.[63] He now insisted that the Turks must agree by 14 May to a formal guarantee of Russia's right to protect some twelve million Orthodox Christians in the Ottoman Empire.[64] All that Menshikov had received from Turkish statesmen by that fateful evening, however, was a request to wait another six days for a final answer,[65] for on 9 May the Sultan had learned a most vital piece of news. He already knew that the French fleet had left Toulon for the island of Salamis, but had now been told that the British had refused to send their fleet to join the French. He now learned from Lord Redcliffe 'that in the event of imminent danger, I [Redcliffe] am instructed to request the commander of Her Majesty's forces in the Mediterranean to hold his squadron in readiness'.[66] Redcliffe specified that 'imminent danger' did not mean a Russian invasion of the Balkans, but an actual threat to Constantinople itself.[67] But the Sultan now knew that if faced by the last extremity – a Russian attack upon his capital – Britain would come to his aid. It had been precisely the lack of any such British commitment in 1829 which had forced Turkey to sign the peace of Adrianople. This time the Sultan could hope for a different outcome. He was therefore more inclined to resist Menshikov's demands and to force Nicholas's hand if necessary. One brief phrase from Lord Redcliffe had assured the failure of Menshikov's mission.[68] And it brought Russia, the Ottoman Empire and Europe closer to war.

When Menshikov received no satisfactory reply from the Sultan by the evening of 14 May, he formally broke relations with the Ottoman Empire and took part of the Russian Embassy's personnel aboard the *Thunderer*.[69] He remained in port for a week more, however, in case the Turks should decide to accede. It was a vain hope. Precisely at noon on 21 May, the *Thunderer* steamed away from Constantinople, en route to the Russian Black Sea port of Odessa.[70] War between Russia and Turkey seemed very possible. By the end of the following month, it would be almost inevitable.

Two decisions taken independently – one in St Petersburg, the other in London – brought war much closer in June 1853. At the beginning of the month, the British decided to send their fleet to Besika Bay, a port just outside the Dardanelles, where they would be supported by the French squadron from Toulon. Then, on 14 (26) June, Nicholas ordered Russia's southern armies to cross the Pruth and to occupy the Danubian principalities.[71] There were now a Russian army, a British fleet and a French squadron all in close geographical proximity. As Nicholas had lamented to Aberdeen in 1844, in foreseeing just such a situation, 'so many powder barrels close to the fire; how shall one prevent the sparks from catching?'[72] Equally important, could they all be withdrawn with honour by their respective governments?

An effort to find a way out of this seemingly insoluble dilemma was made by Austria during the summer of 1853, when the Habsburg Foreign Minister, Count Buol-Schauenstein, arranged for the French, British and Prussian ambassadors to meet him in Vienna in late June. From these meetings, which Russia's ambassador, Count Meiendorf, did not attend 'because no instructions were sent' from St Petersburg,[73] there emerged the famous 'Vienna Note'. This document, incorporating the best efforts of the new head of the British Foreign Office, the Earl of Clarendon, Napoleon III and Count Buol, was basically a restatement and reaffirmation of the 'letter and spirit of the treaties of Kuchuk-Kainardji [1774] and Adrianople [1829]'[74] upon which Nicholas had based a major portion of his claim as protector of the Orthodox Church in the Ottoman Empire. It also obliged Turkey to undertake no change in the present state of affairs regarding any Christian communities without the specific advance approval of Russia and France.[75] The Vienna Note, acceptable to Britain, Austria, Prussia, France and even Nicholas himself (to whom it had been shown secretly),[76] affirmed Russia's right as protector of Orthodox Christians in the Ottoman Empire, but proposed a forced settlement which the Sultan could not accept without loss of honour. On 20 August he and his Grand Council therefore rejected Europe's effort at mediation and proposed amendments to the Vienna Note which Nicholas would not agree to.[77]

European diplomatic opinion turned against the Sultan, but only briefly. In early September, the Western press published Nesselrode's private interpretation of the Vienna Note, which seemed to indicate that Nicholas and his Vice-Chancellor would be satisfied with no less than a full recognition by Turkey of Russia's 'active solicitude' for some twelve million Orthodox Christians in Ottoman domains.[78] Believing that Nicholas and his ministers had betrayed them, France and Britain withdrew their support of the Vienna Note in mid September, and the European (especially the British) press launched a vitriolic campaign against Nicholas and Russia. Time had nearly run out. By 24 September, Clarendon wrote to Lord Redcliffe that 'the only real likelihood now is war'.[79]

One chance remained, and it was a slim reed indeed upon which to hang the question of war or peace. Nicholas and Franz Josef were to meet at Olmütz in late September in a last effort to avoid conflict. Nicholas reportedly was in a conciliatory mood;[80] the Austrian Emperor, and especially Count Buol, were prepared to meet him more than half-way. Buol drafted the so-called 'Buol Project', which specified that Russia would adhere to the original text and interpretation of the Vienna Note, and evidently not only Nicholas and Franz Josef, but also Napoleon III, agreed to this new statement. But Britain's cabinet, convinced that Nicholas's protestations of moderation could not be trusted because they suspected him of territorial designs upon the Ottoman Empire and even Constantinople itself, pressed for a rejection of Buol's plan and convinced the French to do likewise.[81] By that point, the acceptance or rejection of Buol's plan had become irrelevant. On 4 October the Sultan had declared war on Russia, and the first clash between Russians and Turks occurred on 23 October (9 October, OS). On 27 November, France and Britain concluded an offensive and defensive alliance with the Ottoman Empire against Russia, and on 3 January 1854, an Anglo-French fleet entered the Black Sea.[82] France and Britain officially declared war on Russia on 28 March 1854.

There was, of course, more to the outbreak of war than simply the failure of diplomatic negotiations. Russia's expanding economic activities in the Near East and Central Asia, and the growing size and power of her fleet, posed a threat to British sea power and imperial economic interests which English statesmen could not ignore. As General Castelbajac, the French ambassador to St Petersburg, wrote to M. Thouvenel: '[Britain] has two further interests which we do not share:

the destruction of the fleets of all nations and the diversion of the Russian march towards India.'[83] Even had they wished to follow a peaceful course, Britain's ministers were being pressed into war by the nation's very articulate banking and commercial interests. As Clarendon wrote in July 1853, 'Our [the cabinet's] pacific policy is at variance with public opinion, so it cannot long be persisted in.'[84] Likewise, France had significant trading and financial interests in Turkey which she would defend.[85] For Austria, the threat was even more immediate since, to stimulate exports from the port of Odessa, Russia had sought to hinder navigation on the Danube. Further, Austrian and Russian interests in other areas of the Balkans were beginning to conflict more sharply. Alone, none of these powers stood ready to challenge Russia. But together, as they stood in late 1853, it was in their interest to do so, although Austria would not engage in actual military operations against the Russians. For, as Marx wrote in the spring of 1854, if Russia were deprived of her outlets on the Baltic and Black Seas, she would become 'a colossus without arms and without eyes'.[86] Prussia, of course, had no immediate interests in the Balkans, but she was hardly likely to follow a policy contrary to that taken by Austria, France and Britain. At best she could be relied upon to maintain a 'benevolent neutrality'.[87] Russia stood alone. For Nicholas, the time of reckoning had come.

3. The Commander's Last Campaign

As in 1828, Nicholas had not expected war with Turkey in the autumn of 1853. Yet come it had, and as a result of his own serious misjudgements. 'The Emperor Nicholas has in himself something of Peter the Great, of Paul I, and of a medieval knight. But, as the years have passed, it is now the qualities of Paul I which rise more to the fore,' wrote General Castelbajac in mid September 1853.[88] Castelbajac did not mean, of course, that Nicholas was mad, or even on the verge of madness. But, like all autocrats, and especially like his father, his judgement had been impaired by the absolute nature of his power. 'This sovereign, born with the best possible qualities, has been spoiled by adulation, by success, and by the religious and political prejudices of the Muscovite nation,' Castelbajac added somewhat later.[89]

Nicholas had ruled too long. He had come to believe too much in his and Russia's God-given mission, which the disciples of Official Nationality had lauded for some two decades. As the young maid-of-honour A. F. Tiutcheva confided in her diary in early October 1853:

A terrible struggle has burst upon us. Monumental and contradictory forces are on a collision course: the East and the West, the Slavic world and the Latin world . . . Filled with dread and anguish, one asks, what will be the outcome of this struggle between two worlds? There can be no doubt. We, Russia, are on the side of truth and ideals: Russia fights not for material gain and worldly interest, but for eternal ideas.[90]

For this tragic confrontation, first between Russia and the Ottoman Empire, and then between Russia and the West, Nicholas summoned his remaining reserves of physical and spiritual strength. He seemed, as we have said, considerably older than his fifty-seven years; he was ill, and a strong fatalism had set into his manner of thinking. As General Castelbajac wrote at the beginning of 1854:

In his painful indecision, his religious scruples on one hand, and his humanitarian scruples on the other; in his wounded pride, in the face of national feeling and the dangers which pursue his Empire; in the violent struggle with these various feelings, the Emperor Nicholas has aged ten years. He is truly sick, physically and morally.[91]

Despite his own weakened reserves, despite the fact that Russia's armies were armed with antiquated weapons, despite even the ever-present supply problems which plagued the Russian army, Nicholas and Russia were still powerful forces to be reckoned with, as the battles of late 1853 and the campaign of 1854 would show. Russia's major fault in the war would be miscalculations in the diplomatic arena and in the high reaches of her military command. Here lay perhaps the greatest shortcoming of the Nicholas system, and the one that contributed most directly to Russia's ultimate defeat. For not only Nicholas, but also his advisers, had commanded too long. Nicholas had ruled Russia since 1825, and his decisions in 1853–4 lacked that creative and dynamic quality which had been characteristic of those taken in 1828, 1830 or even 1848.

Set in patterns of behaviour that had become rigidly established over the course of nearly three decades, Nicholas could not alter his views or his evaluations of diplomatic alignments. He expected the animosity of France; but as we have seen, he did not anticipate, nor could he understand, the hostility of Britain. As for Austria and Prussia, nearly three decades of following a common policy of defence against the menace of revolution by a conservative coalition in which Russia had always been the dominant power had made it nearly impossible for Nicholas to realize that these were new times and that central Europe faced other problems. Nicholas had saved Austria from revolution by his invasion of Hungary in 1849; he had also been willing to defend Prussia should she need his aid. In 1853, he could not be convinced that these powers might forget his efforts for them in the past; and Nicholas forgot that a friend in one's debt often ceases to be a friend.

For advice in 1853–4, Nicholas relied upon men who were equally set in their ways. Field-Marshal Prince Paskevich, too long an administrator in Poland, had lost the art of combat command, and more than two decades in Warsaw had conditioned him to think in Poland-centred terms. Not that Paskevich's outlook and sentiments were pro-Polish – far from it. But his long service in Poland, where any attack upon the area he governed could come only from Austria or Prussia, led him to emphasize too heavily the Austrian threat to Russia's frontiers. In late 1853, and during the first half of 1854, Paskevich was convinced that the major Allied attack would come from the Balkans or in combination with an attack from Austria.[92] Even after the Allies had settled upon the Crimea as the main focus of their attack, and even after Russian troops had withdrawn from the Balkans to positions behind the Pruth River by late summer 1854, Paskevich still insisted that large concentrations of troops, which might well have turned the tide in the Crimea, remain committed to a defence of the Empire's Western frontiers.[93]

Like Paskevich, Admiral Menshikov, twenty-five years the Head of the Russian Navy, had spent far too much time in the company of committees and official papers, and far too little with fighting men and ships. Menshikov's failure in Constantinople in 1853 was only the beginning of a series of failures in Nicholas's service, for the Emperor would entrust his admiral, who had never held a naval combat command in his entire life, with the defence of Russia's most vital Black Sea stronghold: the naval base of Sevastopol. As a result, when the Allies landed at Eupatoria at the beginning of September, the Russians were in no way prepared to stop them. Menshikov made no effort to attack the Allies while their landings were being carried out, but retired behind the Alma River to await their advance. And while Russia's armies waited, Menshikov made no effort to improve their defensive position. He took no measures to strengthen his left flank; he did not even make a reconnaissance of his position and hence did not know about a road which the Allies would use to bring troops and artillery up the steep river bank to outflank his defences.[94]

Finally, if Menshikov and Paskevich had been at their posts for too long, Nesselrode had been Russia's Foreign Minister for even longer. He had directed the Empire's foreign affairs for four decades, and simply failed to understand that much had changed. The men with whom he had laboured to construct the Concert of Europe and the Nicholas system abroad – Metternich, Castlereagh, Talleyrand, Canning, Wellington, Friedrich Wilhelm III and others – had long since left the scene for retirement or the grave. A second generation – even a third generation – of diplomats had replaced them, and though Nesselrode had always understood Britain better than had his masters, he still miscalculated in judging the contours of European diplomacy during those years.

These men dominated Nicholas's councils during the early stages of the war, and it was their advice which usually carried the day. Younger officers might win victories, as did Prince Bariatinskii in the Caucasus, but they could not get the troops or supplies to follow them up. A genius at military fortification, such as Colonel E. I. Todleben, might construct a brilliantly conceived system of fortifications to strengthen the shockingly poor defences at Sevastopol, but Paskevich's urgings would keep Sevastopol's commanders perpetually short of reinforcements for most of 1854.

Yet, despite these shortcomings in Russia's command structure and in Nicholas's inner councils, there was no question but that Russia's forces were more than a match for the Turks when war began. During the last months of 1853, the Russians won victories on all fronts: in the Caucasus, in the Danube theatre of operations and on the Black Sea. On 14 (26) November, General Prince I. M. Andronikov, with some 7,000 men, attacked the Turkish army of Ali Pasha at Akhaltsike. Although outnumbered nearly three to one, Andronikov directed a brilliant bayonet charge which forced the Turks to retreat.[95] Five days later, General Prince V. O. Bebutov won a much greater victory over Ahmed Pasha, the Turkish commander-in-chief in Anatolia. At Başgedikler, Bebutov, with some 7,000 infantry and 2,800 cavalry, routed Ahmed's forces which included regular infantry, cavalry and a large contingent of Kurds and numbered over 30,000. The Russians captured Ahmed's camp and twenty-six cannon. Turkish losses were more than 8,000, while Bebutov's own were just over 1,200.[96] Just one day before Bebutov's victory, on 18 (30) November, the Russians won an even more dramatic victory on the Black Sea itself. Commanded by a brilliant tactician and strategist, Admiral P. S. Nakhimov, Nicholas's Black Sea fleet destroyed the Turkish fleet in Sinope Harbour. It was Russia's greatest naval victory of the war.[97] On the Danube front, too, Nicholas's armies won the only major battle of 1853 at Cetate where, on 25 December (6 January 1854), a force of Russians under General A. K. Baumgarten was attacked by a much stronger Turkish force and drove them back.[98]

At the beginning of 1854, then, Nicholas's armies were victorious against the Turks on all fronts. But he would have to face a vastly different enemy from here onwards. On 3 January 1854, the Anglo-French fleet passed through the Dardanelles and the Bosphorus into the Black Sea, and when Nicholas ignored their ultimatum to evacuate the Danubian principalities, Britain and France declared war on Russia on 28 March.

Nicholas had led Russia into war in 1853 with a regular peacetime army which numbered 27,745 officers and 1,123,583 men. Coupled with her 'irregular' troops (mainly Cossack units), Russia's total land forces thus numbered nearly one and a half million. Further, the Russian navy numbered some 3,447 officers and 87,238 men.[99] This was the colossal Russian military machine which the West had so feared since the Napoleonic wars. But, as we noted in discussing the Hungarian campaign of 1849, Nicholas's armies were poorly equipped and often led by inept commanders. There were only three weapons factories in all of Russia at the time, and these were at best capable of producing only 61,000 smooth-bore muskets a year. The result, as the future War Minister, D. A. Miliutin, noted, was that Russia could not even equip her infantry with smooth-bore flintlock muskets, let alone more accurate longer-range percussion rifles.[100] As early as the beginning of 1851, the War Ministry had begun to order percussion rifles in Belgium, but the first shipments arrived only after the war had started. Orders placed in the United States in 1854 were not ready until after the war had ended. As a result, while 33 per cent of the French army, and 50 per cent of the British troops in the Crimea carried percussion rifles, only 4 per cent of Nicholas's soldiers had been issued such weapons in 1854.[101]

According to regulations, at the beginning of 1853 Russian arsenals were authorized to contain 1,014,959 infantry muskets, 71,038 dragoon muskets, 69,199 carbines, 37,318 rifles and 43,248 pistols. In fact there were 532,835 infantry muskets (a shortage of 482,124); 20,849 dragoon muskets (a shortage of 50,189); 21,167 carbines (a shortage of 48,032); 6,198 rifles (a shortage of 31,120); and 7,704 pistols (a shortage of 35,544). In all, Russian arsenals contained some 647,000 fewer weapons than were authorized by regulations.[102] Perhaps most important, there were only 52·5 per cent of the authorized weapons for the rank and file of the infantry.

Dramatic as these shortages were, they were only part of the problem. Many of the weapons that Nicholas's soldiers carried were in such poor condition as to be dangerous or even totally useless. This was partly due to neglect, but also to an effort by the rank-and-file infantry to make their weapons more effective for performing the manual of arms on parade. As one report stated: 'Sometimes soldiers, in order that the musket should rattle more during the actions of the manual of arms, loosened the ramrod in its seat, by burning the opening with a heated ramrod . . . and they scrape out the stock under the keeper-rings and other parts, wherever it is possible to make the musket rattle more.'[103] Most tragic of all, perhaps, was that even those Russian infantry weapons which were in workable condition simply did not have the range of those carried by the Allies. As a result, Russian troops were cut down by enemy infantry fire before they could come within musket range. As one staff officer wrote in late 1854: 'In the Inkerman action, whole regiments melted . . . losing a fourth of their men, while *they* were coming into musket range. I am convinced that they [the Allied infantry] will cut us down as soon as we fight in the open.'[104] Beyond this, some troops were issued cartridges filled with millet rather than gunpowder. Others were issued bullet moulds which cast balls too large to fit the standard-bore infantry musket. Still others carried muskets with broken triggers, faulty locks, cracked barrels or without ramrods.[105] And newly made weapons were often so badly manufactured as to be useless; of 1,500 rifles made in the Warsaw Citadel armoury in 1854, a total of 1,490 were found to be defective when they reached the troops at Sevastopol in mid 1855.[106]

These and many other tragic shortcomings in ordnance, supply and command led, in September 1855, to the fall of Sevastopol and to what is almost universally regarded as a disastrous Russian defeat by the Allies. The ignominious failure of Nicholas's armies in 1853–5, it is usually argued, crushed him, and perhaps even led to his sudden and unexpected death in February 1855. Yet during the eighteen months of war that Nicholas witnessed, the situation was nowhere so desperate as it became during the last six months of fighting, and at the time of his death Nicholas had no reason to foresee Russia's defeat. While the first months of war saw the Russian victories in the Balkans, the Caucasus and on the Black Sea, the next ten months of fighting after the Allies declared war did not look significantly worse.

The Allies did not land at Eupatoria until September 1854. Admiral Menshikov did not oppose their landing in any way – a serious tactical error – and through carelessness, lack of proper fortification and reconnaissance, Menshikov's army suffered a defeat at the Battle of Alma a week later. But this defeat could hardly have been seen as particularly disastrous in St Petersburg. As one official historian commented in retrospect, 'The Alma battle . . . had for us [Russia] no strategic or tactical significance whatsoever.'[107] The Anglo-French army had outnumbered the Russians by nearly two to one,[108] and Nicholas's military planners, led by Field-Marshal Paskevich, still thought that the major attack would come from the Balkans or be launched by Austria. As Paskevich pointed out to General M. D. Gorchakov in early October, the Russian army on the Danube was threatened by some 200,000 Austrians and perhaps by as many as 80,000 Turks.[109] Others, such as the now-aged Baron Jomini, who had served under Napoleon's marshals Ney and Berthier, and who had been in the Russian service for some four decades, also stressed the Austrian threat and continued to insist that only a holding action need be fought in the Crimea.[110]

Neither were the battles of Balaklava and Inkerman, which followed a few weeks later in the Crimea, seen as serious defeats. Balaklava had been inconclusive, the Allied position saved only by the brilliant counter-attack led by General Sir James Scarlatt. On the other hand, the Russians had enjoyed some measure of success, having annihilated a portion of the British cavalry in the disastrous and heroic 'Charge of the Light Brigade'.[111] At Inkerman, with heavy reinforcements, Menshikov's commanders Gorchakov and Dannenberg nearly drove the British from the heights east of Sevastopol, and only failed to do so because they failed to commit their very sizeable reserves to action at a critical moment.[112] Again, it was a defeat for Nicholas's armies, but by no means a decisive or ruinous one. By late 1854, the Russians and their adversaries had settled down to a winter of inconclusive siege operations at Sevastopol.

On all other fronts in 1854, the action was either inconclusive or brought Russian victories. In the Baltic, where the first clashes between Allies and Russians had taken place in the summer of 1854, there was no serious threat. In mid June Admiral Sir Charles Napier's fleet appeared briefly off Kronstadt, Russia's main naval fortress in the Baltic, but it posed no real danger, and Napier himself had already told the British Admiralty flatly that the fortress was impregnable to attack by sea.[113] Indeed, when Napier's fleet appeared, some of the Court, including Nicholas's heir Aleksandr Nikolaevich, his wife and a number of ladies-in-waiting, simply regarded it as an excuse for an outing on a pleasant summer day. As the young maid-of-honour Anna Tiutcheva, who was usually very sensitive to tensions at Court, remarked in her diary, 'I am very grateful indeed to the English for providing us with an excuse for such a pleasant outing.'[114] By the end of the year, Napier and the French admiral Parseval had done little more than attack a Russian garrison in the Åland Islands, and the French, with vastly superior forces, had finally succeeded in taking the Russian fortress of Bomarsund after a long bombardment in August.[115]

In the Far East, an Anglo-French fleet attacked the Russian garrison in Kamchatka. The assault, including naval bombardments and attacks by land, lasted an entire week, from 17 to 24 August, but the Allies were beaten off.[116] In the north Caucasus and Transcaucasus, the news was even more promising for Nicholas, for 1854 brought a series of important victories. In early July, General Prince Andronikov drove the Turks from their fortified positions on the Cholok River, and forced them to fall back upon Batum. Two weeks later, General Wrangel captured Bayazit. And, in late July, General Bebutov defeated the main Turkish army of the Caucasus under Mustafa Zarif Pasha, a victory which convinced Persia to conclude a treaty of neutrality with Russia thereby removing the threat of a Persian attack on Russia's frontiers.[117]

By the end of 1854, the military situation which Nicholas faced was scarcely hopeless, and in a number of areas there were grounds for cautious optimism. In the Baltic, the Allied campaign had achieved little except for the capture of Bomarsund, and the 200,000 troops stationed at various strategic centres on the Baltic[118] would be enough to foil any major landing the Allies might plan for the following year. In the Far East, an Allied force had been defeated at Petropavlovsk, and in the Caucasus and Transcaucasus, Russian arms had won a series of important victories. Only in the Crimea had Nicholas's armies suffered defeats, but none of them had been conclusive or irreparable. There was at least some good reason to hope that the situation might improve by spring. Sevastopol had been fortified by the engineering genius of Colonel Todleben, and extensive arms orders had been placed abroad which, when they arrived, would put Russia's infantry weapons on a par with those of the Allies. Admiral Nakhimov, in charge of the defence of Sevastopol, was proving as brilliant an officer on land as he had been at sea when he had destroyed the Turkish fleet at Sinope. And, if some of Nicholas's senior officers had proved incompetent in the Crimean battles of 1854, there was some comfort to be taken from the fact that the Allies were having their own squabbles and command difficulties. By late autumn, the forces of nature also turned against the Allies. Early in the winter, a great storm had destroyed a number of their supply ships and the British, still living in tents, were left with almost no shelter. There were serious supply problems as well, and as a result, in November and December, the Allies, especially the British, were in dire straits indeed. Finally, recent developments on the diplomatic scene, while not promising an immediate end to the war, gave cause for cautious optimism. Discussions between the Habsburg Foreign Minister, Count Buol, and the English, French and Russian ambassadors, had begun in Vienna in late December in an effort to find a way to end the conflict.[119]

Although the campaigns of 1854 hardly presented a hopeless or even very threatening picture, the strain had taken a great toll upon Nicholas. In his twenty-nine years on the throne, he had never known defeat in battle. Only once, in February 1831, at the bloody battle of Grochów, had he known a major Russian force even to withdraw, and he had attributed that directly to the incompetence of his commander, General Count Dibich. Throughout his reign, Nicholas's soldiers had advanced. His soldiers had attacked. They had died for the faith, their Tsar and their motherland. With them, behind a wall of a million bayonets, Russia had seemed safe from all attacks. Therefore news that Russian arms were not everywhere victorious was bitter for Nicholas to hear.

Perhaps equally important in explaining the toll which the war took upon him was the fact that, by late 1854, all of the major powers of

Europe were arrayed against Russia. Nicholas had expected the animosity of France; he had reluctantly come to accept the hostility of Britain. But for Austria to turn against him, and for Prussia to maintain, at best, a benevolent neutrality, was something he found offensive and impossible to understand. 'I love the Emperor of Austria as if he were my son; I know that he will be my ally in putting an end to this foul administration of the Bosphorus and the oppression of poor Christians by these damned infidels,' Nicholas had declared to an assemblage of diplomats in 1853.[120] But, in mid 1854, Austria had demanded that he evacuate the Danubian principalities under the threat of war, and Nicholas then knew the full misery of his and Russia's isolation. As one observer noted, when Nicholas arrived to inspect the Imperial Guards on that day, he was unlike anyone had ever seen him before. 'When the Emperor appeared,' an officer recalled, 'he was unrecognizable, his face had a greenish pallor, his profile had lengthened, and his eyes had a fixed expression: only his step was firm.' In his rage, Nicholas turned the Emperor Franz Josef's portrait to the wall and scrawled in fury on the back '*Du Undankbarer!*'[121] But there was no escaping the hard fact that Nicholas and Russia were alone against the West. Even during the darkest days of the Napoleonic Wars, when Napoleon was actually in Moscow, Russia still had one ally in the West – Britain. But now there were none whatsoever who would side with her. And the strain of isolation told upon Nicholas. 'His tall figure is beginning to bend. He has a sort of lifeless stare, his face a leaden colour. His brow, haughty not long ago, each day is lined with new furrows,' wrote the young maid-of-honour Tiutcheva in October. 'In general, his nerves are in an absolutely lamentable state.'[122] A month later, Tiutcheva added that 'he is like an oak, broken by a whirlwind, an oak which can never bend and can only die in the midst of a storm'.[123]

If the strain of hearing that his troops had suffered defeat in battle and that the Austrians had turned against him was hard to bear, this was only the beginning of the physical and psychological strains which weakened Nicholas in late 1854 and early 1855. Late in 1854 many feared that the Empress, his 'Mouffy', was at death's door. 'The Empress is critically ill,' wrote Tiutcheva. 'For several days her life was in danger . . . The slightest upset could cause the illness to return.'[124] During these days, most of Nicholas's concern was for his wife. 'He neither sleeps nor eats,' one observer noted.[125] The illness of his Empress, the defeats of his armies in the Crimea, the loneliness of standing alone against the Allies, the gruelling strain of ruling Russia for nearly three decades – all of this placed a tremendous psychological and physical burden upon Nicholas during the winter of 1854–5. And the strain exacted a higher price than had been the case in the past: it would cost him his life.

At the beginning of 1855, no one could have imagined that, in less than two months, Nicholas would be dead. As late as 2 February, when he had just more than two weeks to live, there was nothing in Nicholas's manner that hinted at anything unusual. He continued to fume about Menshikov's failure to mount an offensive against the Allies while they suffered from cold and hunger in their flimsy winter quarters, but he seemed quite confident that the reinforcements he had ordered to Sevastopol would be sufficient for its defence and had no serious thoughts that it would fall.[126] He was equally confident that Russia's western frontier could be defended should the Austrians attack, even if the French joined with Habsburg forces in an offensive against Russia through Poland.[127]

On 15 February, Nicholas finally relieved Menshikov from his command and named General Prince M. D. Gorchakov, a younger and more energetic commander, to replace him. Even then no one realized that this would be his last major act as Russia's supreme commander. Nicholas had caught a slight cold on 12 February, at the wedding of Count Kleinmichel's daughter, but, as he had often done in the past, he ignored his doctors' advice and went about his daily tasks. The next day, in freezing temperatures, he reviewed troops at the Riding School who were about to leave for the Crimea. His cold became worse, but no one was particularly concerned; heavy colds were common in St Petersburg's damp, cold climate. Even on the evening of Wednesday, 16 February, one of Aleksandra Fedorovna's ladies-in-waiting would recall in her memoirs that 'the Empress was still calm in view of the assurances of Doctor Mandt that there was *absolutely nothing dangerous about the condition of His Majesty*'.[128] Mandt repeated his assurance as late as nine o'clock in the evening of 17 February, when Nicholas, in fact, had just over twelve hours to live.

Very early in the morning of 18 February, Mandt suddenly realized that Nicholas's illness was most serious. Just after 1 a.m., he urged him to summon a priest because paralysis was setting into his lungs. Nicholas fixed an imperious and penetrating stare upon his doctor: 'Then I am dying?' Recalling a promise that he had once made to his sovereign, Mandt replied, 'Your Majesty, you have only a few hours left.'[129] Nicholas accepted the news with imperial dignity. He took the sacraments and bade farewell to those servants, close friends and family who were with him. He then turned to affairs of state once again; until his last hour he would do his duty. As Anna Tiutcheva recorded the scene after hearing the details from the Empress:

He instructed his heir [Alexander II] to say farewell for him to the Guards, to the entire army, and, most of all, to the heroic defenders of Sevastopol. 'Tell them that I shall continue to pray for them in the next world ...' At five o'clock in the morning, he personally dictated a dispatch to Moscow in which he said that he was dying and bade farewell to his ancient capital ... He ordered a message telegraphed to Warsaw and dictated a dispatch to the King of Prussia in which he begged him always to remember his father's testament and never to alter the alliance with Russia.[130]

Nicholas ordered all the Guards regiments to be brought to the palace so they would be on hand to swear allegiance to his son the moment that he breathed his last, for, even in death, Nicholas could not forget the tragic circumstances of his own accession. His suffering grew worse as the night drew to a close. 'If this is the beginning of the end, it is very painful,' he told Mandt.[131] To his son, about to become Alexander II, Nicholas spoke his last words:

I wanted to take everything difficult, everything serious, upon my shoulders and to leave to you a peaceful, well-ordered, and happy realm. Providence decreed otherwise. Now I go to pray for Russia and for you all. After Russia, I loved you [his family] more than anything else in the world. Serve Russia.[132] Never have I seen anyone die like this [wrote Mandt]. There was something superhuman in this carrying out of duty to the very last breath.[133]

Nicholas had done his duty to the end. Therein lay the true meaning of all earthly existence for him. As he had written in one of his letters:

How strange is my fate! They tell me that I am one of the mightiest Princes on earth. And, one must admit that anything – that is, anything which is permissible – ought to be possible for me, that I could in fact be anywhere and do anything that I desired. But, in fact, for myself in particular, however, just the reverse is true. And, should I be asked the reason for this anomaly, there is only one possible reply: Duty! Yes, that is not a meaningless word for one who from childhood was taught to understand it as I was. This word has a sacred meaning before which every personal impulse must give way. All must fall silent in the face of this feeling and must yield to it until one vanishes into the grave. Such is my watchword. It is harsh, I tell you truly. Beneath its weight, it is more agonizing than I can possibly tell you. But, then, I was born to suffer.[134]

4. Epilogue

News of Nicholas's death stirred intense sentiments in the breasts of all who heard it. In London, the émigré radical Aleksandr Herzen uncorked his best champagne, summoned his friends, and gave silver coins 'for beer and candy' to the street urchins to shout, 'Hurrah! Hurrah! Impernikel is dead! Impernikel is dead!'[135] In St Petersburg, the censor A. V. Nikitenko wrote that 'the main shortcoming of the reign of Nikolai Pavlovich consisted in the fact that it was all a mistake'.[136] The publicist and jurist K. D. Kavelin called it 'a thirty-year tyranny of madness, brutality, and misfortunes of all sorts, the likes of which history has never seen'.[137] But there were also those who felt a deep emptiness, an intense sense of loss, as if a vast chasm had opened. Who would chart their course and guide their steps along it? As Anna Tiutcheva recorded the events of Nicholas's death, she confided to her diary that 'only two days have passed since all this occurred, but it seems to me that, after these two days, the world has come tumbling down'. 'I went to dine with my parents,' she added, 'and Papa said "it is as if we had been told that a god had died".'[138] 'He wanted to do everything himself. He laboured for nearly thirty years, never thinking of himself, and finally fell, a victim to the royal duty which he had imposed upon himself,' wrote the historian Pogodin.[139] 'What crushing news!' mourned the Princess Lieven. 'In the twenty-four hours since I learned of it, I have been completely unable to collect my wits.'[140] 'My God, what frightful, unexpected news! We were staggered, absolutely and utterly stunned,' Vera Aksakova, sister of the Slavophiles Ivan and Konstantin, wrote in her diary.[141] Count P. D. Kiselev, for nearly two decades Nicholas's 'Chief of Staff for Peasant Affairs', perhaps summed up such reactions best:

History will give him his due. I shall only say in this initial surge of my soul's grief, that in his valiant heart were reflected all the noble feelings with which the Almighty in his mercy adorns man.[142]

Whether they despised him or worshipped him, mid-nineteenth-century Russians could not remain unmoved or indifferent to Nicholas's death, for he and the system he had forged had a profound and lasting impact upon their lives. A. V. Golovnin, Minister of Public Instruction from 1861 to 1866, regarded the experience of maturing during the last decade of the reign as an almost crippling psychological one from which few, if any, fully recovered.[143] As Emperor, Nicholas had sought to create the epitome of an eighteenth-century Western European police state, an absolute monarchy such as that fashioned in France by Louis XIV. But the world in which Nicholas lived was a very different one from France in the late seventeenth and early eighteenth centuries, for the French Revolution of 1789 and the Industrial Revolution had given birth to a vastly different social, economic and political order in the West.

In the manner of an enlightened despot, Nicholas sought to take all power, and the resolution of all problems, into his hands alone. Such had been a vastly difficult task within the relatively manageable geographical limits of Western European states; it was utterly impossible in Russia. True, in a country as vast and diverse as the Russian Empire, where the overwhelming mass of inhabitants were illiterate and in bondage, it could be argued (and often was) that only an absolute ruler could rise above the various narrow interests of diverse classes and groups and work for the welfare of Russia as a whole. But the area was too vast, and, especially in the nineteenth century, the problems too complex for one man to resolve or even fully comprehend. As the academician Georg Friedrich Parrot told Nicholas early in his reign, an autocrat must have enlightened councillors with the power and will to act independently, and he must have some contact with educated public opinion so as to learn the true nature of the needs of his subjects and the problems which faced them.[144] In a word, the state which Nicholas ruled, and the world in which he lived in the second quarter of the nineteenth century, was too multi-faceted and too complex for one man to face alone. Devotion to duty and confidence in the rightness of his purpose were not enough, and the phenomenon of eighteenth-century absolutism, expressed in the person of the Russian autocrat, was an anachronism in the post-Napoleonic world. As Pogodin put it, 'Carried away by the brilliant example of his ancestor [Peter the Great], he [Nicholas] did not realize that since the time of Peter conditions had changed, and that Petrine activities, transposed into our era, simply became an optical illusion.'[145]

Nicholas was the last ruler of Russia to hold undivided power. He was, in a real sense, Russia's last absolute monarch, for the collapse of his system, which became so dramatically and painfully obvious in the year after his death, forced Russia on to a new course. A multitude of problems had arisen in the first half of the nineteenth century, and they demanded solutions which Nicholas and his system could not provide. The lack of legality in Russia, the Empire's continuing financial crisis, her economic backwardness and lack of industry, the inefficient administration and, underlying all of these problems, the institution of serfdom, all needed to be dealt with. Nicholas and his advisers dealt partially with the first of these problems, and forged a tenuous and fragile solution to the second; the rest went unresolved.

During the first year of his reign, Alexander II thus faced the full collapse of his father's system. Although the Russian army continued to win victories in the Caucasus and Transcaucasus, the war in the Crimea turned into a disaster and, by July 1855, Prince Gorchakov considered the defence of Sevastopol hopeless.[146] A defeat in the Crimea did not pose any direct threat to Russia's security, for the Anglo-French armies, even if joined by Austria, were not going to march upon Moscow. The

Allies had not gone to war to conquer Russia, after all, but only to foil what they regarded as Nicholas's improper designs upon the Ottoman Empire. But a defeat in the Crimea (and such became a certainty with the fall of Sevastopol in September 1855), did pose a serious threat to Russia in a different sense. Ever since Peter the Great had thrust his Empire upon the European political scene with his dramatic defeat of Charles XII and the Swedish armies at Poltava in 1709, Russia's only claim to membership in the European community of Great Powers was her military strength. Particularly after the defeat of Napoleon, Russia could make no claim to being a great industrial power. Nor was she a major maritime power. She was not even a major cultural force in European life, and the novelist Ivan Turgenev, who lived the last three decades of his life mostly in the West, was the first major Russian novelist to see his works become well known outside Russia. Russia as the nation which produced such literary giants as Tolstoi and Dostoevskii, was still a phenomenon of the future in the mid nineteenth century; indeed, even Turgenev's recognition in the West would not come till after that date.

Russia's only claim to Great Power status thus lay in the fact that she possessed the largest and most powerful army in Europe. A defeat in the Crimea seriously undermined that claim, and as a result she faced a very pressing choice in the mid 1850s: modernize along European lines or be pushed back into Asia.[147] The second alternative was not a remote possibility in 1856, and was one which a number of Western Europeans found attractive. Count Reiset, a former First Secretary of the French Embassy in St Petersburg, made the point with dramatic force in early 1854 when he told a Russian acquaintance in Paris:

I am resolved to direct all of my efforts towards a struggle against your influence [in European affairs] and to drive you back into Asia whence you came. You are not a European Power; you ought not to be, and you will not be if France remembers the part which she should play in Europe. Our government knows very well your weak points and they are precisely the ones by which you are tied to Europe; let those ties be weakened and, of your own accord, you will flow back towards the East and you will become once again an Asiatic Power.[148]

If Russia were to be restored to her position as a major European Power, much would have to be changed. With the possible exception of the cotton textile industry, Russia's industrial forces were underdeveloped, her economy backward. State finances were in a parlous state, the fragile balance which had been created by Count Kankrin's reforms having been destroyed by the ruinous financial drain of the Crimean War. No nation could bear the financial burden of maintaining an army of nearly one and a half million men in peacetime. But to create a smaller standing army, which could be expanded in wartime by a system of reserves such as existed in Prussia, was an impossibility in a country where the military rank and file were drawn from a servile class.[149] At the root of Russia's difficulties, of course, was the institution of serfdom, a system which held nearly fifty million of her inhabitants in bondage to the state or to noble landowners. Nicholas himself had been aware of that to some extent but had hoped for a gradual resolution of the problem. The major difficulty was to determine how serfdom could be abolished and yet not destroy the economic base of the nobility, the pillar of the Russian throne and the traditional social base of autocratic power. Equally important, a means had to be found by which serfdom could be done away with while order was maintained in the countryside and abolition not be followed by mass peasant uprisings. Further, some means had to be found to maintain local government and administration throughout the Empire once the power of the aristocracy over its peasants was ended.

Such problems would have presented immense difficulties to the government of any state. In Russia they appeared overwhelming. As one observer commented in September 1855: 'Administration is in a chaos; moral feelings are crushed; intellectual development has been abandoned; abuses and thievery have grown to prodigious proportions. All this is the fruit of a contempt for the truth and a blind, barbaric faith in material force alone.'[150] But such was only an external symptom of a deeper and far more malignant disease. For one of the most critical shortcomings of the Nicholas system had been that it had not produced any politically or socially responsible group upon which the Emperor could rely for advice in planning change and for assistance in carrying out any programme of reform. The censor A. V. Nikitenko described the problem vividly in his diary in April 1855. 'Our qualities as responsible citizens,' he wrote, 'have not yet been formed because we do not yet have the essential element, without which there can be only civic cohabitation but not civic virtue, namely public-spiritedness, a sense of legality, and honour.'[151] Nor were there the means for consulting and communicating with any such group had it existed. Russia lacked any sort of national consultative body, for such was inconsistent with the premises upon which autocracy, and particularly the Nicholas system, had been based. And the rigid censorship of Russia's press meant that public debate or even commentary upon the pressing problems which the Empire faced was impossible. The major problem which Alexander II thus faced at the beginning of his reign was to stimulate such a body of public opinion into being, and to create with it the means of a dialogue. At the same time, such a dialogue and expression of opinion had to be controlled and kept within bounds acceptable to autocracy.

Alexander's first steps in this direction were halting and uncertain. Above all, he wanted to preserve the prerogatives and essence of autocratic power. To do so, but at the same time to undertake the beginnings of the modernization which his Empire so desperately required, he needed to create the conditions for bourgeois economic (and even social) development while withholding all the political apparatus, such as parliaments and representative institutions, which had accompanied that phenomenon in the West. Russia's new Emperor sought to achieve this end by creating an intricate system of what at the time was called 'artificial publicity', which he sought to integrate with the mediatory function of autocracy about which his father's senior statesman M. M. Speranskii had lectured him in 1836. Such a system of artificial publicity was neither unknown nor even untried in Russia. The academician Georg-Friedrich Parrot had urged it upon Nicholas in the late 1820s,[152] and Alexander's younger brother, the Grand Duke Konstantin Nikolaevich, had used it with some effect in the discussions surrounding the reform of Russian naval regulations in 1853.[153]

In an effort to create artificial publicity, a discussion of Russia's problems kept within limits acceptable to the preservation of autocratic power, Alexander II turned first to the nobility, the best educated and most articulate class in his Empire. But, as he found during the two years after he first asked them to consider the emancipation question in March 1856, the nobility was self-interested and self-centred; it was hardly the socially and politically responsible body of opinion which he needed. To turn to the intelligentsia, that group in Russian society which his father had regarded as partially responsible for the Decembrist revolt, and which, during the 1840s and first half of the 1850s, had been continually at odds with Russia's censors (and thus seen by Nicholas and his son as politically dangerous), was more than Alexander II could do, even when faced by the Crimean defeat. He therefore turned to the bureaucracy, the group which he felt most able to control, and the group within which his younger brother, the Grand Duke Konstantin Nikolaevich, had, in a sense, already tested artificial publicity earlier in the decade.

Alexander's turn to the bureaucracy as a source of public opinion, however, was more complex than appeared at first glance, for the end result was to utilize a unique interaction between enlightened officials, progressive aristocrats and moderate segments of the intelligentsia to advance the cause of limited change within the Russian Empire. In an important sense, Alexander drew upon those segments of the nobility and the intelligentsia which he regarded as least threatening to his autocratic power, and then made an effort to ensure their reliability by coopting them into essentially bureaucratic bodies, thereby controlling them through the natural (and essentially limiting) forces of bureaucratic caution. At the same time, by splitting the ranks of the intelligentsia, which had joined in a united front to advance the cause of reform in 1857, Alexander ensured that they would not succeed in presenting any sort of broad challenge to autocratic power. Alexander thus created within the nobility, the intelligentsia and even the bureaucracy a small group which he coopted into his service and split away from the broader social or intellectual groups which they might have led in a campaign against his refusal to grant them those means of political expression which had accompanied the emergence of a bourgeois economic and social order in the West.

The Great Reforms of the 1860s – the emancipation of the serfs, the new judicial system, the new institutions of local government – which Alexander posed as a solution to the collapse of the Nicholas system, were imperfect to say the least. Russia's peasants continued to be crushed by economic hardships. The *zemstva*, the new institutions of self-government in the districts and provinces of the Empire, ultimately came to provide a forum for the development and expression of public opinion which the autocrat could not control. Finally, the creation of judges with life tenure, a product of the judicial reforms of 1864, removed the dispensation of justice, one of the most cherished prerogatives of the autocrat, from the Emperor's control, and from that moment his power was neither undivided nor absolute. True, these reforms and new institutions created a climate in which considerable industrial development could and did occur in Russia, and the half-century after Alexander II's accession brought the development of railways and industry, the growth of cities, the emergence of an industrial labour force: in a word, all of the economic and social phenomena which had accompanied the Industrial Revolution in the West.

It had taken a shocking military defeat to bring these aspects of nineteenth-century life to Russia, but the society upon which they were imposed continued to lack any means of political expression. The dialogue between state and society, established through the medium of essentially bureaucratic bodies, had been of brief duration, though its further extension was an essential factor in the development of a modern industrialized society in Russia. Only another war and another crushing defeat at the hands of Japan's armies in the Russo–Japanese War of 1904–5 would force Russia's Emperor to grant his Empire the political institutions the Great Reforms had made a necessity. But these concessions were too little, and came too late. In the event, the fragile and delicate bloom of a modern, constitutional, industrialized Russian state was destroyed by the violent upheaval of the First World War.

The cataclysm of world war would destroy not only the 'sick man of Europe', whose demise Nicholas had so feared, but also the Habsburg and Russian Empires. In 1917, Russia felt the full force of the revolutionary tempest from which Nicholas had sought to protect her, the ultimate expression of all the tensions and conflicts which Russia had known since his death. For the reign of Nicholas I was the last period of calm and certainty that Russia was to know for the remainder of the imperial period. As one historian would write in the early twentieth century, Nicholas's reign had been the 'apogee of autocracy'.[154] There was a certain nostalgia, even pathos, in an epitaph for Nicholas's Russia which Baroness M. P. Frederiks, who had lived at his Court as a child, would write in the 1880s:

I only know that during the lifetime of Nikolai Pavlovich, Russia had great and noble stature. He knew how to preserve that enchantment which she possessed before his time and, by his chivalrous, firm, and undaunted character, he heaped still greater glory upon her. Everyone and everything bowed down before him and before Russia![155]

Notes and References

Key to abbreviations

GPB: Gosudarstvennaia Publichnaia Biblioteka imeni M. E. Saltykova-Shchedrina, g. Leningrad. Otdel Rukopisei.

Grunwald: Constantin de Grunwald, *Tsar Nicholas I*, translated from the French by Brigit Patmore (London, 1954).

IV: Istoricheskii vestnik (St Petersburg, 1880–1917).

KA: Krasnyi arkhiv (Moscow, 1922–41).

Korf, *Materialy*: M. A. Korf, 'Materialy i cherty k biografii Imperatora Nikolaia I i k istorii ego tsarstvovaniia. Rozhdenie i pervyia dvadtsat' let zhizni (1797–1917 gg.)'. in N. F. Dubrovin (ed.), *Materialy i cherty k biografii Imperatora Nikolaia I i k istorii ego tsarstvovaniia* (St Petersburg, 1896).

LaCroix: Paul LaCroix, *Histoire de la vie et du règne de Nicholas Ier*, 8 vols. (Paris, 1864–9).

Martens: F. Martens, *Sobranie traktatov i konventsii zakliuchennykh Rossieiu s inostrannymi derzhavami*, 15 vols. (St Petersburg, 1874–1908).

Mezhdutsarstvie: B. E. Syroechkovskii (ed.), *Mezhdutsarstvie 1825 goda i vosstanie dekabristov v perepiske i memuarakh chlenov tsarskoi sem'i* (Moscow-Leningrad, 1926).

ORGBL: Gosudarstvennaia Biblioteka S.S.S.R. imeni V. I. Lenina, g. Moskva. Otdel Rukopisei.

Polievktov: M. Polievktov, *Nikolai I: Biografiia i obzor tsarstvovaniia* (Moscow, 1918).

RA: Russkii arkhiv (Moscow, 1863–1917).

RS: Russkaia starina (St Petersburg, 1870–1918).

RV: Russkii vestnik (Moscow-St Petersburg, 1856–1906).

Riasanovsky: N. V. Riasanovsky, *Nicholas I and Official Nationality in Russia, 1825–1855* (Berkeley and Los Angeles, 1959).

Schiemann: Th. Schiemann, *Geschichte Russlands unter Kaiser Nikolaus I*, 4 vols. (Berlin, 1908–19).

Shilder: N. K. Shilder, *Imperator Nikolai Pervyi: Ego zhizn' i tsarstvovanie*, 2 vols. (St Petersburg, 1903).

SIRIO: Sbornik imperatorskago russkago istoricheskago obshchestva (St Petersburg, Iur'ev, Moscow, 1867–1916).

Temperley: Harold Temperley, *England and the Near East: The Crimea* (London-New York, 1936).

TsGIAL: Tsentral'nyi Gosudarstvennyi Istoricheskii Arkhiv S.S.S.R., g. Leningrad.

TsGAOR: Tsentral'nyi Gosudarstvennyi Arkhiv Oktiabr'skoi Revoliutsii, g. Moskva.
'Zapiski Benkendorfa', *KA*: A. Kh. Benkendorf, 'Graf A. Kh. Benkendorf o Rossii v 1827–1830 gg.,' *Krasnyi arkhiv*, XXXVII (1929), XXXVIII (1930).
'Zapiski Benkendorfa', *RS*: A. Kh. Benkendorf, 'Imperator Nikolai v 1828–1829 i v 1830–1831 gg. (Iz zapisok grafa A. Kh. Benkendorfa)', *Russkaia starina*, LXXXVI, No. 6 (June 1896); LXXXVII, No. 7 (July 1896); LXXXVIII, No. 10 (October 1896).
'Zapiski Benkendorfa' (Shilder): A. Kh. Benkendorf, 'Zapiski grafa A. Kh. Benkendorfa, 1832–1837 gg.', in N. K. Shilder, *Imperator Nikolai Pervyi: Ego zhizn' i tsarstvovanie* (St Petersburg, 1903), II, pp. 647–764.

PREFACE

1. Baroness M. P. Frederiks, 'Iz vospominanii baronessy M. P. Frederiks', *IV*, LXXI, No. 1 (January 1898), p. 55.

CHAPTER I

1825: THE EMPEROR IS DEAD! LONG LIVE THE EMPEROR!

1. Heinrich Storch, *The Picture of Petersburg* (London, 1801), pp. 509–14.
2. W. Bruce Lincoln, 'The Daily Life of St Petersburg Officials in the Mid-Nineteenth Century', *Oxford Slavonic Papers*, VIII (1975), pp. 82–100.
3. Quoted in Allen McConnell, *Tsar Alexander I: Paternalistic Reformer* (New York, 1970), p. 180.
4. ibid., pp. 180–81.
5. ibid., pp. 182–4.
6. ibid., p. 185.
7. Quoted in J. H. Schnitzler, *Secret History of the Court and Government of Russia under the Emperors Alexander and Nicholas* (London, 1847), I, 133.
8. 'Iz dnevnikov Marii Fedorovny', in *Mezhdutsarstvie*, entry for 25 November 1825, p. 97.
9. Quoted in Schnitzler, I, pp. 135–6.
10. 'Iz dnevnikov Marii Fedorovny', in *Mezhdutsarstvie*, entries for 25 November 1825, p. 97; and 26 November 1825, p. 68.
11. N. K. Shilder, *Imperator Nikolai Pervyi: Ego zhizn' i tsarstvovanie* (St

Petersburg, 1903), I, pp. 183–4; M. Polievktov, *Nikolai I: Biografiia i obzor tsarstvovaniia* (Moscow, 1918), p. 45.
12. 'Iz dnevnikov Nikolaia Pavlovicha', in *Mezhdutsarstvie*, entry for 27 November 1825, p. 68.
13. Schnitzler, I, p. 164.
14. 'Pis'mo Nikolaia Pavlovicha k bratu Konstantinu Pavlovichu', early December (probably 3 December), 1825, in *Mezhdutsarstvie*, p. 130.
15. 'Iz dnevnikov Nikolaia Pavlovicha', in *Mezhdutsarstvie*, entry for 27 November 1825, p. 68.
16. Polievktov, p. 45.
17. ibid.
18. Shilder, I, p. 187.
19. ibid., p. 38.
20. ibid.; and Polievktov, p. 41.
21. A. Korsakov, 'Detstvo i otrochestvo Nikolaia Pavlovicha', *RA*, XXXIV, No. 6 (1896), p. 285, n. 2. Konstantin Pavlovich also bore the title Tsesarevich, but this was specifically awarded to him in 1799 by his father Paul I as a reward for valour in the Italian Campaign of that year. See A. E. Presniakov, *14 dekabria 1825 goda* (Moscow–Leningrad, 1926), p. 54; Schnitzler, I, pp. 145, 314.
22. Shilder, I, p. 38.
23. 'Vospominaniia imperatritsy Aleksandry Fedorovny s 1817 po 1820 g.', *RS*, No. 10 (October 1896), pp. 53–4; 'Zapiski Nikolaia I o vstuplenii ego na prestol', in *Mezhdutsarstvie*, p. 13; 'Pis'mo Nikolaia Pavlovicha k bratu

Konstantinu Pavlovichu', early December (probably 3 December), 1825, in ibid., p. 131.

24. 'Zapiski Nikolaia I o vstuplenii ego na prestol', in ibid., p. 14.

25. Shilder, I, p. 187.

26. 'Pis'mo Nikolaia Pavlovicha k Konstantinu Pavlovichu', 3 December 1825, in *Mezhdutsarstvie*, p. 143.

27. G. Vasilich, *Vosshestvie na prestol Imperatora Nikolaia I* (Moscow, 1909), pp. 30–32.

28. 'Iz dnevnikov Nikolaia Pavlovicha', entry for 27 November 1825, p. 69.

29. 'Pis'mo Nikolaia Pavlovicha k bratu Konstantinu Pavlovichu', early December (probably 3 December), 1825, in *Mezhdutsarstvie*, pp. 131–2.

30. D. V. Davydov, 'Vospominaniia o tsesareviche Konstantine Pavloviche', *Golos Minuvshego*, No. 5–6 (May–June 1917), p. 36.

31. *Secret Memoirs of the Court of St Petersburg*, pp. 191–2.

32. Marquis de Custine, *La Russie en 1839*, Paris, 1843, III, p. 210.

33. Shilder, I, p. 203.

34. Presniakov, *14 dekabria*, p. 54.

35. ibid., p. 55; Shilder, I, p. 134.

36. Shilder, I, pp. 134–5.

37. ibid., p. 214.

38. P. A. Kolzakov, 'Zametki P. A. Kolzakova', *RS*, I, No. 6 (June 1870), p. 496.

39. Davydov, 'Vospominaniia o tsesareviche Konstantine Pavloviche', p. 36.

40. ibid.

41. ibid., p. 39.

42. Schnitzler, I, p. 161.

43. ibid., p. 160.

44. Shilder, I, pp. 216, 227.

45. 'Pis'mo Konstantina Pavlovicha k Nikolaiu Pavlovichu', 2 December 1825, in Th. Schiemann, *Die Ermordung Pauls und die Thronbesteigung Nikolaus I. Neue Materialien* (Berlin, 1902), p. 94.

46. Presniakov, *14 dekabria*, pp. 66–78.

47. 'Iz dnevnikov Aleksandry Fedorovny', in *Mezhdutsarstvie*, entry for 3 December 1825, p. 85.

48. S. B. Okun', *Dekabrist M. S. Lunin* (Leningrad, 1962), pp. 79–91.

49. 'Iz dnevnikov Nikolaia Pavlovicha', entries for 9 December 1825, p. 77; and 12 December 1825, p. 79.

50. Schiemann (Berlin, 1908), II, p. 31.

51. 'Zapiski Nikolaia I o vstuplenii ego na prestol', p. 19.

52. See N. I. Lorer, *Zapiski dekabrista* (Moscow, 1931), pp. 437–8; Presniakov, *14 dekabria*, pp. 78–9; and M. V. Nechkina, *Dvizhenie dekabristov* (Moscow, 1955), II, p. 219.

53. 'Iz dnevnikov Aleksandry Fedorovny', entry for 12 December 1825, p. 87.

54. Speranskii's career has received masterful and definitive treatment in Marc Raeff, *Michael Speransky: Statesman of Imperial Russia, 1772–1839* (The Hague, 1957).

55. 'Iz dnevnikov Nikolaia Pavlovicha', in *Mezhdutsarstvie*, entries for 27 November 1825, p. 69; and for 11 and 12 December 1825, pp. 78–9.

56. ibid., entry for 12 December 1825, p. 79.

57. Aleksandr Murav'ev, 'Mon Journal ou Mémoires d'Alexandre Mouravieff', in Schiemann, *Die Ermordung Pauls und die Thronbesteigung Nikolaus I*, pp. 168–9.

58. *Vospominaniia Bestuzhevykh*, edited by M. K. Azadovskii and I. M. Trotskii (Moscow, 1931), p. 83.

59. ibid., p. 82.

60. Quoted in Presniakov, *14 dekabria*, p. 78.

61. Baron M. A. Korf, *The Accession of Nicholas I*, 3rd impression (first published), (London, 1857), pp. 156–63.

62. A. D. Borovkov, 'A. D. Borovkov i ego avtobiograficheskie zapiski', *Russkaia starina*, XCVI, No. 11 (November 1898), p. 333.

63. *Vospominaniia Bestuzhevykh*, p. 141.

64. Baron M. A. Korf, *The Accession of Nicholas I*, p. 163.

65. Shilder, I, p. 266.

66. ibid.

67. 'Dnevnik Barona M. A. Korfa za

1847 g.', TsGAOR, fond 728, opis' 1, delo No. 1817/x/140.

68. A useful summary of this problem can be found in Marc Raeff, *The Decembrist Movement* (Englewood Cliffs, 1966), pp. 1–29. See also Anatole Mazour, *The First Russian Revolution 1825: The Decembrist Movement, Its Origins, Development, and Significance* (Berkeley, 1937), pp. 46–65.

69. V. I. Semevskii, *Politicheskiia i obshchestvennyia idei dekabristov* (St Petersburg, 1909), pp. 286–377.

70. Richard Pipes, 'The Russian Military Colonies 1810–1831', *Journal of Modern History*, XXII, No. 3 (September 1950), pp. 205–19.

71. Nechkina, *Dvizhenie dekabristov*, I, pp. 308–12.

72. ibid., pp. 304–42.

73. N. M. Druzhinin, *Dekabrist Nikita Murav'ev* (Moscow, 1933), pp. 117–76; Nechkina, *Dvizhenie dekabristov*, I, pp. 376–426; V. I. Semevskii, *Politicheskiia i obshchestvennyia idei dekabristov*, pp. 447–499.

74. For the development of Murav'ev's constitutional views, see the different drafts of his constitutions in N. M. Druzhinin, *Dekabrist Nikita Murav'ev*, pp. 303–46.

75. P. I. Pestel', 'Russkaia Pravda, II redaktsiia', *Vosstanie Dekabristov: Dokumenty* (Moscow, 1958), VII, pp. 118–19.

76. 'Konstitutsiia N. Murav'eva', in N. M. Druzhinin, *Dekabrist Nikita Murav'ev*, p. 303.

77. Quoted in A. Mazour, *The First Russian Revolution*, p. 165.

78. 'Delo o polkovnike Leib-Gvardii Preobrazhenskago Polka Kniaze Trubetskom', *Vosstanie Dekabristov: Materialy* (Moscow-Leningrad, 1925), I, p. 19.

79. *Vospominaniia Bestuzhevykh*, p. 83.

80. ibid.

81. Quoted in Shilder, I, p. 281.

82. Presniakov, *14 dekabria*, pp. 101–102.

83. Quoted in Shilder, I, p. 281.

84. Schiemann, II, p. 44.

85. ibid., p. 45; 'Zapiski Nikolaia I o vstuplenii ego na prestol', pp. 21–2.

86. ibid.

87. ibid., p. 22.

88. Presniakov, *14 dekabria*, pp. 106–107.

89. Nechkina, *Dvizhenie dekabristov*, II, pp. 268–9.

90. Baroness M. P. Frederiks, 'Iz vospominanii baronessy M. P. Frederiks', *IV*, LXXI, No. 1 (January 1898), p. 53.

91. *Vospominaniia Bestuzhevykh*, p. 142.

92. Presniakov, *14 dekabria*, p. 116.

93. 'Zapiski Nikolaia I o vstuplenii ego na prestol', p. 23.

94. ibid., p. 22.

95. ibid., p. 23.

96. ibid.; Presniakov, *14 dekabria*, p. 116.

97. Baron M. A. Korf, *The Accession of Nicholas I*, p. 204.

98. 'Pis'ma P. G. Kakhovskago ot 11-go i 14-go maia 1826 g. k G. General-ad'iutantu Levashovu', *Vosstanie Dekabristov: Materialy*, I, pp. 369, 377.

99. Presniakov, *14 dekabria*, p. 119. 'Zapiski Nikolaia I o vstuplenii ego na prestol', pp. 24–5.

100. Shilder, I, 287; 'Zapiski Nikolaia I o vstuplenii ego na prestol', p. 25.

101. ibid.

102. ibid.

103. Presniakov, *14 dekabria*, p. 119.

104. 'Iz vospominanii printsa Evgenii Virtembergskago', in *Mezhdutsarstvie*, p. 120.

105. 'Zapiski Nikolaia I o vstuplenii ego na prestol', p. 27.

106. Schnitzler, I, p. 421.

107. Presniakov, *14 dekabria*, p. 123.

108. 'Zapiski Nikolaia I o vstuplenii ego na prestol', p. 27.

109. Quoted in Korf, *The Accession of Nicholas I*, p. 254.

110. ibid., p. 255; Shilder, I, 290.

111. ibid.; Korf, *The Accession of Nicholas I*, p. 255.

112. G. Vasilich, *Vosshestvie na prestol Imperatora Nikolaia I*, I, pp. 88–9.

113. Quoted in Korf, *The Accession of Nicholas I*, p. 258.

114. Presniakov, *14 dekabria*, pp. 130–132.

115. Shilder, I, 291.

116. 'Iz vospominanii printsa Evgenii Virtembergskago', p. 119.

117. 'Zapiski Nikolaia I o vstuplenii ego na prestol', p. 28.

118. 'Iz vospominanii printsa Evgenii Virtembergskago', p. 119.

119. 'Zapiski Nikolaia I o vstuplenii ego na prestol', p. 29.

120. 'Vospominanii Mikhaila Pavlovicha o sobytiiakh 14 dekabria 1825 g.', in *Mezhdutsarstvie*, p. 62.

121. 'Pis'mo Nikolaia I k Konstantinu Pavlovichu', 14–16 December, 1925, in Schiemann, *Die Ermordung Pauls und die Thronbesteigung Nikolaus I*, p. 103.

CHAPTER 2

THE EDUCATION OF A DRILL-MASTER

1. De Custine, *La Russie en 1839*, I, pp. 317–19.

2. Baron C. F. von Stockmar, *The Memoirs of Baron Stockmar*, translated from the German by G. A. M., edited by F. Max Müller (London, 1872), I, p. 57.

3. 'Pis'mo Imperatritsy Ekateriny II k baronu Mel'khioru Grimmu', 25 June 1796, *SIRIO*, XXIII, (1878), p. 679.

4. 'Pis'mo Imperatritsy Ekateriny II k baronu Mel'khioru Grimmu', 5 June 1796, *SIRIO*, XXIII, (1878), p. 681.

5. Korf, *Materialy*, p. 17.

6. ibid., p. 16.

7. ibid., pp. 12–14.

8. Shilder, I, p. 4.

9. ibid.

10. Korf, *Materialy*, p. 11.

11. See Chapter 1, pp. 24–5.

12. A. E. Presniakov, *Apogei samoderzhaviia: Nikolaia I* (Leningrad, 1925), pp. 6–7.

13. See Korf, *Materialy*, pp. 17–18, 20, 21.

14. ibid., p. 14.

15. ibid., p. 15.

16. ibid., pp. 11–12.

17. Quoted in Presniakov, *Apogei samoderzhaviia*, p. 9.

18. Letter of Queen Victoria to King Leopold, 4 June 1844, in A. C. Benson and Viscount Esher (eds.), *The Letters of Queen Victoria: A Selection of Her Majesty's Correspondence between the Years 1837–1861* (London, 1907), II, p. 14.

19. De Custine, *La Russie en 1839*, I, p. 319.

20. Korf, pp. 22–3.

21. ibid., p. 26.

22. Shilder, I, p. 11.

23. Korf, *Materialy*, p. 26.

24. 'Zapiski Nikolaia I o vstuplenii ego na prestol', p. 11.

25. Korf, *Materialy*, p. 31.

26. 'Imperatritsa Aleksandra Fedorovna v svoikh vospominaniiakh', *RS*, No. 10 (October 1896), p. 51.

27. Quoted in Korf, *Materialy*, pp. 85–86.

28. Shilder, I, p. 26.

29. Korf, *Materialy*, pp. 27–8.

30. Quoted in LaCroix, I, pp. 37, 39.

31. Quoted in ibid., p. 39.

32. Both quotes from Shilder, I, p. 22.

33. Quoted in Korf, *Materialy*, p. 30.

34. Quoted in ibid., p. 29.

35. 'Imperator Nikolai I v doneseniiakh shvedskago poslannika', *RS*, CXVI, No. 10 (October 1903), p. 206.

36. 'Zapiski Nikolaia I o vstuplenii ego na prestol', p. 11.

37. Shilder, I, p. 22.

38. Korf, *Materialy*, p. 36.

39. Grunwald, p. 23.

40. Korf, *Materialy*, p. 30.

41. Quoted in ibid., p. 36.

42. 'Zapiski Nikolaia I o vstuplenii ego na prestol', p. 12.

43. LaCroix, I, 54.

44. 'Zapiski Nikolaia I o vstuplenii ego na prestol', p. 12.

45. Korf, *Materialy*, p. 72.

46. Quoted in Presniakov, *Apogei samoderzhaviia*, p. 14. (Italics mine.)

47. 'Zapiski Nikolaia I o vstuplenii ego na prestol', p. 12.

48. Quoted in Korf, *Materialy*, pp. 79–80.

49. Shilder, II, p. 22.

50. See, for example, 'Imperator Nikolai Pavlovich v ego pis'makh k kniaziu Paskevich', *RA*, No. 1 (January 1897), pp. 5–44.

51. Shilder, I, p. 48.

52. See Korf, *Materialy*, pp. 84–6.

53. During these days and for the next two years, Charlotte wrote Nicholas a number of letters which he treasured. In 1837, when the Winter Palace burned, he reportedly told an aide-de-camp, 'Let everything burn up, only just save for me the small case of letters in my study which my wife wrote to me when she was my betrothed.' See I. N. Bozherianov, *Zhizneopisanie imperatritsy Aleksandry Fedorovny, suprugi Imperatora Nikolaia I* (St Petersburg, 1898), I, p. 37.

54. Grunwald, p. 29.

55. Quoted in Korf, *Materialy*, p. 30.

56. 'Doklad M. A. Balugianskago', in ibid., p. 87.

57. Shilder, I, p. 64.

58. 'Dnevnik Nikolaia Pavlovicha', in Korf, *Materialy*, p. 91.

59. Shilder, I, p. 68.

60. 'Dnevnik Nikolaia Pavlovicha', in Korf, *Materialy*, p. 95.

61. Quoted in Korf, *Materialy*, pp. 79–80.

62. Korf, *Materialy*, p. 96. (Italics in original.)

63. Quoted in ibid., p. 96.

64. K. V. Nesselrode, 'Mémoire destiné à Son Altesse Impériale, Monseigneur le grand duc Nicolas à l'occasion de son voyage dans les pays étrangers,' in Shilder, I, pp. 586–90.

65. Polievtkov, p. 19.

66. Baron von Stockmar, *Memoirs*, I, pp. 55–7.

67. Quoted in Shilder, I, p. 80.

68. Polievktov, pp. 23–4.

69. 'Imperatritsa Aleksandra Fedorovna v svoikh vospominaniiakh', *RS*, LXXXVIII, No. 10 (October 1896), pp. 13–16.

70. ibid., p. 17.

71. ibid., p. 51.

72. F. F. Vigel', *Zapiski* (Moscow, 1891–3), V, p. 70.

73. P. M. Daragan, 'Vospominaniia pervago kamer-pazha velikoi kniagini (imperatritsy) Aleksandry Fedorovny, 1817–1819 gg.', *RS*, XII, No. 4 (April 1875), pp. 793–5.

74. 'Imperatritsa Aleksandra Fedorovna v svoikh vospominaniiakh', p. 21; Bozherianov, *Zhizneopisanie*, I, pp. 51–3.

75. Quoted in Presniakov, *Apogei Samoderzhaviia*, p. 87.

76. Letter of Queen Victoria to King Leopold, 4 June 1844, in Bensen and Esher (eds.), *The Letters of Queen Victoria*, II, p. 14.

77. 'Imperatritsa Aleksandra Fedorovna v svoikh vospominaniiakh', p. 25.

78. ibid, p. 32.

79. ibid., pp. 46–8.

80. Quotes from Shilder, I, p. 100.

81. ibid., p. 114.

82. This position is taken by the following scholars: Grunwald; A. A. Kornilov, *Kurs istorii rossii XIX veka* (Moscow, 1912), II; Polievktov; and Shilder.

83. 'Zapiski Nikolaia I o vstuplenii ego na prestol', p. 15.

84. Catherine II, *Mémoires de l'impératrice Catherine II*, edited by A. Herzen (London, 1859).

85. Quoted in Shilder, II, p. 407.

86. ibid., I, p. 126.

87. Quotes from LaCroix, I, pp. 112, 111.

88. S. S. Tatishchev, 'Votsarenie imperatora Nikolaia', *RV*, CCXXIV, No. 4 (April 1893), p. 9.

89. Quotes from Shilder, I, p. 59.

90. A. D. Borovkov, 'Zapiski', pp. 331, 353, 360.

CHAPTER 3

THE GENESIS OF THE NICHOLAS SYSTEM

1. Presniakov, *Apogei samoderzhaviia*, p. 46.

2. F. F. Vigel', *Zapiski*, V, p. 70.

3. Shilder, I, p. 312.

4. S. Frederick Starr, *Decentralization and Self-Government in Russia, 1830–1870* (Princeton, 1972), p. 48.

5. Marc Raeff, *The Origins of the Russian Intelligentsia: The Eighteenth-Century Nobility* (New York, 1966), pp. 34–121.

6. W. Bruce Lincoln, 'The Genesis of an "Enlightened" Bureaucracy in Russia, 1825–1855', *Jahrbücher für Geschichte Osteuropas*, XX, No. 3 (September 1972), pp. 322–3; Marc Raeff, 'The Russian Autocracy and Its Officials', *Harvard Slavic Studies*, IV (1957), pp. 77–92.

7. 'Zapiski Benkendorfa', *RS*, LXXXVIII, No. 10 (October 1896), p. 88.

8. W. Bruce Lincoln, 'The Emperor Nicholas I in England', *History Today*, XXV, No. 1 (January 1975), p. 27.

9. Nicholas I, 'Zaveshchanie Nikolaia I synu', *KA*, III (1923), pp. 291–3.

10. Baron M. A. Korf, 'Dnevnik barona M. A. Korfa za 1841 g.', TsGAOR, fond 728, opis' 1, delo No. 1817/iv/167.

11. De Custine, *La Russie en 1839*, I, pp. 316–7.

12. 'Zapiski Benkendorfa' (Shilder), p. 665.

13. These figures are taken from a survey of *Vosstanie dekabristov. Materialy* (Leningrad, 1925), VIII, *passim*.

14. Quoted in Shilder, I, p. 270.

15. Quoted in Grunwald, p. 61. (Italics mine.)

16. Quoted in ibid., p. 58.

17. 'Pis'mo Imperatora Nikolaia I k Konstantinu Pavlovichu', 23 December 1825, in *Mezhdutsarstvie*, p. 168.

18. Shilder, I, p. 329.

19. These figures are taken from a survey of *Vosstanie dekabristov. Materialy*, VIII, *passim*.

20. V. I. Semevskii and P. E. Shchegolov (eds.), *Obshchestvennye dvizheniia v Rossii v pervuiu polovinu XIX veka* (St Petersburg, 1905), I, pp. 197–8.

21. A. D. Borovkov, 'A. D. Borovkov i ego avtobiograficheskie zapiski', *Russkaia starina*, No. 11 (November, 1898), p. 353.

22. Shilder, I, p. 442.

23. Quoted in I. D. Iakushkin, *Zapiski, stat'i, pis'ma dekabrista I. D. Iakushkina* (Moscow, 1951), pp. 82–3.

24. Quoted in Shilder, I, p. 440.

25. 'Pis'mo Imperatora Nikolaia I k Marii Fedorovne', 30 June–1 July 1826, in *Mezhdutsarstvie*, p. 207.

26. ibid., 16 January 1826.

27. Quoted in Shilder, I, p. 454. Italics mine.

28. K. F. Ryleev, *Polnoe sobranie sochineniia* (Moscow, 1934), pp. 501, 518.

29. 'Pis'mo Imperatora Nikolaia i Marii Fedorovne', 5 June 1826, in *Mezhdutsarstvie*, p. 204.

30. A. Mazour, *The First Russian Revolution*, p. 219.

31. 'Pis'ma Imperatora Nikolaia I k Konstantinu Pavlovichu', 22 January, 22 March and 6 June 1826, in *Mezhdutsarstvie*, pp. 184, 192, and 195.

32. Quoted in LaCroix, I, p. 39.

33. Quoted in Shilder, I, p. 292.

34. Quoted in ibid., p. 372.

35. Borovkov, 'A. D. Borovkov i ego avtobiograficheskie zapiski', p. 354.

36. ibid., No. 12 (December 1898), p. 608.

37. A. A. Kiesewetter, 'Vnutreniaia politika Imperatora Nikolaia Pavlovicha', *Istoricheskie ocherki* (Moscow, 1912), p. 422.

38. Quoted in Shilder, I, p. 311.

39. Quoted in ibid.

40. N. M. Karamzin, *Karamzin's Memoir on Ancient and Modern Russia*, translated and edited by Richard Pipes (Cambridge, Mass., 1959), p. 166.

41. A. A. Kornilov, *Kurs*, II, pp. 24, 28, 101.

42. Polievktov, pp. 65–8.

43. Kornilov, *Kurs*, II, p. 18.

44. These quotations are taken from 'Zaveshchanie Nikolaia I synu', pp. 291–293.

45. See Karamzin, *Memoir on Ancient and Modern Russia*, pp. 197 and 198.

46. Quoted in Polievktov, p. 376.

47. Karamzin, *Memoir on Ancient and Modern Russia*, pp. 196, 200, 204.

48. Quoted in Korf, *Materialy*, pp. 79–80.

49. 'Zapiski Nikolaia I o vstuplenii ego na prestol', p. 15.

50. M. P. Pogodin, *Nikolai Mikhailovich Karamzin* (Moscow, 1866), II, p. 498.

51. Kornilov, *Kurs*, II, p. 22.

52. A. V. Golovnin, 'Zapiski Aleksandra Vasil'evicha Golovnina s marta 1867 goda', TsGIAL, fond 851, opis' 1, delo No. 7/2.

53. Riasanovsky, p. 47.

54. Sidney Monas, *The Third Section: Police and Society in Russia under Nicholas I* (Cambridge, Mass., 1961), p. 63. The Third Section is in the West by far the best-studied of Nicholas's institutions. Apart from Monas's more general work, there is P. G. Squire, *The Third Department* (Cambridge, 1968), a careful and highly useful study which discusses in some detail the organization of the Third Section throughout the Empire. Squire's treatment of the careers of Third Section officials also provides a valuable chapter in the far too scanty literature on the Russian bureaucracy.

55. Monas, *The Third Section*, pp. 62–63.

56. Quoted in Shilder, I, p. 467.

57. Quoted in Monas, *The Third Section*, p. 65.

58. 'Zapiski Benkendorfa', *KA*, XXXVIII (1930), p. 132.

59. V. Bogucharskii, 'Tret'e otdelenie sobstvennago ego imperatorskago velichestva kantseliarii o sebe samom', *Vestnik evropy*, No. 3 (March 1917), p. 99.

60. A. V. Golovnin, 'Prodolzhenie zapisok A. V. Golovnina s dekabria 1870 g. po fevral' 1871 g.', TsGIAL, fond 851, opis' 1, delo No. 9/7–8.

61. Presniakov, *Apogei samoderzhaviia*, p. 7.

62. Shilder, I, p. 428.

63. Quoted in ibid.

64. Quoted in ibid., p. 429.

65. ibid.

66. Kornilov, *Kurs*, II, p. 26.

67. 'Pis'mo Imperatora Nikolaia I k Konstantinu Pavlovichu', 4 January 1826, in *Mezhdutsarstvie*, p. 175.

68. 'Pis'mo Imperatora Nikolaia I k Konstantinu Pavlovichu', 17 December 1825, in ibid., p. 166.

69. ibid., 11 January 1826, p. 180.

70. A. V. Nikitenko, *Dnevnik* (Moscow, 1955), I, pp. 328–9.

71. Quoted in Michael Florinsky, *Russia: A History and an Interpretation* (New York, 1968), II, p. 1115.

72. Quoted in Shilder, II, p. 32.

73. ibid., pp. 32–3.

74. Quoted in ibid., p. 407.

75. I. N. Borozdin, 'Universitety v Rossii v pervoi polovine XIX veka', *Istoriia Rossii v XIX vek* (St Petersburg, 1907), II, p. 370.

76. Raeff, *Michael Speranskii*, pp. 83–167.

77. Kiesewetter, 'Vnutrenniaia politika', p. 428.

78. 'Zhurnaly komiteta uchrezhdennago Vysochaishim reskriptom 6 dekabria 1826 goda', *SIRIO*, LXXIV (1891), p. 264.

79. Kiesewetter, 'Vnutrenniaia politika', p. 433.

80. 'Zhurnaly komiteta uchrezhdennago Vysochaishim reskriptom 6 dekabria 1826 goda', p. 92.

81. Nikitenko, *Dnevnik*, I, p. 5.

82. H.-J. Torke, 'Das russische Beamtentum in der ersten Hälfte des 19. Jahrhunderts', *Forschungen zur osteuropäischen Geschichte*, XIII (Berlin-Wiesbaden, 1967), pp. 7–345.

83. For a discussion of this problem, see S. M. Troitskii, *Russkii absoliutizm i dvorianstvo v XVIII v.: Formirovanie biurokratii* (Moscow, 1974), pp. 267–95.

84. 'Zhurnaly komiteta uchrezhdennago Vysochaishim reskriptom 6 dekabria 1826 goda', pp. 92, 107.

85. ibid., pp. 379–80.

86. Starr, *Decentralization*, pp. 29–30.

87. Quote from ibid., p. 45.

88. Kiesewetter, 'Vnutrenniaia politika', p. 444.

89. Marc Raeff, *The Origins of the Russian Intelligentsia*, pp. 64–70.

90. Kiesewetter, 'Vnutrenniaia politika', p. 442.

91. Nicholas I, 'Zaveshchanie Nikolaia I synu', p. 293.

92. Shilder, II, p. 64.

93. W. Bruce Lincoln, 'The Ministers of Nicholas I: A Brief Inquiry Into Their Backgrounds and Service Careers', *Russian Review*, XXIV, No. 3 (July 1975), p. 316.

94. M. M. Speranskii, 'Predpolozheniia okonchatel'nomu sostavleniiu zakonov', *RS*, XV (1876), pp. 434–41.

95. M. Raeff, *Michael Speransky*, p. 324.

96. A. F. Bychkov (ed.), 'K piatidesiatiletiiu II-go otdeleniia sobstvennoe E. I. V. Kantseliarii', *RS* (1876), p. 431.

97. Raeff, *Michael Speransky*, p. 322.

98. *Gosudarstvennyi sovet, 1801–1901 gg.* (St Petersburg, 1902), p. 19.

99. Raeff, *Michael Speransky*, pp. 322–323.

100. ibid., p. 323.

101. ibid., pp. 321–2.

102. Polievktov, p. 257.

103. Raeff, *Michael Speransky*, p. 325.

104. G. Tel'berg, 'Uchastie Imperatora Nikolaia I v kodifikatsionnoi rabote ego tsarstvovaniia', *Zhurnal Ministerstva Iustitsii*, XXII, No. 1 (January, 1916), pp. 233–44.

105. Raeff, *Michael Speransky*, p. 325.

106. ibid., p. 330.

107. Raeff, *Michael Speransky*, pp. 332 and 342.

108. Kiesewetter, 'Vnutrenniaia politika', p. 426.

CHAPTER 4

THE HERITAGE OF THE HOLY ALLIANCE

1. Quoted in Shilder, I, p. 349.

2. H. Nicolson, *The Congress of Vienna: A Study in Allied Unity, 1812–1822* (New York, 1946), p. 249.

3. McConnell, *Tsar Alexander I*, p. 58; S. S. Tatishchev, *Vneshniaia politika imperatora Nikolaia I* (St Petersburg, 1887), p. 4.

4. Quoted in Nicolson, *The Congress of Vienna*, p. 249.

5. Quoted in C. K. Webster (ed.), *British Diplomacy, 1813–1815* (London, 1921), p. 383.

6. Quoted in Nicolson, *The Congress of Vienna*, p. 250.

7. Quoted in Tatishchev, *Vneshniaia politika*, p. 7.

8. Quotes from Nicolson, *The Congress of Vienna*, pp. 250, 252.

9. Quotes from ibid., pp. 253, 254.

10. ibid.

11. Quotes from ibid., pp. 271, 272.

12. Shilder, I, p. 466.

13. Nicholas to Konstantin Pavlovich, 4 January 1826, in *Mezhdutsarstvie*, p. 175.

14. Nicholas to Konstantin Pavlovich, 16 January 1826, in ibid., p. 181.

15. See, especially, Grunwald, *passim*.

16. Quoted in Presniakov, *Apogei samoderzhaviia*, p. 60.

17. Count K. V. Nesselrode, *Lettres et papiers du Chancelier Comte de Nesselrode, 1760–1850* (Paris, 1905–12), VI, p. 270.

18. S. S. Tatishchev, 'Votsarenie Imperatora Nikolaia', *RV*, CCXXIV, Nos. 3–4 (1893), pp. 9–14.

19. Comte de la Ferronnays au Baron de Damas, 24 December 1825/5 January 1826, in Nesselrode, *Lettres et papiers*, VI, p. 295.

20. Nesselrode, *Lettres et papiers*, VI, pp. 274–5.

21. V. R. Zotov, 'Peterburg v sorokovykh godakh', *IV*, XXXIX, No. 1 (January 1890), p. 325.

22. Quoted in Tatishchev, 'Votsarenie Imperatora Nikolaia', *RV*, CCXXV, No. 5 (May 1893), p. 97.

23. Quoted in Tatishchev, *Vneshniaia politika*, p. 137.

24. J. F. Baddeley, *The Russian Conquest of the Caucasus* (London, 1908), pp. 154–5; Polievktov, p. 103.

25. Nicholas to Konstantin Pavlovich, 5 September 1825, in Shilder, II, p. 20.

26. 'Zapiski I. F. Paskevicha', in Kniaz' A. Shcherbatov, *General-Fel'd-marshal kniaz' Paskevich. Ego zhizn' i deiatel'nost'* (St Petersburg, 1888), I, p. 394.

27. A. Kh. Benkendorf, 'Zapiska A. Kh. Benkendorfa k Nikolaiu I', in Shilder, II, p. 28.

28. Baron I. I. Dibich to Nicholas I, 22 December 1825, in ibid., II, p. 22.

29. For a discussion of the Decembrists in the Caucasus, see Lauren Leighton, *Alexander Bestuzhev-Marlinsky* (Boston, 1975), pp. 30–36, and D. Davydov, *Voennye zapiski* (Moscow, 1940), I, *passim.*

30. A. P. Ermolov, 'Dnevnik Alekseia Petrovicha Ermolova v prodolzhenie komandirovaniia v Gruzii do konchiny Imperatora Aleksandra', in M. P. Pogodin, *Aleksei Petrovich Ermolov: Materialy dlia ego biografii* (Moscow, 1864), p. 252.

31. Nicholas I to General A. P. Ermolov, 1 and 11 August 1826, in ibid., pp. 359, 362–3.

32. F. M. Umanets, 'Prokonsul Kavkaza', *IV*, XXXIII (1888), p. 492.

33. Nicholas I, 'Ermolov, Dibich, i Paskevich na Kavkaze v 1826–1827 gg. Perepiska Imperatora Nikolaia', *RS*, XXIX, No. 11 (November 1880), p. 617.

34. 'Zapiski Paskevicha', in Shcherbatov, *General-Fel'dmarshal kniaz' Paskevich*, I, p. 393.

35. Nicholas I to General A. P. Ermolov, 11 August 1826, in Pogodin, *Ermolov: Materialy*, p. 362.

36. Nicholas I to General A. P. Ermolov, 24 October 1826, in ibid., pp. 364–5.

37. Nicholas I to General I. F. Paskevich, 31 January 1827, in Shilder, II, p. 68.

38. Umanets, 'Prokonsul Kavkaza', p. 495.

39. Nicholas I to Baron Dibich, 27 March 1827, in 'Ermolov, Dibich, i Paskevich', *RS*, XXIX, No. 11 (November 1880), p. 623.

40. General A. P. Ermolov to Nicholas I, 3 March 1827, in Pogodin, *Ermolov: Materialy*, p. 378.

41. Quotes from A. P. Ermolov, 'Dnevnik A. P. Ermolova', in ibid., pp. 352, 353.

42. General I. F. Paskevich to Nicholas I, 3 October 1827, in Shilder, II, p. 86.

43. Baddeley, *The Russian Conquest of the Caucasus*, p. 175.

44. Shilder, II, p. 90.

45. I. F. Paskevich, 'Vsepoddanneishii raport general-ad'iutanta Paskevicha ot 29-go oktiabria 1827 goda', in Shilder, II, p. 88.

46. Shcherbatov, *General-Fel'dmarshal kniaz' Paskevich*, III, p. 23.

47. 'Ukaz pravitel'stvuiushchemu senata ot 15-go marta 1828 goda', in Shilder, II, p. 420.

48. Quoted in Grunwald, p. 85.

49. Polievktov, p. 97.

50. Nicholas gave a further hint at what Alexander's intentions had been in early January 1826 when he told the Comte de Saint-Priest that his brother had been 'ready to put an end to the problem when his premature death took him from us' – Tatishchev, *Vneshniaia politika*, p. 137.

51. Quoted in ibid., pp. 137–8.

52. Quoted in ibid., p. 138.

53. W. Bruce Lincoln, 'The Emperor Nicholas I in England', *History Today*, XXV, No. 1 (January 1975), p. 29.

54. S. Zhigarev, *Russkaia politika v vostochnom voprose: Istoriko-Iuridicheskie ocherki* (Moscow, 1896), p. 327.

55. ibid.

56. Tatishchev, *Vneshniaia politika*, p. 145.

57. ibid., p. 149.

58. Quoted in ibid.,

59. Zhigarev, *Russkaia politika*, p. 330.

60. Tatishchev, *Vneshniaia politika*, p. 150.

61. Quoted in ibid., p. 151.

62. ibid., pp. 152–3.

63. Count Zichy to Prince Metternich, 24 April 1828 (NS), in *Memoirs of Prince Metternich* (New York, 1879–82), IV, p. 489.

64. Grunwald, p. 86.

65. Polievktov, pp. 99–100.

66. Tatishchev, *Vneshniaia politika*, p. 170.

67. ibid., p. 168.

68. Quotes from J. A. R. Marriott, *The Eastern Question: An Historical Study in European Diplomacy*, 4th ed. (Oxford, 1940), p. 219.

69. Quotes from ibid., p. 220.

70. Quotes from A. I. Ribop'er, 'Zapiski grafa Aleksandra Ivanovicha Ribop'era', *RA*, XV, No. 2 (1877), pp. 23, 24–5.

71. Nicholas I to Grand Duke Konstantin Pavlovich, 12 November 1827, in 'Perepiska Imperatora Nikolaia Pavlovicha s velikim kniazem tsesarevichem Konstantinom Pavlovichem, 1825–1829 gg.', *SIRIO*, CXXXI (1910), p. 193.

72. Grand Duke Konstantin Pavlovich to Nicholas I, in ibid., p. 193.

73. Prince Metternich to Count Apponyi, 13 November 1827 (NS), in *Memoirs of Prince Metternich*, IV, pp. 418–19.

74. Grand Duke Konstantin Pavlovich to Nicholas I, 7 December 1827, in Shilder, II, p. 427.

75. Metternich to the Emperor Franz, 26 November 1827 (NS), in *Memoirs of Prince Metternich*, IV, p. 426.

76. Metternich to Count Werner, in Berlin, 29 November 1827 (NS), in ibid., pp. 427–8.

77. Metternich to Count Werner, 29 November 1827 (NS), in ibid., IV, p. 428.

78. Metternich to the Emperor Franz, 30 November 1827 (NS), in ibid., p. 429.

79. Metternich to the Emperor Franz, 9 December 1827 (NS), in ibid., p. 432.

80. Marriott, *The Eastern Question*, p. 221.

81. Tatishchev, *Vneshniaia politika*, pp. 174–5.

82. Polievktov, p. 104; Prince Metternich, *Memoirs of Prince Metternich*, IV, p. 452.

83. Quoted in Tatishchev, *Vneshniaia politika*, p. 179.

84. Nicholas I to Grand Duke Konstantin Pavlovich, 15 March 1828, *SIRIO*, CXXXI, p. 215.

85. Count Zichy to Metternich, 12 (24) April 1828, in *Memoirs of Prince Metternich*, IV, p. 493.

86. Metternich to Count Esterhazy, 24 March 1828 (NS), in ibid., p. 478.

87. Metternich to Count Apponyi, 9 May 1828 (NS), in ibid., p. 497.

88. Count Zichy to Metternich, 12 (24) April 1828, in ibid., p. 490.

89. ibid., p. 493.

90. Metternich to Count Ottenfels, 4 September 1828 (NS), in ibid., pp. 514–515.

91. Shilder, II, pp. 122, 432.

92. ibid., p. 123.

93. V. Ia. Grosul, *Reformy v Dunaiskikh kniazhestvakh i Rossiia* (Moscow, 1966), pp. 150–72.

94. Polievktov, p. 106.

95. Nicholas I to Baron I. I. Dibich, 3 May 1828, 'Imperator Nikolai Pavlovich i graf Dibich-Zabalkanskii: Perepiski, 1828–1829 gg', *RS*, XXVII, No. 1 (January 1880), p. 102.

96. Shilder, II, p. 125.

97. I. P. Dubetskii, 'Zapiski I. P. Dubetskago', *RS*, LXXXIV, No. 5 (May 1895), p. 87.

98. Le comte Charles de Nesselrode à sa femme, juin 29, 1828, in Nesselrode, *Lettres et papiers*, VII, p. 39.

99. Nicholas I to Grand Duke Konstantin Pavlovich, 9 June 1828, *SIRIO*, CXXXI, p. 241.

100. Nesselrode à sa femme, juillet 18, 1828, in Nesselrode, *Lettres et papiers*, VII, p. 65.

101. Nicholas I to Grand Duke Konstantin Pavlovich, 16 May 1828, *SIRIO*, CXXXI, p. 230.

102. A. P. Zablotskii-Desiatovskii, *Graf P. D. Kiselev*, I, p. 277.

103. Shilder, II, p. 143.

104. Nicholas I to Grand Duke Konstantin Pavlovich, 30 June 1828, *SIRIO*, CXXXI, p. 247.

105. Dubetskii, 'Zapiski', p. 87.

106. Nicholas I to Grand Duke Konstantin Pavlovich, 16 May 1828 *SIRIO*, CXXXI, p. 230

107. Grunwald, pp. 89–90.

108. Quoted in Shilder, II, p. 435.

109. 'Zapiski Benkendorfa', *RS*, LXXXVI, No. 6 (June 1896), p. 487.

110. General A. A. Zakrevskii to General P. D. Kiselev, 9 February 1828, in N. Dubrovnin (ed.), 'Bumagi grafa Arseniia Andreevicha Zakrevskago', *SIRIO*, LXXVIII, (1981), p. 304.

111. General P. D. Kiselev to General A. A. Zakrevskii, 22 January 1828, in ibid., p. 154.

112. 'Zapiski Benkendorfa', *KA*, XXXVII (1929), p. 157.

113. Metternich to Count Esterhazy, 31 May 1828 (NS), in *Memoirs of Prince Metternich*, IV, pp. 501–2.

114. 'Zapiski Benkendorfa', *KA*, XXXVII (1929), pp. 157–8.

115. ibid., pp. 159, 160,

116. A. A. Zakrevskii, 'Zapiski A. A. Zakrevskago', *SIRIO*, LXXVIII, p. 542.

117. Quoted in Grunwald, p. 91.

118. A. V. Fadeev, *Rossiia i vostochnyi krizis 20-kh godov XIX veka* (Moscow, 1958), p. 291.

119. I. V. Vasil'chikov, 'Aperçu sur la campagne de l'année 1828', in Shilder, II, pp. 546–7.

120. General A. A. Zakrevskii to General P. D. Kiselev, 17 March 1820, in A. P. Zablotskii-Desiatovskii, *Graf P. D. Kiselev*, I, p. 129.

121. D. Davydov, *Voennye zapiski*, I, p. 247.

122. Polievktov, p. 109; Fadeev, *Rossiia i vostochnyi krizis*, pp. 299–301.

123. K. I. Zeidlits, 'Vospominaniia o turetskoi pokhode 1829 g.', *RA*, No. 4 (1878), p. 428.

124. ibid., p. 434.

125. Princess Daria Lieven to General A. Kh. Benkendorf, 10 (22) October 1829, in L. G. Robinson (ed.), *Letters to Dorothea, Princess Lieven, during Her Residence in London, 1812–1834* (London, 1902), p. 199.

126. Metternich to Count Esterhazy, 14 September 1828 (NS), in *Memoirs of Prince Metternich*, IV, p. 523.

127. Prince Metternich to the Emperor Franz, 9 October 1828 (NS), in ibid., p. 638.

128. S. S. Tatishchev, *Imperator Nikolai i inostrannye dvory: istoricheskie ocherki* (St Petersburg, 1889), p. 142.

129. Nicholas I, Écrit autographe de sa majesté l'empereur Nicolas (n.d.), in Shilder, II, p. 563.

130. Nicholas I to Count I. I. Dibich, 3 April 1830, in ibid., p. 284.

131. 'Zapiski Benkendorfa', *KA*, XXXVIII (1930), p. 138.

132. Nicholas I to Grand Duke Konstantin Pavlovich, 6 (18) August 1830, *SIRIO*, CXXXII (1911), p. 36.

133. A. A. Kiesewetter, 'Imperator Nikolai I kak konstitutsionnyi monarkh', *Istoricheskie ocherki* (Moscow, 1912), pp. 402–3.

134. Nicholas I to Grand Duke Konstantin Pavlovich, 6 (18) August 1830, *SIRIO*, CXXXII, p. 36.

135. ibid.

136. ibid.

137. ibid., p. 37.

138. See, e.g., Polievktov, p. 115.

139. Quoted in Shilder, II, p. 290.

140. Metternich's notes of his interview with General Belliard, 30 August 1830 (NS), in *Memoirs of Prince Metternich*, V, p. 26.

141. Nicholas I to Grand Duke Konstantin Pavlovich, 6 (18) October 1830, *SIRIO*, CXXXII, pp. 55–6.

142. Polievktov, p. 118.

143. Metternich to Count Ficquelmont, 13 October 1830 (NS), in *Memoirs of Prince Metternich*, V, p. 55.

144. 'Zapiski Benkendorfa', *KA*, XXXVIII (1930), p. 138.

145. A. I. Herzen, *Polnoe sobranie*

sochinenii i pisem A. I. Gertsena, M. K. Lemke (ed.), (Petersburg-Leningrad, 1919–25), XII, p. 125.

146. A. E. Tsimmermana, 'Vospominaniia Generala A. E. Tsimmerman, 1825–1856 gg.', ORGBL, fond 325, karton 1, papka 2/7.

147. Metternich to the Emperor Franz, 11 October 1830 (NS), in *Memoirs of Prince Metternich*, V, p. 38.

148. Nicholas I, 'Ma confession', in Shilder, II, p. 310.

149. A. I. Herzen, *Polnoe sobranie sochinenii i pisem*, XII, p. 125.

150. A detailed examination of the causes and events of the revolt of 1830–31 are, regrettably, far beyond the scope of this present study. For further information about these questions, the reader may refer to a number of works. One lengthy account, written by a participant in the revolt, and a member of the Polish National Government of 1831, is S. Barzykowski, *Historia powstania listopadowego* (Poznań, 1883–4), 5 vols. To my knowledge, the most balanced account yet to appear – and one that is almost totally devoid of any nationalistic bias – is R. F. Leslie, *Polish Politics and the Revolution of November 1830* (London, 1956). The brief account on the following pages is much indebted to Leslie's analysis.

151. Raeff, *The Decembrists*, p. 4.

152. R. F. Leslie, *Polish Politics*, pp. 51–95.

153. Nicholas I, 'Zapiska Nikolaia o Pol'skom voprose', in Shilder, II, p. 582.

154. W. A. White to Earl John Russell, Warsaw, 8 December 1864 (NS), No. 4, Public Records Office, FO 65/665/286–7.

155. A. A. Kiesewetter, 'Imperator Nikolai I kak konstitutsionnyi monarkh', pp. 405–7.

156. Polievktov, p. 124.

157. R. F. Leslie, *Polish Politics*, pp. 114–15.

158. P. Wysocki, *Pamiętnik o powstaniu 29 listopada r. 1830*, 2 vols. (Paris, 1867).

159. R. F. Leslie, *Polish Politics*, p. 115.

160. W. Tokarz, *Sprzysężenie Wysockiego i noc listopadowa* (Warsaw, 1925), pp. 16–17.

161. 'Zapiski Benkendorfa', *RS*, October 1896), No. 10, LXXXVIII, pp. 68–9.

162. A. A. Kiesewetter, 'Imperator Nikolai I kak konstitutsionnyi monarkh', pp. 402–12.

163. A. A. Kornilov, *Kurs*, II, p. 36.

164. Leslie, *Polish Politics*, p. 122.

165. S. Siegel, *Ceny w Warszawie w latach 1816–1914* (Poznan, 1949), *passim*; Leslie, *Polish Politics*, p. 122.

166. Leslie, *Polish Politics*, pp. 120–23.

167. W. Zamoyski, *Jenerał Zamoyski* (Poznan, 1910), I, p. 376; P. Popiel, *Pamiętniki Pawła Popiela, 1807–1892* (Cracow, 1927), p. 59.

168. Quoted in Leslie, *Polish Politics*, p. 123.

169. L. Dembowski, *Moje wspomnienia* (St Petersburg, 1898), II, p. 28.

170. ibid.

171. Quoted in Shilder, II, p. 324.

172. Nicholas I to Grand Duke Konstantin Pavlovich, 8 December 1830, *SIRIO*, CXXXII, p. 69.

173. ibid.

174. 'Pamiętnik A. Młockiego', in A. Hirschberg (ed.), *Zbiór pamiętników do historyi powstania polskiego z roku 1830–1831* (Lwow, 1882), p. 271.

175. Leslie, *Polish Politics*, pp. 130–42.

176. 'Zapiski Benkendorfa', *RS* (October 1896), No. 10, LXXXIII, p. 81.

177. 'Entretien de S. M. L'Empereur Nicolas Ier avec le Prince Lubetski', in Nesselrode, *Lettres et papiers*, VII, p. 167.

178. Nicholas I to Grand Duke Konstantin Pavlovich, 27 December 1830, *SIRIO*, CXXXII, p. 93.

179. 'Zapiski Benkendorfa', *RS* (October 1896), No. 10, LXXXVIII, p. 83.

180. Shilder, II, 332.

181. Quoted in ibid., p. 340.

182. Nicholas I to Count I. I. Dibich, 13 (25) April 1831, in ibid., p. 478.

183. Nicholas I to Count I. I. Dibich, 27 May (7 June) 1831, in ibid., p. 483.

184. Princess Lowicza to Nicholas I,

15 (27) June 1831, *SIRIO*, CXXXII, p. 243.

185. Leslie, *Polish Politics*, p. 250.

186. Quoted in LaCroix, V, p. 518.

187. Quoted in Shilder, II, p. 375.

188. Schiemann, III, p. 139.

189. Leslie, *Polish Politics*, pp. 262–3.

190. Tatishchev, *Imperator Nikolai I i inostrannye dvory*, p. 248.

191. Nicholas I to Count I. I. Dibich, 26 May (7 June) 1830, in Tatishchev, *Imperator Nikolai I i inostrannye dvory*, p. 247.

192. Tatishchev, *Imperator Nikolai I i inostrannye dvory*, p. 247.

193. Metternich to Count Werner, 31 July 1831 (NS), in *Memoirs of Prince Metternich*, V, p. 133.

194. Metternich to Count Apponyi, 25 January 1832 (NS), in ibid., p. 180.

195. Metternich to Count Apponyi, 14 May 1832 (NS), in ibid., p. 189.

196. *Memoirs of Prince Metternich*, V, p. 19.

197. Prince Metternich to Count Ficquelmont, 13 October 1830 (NS), in ibid., pp. 54–5.

198. ibid., p. 55.

199. Metternich to Baron Hügel. 22 October 1833 (NS), in ibid., pp. 370–371.

200. Metternich to Count Apponyi, 14 May 1832 (NS), in ibid., p. 189.

201. Polievktov, *Nikolai I*, p. 157; Diary of Princess Melanie Metternich (formerly Countess Melanie Zichy-Ferraris), in *Memoirs of Prince Metternich*, V, pp. 302–3.

202. 'Zapiski Benkendorfa' (Shilder), p. 671. Benkendorf's account lists incorrect dates for the entire journey. For correct dates, see Schiemann, III, pp. 231–3, and Princess Melanie Metternich's diary in *Memoirs of Prince Metternich*, V, pp. 300–312.

203. Schiemann, III, pp. 231–3.

204. 'Zapiski Benkendorfa' (Shilder), p. 674.

205. Schiemann, III, pp. 232, 234.

206. Princess Melanie Metternich's

Diary, 10 September 1833 (NS), in *Memoirs of Prince Metternich*, V, p. 307.

207. 'Zapiski Benkendorfa' (Shilder), p. 677.

208. See Nicholas's comments on Baron Brunnov's report in late 1839, in Martens, XII, p. 112.

209. Princess Melanie Metternich's Diary, 10, 11 and 12 September 1833 (NS), in *Memoirs of Prince Metternich*, V, pp. 307–11.

210. Prince Metternich to Baron Hügel, 22 October 1833 (NS), in *Memoirs of Prince Metternich*, V, p. 371.

211. Martens, IV, Pt 1, pp. 445–9.

212. ibid., pp. 454–60.

213. Prince Metternich to Baron Hügel, 22 October 1833 (NS), in *Memoirs of Prince Metternich*, V, p. 369.

214. Martens, IV, Pt. 1, pp. 460–62.

215. Nicholas I to King Friedrich Wilhelm III, 6 (18) September, in Schiemann, III, pp. 436–7. (Italics mine.)

216. Count Esterhazy to Prince Metternich, 29 November 1834 (NS), quoted in Grunwald, p. 188.

CHAPTER 5

THE APOGEE OF AUTOCRACY

1. A. E. Tsimmerman, 'Vospominaniia Generala A. E. Tsimmermana, 1825–1856 gg.', ORGBL, fond 325, karton 1, papka 1/142.

2. Baroness M. P. Frederiks, 'Iz vospominanii', *IV*, LXXI (January 1898), p. 55.

3. A. E. Tsimmerman, 'Vospominaniia', ORGBL, fond 325, karton 1, papka 1/41–2.

4. Baron M. A. Korf, 'Iz zapisok barona Korfa', *RS*, XCVIII (1899), pp. 373–4.

5. *Gosudarstvennyi sovet, 1801–1901 gg.* (St Petersburg, 1902), p. 64.

6. A. I. Herzen, *Polnoe sobranie sochinenii i pisem A. I. Gertsena*, M. K. Lemke (ed.) (St Petersburg, 1919), VII, pp. 279–80.

7. Quoted in M. Florinsky, *Russia: A*

History and an Interpretation (New York, 1968), II, p. 799.

8. M. P. Veselovskii, 'Zapiski M. P. Veselovskago', GPB, fond 550. F. IV, 861/390.

9. N. A. Miliutin to D. A. Miliutin, 10 avgusta 1838 g., ORGBL, fond 169, karton 69, papka No. 6.

10. Queen Victoria to Leopold, King of the Belgians, 4 June 1844 (NS), in Benson and Esher (eds.), *Letters of Queen Victoria*, II, p. 14.

11. Baroness M. P. Frederiks, 'Iz vospominanii', p. 61.

12. 'Zapiski Benkendorfa', (Shilder), pp. 737–8.

13. 'Zapiski Benkendorfa', *RS*, LXXXVII, No. 7 (July 1896), pp. 6–7.

14. Nicholas I, 'Perepiska Imperatora Nikolaia Pavlovicha s velikim kniazem tsesarevichem Konstantinom Pavlovichem, 1825–1829, 1830–1831', *SIRIO*, CXXXI–CXXXII (1910–11), *passim*.

15. S. V. Bakhrushin, 'Velikaia kniaginia Elena Pavlovna', in *Osvobozhdenie krest'ian: deiateli reformy* (Moscow, 1911), pp. 116–17.

16. A. G. Rubinshtein, 'Vospominaniia', *RS*, C, No. 11 (November 1899), pp. 542–543.

17. W. Bruce Lincoln, 'The Composition of the Imperial Russian State Council under Nicholas I', *Canadian-American Slavic Studies*, X, No. 3 (1976), p. 370.

18. LaCroix, VII, p. 4.

19. ibid., p. 5.

20. S. V. Bakhrushin, 'Velikaia kniaginia Elena Pavlovna', p. 131.

21. LaCroix, VII, p. 12.

22. Th. Schiemann, 'Imperator Nikolai Pervyi (iz zapisok i vospominanii sovremennikov)', *RA*, No. 2 (February 1902), pp. 464–5; Grunwald, pp. 139–40.

23. Quoted in Schiemann, III, pp. 317–18.

24. Quoted in I. N. Bozherianov, *Zhizneopisanie*, I, p. 37.

25. Grunwald, p. 216.

26. M. Mandt, *Ein deutscher Arzt am Hofe Kaiser Nikolaus I von Russland* (Munich-Leipzig, 1917), p. 437.

27. Schiemann, III, p. 318; see also II, pp. 366–80, 318.

28. Empress Aleksandra Fedorovna, 'Imperatritsa Aleksandra Fedorovna v svoikh vospominaniiakh', *RS*, No. 10 (October 1896), pp. 21, 25.

29. Quoted in Grunwald, p. 142.

30. Empress Aleksandra Fedorovna, 'Iz dnevnikov Aleksandry Fedorovny', in *Mezhdutsarstvie*, entry for 22 December 1825, p. 92.

31. Baroness M. P. Frederiks, 'Iz vospominanii', pp. 58–60.

32. A. P. Zablotskii-Desiatovskii, *Graf P. D. Kiselev*, II, p. 11.

33. The Prussian envoy Liebermann to Friedrich Wilhelm III, 18 February (2 March) 1839, in Schiemann, III, p. 495.

34. ibid., p. 496.

35. Coronation manifesto of Emperor Nicholas I, quoted in A. A. Kornilov, *Kurs*, II, p. 18.

36. W. Bruce Lincoln, 'The Last Years of the Nicholas "System"', The Unpublished Diaries and Memoirs of Baron Korf and General Tsimmerman', *Oxford Slavonic Papers*, VI (1973), pp. 22–3.

37. LaCroix, VII, pp. 1–20.

38. Quoted in Grunwald, p. 154.

39. Quoted in ibid., p. 154.

40. Riasanovsky, p. 42.

41. Schiemann, IV, p. 233.

42. Grunwald, p. 138.

43. Baron M. A. Korf, 'Imperator Nikolai I v soveshchatel'nykh sobraniiakh', in N. F. Dubrovin (ed.), *Materialy i cherty k biografii Imperatora Nikolaia I*, p. 237.

44. Kn. D. A. Obolenskii, 'Moi vospominaniia o velikoi kniagine Elene Pavlovne', *RS*, CXXXVIII, No. 3 (March 1909), pp. 506–7.

45. L. A. Perovskii, 'O prichinakh umnozheniia deloproizvodstva vo vnutrennem upravlenii', (mart' 1851 g.), TsGIAL, fond 1284, opis' 36, delo No. 137/15.

46. ibid., delo No. 137/14–23; L.

Tengoborskii, 'Extraits du Mémoire sécret du Conseiller Privé Actuel Tengoborskii (ianvar' 1857), TsGIAL, fond 851, opis' 1, delo No. 50/288–91.

47. N. Kutuzov, 'Zapiska: Sostoianie gosudarstva v 1841 godu', *RS*, No. 9 (September 1898), p. 517.

48. Nicholas I to Aleksandra Fedorovna, 18 August 1836, in Schiemann, III, p. 475.

49. Baron M. A. Korf, 'Dnevnik za 1840 g.', TSGAOR, fond 728, opis' 1, delo No. 1817/iii/264.

50. Quoted in Presniakov, *Apogei samoderzhaviia*, p. 14.

51. W. Bruce Lincoln, 'The Ministers of Nicholas I', pp. 319, 320.

52. ibid., p. 320.

53. ibid.

54. ibid., p. 321.

55. ibid., pp. 322–3.

56. *Gosudarstvennyi sovet, 1801–1901 gg.*, p. 19.

57. Baron M. A. Korf, 'Dnevnik za 1847 g.', TsGAOR, fond 728, opis' 1, delo No. 1817/x/140.

58. W. Bruce Lincoln, 'The Composition of the Imperial Russian State Council under Nicholas I', pp. 371–2.

59. Michel Crozier, *The Bureaucratic Phenomenon* (Chicago, 1967), pp. 189–90.

60. Presniakov, *Apogei samoderzhaviia*, p. 46.

61. Marc Raeff, 'The Russian Autocracy and Its Officials', *Harvard Slavic Studies*, IV (1957), pp. 77–92; S. Frederick Starr, *Decentralization*, pp. 44–50; W. Bruce Lincoln, 'The Genesis of an "Enlightened" Bureaucracy in Russia, 1825–1856', pp. 321–30.

62. 'Kratkii obzor deistvii Ministerstva Vnutrennikh Del s 1825 po 1850 god', TsGAOR, fond 722, opis' 1, delo No. 599/104.

63. Hans-Joachim Torke, 'Das russische Beamtentum in der ersten Hälfte des 19. Jahrhunderts', pp. 214–15.

64. W. Bruce Lincoln, 'N. A. Miliutin and the St. Petersburg Municipal Act of 1846: A Study in Reform under Nicholas I', *Slavic Review*, XXXIII, No. 1 (March 1974), p. 58.

65. Zapiski Benkendorfa' (Shilder), pp. 698–9.

66 M. P. Veselovskii, 'Zapiski M. P. Veselovskago, s 1828 po 1882 g.', GPB, fond 550.f.IV.861/390.

67. A. S. Zarudnyi (ed.), 'Pis'mo opytnago chinovnika sorokovykh godov mladshemu sobratu, postupaiushchemu na sluzhbu', *RS*, C, No. 12 (December 1899), pp. 455–6.

68. L. A. Perovskii, 'O prichinakh umnozheniia deloproizvodstva vo vnutrennem upravlenii', (mart' 1851 g.), TsGIAL, fond 1284, opis' 36, Delo No. 137/15.

69. There were a number of committees devoted to this problem during the reign of Nicholas I. For a discussion of the most important one, established in 1852, see S. Frederick Starr, *Decentralization*, pp. 111ff.

70. 'Tsenzura v tsarstvovanie imperatora Nikolaia I', *RS*, CXIV, No. 4 (April 1903), pp. 172–3.

71. ibid., CXIII, No. 2 (February 1903), pp. 305–7.

72. A. V. Golovnin, 'Prodolzhenie zapisok 1868–1870 gg.', TsGIAL, fond 851, opis' 1, delo No. 8/29.

73. 'Imperator Nikolai I i akademik Parrot', *RS*, No. 7 (July 1898), pp. 140–142.

74. N. A. Miliutin, 'Istoricheskaia zapiska o raznykh predpolozheniiakh po predmetu osvobozhdeniia krest'ian', in P. Bartenev (ed.), *Deviatnadtsatyi vek* (Moscow, 1872), II, pp. 145–208; N. M. Druzhinin, *Gosudarstvennye krest'iane i reformy P. D. Kiseleva* (Moscow, 1946), I, pp. 121–96.

75. *Istoriia pravitel'stvuiushchago Senata za dvesti let, 1711–1911 gg.* (St Petersburg, 1911), IV, pp. 513–16.

76. One prominent example was Count Kiselev's survey of a number of areas for which his Ministry of State Domains was responsible in 1836. N. M. Druzhinin, *Gosudarstvennye krest'iane*, I, p. 476.

77. On Benkendorf's death in 1844, Count Orlov, Benkendorf's successor as Head of the Third Section, brought these accounts to Nicholas and, after reading them, Nicholas commented that 'one finds here a very accurate and lively portrayal of my reign' – 'Zapiski Benkendorfa', *RS*, LXXXVI, No. 6 (June 1896), p. 474.

78. ibid., *RS*, LXXXVIII, No. 10 (October 1896), p. 67.

79. One need only recall some of the scenes in N. V. Gogol's play, *The Inspector General*, to see in microcosm how officials in Russia conspired to conceal abuses from imperial adjutants, and even from the Emperor. See N. V. Gogol, *Sobranie sochinenii* (Moscow 1959), IV, pp. 5–96.

80. A. S. Zarudnyi (ed.), 'Pis'mo opytnago chinovnika', *RS*, C, No. 12 (December 1899), pp. 543–4.

81. Aleksandr Kamenskii, 'Vsepoddanneishaia zapiska Kamenskago 1850 goda', *RS*, CXII, No. 6 (June 1905), p. 631.

82. W. Bruce Lincoln, 'The Composition of the Imperial Russian State Council under Nicholas I', pp. 376–8.

83. A. V. Nikitenko, *Dnevnik* (Moscow, 1955), I, pp. 126–7.

84. A. D. Borovkov, 'Avtobiograficheskiia zapiski A. D. Borovkova', *RS*, XCV, No. 12 (December 1898), pp. 591–616.

85. Even relatively progressive ministers shared this failing. Count Kiselev, for example, refused to allow his nephew N. A. Miliutin to take part in a Ministry of State Domains fact-finding survey in the summer of 1839 because Miliutin was serving in a different ministry – Pis'mo N. A. Miliutina k D. A. Miliutinu, 10 avgusta 1839 g., ORGBL, fond 169, karton 69, papka No. 6.

86. A. N. Radishchev, *A Journey from St Petersburg to Moscow*, translated by Leo Wiener (Cambridge, Mass., 1958), p. 68.

87. 'Otchet inspektorskomu departamentu grazhdanskomu vedomstva za 1847, 1850, i 1855 gg.', TsGIAL, fond 1409, opis' 2, delo No. 6829.

88. A. I. Herzen, *My Past and Thoughts*, trans. by C. Garnett (New York, 1968), II, pp. 433–7.

89. Arkhiv tret'ego otdeleniia Sobstvennogo Ego Imperatorskago Velichestva. TsGAOR, fond 109, opis' 440, delo No. 1849/1–20.

90. LaCroix, VII, pp. 22–4.

91. ibid., pp. 47–9.

92. Grunwald, p. 135.

93. LaCroix, VII, p. 25.

94. Quoted in Grunwald, p. 136.

95. A. Korsakov, 'Detstvo i otrochestvo Nikolaia Pavlovicha', *RA*, No. 2 (June 1896), p. 282.

96. A. E. Tsimmerman, 'Vospominaniia Generala A. E. Tsimmermana', ORGBL, fond 325, karton 1, papka, 2/168.

97. A. V. Nikitenko, *Dnevnik*, I, pp. 328–9.

98. 'Imperator Nikolai I i akademik Parrot', *RS*, No. 7 (July 1898), pp. 145–6; A. V. Golovnin, 'Kratkii ocherk deistvii Velikago Kniazia Konstantina Nikolaevicha po Morskomu Vedomstvu, so vremeni vstupleniia v upravlenie onym po ianvar' 1858 g.', GPB, fond 208, No. 2/269–70.

99. This material, and the discussion of Russian economic policy which follows, is much indebted to Professor Walter Pintner's *Russian Economic Policy under Nicholas I* (Ithaca, 1967), which is one of the best analyses available. A broader, and also important, study of Russian industrial development and economic policy in the first six decades of the nineteenth century is W. L. Blackwell, *The Beginnings of Russian Industrialization, 1800–1861* (Princeton, 1968).

100. W. M. Pintner, *Russian Economic Policy*, p. 3.

101. Blackwell, *The Beginnings of Russian Industrialization*, p. 431.

102. M. M. Speranskii, 'O zakonakh. Besedy grafa M. M. Speranskago s Ego Imperatorskim Vysochestvom Gosudarem

Naslednikom Tsesarevichem Velikim Kniazem Aleksandrom Nikolaevichem, s 12 oktiabria 1835 po 10 aprelia 1837 goda', *SIRIO*, XXX (1880), p. 371.

103. B. N. Liddell Hart, 'Armed Forces: Armies', in J. P. T. Bury (ed.), *New Cambridge Modern History* (Cambridge, 1960), X, pp. 302–31; and Michael Lewis, 'Armed Forces: Navies', in ibid., pp. 274–301.

104. See Pintner, *Russian Economic Policy*, p. 253.

105. ibid., p. 184.

106. There were also, for a brief time in the 1830s, platinum coins issued in Russia.

107. P. A. Shtorkh, 'Materialy dlia istorii gosudarstvennykh denezhnykh znakov v Rossii s 1653 po 1840 god', *Zhurnal Ministerstva Narodnago Prosveshcheniia*, CXXXVII (1868), pp. 822–823.

108. For a very perceptive summary of this question, see Pintner, *Russian Economic Policy*, pp. 187–96.

109. ibid., p. 193.

110. I. I. Kaufman, *Iz istorii bumazhnykh deneg v Rossii* (St Petersburg, 1909), pp. 97–8.

111. P. E. Mosely, *Russian Diplomacy and the Opening of the Eastern Question* (Cambridge, Mass., 1934), pp. 37–8.

112. P. P. Mel'nikov, 'Svedeniia o russkikh zheleznykh dorog', *KA*, XCIV (1940), pp. 164–5; Blackwell, *The Beginnings of Russian Industrialization*, p. 280; R. M. Haywood, *The Beginnings of Railway Development in Russia in the Reign of Nicholas I, 1835–1842* (Durham, 1969), pp. 201–3.

113. Pintner, *Russian Economic Policy*, pp. 207–8, 209.

114. A summary of these decrees is available in ibid., p. 210.

115. Baron M. A. Korf, 'Imperator Nikolai v soveshchatel'nykh sobraniiakh', in N. F. Dubrovin (ed.), *Materialy i cherty k biografii Imperatora Nikolaia I*, pp. 124–8.

116. Blackwell, *The Beginnings of*

Russian Industrialization, p. 273; Haywood, *The Beginnings of Railway Development in Russia*, pp. 182–7.

117. V. S. Virginskii, *Vozniknovenie zheleznykh dorog v Rossii do nachala 40-kh godov XIX v.* (Moscow, 1949), pp. 130–131.

118. Haywood, *The Beginnings of Railway Development in Russia*, pp. 92–9; Blackwell, *The Beginnings of Russian Industrialization*, pp. 275–7; Pintner, *Russian Economic Policy*, pp. 140–41.

119. Pintner, *Russian Economic Policy*, p. 140.

120. Virginskii, *Vozniknovenie zheleznykh dorog v Rossii*, pp. 140–43.

121. N. A. Kislinskii, *Nasha zheleznodorozhnaia politika po dokumentam arkhiva Komiteta Ministrov* (St Petersburg, 1902), I, pp. 18–19; Virginskii, *Vozniknovenie zheleznykh dorog v Rossii*, pp. 189–90.

122. Virginskii, *Vozniknovenie zheleznykh dorog v Rossii*, pp. 222–3.

123. J. H. Clapham, *The Economic Development of France and Germany, 1815–1914* (Cambridge, 1951), p. 146.

124. H. Heaton, 'Economic Change and Growth', in *New Cambridge Modern History*, X, p. 33.

125. W. L. Langer, *Political and Social Upheaval, 1832–1852* (New York and London, 1969), p. 28.

126. Heaton, 'Economic Change and Growth', p. 32.

127. *Gosudarstvennyi sovet, 1801–1901 gg.*, p. 64.

128. P. I. Liashchenko, *Istoriia narodnago khoziaistva SSSR* (Moscow, 1956), I, p. 570. See also P. Péchoux, 'L'Ombre de Pugačev', in R. Portal (ed.), *Le Statut des paysans libérés du servage, 1861–1961* (Paris and The Hague, 1963), pp. 128–52.

129. *Gosudarstvennyi sovet, 1801–1901 gg.*, p. 64.

130. A summary of the work of these committees can be found in N. A. Miliutin, 'Istoricheskaia zapiska o raznykh predpolozheniiakh po predmetu osvobozhdeniia krest'ian', in P. Bartenev,

Deviatnadtsatyi vek: istoricheskii sbornik, II, pp. 145–208; N. M. Druzhinin, *Gosudarstvennye krest'iane*, I, pp. 121–95; V. I. Semevskii, *Krest'ianskii vopros v Rossii v XVIII i pervoi polovine XIX veka* (St Petersburg, 1888), II, pp. 1–162.

131. M. Florinsky, *Russia: A History and An Interpretation*, II, p. 778.

132. A. P. Zablotskii-Desiatovskii, *Graf P. D. Kiselev*, I, pp. 47, 83, 205–29.

133. ibid., p. 324.

134. W. Bruce Lincoln, *Nikolai Miliutin: An Enlightened Russian Bureaucrat* (Newtonville, Mass., 1977), pp. 75–100; I. I. Kostiushko, *Krest'ianskaia reforma 1864 goda v tsarstve Pol'skom* (Moscow, 1962), pp. 75–183.

135. See V. Ia. Grosul, *Reformy v Dunaiskikh kniazhestvakh i Rossiia* (Moscow, 1966), pp. 206–10, 212–36.

136. The text of this memorandum is supplied in A. P. Zablotskii-Desiatovskii, *Graf P. D. Kiselev*, IV, pp. 197–9.

137. N. M. Druzhinin, *Gosudarstvennye krest'iane*, I, pp. 275–7.

138. This statute was implemented in Wallachia on 1 July 1831, and in Moldavia on 1 January 1832 – Grosul, *Reformy*, pp. 261, 322.

139. ibid., pp. 284–8.

140. ibid., pp. 374–8.

141. A. O. Smirnova Rosset, *Avtobiografiia*, edited by L. V. Krestov (Moscow, 1931), p. 154.

142. This account is published in A. P. Zablotskii-Desiatovskii, *Graf P. D. Kiselev*, IV, see also II, p. 2.

143. ibid., p. 11.

144. 'Graf P. D. Kiselev', *Russkii biograficheskii slovar'* (Moscow and St Petersburg, 1896–1918), VII, p. 713.

145. See N. M. Druzhinin, *Gosudarstvennye krest'iane*, I, on which this and following paragraph are based, esp. pp. 45, 182–3, 295, 299–475, 476, 480–81.

146. P. Dukes, *Catherine the Great and the Russian Nobility* (Cambridge, 1967), *passim*; M. Polievktov, pp. 210–13; A. A. Kiesewetter, *Istoricheskie ocherki*, pp. 273–86.

147. Quoted in 'Graf P. D. Kiselev', *Russkii biograficheskii slovar'*, VIII, p. 713.

148. N. M. Druzhinin, *Gosudarstvennye krest'iane*, I, pp. 476–610.

149. W. Bruce Lincoln, 'The Circle of Grand Duchess Elena Pavlovna, 1847–1861', *Slavonic and East European Review*, XLVIII, No. 112 (July 1970), pp. 373–87.

150. N. M. Druzhinin, *Gosudarstvennye krest'iane*, I, pp. 476–531.

151. A. P. Zablotskii-Desiatovskii, *Graf P. D. Kiselev*, II, pp. 229–59; V. I. Semevskii, *Krest'ianskii vopros v Rossii v XVIII i pervoi polovine XIX veke*, II, pp. 111–15, 118–31, 154–9, 190–2.

152. I. Engelman, *Istoriia krepostnago prava v Rossii* (Moscow, 1906), pp. 277–8.

153. These figures are approximate. According to the census of 1858, there were 22,846,054 serfs of both sexes in the Empire, and there were 27,397,289 state peasants of both sexes. See Jerome Blum, *Lord and Peasant in Russia from the Ninth to the Nineteenth Century* (Princeton, 1961), p. 477.

154. N. M. Druzhinin, *Gosudarstvennye krest'iane*, I, pp. 275–7.

155. 'Pamiati Andreia Parfenovicha Zablotskago', *RS*, XXXIII, No. 2 (February 1882), p. 520.

156. W. Bruce Lincoln, 'Russia's "Enlightened" Bureaucrats and the Problem of State Reform, 1848–1856', *Cahiers du monde russe et soviétique*, XII, No. 4 (October–December 1971), pp. 418–21.

CHAPTER 6

EUROPE'S GENDARME EMERGES

1. Count Ficquelmont to Metternich, 2 January 1835 (NS), quoted in Grunwald, p. 191.

2. Quoted in S. S. Tatishchev, *Vneshniaia politika*, p. 307.

3. Metternich to Baron Neumann, 15 February 1833 (NS), in *Mémoires, documents, et écrits divers laissés par le Prince de Metternich, Chancelier de cour et d'état* (Paris, 1882), V, p. 491.

4. Baron F. I. Brunnov, 'Obzor politiki russkago dvora v nvneshnee

tsarstvovanie', quoted in S. S. Tatishchev, *Vneshniaia politika*, p. 307.

5. S. Zhigarev, *Russkaia politika*, p. 327; Tatishchev, *Vneshniaia politika*, p. 145.

6. M. Florinsky, *Russia: A History and An Interpretation*, I, p. 564.

7. Quoted in Tatishchev, *Vneshniaia politika*, p. 138.

8. Martens, IV, p. 440.

9. A. V. Fadeev, *Rossiia i vostochnyi krizis 20-kh godov XIX veka* (Moscow, 1958), pp. 337–53.

10. J. A. R. Marriott, *The Eastern Question*, p. 231.

11. S. S. Tatishchev, *Vneshniaia politika*, p. 343.

12. ibid., pp. 343–4.

13. Frederick S. Rodkey, *The Turko–Egyptian Question in the Relations of England, France, and Russia, 1832–1841* (Urbana, 1924), p. 14.

14. H. Seton-Watson, *The Russian Empire*, p. 302.

15. Marriott, *The Eastern Question*, p. 233.

16. Metternich to Count Prokesch-Osten, 3 February 1833 (NS), in *Mémoires, documents, et écrits divers*, V, pp. 495–500.

17. Quoted in S. M. Goriainow, *Le Bosphore et les Dardanelles* (Paris, 1910), pp. 30, 29.

18. Quoted in ibid., p. 30.

19. Nicholas's instruction to General N. N. Murav'ev, quoted in Tatishchev, *Vneshniaia politika*, p. 352.

20. Pis'mo A. P. Buteneva k Lavizonu, 18 (30) July 1832, in Tatishchev, *Vneshniaia politika*, p. 346.

21. Nesselrode to Prince Lieven, 10(22) September, 1829, in Martens, XI, p. 412.

22. Quoted in Tatishchev, *Vneshniaia politika*, p. 352.

23. Goriainow, *Le Bosphore*, p. 31; Tatishchev, *Vneshniaia politika*, p. 359.

24. Tatishchev, *Vneshniaia politika*, pp. 361–2.

25. Goriainow, *Le Bosphore*, p. 31.

26. Tatishchev, *Vneshniaia politika*, p. 367.

27. Goriainow, *Le Bosphore*, p. 32.

28. Metternich to Count Prokesch-Osten, 3 February 1833 (NS), in *Mémoires, documents, et écrits divers*, V, p. 496.

29. Tatishchev, *Vneshniaia politika*, p. 353.

30. Baron von Stockmar, *Memoirs*, II, p. 107.

31. Tatishchev, *Vneshniaia politika*, p. 374.

32. Goriainow, *Le Bosphore*, p. 33.

33. Nicholas's instructions to Count Orlov, 8 April 1833, quoted in ibid., pp. 33–4.

34. ibid., p. 33.

35. H. Seton-Watson, *The Russian Empire*, p. 303.

36. Count Orlov to Count Nesselrode, 17 May 1833, quoted in Goriainow, *Le Bosphore*, p. 37.

37. Tatishchev, *Vneshniaia politika*, p. 378.

38. Quoted in Goriainow, *Le Bosphore*, p. 34.

39. Quotes from ibid., pp. 38–9, 40.

40. F. Guizot, *Mémoires pour servir à l'histoire de mon temps* (Paris-Leipzig, 1861), IV, p. 49.

41. Harold Temperley, *England and the Near East: The Crimea* (London-New York, 1936), p. 72.

42. 'Admiral A. S. Menshikov to Nesselrode', *Reports to the Emperor*, 4 January 1838, published in P. E. Mosely, *Russian Diplomacy and the Opening of the Eastern Question*, Appendix A, p. 141.

43. 'Nesselrode's Report to the Emperor, January 16, 1838', published in ibid., p. 147.

44. See Martens, XV, pp. 147, 148–9.

45. ibid., IV, p. 440.

46. Quoted in Temperley, p. 73.

47. ibid., pp. 73–4.

48. ibid., p. 77.

49. See ibid., pp. 75, 76, for this and following quotes.

50. Grosul, *Reformy*, pp. 374–9.

51. Seton-Watson, *The Russian Empire*, p. 304.

52. Quoted in Temperley, p. 75.

53. Lord Palmerston to Sir William Temple, 21 November (3 December) 1833, quoted in Tatishchev, *Vneshniaia politika*, p. 397.

54. Temperley, p. 80.

55. Martens, IV, pp. 464–5.

56. Mosely, *Russian Diplomacy and the Opening of the Eastern Question*, pp. 48–9.

57. Quoted in Tatishchev, *Vneshniaia politika*, p. 352.

58. Mosely, *Russian Diplomacy and the Opening of the Eastern Question*, p. 50.

59. Lord Palmerston to Granville, 8 June 1838 (NS), in Baron Henry Lytton Bulwer, *Life of Henry John Temple, Viscount Palmerston* (London, 1871–4), II, p. 269.

60. The literature on this problem is voluminous. Some of the most useful studies include: Temperley, *England and the Near East*; Goriainow, *Le Bosphore et les Dardanelles*; C. K. Webster, *The Foreign Policy of Palmerston, 1830–1841* (London, 1951); Eugène de Guichen, *La Crise d'orient de 1839 à 1841 et l'Europe* (Paris, 1921); F. S. Rodkey, *The Turko-Egyptian Question*; Mosely, *Russian Diplomacy and the Opening of the Eastern Question*; and S. S. Tatishchev, *Vneshniaia politika imperatora Nikolaia I.*

61. Helmuth C. B. von Moltke, 'Briefe über Zustände und Begebenheiten in der Türkei aus den Jahren 1835 bis 1839', in *Gesammelte Schriften und Denswürdigseiten bis General-Feldmarschalls Grafen Helmuth von Molkte* (Berlin, 1893), VIII, pp. 207–397.

62. Tatishchev, *Vneshniaia politika*, p. 421.

63. Moltke, 'Briefe über Zustände und Begebenheiten in der Türkei aus den Jahren 1835 bis 1839', pp. 357–442.

64. Rodkey, *The Turko–Egyptian Question*, p. 105.

65. ibid., p. 109.

66. Mosely, *Russian Diplomacy and the Opening of the Eastern Question*, pp. 40–43.

67. Metternich to his wife, the Princess Melanie, 22 July 1838 (NS), in *Mémoires, documents, et écrits divers*, VI, p. 296.

68. Metternich to his wife, the Princess Melanie, 19 July 1838 (NS), in ibid., p. 294.

69. Mosely, *Russian Diplomacy and the Opening of the Eastern Question*, pp. 56–7.

70. For a discussion of this incident, see Martens, XII, pp. 62–3.

71. ibid., pp. 70–71.

72. Quotes from ibid., p. 73.

73. Mosely, *Russian Diplomacy and the Opening of the Eastern Question*, p. 57.

74. ibid., p. 52.

75. Quoted in ibid., p. 60.

76. Quotes from Martens, XII, p. 112.

77. Quoted in ibid., p. 107.

78. ibid., p. 108.

79. Mosely, *Russian Diplomacy and the Opening of the Eastern Question*, pp. 134–8.

80. Nicholas's instructions to Brunnov, 16 August 1839, in Martens, XII, p. 109.

81. ibid., p. 110.

82. Baron Brunnov to Count Nesselrode, 12 (24) September 1839, in Martens, XII, p. 111.

83. ibid., p. 114.

84. ibid.

85. Quoted in ibid., p. 119.

86. ibid., p. 115.

87. 'Zapiski Benkendorfa' (Shilder), pp. 652–3.

88. Quoted in Martens, XII, p. 114.

89. ibid., p. 115.

90. Quoted in ibid., p. 116.

91. Baron von Stockmar, *Memoirs*, II, p. 106.

92. See Martens, XII, pp. 117, 119, 120.

93. Goriainow, *Le Bosphore*, p. 73.

94. ibid., p. 74; Martens, XII, p. 125.

95. ibid., p. 128.

96. For the text of this document, see ibid., pp. 130–41.

97. Rodkey, *The Turko–Egyptian Question*, pp. 164–94.

98. Quoted in Martens, XII, p. 146.

99. Temperley, p. 118.

100. Martens, XII, pp. 155–9.

101. Marriott, *The Eastern Question*, pp. 244–5.

102. Martens, XII, p. 154.

103. Tatishchev, 'Imperator Nikolai I v Londone', *IV*, XXIII, No. 2 (February 1886), p. 351; V. Puryear, *England, Russia, and the Straits Question, 1844–1856* (Berkeley, 1931), p. 41.

104. Tatishchev, 'Imperator Nikolai I v Londone', p. 353.

105. Queen Victoria to Leopold, King of the Belgians, 11 June 1844 (NS), in Benson and Esher (eds.), *Letters of Queen Victoria*, II, p. 16.

106. Tatishchev, 'Imperator Nikolai I v Londone', *IV*, XXIII, No. 3 (March, 1886), pp. 602–3.

107. 'Zapiski Benkendorfa' (Shilder), p. 693.

108. Nicholas I, 'Zaveshchanie Nikolaia I synu', *KA*, III (1923), pp. 291–3.

109. *The Times* (London), 3 June 1844, p. 6.

110. Tatishchev, 'Imperator Nikolai I v Londone', No. 3, p. 603.

111. Baron von Stockmar, *Memoirs*, II, p. 110.

112. Puryear, *England, Russia, and the Straits Question*, p. 44.

113. Baron von Stockmar, *Memoirs*, II, pp. 107–8.

114. Queen Victoria to Leopold, King of the Belgians, 11 June 1844 (NS), in Benson and Esher (eds.), *Letters of Queen Victoria*, II, p. 17.

115. Puryear, *England, Russia, and the Straits Question*, pp. 50–51.

116. Queen Victoria to Leopold, King of the Belgians, 11 June 1844 (NS), in Benson and Esher (eds.), *Letters of Queen Victoria*, II, pp. 16–17.

117. Dispatch to Tatishchev (Russian Ambassador in Vienna), 13 (25) April 1839, in Martens, IV, p. 477.

118. ibid., p. 463.

119. Dispatch of Brunnov, 26 August (7 September) 1839, in ibid., VIII, p. 242.

120. Polievktov, pp. 159–60.

121. Quoted in Martens, VIII, p. 229,

122. Report of Ribeaupierre, 11 (23) March 1834, in ibid.

123. ibid., IV, p. 468.

124. Dispatch to Tatishchev, 13 (25) May 1837, in ibid., p. 477.

125. See, for example, the dispatches of Peter von Meiendorf from Stuttgart and Berlin, in Meiendorf, *Politischer und privater briefweschel, 1826–1863* (Berlin and Leipzig, 1923), I, *passim*.

126. 'Zapiski Benkendorfa' (Shilder), pp. 720–21.

127. ibid., p. 693.

128. Tatishchev, *Imperator Nikolai I i inostrannye dvory: Istoricheskie ocherki* (St Petersburg, 1889), p. 256.

129. 'Zapiski Benkendorfa', (Shilder), p. 693.

130. Prince Metternich, *Mémoires, documents, et écrits divers*, VI, p. 86.

131. Grunwald, p. 191.

132. Princess Melanie's Diary, entry for 12 October 1835 (NS), in Metternich, *Mémoires, documents, et écrits divers*, VI, p. 23.

133. Tatishchev, *Imperator Nikolai I i inostrannye dvory*, pp. 344–70.

134. ibid., p. 268; W. Bruce Lincoln, 'The Emperor Nicholas I in England', p. 27.

135. This was Baron Stockmar's view. Quoted in Tatishchev, *Imperator Nikolai I i inostrannye dvory*, p. 258.

136. Martens, VIII, p. 229.

137. ibid., pp. 364–7.

138. Letter of Nicholas to Aleksandra Fedorovna, 19 December 1845, in Schiemann, IV, p. 380.

139. Martens, IV, pp. 533–6; VIII, 368–70.

140. ibid., p. 229; IV, pp. 468, 477.

141. Polievktov, pp. 159–60.

142. J. S. Curtiss, *The Russian Army under Nicholas I, 1825–1855* (Durham, 1965), pp. 212–32.

143. W. Bruce Lincoln, 'The Daily Life of St Petersburg Officials', pp. 97–8.

144. See P. A. Zaionchkovskii, *Voennye reformy 1860–1870 godov v Rossii* (Moscow, 1952), pp. 17, 38.

145. Curtiss, *The Russian Army*, pp. 120, 121.

146. Comment by Major-General N. Gerasevanov, quoted in ibid., p. 121.

CHAPTER 7

NICHOLAS AND RUSSIA'S
INTELLECTUALS

1. K. D. Kavelin to T. N. Granovskii, 4 March 1855, in Sh. M. Levin, 'K. D. Kavelin o smerti Nikolaia I', *Literaturnoe nasledstvo*, LXVII (Moscow, 1959), p. 610.

2. 'Tsenzura v tsarstvovanie imperatora Nikolaia I', *RS*, CVII, No. 8 (August, 1901), pp. 395–7.

3. Monas, *The Third Section*, p. 139.

4. *Russkaia periodicheskaia pechat'*, *1702–1894 gg.* (Moscow, 1959), pp. 746–782.

5. Quoted in Monas, *The Third Section*, p. 140.

6. Quoted in ibid., p. 141.

7. K. Sivkov, 'S. N. Glinka', *Russkii biograficheskii slovar'*, V, p. 294.

8. Quoted in Monas, *The Third Section*, p. 142.

9. 'Tsenzura v tsarstvovanie imperatora Nikolaia I', *RS*, CVII, No. 9 (September 1901), pp. 643–5.

10. Quoted in Monas, *The Third Section*, p. 142.

11. 'Tsenzura v tsarstvovanie imperatora Nikolaia I', *RS*, CVII, No. 9 (September 1901), pp. 643–5.

12. ibid., p. 644.

13. Monas, *The Third Section*, p. 145.

14. Quoted in ibid., p. 146.

15. I. Miklashevskii, 'Statistika', *Entsiklopedicheskii slovar' Brokgauza-Eifrona* (St Petersburg, 1901), LXII, pp. 476–505.

16. P. P. Semenov-Tian-Shanskii, *Istoriia poluvekovoi deiatel'nosti imperatorskago russkago geograficheskago obshchestva, 1845–1895* (St Petersburg, 1896), I, pp. 19–31, 70–87, 88–95.

17. Th. Dan, *The Origins of Bolshevism*, translated by J. Carmichael (New York, 1964), pp. 39–55.

18. The best treatment of the question of Official Nationality by far is N. Riasanovsky, *Nicholas I and Official Nationality in Russia, 1825–1855* (Berkeley and Los Angeles, 1959), a work not likely to be superseded in the near future. Portions of the following section are much indebted to Professor Riasanovsky's excellent study.

19. Tsar Ivan IV to Prince Andrei Kurbskii, 5 July 1564, in J. L. I. Fennell, *The Correspondence between Prince A. M. Kurbskii and Tsar Ivan IV of Russia, 1564–1579* (Cambridge, 1955), pp. 13–15.

20. Presniakov, *Apogei samoderzhaviia*, p. 4.

21. P. Miliukov, *Ocherki po istorii russkoi kul'tury* (St Petersburg, 1901), III, pp. 408–23.

22. N. M. Karamzin, *Karamzin's Memoir on Ancient and Modern Russia*, translated and edited by Richard Pipes (Cambridge, Mass., 1959), pp. 5–6.

23. Quoted in Riasanovsky, p. 74.

24. S. S. Uvarov, 'Tsikuliarnoe predlozhenie G. Upravliaiushchego Ministerstva Narodnago Prosveshcheniia Nachal'stvam Uchevnykh Okrugov 'O vstuplenii v upravlenie Ministerstvom'', 21 March 1833, *Zhurnal Ministerstva Narodnago Prosveshcheniia*, I, part 1, (1834), p. 49.

25. Quoted in Riasanovsky, p. 75.

26. Quoted in S. F. Starr, *Decentralization*, p. 53.

27. S. P. Shevyrev, 'Vzgliad russkago na sovremennoe obrazovanie Evropy', *Moskvitianin*, No. 1 (1841), pp. 292–3.

28. Riasanovsky, p. 78.

29. Nicholas to Prince Gorchakov, 25 November 1854, in Polievktov, p. 376.

30. Nicholas to King Friedrich Wilhelm IV, 26 August 1854, in Schiemann, IV, pp. 434–5.

31. Riasanovsky, p. 85.

32. Quoted in Schiemann, III, pp. 327–8.

33. Quoted in Presniakov, *Apogei samoderzhaviia*, p. 14.

34. Quoted in Schiemann, IV, p. 209.

35. Nicholas I to Prince Paskevich, 17 January 1854, in Schiemann, IV, p. 305.

36. See Riasanovsky, pp. 79–96, for an excellent summary of some of the most important of these works.

37. ibid., p. 84.

38. N. V. Gogol', *Polnoe sobranie sochinenii N. V. Gogolia* (Moscow, 1913), VIII, p. 107.

39. Baron August Ludwig Maria von Haxthausen Abbenberg, *The Russian Empire: Its People and Resources*, translated by Robert Farie (London, 1856), I, p. 335.

40. 'Svod osnovykh gosudarstvennykh zakonov', article I, *Svod zakonov rossiiskoi imperii* (St Petersburg, 1897), I, pt. 1.

41. ibid., article 47.

42. Quoted in Riasanovsky, pp. 97, 98.

43. N. V. Gogol', *Polnoe sobranie sochinenii N. V. Gogolia* (Moscow, 1913), VIII, p. 42.

44. ibid., p. 41.

45. Baron M. A. Korf, 'Dnevnik za 1841 g.', TsGAOR, fond 728, opis' 1, delo No. 1817/iv/167.

46. See above, pp. 178–9.

47. Riasanovsky, p. 98.

48. ibid., p. 99.

49. Baron Haxthausen, *The Russian Empire*, I, p. 335.

50. Quoted in Riasanovsky, p. 99.

51. 'Tsenzura v tsarstvovanie imperatora Nikolaia I', *RS*, CVII, No. 9 (September 1901), p. 664.

52. Quoted in Presniakov, *Apogei samoderzhaviia*, p. 13.

53. Quoted in ibid., p. 13.

54. Quoted in Riasanovsky, p. 100.

55. See, for example, 'Alfavitnyi spisok knigam zapreshchennym komitetom tsenzury inostrannoi v 1849 i 1850 gg.', TsGIAL, fond 1284, Opis' 34, delo Ho. 46 and opis' No. 35, Delo No. 3.

56. 'Tsenzura v tsarstvovanie imperatora Nikolaia I', *RS*, CVII, No. 19 (September 1901), pp. 649–50.

57. Nikitenko, *Dnevnik*, I, pp. 328–9.

58. Nicholas I, 'Rech' Imperatora Nikolaia k deputatam peterburgskago dvorianstva', 21 marta 1848 g., in M. Gershenzon (ed.), *Epokha Nikolaia I*, (Moscow, 1910), p. 10.

59. Riasanovsky, p. 124.

60. N. D. Chechulin (ed.), *Nakaz Imperatritsy Ekateriny II, dannyi kommissii o sochinenii proekta novago ulozheniia* (St Petersburg, 1907), p. 2.

61. Baron M. A. Korf, *The Accession of Nicholas I*, 3rd impression (first published) (London, 1857), pp. 275–6.

62. ibid, p. 276.

63. Quoted in Grunwald, p. 154.

64. S. P. Shevyrev, 'Vzgliad russkago na sovremennoe obrazovanie Evropy', *Moskvitianin*, No. 1 (1841), p. 219.

65. M. P. Pogodin, *Istoriko-politicheskie pis'ma i zapiska v prodolzhenii Krymskoi voiny, 1853–1856* (Moscow, 1874), p. 254.

66. S. P. Shevyrev, 'Lektsii o russkoi literature', *Sbornik otdeleniia russkago iazkya i slovesnosti Imperatorskoi Akademii Nauk*, XXXIII, No. 5 (St Petersburg, 1884), p. 5.

67. F. I. Tiutchev, 'La Russie et la Révolution', *Polnoe sobranie sochinenii F. I. Tiutcheva* (St Petersburg, 1913), p. 344.

68. 'Manifest 14 marta 1848 g.', in Gershenzon (ed.), *Epokha Nikolaia I*, p. 9.

69. Quoted in Schiemann, IV, p. 235.

70. M. P. Pogodin, 'Pis'mo k Gosudariu Tsesarevichu, Velikomu Kniaziu Aleksandru Nikolaevichu, v 1838 godu', *Istoriko-politicheskie pis'ma*, p. 2.

71. Riasanovsky, p. 78.

72. This is a subject which has long occupied the attention of scholars, and one on which considerable excellent work has been done. Even a listing of the important works in English would be far too lengthy. For a brief, and excellent survey of the problem, see Sir Isaiah Berlin, 'The Marvellous Decade', *Encounter*, 1955–1956. Citations to further materials can be found in the bibliographies of M. Malia, *Alexander Herzen and the Origins of Russian Socialism*

(Cambridge, Mass., 1961), and N. Riasanovsky, *Russia and the West in the Teachings of the Slavophiles. A Study of Romantic Ideology* (Cambridge, Mass., 1952).

73. See, for example, D. A. Korsakov, 'Artemii Petrovich Volynskii i ego konfidenty', *RS*, No. 10 (October, 1885), pp. 22–4; 'Zapiski ob Artemii Volynskom', *Chteniia v Imperatorskom obshchestve istorii i drevnostei rossiiskikh pri Moskovskom Universitete* (1858), bk 2, section 5. Iu. V. Got'e, 'Proekt o popravlenii gosudarstvennykh del Artemiia Petrovicha Volynskago', *Dela i Dni*, III (1922), pp. 1–31; P. N. Miliukov, *Ocherki po istorii russkoi kul'tury*, III, pp. 209–17.

74. M. M. Shcherbatov, 'Puteshestvie v zemliu Ofirskuiu g-na S . . . shvetskago dvorianina', *Sochineniia kniazia M. M. Shcherbatova* (St Petersburg, 1896), I, pp. 793–5.

75. For a thoughtful discussion of this problem, see Hans Rogger, *National Consciousness in Eighteenth-Century Russia* (Cambridge, Mass., 1960).

76. P. N. Miliukov, *Ocherki po istorii Russkoi kul'tury*, III, pp. 248–79; 335–41.

77. G. P. Makogonenko, *Nikolai Novikov*, pp. 419–84.

78. See the following studies for useful treatments of freemasonry in eighteenth-century Russia: A. N. Pypin, *Russkoe masonstvo – XVIII i pervaia chervert' XIX v.* (Petrograd, 1918); G. V. Vernadskii, *Russkoe masonstvo XVIII v.* (Petrograd, 1918).

79. A. N. Radishchev, *Izbrannye filosofskie i obshchestvenno-politicheskie proizvedeniia* (Moscow, 1952).

80. V. G. Belinskii, *Sobranie sochinenii V. G. Belinskago*, edited by Ivanov-Razumnik (Petrograd, 1919), III, p. 827.

81. Richard Pipes, *Russia under the Old Regime* (New York, 1974), p. 259.

82. M. Malia, *Alexander Herzen*, p. 41. Malia's work is a model of an intellectual biography, and is fundamental for the study of this problem.

83. B. N. Chicherin, *Vospominaniia Borisa Nikolaevicha Chicherina: Moskva sorokovykh godov* (Moscow, 1929), pp. 5–6; Malia, *Alexander Herzen*, p. 279.

84. Quoted by Ivanov-Razumnik, 'Obshchestvennye i umstvennye techeniia 30-kh godov', in D. N. Ovsianniko-Kulikovskii (ed.), *Istoriia russkoi literatury XIX veka* (Moscow, 1909), I, p. 247.

85. V. G. Belinskii to V. P. Botkin, 13 June, 1840, in E. A. Liatskii (ed.), *Belinskii: Pis'ma* (St Petersburg, 1914), II, p. 129.

86. Malia, *Alexander Herzen*, p. 64.

87. Quoted in Ivanov-Razumnik, 'Obshchestvennye i umstvennye techeniia 30-kh godov', I, p. 260.

88. E. Brown, *Stankevich and His Moscow Circle, 1830–1840* (Stanford, 1961), pp. 7–8.

89. Ivanov-Razumnik, 'Obshchestvennye i umstvennye techeniia 30-kh godov', p. 261.

90. P. N. Miliukov, 'Liubov' u idealistov tridtsatykh godov', *Iz istorii russkoi intelligentsii* (St Petersburg, 1903), pp. 84–94.

91. V. G. Belinskii to V. P. Botkin, April 1840, in Liatskii, *Belinskii: Pis'ma*, II, p. 121.

92. V. G. Belinskii to V. P. Botkin, 11 December 1840, in ibid., p. 190.

93. Malia, *Alexander Herzen*, p. 211.

94. Herbert E. Bowman, *Vissarion Belinskii, 1811–1848: A Study in the Origins of Social Criticism in Russia* (Cambridge, Mass., 1854), pp. 127–30.

95. P. V. Annenkov, *Literaturnye vospominaniia* (Moscow, 1960), pp. 209–212.

96. Quoted in Ch. Vetrinskii, 'Umstvennoe i oshchestvennoe dvizhenie sorokovykh godov', in Ovsianniko-Kulkovskii, *Istoriia russkoi literatury XIX veka*, II, p. 100.

97. N. Riasanovsky, *Russia and the West in the Teachings of the Slavophiles* (Cambridge, Mass., 1952), pp. 29–34.

98. Malia, *Alexander Herzen*, p. 209.

99. B. N. Chicherin, *Moskva soroko-vykh godov*, p. 5.

100. M. Gershenzon, *Sochineniia i Pis'ma P. Ia. Chaadaeva* (Moscow, 1913), I, pp. 104–7.

101. P. S. Shkurinov, *P. Ia. Chaadaeva* (Moscow, 1960), p. 24.

102. P. N. Miliukov, *Glavnye techeniia russkoi istoricheskoi mysli* (Moscow, 1898), I, pp. 374–8.

103. Gershenzon, *Sochineniia i pis'ma P. Ia. Chaadaeva*, p. 79.

104. N. Rusanov, 'Vliianie zapadno-evropeiskago sotsializma na russkii', *Minuvshie gody* (May–June 1908), p. 14.

105. Malia, *Alexander Herzen*, p. 207.

106. A great deal has been written about the Slavophiles, and their most important works have long been published. The best summaries of their views can be found in the following: Ch. Vetrinskii, 'Umstvennoe i obshchest-vennoe dvizhenie sorokovykh gg.', pp. 67–130; Ivanov-Razumnik, *Istoriia russ-koi obshchestvennoi mysli* (St Petersburg, 1908), I, pp. 290–331; V. V. Zenkovskii, *Istoriia russkoi filosofii* (Paris, 1948), I, pp. 180–245; N. Riasanovskii, *Russia and the West in the Teachings of the Slavophiles*, pp. 91–187; M. Malia, *Alexander Herzen*, *passim*, but esp. pp. 279–312. In addition, a number of more detailed studies on individual Slavophiles and their ideas are listed in the bibliography of this present study.

107. V. G. Belinskii, *Sobranie sochinenii V. G. Belinskago*, edited by Ivanov-Razumnik, III, p. 822.

108. ibid., p. 824.

109. For a summary of this debate, see A. A. Kiesewetter, 'Krest'ianstvo v russkoi nauchno-istoricheskoi literature', *Krest'ianskaia rossiia*, V (1923), pp. 23–43.

110. Pipes, *Russia under the Old Regime*, p. 269.

111. Malia, *Alexander Herzen*, p. 332.

112. This phrase was coined by P. V. Annenkov. See P. V. Annenkov, *Literaturnye Vospominaniia*, pp. 135–377.

113. W. Bruce Lincoln, 'Russia's "Enlightened" Bureaucrats and Problems of State Reform, 1848–1856', pp. 410–13.

CHAPTER 8

THE YEAR 1848

1. Quoted in Th. Dan, *The Origins of Bolshevism*, p. 27.

2. N. Shchedrin (M. E. Saltykov), *Izbrannye proizvedeniia* (Moscow, 1947), III, p. 241.

3. V. R. Zotov, 'Peterburg v soroko-vykh godakh', *IV*, XXXIX, No. 1 (February 1890), p. 325.

4. A. E. Tsimmerman, 'Vospominaniia Generala A. E. Tsimmermana', ORGBL, fond 325, karton 1, papka 1/142.

5. Polievktov, pp. 280–89; Pintner, *Russian Economic Policy*, p. 221.

6. Blum, *Lord and Peasant in Russia*, p. 296.

7. P. Khromov, *Ekonomicheskoe razvi-tie Rossii v XIX–XX vekakh, 1800–1917* (Moscow, 1950), pp. 437–9.

8. M. Tugan-Baranovskii, *Russkaia fabrika v proshlom i nastoiashchem* (Moscow, 1938), p. 65.

9. Blackwell, *The Beginnings of Russian Industrialization*, p. 431.

10. Quoted in A. S. Nifontov, *Rossiia v 1848 godu* (Moscow, 1949), p. 19.

11. Baron M. A. Korf, 'Dnevnik za 1848 g.', TsGAOR, fond 728, opis' 1, delo No. 1817/xi/144.

12. The Austrian ambassador Collo-redo to Metternich, 31 August 1846 (NS), quoted in Grunwald, pp. 228–9.

13. ibid., p. 229, n. 1.

14. See, for example, A. F. Tiutcheva (Aksakova), *Pri dvore dvukh imperatorov. Vospominaniia-Dnevnik* (Moscow, 1928), I, p. 168.

15. Custine, *La Russie en 1839*, I, pp. 316–17.

16. Quoted in Schiemann, III, p. 318.

17. Memoirs of Captain Haffner, quoted in Grunwald, p. 216.

18. See 'Obozrenie khoda i deistvii kholernoi epidemii v Rossii v techenie

1848 goda', *Zhurnal Ministerstva Vnutrennikh Del*, XXVII, No. 9 (September 1849), pp. 316–17.

19. Nikitenko, *Dnevnik*, I, p. 312.

20. ibid.

21. V. P. Bykova, *Zapiski staroi smolianki* (St Petersburg, 1898), p. 180.

22. See 'Obozrenie khoda i deistvii kholernoi epidemii', pp. 319–28.

23. A. V. Golovnin to M. P. Pogodin, 25 July 1848, in N. Barsukov, *Zhizn' i trudy M. P. Pogodina* (St Petersburg, 1895), IX, p. 325.

24. 'Statistika pozharov v Rossii v 1848 god', *Zhurnal Ministerstva Vnutrennikh Del*, XXVII, No. 7 (July 1849), pp. 7–44.

25. Shilder, II, p. 362.

26. 'Zapiski Benkendorfa', *RS*, LXXXVIII, No. 10 (October 1896), pp. 88–9.

27. Nifontov, p. 27.

28. ibid., p. 19.

29. A. P. Zablotskii-Desiatovskii, 'Prichiny kolebaniia tsen na khleb v Rossii', *Otechestvennye zapiski*, LII, No. 5 (May 1847), p. 11.

30. ibid., pp. 12–13.

31. N. A. Miliutin, 'Donesenie Gospodinu Upravliaiushchemu Ministerstvom Vnutrennikh Del ot sluzhashchago v khoziaistvennom departamente tituliarnago sovetnika Miliutina, aprel' 1841 g.', TsGIAL, fond 869, opis' 1, delo No. 725/88.

32. Nifontov, p. 19.

33. ibid., p. 20.

34. Quoted in ibid., pp. 28–9.

35. Statistics from ibid., pp. 32, 33.

36. N. D. Kiselev's report of 7 (19) January 1848 in Martens, XV, p. 224.

37. Quoted in Nifontov, p. 196.

38. W. L. Langer, *Political and Social Upheaval*, p. 255.

39. Grand Duke Konstantin Nikolaevich, 'Dnevnik', entry for 21 February 1848, TsGAOR, fond 722, opis' 1, delo No. 89/29.

40. ibid., delo No. 89/29–30.

41. ibid., delo No. 89/30.

42. Quoted in Nifontov, p. 69.

43. Emperor Nicholas I to Friedrich Wilhelm IV, 29 February (12 March) 1848, in Schiemann, IV, p. 392.

44. ibid.

45. Baron M. A. Korf, 'Dnevnik za 1848 g.', entry for 23 February 1848, TsGAOR, fond 728, opis' 1, delo No. 1817/xi/135.

46. Nicholas I, 'Zapiska o polozhenii del v Evrope', *KA*, LXXXIX–XC (1938), p. 163.

47. Letter of Count Nesselrode to Metternich, 7 February 1848, in Martens, IV, p. 581.

48. Emperor Nicholas I to Friedrich Wilhelm IV, 24 February 1848, *KA*, LXXXIX–XC (1938), p. 170.

49. ibid., pp. 169–70. (Italics mine.)

50. ibid., p. 170.

51. N. K. Shilder, 'Imperator Nikolai I v 1848 i 1849 godakh', in *Imperator Nikolai Pervyi*, II, p. 622.

52. Nicholas I, 'Rech' Nikolaia I k deputatam peterburgskago dvorianstva', in Gershenzon, *Epokha Nikolaia I*, p. 10.

53. V. R. Zotov, 'Peterburg v sorokovykh godakh', p. 305.

54. A. E. Tsimmerman, 'Vospominaniia Generala A. E. Tsimmermana', ORGBL, fond 325, karton 1, papka 2/9.

55. Baron M. A. Korf, 'Dnevnik za 1848 g.', TsGAOR, fond 728, opis' 1, delo No. 1817/xi/137.

56. A. E. Tsimmerman, 'Vospominaniia Generala A. E. Tsimmermana', ORGBL, fond 325, karton 1, papka, 2/8.

57. Quoted in Nifontov, p. 61.

58. Quoted in ibid., p. 62.

59. Nicholas I to Aleksandra Fedorovna, 19 December 1845 (1 January 1846), in Schiemann, IV, p. 380.

60. Emperor Nicholas I to Friedrich Wilhelm IV, 29 February (12 March) 1848, in ibid., p. 392.

61. Dispatch of Baron Meiendorf from Berlin, 24 February 1848, Martens, VIII, p. 370.

62. Quoted in ibid.

63. Emperor Nicholas I to Friedrich Wilhelm IV, 6 (18) January 1848, in ibid., p. 367.
64. Quoted in ibid., p. 368.
65. Baron Meiendorf, dispatch of 8 (20) March 1848, in ibid., pp. 370–71.
66. Langer, *Political and Social Upheaval*, p. 351.
67. ibid., p. 354.
68. A. E. Tsimmerman, 'Vospominaniia Generala A. E. Tsimmermana', ORGBL, fond 325, karton 1, papka 2/8.
69. Baron Meiendorf, dispatch of 8 (20) March 1848, in Martens, VIII, 371.
70. Baron Meiendorf, dispatch of 17 (29) March, 1848, in ibid., p. 371.
71. 'Manifest 14 marta 1848 g.', in Gershenzon (ed.), *Epokha Nikolaia I*, p. 9.
72. Quoted in Grunwald, p. 232.
73. Nifontov, pp. 76, 77.
74. ibid., p. 91.
75. Published in ibid., p. 82.
76. Quoted in ibid., p. 87.
77. Korf, *Materialy*, p. 93.
78. ibid.
79. S. W. Baron, *The Russian Jew* (New York, 1961), pp. 35–8.
80. Schiemann, II, p. 238.
81. Baron, *The Russian Jew*, pp. 38–46.
82. Nifontov, p. 98.
83. Emperor Nicholas I to Prince Paskevich, 4 (16) December 1848, in S. Z., 'Imperator Nikolai I i evropeiskiia revoliutsiia', *RS*, CXVIII, No. 5 (May 1904), p. 284.

CHAPTER 9
THE LAST YEARS OF THE NICHOLAS SYSTEM

1. This is General Tsimmerman's appraisal of Korf's view – Tsimmerman, 'Vospominaniia', ORGBL, fond 325, karton 1, papka 2/168. That Tsimmerman was accurate in this statement is evident from even the most cursory reading of Korf's unpublished diary in TsGAOR, fond 728, opis' 1, dela Nos. 1817/i–xiv.
2. Tsimmerman, 'Vospominaniia', ORGBL, fond 325, karton 1, papka 1/42; karton 2, papka 1/243.
3. ibid., papka 1/243.
4. W. Bruce Lincoln, 'The Ministers of Nicholas I', pp. 321–2.
5. Baron M. A. Korf, 'Dnevnik za 1840 g.', TsGAOR, fond 728, opis' 1, delo No. 1817/iii/264.
6. Nikitenko, *Zapiski i dnevnik, 1826–1877* (St Petersburg, 1893), I, p. 577.
7. Nikitenko, *Dnevnik*, I, pp. 421–2.
8. M. Lemke, *Ocherki po istorii russkoi tsenzury i zhurnalistiki XIX stoletiia* (St Petersburg, 1904), pp. 183–308.
9. ibid., p. 239.
10. 'Otnoshenie Deistvitel'nago Tainago Sovetnika Dmitriia Buturlina 17-go marta 1849 g., k Ministru Narodnago Prosveshcheniia Grafu Uvarovu' (konfidential'no), TsGIAL, fond 772, opis' 1, delo No. 2242/1–2.
11. Nikitenko, *Dnevnik*, I, p. 338.
12. Nicholas I, 'Zaveshchanie Nikolaia I synu', *KA*, III (1923), p. 292.
13. Quoted in Presniakov, *Apogei samoderzhaviia*, p. 13.
14. Nicholas I to Prince Paskevich, 30 March 1848, in Shcherbatov, *General Fel'dmarshal Kniaz Paskevich*, VI, p. 214.
15. Nicholas I to Prince M. P. Gorchakov, 25 November 1854, in Polievktov, p. 376.
16. Lemke, *Ocherki po istorii russkoi tsenzury*, p. 224.
17. Schiemann, III, p. 318.
18. This was very evident in Nicholas's speech to the assembled St Petersburg nobility in March 1848; see 'Rech' Nikolaia I, 21 marta 1848', in Gershenzon, *Epokha Nikolaia I*, pp. 9–11.
19. A. P. Zablotskii-Desiatovskii, *Graf P. D. Kiselev*, IV, pp. 197–9.
20. Druzhinin, *Gosudarstvennye krest'iane*, I, pp. 275–7, 476–521.
21. Engelman, *Istoriia krepostnago prava v Rossii*, p. 276.
22. ibid., p. 277.
23. N. A. Miliutin, 'Istoricheskaia zapiska o raznykh predpolozheniiakh po

predmetu osvobozhdeniia krest'ian', in Bartenev (ed.), *Deviatnadtsatyi vek*, II, pp. 194–5.

24. ibid., pp. 195–6; Engelman, *Istoriia krepostnago prava v Rossii*, p. 261.

25. Engelman, *Istoriia krepostnago prava v Rossii*, p. 277.

26. Nicholas I, 'Rech' Nikolaia I, 21 marta 1848 g.', in Gershenzon, *Epokha Nikolaia I*, p. 10.

27. Nifontov, p. 226.

28. W. Bruce Lincoln, 'The Daily Life of St Petersburg Officials', pp. 87–8.

29. I. P. Liprandi, 'Kratkii obzor sluzhebnykh zaniatii Deistvitel'nago Statskago Sovetnika Liprandi po Ministerstvu Vnutrennikh Del, s nachala 1840 g. po nastoiashchee vremia, s pokazaniem soputstvovavshikh nekotorym delam obstoiatel'stv (1853 g.)', GPB, fond 72, delo No. 9/3–51.

30. See Nifontov, pp. 223, 227.

31. 'Zapiski Benkendorfa', *KA*, XXXVIII (1930), p. 132.

32. Tsimmerman, 'Vospominaniia', ORGBL, fond 325, karton 1, papka 2/8.

33. Squire, *The Third Department*, pp. 215–25; Monas, *The Third Section*, p. 245.

34. M. A. Korf, 'Dnevnik za 1849 g.', TsGAOR, fond 728, opis' 1, delo No. 1817/xii/163.

35. M. A. Korf, 'Dnevnik za 1848 g.', TsGAOR, fond 728, opis' 1, delo No. 1817/xi/144.

36. M. P. Pogodin, *Istoriko-politicheskie pis'ma i zapiski*, p. 257.

37. For a discussion of the changing social and economic position of the bureaucracy, see W. M. Pintner, 'The Social Characteristics of the Early Nineteenth-Century Russian Bureaucracy', *Slavic Review*, XXIX, No. 3 (September 1970), pp. 429–43.

38. A. Romanovich-Slavatinskii, *Dvorianstvo v Rossii ot nachala XVIII veka do otmeny krepostnago prava* (St Petersburg, 1870), p. 435; G. Evreinov, *Proshloe i nastoiashchee znachenie russkago dvorianstva* (St Petersburg, 1898), p. 49.

39. Nicholas I, 'Rech' Nikolaia I', in Gershenzon, *Epokha Nikolaia I*, p. 11.

40. Quoted in Nifontov, p. 227.

41. See, for example, K. S. Veselovskii, 'Vospominaniia K. S. Veselovskago', *RS*, CXVI, No. 10 (October 1903), pp. 5–42, and A. V. Golovnin, 'Zapiski A. V. Golovnina', GPB, fond 208, delo No. 1/11–22; K. S. Veselovskii, 'Vospominaniia o tsarskosel'skom litsee', *RS*, CIV, No. 10 (October 1900), pp. 3–29.

42. See, for example, Pis'ma N. A. Miliutina k D. A. Miliutinu, 1835–1837 gg., ORGBL, fond 169, karton 69, papka 5, and Pis'mo N. A. Miliutina k D. A. Miliutinu, 10 avgusta 1839 g., ORGBL, fond 169, karton 69, papka 6.

43. A. S. Zarudnyi (ed.), 'Pis'mo opytnago chinovnika sorokovykh godov mladshemu sobratu postupaiushchemu na sluzhbu', *RS*, C, No. 12 (December 1899), pp. 543–5.

44. V. R. Zotov, 'Peterburg v sorokovykh godakh', *IV*, XXXIX (January 1890), p. 31; A. K., 'Mezhdu strokami odnago formuliarnago spiska', *RS*, XXXIII, No. 12 (December 1881), pp. 820–21; Pis'mo N. A. Miliutina k D. A. Miliutinu 10 avgusta 1838 g., ORGBL, fond 169, karton 69, papka 6.

45. See, for example, Pis'ma N. A. Miliutina k D. A. Miliutinu, 29 dekabria 1836, 8 ianvaria 1837, i 14 fevralia 1837 gg., ORGBL, fond 169, karton 69, papka 5.

46. V. I. Semevskii, *M. V. Butashevich-Petrashevskii i Petrashevtsy* (Moscow, 1922), I, pp. 39–50.

47. ibid., p. 171.

48. ibid., pp. 52–3.

49. R. E. MacMaster, *Danilevskii: A Russian Totalitarian Philosopher* (Cambridge, Mass., 1967), p. 48.

50. V. I. Semevskii, *M. V. Butashevich-Petrashevskii*, pp. 166–86; V. Desnitskii (ed.), *Delo Petrashevtsev* (Moscow-Leningrad, 1937), I, pp. 152–3.

51. P. P. Semenov-Tian-Shanskii, *Memuary* (Petrograd, 1915), I, p. 195.

52. D. D. Akhsharumov, *Iz moikh*

vospominanii, 1849–1851 gg. (St Petersburg, 1905), pp. 15–16.

53. Semevskii, *M. V. Butashevich-Petrashevskii*, p. 109.

54. ibid., pp. 109–10.

55. ibid., p. 111.

56. V. Desnitskii (ed.), *Delo Petrashevtsev*, I, p. 150.

57. S. N. Valk (ed.), *Delo Petrashevtsev* (Moscow-Leningrad, 1951), III, p. 115.

58. Franco Venturi, *Roots of Revolution* (New York, 1960), pp. 86–8.

59. ibid., pp. 85–6.

60. ibid., pp. 87–8.

61. Semevskii, *M. V. Butashevich-Petrashevskii*, p. 151.

62. F. M. Dostoevskii, *Pis'ma* (Moscow-Leningrad, 1928), I, p. 128.

63. The memoirs about this period stress over and over again the monumental stature of Belinskii in St Petersburg intellectual circles. See esp. S. N. Golubov, *et al.* (eds.), *V. G. Belinskii v vospominaniiakh sovremennikov* (Moscow, 1962), *passim.*

64. W. Bruce Lincoln, 'Russia's "Enlightened" Bureaucrats and the Problem of State Reform, 1848–1856', pp. 410–21.

65. W. Bruce Lincoln 'The Circle of Grand Duchess Elena Pavlova, 1847–1861', pp. 373–87.

66. Roger Ikor, *Insurrection ouvrière de juin, 1848* (Paris, 1936), p. 58.

67. Quoted in E. H. Carr, *The Romantic Exiles* (Boston, 1961), p. 43.

68. Langer, *Political and Social Upheaval*, pp. 469–82.

69. ibid., pp. 436–44; H. M. Smyth, 'The Armistice of Novara: A Legend of A Liberal King', *Journal of Modern History*, VII (1935), pp. 141–52.

70. Nicholas I to Friedrich Wilhelm IV, 24 February 1848, *KA*, LXXXIX–XC, Nos. 4–6 (1938), p. 170.

71. Nifontov, pp. 269–70.

72. Nicholas I to Prince Paskevich, 16 March 1848, quoted in ibid., p. 247.

73. ibid., p. 256.

74. Nicholas I to Friedrich Wilhelm

IV, 3 (15) July 1848, quoted in Martens, VIII, p. 274. (Italics in original.)

75. *Polnoe sobranie zakonov rossiiskoi imperii*, 2nd ed., XXIII, No. 22,449.

76. Schiemann, IV, pp. 176–7.

77. Langer, *Political and Social Upheaval*, p. 489.

78. Nifontov, p. 270.

79. E Andics, *Das Bündnis Habsburg-Romanow. Vorgeschichte der zaristischen intervention in Ungarn im Jahre 1849* (Budapest, 1963), pp. 106–36.

80. Langer, *Political and Social Upheaval*, pp. 488–9.

81. Nicholas I to Prince Paskevich, 13 April 1849, in Shcherbatov, *General Fel'dmarshal Kniaz' Paskevich*, VI, p. 285.

82. Quoted in Grunwald, p. 251n.

83. *Polnoe sobranie zakonov Rossiiskoi imperii*, 2nd ed., XXIV, No. 23,200.

84. 'Gustav du Plat über Franz-Josephs Aufenthalt in Warschau', 24 May 1849, in Schiemann, IV, p. 397.

85. Martens, IV, pp. 585–8.

86. R. A. Averbukh, *Tsarskaia interventsiia v bor'be s vengerskoi revoliutsiei* (Moscow, 1935), pp. 122–4.

87. I. Oreus, *Opisanie vengerskoi voiny 1849 g.* (St Petersburg, 1880), pp. 71, 105–15.

88. ibid., p. 539.

89. J. S. Curtiss, *The Russian Army*, pp. 297–8.

90. Oreus, *Opisanie vengerskoi voiny*, pp. 275–8.

91. Curtiss, *The Russian Army*, p. 302.

92. Nicholas I to Prince Paskevich, 29 July (10 August) 1849, Shcherbatov, *General Fel'dmarshal Kniaz' Paskevich*, VI, pp. 321–3.

93. Nifontov, p. 296.

94. R. A. Averbukh, *Revoliutsiia i natsional'no-osvoboditel'naia bor'ba v Vengrii, 1848–1849* (Moscow, 1965), pp. 309–10.

95. Graf Otto von Bray-Steinberg, 'Imperator Nikolai i ego spodvizhniki', *RS*, CIX, No. 1 (January 1890), p. 121.

96. Quoted in Grunwald, p. 252n.

97. Curtiss, *The Russian Army*, p. 306.

98. Quoted in ibid., p. 305.

99. Shcherbatov, *General Fel'dmarshal Kniaz' Paskevich*, VI, p. 330; Nifontov, p. 296.

100. Nicholas I to Prince Paskevich, 4 (16) August 1849, in Shcherbatov, *General Fel'dmarshal Kniaz' Paskevich*, VI, p. 329.

101. P. Men'kov, *Zapiski ('Dunai i nemtsy-vostochnyi vopros, 1853–1855 gg') i Dnevnik* (St Petersburg, 1898), II, pp. 169–70.

102. Nicholas I to Prince Paskevich, 11 July 1848, in Shcherbatov, *General Fel'dmarshal Kniaz' Paskevich*, VI, p. 248.

103. *Polnoe sobranie zakonov rossiiskoi imperii*, 2nd ed., XXIII, No. 22,053.

104. Graf Otto von Bray-Steinberg, 'Imperator Nikolai I i ego spodvizhniki', p. 121.

105. V. G. Fedorov, *Vooruzhenie russkoi armii v krymskuiu kampaniiu* (St Petersburg, 1904), pp. 14–21; L. Gorev, *Voina 1853–1856 gg. i oborona Sevastopolia* (Moscow, 1955), p. 15.

106. Quoted in Curtiss, *The Russian Army*, p. 120.

107. ibid., p. 119.

108. ibid., pp. 119, 136–9.

109. Quoted in E. Willis Brooks, *D. A. Miliutin: Life and Activity to 1856* (unpublished Ph.D. dissertation, Stanford University, 1970), p. 144.

110. Quoted in ibid., p. 144.

111. S. M. Solov'ev, *Zapiski Sergeia Mikhailovicha Solov'eva* (St Petersburg, n.d.), p. 121.

112. P. A. Valuev, 'Dnevnik grafa Petra Aleksandrovicha Valueva, 1847–1860 gg.', *RS*, LXX, No. 4 (April 1891), pp. 172–3.

113. M. Lemke, *Nikolaevskie zhandarmy i literatura, 1826–1855 gg.* (St Petersburg, 1909), pp. 300–310.

114. ibid., p. 300.

115. ibid., p. 303.

116. V. E. Evgenev-Maksimov, *Ocherki po istorii sotsialisticheskoi zhurnalistiki v Rossii XIX veka* (Moscow-Leningrad, 1927), p. 46.

117. ibid., p. 47.

118. A. G. Dement'ev, *Ocherki po istorii russkoi zhurnalistiki 1840–1850 gg.* (Moscow-Leningrad, 1951), p. 93.

119. ibid.

120. Shilder, 'Imperator Nikolai I v 1848–1849 godakh', *Imperator Nikolai Pervyi*, II p. 633; Lemke, *Ocherki po istorii russkoi tsenzury*, pp. 192–3.

121. A. G. Dement'ev, *Ocherki*, p. 94.

122. Lemke, *Ocherki po istorii russkoi tsenzury*, p. 194.

123. ibid., pp. 201–2.

124. ibid., p. 201.

125. ibid., p. 206.

126. Nikitenko, *Dnevnik*, I, p. 336.

127. ibid., p. 326.

128. 'Otnoshenie Deistvitel'nago Tainago Sovetnika Dmitriia Buturlina, 29 ianvaria 1849 g. k Ministru Narodnago Prosveshcheniia Grafu S. S. Uvarovu, (konfidential'no)', TsGIAL, fond 772, opis' 1, delo No. 2209/2.

129. 'Otnoshenie Deistvitel'nago Tainago Sovetnika Dmitriia Buturlina 17-go marta 1849 g., k Ministru Narodnago Prosveshcheniia Grafu S. S. Uvarovu', (konfidential'no), TsGIAL, fond 772, opis' 1, delo No. 2242/1–3.

130. 'Vsepoddanneishaia dokladnaia zapiski grafa Uvarova' [k Ego Imperatorskomu Velichestvu Nikolaiu Pavlovichu] 21 marta 1849 g. TsGIAL, fond 772, opis' 1, delo No. 2242/6–42; see Nicholas's marginal comments.

131. Nikitenko, *Dnevnik*, I, p. 326.

132. N. Rodzianko, 'Nabliudeniia za dukhom i napravleniem zhurnala *Biblioteka dlia Chteniia*', (mai 1850), TsGIAL, fond 772, opis' 1, delo No. 2423/16.

133. Nikitenko, *Dnevnik*, I, p. 348.

134. M. P. Pogodin, *Istorikopoliticheskiia pis'ma i zapiski*, p. 257.

135. Lemke, *Ocherki po istorii russkoi tsenzury*, pp. 266–7.

136. See, for example, Lemke, *Ocherki po istorii russkoi tsenzury*, pp. 268–9; 'Konfidential'noe pis'mo Barona Korfa Ministru Vnutrennikh Del L. A. Perovskomu', 21 iiunia 1850 g., TsGIAL,

fond 1287, opis' 35, delo No., 97/1–2.

137. Nikitenko, *Dnevnik*, I, pp. 312–13.

138. Lemke, *Ocherki po istorii russkoi tsenzury*, p. 239.

139. ibid.

140. Dement'ev, *Ocherki*, p. 100.

141. ibid., pp. 98–100.

142. ibid., pp. 105, 106.

143. Quoted in ibid., p. 106.

144. T. N. Granovskii to E. F. Korsh, in *T. N. Granovskii i ego perepiska* (Moscow, 1897), II, p. 470.

145. Evgenev-Maksimov, *Ocherki po istorii sotsialisticheskoi zhurnalistiki*, pp. 58–9.

146. Quoted in P. S. Popov (ed.), *Pis'ma k A. V. Druzhininu (1850–1863 gg.)* (Moscow, 1948), p. 11.

147. ibid., p. 10; A. E. Tsimmerman, 'Vospominaniia', ORGBL, fond 325, karton 1, papka, 2/7–8.

148. Tsimmerman, 'Vospominaniia', ORGBL, fond 325, karton 1, papka 1/209.

149. K. D. Kavelin to T. N. Granovskii, 4 marta 1855 goda, in Sh. M. Levin, 'K. D. Kavelin o smerti Nikolaia I', *Literaturnoe nasledstvo*, LXVII (Moscow, 1959), p. 610.

150. Nikitenko, *Dnevnik*, I, p. 419.

151. Aleksandr Kamenskii, 'Vsepoddanneishaia zapiska Kamenskago 1850 goda', CXXII, No. 6 (June 1905), p. 629.

CHAPTER 10

THE LAST ACT: THE CRIMEAN WAR

1. Quoted in Grunwald, p. 253n.

2. Langer, *Political and Social Upheaval*, p. 495.

3. A. Rapp, *Grossdeutsch-Kleindeutsch* (Munich, 1922), xxii–xxiv. See also Hans G. Telle, *Das Österreichische Problem im Frankfurter Parlament im Sommer und Herbst 1848* (Marburg, 1933).

4. Langer, *Political and Social Upheaval*, p. 497.

5. Quotes from ibid., pp. 500, 505.

6. See Egmont Zechlin, *Die deutsche Einheitsbewegung* (Frankfurt, 1967), pp. 157–66.

7. W. O. Henderson, *The Zollverein* (London, 1959), pp. 203–13; Henry C. Meyer, *Mitteleuropa in German Thought and Action* (The Hague, 1955), pp. 11–15; Franz J. Schoeningh, 'Karl Ludwig Bruck und die Idee Mitteleuropas', *Historisches Jahrbüch*, LVI (1936).

8. Baron Meiendorf to Count Nesselrode, 25 November (7 December) 1849 in Meiendorf, II, p. 242.

9. Dispatches of Baron Meiendorf to Nesselrode, 23 February (7 March), and 15 (27) September 1850, quoted in Martens, VIII, p. 381.

10. Dispatch of Meiendorf to Nesselrode, 15 (27) September 1850, in Martens, VIII, p. 381.

11. Quoted in ibid., p. 382.

12. ibid., p. 381.

13. Dispatch of Meiendorf to Nesselrode, 9 (21) June 1850, in ibid., p. 382.

14. Dispatch of Meiendorf to Nesselrode, 7 (19) July 1850, in ibid., p. 382.

15. Langer, *Political and Social Upheaval*, pp. 506–10.

16. ibid., p. 510.

17. ibid., pp. 509–10.

18. E. Bapst, *Les Origines de la guerre de Crimée. La France et la Russie de 1848–1854* (Paris, 1912), pp. 178–9.

19. Martens, VIII, p. 386.

20. Joachim Hoffmann, 'Russland und die Olmützer Punktation', *Forschungen zur osteuropäischen Geschichte*, VII (1959), pp. 59–71; Meiendorf to Nesselrode, 17 (29) November 1850, in Meiendorf, II, pp. 346–7; Charles Pouthas, *Démocraties et capitalisme, 1848–1860* (Paris, 1961), pp. 161–3; Martens, VIII, pp. 386–8.

21. Le comte Charles de Nesselrode au baron de Meyendorff, 11 décembre 1850, in Nesselrode, *Papiers et lettres*, X, pp. 16–19.

22. Joachim Hoffmann, 'Russland und die Olmützer Punktation', pp. 59–71.

23. Martens, VIII, p. 388.

24. ibid., p. 421.

25. Quoted in Grunwald, p. 255.

26. 'Rapport presenté par le comte

Charles de Nesselrode à S. M. l'Empereur Nicolas Ier, au jubilé de sa 25e année de règne', 20 November 1850, in Nesselrode, *Lettres et papiers*, X, pp. 2–3.

27. Memoirs of Count Beust relating to 1852, both quotes in Grunwald, p. 255.

28. Palmerston once said in 1853 that 'the Emperor of Russia is ambitious and grasping, but he is a gentleman, and I should be slow to disbelieve his positive denial of such things as those in question' – quoted in Temperley, p. 270.

29. A. M. Zaionchkovskii, *Vostochnaia voina v sviazi s sovremennoi ei politicheskoi obstanovkoi* (St Petersburg, 1908), Appendix to vol. I, p. 357.

30. Quoted in Temperley, p. 272.

31. ibid.

32. Seymour's account of conversations with Count Nesselrode in early 1853, quoted in Temperley, p. 272.

33. Quoted in ibid., p. 273.

34. ibid., p. 276; Schiemann, IV, pp. 276–8.

35. Seymour to Malmesbury, 4 December 1852 (NS), in Schiemann, IV, pp. 421–3.

36. ibid., pp. 281–2.

37. Quoted in Temperley, p. 275.

38. Zaionchkovskii, *Vostochnaia voina*, Appendix to vol. I, p. 362.

39. Temperley, p. 283.

40. Leonid Strakhovsky, *Alexander I of Russia* (New York, 1947), pp. 236–7.

41. Temperley, p. 284.

42. ibid.

43. Quoted in L. Thouvenel, *Nicolas Ier et Napoleon III* (Paris, 1891), p. 11.

44. Zaionchkovskii, *Vostochnaia voina*, Appendix to vol. I, p. 333.

45. Quoted in Temperley, p. 290.

46. Zaionchkovskii, *Vostochnaia voina*, Appendix to vol. I, p. 277.

47. ibid.; Martens, XII, p. 292.

48. Quoted in Martens, XII, p. 303.

49. Temperley, p. 300.

50. E. V. Tarle, *Sochineniia* (Moscow, 1959), VIII, p. 16.

51. Quoted in Martens, XII, p. 309.

52. Quoted in ibid., p. 311.

53. ibid., p. 309.

54. Nesselrode to Brunnov, January 1853, quoted in ibid., p. 310. Tarle, *Sochineniia*, VIII, p. 156.

55. Schiemann, IV, pp. 282–5.

56. Quoted in Tarle, *Sochineniia*, VIII, p. 158.

57. N. Putilov, *Sbornik izvestii otnosiashchikhsia do nastoiashchei voiny* (St Petersburg, 1854), I, 'Politicheskii otdel', p. 1; Bapst, *Les origines de la guerre*, pp. 345–7; Tarle, *Sochineniia*, VIII, p. 162.

58. Tarle, *Sochineniia*, VIII, p. 176.

59. Quoted in Temperley, p. 310.

60. There has been considerable controversy about Lord Redcliffe's role during this time. The most thorough treatment is by Temperley, *England and the Near East*. A view dramatically opposed to Temperley's is the work by the distinguished Soviet historian, the late Professor E. V. Tarle, who insists that Temperley's treatment of Redcliffe is 'a crude, inadmissible, historical falsification, a scandalous violation of the known facts, and a perversion of historical truth' – Tarle, *Sochineniia*, VIII, p. 183.

61. Quoted in Temperley, p. 316.

62. Zaionchkovskii, *Vostochnaia voina*, Appendix to vol. I, p. 401.

63. ibid., pp. 399–400.

64. Tarle, *Sochineniia*, VIII, p. 177; Putilov, *Sbornik izvestii*, I, 'Politicheskii otdel', pp. 14–16.

65. Tarle, *Sochineniia*, VIII, p. 181.

66. Temperley, p. 323.

67. ibid.

68. Tarle, *Sochineniia*, VIII, p. 186.

69. ibid., p. 182.

70. Putilov, *Sbornik izvestii*, I, 'Politicheskii otdel', pp. 22–3.

71. ibid., pp. 28–9, 30–31.

72. Baron von Stockmar, *Memoirs*, II, pp. 107–8.

73. Tarle, *Sochineniia*, VIII, p. 295.

74. Bapst, *Les Origines de la guerre*, p. 427.

75. Temperley, p. 344.

76. Putilov, *Sbornik izvestii*, I, 'Politi-

cheskii otdel', p. 43; Tarle, *Sochineniia*, VIII, p. 296.

77. Putilov, *Sbornik izvestii*, I, 'Politi- cheskii otdel', pp. 43–4, 47; Bapst, *Les Origines de la guerre*, pp. 436–7.

78. Temperley, pp. 349–50.

79. Quoted in ibid., p. 354.

80. Bapst, *Les Origines de la guerre*, p. 421.

81. Temperley, p. 355.

82. Martens, VIII, p. 429.

83. General Castelbajac to M. Thouve- nel, 19 October 1855, in L. Thouvenel, *Nicolas Iᵉʳ et Napoléon III*, pp. 250–51.

84. Temperley, p. 344.

85. Tarle, *Sochineniia*, VIII, p. 16.

86. Quoted in Grunwald, p. 263n.

87. Martens, VIII, p. 430.

88. General Castelbajac to M. Thouve- nel, 16 September 1853, in L. Thouvenel, *Nicolas Iᵉʳ et Napoléon III*, p. 218.

89. General Castelbajac to M. Thouve- nel, 11 February 1854, in ibid., p. 334.

90. A. F. Tiutcheva, *Pri dvore dvukh imperatorov*, I, entry for 4 October 1853, p. 124.

91. General Castelbajac to M. Thouve- nel, 11 February 1854, in L. Thouvenel. *Nicolas Iᵉʳ et Napoleon III*, p. 333.

92. Zaionchkovskii, *Vostochnaia voina*, Appendix, to vol. II, pp. 338–41; Shcherbatov, *General Fel'dmarshal Kniaz' Paskevich*, VII, pp. 97–102.

93. N. Dubrovin, *Istoriia krymskoi voiny i oborony Sevastopolia* (St Peters- burg, 1900), I, pp. 118–19.

94. Dubrovin, *Istoriia krymskoi voiny*, I, pp. 198–202.

95. Tarle, *Sochineniia*, VIII, pp. 283– 284.

96. ibid., pp. 285–7.

97. ibid., pp. 353–64; Zaionchkovskii, *Vostochnaia voina*, II, Pt 1, pp. 299–303.

98. Tarle, *Sochineniia*, VIII, pp. 273– 279.

99. Gorev, *Voina 1853–1856 gg. i oborona Sevastopolia*, pp. 21, 35.

100. ibid., p. 14.

101. ibid., p. 15.

102. ibid., p. 16.

103. Quoted in Curtiss, *The Russian Army*, p. 124.

104. Quoted in ibid., p. 127.

105. ibid., pp. 125–8.

106. ibid, p. 127.

107. Dubrovin, *Istoriia krymskoi voiny*, I, p. 267.

108. ibid., pp. 232–60; Tarle, *Sochineniia*, IX, p. 107.

109. Shcherbatov, *General Fel'd- marshal Kniaz Paskevich*, VII, p. 210.

110. ibid., pp. 212–20.

111. Tarle, *Sochineniia*, IX, pp. 157– 162; Dubrovin, *Istoriia krymskoi voiny*, II, pp. 136–51.

112. Tarle, *Sochineniia*, IX, pp. 173–84.

113. ibid., p. 57.

114. Tiutcheva, *Pri dvore dvukh imperatorov*, entry for 14 June 1854, I, p. 145.

115. Tarle, *Sochineniia*, IX, pp. 72–92; M. Borodkin, *Voina 1854–1855 gg. na finskom poberezhe* (St Petersburg, 1904), pp. 126–64.

116. Tarle, *Sochineniia*, IX, pp. 205– 212.

117. ibid., 479–80.

118. ibid., p. 90.

119. ibid., pp. 328–34.

120. Quoted in Grunwald, p. 271.

121. Quoted in ibid., p. 273.

122. Tiutcheva, *Pri dvore dvukh imperatorov*, entry for 19 October 1854, I, p. 160.

123. ibid., entry for 24 November 1854, I, p. 168.

124. ibid., p. 167.

125. ibid., p. 168.

126. Nicholas I, 'Predsmertnoe pis'mo Imperatora Nikolaia k kniaziu M. D. Gorchakovu, 2 fevralia 1855 g.', *RS*, No. 12 (December 1881), pp. 895–6.

127. Nicholas I, 'Sobstvennoruchnaia zapiska Imperatora Nikolaia o pred- stoiashchikh vsennykh deistviiakh ot 1-go fevralia 1855 g. dlia kniazia Varshavskago', *RS*, No. 12 (1881), pp. 896–9.

128. Baroness M. P. Frederiks, 'Iz vospominanii', *IV*, LXXI, No. 2 (Feb- ruary 1898), p. 477. (Italics in original.)

129. Tiutcheva, *Pri dvore dvukh imperatorov*, entry for 19 February 1855, I, p. 184.

130. ibid., p. 178.

131. ibid., p. 180.

132. Quoted in Polievktov, p. 376.

133. Quoted in Grunwald, p. 286.

134. Quoted in Presniakov, *Apogei samoderzhaviia*, pp. 93–4.

135. Aleksandr Herzen, *Polnoe sobranie sochinenii i pisem*, XIII, p. 616.

136. Nikitenko, *Zapiski i dnevnik* (St Petersburg, 1904), I, p. 553.

137. K. D. Kavelin to T. N. Granovskii, 4 March 1855, in Sh. M. Levin 'K. D. Kavelin o smerti Nikolaia I', in *Literaturnoe nasledstvo*, LXVII (Moscow, 1959), p. 610.

138. Tiutcheva, *Pri dvore dvukh imperatorov*, entry for 19 February 1855, pp. 179, 185.

139. M. P. Pogodin, 'Tsarskoe vremia', *Istoriko-politicheskie pis'ma*, p. 312.

140. Princess Lieven to Baron Meiendorf, 3 March 1855, in Meiendorf, III, p. 205.

141. V. Aksakova, *Dnevnik Very Sergeevny Aksakovoi*, edited by Kniaz' N. V. Golitsyn and P. E. Shchegolev (St Petersburg, 1913), entry for 20 February 1855, p. 59.

142. Quoted by N. S. Shtakel'berg, 'Zagadka smerti Nikolaia I', *Russkoe proshloe*, I (1923), p. 60.

143. A. V. Golovnin, 'Prodolzhenie zapisok, 1868–1870 gg.', TsGIAL, fond 851, opis' 1, delo No. 8/24.

144. 'Imperator Nikolai I i akademik Parrot', *RS*, XCV (1898), pp. 140–43.

145. M. P. Pogodin, 'Tsarskoe vremia', *Istoriko-politicheskie pis'ma*, p. 312.

146. Tarle, *Sochineniia*, IX, pp. 441–443.

147. A. J. Rieber (ed.), *The Politics of Autocracy: Letters of Alexander II to Prince A. I. Bariatinskii, 1857–1864* (Paris-The Hague, 1966), pp. 23–4.

148. M. Poggenpohl au Directeur de la Chancellerie de St Petersbourg, 20 mars 1854, in Nesselrode, *Papiers et lettres*, XI, pp. 30–31.

149. This was precisely the argument set forth in a memorandum to Alexander II in March 1856 by D. A. Miliutin, to become Russia's Minister of War in 1861. See P. A. Zaionchkovskii, 'D. A. Miliutin: Biograficheskii ocherk', *Dnevnik D. A. Miliutina, 1873–1875 gg.* (Moscow, 1947), I, p. 17.

150. Nikitenko, *Dnevnik*, I, p. 421.

151. ibid., p. 411.

152. 'Imperator Nikolai I i akademik Parrot', *RS*, XCV (1898), p. 145.

153. A. V. Golovnin, 'Kratkii obzor deistvii Velikago Kniazia Konstantina Nikolaevicha po Morskomu Vedomstvu so vremeni vstupleniia v upravlenie onym po ianvar' 1858', GPB, fond 208, No. 2/269.

154. Presniakov, *Apogei samoderzhaviia*, passim.

155. Baroness M. P. Frederiks, 'Iz vospominanii baronessy', *IV*, LXXI, No. 1 (January 1898), p. 55.

Selected Bibliography

This bibliography is not intended to be an exhaustive compilation of all materials available about the Emperor Nicholas I, or even a comprehensive listing of all materials consulted in the research for this book. It contains mainly materials which have been cited in the notes of the present work, and those which I have found particularly useful in my studies about this period.

ARCHIVAL SOURCES

Gosudarstvennaia Publichnaia Biblioteka imeni M. E. Saltykova–Shchedrina, g. Leningrad. Otdel Rukopisei [GPB]. Saltykov–Shchedrin State Public Library, Leningrad, Manuscript Section.
    Collection   208 A. V. Golovnin archive.
    Collection   380 Baron M. A. Korf archive.
    Collection   833 V. A. Tsie archive.
Gosudarstvennaia Biblioteka S.S.S.R. imeni V. I. Lenina, g. Moskva. Otdel Rukopisei [ORGBL]. The V. I. Lenin State Library of the U.S.S.R., Moscow. Manuscript Section.
    Collection   169 Miliutin archive.
    Collection   325 A. E. Tsimmerman archive.
Tsentral'nyi Gosudarstvennyi Istoricheskii Arkhiv S.S.S.R., g. Leningrad. [TsGIAL]. The Central State Historical Archive of the U.S.S.R., Leningrad.
    Collection   673 I. P. Liprandi archive.
    Collection   772 Chief Directorate of Censorship archive.
    Collection   775 Central Directorate of Censorship archive.
    Collection   851 A. V. Golovnin archive.
    Collection   869 N. A. Miliutin archive.
    Collection   908 P. A. Valuev archive.
    Collection   940 A. P. Zablotskii-Desiatovskii archive.
    Collection 1159 State Council archive: memoranda of the State Council General Sessions and of its various departments.
    Collection 1284 Department of General Affairs of the Ministry of the Interior archive.
    Collection 1287 Economic Department of the Ministry of the Interior archive.
Tsentral'nyi Gosudarstvennyi Arkhiv Oktiabr'skoi Revoliutsii, g. Moskva. [TsGAOR] Central State Archive of the October Revolution, Moscow.
    Collection   109 Secret archive of the Third Section of His Majesty's Own Chancery.
    Collection 647 Grand Duchess Elena Pavlovna archive

Collection 722 Marble Palace (Grand Duke Konstantin Nikolaevich) archive.
Collection 728 Baron M. A. Korf archive.
The Public Records Office, London.
FO. 65. Volumes 583–4, 612, 641–4, 665, 686, 708.
Sterling Memorial Library, Yale University, New Haven, Connecticut.
The Osborn Collection (Miliutin Papers).

PUBLISHED SOURCES

Akhsharumov, D. D., *Iz moikh vospaminanii, 1849–1851 gg*, St Petersburg, 1905.
Aksakova, V. S., *Dnevnik Very Sergeevny Aksakovoi*, edited by Kniaz' N. V. Golitsyn and P. E. Shchegolev, St Petersburg, 1913.
Aksenov, K., *Severnoe obshchestvo dekabristov*, Leningrad, 1851.
Aleksandra Fedorovna, Empress, 'Imperatritsa Aleksandra Fedorovna v svoikh vospominaniiakh', *Russkaia starina*, No. 10 (October 1896), pp. 5–60.
—, 'Iz dnevnikov Aleksandry Fedorovny', in B. E. Syroechkovskii (ed.), *Mezhdutsarstvie 1825 goda i vosstanie dekabristov v perepiske i memuarakh chlenov tsarskoi sem'i*, Moscow-Leningrad, 1926.
Alston, Patrick L., *Education and the State in Tsarist Russia*, Stanford, 1969.
Andics, Erzsébet (ed.), *A Habsburgok és Románovok szövetsége*, Budapest, 1961.
—, *Das Bündnis Habsburg-Romanow. Vorgeschichte der zaristischen Intervention in Ungarn im Jahre 1849*, Budapest, 1963.
Annenkov, P. A., *Literaturnye vospominaniia*, Moscow, 1960.
Artz, F. B., *France under the Bourbon Restoration*, Cambridge, 1931.
Averbukh, R. A., 'Avstriiskaia revoliutsiia 1848 g. i Nikolai I', *Krasnyi arkhiv*, LXXXIX–XC (1938), pp. 155–207.
—, *Revoliutsiia i natsional'no-osvoboditel'naia bor'ba v Vengrii, 1848–1849 gg.*, Moscow, 1965.
—, *Tsarskaia interventsiia v bor'be s vengerskoi revoliutsiei*, Moscow, 1935.
—, *Revoliutsiia v Avstrii (1848–1849 gg.)*, Moscow, 1970.
Baddeley, J. F., *The Russian Conquest of the Caucasus*, London, 1908.
Balmuth, D., 'The Origins of the Tsarist Epoch of Censorship Terror', *American Slavic and East European Review*, XIX (1960), pp. 497–520.
Bapst, Edmond, *Les Origines de la Guerre de Crimée. La France et la Russie de 1848–1854*, Paris, 1912.
Baranovskaia, M. Iu., *Dekabrist Nikolai Bestuzhev*, Moscow, 1954.
Baron, S. W., *The Russian Jew*, New York, 1961.
Barsukov, N., *Zhizn' i trudy M. P. Pogodina*, 22 vols., St Petersburg, 1888–1910.
Bartenev, P. I. (ed.), *Deviatnadtsatyi vek. Istoricheskii sbornik*, 2 vols., Moscow, 1872.
Barzykowski, S., *Historia powstania listopadowego*, 5 vols., Poznań, 1883–4.
Bazancourt, Baron de, *L'Expédition de Crimée, jusqu'à la prise de Sévastopol*, 2 vols., Paris, 1856.
Bekmakhanov, E. V., *Prisoedinenie Kazakhstana k Rossii*, Moscow, 1957.

Belinskii, V. G., *Sobranie sochinenii V. G. Belinskago*, 3 vols., St Petersburg, 1919.

Benkendorf, A. Kh., 'Graf A. Kh. Benkendorf o Rossii v 1827–1830 gg.', *Krasnyi arkhiv*, XXXVII (1929), pp. 138–74; XXXVIII (1930), pp. 109–47.

—, 'Imperator Nikolai I v 1828–1829 gg. (Iz zapisok grafa A. Kh. Benkendorfa)', *Russkaia starina*, LXXXVI, No. 6 (June 1896), pp. 471–510; LXXXVII, No. 7 (June 1896), pp. 3–27.

—, 'Imperator Nikolai I v 1830–1831 gg. (Iz zapisok grafa A. Kh. Benkendorfa)', *Russkaia starina*, LXXXVIII, No. 10 (October 1896), pp. 65–96.

—, 'Zapiski grafa A. Kh. Benkendorfa, 1832–1837 gg.', in N. K. Shilder, *Imperator Nikolai Pervyi: Ego zhizn' i tsarstvovanie*, II, St Petersburg, 1903, pp. 647–764.

Benois, A. and N. Lanceray, 'Dvortsovoe stroitel'stvo Imperatora Nikolaia I', *Starye gody* (July–September 1913), pp. 173–97.

Benson, A. C., and Viscount Esher (eds.), *The Letters of Queen Victoria: A Selection of Her Majesty's Correspondence between the Years 1837–1861*, vol. II, London, 1907.

Berlin, Sir Isaiah, 'The Marvellous Decade', *Encounter*, 1955–6.

—, 'Russia and 1848', *Slavonic Review*, XXVI (1948), pp. 341–60.

Blackwell, W. L., *The Beginnings of Russian Industrialization, 1800–1860*, Princeton, 1968.

Bogdanovich, M. I., *Vostochnaia voina, 1853–1856 gg.*, 4 vols., St Petersburg, 1876.

Bogucharskii, V. (Pseudonym of V. Iakovlev,) 'Tret'e otdelenie sobstvennago ego imperatorskago velichestva kantseliarii o sebe samom', *Vestnik evropy*, No. 3 (March 1917).

Bologne, M., *L'Insurrection prolétarienne de 1830 en Belgique*, Brussels, 1929.

Bolsover, G. H., 'Nicholas I and the Partition of Turkey', *Slavonic Review*, XXVII, No. 68 (1948), pp. 115–45.

Borodkin, M., *Istoriia Finlandii. Vremia Imperatora Nikolaia I*, Petrograd, 1915.

—, *Voina 1854–1855 gg. na Finskom Poberezh'e*, St Petersburg, 1904.

Borovkov, A. D., 'A. D. Borovkov i ego avtobiograficheskie zapiski', *Russkaia starina*, No. 11 (November 1898), pp. 331–63; No. 12 (December 1898), pp. 591–616.

Borozdin, I. N., 'Universitety v Rossii v pervoi polovine XIX veka', *Istoriia Rossii v XIX vek*, II, St Petersburg, 1907, pp. 349–79.

Bowman, Herbert E., *Vissarion Belinskii, 1811–1848: A Study in the Origins of Social Criticism in Russia*, Cambridge, Mass., 1954.

Bozherianov, I. N., *Zhizneopisanie imperatritsy Aleksandry Fedorovny suprugi Imperatora Nikolaia I*, 2 vols., St Petersburg, 1898.

Bray-Steinberg, Graf Otto von, 'Imperator Nikolai I i ego spodvizhniki', *Russkaia starina*, CIX, No. 1 (January 1901), pp. 115–39.

Brioni, P. I. (ed.), 'Ermolov, Dibich, i Paskevich na Kavkaze v 1826–1827 gg.: Doneseniia i pis'ma', *Russkaia starina*, V, No. 5 (May 1872), pp. 706–26; VI, No. 7 (July 1872), pp. 39–69; VI, No. 8 (August 1872), pp. 243–80.

Brodskii, N. L., *Rannye slavianofily*, Moscow, 1910.

Brooks, E. W., 'D. A. Miliutin: Life and Activity to 1856' (unpublished Ph. D. Dissertation, Stanford University, 1970).

Brown, E., _Stankevich and His Moscow Circle, 1830–1840_, Stanford, 1961.

Bulwer, Baron Henry Lytton, _Life of Henry John Temple, Viscount Palmerston_, 3 vols., London, 1871–4.

Bychkov, A. F. (ed.), 'K piatidesiatiletiiu II-go otdeleniia Sobstvennoi E. I. V. Kantseliarii', _Russkaia starina_ (1876).

Bykova, V. P., _Zapiski staroi smolianki_, St Petersburg, 1898.

Carpathinus, '1848 and Roumanian Unification', _Slavonic Review_, XXVI, No. 67 (April 1948), pp. 390–421.

Carr, E. H., _Michael Bakunin_, 2nd ed., New York, 1961.

—, _The Romantic Exiles_, Boston, 1961.

Catherine II, Empress, _Mémoires de l'impératrice Catherine II_, edited by A. Herzen, London, 1859.

—, 'Pis'ma Imperatritsy Ekateriny II baronu Mel'khioru Grimmu, 1774–1796 gg.', _Sbornik Imperatorskago Russkago Istoricheskago Obshchestva_, XXIII, St Petersburg, 1878.

Cattain, René, _Le Règne de Mohammed-Ali d'après les archives russes en Egypte_, 3 vols. in 2, Cairo, 1931–5.

Chaadaev, P. Ia., _Sochineniia i pis'ma P. Ia. Chaadaeva_, edited by M. O. Gershenzon, vol. I, Moscow, 1913.

Charles-Roux, François, _Thiers et Méhémet-Ali_, Paris, 1951.

Charléty, S., _La Restauration_, Paris, 1921.

Chicherin, B. N., _Vospominaniia Borisa Nikolaevicha Chicherina: Moskva sorokovykh godov_, Moscow, 1929.

Chmielewski, Edward, _Tribune of the Slavophiles: Konstantin Aksakov_, Gainesville, Fla., 1961.

Christoff, P. K., _An Introduction to Nineteenth-Century Russian Slavophilism_, 2 vols., The Hague, 1961, 1972.

Christoff, P. K., _The Third Heart_, The Hague, 1970.

Clapham, J. H., _The Economic Development of France and Germany, 1815–1914_, Cambridge, 1951.

Crisp. O., 'The State Peasants under Nicholas I', _Slavonic and East European Review_, XXXVII (1959), pp. 387–412.

Curtiss, J. S., _The Russian Army under Nicholas I, 1825–1855_, Durham, 1965.

Custine, Marquis de, _La Russie en 1839_, 4 vols., Paris, 1843.

Dan, Th., _The Origins of Bolshevism_, translated by J. Carmichael, New York, 1964.

Daragan, P. M., 'Vospominaniia pervago kamer-pazha velikoi kniagini (imperatritsy) Aleksandry Fedorovny, 1817–1819 gg.', _Russkaia starina_, XII, No. 4 (April 1875), pp. 769–96; XIII, No. 5 (May 1875), pp. 1–19.

Davydov, D., _Voennye zapiski_, vol. I, Moscow, 1940.

Davydov, D. V., 'Vospominaniia o tsesareviche Konstantine Pavloviche', _Golos minuvshego_, No. 5–6 (May–June 1917), pp. 36–46.

Dembowski, L., _Moje wspomnienia_, 2 vols., St Petersburg, 1898.

Dement'ev, A. G., *Ocherki po istorii russkoi zhurnalistiki, 1840–1850 gg.*, Moscow-Leningrad, 1951.

Dement'ev, A. G., A. V. Zapadov, and M. S. Cherepakhov, *Russkaia periodicheskaia pechat', 1702–1894 gg.*, Moscow, 1959.

Demoulin, R., *La Révolution de 1830*, Brussels, 1950.

Desnitskii, V., *et al.* (eds.), *Delo Petrashevtsev*, 3 vols., Moscow-Leningrad, 1937–51.

Dostoevskii, F. M., *Pis'ma*, vol. I, Moscow-Leningrad, 1928.

Dovnar-Zapol'skii, M. V., *Memuary Dekabristov*, Kiev, 1906.

Druzhinin, N. M., *Dekabrist Nikita Murav'ev*, Moscow, 1933.

—, *Gosudarstvennye krest'iane i reforma P. D. Kiseleva*, 2 vols., Moscow-Leningrad, 1946, 1958.

Dubetskii, I. P., 'Zapiski I. P. Dubetskago', *Russkaia starina*, LXXXIII, No. 4 (April 1895), pp. 113–44; LXXXIV, No. 5 (May 1895), pp. 87–110; No. 6 (June 1895), pp. 107–41.

Dubrovin, N. F. (ed.), 'Bumagi Grafa Arseniia Andreevicha Zakrevskago', *Sbornik Imperatorskago Russkago Istoricheskago Obshchestva*, LXXVIII, St Petersburg, 1891.

—, *Istoriia Krymskoi voiny i oborony Sevastopolia*, 3 vols., St Petersburg, 1900.

—, *Istoriia voiny i vladichestva russkikh na Kavkaze*, St Petersburg, 1888.

Dziewanowski, M. K., '1848 and the Hotel Lambert', *Slavonic Review*, XXVI, No. 67 (April 1948), pp. 361–73.

Emmons, T., *The Russian Landed Gentry and the Peasant Emancipation of 1861*, Cambridge, 1968.

Engleman, I., *Istoriia krepostnago prava v Rossii*, Moscow, 1906.

Epanchin, N., *Takticheskaia podgotovka russkoi armii pered pokhodom 1828–1829 gg.*, St Petersburg, 1904.

Ermolov, A. P., 'Dnevnik Alekseia Petrovicha Ermolova v prodolzhenie komandirovaniia v Gruzii do konchiny Imperatora Aleksandra', in M. P. Pogodin, *Aleksei Petrovich Ermolov: Materialy dlia ego biografii*, Moscow, 1864, pp. 235–54.

Ermolov, Aleksandr, *A. P. Ermolov: Biograficheskii ocherk*, St Petersburg, 1912.

Evgenev-Maksimov, V. E., *Ocherki po istorii sotsialisticheskoi zhurnalistiki v Rossii XIX veka*, Moscow-Leningrad, 1927.

Evreinov, G., *Proshloe i nastoiashchee znachenie russkago dvorianstva*, St Petersburg, 1898.

Fadeev, A. V., *Rossiia i Kavkaz pervoi treti XIX v*, Moscow, 1960.

—, *Rossiia i vostochnyi krizis 20-kh godov XIX veka*, Moscow, 1958.

Ficquelmont, Comte Karl Ludwig de, *La Politique de la Russie et les principautés danubiennes*, Paris, 1854.

Filippov, A., 'K voprosu o sostave pervago Polnago Sobraniia Zakonov Rossiiskoi Imperii', *Otchet Imperatorskago Moskovskago Universiteta za 1915 g.*, vol I, Moscow, 1916.

Florinsky, M., *Russia: A History and an Interpretation*, 2 vols., New York, 1968.

Flynn, J. E., 'The Universities, the Gentry, and the Russian Imperial Services, 1815–1825', *Canadian Slavic Studies*, II (Winter, 1968), pp. 486–503.

Frederiks, Baroness M. P., 'Iz vospominanii baronessy M. P. Frederiksa', *Istoricheskii vestnik*, LXXI (January 1898), pp. 52–88; LXXI (February 1898), pp. 454–84.

Gershenzon, M. O. (ed.), *Epokha Nikolaia I*, Moscow, 1910.

Gogol', N. V., *Polnoe sobranie sochineniia N. V. Gogolia*, 8 vols., Moscow, 1913.

Golovine, Ivan, *Russia under the Autocrat Nicholas the First*, 2 vols., London, 1846.

Golubov, S. N., *et al.* (eds.), *V. G. Belinskii v vospominaniiakh sovremennikov*, Moscow, 1962.

Gorbachevskii, I. I., *Zapiski dekabrista I. I. Gorbachevskago*, Moscow, 1916.

Gorev, L., *Voina 1853–1856 gg. i oborona Sevastopolia*, Moscow, 1955.

Goriainow, S. M., *Le Bosphore et les Dardanelles*, Paris, 1910.

Gosudarstvennyi sovet, 1801–1901 gg., St Petersburg, 1902.

Granovskii, T. N., *T. N. Granovskii i ego perepiska*, 2 vols., Moscow, 1897.

Gratieux, A., *A. S. Khomiakov et le mouvement Slavophile*, 2 vols., Paris, 1939.

Grimm, A. Th. von, *Alexandra Feodorowna Kaiserin von Russland*, 2 vols., Leipzig, 1866.

Grosul, V. Ia., *Reformy v Dunaiskikh kniazhestvakh i Rossiia*, Moscow, 1966.

Grunwald, Constantin de, *Tsar Nicholas I*, translated from the French by Brigit Patmore, London, 1954.

Grynwaser, H., *Demokracja szlachecka, 1795–1831*, Warsaw, 1918.

Guichen, Eugène de, *La Crise d'Orient de 1839 à 1841 et l'Europe*, Paris, 1921.

—, *La Guerre de Crimée (1854–1856) et l'attitude des puissances Européennes*, Paris, 1936.

Guizot, F., *Mémoires pour servir à l'histoire de mon temps*, vol. IV, Paris-Leipzig, 1861.

Gulick, E. V., *Europe's Classical Balance of Power*, New York, 1967.

Haywood, Richard N., *The Beginnings of Railway Development in Russia in the Reign of Nicholas I, 1835–1842*, Durham, 1969.

Haxthausen-Abbenburg, Baron August Ludwig Maria von, *The Russian Empire: Its People and Resources*, translated by Robert Farie, 2 vols., London, 1856.

Heaton, H., 'Economic Change and Growth', in J. P. T. Bury (ed.), *New Cambridge Modern History*, vol. X. Cambridge, 1960, pp. 22–48.

Henderson, W. O., *The Zollverein*, London, 1959.

Herzen, A. I., *Polnoe sobranie sochinenii i pisem*, M. K. Lemke (ed.), 22 vols., Petersburg/Leningrad, 1919–25.

Hoffman, Joachim, 'Russland und die Olmützer Punktation', *Forschungen zur osteuropäischen Geschichte*, VII (1959), pp. 59–71.

Horváth, Eugene, 'Russia and the Hungarian Revolution, 1848–1849', *Slavonic Review*, XII, No. 36 (April 1934), pp. 628–45.

Iakhontov, A. H., 'Vospominaniia tsarskosel'skago litseista', *Russkaia starina*, LX, No. 10 (October 1888).

Iakushkin, I. D., *Zapiska, stat'i, pis'ma dekabrista I. D. Iakushkina*, Moscow, 1951.

Ikor, Roger, *Insurrection ouvrière de juin 1848*, Paris, 1936.

'Imperator Nikolai I i akademik Parrot', *Russkaia starina*, No. 7 (July 1898), pp. 139–52.

'Imperator Nikolai I i Napoleon III (iz bumag generala de-Kastel'bazhaka)', *Russkaia starina*, CVII, No. 7 (July 1901), pp. 67–76.

'Imperator Nikolai I v doneseniiakh shvedskago poslannika', *Russkaia starina*, CXVI, No. 10 (October 1903), pp. 205–19.

Istoricheskoe obozrenie piatidesiatiletnei deiatel'nosti Ministerstva Gosudarstvennykh Imushchestv, 1837–1887 gg., 5 vols., St Petersburg, 1888.

Istoriia leib-gvardii Egerskago polka za sto let, 1796–1896 gg., 3 vols., St Petersburg, 1896.

Istoriia Pravitel'stvuiushchego senata za dvesti let, 1711–1911 gg., 5 vols., St Petersburg, 1911.

Ivanov-Razumnik, 'Obshchestvennye i umstvennye techeniia 30-kh godov', in D. N. Ovsianniko-Kulikovskii (ed.), *Istoriia russkoi literatury XIX v*, I, Moscow, 1909, pp. 247–75.

'Iz ofitsial'noi perepiski chlenov tsarskoi sem'i', in B. E. Syroechkovskii (ed.), *Mezhdutsarstvie 1825 goda i vosstanie dekabristov v perepiske i memuarakh chlenov tsarskoi sem'i*, Moscow-Leningrad, 1926.

Jelavich, Charles and Barbara (eds.), The *Education of a Russian Statesman: The Memoirs of Nicholas Karlovich Girs*, Berkeley and Los Angeles, 1962.

Kalken, F. van, *Histoire du royaume des Pays-Bas et de la Révolution belge de 1830*, Brussels, 1910.

Kamenskii, Aleksandr, 'Vsepoddanneishaia zapiska A. Kamenskago 1850 goda', *Russkaia starina*, CXXII, No. 6 (June 1905), pp. 629–57.

Kamiński, Aleksander, *Polskie związki młodzieży, 1831–1848*, Warsaw, 1968.

—, *Prehistoria polskich związków młodzieży*, Warsaw, 1959.

Kaplan, F. I., 'Russian Fourierism of the 1840s: A Contrast to Herzen's Westernism', *American Slavic and East European Review*, XVII (April 1958), pp. 161–72.

Karamzin, N. M., *Karamzin's Memoir on Ancient and Modern Russia*, translated and edited by Richard Pipes, Cambridge, Mass., 1959.

Kaufman, I. I., *Iz istorii bumazhnykh deneg v Rossii*, St Petersburg, 1909.

Kharitonov, A. A., 'Iz vospominanii A. A. Kharitonova', *Russkaia starina*, LXXXI, No. 1 (January 1894), pp. 101–32.

Khromov, P., *Ekonomicheskoe razvitie Rossii v XIX–XX vekakh, 1800–1917 gg.*, Moscow, 1950.

Kieniewicz, S., *Konspiracje galicyjskie (1831–1845)*, Warsaw, 1950.

—, 'The Social Visage of Poland in 1848', *Slavonic Review*, XXVII, No. 68 (December 1948), pp. 91–105.

Kiesewetter, A. A., 'Imperator Nikolai I, kak konstitutsionnyi monarkh', in A. A. Kiesewetter, *Istoricheskie ocherki*, Moscow, 1912, pp. 402–18.

—, 'Krest'ianstvo v russkoi nauchno-istoricheskoi literature', *Krest'ianskaia rossiia*, V (1923), pp. 23–43.

—, 'Vnutrenniaia politika Imperatora Nikolaia Pavlovicha', in A. A. Kiesewetter, *Istoricheskie ocherki*, Moscow, 1912, pp. 419–502.

Kinglake, A. W., *The Invasion of the Crimea: Its Origins, and an Account of Its Progress Down to the Death of Lord Raglan*, 8 vols., Edinburgh, 1863–1887.

Kislinskii, N. A., *Nasha zheleznodorozhnaia politika po dokumentam arkhiva Komiteta Ministrov*, 4 vols., St Petersburg, 1902.

Kolmakov, N. M., 'Ocherki i vospominaniia N. M. Kolmakova', *Russkaia starina*, LXX, No. 6 (June 1891), pp. 657–80.

Kolzakov, P. A., 'Zametki P. A. Kolzakova', *Russkaia starina*, I, No. 6 (June 1870), pp. 495–9.

Konstantin Pavlovich, Grand Duke, 'Iz perepiski Konstantina Pavlovicha i Marii Fedorovny', in B. E. Syroechkovskii (ed.), *Mezhdutsarstvie 1825 goda i vosstanie dekabristov v perepiske i memuarakh chlenov tsarskoi sem'i*, Moscow-Leningrad, 1926.

—, 'Iz perepiski Nikolaia I i Konstantina Pavlovicha (26/xi–16/xii 1825)', in B. E. Syroechkovskii (ed.), *Mezhdutsarstvie 1825 goda i vosstanie dekabristov v perepiske i memuarakh chlenov tsarskoi sem'i*, Moscow-Leningrad, 1926.

—, Iz perepiski Nikolaia I i Konstantina Pavlovicha (17/xii 1825–21/vii 1826)', in B. E. Syroechkovskii (ed.), *Mezhdutsarstvie 1825 goda i vosstanie dekabristov v perepiske i memuarakh chlenov tsarskoi sem'i*, Moscow-Leningrad, 1926.

—, 'Iz perepiski Nikolaia I i Konstantina Pavlovicha (1/xi 1826–26/i 1827)', in B. E. Syroechkovskii (ed.), *Mezhdutsarstvie 1825 goda i vosstanie dekabristov v perepiske i memuarakh chlenov tsarskoi sem'i*, Moscow-Leningrad, 1926.

—, 'Perepiska Imperatora Nikolaia Pavlovicha s velikim kniazem tsesarevichem Konstantinom Pavlovichem, 1825–1829 gg.', *Sbornik Imperatorskago Russkago Istoricheskago Obshchestva*, CXXXI, St Petersburg, 1910.

—, 'Perepiska Imperatora Nikolaia Pavlovicha s velikim kniazem tsesarevichem Konstantinom Pavlovichem, 1830–1831 gg.', *Sbornik Imperatorskago Russkago Istoricheskago Obshchestva*, CXXXII, St Petersburg, 1911.

Korf, M. A., *The Accession of Nicholas I*, 3rd impression (first published), London, 1857.

—, 'Imperator Nikolai v soveshchatel'nykh sobraniiakh', in N. F. Dubrovin (ed.), *Materialy i cherty k biografii Imperatora Nikolaia I i k istorii ego tsarstvovaniia*, St Petersburg, 1896, pp. 101–286.

—, 'Materialy i cherty k biografii Imperatora Nikolaia I i k istorii ego tsarstvovanie. Rozhdenie i pervyia dvadtsat' let zhizni (1796–1817 gg.)', in N. F. Dubrovin (ed.), *Materialy i cherty k biografii Imperatora Nikolaia I i k istorii ego tsarstvovaniia*, St Petersburg, 1896, pp. 1–100.

—, 'Iz zapisok barona Korfa', *Russkaia starina*, XCVII–CII (1899–1900).

Kornilov, A. A., *Kurs istorii Rossii XIX v*, 3 vols., Moscow, 1918.

Korsakov, A., 'Detstvo i otrochestvo Nikolaia Pavlovicha', *Russkii arkhiv*, XXXIV, No. 6 (1896), pp. 278–90.

Kostiushko, I. I., *Krest'ianskaia reforma 1864 goda v tsarstve pol'skom*, Moscow, 1962.

Koyré, A., *La Philosophie et le problème national en Russie au début du XIXᵉ siècle*, Paris, 1929.

Kosłowski, W. M., *Autonomia królestwa polskiego, 1815–1831*, Warsaw, 1907.

Kraushar, A., *Świętokrzyżcy – pierwsze tajne towarzystwo demokratyczne w Warszawie*, Warsaw, 1916.

Kucharzewski, J., *Epoka paskiewicziwska w Królestwie Polskim*, Warsaw, 1914.

Kutuzov, N., 'Zapiska: Sostoianie gosudarstva v 1841 godu', *Russkaia starina*, No. 9 (September 1898), pp. 517–31.

LaCroix, Paul, *Histoire de la vie et du règne de Nicolas Ier*, 8 vols., Paris, 1864–9.

Lander, K., 'Pribaltiiskii krai v pervoi polovine XIX veka', in *Istoriia Rossii v XIX veke*, II, St Petersburg, 1907, pp. 327–49.

Langer, W. L., *Political and Social Upheaval, 1832–1852*, New York-London, 1969.

Lednicki, Wacław, *Russia, Poland, and the West: Essays in Literary and Cultural History*.

Leighton, Lauren, *Alexander Bestuzhev-Marlinsky*, Boston, 1975.

Leikina-Svirskaia, V. R., *Intelligentsiia v Rossii vo vtoroi polovine XIX veka*, Moscow, 1971.

Lemke, M., *Nikolaevskie zhandarmy i literatura, 1826–1855 gg.*, St Petersburg, 1909.

—, *Ocherki po istorii russkoi tsenzury i zhurnalistiki XIX stoletiia*, St Petersburg, 1904.

Lenskii, Z., 'Pol'sha v pervoi polovine XIX veka', *Istoriia Rossii v XIX veke*, I, St Petersburg, 1907, pp. 260–327.

Leslie, R. F., *Polish Politics and the Revolution of November 1830*, London, 1956.

Levin, Sh. M., 'K. D. Kavelin o smerti Nikolaia I', *Literaturnoe Nasledstvo*, LXVII, Moscow, 1959, pp. 596–612.

Lewis, Michael, 'Armed Forces and the Art of War: Navies', in J. P. T. Bury (ed.), *New Cambridge Modern History*, Cambridge, 1960, pp. 274–301.

Liashchenko, P. I., *Istoriia narodnago khoziaistva SSSR*, 2 vols., Moscow, 1956.

Liatskii, E. A. (ed.), *Belinskii. Pis'ma*, 3 vols., St Petersburg, 1914.

Liddell Hart, B. H., 'Armed Forces and the Art of War: Armies', in J. P. T. Bury (ed.), *New Cambridge Modern History*, Cambridge, 1960, pp. 302–30.

Lincoln, W. Bruce, 'The Circle of Grand Duchess Elena Pavlovna, 1847–1861', *Slavonic and East European Review*, XLVIII, No. 112 (July 1970), pp. 373–87.

—, 'The Circle of M. V. Butashevich-Petrashevskii: Some Comments on the Social and Intellectual Climate of St Petersburg in the 1840s', *Australian Journal of Politics and History*, XIX, No. 3 (December 1973), pp. 366–76.

—, 'Count P. D. Kiselev: A Reformer in Imperial Russia', *Australian Journal of Politics and History*, XVI, No. 2 (August 1970), pp. 177–88.

—, 'The Daily Life of St Petersburg Officials in the Mid-Nineteenth Century', *Oxford Slavonic Papers*, VIII (1975), pp. 82–100.

—, 'The Emperor Nicholas I in England', *History Today*, XXV, No. 1 (January 1975), pp. 24–30.

—, 'The Genesis of an "Enlightened" Bureaucracy in Russia, 1825–1855', *Jahrbücher für Geschichte Osteuropas*, XX, No. 3 (September 1972), pp. 321–330.

—, 'The Ministers of Nicholas I: A Brief Inquiry into Their Backgrounds and Service Careers', *Russian Review*, XXXIV, No. 3 (July 1975), pp. 308–23.

Lincoln, W. Bruce, 'N. A. Miliutin and the St Petersburg Municipal Act of 1846: A Study in Reform under Nicholas I', *Slavic Review*, XXXIII, No. 1 (March 1974), pp. 55–68.

—, 'Nicholas I: Russia's Last Absolute Monarch', *History Today*, XXI, No. 2 (February 1971), pp. 79–88.

—, *Nikolai Miliutin: An Enlightened Russian Bureaucrat*, Newtonville, Mass., 1977.

—, 'Russia and the Revolutions of 1848', *History Today*, XXIII, No. 1 (January 1973). pp. 53–60.

—, 'Russia's "Enlightened" Bureaucrats and Problems of State Reform, 1848–1856', *Cahiers du monde russe et soviétique*, XII, No. 4 (October–December 1971), pp. 410–21.

—, 'The Composition of the Imperial Russian State Council under Nicholas I', *Canadian-American Slavic Studies*, X, No. 3 (1976), pp. 369–81.

—, 'The Last Years of the Nicholas System: The Unpublished Diaries and Memoirs of Baron Korf and General Tsimmerman', *Oxford Slavonic Papers*, VI (1973), pp. 12–27.

—, 'Reform and Reaction in Russia: A. V. Golovnin's Critique of the 1860s', *Cahiers du monde russe et soviétique*, XVI, No. 2 (April–June 1975), pp. 167–179.

Lubomirski, Prince Joseph, *Souvenirs d'un page du tzar Nicolas*, Paris, 1869.

Lucas-Dubreton, J., *La Restauration et la monarchie de juillet*, Paris, 1926.

Lukashevich, Stephen, *Ivan Aksakov, 1823–1886: A Study in Russian Thought and Politics*, Cambridge, Mass., 1965.

McGrew, R. E., *Russia and the Cholera, 1823–1832*, Madison, 1965.

MacMaster, R. E., *Danilevskii: A Russian Totalitarian Philosopher*, Cambridge, Mass., 1967.

Maikov, P. M., *Vtoroe otdelenie sobstvennoi ego imperatorskago velichestva kantseliarii, 1826–1882 gg.*, St Petersburg, 1906.

Makogonenko, G. P., *Nikolai Novikov i russkoe prosveshchenie XVIII veka*, Moscow-Leningrad, 1952.

—, *Radishchev i ego vremia*, Moscow, 1956.

Malia, M., *Alexander Herzen and the Birth of Russian Socialism*. Cambridge, Mass., 1961.

Mardar'ev, M., 'Pis'ma i zapiski Georga-Fridrika Parrota k Imperatoram Aleksandru I i Nikolaiu I', *Russkaia starina*, LXXXIII, No. 4 (April 1895), pp. 191–219.

Mariia Fedorovna, Dowager Empress, 'Iz dnevnikov Marii Fedorovny', in B. E. Syroechkovskii (ed.), *Mezhdutsarstvie 1825 goda i vosstanie dekabristov v perepiske i memuarakh chlenov tsarskoi sem'i*, Moscow-Leningrad, 1936.

—, 'Iz perepiski Konstantina Pavlovicha i Marii Fedorovny', in B. E. Syroechkovskii (ed.), *Mezhdutsarstvie 1825 goda i vosstanie dekabristov v perepiske i memuarakh chlenov tsarskoi sem'i*, Moscow-Leningrad, 1936.

Marriott, J. A. R., *The Eastern Question: An Historical Study in European Diplomacy*, 4th ed., Oxford, 1940.

Martens, F., *Sobranie traktatov i konventsii zakliuchennykh Rossieiu s inostrannymi derzhavami*, 15 vols., St Petersburg, 1874–1908.

Materialy dlia istorii tsarstvovaniia Imperatora Nikolaia Pavlovicha, Leipzig, 1880.

Mazour, Anatole, *The First Russian Revolution, 1825: The Decembrist Movement: Its Origins, Development, and Significance*, Berkeley, 1937.

McConnell, Allen, *Tsar Alexander I: Paternalistic Reformer*, New York, 1970.

Meiendorff, Peter von, *Politischer und privater briefweschel, 1826–1863*, 3 vols., Berlin and Leipzig, 1923.

Men'kov, *Zapiski ('Dunai i nemtsy-vostochnyi vopros, 1853–1855') i dnevnik*, 2 vols., St Petersburg, 1898.

Metternich, Prince Clemens von, *Mémoires, documents, et écrits divers laissés par le Prince de Metternich, Chancelier de cour et d'état*, vols. V–VIII, Paris, 1882.

—, *Memoirs of Prince Metternich*, 5 vols., New York, 1879–82.

Meyer, Henry C., *Mitteleuropa in German Thought and Action*, The Hague, 1955.

Mierosławski, L., *Powstanie narodu polskiego w r. 1830 i 1831*, 2 vols., Paris, 1834.

Mikhail Pavlovich, Grand Duke, 'Iz perepiski Nikolaia I i Mikhaila Pavlovicha (27/xi–16/xii 1825)', in B. E. Syroechkovskii (ed.), *Mezhdutsarstvie 1825 goda i vosstanie dekabristov v perepiske i memuarakh chlenov tsarskoi sem'i*, Moscow-Leningrad, 1926.

—, 'Iz perepiski Nikolaia I i Mikhaila Pavlovicha (9/v–16/vii 1826 g)', in B. E. Syroechkovskii (ed.), *Mezhdutsarstvie 1825 goda i vosstanie dekabristov v perepiske i memuarakh chlenov tsarskoi sem'i*, Moscow-Leningrad, 1926.

—, 'Vospominaniia Mikhaila Pavlovicha o sobytiiakh 14 dekabria 1825 g.', in B. E. Syroechkovskii (ed.), *Mezhdutsarstvie 1825 goda i vosstanie dekabristov v perepiske i memuarakh chlenov tsarskoi sem'i*, Moscow-Leningrad, 1926.

Miklashevskii, I., 'Statistika', *Entsiklopedicheskii slovar' Brokgauza-Eifrona*, St Petersburg, 1901, LXII, pp. 476–505.

Miliukov, P. N., *Glavnye techeniia russkoi istoricheskoi mysli*, Moscow, 1898.

—, 'Liubov' u idealistov tridtsakykh godov', *Iz istorii russkoi intelligentsii*, St Petersburg, 1903.

—, *Ocherki po istorii russkoi kul'tury*, vol. III, St Petersburg, 1901.

Miliutin, N. A., 'Istoricheskaia zapiska o raznykh predpolozheniiakh po predmetu osvobozhdeniia krest'ian', in P. Bartenev (ed.), *Deviatnadtsatyi vek: istoricheskii sbornik*, Moscow, 1972, II, pp. 145–208.

Ministerstvo Finansov, 1802–1902 gg., 2 vols., St Petersburg, 1902.

Ministerstvo iustitsii za sto let, 1802–1902 gg., St Petersburg, 1902.

Molok, A., 'Tsarskaia Rossiia i iiul'skaia revoliutsiia 1830 g.', *Literaturnoe Nasledstvo*, XXIX/XXX, Moscow, 1937, pp. 727–62.

—, 'K istorii revoliutsii 1830 g. v Bel'gii', *Krasnyi arkhiv*, CIV (1941), pp. 199–247.

Moltke, Helmuth C. B. von, 'Briefe über Zustände und Begebenheiten in der Türkei aus den Jahren 1835 bis 1839', in *Gesammelte Schriften und Denswürdigseiten bis General-Feldmarschalls Grafen Helmuth von Moltke*, vol. VIII, Berlin, 1893.

Monas, S., 'Bureaucracy in Russia under Nicholas I', in M. Cherniavsky (ed.), *The Structure of Russian History: Interpretative Essays*, New York, 1970, pp. 269–81.

406   *Selected Bibliography*

Monas, S., *The Third Section: Police and Society in Russia under Nicholas I*, Cambridge, Mass., 1961.

Mosely, P. E., *Russian Diplomacy and the Opening of the Eastern Question*, Cambridge, Mass., 1934.

Nechkina, M. V., *Dvizhenie dekabristov*, 2 vols., Moscow, 1955.

—, *Obshchestvo soedinennykh slavian*, Moscow-Leningrad, 1927.

Nesselrode, Count K. V., *Lettres et papiers du Chancelier Comte de Nesselrode, 1760–1850*, 11 vols., Paris, 1905–12.

—, 'Mémoire destiné à Son Altesse Impériale, Monseigneur le grand duc Nicolas à l'occasion de son voyage dans les pays étrangers', in N. K. Shilder, *Imperator Nikolai Pervyi: Ego zhizn' i tsarstvovanie*, I, St Petersburg, 1903, pp. 585–91.

Nicholas I, Emperor, 'Chetyre pis'ma Imperatora Nikolaia Pavlovicha k grafu P. A. Kleinmikheliu', *Russkaia starina*, No. 4 (April 1895), pp. 461–5.

—, 'Ermolov, Dibich i Paskevich na Kavkaze v 1826–1827 gg., Perepiska Imperatora Nikolaia', *Russkaia starina*, XXIX, No. 11 (November 1880), pp. 617–26.

—, 'Imperator Nikolai Pavlovich i graf Dibich Zabalkanskii. Perepiska, 1828–1830 gg.', *Russkaia starina*, XXVII, No. 1 (January 1880), pp. 95–110; No. 3 (March 1880), pp. 511–26; No. 4 (April 1880), pp. 765–80; XXVIII, No. 6 (June 1880), pp. 409–28; XXIX, No. 12 (1880), pp. 891–934.

—, 'Imperator Nikolai Pavlovich v Ego pis'makh k Kniaziu Paskevichu', *Russkii arkhiv*, No. 1 (January 1897), pp. 5–44.

—, 'Iz dnevnikov Nikolaia Pavlovicha', in B. E. Syroechkovskii (ed.), *Mezhdutsarstvie 1825 goda i vosstanie dekabristov v perepiske i memuarakh chlenov tsarskoi sem'i*, Moscow-Leningrad, 1926.

—, 'Iz perepiski Nikolaia I i Konstantina Pavlovicha (26/xi–16/xii 1825)', in B. E. Syroechkovskii (ed.), *Mezhdutsarstvie 1825 goda i vosstanie dekabristov v perepiske i memuarakh chlenov tsarskoi sem'i*, Moscow-Leningrad, 1926.

—, 'Iz perepiski Nikolaia I i Konstantina Pavlovicha (17/xii 1825–21/vii 1826)', in B. E. Syroechkovskii (ed.), *Mezhdutsarstvie 1825 goda i vosstanie dekabristov v perepiske i memuarakh chlenov tsarskoi sem'i*, Moscow-Leningrad, 1926.

—, 'Iz perepiski Nikolaia I i Konstantina Pavlovicha (1/xi 1826– 26/i 1827)', in B. E. Syroechkovskii (ed.), *Mezhdutsarstvie 1825 goda i vosstanie dekabristov v perepiske i memuarakh chlenov tsarskoi sem'i*, Moscow-Leningrad, 1926.

—, 'Iz perepiski Nikolaia I i Mikhaila Pavlovicha (27/xi–16/xii 1825)', in B. E. Syroechkovskii (ed.), *Mezhdutsarstvie 1825 goda i vosstanie dekabristov v perepiske i memuarakh chlenov tsarskoi sem'i*, Moscow-Leningrad, 1926.

—, 'Iz perepiski Nikolaia I i Mikhaila Pavlovicha (9/v–16/vii 1826 g.)', in B. E. Syroechkovskii (ed.), *Mezhdutsarstvie 1825 goda i vosstanie dekabristov v perepiske i memuarakh chlenov tsarskoi sem'i*, Moscow-Leningrad, 1926.

—, 'Iz zapisok Imperatora Nikolaia I', *Byloe*, bk 10 (1910), pp. 76–100.

—, 'Ma confession', in N. K. Shilder, *Imperator Nikolai Pervyi: Ego zhizn' i tsarstvovanie*, II, St Petersburg, 1903, pp. 310–12.

—, 'Perepiska Imperatora Nikolaia Pavlovicha s velikim kniazem tsesarevichem

Konstantinom Pavlovichem, 1825–1829 gg.', *Sbornik Imperatorskago Russkago Istoricheskago Obshchestva*, CXXXI, St Petersburg, 1910.

—, 'Perepiska Imperatora Nikolaia Pavlovicha s velikim kniazem tsesarevichem Konstantinom Pavlovichem, 1830–1831 gg.', *Sbornik Imperatorskago Russkago Istoricheskago Obshchestva*, CXXXII, St Petersburg, 1911.

—, 'Pis'ma Imperatora Nikolaia I i velikago kniazia Mikhaila Pavlovicha', *Russkaia starina*, No. 5 (May 1902), pp. 225–30.

—, 'Predsmertnoe pis'mo Imperatora Nikolaia k kniaziu M. D. Gorshakovu, 2 fevralia 1855 g.', *Russkaia starina*, No. 12 (December 1881), pp. 895–6.

—, 'Rech' Nikolaia k deputatam Peterburgskago dvorianstva', in M. O. Gershenzon (ed.), *Epokha Nikolaia I*, Moscow, 1910, pp. 10–11.

—, 'Sobstvennoruchnaia zapiska Imperatora Nikolaia o pol'skom voprose', in N. K. Shilder, *Imperator Nikolai Pervyi: Ego zhizn' i tsarstvovanie*, II, St Petersburg, 1903, pp. 582–4.

—, 'Sobstvennoruchnaia zapiska Imperatora Nikolaia o predstoiashchikh vsennykh deistviiakh ot l-go fevralia 1855 g. dlia kniazia Varshavskago', *Russkaia starina*, No. 12 (December 1881), pp. 896–9.

—, 'Zapiska Nikolaia I o polozhenii del v Evrope, 1848 g.', *Krasnyi arkhiv*, LXXXIX–XC (1938), pp. 160–64.

—, 'Zapiski Nikolaia I o vstuplenii na prestol', in B. E. Syroechkovskii (ed.), *Mezhdutsarstvie 1825 goda i vosstanie dekabristov v perepiske i memuarakh chlenov tsarskoi sem'i*, Moscow-Leningrad, 1926.

—, 'Zaveshchanie Nikolaia I synu', *Krasnyi arkhiv*, III (1923), pp. 291–3.

Nicolson, Harold, *The Congress of Vienna: A Study in Allied Unity, 1812–1822*, New York, 1946.

Nifontov, A. S., *Rossiia v 1848 godu*, Moscow, 1949.

Nikitenko, A. V., *Dnevnik*, 3 vols., Moscow, 1955.

—, *Moia povest' o samom sebe i o tom, 'chemu svidetel' v zhizn' byl': Zapiski i dnevnik (1804–1877 gg.)*, 2 vols., St Petersburg, 1904–5.

'Obozrenie khoda i deistvii kholernoi epidemii v Rossii v techenie 1848 goda', *Zhurnal Ministerstva Vnutrennikh Del*, XXVII, No. 9 (September 1849), pp. 314–28.

Oksman, Iu. G., 'Mery nikolaevskoi tsenzury protiv fur'erizma i kommunizma', *Golos minuvshego*, No. 5–6 (May–June 1917), pp. 69–73.

—, *Vospominaniia i rasskazy deiatelei tainykh obshchestv 1820-kh godov*, vol. 2, Moscow, 1933.

Okun, S. B., *Dekabrist M. S. Lunin*, Leningrad, 1962.

Oppman, E., *Warszawskie 'Towarzystwo Patriotyczne' 1830–1831*, Warsaw, 1937.

Oreus, I., *Opisanie vengerskoi voiny 1849 g.*, St Petersburg, 1880.

'Otchety Ministerstv za dvadtsatipiatiletie tsarstvovaniia Imperatora Nikolaia I', in N. F. Dubrovin (ed.), *Materialy i cherty biografii Imperatora Nikolaia I i k istorii ego tsarstvovaniia*, St Petersburg, 1896, pp. 287–695.

P——, 'Imperator Nikolai I', *Russkaia starina*, CXV, No. 9 (September 1903), pp. 541–57; CXVI, No. 10 (October 1903), pp. 87–104; No. 11 (November 1903), pp. 295–306.

'Pamiati Andreia Parfenovicha Zablotskago', *Russkaia starina*, XXXIII, No. 2 (February 1882), pp. 520–24.

Pavlova, L. Ia., *Dekabrist M. F. Orlov*, Moscow, 1964.

Pechoux, P., 'L'Ombre de Pugačev', in R. Portal (ed.), *Le Statut des paysans libérés du servage, 1861–1961*, Paris-The Hague, 1963, pp. 128–52.

Pel'chinskii, V. S., *La Russie en 1844: Système de Législation, d'Administration, et de Politique de la Russie en 1844*, Paris-Leipzig, 1845.

Pintner, W. M., *Russian Economic Policy under Nicholas I*, Ithaca, 1967.

—, 'The Social Characteristics of the Early Nineteenth-Century Russian Bureaucracy', *Slavic Review*, XXIX, No. 3 (September 1970), pp. 429–43.

Pipes, Richard, *Russia under the Old Regime*, New York, 1974.

Pirogov, N. I., *Sevastopol'skiia pis'ma, 1854–1855*, St Petersburg, 1899.

Pogodin, M. P., *Aleksei Petrovich Ermolov: Materialy dlia ego biografii*, Moscow, 1864.

—, *Istoriko-politicheskie pis'ma i zapiski v prodolzhenii krymskoi voiny, 1853–1856 gg.*, Moscow, 1874.

—, *Nikolai Mikhailovich Karamzin*, 2 vols., Moscow, 1866.

Polievktov, M., *Nikolai I: Biografiia i obzor tsarstvovaniia*, Moscow, 1918.

Polnoe Sobranie Zakonov Rossiiskoi Imperii, 2nd ed., 55 vols., St Petersburg, 1830–84.

Polovtsov, A. A. (ed.), 'Bumagi Vysochaisha utverzhdennago, 6 dekabria 1826 g., "Osobago sekretnago komiteta"', *Sbornik Imperatorskago Russkago Istoricheskago Obshchestva*, LXXIV, XC, St Petersburg, 1891, 1902.

Ponteil, F., *L'Éveil des nationalités et le mouvement libéral, 1815–1848*, Paris, 1960.

Popiel, P., *Pamiętniki Pawła Popiela, 1807–1892*, Cracow, 1927.

Popov, P. S., (ed.), *Pis'ma k A. V. Druzhininu, 1850–1863*, Moscow, 1948.

Pouthas, C. H., *Démocraties et capitalisme, 1848–1860*, Paris, 1961.

Presniakov, A. E., *14 Dekabria 1825 goda*, Moscow-Leningrad, 1926.

—, *Apogei samoderzhaviia: Nikolai I*, Leningrad, 1925. Also available in English as *Emperor Nicholas I of Russia: The Apogee of Autocracy, 1825–1855*, edited and translated by Judith C. Zacek, with an introductory essay, 'Nicholas I. and the Course of Russian History', by N. V. Riasanovsky, Gulf Breeze, 1974.

Prokesch von Osten, Count Anton, *Zur Geschichte der orientalischen Frage*, Vienna, 1877.

Puryear, V., *England, Russia, and the Straits Question, 1844–1856*, Berkeley, 1931.

Putilov, N., (ed.), *Sbornik izvestii otnosiashchikhsia do nastoiashchei voiny*, vols. 1–16, St Petersburg, 1854–5.

Puzyrevskii, A. K., *Pol'sko-russkaia voina 1831 goda*, 2 vols., St Petersburg, 1886.

Quénet, Charles, *Tchaadaev et les lettres philosophiques*, Paris, 1931.

Radishchev, A. N., *Izbrannye filosofskie i obshchestvenno-politicheskie proizvedeniia*, Moscow, 1952.

Raeff, M., *Michael Speranskii: Statesman of Imperial Russia, 1772–1839*, The Hague, 1957.

Raeff, M., *The Origins of the Russian Intelligentsia: The Eighteenth-Century Nobility*, New York, 1966.

—, *The Decembrist Movement*, Englewood Cliffs, 1966.

—, 'The Russian Autocracy and Its Officials', *Harvard Slavic Studies*, IV, (1957), pp. 77–92.

Ramazanov, N. A., 'Imperator Nikolai I v Rime v 1845 g.', *Russkaia starina*, CVII, No. 9 (September 1901), pp. 465–79.

Ramotowska, F., *Rząd carski wobec manifestacji patriotycznych w Królestwie Polskim w Latach 1860–1862*, Warsaw, 1971.

Rapp, Adolf, *Grossdeutsch-Kleindeutsch*, Munich, 1922.

Riasanovsky, N. V., 'Fourierism in Russia: An Estimate of the Petrashevtsy', *American Slavic and East European Review*, XII (October 1953), pp. 289–302.

—, *Nicholas I and Official Nationality in Russia, 1825–1855*, Berkeley and Los Angeles, 1959.

—, *Russia and the West in the Teaching of the Slavophiles. A Study of Romantic Ideology*, Cambridge, Mass., 1952.

Ribop'er, A. I., 'Zapiski grafa Aleksandra Ivanovicha Ribop'era', *Russkii arkhiv*, XV, No. 1 (1877), pp. 460–96; No. 2 (1877), pp. 5–36.

Rieber, A. J. (ed.), *The Politics of Autocracy: Letters of Alexander II to Prince A. I. Bariatinskii, 1857–1864*, Paris-The Hague, 1966.

Robinson, L. G. (ed.), *Letters of Dorothea, Princess Lieven, during Her Residence in London, 1812–1834*, London, 1902.

Rodkey, F. S., *The Turko-Egyptian Question in the Relations of England, France, and Russia, 1832–1841*, Urbana, 1924.

Rogger, Hans, *National Consciousness in Eighteenth Century Russia*, Cambridge, Mass., 1960.

Romanovich-Slavatinskii, A., *Dvorianstvo v Rossii ot nachala XVIII veka do otmeny krepostnago prava*, St Petersburg, 1870.

Roskovshenko, I. V., 'Peterburg v 1831–1832 gg.', *Russkaia starina*, CI, No. 2 (February 1900), pp. 477–90.

Rozhdestvenskii, S. V., *Istoricheskii obzor deiatel'nosti Ministerstva Narodnago Prosveshcheniia, 1802–1902 gg.*, St Petersburg, 1902.

—, 'Posledniaia stranitsa iz istorii politiki narodnago prosveshcheniia imperatora Nikolaia I', *Russkii istoricheskii zhurnal*, bks 3–4, 1917, pp. 37–59.

Rusanov, N., 'Vliianie zapadnoevropeiskago sotsializma na russkii', *Minuvshie gody*, May-June 1908.

Rutkowska, Janina, *Warszawa*, Warsaw, 1972.

Ryleev, K. F., *Polnoe sobranie sochineniia*, Moscow, 1934.

Ryndziunskii, P. G., *Gorodskoe grazhdanstvo doreformennoi Rossii*, Moscow, 1958.

Saltykov-Shchedrin, M. E., *Izbrannye proizvedeniia*, 7 vols., Moscow, 1939–49.

Sbornik rasporiazhenii po Ministerstvu Narodnago Prosveshcheniia, 3 vols., St Petersburg, 1866–7.

Schapiro, Leonard, *Rationalism and Nationalism in Russian Nineteenth-Century Political Thought*, New Haven and London, 1967.

Schiemann, Th., *Die Ermordung Paul und die Thronbesteigung Nikolaus I. Neue Materialen*, Berlin, 1902.

—, *Geschichte Russlands unter Kaiser Nikolaus I*, 4 vols., Berlin, 1908–19.

—, 'Imperator Nikolai Pavlovich (iz zapisok i vospominanii sovremennikov)', *Russkii arkhiv*, No. 2 (February 1902), pp. 459–75.

Schnitzler, J. H., *Secret History of the Court and Government of Russia under the Emperors Alexander and Nicholas*, 2 vols., London, 1847.

Schoeningh, Franz J., 'Karl Ludwig Bruck und die Idee Mitteleuropas', *Historisches Jahrbüch*, LVI (1936).

Secret Memoirs of the Court of St Petersburg, Particularly Towards the End of the Reign of Catherine II and the Commencement of that of Paul I, London, 1895.

Semenov-Tian-Shanskii, P. P., *Istoriia poluvekovoi deiatel'nosti imperatorskago russkago geograficheskago obshchestva, 1845–1895*, 3 vols., St Petersburg, 1896.

Semevskii, V. I., *Krest'ianskii vopros v Rossii v XVIII i pervoi polovine XIX veka*, 2 vols., St Petersburg, 1888.

—, *M. V. Butashevich-Petrashevskii i Petrashevtsy*, Pt 1 (all published), Moscow, 1922.

—, *Politicheskiia i obshchestvennyia idei dekabristov*, St Petersburg, 1909.

—, and P. E. Shcheglov (eds.), *Obshchestvennye dvizheniia v Rossii v pervuiu polovinu XIX veka*, vol. I, St Petersburg, 1905.

Seredonin, S. M., *Istoricheskii obzor deiatel'nosti komiteta ministrov*, 3 vols., St Petersburg, 1902.

Shapiro, O., 'Vneshniaia politika Kanninga i grecheskii vopros', *Voprosy istorii*, No. 12 (1947), pp. 43–61.

Shcherbatov, Kniaz' A., *General-Fel'dmarshal kniaz' Paskevich. Ego zhizn' i deiatel'nost'*, 7 vols., St Petersburg, 1888–1904.

Shcherbatov, M. M., 'Puteshestvie v zemliu Ofirskuiu G-na S . . . shvetskago dvorianina', in *Sochineniia kniazia M. M. Shcherbatova*, vol. I, St Petersburg, 1898.

Shevyrev, S. P., 'Lektsii o russkoi literature', *Sbornik otdeleniia russkago iazyka i slovesnosti imperatorskoi akademii nauk*, XXXIII, No. 5, St Petersburg, 1884.

—, 'Vzgliad russkago na sovremennoe obrazovanie Evropy', *Moskvitianin*, No. 1 (1841), pp. 219–96.

Shilder, N. K., *Imperator Nikolai Pervyi: Ego zhizn' i tsarstvovanie*, 2 vols., St Petersburg, 1903.

Shkurinov, P. S., *P. Ia. Chaadaev*, Moscow, 1960.

Shtakel'berg, N. S., 'Zagadka smerti Nikolaia I', *Russkoe proshloe*, I (1923), pp. 58–73.

Siegel, Stanisław, *Ceny w Warszawie w latach 1816–1914*, Poznań, 1949.

Sivkov, K., 'S. N. Glinka', *Russkii biograficheskii slovar'*, V, Moscow, 1916, pp. 290–97.

Sliwowska, Wiktoria, *Mikołaj I i jego czasy (1825–1855)*, Warsaw, 1965.

—, *Sprawa Pietraszewców*, Warsaw, 1964.

Smirnova-Rosset, A. O., *Avtobiografiia*, Moscow, 1931.

Solov'ev, S. M., *Zapiski Sergeia Mikhailovicha Solov'eva*, Petrograd, n.d.

Speranskii, M. M., 'O zakonakh. Besedy grafa M. M. Speranskago s Ego Imperatorskim Vysochaishestvom Gosudarem Naslednikom Tsesarevichem Velikim Kniazem Aleksandrom Nikolaevichem, s 12 oktiabria 1835 po 10 aprelia 1837 goda', *Sbornik Imperatorskago Russkago Istoricheskago Obshchestva*, XXX, St Petersburg, 1880.

Speranskii, M. M., 'Predpolozheniia okonchatel'nomu sostavleniiu zakonov', *Russkaia starina*, XV (1876), pp. 434–41.

Squire, P. S., *The Third Department. The Establishment and Practices of the Political Police in the Russia of Nicholas I*, Cambridge, 1968.

Starr, S. Frederick, *Decentralization and Self-Government in Russia, 1830–1870*, Princeton, 1972.

Stasov, V. V., 'Uchilishche pravovedeniia sorok let tomu nazad, 1836–1842 gg.', *Russkaia starina*, XXIX (1880), pp. 1015–42.

'Statistika pozharov v Rossii v 1848 god', *Zhurnal Ministerstva Vnutrennikh Del*, No. 7 (July 1849), pp. 7–44.

Stockmar, Baron C. F. von, *Memoirs of Baron Stockmar*, translated from the German by G. A. M., edited by F. Max Müller, 2 vols., London, 1872.

Stoiunin, V. Ia., 'Konservatory sorokovykh godov', *Istoricheskii vestnik*, VII, No. 1 (January 1882), pp. 5–28.

Storch, Heinrich, *The Picture of Petersburg*, London, 1801.

Strakhovsky, Leonid, *Alexander I of Russia*, New York, 1947.

—, *L'Empereur Nicolas Ier et l'ésprit national russe*, Louvain, 1928.

Stroev, V. I., *Stoletie sobstvennoi ego imperatorskago velichestva kantseliarii*, St Petersburg, 1912.

Struve, P. B., *Krepostnoe khoziaistvo*, Moscow, 1913.

Svod Zakonov Rossiiskoi Imperii, 1892 ed., 16 vols. in 1, St Petersburg, 1897.

Tarle, E. V., *Krymskaia voina* (vols. VIII and IX of *Sochineniia v dvenadtsati tomakh*), Moscow, 1959.

—, 'Samoderzhavie Nikolaia I i frantsuzskoe obshchestvennoe mnenie', *Byloe*, No. 9 (September 1906), pp. 12–42; No. 10 (October 1906), pp. 138–59.

Tatishchev, S. S., *Imperator Nikolai i inostrannye dvory: istoricheskie ocherki*, St Petersburg, 1889.

—, 'Imperator Nikolai I v Londone v 1844 godu', *Istoricheskii vestnik*, XXIII, No. 2 (February 1886), pp. 343–59; No. 3 (March 1886), pp. 602–21.

—, *Vneshniaia politika Imperatora Nikolaia I*, St Petersburg, 1887.

—, 'Votsarenie Imperatora Nikolaia', *Russkii vestnik*, CCXXV (1893), No. 5, pp. 89–113.

Tel'berg, G., 'Uchastie imperatora Nikolaia I v kodifikatsionnoi rabote ego tsarstvovaniia', *Zhurnal Ministerstva Iustitsii*, XXII, No. 1 (January 1916), pp. 233–44.

Telle, Hans G., *Das Österreichische Problem im Frankfurter Parlament im Sommer und Herbst 1848*, Marburg, 1933.

Temperley, Harold, *England and the Near East: The Crimea*, London and New York, 1936.

Testa, Le Baron I. de, *Recueil des traités de la Porte Ottomane avec les puissances étrangères*, vols. II, III, IX, X, Paris, 1865–1901.

Thaden, E. W., *Conservative Nationalism in Nineteenth-Century Russia*, Seattle 1964.
Thouvenel, L., *Nicolas Ier et Napoléon III. Les preliminaires de la guerre de Crimée*, Paris, 1891.
The Times (London), 1–10 June 1844.
Tiutchev, F. I., *Polnoe sobranie sochinenii F. I. Tiutcheva*, St Petersburg, 1913.
Tiutcheva (Aksakova), A. F., *Pri dvore dvukh imperatorov. Vospominaniia, Dnevnik*, vol. I, Moscow, 1928.
Tokarz, W., *Sprzysiężenie Wysockiego i noc listopadowa*, Warsaw, 1925.
—, *Wojna polsko-rosyjska 1830–1831*, Warsaw, 1930.
Torke, H-J., 'Continuity and Change in the Relations between Bureaucracy and Society in Russia, 1613–1861', *Canadian Slavic Studies*, V, No. 4 (Winter, 1971), pp. 457–76.
—, 'Das russische Beamtentum in der ersten Hälfte des 19. Jahrhunderts', *Forschungen zur osteuropäischen Geschichte*, XIII (Berlin-Wiesbaden, 1967), pp. 7–345.
Troitskii, S. M., *Russkii absoliutizm i dvorianstvo v XVIII v.: Formirovanie biurokratii*, Moscow, 1974.
'Tsenzura v tsarstvovanie imperatora Nikolaia I', *Russkaia starina*, CVII, No. 8 (August 1901), pp. 395–404; No. 9 (September 1901), pp. 643–68; CXIII, No. 2 (February 1903), pp. 305–28; No. 3 (March 1903), pp. 571–91; CXIV, No. 4 (April 1903), pp. 163–82; No. 5 (May 1903), pp. 379–96; No. 6 (June 1903), pp. 643–71.
Tugan-Baranovskii, M., *Russkaia fabrika v proshlom i nastoiashchem*, Moscow, 1938.
Umanets, F. M., 'Prokonsul Kavkaza', *Istoricheskii vestnik*, XXXIII (1888), pp. 258–95; 477–506.
Uvarov, S. S., 'Tsirkuliarnoe predlozhenie G. Upravliaiushchago Ministerstvom Narodnago Prosveshcheniia Nachal'stvam Uchebnykh Orkugov "O vstuplenii v upravlenie Ministerstvom"', 21 March 1833, *Zhurnal Ministerstva Narodnago Prosveshcheniia*, Pt I (1834), pp. 49–60.
Valuev, P. A., 'Dnevnik grafa Petra Aleksandrovicha Valueva, 1847–1860 gg.', *Russkaia starina*, LXX, No. 4 (April 1891), pp. 167–82.
—, 'Duma russkago', *Russkaia starina*, LXX, No. 5 (May 1891), pp. 349–59.
Varadinov, N., *Istoriia Ministerstva Vnutrennikh Del*, 8 vols., St Petersburg, 1858–63.
Vasilich, G., *Vosshestvie na prestol Imperatora Nikolaia I*, 2 vols., Moscow, 1909.
Velikin, B., *Peterburg-Moskva: Iz istorii oktiabr'skoi zheleznoi dorogi*, Leningrad, 1934.
Venturi, Franco, *The Roots of Revolution*, New York, 1960.
Veselovskii, K. S., 'Vospominaniia K. S. Veselovskago', *Russkaia starina*, CXVI, No. 10 (October 1903), pp. 5–42.
Vetrinskii, Ch., *T. N. Granovskii i ego vremia*, St Petersburg, 1905.
—, 'Umstvennoe i obshchestvennoe dvizhenie sorokovykh gg.', in D. N. Ovsianniko-Kulikovskii (ed.), *Istoriia russkoi literatury*, Moscow, 1909, II, pp. 66–130.

Victoria, Queen of England, *The Letters of Queen Victoria: A Selection of Her Majesty's Correspondence between the Years 1837–1861*, A. C. Benson and Viscount Esher (eds.), 3 vols., London, 1907.

Vigel', F. F., *Zapiski*, 2 vols., Moscow, 1928.

—, *Zapiski F. F. Vigelia*, 7 vols., Moscow, 1891–3.

Villamov, G. I., 'Votsarenie Imperatora Nikolaia I-go: Iz dnevnika G. I. Villamova', *Russkaia starina*, No. 1 (January 1899), pp. 90–108; No. 2 (February 1899), pp. 315–31; No. 3 (March 1899), pp. 665–89.

Virginskii, V. S., *Vozniknovenie zheleznykh dorog v Rossii do nachala 40-kh godov XIX v*, Moscow, 1949.

Vospominaniia Bestuzhevykh, Moscow, 1931.

Vosstanie dekabristov. Materialy, 12 vols., Moscow-Leningrad, 1925–69.

Vucinich, Alexander, *Science in Russian Culture: A History to 1860*, Stanford, 1963.

Webster, C. K. (ed.), *British Diplomacy, 1813–1815*, London, 1921.

—, *The Foreign Policy of Palmerston, 1830–1841*, London, 1951.

Württemberg, Prince Eugene, 'Iz vospominanii printsa Evgeniia Virtembergskogo', in B. E. Syroechkovskii (ed.), *Mezhdutsarstvie 1825 goda i vosstanie dekabristov v perepiske i memuarakh chlenov tsarskoi sem'i*, Moscow-Leningrad, 1926.

—, 'Zapiski printsa Virtembergskago: Turetskii pokhod 1828 goda i sobytiia, za nim sledovavshiia', *Russkaia starina*, XXVII, No. 1 (January 1880), pp. 79–94; No. 3 (March 1880), pp. 527–44; No. 4 (April 1880), pp. 781–800; XXVIII, No. 6 (June 1880), pp. 429–48; XXIX, No. 9 (September 1880), pp. 43–56.

Wysocki, P., *Pamiętnik o powstaniu 29 listopada r. 1830*, 2 vols., Paris, 1867.

Z. S., 'Imperator Nikolai I i evropeiskaia revoliutsiia', *Russkaia starina*, CXVII, No. 3 (March 1904), pp. 517–51; CXVIII, No. 4 (April 1904), pp. 35–63; No. 5 (May 1904), pp. 265–89.

Zablotskii-Desiatovskii, A. P., *Graf P. D. Kiselev i ego vremia*, 4 vols., St Petersburg, 1881.

—, 'Prichiny kolebaniia tsen na khleb v Rossii', *Otechestvennye zapiski*, LII, No. 5 (May 1847).

Zaionchkovskii, A. M., *Vostochnaia voina v sviazi s sovremennoi ei politicheskoi obstanovkoi*, 4 vols. in 5, St Petersburg, 1908–13.

Zaionchkovskii, P. A., 'Dmitrii Alekseevich Miliutin: Biograficheskii ocherk', *Dnevnik D. A. Miliutina, 1873–1875 gg.*, I, Moscow, 1947, pp. 1–68.

—, *Otmena krepostnogo prava v Rossii*, Moscow, 1954.

—, *Voennye reformy 1860–1870 godov v Rossii*, Moscow, 1952.

—, 'Vysshaia biurokratiia nakanune Krymskoi Voiny', *Istoriia SSSR*, No. 4 (July-August 1974), pp. 154–65.

Zamoyski, W., *Jenerał Zamoyski, 1803–1868*, 5 vols., Poznan, 1910–14.

Zechlin, Egmont, *Die deutsche Einheitsbewegung*, Frankfurt, 1967.

Zeidlits, K. I., 'Vospominaniia o turetskoi pokhode 1829 g.', *Russkii arkhiv*, No. 4 (1878), pp. 412–35; No. 5 (1878), pp. 88–113.

Zenkovskii, V. V., *Istoriia russkoi filosofii*, 2 vols., Paris, 1948.

Zhigarev, S., *Russkaia politika v vostochnom voprose: Istoriko-Iuridicheskie ocherki*, Moscow, 1896.

Zotov, V. R., 'Peterburg v sorokovykh godakh', *Istoricheskii vestnik*, XXXIX, No. 1 (January 1890), pp. 29–53.

Index